THE BOOK OF ACTS

A COMMENTARY

C. PETER WAGNER

Chosen
a division of Baker Publishing Group
Minneapolis, Minnesota

Published by Chosen Books
11400 Hampshire Avenue South
Bloomington, Minnesota 55438
www.chosenbooks.com

Chosen Books is a division of
Baker Publishing Group, Grand Rapids, Michigan

Chosen Books edition published 2017
ISBN 978-0-8007-9734-8

First edition published as *The Acts of the Holy Spirit Series: Spreading the Fire, Blazing the Way* and *Lighting the World* in 1995.
Second edition published as *The Acts of the Holy Spirit* in 2000.
Third revised and updated edition published by Regal Books as *The Book of Acts* in 2008.

Printed in the United States of America

Library of Congress Catalog Number: 2017937766

CONTENTS

Foreword 5
By Ralph Winter

Our Timeline for Understanding Acts 7

1. God's Training Manual for Modern Christians 11
2. How Jesus Attracted 120 Followers 27
3. History's Most Powerful Prayer Meeting (Acts 1) 43
4. The Spiritual Explosion at Pentecost (Acts 2) 60
5. One Hundred Thirty Converts a Day Can Shake a City (Acts 3 and 4) . . 80
6. Follow These Signs to Salvation (Acts 4 and 5) 100
7. Should Foreigners Run the Church? (Acts 6) 122
8. Samaria: Preaching on the Other Side of the Tracks (Acts 6, 7 and 8) . . 143
9. Meet Paul—The Greatest Missionary of All Time (Acts 9) 166
10. Peter Blazes the Trail to the Gentiles (Acts 9, 10 and 11) 194
11. Planting the First Gentile Church (Acts 11) 220
12. The Power of Herod Versus the Power of Prayer (Acts 12) 239
13. Onward to the Nations (Acts 13) 259
14. Extending God's Kingdom Upsets the Enemy (Acts 14) 282
15. Solving Conflicts in a Multicultural Church (Acts 15 and Galatians) . . 305
16. The Famous Jerusalem Council (Acts 15) 322
17. Goodbye, Barnabas; Hello, Silas: Reorganizing the Mission (Acts 15 and 16) 340
18. To Europe with Power (Acts 16) 355
19. You Win Some and You Lose Some (Acts 17) 381
20. Corinth to Antioch to Ephesus (Acts 18 and 19) 405
21. Invading Diana's Territory (Acts 19) 428

22. A Long Trip Toward the Jerusalem Jail (Acts 20 and 21) 449
23. What to Do with This Troublemaker? (Acts 21 to 26) 467
24. Destination: Rome (Acts 27 and 28) 483

Endnotes 497
Scripture Index 507
Subject Index 511

FOREWORD

In this remarkable book, C. Peter Wagner concedes up front that his commentary is not the first ever written on the book of Acts. By his count, his book is commentary number 1,339 of the commentaries on Acts that have been produced in English! However, what Wagner does with Acts could hardly have been done before; never has an internationally known missiologist turned his heart and mind to such a task.

In Wagner's hands this unique book of the Bible is seen as the very hinge (the one full-blown biblical description) of a mighty move of God—a move that had been foreshadowed from the time of Abraham, but not fully unleashed until the events chronicled in Acts. From that point on, the rest of history would continue to reveal the kind of transitions that we read about in *The Book of Acts.*

Acts explains how a true heart faith in a living, loving, self-sacrificing, forgiving, holy heavenly Father would expand as the kingdom of God encompassed more and more of the world's diverse cultures. But it is much more complicated than that. Acts portrays the consternation of the holdouts, in addition to the amazement and joy of the recipients of God's blessing. It shows the legalists on both sides who could not see the need for true faith within the cultural forms of either Jew or Greek. Wagner's commentary clearly demonstrates the excitement that can result when a heart faith is transmitted by earthen vessels (men and women) of one nation to another. This extraordinary commentary provides a stirring account of those specific events that took place after centuries of Jewish witness had attracted maybe a million Gentiles to the back row—a mere second-class status—in the thousands of Jewish synagogues throughout the Roman Empire and places beyond. In Wagner's book we see and feel the exuberant delight of those astounded and grateful Gentiles who allowed Paul's gospel to sink into their hearts. The explosive implication, which was revealed earlier to Abraham, was that all the world was, and is, invited to receive this faith, this fellowship with the Almighty, regardless of the clothing and cultural specifics of those who desire to receive it.

We also see the perplexity and fury of those Jews—devout and otherwise—who could not for the life of them perceive the continuities of their faith in the detested Gentile outer garments any more than many of us today can readily identify our version of that same faith in the many astounding garments that it already wears throughout today's global reality.

In this volume, the book of Acts is clearly exposited as illuminating other writings of Paul, such as his loyal defense of the Jewish tradition in both Romans 9-11 and Romans 14. Above all, the way that Wagner handles these events relentlessly presses home the vibrancy and authenticity of the work of the Holy Spirit both then and now. The result is that we cannot help but catch the warm encouragement of that same spiritual reality in our own lives today.

The book of Acts rightly understood—and Wagner's work excels all others in this—throws penetrating light on the present enigmas of missionary outreach to the last people, tribe and tongue on Earth. It helps us cope with the major "resistant" blocks of Hindus, Muslims, Buddhists, Japanese and others, as well as with the smallest human community anywhere at all.

The Book of Acts dispels once and for all the thought that the New Testament tells how a true faith was developed out of a defunct Jewish tradition. Rather, it portrays with great accuracy how a true faith in Jewish clothes, often invisible, could become an equally true faith in a radically different form. It also provides a paradigm to understand how that same true faith could become highly visible, and also how it could wane drastically from time to time as subsequent history unfolded.

Acts, as Wagner sees it, is not the end of the story, but rather the most definitive biblical account of exactly how our faith, with all its complexity, can and will engage and encompass every people, tribe and tongue in this generation.

I cannot think of any single biblical commentary that deserves more praise or more serious attention than *The Book of Acts.* Peter Wagner gives us all a new Acts for new times, one of crucial value and of almost unique significance in biblical literature.

Ralph D. Winter
Director, U.S. Center for World Mission
Pasadena, California

OUR TIMELINE FOR UNDERSTANDING ACTS

Not all scholars agree on the dates for the sequence of events in the book of Acts. Although the matter has been thoroughly researched by competent specialists, there is not yet consensus. I will not repeat the arguments for different timelines that are readily accessible in the various critical commentaries, but it is necessary to form an opinion. Here are some of the chief dates that I am adopting (all dates are A.D.):

30	Pentecost
31	Persecution from fellow Jews becomes severe
32	The gospel moves from the Hebrews to the Jewish Hellenists
	Philip evangelizes Samaria
	The gospel enters North Africa
33	Saul (Paul) is converted, travels to Jerusalem
34-36	Paul in Damascus, Arabia, Jerusalem
	Peter evangelizes Judea
37-45	Paul in Cilicia and Syria
	Peter continues in Judea
	The missionaries from Cyprus and Cyrene begin to win Gentiles in Antioch
46	Paul goes to Antioch
	James takes leadership of the Jerusalem church
47-48	Paul's first missionary term
49	Paul's furlough
	The Jerusalem Council
50-52	Paul's second term
52-53	Paul's second furlough
53-57	Paul's third term
57	Paul's furlough and arrest
58-61	Paul in Rome (where he eventually dies)
61-62	Paul's possible release (acquittal)
63-64	Paul's final arrest

THE BOOK OF ACTS

1

GOD'S TRAINING MANUAL FOR MODERN CHRISTIANS

Many modern Christians are not satisfied with Christianity as usual. They are fed up with playing church. The status quo has little appeal. Their desire is to look back at the end of the day, or the end of the year, and say, "Praise God! His kingdom has advanced, and He has allowed me to be a part of it!" They don't want to be spectators; they want to be participants in the great work that God is doing today.

For those desiring to be a part of God's action both in their churches and in the workplace, I know of nothing that will help more than thoroughly understanding the book of Acts and applying what we learn from it. Acts was designed to be God's training manual for modern Christians. Seeing and understanding what worked so well almost 2,000 years ago can directly apply to your service to God today, and it can provide a welcome power boost to your Christian life. Your serious study of Acts will bring new intimacy with the Father and new joy in doing His will.

STUDYING ACTS AND LIVING IT

Acts has been an important book to me from the start of my Christian life, which began in 1950. On the very day I accepted Jesus Christ as my Lord and Savior, I committed my life to world evangelization. Because I was not raised in a Christian home, I knew virtually nothing of the Christian life and much less about Christian ministry when I became a Christian at age 19. Nevertheless, from the moment I was born again, I knew that I was going to be a missionary.

By God's grace, my wife, Doris, and I were permitted to spend the first 16 years of our active ministry as field missionaries to Bolivia. In 1971, we returned to the United States, where I accepted a position on the faculty of the Fuller Seminary School of World Mission (now the School of

Intercultural Studies) and began my career as a professional missiologist. All of my Christian activities have been centered around obeying Jesus' Great Commission to make disciples of all nations (see Matt. 28:19-20).

Because I was one of those who are called to the front lines of God's work in the world, I soon discovered that the book of Acts was written for me. Not only did I spend considerable time in Acts during my personal Bible study, but I also began teaching it whenever I could.

My greatest opportunity for serious study and teaching of Acts came when I participated in founding a new adult Sunday School class at Lake Avenue Church in Pasadena, California. I taught the class for 13 years. One hundred adults, of all ages, joined me to be part of something new. The book of Acts was declared our textbook from the outset, and week after week we drank from its well of spiritual nourishment. Together we learned how to apply what it taught to our daily lives and to our service for God.

We took our class name, 120 Fellowship, from the band of 120 disciples in the Upper Room, reported in Acts 1:15. We prayed that what had happened to them on the Day of Pentecost, and afterward, would also happen to us. By God's grace, to some degree at least, it did. Our goal was not only to study the book of Acts but also to live it!

WHY ANOTHER COMMENTARY ON ACTS?

Through the years, I did what scholars are expected to do; I built up a substantial library of reference material on Acts. I acquired commentaries; various theologians' studies on the life of Paul, and on the life of Peter; histories of early Christianity; sociological and archaeological studies of the first-century world; expositions of Pauline theology; sermons on Acts and specific applications of Acts to certain areas of ministry, such as evangelism, small groups and church growth. Many others have gone before me in deciding that their principal field of biblical research would also be the Acts of the Apostles.

Of the collection of books I have, measuring more than 6 feet in length, 16 of the volumes are verse-by-verse commentaries on Acts. The authors of these volumes include household names in the field of New Testament studies: F. F. Bruce, Ernst Haenchen, Everett Harrison, Simon J. Kistemaker, R. C. H. Lenski, Howard Marshall, Johannes Munck, John R. W. Stott and others. To supplement these, I had access to the Fuller Seminary McAlister Library, which catalogues no fewer than 86 commentaries on Acts. A computer search discovered that 1,398 commentaries on Acts have been published in English.

Why, then, write commentary number 1,399?

I want to say up front that I do not pretend to be a professional biblical scholar, as were many of my colleagues at Fuller Seminary. I hold them in the highest esteem. I once overheard my friend Leslie Allen comment that he had read every known scholarly work on Ezekiel 18. I then asked him how many scholarly works that might include, and I was amazed when he told me he had studied the opinions of more than 150 authors on Ezekiel 18. No wonder Allen has gained the reputation among peers as the top living expert on Ezekiel. He can probably recite much of Ezekiel 18 in the original Hebrew. The late F. F. Bruce gained a similar reputation for expertise on the book of Acts during his lifetime.

I would be foolish to claim that this volume competes with the biblical scholarship of Allen, Bruce and many others. Not only do I lack their critical and linguistic acumen, but I also lack the patience to read what perhaps 150 others might have to say about one chapter of the Bible. I do read the writings of many such scholars, however, and I attempt to reflect in my own writings all the insights that I can glean from them in terms of grammar, theology and historical context. I am deeply grateful for their exegesis and I, as do many others, lean heavily upon it.

My strongest personal gifts are in other areas. I am essentially an activist. Most of my research in church growth and missiology, and in spiritual warfare and prayer, is field research as opposed to library research. History is vitally important, but I am not as personally interested in the past as I am in the present and future. I keep reminding myself that yesterday ended last night. I am enough of a pragmatist to have drawn a rather steady flow of criticism over the years. My passion is to get the job done—in this case, fulfilling the Great Commission—as well and as quickly as possible. As a theoretician, I have discovered that the theories I like best are the ones that work!

I am also a communicator. Although I appreciate the complexity of many issues relating to our Christian faith and practice, I see my role as communicating them to the Body of Christ in terms that common people can understand and act upon. This trait also draws its share of criticism, much of it undoubtedly deserved. But one of my worst fears is the risk of boring both myself and my audience with deep, complicated, accurate material that no one really cares about. This is why I may at times go to the opposite extreme.

THE WORLD IS CHANGING RAPIDLY

What, then, can an activist and a communicator hope to add to the shelves of solid, biblical scholarship on Acts?

The answer lies in the fact that Christianity at the outset of the twenty-first century is dramatically different from anything that has been seen in the past. Rapid changes in the fields of science and technology are commonly recognized. Relatively few, however, realize that equally startling changes have recently been taking place in world Christianity. Some of these changes can be traced back to the dawn of the last century. Many more changes have taken place during the last 50 years. But even more rapid changes have occurred in our own generation. My assignment as a missiologist is to stay as well informed as possible about what God is currently doing around the globe.

My purpose in writing "Acts commentary number 1,399," therefore, is to attempt to apply the eternal truths of the book of Acts to our contemporary situation, something that, obviously, no one who has written about Acts in the past would have been able to do. This does not mean that the insights of the past are obsolete; much of what has been said in the past still applies, and I will draw on it. But questions are being raised in world Christianity today that never entered the minds of commentators of yesteryear.

What might these questions be?

THE TWO CRUCIAL ISSUES

As we go through Acts chapter by chapter, I will highlight these questions. But to set the stage, two crucial issues have been subject to more study, innovation and creative application during the past 10 to 20 years than could previously have been imagined. These can be summarized as follows:

- Issues of *power ministries* characterized by supernatural healings, deliverances, miracles and spiritual warfare, and
- *Missiological* issues involved in the cross-cultural expansion of the Christian faith

I heard one observer conjecture that we have learned more about missiology and power ministries in this current generation than in all previous generations combined. This may be an overstatement, but it highlights a very important contemporary phenomenon directly related to the central message of the book of Acts.

THE THEME OF ACTS

Most commentators would agree with Simon Kistemaker, who says that in Acts 1:8, "Luke presents the theme for the entire book."[1] Let's take a look at the verse:

> But you shall receive power when the Holy Spirit has come upon you; and you shall be witnesses to Me in Jerusalem, and in all Judea and Samaria, and to the end of the earth.

Very simply, in His last recorded words spoken on this earth, Jesus highlights two themes: power ministries and missiology. Of the 16 commentaries on Acts that I have used the most, only Stanley M. Horton, a Pentecostal, seems to recognize how the power (*dunamis*) would relate to contemporary power ministries, although he does not make a specific application at this juncture.[2] Likewise, only Paul E. Pierson, a professional missiologist, relates material in Acts to contemporary insights on cross-cultural ministry.[3] This means that, unless I am mistaken, very few of the existing 1,398 commentaries on Acts deal with, in any notable depth or with specifically professional expertise, the interaction of the two major themes of the book. Most commonly, the authors take Acts 1:8 as a chronological table of contents for the book, but not as an all-pervasive warp and woof through which to interpret each one of the subsequent scenarios described by Luke, applying them to the contemporary Church.

It is in these two areas—power ministry and missiology—that I feel I can make enough of a contribution to justify adding yet another commentary on Acts to our library shelves. I bring a degree of expertise in these areas that few of the biblical scholars who have produced the classical works on Acts could provide. In doing so, I have no illusions of grandeur. The classical works have a well-deserved reputation as classics.

POWER MINISTRIES AND MISSIOLOGY

My experience in power ministries began through the framework of what has been called the Third Wave. This refers to the third wave of the power of the Holy Spirit experienced through the Body of Christ in the twentieth century—the first being the Pentecostal movement starting at the beginning of the twentieth century, and the second, the Charismatic movement dating back to 1960. The Third Wave does not replace the other two waves but flows into the same stream of Holy Spirit renewal. The form this progression has taken in the twenty-first century is what I have called The New Apostolic Reformation.[4]

I began to research and write on this phenomenon in the early 1970s with my book *Spiritual Power and Church Growth* (1986), first titled *Look Out! The Pentecostals Are Coming.* I later published *The Third Wave of the Holy Spirit* (1988) and *How to Have a Healing Ministry in Any Church* (1988). My more recent research on prayer and spiritual warfare is reported in the six-volume Prayer Warrior Series: *Warfare Prayer* (1992), *Prayer Shield* (1992), *Breaking Strongholds in Your City* (1993), *Churches That Pray* (1993), *Confronting the Powers* (1996) and *Praying with Power* (1997). Some 25 years of research, mostly field research, into power ministries has given me a substantial foundation upon which to make contemporary applications of the incidents recorded in the book of Acts.

Likewise, more than 30 years of participation on what some have regarded as the premier missiological faculty of recent times has allowed me to absorb knowledge from some of the finest minds in the field. My Fuller School of Intercultural Studies colleagues and I all served as professional field missionaries before joining the faculty. We travel frequently to every continent and share our experiences in depth with the others. This is an enviable position, for which I give God all the thanks, allowing me to see some of the dynamics of the spread of the gospel in Acts that others may have missed.

I have shared this autobiographical information so that you will know that some of the interpretations I suggest for many passages in Acts are based on careful and reasonable assumptions, even if they might differ considerably from more classical interpretations of the same passages. I have no desire to attempt to prove that others are wrong and that I am right. But, in many cases, I will offer some seemingly novel suggestions that at least may merit careful consideration by thoughtful readers. And my hope is that commentary number 1,399 on Acts will help spark a fire of the Holy Spirit that will not die until "this gospel of the kingdom will be preached in all the world as a witness to all the nations" (Matt. 24:14).

WHY ACTS IS IN THE BIBLE

Well over half (56 percent) of the New Testament is dedicated to explaining the origins and growth of the Christian movement. These are the Gospels and the book of Acts. Another 38 percent deals with the nurture of existing Christians (the Epistles); and Revelation comprises the remaining 6 percent. This clearly shows us that the primary emphasis of the New Testament is directed toward understanding why and how unbelievers can become believers. Communicating the gospel to the lost is the major theme, and the Gospels and Acts are designed to inform us how it happened in the past and, in most cases, how it should happen today.

The four Gospels—Matthew, Mark, Luke and John—record the beginnings of the Christian movement, and they tell us of remarkable church growth. Jesus began His three years of earthly ministry, according to some calculations, in A.D. 27. He attracted 12 disciples, plus some other men and women. This group soon grew to 70, according to Luke 10. By the time we get to Acts, 120 people are meeting in the Upper Room after Jesus' ascension to heaven (see Acts 1:15). We later read in 1 Corinthians 15:6 that 500 believers saw the risen Christ at once, a number that may be over and above the 120, giving a possible total of 620.

Some may wonder why I refer to this as "remarkable" growth. I have trained thousands of new church planters over the years, and very few of them have started with nothing and seen their church grow to 620 members in only three years. In fact, something less than 3 percent of all churches *ever* grow to 620. "Remarkable growth" is an accurate phrase.

The Gospels are foundational. The book of Acts follows the Gospels to show how Christians built on the solid foundation laid by Jesus after He departed from the earth. It is intended to be a paradigm of how the kingdom of God would be spread worldwide through the centuries until Jesus returns. In planning our service to God today, we draw deeply on the Gospels and the later Epistles; but Acts, more than any other book, is our primary training manual.

The book of Acts records another era of spectacular church growth, which I will detail later on. In general, however, some scholars estimate that over the 30-year span of Acts, the Christian movement grew from 120 to 100,000 among Jews alone. If this is the case, the decadal growth rate would figure to be more than 800 percent, an astronomically high rate sustained over such a period of time. The total growth rate would be even greater if the Gentiles were added. Therefore, if taken only as a church growth case study, Acts would qualify as a valuable source for discovering principles and procedures for spreading the gospel.

The Epistles comprise 38 percent of the New Testament. These are designed as guides for the nurture of existing Christians, and they do not particularly focus on reaching the lost for Christ. Interestingly enough, nothing in the Epistles directly admonishes Christians to evangelize their neighbors, even though there are many indications that it was, in fact, being done and that evangelizing the lost was a commendable thing for Christians to do.

Most of the Epistles were written while the evangelistic ministry of the book of Acts was unfolding. The Epistles of Peter, John and Hebrews are the exceptions, and possibly Paul's apostolic Epistles to Timothy and Titus as well.

DR. LUKE: A WORLD CHRISTIAN

Luke, whom Paul calls "the beloved physician" (Col. 4:14), wrote the book of Acts. It was the second volume in his two-volume series on the origins and expansion of Christianity. The opening of the first volume, The Gospel According to Luke, states that "it seemed good . . . to write to you an orderly account, most excellent Theophilus" (Luke 1:3). Then the first verse of Acts picks it up by saying, "The former account I made, O Theophilus" (Acts 1:1).

No one seems to know exactly who Theophilus might have been, but the tie between Acts and the Gospel of Luke is evident. F. F. Bruce says that Luke's description of his first volume as "all that Jesus began both to do and teach, until the day he was taken up . . . until the day when, by the Holy Spirit, he commissioned the apostles whom he had chosen, and charged them to proclaim the gospel [Acts 1:1-2] exactly summarizes the scope of Luke's Gospel."[5] The Gospel of Luke tells what Jesus did, and Acts tells what He expects His followers to do, both then and now.

Luke was well educated and cultured. Biblical scholars agree that he was "a man possessed of remarkable literary skill, with a fine sense of form and a beautiful style."[6] He was exceptionally well qualified to write these two historical books. Edmund Hiebert describes him as "a competent scholar and first-rate literary historian. . . . His work was characterized by comprehensiveness, thoroughness, accuracy, and orderliness."[7]

Above all, it is important to recognize that Luke was what we would call today a "world Christian." He was dedicated to spreading Christianity not only in his hometown of Antioch of Syria, or in the city where he later may have settled, Philippi, but also to the unreached peoples of the first-century world. Luke is, in fact, the only Gentile writer of the New Testament—or of the whole Bible, for that matter. This person, whom we would see today as a "mission field convert," actually wrote more words in the New Testament than anyone else. In Acts, Luke shows how the cultural walls of separation between Jew and Gentile were surmounted and, thus, he writes more about true missiology than any other biblical author.

One of the reasons the book of Acts is such a practical book is that Luke was also an active member of Paul's missionary team in the role of what we would call a "national worker." As we will see, Luke writes several sections of Acts using the first person "we," indicating that he himself may have drawn from his own diary, which he would have kept when he was part of Paul's missionary activities (see Acts 16:10-18; 20:5-21; 27:1–28:16). We are not told how Luke came to know Christ. It does not appear, however, that he was a convert of Paul's. He enters the picture on Paul's second term at Troas, presumably as a mature national Christian worker. Paul indicates that Luke was with him in his letters to the Colossians (see Col. 4:14), to Philemon (see Philem. 24) and to Timothy (see 2 Tim. 4:11). It was likely that Luke, a physician and not what we might regard as an "ordained minister," was a person of some financial means. As I explain in my book *The Church in the Workplace*, I regard Luke as the prototype of "Workplace" apostles.

With an author possessing the qualifications of Dr. Luke, it is no surprise that in the Acts of the Apostles we have a book that we can characterize as a training manual for modern Christians.

THE KINGDOM OF GOD ON THE BIG SCREEN

A major theological framework for understanding the book of Acts is the kingdom of God. Acts starts with the kingdom of God and ends with it. It opens with a description of the ministry of Jesus during the 40 days between His resurrection and His ascension to heaven, saying that Jesus spoke to His apostles "of the things pertaining to the kingdom of God" (Acts 1:3). At the end of the book, we find the apostle Paul under house arrest in Rome, receiving visitors and "preaching the kingdom of God" (Acts 28:31).

What is the kingdom of God?

The kingdom of God is present, first and foremost, wherever Jesus Christ is acknowledged and served as King. It is not a geopolitical territory with recognized boundaries. It could not join the United Nations. It is a kingdom not *of* this world but nevertheless *in* this world. It is essentially a spiritual kingdom; but it also has tangible, visible manifestations.

In another sense, the kingdom of God is future as well as present. There will be a day when Jesus "delivers the kingdom to God the Father, when He puts an end to all rule and all authority and power. For He must reign till He has put all enemies under His feet. The last enemy that will be destroyed is death" (1 Cor. 15:24-26). As long as death is with us, the *future* Kingdom has not yet arrived. When it does come, we will see the "new heaven and new earth" (Rev. 21:1), which we have not yet seen in their fullness.

Until that day, however, we live in a world where many enemies of God and of His people are still present. Satan, the supreme enemy, is spoken of as "the god of this age" (2 Cor. 4:4). John affirms that "the whole world lies under the sway of the wicked one" (1 John 5:19). The devil is known as "the prince of the power of the air" (Eph. 2:2). This language must not be taken lightly. It is used of Satan by those writing on this side of the Cross and the Resurrection. Before Jesus came, things were even worse!

Whereas, in Old Testament times, bright reflections of God's kingdom were seen from time to time, Satan's control, apart from the small segment of humanity descended from Abraham, was almost total. This world never rightfully belonged to Satan, but to its Creator: "The earth is the LORD's, and all its fullness, the world and those who dwell therein" (Ps. 24:1).

Nevertheless, as a result of the strongholds provided through the disobedience of Adam and Eve, Satan succeeded in usurping the dominion over creation that God had originally planned for Adam. Satan had become so powerful that in the temptation he could offer Jesus the kingdoms of this world, claiming that "this has been delivered to me, and I give it to whomever I wish" (Luke 4:6). This would have included the Egyptians, the Pygmies, the Mayans, the Mongols, the Arabs, the Chinese and thousands of other people groups. Interestingly enough, Jesus never denied that Satan actually had such power. In fact, if Satan did not have control of the kingdoms, the temptation itself would have been a farce. No wonder Jesus would later call him "the ruler of this world" (John 12:31).

Jesus Invades Satan's Kingdom

The situation changed radically through Jesus' life, death and resurrection. When Jesus first came, John the Baptist declared, "The kingdom of heaven is at hand!" (Matt. 3:2). Jesus was also accustomed to "preaching the gospel of the kingdom" (Matt. 4:23), and He later sent out His disciples to "preach, saying, 'The kingdom of heaven is at hand' " (Matt. 10:7). These statements amounted to a declaration of war. Satan's kingdom, referred to in Matthew 12:26, had existed up to that time virtually unthreatened. No longer! Jesus' purpose in coming to Earth was clear: "The Son of God was manifested, that He might destroy the works of the devil" (1 John 3:8). The kingdom of God had invaded the kingdom of the enemy!

Much to Satan's dismay, Jesus' death on the cross sealed His ultimate victory over the realm of darkness and assured the world that God's kingdom would continue to expand until the day it would arrive in all fullness and perfection. His death "disarmed principalities and powers" and "made a public spectacle of them, triumphing over them in it" (Col. 2:15).

The radical difference between New Testament times and Old Testament times is described clearly by Jesus' reference to John the Baptist. Jesus affirmed that no greater man was born of woman than John the Baptist. But John symbolized the ending of the Old Testament age, and Jesus said, "He who is least in the kingdom of heaven is greater than he" (Matt. 11:11). Immediately afterward, Jesus announced His declaration of war. He said that from the days of John the Baptist, the kingdom of heaven comes with violence "and the violent take it by force" (Matt. 11:12). With this, Jesus was establishing the pattern of things to come. His people would be recruited, mobilized and empowered to move with force against Satan and on behalf of the kingdom of God. Jesus' desire is that His people regain the dominion over creation originally intended for Adam.

Spiritual Warfare

The weapons to conduct this warfare destined to retake dominion would be spiritual, not carnal. In the Lord's Prayer, Jesus taught His disciples to pray daily, "Your kingdom come. Your will be done on earth as it is in heaven" (Matt. 6:10). He said, "My kingdom is not of this world" (John 18:36).

What would Jesus' kingdom look like? At the outset of His public ministry, Jesus went into the synagogue of his hometown of Nazareth and answered this question. Quoting Isaiah 61, He said He had come to:

- preach the gospel to the poor;
- heal the brokenhearted;
- preach deliverance to the captives;
- preach recovery of sight to the blind;
- set at liberty those who are oppressed; and
- preach the acceptable year of the Lord (Luke 4:18-19).

Satan and his kingdom receive a setback every time a sick person is healed, every time a demon is cast out, every time a lost soul is saved, every time people of different races live together in love and harmony, every time injustice is exposed and punished, every time families maintain standards of holiness and purity. Satan, the thief, comes "to steal, and to kill, and to destroy"; but Jesus comes "that they may have life, and that they may have it more abundantly" (John 10:10).

When Jesus left the earth, He left the task of extending His kingdom in the hands of His followers empowered by the Holy Spirit. The first time Jesus sent them out, He "gave them power over unclean spirits, to cast them out, and to heal all kinds of sickness and all kinds of disease" (Matt. 10:1). He later told an expanded group of disciples, "Behold, I give you the authority to trample on serpents and scorpions, and over all the power of the enemy" (Luke 10:19). By using that power, they were to declare and manifest the kingdom of God. They were to "Go . . . and make disciples of all the nations, baptizing them in the name of the Father and of the Son and of the Holy Spirit, teaching them to observe all things that I have commanded you" (Matt. 28:19-20).

This brings us to the book of Acts, for there, more than anywhere else in the Bible, we find exactly how Jesus' disciples went about implementing their Master's desire that the kingdom of God be extended.

PRINCIPLES AND PRACTICE OF CHURCH GROWTH

F. F. Bruce says that the alternate Western reading of Acts 1:2 is slightly different from the one we ordinarily use. According to this text, Luke's Gospel had told of all that Jesus did and taught, "until the day when he by the Holy Spirit commissioned the apostles whom he had chosen, and *commanded them to proclaim the gospel.*"[8] This is interesting, because it even more specifically casts the book of Acts into an evangelistic mode. An important part of what Jesus taught was that He had come to "build [His] church" (Matt. 16:18).

Building the Church of Jesus Christ, as described by Jesus and implemented by His followers in the book of Acts, involves the key elements of both missiology and power ministries. This is mirrored in Jesus' final words to the disciples, which we have cited previously: "But you shall receive power when the Holy Spirit has come upon you; and you shall be witnesses to Me in Jerusalem, and in all Judea and Samaria, and to the end of the earth" (Acts 1:8).

It is not easy for us today to fully comprehend what a radical concept this was to first-century Jews. Although Jesus' disciples had recollections of brief episodes when He ministered to a Samaritan woman and a Syrophoenician woman and a Roman centurion, their idea of the kingdom of God was still limited to the Jews, God's chosen people. They should have known better, but they didn't, and most of them wouldn't, at least for another 20 years or so.

I like the way Paul Pierson describes the implications of "Jerusalem, Judea, Samaria, and the end of the earth":

> These words symbolized the breaking of an almost infinite number of barriers in order that men and women everywhere might hear and respond to the Good News. Just as God in Christ had broken through the barriers which separated eternity from time, divinity from humanity, holiness from sin, so His people were to break through geographical, racial, linguistic, religious, cultural and social barriers in order that people of every race and tongue might receive the Good News.[9]

The missiological task was clear, and it was magnificently implemented in the book of Acts. But it could not be implemented with human power alone.

After three years of personal instruction, Jesus had told His disciples to "tarry in the city of Jerusalem until you are endued with power from on high" (Luke 24:49). Three years with Jesus Himself had only partially equipped them for what was ahead. They needed much more than that to engage in the spiritual warfare necessary to take the Kingdom by force (see Matt. 11:12).

The Gates of Hades

Jesus did not tell His disciples that their task was to build His Church without first warning them of the spiritual warfare it would entail. He said, "I will build My church, and the gates of Hades shall not prevail against it" (Matt. 16:18). He didn't say that the gates of Hades wouldn't do whatever they could to *hinder* the growth of the Church; He just said they wouldn't *prevail*.

Jesus also said that He would give His disciples "the keys of the kingdom of heaven" (Matt. 16:19). These keys would help open the opposing gates of Hades. What were the keys? "Whatever you bind on earth will be bound in heaven, and whatever you loose on earth will be loosed in heaven" (Matt. 16:19). The Greek word for bind, *deo*, is the same word Jesus used when He spoke of binding the strongman in Matthew 12:29.

Binding the strongman, in this case Beelzebub, ruler of the demons, is a description of what we call in today's language strategic-level spiritual warfare. Paul says, "We do not wrestle against flesh and blood, but against principalities, against powers, against the rulers of the darkness of this age, against spiritual hosts of wickedness in the heavenly places" (Eph. 6:12). Time after time in the book of Acts we will see strategic-level spiritual warfare in action. Examples will include western Cyprus with Bar-Jesus the sorcerer; Philippi with the Python spirit; Ephesus with Diana of the Ephesians; and others.

A New Advantage?

Immediately after giving them the keys of the kingdom of heaven, Jesus told His disciples that He was going to leave them. This was such a shock that Peter inadvisably argued with the Master, and Jesus said, "Get behind Me, Satan!" (Matt. 16:23). Later He explained to them that His departure would be to their *advantage*: "I tell you the truth. It is to your advantage that I go away; for if I do not go away, the Helper will not come to you; but if I depart, I will send Him to you" (John 16:7).

Note the rather astounding implication of what Jesus said to His disciples. For the task of evangelizing the world, building His church and expanding His kingdom, the immediate presence of the Third Person of the Trinity would be more important to them than the immediate presence of the Second Person of the Trinity! The book of Acts is as much about the acts of the Holy Spirit as it is about the acts of the apostles.

CHURCH GROWTH REPORTS

Obviously, Jesus' disciples ended up doing what was expected of them in the power of the Holy Spirit, because Luke peppers his historical account with these reports of the growth of churches:

- The original nucleus was 120 (see Acts 1:15).
- Three thousand more came on Pentecost (see Acts 2:41).
- People were subsequently being added to the Church daily (see Acts 2:47).
- Soon there were 5,000 men plus women and children (see Acts 4:4).
- Multitudes were being saved (see Acts 5:14).
- Addition changed to multiplication (see Acts 6:1).
- Religious leaders began to be converted (see Acts 6:7).
- Samaritans came to Christ (see Acts 8:12).
- An Ethiopian was saved (see Acts 8:38).
- Entire towns committed to Christ (see Acts 9:35).
- A great number of Gentiles became Christians (see Acts 11:21).
- A Roman proconsul believed (see Acts 13:12).
- Large multitudes of Jews and Greeks accepted the faith (see Acts 14:1).
- Churches increased in number daily (see Acts 16:5).
- Prominent women followed Jesus (see Acts 17:12).
- A ruler of the synagogue became a Christian with his household (see Acts 18:8).
- The word of the Lord grew mightily and prevailed (see Acts 19:20).

Furthermore, Luke specifically mentions power ministries as a means toward the conversion of many individuals and communities in Acts. The complete list would be too long to reproduce, but here are a few samples:

- On Pentecost, 3,000 people were attracted through the miracle of tongues.
- The process leading to the 5,000 began with Peter and John healing the lame man at the Temple gate.
- Believers were added when Peter's shadow healed some and demons were cast out.
- The gospel broke through to the Samaritans because of the miracles done through Philip.
- Many believed in Joppa because Peter raised Dorcas from the dead.
- The proconsul believed when Paul had a power encounter with Elymas the sorcerer.

- The Word of the Lord spread through Ephesus when demons were cast out through handkerchiefs blessed by Paul.

It must be clear that none of these signs and wonders by themselves saved anyone. They were accompanied by the persuasive preaching of the gospel of the death and resurrection of Jesus Christ, the promised Messiah and the Son of God. Paul says, "For I am not ashamed of the gospel of Christ, for it is the power of God to salvation for everyone who believes" (Rom. 1:16). People are born again because they put their faith in Jesus as Savior and Lord, not because they are healed or delivered. But healing and deliverance make many more open to consider the claims of Jesus Christ than they would be without them, as we see clearly from the book of Acts.

REFLECTION QUESTIONS

1. From what you have read in this chapter, express in your own words what "missiology" and "missiologist" mean. Name some individuals known to you who might see themselves as missiologists.
2. Read Acts 1:8. Do you agree that its two major themes are power ministries and cross-cultural missions? Are you familiar with other commentaries on Acts that stress these things?
3. How important do you think Acts is as compared to the Gospels? As compared to the Epistles?
4. Do you agree that Jesus invaded Satan's kingdom? If so, name some of the ways this can affect your family, your church or your community.
5. Talk about the "gates of Hades." How do they enter the picture of evangelism and church growth in Acts, and today?

2

HOW JESUS ATTRACTED 120 FOLLOWERS

The book of Acts opens with Jesus instructing His 11 apostles. Remarkably, they were all Jews. Later, 120 people gathered in the Upper Room. They also were all Jews.

Apart from an isolated exception here and there, such as the Samaritan woman at the well and her friends, virtually every one of the early believers was a Jew. No intentional effort to evangelize non-Jews is recorded in the Gospels or in Acts until we come to chapter 8. There, Philip began to evangelize the half-breed Samaritans. Then in Acts 10, Peter visits the home of a Gentile named Cornelius. However, a systematic mission to plant churches among Gentiles is not recorded until Acts 11:20 where, 15 years after Pentecost, missionaries from Cyprus and Cyrene traveled to Antioch. The apostle Paul later went out from Antioch to plant churches among Gentiles, but his radical ministry became so controversial among the Jews that a summit meeting, the Council of Jerusalem, had to be convened to help resolve the arising tensions. In the minds of most church leaders of that day, only Jews were qualified to follow the Messiah; if Gentiles wanted to be included, they would first have to agree to become Jewish proselytes.

The apostle Paul said that the gospel was "for the Jew first and also for the Greek" (Rom. 1:16). Why was this? Why is it that Jesus would say, "I was not sent except to the lost sheep of the house of Israel" (Matt. 15:24)? It will not be possible to adequately comprehend the radical nature of the cross-cultural missiology unfolding in the book of Acts without first going back to the Gospels and understanding how, and why, Jesus built a nucleus of 120 Jews to initiate what has now become 20 centuries of trans-cultural world missions aimed at all peoples of the earth.

This is one of those extremely significant missiological issues that are largely ignored by the classical commentaries on Acts. Why were the 120 in the upper room all Jews?

A THEOLOGICAL YES

Paul had some good theological reasons for saying that the gospel is for the Jews first. He had personal reasons as well. Paul himself was a Jew, a Hebrew of the Hebrews, who dearly loved his own people. He personally had such a burden for them that he once declared that he would give up his own salvation if by doing so the Jewish people would follow Jesus as their Messiah (see Rom. 9:1-5).

The covenant that God made with Abraham 4,000 years ago was a clear expression of God's heart for the world. He chose Abraham to be the progenitor of His special people, Israel. God's intention was not only to bless Israel, but much more. He said to Abraham, "In you *all the families of the earth* shall be blessed" (Gen. 12:3). If the Jewish people had been faithful to God's commission in the Old Testament times, the world would have been different. Many Jews, even today, do not understand why history changed so radically for them when Jesus Christ came.

Paul, who eventually became a Jewish apostle to the Gentiles, struggled much of his life, attempting to comprehend why history did change and why the focus of God's activity, in His perspective, apparently shifted from the Jews to the Gentiles. Most of His people had not grasped that fact due to unbelief in their daily lives. It took Paul almost 25 years after his conversion to be able to articulate it in detail, which he does in his letter to the Romans. There he says that God, true to His covenant with Abraham, brought the Messiah into the world through Jews and to the Jewish community. But Judaism, as an institution, would not accept the Messiah. They were like an olive tree whose natural branches had to be broken off and wild branches grafted in. Why? "Because of unbelief they were broken off" (Rom. 11:20). The root remained a Jewish root, but the subsequent branches of the olive tree for two millennia have been largely Gentiles. And, Paul adds, this hardening on the part of Israel will continue "until the fullness of the Gentiles has come in" (Rom. 11:25).

That is the theological yes, a clear reason to expect that the first believers in Jesus the Messiah would be Jews.

A THEOLOGICAL NO

But there is also a theological no, a side of theology that would raise questions about whether such a thing is legitimate.

Part of the nature of God is that He is "not willing that any should perish but that all should come to repentance" (2 Pet. 3:9). For God, "There is neither Jew nor Greek, there is neither slave nor free, there is neither male nor female" (Gal. 3:28). The clear intentions of Jesus Himself were that the gospel should spread among Gentiles as well as Jews. When He was about to depart, the Great Commission He left with His disciples was, "Go therefore and make disciples of all the nations" (Matt. 28:19). The word Jesus used for "nations" was *ethne,* which today we call peoples or people groups. In the minds of first-century Jews, *ethne* was also a synonym for Gentiles.

Jesus, of course, knew this. He was very much aware that He was the Son of God, the long-awaited Messiah. He knew that when He died on the cross, the blood He shed was to be for remission of sins of whomsoever believes, Gentiles as well as Jews. Jesus knew that He was beginning a process of redemption that would end with a great multitude in heaven composed of "all nations, tribes, peoples, and tongues standing before the throne and before the Lamb" (Rev. 7:9).

So the question persists: Why were the 120 who surrounded Jesus all Jews? Why didn't Jesus follow the pattern of one modern pastor who said he was praying for "a heterogeneous church, a group of believers that was a microcosm of the church universal. If persons from all walks of life, cultures, races, church affiliations, and doctrinal divergences make up the true Body of Christ . . . why could we not in one local church have the same diversity?" Why, during the three years of His public ministry, did Jesus not win some Jews first to honor the Abrahamic covenant, but also include some Ethiopians or Lystrans or Samaritans or Macedonians or Venelli or Vercingetorix or Atuatuci, just to name a few of the diverse non-Jewish people groups of that time and place?

Presumably, Jesus' reasons for maintaining Jewish homogeneity, rather than attempting multicultural heterogeneity, could not have been entirely theological. Theologically, He had come to announce the kingdom of God not only for Jews, but also for all of the above people groups and many more as well. Having a mixture in His own nucleus that represented the diversity of the ethnic multitude around the throne in heaven would seem to have been more politically correct and theologically correct than having a nucleus of all Jews.

If the underlying reasons were, therefore, not primarily *theological*, it could well be that they could be interpreted as *methodological*. Under the assumption that Jesus had planned a systematic strategy for His three short years of ministry, as opposed to relying on happenstance, could it be that He intended to set a pattern for the future of Christian missions? If so, Jesus might have been modeling a principle that plays a key role in contemporary missiology called "the people approach to world evangelization."

THE PEOPLE APPROACH TO WORLD EVANGELIZATION

The people approach to world evangelization is based on a high appreciation of culture. As Donald McGavran says, "People like to become Christians without crossing racial, linguistic, or class barriers."[1] Culture is something that most people do not take lightly, as anthropologists are quick to inform us. Violating or denigrating the way of life or the way of thinking of a people group has proven to be a poor way of subsequently attracting them to the gospel of Christ, even though the gospel has clearly trans-cultural dimensions.

Although there may be some variations and exceptions, modern missiology teaches that the most viable strategy for extending the kingdom of God throughout the world is to set targets, people group by people group. What is a people group? Contemporary missiologists have agreed on the following definition:

> A people group is a significantly large sociological grouping of individuals who perceive themselves to have a common affinity for one another. From the viewpoint of evangelization, this is the largest possible group within which the gospel can spread as a church-planting movement without encountering barriers of understanding or acceptance.

Apparently, Jesus considered the Jews of His day as one such people group. Among them, a considerable variety ranged, from Matthew, who was a tax collector for the Roman government, to Simon, who was a Zealot bent on overthrowing the Roman government. But beyond differences in political positions, social class, vocation, age and disposition, Jesus' followers belonged to the same ethnic group, had the same color skin, shared similar cultural values, including prejudices, ate and abstained from the same foods, followed the same dress code, spoke the same language and perceived themselves to have a common affinity for one another.

Jesus knew well that the people approach is the best approach to evangelization. As McGavran says, "It may be taken as axiomatic that whenever becoming a Christian is a *racial* rather than a *religious* decision, there the growth of the church will be exceedingly slow."[2] He then adds, "The great obstacles to conversion are social, not theological."[3] I realize that what I have just said is, to many, a controversial issue. But I can assure them that it is sound missiology.

HOW IMPORTANT IS CULTURE?

If the people approach to world evangelization is based on a high view of culture, how can this be justified? Culture is frequently seen as something that provokes separation and social disharmony. Some think of culture as an evil that needs to be ignored, if not stamped out. Their ideal is to assimilate all peoples into one language and culture, which some unadvisedly would term a "Christian culture."

In today's world, however, such a goal is regarded as unrealistic idealism. A new respect for culture is developing. The United States now thinks of itself as a multicultural society rather than a melting pot. This is a more biblical way of thinking, because God Himself is the creator of human cultures. Three important biblical insights help us understand multiculturalism in a positive light:

The human race is one. All the diverse peoples of the earth ultimately belong to one family. God created Adam and Eve to be the progenitors of all of humankind. Traced back far enough, every human is genetically related to every other. The apostle Paul affirms this in his sermon on Mars Hill in Athens: He [God] has made from one blood every nation of men to dwell on all the face of the earth, and has determined their preappointed times and the boundaries of their habitation (see Acts 17:26). This is the basis for the biblical affirmation that in the community of the Kingdom there is no difference between Jews and Gentiles.

God intended humans to be diverse. Although it is true that the kingdom of God admits Jews and Gentiles on an equal basis, it is equally true that in this present life they are distinct. As I interpret the biblical evidence, I see this distinction and the uniqueness of all people groups as part of God's creative design. Biologically speaking, the genes and chromosomes of Adam and Eve must have contained all the genetic material for the human diversity we see today.

The first biblical list of human people groups occurs in Genesis 10, called by some "The Table of the Nations." Each people was "separated into their lands, everyone according to his own language, according to their families, into their nations" (Gen. 10:5). The way this came about is narrated in Genesis 11, through the well-known story of the Tower of Babel, where, in one fell swoop, God decided to "confuse their language, that they may not understand one another's speech" (Gen. 11:7).

Biblical scholars have at least two opinions about God's underlying motivation for confusing the languages. One of them is expressed by Gerhard von Rad, who sees the outcome of Babel as "disorder in the international world . . . [that] was not willed by God but is punishment for the sinful rebellion against God."[4] This is a very common interpretation, which surfaces frequently in sermons on racial reconciliation.

Von Rad's negative interpretation, however, is not compatible either with a Christian understanding of cultural anthropology or with contemporary views of missiological strategy. Suggesting that cultural diversity is rooted in human sin rather than in the purpose of God's creation is clearly not the only way to understand Genesis 10 and 11. I, for one, see it differently.

The other point of view, which I happen to agree with, regards the sinful rebellion of the human race at the Tower of Babel as an effort to *prevent* the human race from becoming diversified according to God's plan. From the beginning, God had set in motion His design to separate humans into people groups so that they could best fulfill God's command to Adam: "Be fruitful and multiply; fill the earth" (Gen. 1:28). However, the early human race, which still all spoke one language (see Gen. 11:1), rebelled against this plan. They intuitively perceived that as they multiplied, families and clusters of families would need more land for farming and hunting and that if they continued to scatter, their social separation would eventually produce increasing cultural differentiation.

Knowing there was no human way to prevent this, they sought supernatural power to assist them. They could not turn to God, for the scattering was His own plan. Instead, they turned to the satanic powers of darkness to implement their plans for a one-world movement. They built the Tower of Babel, which archaeologists identify as a typical ancient ziggurat, an overtly occultic structure. They wanted the tower to have its "top . . . in the heavens" (Gen. 11:4) in order to commune directly with the demonic principalities they had agreed to serve. And the reason they started building the tower and the city around it was clearly stated: "Lest we be scattered abroad over the face of the whole earth" (Gen. 11:4). Their supreme fear was to allow God to diversify them, and they were willing to make a pact with the devil in order to prevent it.

Their scheme did not work, as we well know. God sovereignly intervened and accomplished in an instant what He might have ordinarily taken centuries or millennia to do—He changed the monolingual society to a multilingual society. This effectively stopped the building of the tower and the city, and rapidly accelerated the geographical scattering of the people groups, each now with its own language.

Bernhard Anderson, professor of Old Testament theology at Princeton Seminary, agrees that God's original will for the human race was dispersion and diversity. He says, "When the Babel story is read in its literary context there is no basis for the negative view that pluralism is God's judgment upon human sinfulness. Diversity is not a condemnation. . . . God's will for His creation is diversity rather than homogeneity. Ethnic pluralism is to be welcomed as a divine blessing."[5]

In my opinion, this high view of human culture and its origins is a valuable building block for formulating a sound biblical and practical missiology.

God is concerned to bring all peoples to Himself. Paul speaks of Jesus Christ as the "only Potentate, the King of kings and Lord of lords" (1 Tim. 6:15). God sent His Son to die so that "this gospel of the kingdom will be preached in all the world as a witness to all the nations" (Matt. 24:14).

The way that God's master plan is and has been implemented most effectively in the world today is through the people approach to world evangelization, the strategy that Jesus used to gather His 120.

NOT ALL EVANGELISM IS THE SAME

In order to sort out the most appropriate evangelistic methodologies for spreading the gospel to all the peoples of the world, some helpful terminology has been developed, using the symbols E-1, E-2 and E-3. The "E" stands for evangelism and the numbers stand for the barriers that must be crossed in order to do it.

E-1 evangelism. E-1 is monocultural evangelism. The only barrier is to move outside the Church, which presumably is a community of believers, into the world, where the unbelievers are found. For many, this "stained-glass barrier" is a formidable one, and all too many Christians fail to cross it. They do not have to learn a new language; they do not have to eat different food; they do not have to adapt to new behavior patterns. Their job is to communicate the good news to people very much like themselves. There are few good excuses for not doing E-1 evangelism.

E-2 and E-3 evangelism. Both of these are cross-cultural, and the difference between the two is one of degree. E-2 implies crossing the same "stained-glass barrier" as E-1, but also one degree of cultural barrier. E-3 involves a more distant cultural barrier. For instance, Anglo-Americans evangelizing Mexican-Americans would be E-2 because the two cultures have comparatively minor differences, although evangelizing Mexican Indians in Chiapas would be E-3. The same Anglo-Americans evangelizing Masai in Kenya would also find themselves in an E-3 situation because the culture there is so radically different from their own.

Keep in mind that the distinction here is cultural, not geographic. In multicultural urban societies in America, for example, opportunities for E-1, E-2 and E-3 can at times be found in the same neighborhood or even on the same city block.

Obviously, most people, year in and year out, are won to Christ through E-1 evangelism. Most evangelists are monocultural evangelists. Most pastors are monocultural pastors. It has always been this way and it always will be. The reason for this is very simple. God has called and equipped most people to minister primarily to those of their own culture. But not all.

God has also called some to minister with whatever spiritual gifts they have in different cultures. If He hadn't, Christianity would never have become a universal religion. Those whom God has called to minister in E-2 and E-3 situations, He also equips with the missionary gift. In my book *Your Spiritual Gifts Can Help Your Church Grow*, I define the missionary gift as follows:

> The gift of missionary is the special ability that God gives to certain members of the Body of Christ to minister whatever other spiritual gifts they have in a second culture.[6]

Given the fact that somewhere between 6,000 and 12,000 people groups are yet to be reached with the gospel, it may come as a surprise to learn, as I indicate in my book *Your Spiritual Gifts Can Help Your Church Grow*, that apparently fewer than 1 percent of committed Christians have been given the missionary gift. Low as this number might sound, considerably fewer than half of this number of Christians around the world are actively engaged in cross-cultural ministries. If as many as 1 percent of the Body of Christ were ever mobilized and trained, the resulting missionary force would be more than adequate to reach all of the unreached peoples in our present generation.

How could it be done with so few?

It goes back to the fact that most evangelism is monocultural. The job for cross-cultural missionaries is to implant the gospel in a new people group by E-2 or E-3 ministry, then to equip the nationals there to continue the task by using E-1. We frequently hear the expression, "Nationals can evangelize better than missionaries." This is true because E-1 is the easiest, most natural and effective kind of evangelism.

But even "national" evangelists are going to have a hard time if they tackle the E-2 and E-3 groups *in their own country*. Keep in mind that E-2 and E-3 missionary work is very tough, whether it is done by nationals within a country or by expatriates from another country. In fact, unreached peoples are often oppressed minorities within a given country, which would make them more likely to trust an expatriate from the outside than someone from an oppressing group within their own country.

JESUS WAS MONOCULTURAL

This brings us back to the main issue of this chapter. Why is it that Jesus' nucleus of 120 were all Jews? It is because Jesus, representing 99 percent of Christian people, was monocultural. In Jesus' human ministry, the Father had called and equipped Him as an E-1 evangelist. I say His *human* ministry because, as the eternal Son of God, Jesus crossed an awesome barrier by taking on a human nature and becoming a servant, as we read in Philippians 2:5-8. This was unique, however; something none of us could ever identify with. Most of us, on the other hand, can easily identify with Jesus' E-1 monocultural human ministry.

As I said before, I believe that Jesus' three years of monocultural ministry to the Jews was more of a *strategic* than a *theological* choice. As far as we know from the Scriptures, Jesus did not train any of His 12 disciples for cross-cultural ministry, although subsequent tradition indicates that some of them may have become missionaries. The possibility that Thomas went to India or that Matthew went to Ethiopia would be examples. Nevertheless, the first E-3 missionary appearing in Acts would be Philip when he preached to the Samaritans (see Acts 8:5). More radical E-3 missionaries would be those who went from Cyprus and Cyrene to the Gentiles in Antioch (see Acts 11:20). And the most outstanding one would be Paul, known as the apostle to the Gentiles. But none of the above was a member of Jesus' nucleus of 120.

Now, let's examine as closely as we can just how Jesus went about His ministry, because 99 percent of us will be using similar methods and strategy.

THE WORLD AS JESUS FOUND IT

The geopolitical world into which Jesus was born and in which He went about His ministry was the Roman Empire. By that time, the central government in Rome had gained political control of about 30 provinces, each with its own ethnic and cultural mixes. The Christian faith began as an insignificant Jewish sect on the eastern end of the Mediterranean Sea. In only 70 years, it had become a prominent feature on the religious landscape of the Roman Empire, and three centuries later it was declared the Empire's official religion!

Looking at the ethnology of the Roman Empire from the perspective of Jesus and the Apostles, the major division was between Jews and Gentiles. It has been estimated that Jews comprised around 8 percent of the population of the Roman Empire of 90 million people. That would calculate to slightly more than 7 million Jews.

Social relationships between Jews and Gentiles were exceedingly strained. A. C. Bouquet comments, "We have perhaps no parallel to it in the world today other than that in India between strict Brahmins and non-Brahmins, and it was more severe in some ways even than this."[7] Jews would tend to alienate Gentiles when, day after day, the Jews would refuse to:

- eat anything but certified kosher food;
- go near a Gentile temple;
- enter a Gentile home;
- drink milk drawn from a cow by a Gentile;
- use Gentile drinking cups;
- leave a Gentile alone in a Jewish home;
- sell cattle to a Gentile.

Gentiles, naturally, would react to such behavior with scorn, ridicule and reverse discrimination. Anti-Semitism was pervasive. Jews were regarded as a despised minority by most Gentiles. It is not difficult, therefore, to understand why Jewish believers would feel that unclean Gentiles should not be admitted to the Church unless they first agreed to become Jewish proselytes through circumcision and they vowed to obey the Jewish law.

The Gentiles, of course, were not all the same. Many people groups, having a great diversity of languages, ethnicity and cultures, were included within the general category of Roman Gentiles.

Jews were not all the same either. Hebrews and Hellenists were quite distinct. Among the Hebrews themselves, Judeans and Galileans had differing cultures. A variety of subgroups of Hellenistic Jews were molded to one degree or another by the particular city or province in which they lived. There were several religious groups such as Pharisees and Sadducees, plus predictable socioeconomic divisions.

Between the Jews and Gentiles were the mixed-blood Samaritans, a community of Jews who had long before intermarried with Gentiles. Jews avoided Samaritans as adamantly as they did Gentiles (see John 4:9).

The world into which God sent His Son, then, was a highly diversified cultural mosaic. It was a formidable evangelistic and missiological challenge.

JESUS GATHERS HIS INNER CIRCLE

After Jesus was baptized by John the Baptist, He began His three years of public ministry. One of the priority items on His agenda was to recruit a ministry team. He naturally began calling His disciples among fellow Jews who had been waiting for generations for the promised Messiah. One of the more devout was Andrew, a disciple of John the Baptist, who was present at Jesus' baptism in the Jordan River. After Andrew met Jesus, he immediately went to his brother, Simon Peter, and said, "We have found the Messiah" (John 1:41).

Soon Philip and Nathanael were added. Nathanael was another Jew who was so receptive that he exclaimed, "Rabbi, You are the Son of God! You are the King of Israel!" (John 1:49). Then Simon Peter's fishing partners, James and John, decided to leave their fishing business to join Jesus' inner circle.

This is the way E-1 evangelism ordinarily happens. For one thing, because all were Jews, they did not consider their decision to follow Jesus a racial issue. This fits with Donald McGavran's statement, cited earlier, that whenever becoming a Christian is seen as a *racial* decision rather than a personal commitment to Jesus or a religious decision, little church growth can be expected. Nothing in the apostles' decision involved a betrayal of their non-Christian kith and kin. By following Jesus, they were not becoming less Jewish than before.

The door was then open for outreach along natural lines. Andrew moved along family lines and found his brother Peter. Peter moved along vocational lines and found fellow fishermen, James and John. Andrew and Peter moved along community lines and found Philip, who lived in their hometown of Bethsaida and who, in all probability, grew up with them as children. In all, the issue was not how Jewish they would continue to be, but whether or not they would recognize Jesus as the Messiah, the Son of God and the King of Israel.

When the apostle Paul says that the gospel is "for the Jew first" (Rom. 1:16), it fits perfectly into the pattern established by Jesus. Missiologically speaking, He could have done it in no other way and seen the same positive results. If, instead of doing this, Jesus had gone back to Egypt where He lived as a baby and attempted to draw together an inner circle of Gentile Egyptians, it is not unreasonable to suspect that little or nothing would have happened.

None of this is to detract in any way from the deity of Jesus Christ or the sovereignty of God. It is simply based on the assumption that Jesus' intent was to model a way of doing evangelism that could be applied through succeeding generations by human individuals who would not have a divine nature such as He had.

What Kind of Jews?

I am familiar with the viewpoint of some idealists that Jesus' inner circle of 12 was characterized by great diversity. This would be true only as far as diversity of age, occupation, formal education, social class, personality types and political preferences might be concerned. It would not be true of race, ethnicity or core culture. Obviously, there were no Gentiles or Samaritans of any kind. But, less obviously, none of the Jews was a *Hellenistic Jew* of the dispersion who might have been raised in Tarsus or Antioch or Pontus. Every one was a *Hebrew Jew* raised in Palestine. Although later on in the fledgling Church all believers were Jews, important differences between Hebrews and Hellenists carried over, as we will clearly see when we come to Acts 6. There we read, "There arose a murmuring against the Hebrews by the Hellenists" (Acts 6:1), showing that even conversion to Christ would not totally erase significant subcultural differences.

Was Jesus a Hillbilly?

But that is not all. No Hebrew Jew of first-century Palestine would have been unaware of the differences between those from Judea to the south as opposed to those from Galilee to the north. Jesus, although born in Bethlehem of Judea and resident for a time in Egypt, was known as a native of Nazareth in Galilee. A common designation for Him was "Jesus of Nazareth." What difference would this make?

I hope I am not interpreted as being irreverent when I report that in those days Galilee was seen much as some Americans see Appalachia in our day. Galileans were commonly regarded as hillbillies by Judeans. If they fit the patterns we are accustomed to, they had their own musical taste, their distinctive foods, their way of life and they spoke Aramaic with a hillbilly accent. They were called *Am ha-aretz*, "people of the land."

Jesus was one of them, and as such, He would have been regarded as culturally challenged by many sophisticated Jerusalemites. Significantly, Jesus selected His inner circle, with one exception, from fellow Galileans. A clear indication that they kept their hillbilly accent occurred when Peter later attempted to deny that he was one of the inner circle, but the people of Jerusalem could not be fooled. They said, "Surely you also are one of them, because your speech betrays you" (Matt. 26:73). Later, those of the Jerusalem Sanhedrin characterized Peter and John as "uneducated and untrained men" (Acts 4:13), not a complimentary remark. None of Jesus' inner circle was a Pharisee, a priest, a scholar or an Essene, although all of them would also have been Hebrew Jews.

The one possible non-Galilean could have been none other than Judas Iscariot. John Broadus points out that "Iscariot" could signify *Ish Kerioth*, Aramaic for "a man of Kerioth." Kerioth was a village in Judea, so Judas may well have been a Judean.[8] It scarcely needs to be mentioned that Judas was the most obvious misfit of the 12.

Who replaced Judas? The two candidates were Matthias, who was another Galilean, and Joseph Barsabas, who was likely a Hellenistic Jew from Cyprus. Matthias, as we know, was selected by casting lots, a method, at that time, apparently regarded as allowing the Holy Spirit to express His will.

So the reorganized 12 still represented a relatively small homogeneous slice of the demographic mix of the day, namely, Galilean Jews.

JESUS MINISTERED TO JEWS

According to E. A. Judge, Jesus' ministry team largely worked with other Aramaic-speaking Jews from the provincial "backwater" of Galilee. Judge says that the area of Galilee was geographically limited and "emotionally the gulf between it and the civilized world was profound. The real division was of course cultural."[9]

When Jesus traveled outside Galilee to Decapolis, a group of Gentile republics, He was declared *persona non grata* even though He had cast a demon out of a man who had been terrorizing the people there. Then an interesting thing happened. The former demoniac was so grateful to Jesus for delivering him that he volunteered his services to his new Master (see Mark 5:18). Some would have expected that Jesus would gladly have received him in order to demonstrate the multicultural nature of the Body of Christ. But Jesus did not allow him to join His band of Galileans and go with them back to Galilee. Rather, He instructed him, "Go home to your friends, and tell them what great things the Lord has done for you" (Mark 5:19). Jesus apparently thought the Gadarene would be more effective doing E-1 evangelism than the E-2 for which he had volunteered.

One of Jesus' more specific statements about the planned scope of His ministry arose in His dialogue with a Gentile Syrophoenician woman who wanted her daughter healed. Jesus graciously healed her daughter, but not until He had made it clear that this would be an exception to His pattern of ministering to Jews. He said, "I was not sent except to the lost sheep of the house of Israel" (Matt. 15:24).

The Gospel of John tells of some Gentiles who had come to Jerusalem to worship Jehovah God and who requested an interview with Jesus. Philip and Andrew related the request to Jesus, but nothing is subsequently said of Jesus ever granting the interview (see John 12:20-22).

It seems that when Jesus had occasion to go to Judea, He frequently stayed in Bethany in the house of His friends Lazarus, Mary and Martha. However, the probability is that they were fellow Galileans who lived in Judea, but who also maintained a second residence in Galilee. For example, some think the well-known incident when Jesus commended Mary for sitting at

His feet occurred in their home in Galilee (see Luke 10:38), not in Judea.

When Jesus first sent out His 12 disciples on their own, He was very specific about the people group they were to seek out for ministry. He said, "Do not go into the way of the Gentiles, and do not enter a city of the Samaritans" (Matt. 10:5). Rather, He instructed them to stick to their own people group, "the lost sheep of the house of Israel" (Matt. 10:6). This clearly was a mandate for E-1 evangelism.

JESUS SO LOVED THE WORLD

None of what I have said should be interpreted to mean that Jesus, the Son of man, was ethnocentric, prejudiced or indifferent to the salvation of non-Jews. He was God, and He loved the whole world. But He was also building a solid nucleus for a movement that would be carried on through centuries to come by human beings, and He was modeling evangelistic strategy for them. He knew that if Christianity were to spread to the whole world, it first must have a firm foundation and that such a foundation could best be established, in His case, among Aramaic-speaking Galilean Jews.

Jesus, on occasion, did cross boundaries. In preparation for His Great Commission to "make disciples of all the nations" (Matt. 28:19), Jesus ministered to a Roman centurion's servant and commended the centurion for his faith, a faith even greater than He had found in Israel (see Matt. 8:5-13). Jesus spent two days in Samaria and demonstrated to His disciples that salvation would also be available for those such as the Samaritan woman and her friends (see John 4:5-43). After the healed Gadarene demoniac had prepared the way, Jesus later went back to Decapolis and fed 4,000 (see Matt. 15:32-39). In a parable, Jesus commended a good Samaritan (see Luke 10:30-37) for crossing a cultural barrier.

These incidents were living demonstrations of the universality of the gospel, but, in actual fact, they were relatively minor episodes on the whole timeline of Jesus' earthly ministry. After each incident, He soon continued His ministry to "the lost sheep of the house of Israel" (Matt. 15:24).

BACK TO JERUSALEM

Jesus ended His ministry, not in Galilee, but in Jerusalem. This brings us into the book of Acts, where we will continue from here on.

It may be that among the 120 Jews who gathered in the Upper Room, several were by then non-Galileans. Barsabas, as we have said, was possibly a Cyprian (see Acts 1:23), and others may also have been non-Galileans. Nevertheless, they were mostly Galileans. How do we know? After Jesus' ascension, two angels appeared and addressed those who had witnessed it as "Men of Galilee" (Acts 1:11). And then, on the Day of Pentecost, part of the amazement of the unbelievers when they heard the gospel being proclaimed in a variety of languages was, "Are not all these who speak Galileans?" (Acts 2:7).

In summary: The reason the 120 in the Upper Room were all Jews was not only that the gospel was to come to "the Jew first." Jesus could have done that by winning 60 Jews and adding another 60 of a multicultural mix of Gentiles and Samaritans. But, instead, He showed us that in order to accomplish His ultimate purpose of making disciples of all nations, a solid foundation needed to be built by using E-1 evangelism within a given people group. That principle is as true today as it was then.

The book of Acts, subsequently, shows how such a committed nucleus can move out in the power of God to break down every possible remaining barrier to world evangelization.

REFLECTION QUESTIONS

1. Discuss the reasons Jesus did not include any non-Jews such as Gentiles or Samaritans in His inner circle or in the 120 disciples He left behind in Jerusalem.
2. Why would the "people approach to world evangelism" be seen by missiologists as the most viable way to plan strategies for world evangelization?
3. Do you agree that God's original design was that the human race would be diversified into many cultural groups and that the incident at the Tower of Babel mainly served to accelerate this process?
4. Discuss the differences between Hebrew Jews and Hellenistic Jews. Then discuss the difference between Judean Hebrews and Galilean Hebrews. Why would God have decided to become a Galilean in His incarnation?
5. Give some biblical illustrations to show that Jesus desired that the gospel eventually would be spread among the world's non-Jews.

3

HISTORY'S MOST POWERFUL PRAYER MEETING

ACTS 1
Bridging from Luke's Gospel to Acts

[1] *The former account I made, O Theophilus, of all that Jesus began both to do and teach,* [2] *until the day in which He was taken up, after He through the Holy Spirit had given commandments to the apostles whom He had chosen.*

I have already explained how we know that Luke is the author of Acts, which, along with Luke's Gospel, comprises a two-volume account of the origins and expansions of the Christian movement. Acts continues what Jesus began. It is true that the book of Acts describes the work of the Holy Spirit, but keep in mind that all this is the outworking of Jesus' foundational ministry. In reality, we could say that we are looking at Phase One and Phase Two of the same mission.

In summarizing his Gospel, Luke mentions that it covers the things Jesus began "both to do and teach." Here, two things are particularly significant.

DOING AND TEACHING GO TOGETHER

When Jesus walked with the two disciples on the road to Emmaus after His resurrection, He asked them what they were talking about. They responded, "The things concerning Jesus of Nazareth, who was a Prophet mighty *in deed and word* before God and all the people" (Luke 24:19). Some people are attracted by philosophers whose ideas are so fascinating that applying their ideas to practical, everyday life is not particularly significant. Other people are attracted by flamboyant wonder-workers, or self-flagellating ascetics, who are not capable of undergirding their lifestyle with sensible explanations of their behavior. Jesus was neither of the above. He preached what He practiced, and He practiced what He preached.

DOING COMES BEFORE TEACHING

I do not think it is an accident that in both Acts and his Gospel, Luke puts practicing before preaching, doing before teaching, deed before word. Whereas some theologians attempt to argue that sound theology must precede fruitful ministry, the opposite is usually the case. It is significant that Jesus never wrote a theology, although His teachings were saturated with theologically significant truths that theologians continue to analyze almost 2,000 years later. Of all the New Testament books, the one that comes closest to a theology is the Epistle to the Romans, which Paul wrote 30 years after gospel preaching began.

The Protestant Reformation was implemented in practice before Luther and Calvin, to say nothing of Kuyper and Barth and Henry and Grudem, who came much later, attempted to systematize its theology. When William Carey decided to go to India as a missionary, he received no encouragement from the recognized theologians of the day. Subsequently, however, excellent, theologically informed missiology has emerged from the modern missionary movement that Carey initiated by taking a risk and moving out in practical ministry. Ministry usually precedes theology.

Even in the world of rapid change in which we now live, it is not unusual for theology to find itself about 10 years behind practice. For example, I was deeply involved with John Wimber through the early and mid-eighties, introducing the signs and wonders movement into mainstream evangelicalism. Thinking back, I realize that I could not have written my book *How to Have a Healing Ministry in Any Church* until I had personally participated in healing ministries for several years. Furthermore, few will consider my book a *theology* of signs and wonders. True, some important, theologically informed books by authors such as Ken Blue[1] and Don Williams[2] were written in the early years. But the more mature theological works, such as Jack Deere's *Surprised by the Power of the Spirit* and Gary Greig and Kevin Springer's *The Kingdom and the Power*, were not published until 1993, more than 10 years after the ministry itself began to spread.

One of the few credentialed theologians who frankly recognizes that deed comes before word is Ray Anderson of Fuller Theological Seminary. His somewhat radical thesis is that "ministry precedes and produces theology, not the reverse." Anderson says that Jesus' "ministry was to do the will of the Father and . . . out of this ministry emerges theological activity."[3]

By this, I do not mean to imply that the theology is incidental or unnecessary. Far from it. Now that sound theologies of signs and wonders and other power ministries are emerging, ministries characterized by supernatural manifestations of the power of the Holy Spirit will spread throughout the Body of Christ even more rapidly and with more integrity than they have previously. My only point is that in this case, as in the life of Jesus, deed usually precedes word.

JESUS USED HOLY SPIRIT POWER

[2] . . . *after He through the Holy Spirit* . . .

How could it be that Jesus would have said to His disciples, "He who believes in Me, the works that I do he will do also; and greater works than these will he do, because I go to My Father" (John 14:12)? The reason certainly cannot be that Jesus will make those of us who follow Him into gods with divine natures such as Jesus had. A much more plausible reason would be that we, as human beings, will have access to the same source of supernatural power that Jesus had, namely, the Holy Spirit.

It is very helpful to understand this before we come to the words of Jesus later in this chapter: "But you shall receive power when the Holy Spirit has come upon you" (Acts 1:8). As we move through Acts, we will see that such was actually the case: Jesus' followers duplicated the power ministries He demonstrated and even did some things that Jesus Himself did not do.

As the Second Person of the Trinity, Jesus was the only individual who ever existed as 100 percent God and 100 percent human. The doctrine of the two natures of Christ is one of biblical Christianity's theological nonnegotiables. Although Jesus was, therefore, never without all the attributes of God, He voluntarily gave up the *use* of these attributes during His incarnation–living, ministering and even thinking with His human nature only. How, then, did He do all the supernatural works and exhibit divine knowledge? It is very simple. He did them "through the Holy Spirit," as Luke indicates in this passage.

This is why Fuller Seminary theologian Colin Brown has coined the term "Spirit Christology." He says, "Jesus' miracles are given a prominent place, but they are not attributed to Jesus as the Second Person of the

Trinity. They are not presented as manifestations of His personal divinity."[4] Thomas A. Smail is also very specific: "If His miracles had nothing to do with His humanity, if divine power was not communicated to His human nature as a charismatic gift, then obviously that power has nothing to do with our humanity either."[5] But a key to understanding the book of Acts, and using it as a training manual for ministry today, is recognizing that the power of the Holy Spirit that operated in Jesus also operated in the apostles and it can and should operate in us as well.

I am fully aware that theologians continue to debate this point, and that here I am giving it an extremely short treatment. Those who wish to know more about my point of view on this can find a complete argument in my book *How to Have a Healing Ministry in Any Church.* But to make one more point, consider Peter's words later in Acts: "God anointed Jesus of Nazareth with the Holy Spirit and with power, who went about doing good and healing all who were oppressed by the devil, for God was with Him" (Acts 10:38). Because God is the source of all power, there is no way that He, *as God*, could have any reason to be anointed, ever. God needs absolutely nothing outside of Himself to do anything at all. It is clear, then, that the reference to Jesus' receiving the anointing of the Holy Spirit and power cannot possibly refer to His divine nature, and, therefore, the anointing must have been performed only on His human nature. It was Jesus' human nature, "through the Holy Spirit," that conducted His ministry, as our text affirms.

THINGS PERTAINING TO THE KINGDOM

[3] ***To whom He also presented Himself alive after His suffering by many infallible proofs, being seen by them during forty days and speaking of the things pertaining to the kingdom of God.***

Between His resurrection and His ascension, Jesus spent about six weeks with His disciples. His topic was the kingdom of God. As I explained in chapter 1, an understanding of the kingdom of God provides a solid theological framework to apply what we learn from the ministry of Jesus, and from the subsequent Acts of the Apostles, to our own churches and communities today.

The most concrete, lasting form of ministry in Acts is church planting. Preaching the gospel, healing the sick, casting out demons, suffering persecution, holding church councils, and the multiple other activities of the apostles and other Christians that unfold before us have, as their goal, multiplying Christian churches throughout the known world. Related to His teaching of the kingdom, I would surmise that Jesus often repeated His purpose statement: "I will build My church" (Matt. 16:18). He had reserved disclosing this to His disciples until in Caesarea Philippi they had finally understood, "You are the Christ, the Son of the living God" (Matt. 16:16). That means that they publicly recognized Him as the Messiah. His resurrection later confirmed forever by "infallible proofs" that Jesus was the true Messiah for whom the Jews had waited for centuries.

For Jesus, the kingdom of God had come, although the kingdom should not be overly identified with the Church. Over the years, many institutional forms of the Christian Church have evolved that are far from what Jesus had in mind as He was instructing His disciples. Without naming names, it is a fact that all too much of what is known as Christianity is actively promulgating both deeds and words that are quite different from what we know of the kingdom of God, and not a reflection of God's will in the world today. Such so-called "churches" are not to be identified with the kingdom of God. But, at the same time, multitudes of churches in many parts of the world, however imperfectly, do accurately reflect the glory of God through Jesus Christ and, as such, can be considered visible outposts of the kingdom of God.

Churches that adhere to biblical standards are not the ultimate, but they are still the most tangible, manifestations we have today of answers to our prayer, "Your kingdom come. Your will be done on earth as it is in heaven" (Matt. 6:10). Our ultimate assignment from God is to retake the dominion over creation that the first Adam lost but the Second Adam came to restore. Meanwhile, believers redeemed by the blood of Jesus Christ, who meet together to worship and praise God on a regular basis, and who minister to others, doing good in Jesus' name, legitimately represent the Kingdom here in this world.

THE PROMISE OF THE FATHER

[4] *And being assembled together with them, He commanded them not to depart from Jerusalem, but to wait for the Promise of the Father, "which," He said, "you have heard from Me."*

Soon after His resurrection, Jesus told His disciples to wait in Jerusalem, as Luke records in his Gospel: "Behold, I send the Promise of My Father upon you; but tarry in the city of Jerusalem until you are endued with power from on high" (Luke 24:49). This was quite an unusual thing. Here were the disciples who had been with Jesus personally for three years. He had thoroughly instructed them through both deed and word in theology, in ethics, in worship, in healing the sick, in casting out demons and in other forms of ministry. He had sent them out on their own for supervised field experience. And yet, this superb training apparently had not fully equipped them for the task Jesus had set before them. Knowing the right thing to do is not enough. Supernatural power is necessary for God's purposes to be fulfilled.

It is easy to get caught up in techniques and methodology, especially when they have produced positive results in the past, such as Jesus' ministry had. The church growth movement, of which I am a part, began to succumb to this tendency toward the end of the 1970s when the movement was around 25 years old. At that time, some of our critics began to complain that we had begun to rely on human technology instead of spiritual power. They were right. The dangers of such a trap are obvious. The kingdom of God cannot successfully invade the kingdom of Satan by human ingenuity and sound missiological principles alone, but only by being "endued with power from on high." Many of us listened to our critics and humbly asked God to correct us, which He has been doing since the beginning of the 1980s.

As God began to change us, He stretched us beyond some of our comfort zones. Many of us had reacted strongly against the Pentecostal movement, for example, saying that what we considered their excesses had taken them far beyond the boundaries of respectable, biblical Christianity. Among other things, we had convinced ourselves that Pentecostals were hyperemotional and uneducated. We scarcely stopped to realize that the Pharisees entertained a similar attitude toward Jesus and His apostles, whom they regarded as uneducated Galilean hillbillies. So, like the Pharisees, we had developed protective, sophisticated theologies, including modern cessationist dispensationalism. Regrettably, I, along with fellow seminary professors, such as Charles Kraft and Jack Deere, had convinced myself and, therefore, many of my students that gifts manifesting supernatural power, such as healings and prophecies and tongues and deliverance, had ceased at the end of the First Apostolic Age.

But God had other things in store for us, and the three of us, along with increasing numbers of traditional evangelicals, subsequently experienced paradigm shifts that have allowed us to begin to understand "the Promise of the Father." Charles Kraft, Jack Deere and I initially began to shift our paradigms through seeing power ministry firsthand from John Wimber, and then attempting to practice it ourselves. You can read about these experiences in our books *Christianity with Power* (Charles H. Kraft) and *How to Have a Healing Ministry in Any Church* (C. Peter Wagner). Jack Deere explains how he changed his point of view, primarily by seriously restudying the Scriptures, in his book *Surprised by the Power of the Spirit.*

I mention these because they represent a widespread trend in the Body of Christ. Although some Christian leaders are still reluctant, the general worldwide trend is toward power ministries, not toward cessationism. Power ministries, and how they should be applied, constitute a crucial theme throughout the book of Acts, as I have mentioned. Unfortunately, almost all of the previous 1,398 commentaries on Acts assume the cessationist point of view.

My parallel theme in interpreting Acts is missiology, by which I mean the more technological and methodological sides of evangelism and church planting. By putting all the stress here on "the Promise of the Father," I do not want to leave the impression that we are to choose between power on the one hand and sound missiological technology on the other. I believe the two must go together like the two wings on a bird. Neither technology nor power *by itself* will effectively fulfill Jesus' Great Commission. We will see multiple examples of this as we continue through the book of Acts.

TARRY—BUT NOT FOREVER

[4] . . . ***wait for the Promise of the Father.***

The disciples never could have become dynamic instruments for the extension of the kingdom of God if they had not obeyed Jesus' command to "wait for the Promise of the Father" or to "tarry . . . until you are endued with power from on high" (Luke 24:49). It is notable that the tarrying took all of 10 days, no longer.

In Christian service, there is a delicate balance between spending time with the Father in worship, praise and intimacy, and in obeying the Father's commands in ministry and outreach. The Upper Room, where the disciples spent a good part of the 10 days, appears to be a place of peace, quiet and security. Undoubtedly, the Holy Spirit was present there in an unusual way. Much time would have been spent in looking back and thanking Jesus for all that His life and ministry had meant to them.

Times such as these, in warm fellowship with other believers in the presence of God, are precious. Through prayer, we are drawn into a close and fulfilling relationship with the Father. I can imagine that in the Upper Room the disciples were discovering "who we are in Christ." Much time, undoubtedly, was spent in worship and praise, pouring out their souls to an audience of One. They could have been telling each other that it was a special time of God receiving them as they *are*, not evaluating them by what they *do*. It must have seemed to them a foretaste of heaven where one day we will all be around God's throne, worshiping Him and exalting His name.

All that for 10 days. But suddenly the "until" took effect and they received the power they had been waiting for. From that time on, it was action, ministry and the practical application of the power they had received. Within 24 hours, they had produced 3,000 unpolished disciples of Christ who needed care and nurture in their Christian faith. And the action sparked that day continued for the 30-year span of the book of Acts, having notable pauses, such as the apostles' desire to "give ourselves continually to prayer and to the ministry of the word" (Acts 6:4); but pauses they were.

Now, nothing is particularly significant in a period of 10 days. The apostle Paul, who had not been with Jesus while He was in the flesh, needed several years as his tarrying time before God launched him into active ministry. But the point is, we must not succumb to the temptation to allow the time spent in preministry spiritual formation to extend indefinitely. God, I know, does call some to a lifetime of Upper Room-style service to Himself, particularly some of those to whom He has given the spiritual gift of intercession. But these probably would not comprise more than 5 percent of the Body of Christ, as I explain in my book *Your Spiritual Gifts Can Help Your Church Grow*. I thank God for these intercessors and feel privileged to know some personally and count them as personal intercessors for my wife, Doris, and me. They may be relatively few, but they are as important to the Body of Christ as the tiny pituitary gland is to the whole human body.

My concern is for many among the other 95 percent who have fallen into a rut and become what I have heard Doris call "professional tarriers." The tarrying is not optional; it is necessary. If we do not have the intimacy with God, we will not have the power. It is as necessary as food is to the human body. But tarrying, like food, can be overdone. Physical obesity can prevent our bodies from being all that God intends them to be. And spiritual obesity can have similar outcomes. If we do not ever get out of the Upper Room and into the marketplace in Jerusalem and elsewhere, God's plans will thereby be stalled. The subtitle of Chuck Pierce and John Dickson's remarkable book, *The Worship Warrior*, says it all: *Ascending in Worship; Descending in War.*

POWER AND MISSION

[5] . . . *for John truly baptized with water, but you shall be baptized with the Holy Spirit not many days from now.* [6] *Therefore, when they had come together, they asked Him, saying, "Lord, will You at this time restore the kingdom to Israel?"* [7] *And He said to them, "It is not for you to know times or seasons which the Father has put in His own authority.* [8] *But you shall receive power when the Holy Spirit has come upon you; and you shall be witnesses to Me in Jerusalem, and in all Judea and Samaria, and to the end of the earth."*

[6] . . . *will You at this time restore the kingdom to Israel?*

Even after Jesus' death and resurrection, the disciples had not yet fully comprehended the nature of the kingdom of God. John Stott says it well: "Their question must have filled Jesus with dismay. Were they still so lacking in perception? . . . the verb *restore* shows they were expecting a political and territorial kingdom; the noun *Israel* that they were expecting a national kingdom; and the adverbial clause *at this time* that they were expecting its immediate establishment."[6]

Jesus had taught His disciples to pray that His kingdom would come and that His will would be done on Earth as it is in heaven. The disciples had not yet sorted out their desire that Jesus would break the political yoke of Rome from the long-range task of the people of God using spiritual weapons to push back the forces of evil and take back the dominion over creation that Adam forfeited to Satan in the Garden of Eden.

THE BAPTISM OF THE HOLY SPIRIT

[5] . . . *you shall be baptized with the Holy Spirit . . .*

The spiritual power for advancing the Kingdom would come through the baptism of the Holy Spirit. Unfortunately, differences of understanding about what is meant by the baptism of the Holy Spirit have been used by the enemy to separate segments of the Body of Christ for more than 100 years. I am glad to report, however, that most differences are rapidly disappearing from the scene, although it may be some time before they are entirely gone, if ever.

Because of this encouraging trend, I do not regard it necessary to analyze the debate about the baptism of the Holy Spirit in any depth. Suffice it to say, sincere believers on all sides are seeking the same thing, namely, the unobstructed power of the Holy Spirit in their lives and ministries. I realize that it is more than a semantic issue; nevertheless, a brief look at semantics may help cool the remaining fires of debate somewhat.

Three separate terms are used for the power-bestowing event Luke is describing here:

- baptized with the Holy Spirit
- the Holy Spirit has come upon you
- filled with the Holy Spirit (2:4)

The verb "baptized" in reference to the Holy Spirit is used only one more time in Acts, namely, when Peter explains that what happened in the house of Cornelius was a fulfillment of Jesus' saying, "John indeed baptized with water, but you shall be baptized with the Holy Spirit" (Acts 11:16).

The verb "filled" with the Holy Spirit is used four other times in Acts. It is used a second time for Peter, who was "filled with the Holy Spirit" (Acts 4:8); the believers were again "filled with the Holy Spirit" when they assembled for a prayer meeting (Acts 4:31); Ananias ministered to Saul to be "filled with the Holy Spirit" in Damascus (Acts 9:17); and Paul again was "filled with the Holy Spirit" for his power encounter with Bar-Jesus the sorcerer (Acts 13:9).

The expression "filled with the Holy Spirit" is used only once in the Epistles, when Paul contrasts it to being "drunk with wine" (Eph. 5:18). And, finally, Paul uses "baptized" only once in his Epistles, when he said, "By one Spirit we were all baptized into one body" (1 Cor. 12:13).

Issues such as whether we are baptized or filled with the Spirit once or many times; whether it occurs at conversion or subsequent to conversion; or whether there is initial physical evidence to certify that it has happened are more important to some Christian leaders today than to others. But the reason the issues are raised is a good one: *We need to receive the supernatural power of the Holy Spirit in our lives and our ministries, to the greatest extent possible, in order to serve God well in our world.* All will agree on this.

RECEIVING THE POWER FOR WITNESSING

[8] . . . *you shall receive power . . . and you shall be witnesses to Me . . .*

Acts 1:8 is the fifth appearance of Jesus' Great Commission, following Matthew, "Make disciples of all the nations" (28:19); Mark, "Preach the gospel to every creature" (16:15); Luke, "Repentance and remission of sins should be preached in His name to all nations" (24:47); and John, "As the Father has sent Me, I also send you" (20:21). Four of the five, John being the exception, specify the international, global scope of the evangelistic task mandated by Jesus.

On another occasion, Jesus said, "And this gospel of the kingdom will be preached in all the world as a witness to all the nations, and then the end will come" (Matt. 24:14). This seems to indicate that world evangelization and establishing the kingdom is not an endless task, but that it is on a divine timeline. A central methodology is to plant the outposts of the kingdom of God, which are principally Christian churches, in every nation or *ethnos*. Today we would say in every "people group."

As I am writing this, missiologists are suggesting for the first time in Christian history that there appears to be light at the end of the Great Commission tunnel! For the first time, there seems to be good reason to believe that the Body of Christ now has the human resources, the material resources and the spiritual resources to complete the task.

Satan's territory has been shrinking steadily over the centuries since the Acts of the Apostles, but never as rapidly as it has in the last few decades. Missiologist George Otis, Jr. says it as well as any: "The soldiers of the Lord of hosts have now encircled the final strongholds of the serpent–the nations and spiritual principalities of the 10/40 Window. While the remaining task is admittedly the most challenging phase of the battle, the armies of Lucifer are faced presently with a community of believers whose spiritual resources–if properly motivated, submitted and unified–are truly awesome."[7]

THE KEYS TO THE KINGDOM

Strategic-level spiritual warfare is one expression of the power given by the Holy Spirit that has been spreading rapidly on all continents over the past few years. As I mentioned in the first chapter, it deals with confronting the principalities and powers described by Paul in Ephesians 6:12. Strategic-level spiritual warfare is significantly different from ground-level spiritual warfare (casting out demons from individuals) and occult-level spiritual warfare (dealing with witches, curses, Eastern religions, New Age channelers and the like). A substantial body of literature has been forthcoming in this relatively new field.[8]

In all probability, part of Jesus' teaching of "things pertaining to the kingdom of God" during the 40 days He was with His disciples had to do with the keys of the Kingdom, mentioned in Matthew 16:19. The keys, directly related to evangelism ("I will build My church"), contain the power to bind and loose.

Jesus speaks of "binding and loosing" in Matthew 12:29, but a clearer picture of what this involves is found in Luke 11, the parallel passage. Referring to Beelzebub, a principality that ranks somewhere near the top of the hierarchy of evil, Jesus says, "When a strong man, fully armed, guards his own palace, his goods are in peace" (Luke 11:21). Obviously, the most prized possession of a ranking principality is unsaved souls. The evangelistic implication is that if the principality's armor remains intact, lost souls will not be saved.

However, it is possible that "a stronger than he comes upon him and overcomes him" (Luke 11:22). When this happens, his armor is ineffective and his spoils, the unsaved souls, can be divided. I take this to mean that overcoming or binding the strongman does not save souls, but it does free them to hear the gospel and make their own decisions about whether to follow Jesus Christ.

Two things are very important here:

1. The word "overcome" (*nikao*) in Luke 11:22 is a parallel expression to "bind" (*deo*) in Matthew 12:29. This indicates that we have here a direct application of the use of the keys of the Kingdom, "Whatever you bind on earth will be bound in heaven" (Matt. 16:19), with presumed evangelistic results.

2. The "stronger than he" cannot be a human being, but it must refer to the "finger of God," or the Holy Spirit, that Jesus said He relied upon to cast a demon out of a mute man in the same passage (see Luke 11:20). But where is the Holy Spirit? He is now in believers who have been filled with the Holy Spirit. This power from the Holy Spirit has a direct relationship to Jesus' ascension. Let's look at it.

ARE WE BETTER OFF WITHOUT JESUS?

[9] *Now when He had spoken these things, while they watched, He was taken up, and a cloud received Him out of their sight.*

This event, called the Ascension, officially ended Jesus' incarnation and His first coming to Earth. He will not appear in person to the world again until His second coming.

During His lifetime, particularly near the end, Jesus attempted as best as He could to prepare His disciples for His leaving them. They loved Him so much, it was not easy for them to accept that He would go away and leave them alone. Peter at one point was so upset that he rebuked Jesus and said, "Far be it from You, Lord; this shall not happen to You!" (Matt. 16:22). But Jesus sharply reprimanded him and said, "Get behind Me, Satan! You are an offense to Me" (Matt. 16:23).

Later, Jesus calmly explained to them, "It is to your *advantage* that I go away" (John 16:7). How could this be? How could anything be an advantage over being with Jesus personally? Very simple. Jesus told them that if He went away, only then could He send the Comforter, the Holy Spirit, who would be with them from then on. In other words, for the purposes of carrying out the task of advancing the kingdom of God, the immediate presence of the Third Person of the Trinity is more helpful than the immediate presence of the Second Person of the Trinity.

One of the advantages of having the Holy Spirit would be that they would have access to the only power source capable of binding or overcoming the strongmen who are out there keeping entire people groups in spiritual darkness.

For the most part, the disciples were ready for Jesus' exit, and by then they had understood it fairly well. Still, they were somewhat stupefied when He actually ascended into heaven from the Mount of Olives. They stared into the clouds so long that two angels had to come to move them along:

[11] *Who also said, "Men of Galilee, why do you stand gazing up into heaven? This same Jesus, who was taken up from you into heaven, will so come in like manner as you saw Him go into heaven."*

This brought the disciples back to their senses, and they went back to Jerusalem, where they joined history's most powerful prayer meeting.

HISTORY'S MOST POWERFUL PRAYER MEETING

[12] *Then they returned to Jerusalem from the Mount called Olivet, which is near Jerusalem, a Sabbath day's journey.* [13] *And when they had entered, they went up into the upper room where they were staying. . . .* [14] *These all continued with one accord in prayer and supplication, with the women and Mary the mother of Jesus, and with His brothers.* [15] . . . *(altogether the number of names was about a hundred and twenty).*

We need to go back to Luke's Gospel to get the whole picture. In Acts, we see that the disciples were meeting for prayer in the Upper Room; but during these 10 days, they also "were continually in the temple praising and blessing God" (Luke 24:53). This combination of praise and worship with sincere prayer and supplication is an unbeatable formula for drawing near to God, opening ourselves to the fullness of the Holy Spirit and hearing the voice of the Father.

Ten days in prayer is a very long prayer meeting. Most of us, including myself, would have a hard time trying to block out 10 straight days for worship and prayer. As I have been participating in coordinating the worldwide prayer movement, however, I have come into contact with some who are actually doing such things. A recent two-week event for prayer only was held in Australia, for example. In Kansas City, Mike Bickel's International House of Prayer (IHOP) has been able to sustain 24/7 prayer for years. Some, particularly orders of nuns, cloister themselves for a lifetime of prayer. Pastoral prayer summits of three or four days each have been popular in many cities of the United States and elsewhere, and Christian leaders who participated in them regarded having done it as a fairly heroic spiritual accomplishment. But we are not looking at three or four days in the Jerusalem Upper Room; we are looking at 10 days.

The agenda of the prayer meeting had been set by the Lord: "Tarry . . . until you are endued with power from on high" (Luke 24:49). They were regrouping to begin the process of advancing the kingdom of God, and they knew from the outset that the task was one that required extraordinary spiritual power. There is no indication that they knew up front that the prayer meeting would last for ten days. They only knew that it was "not many days from now" (Acts 1:5), so they settled in for the long haul. They engaged in *persistent* prayer, and they were prepared to pray the process through until they knew beyond the shadow of doubt that God had responded.

Would God have responded if they had decided to take a break, after all the stress and strain they had been through, and lay out on the beach at Joppa for a few days? This is not a superficial question, because it raises the issue of whether prayer has anything to do with God's actions. I personally believe that if the disciples had vacationed in Joppa or gone fishing in the Sea of Galilee instead of spending their time in the Temple and in the Upper Room, Pentecost, as we know it, would not have come as it did.

I realize that some who hold a very high view of God's sovereignty might say that prayer doesn't change God; it only changes us. And there is a great deal of theological validity in that. God is infinite, eternal. His nature cannot be changed. And certainly the time in the Upper Room worked a deep and significant change in the disciples themselves. But our sovereign God many times has said things such as, "Call to Me, and I will answer you, and show you great and mighty things, which you do not know" (Jer. 33:3). This sounds very much as though God, in His sovereign wisdom, has so arranged reality that, although He might *desire* to do some things, He *will not* do them unless, and until, Christian people are obedient and faithful in their prayer lives. The whole world has been ultimately blessed because the disciples in Jerusalem decided to be obedient to their Lord and give themselves to persistent prayer.

Not only were the disciples persistent and obedient, but they were also unified. They "continued with one accord." One reason corporate prayer is often more effective than solitary prayer is the principle of agreement. Jesus said, "If two of you agree on earth concerning anything that they ask, it will be done for them by My Father in heaven" (Matt. 18:19). The prayer of one person alone is certainly not wasted, but the prayer of two in agreement is better, and presumably the prayer of 120 in agreement is better yet.

In practice, prayer evangelism efforts for cities, if they are to have any lasting effect, must begin with the visible unity of the Christian leaders, especially the pastors, in prayer. This is so difficult to accomplish that it has become widely recognized as a prime target used by the enemy to prevent the kingdom of God from coming to a given city in any significant and tangible way. Keeping Christian leaders apart from each other is one of Satan's most blatant devices.

Knowing the devices of Satan, we can thereby prevent him from taking advantage of us, as Paul says in 2 Corinthians 2:11.

THE WIDER NUCLEUS OF BELIEVERS

[14] . . . with the women and Mary the mother of Jesus, and with His brothers. [26] . . . and the lot fell on Matthias. And he was numbered with the eleven apostles.

The women disciples of Jesus do not first enter the picture here, but they are seen as a key component of His ministry team throughout. Who were they? We do not know the names of many of them, but some we do know. "And certain women who had been healed of evil spirits and infirmities–Mary called Magdalene, out of whom had come seven demons, and Joanna the wife of Chuza, Herod's steward, and Susanna, and many others who provided for Him from their substance" (Luke 8:2-3). Among other things, these faithful women covered what was probably a substantial part of Jesus' ministry expenses.

Jesus' mother, Mary, was also there, and this is the last time she appears in Scripture. There is some debate, particularly from Roman Catholic theologians who hold to the doctrine of the perpetual virginity of Mary, whether Jesus' "brothers" were blood brothers. Most interpreters, however, take the Greek word *adelphoi* to mean natural children of Mary and Joseph. His brothers did not believe in Jesus during His ministry time, as we read in John 7:5, although by the Day of Pentecost they had become disciples. They are identified by name in Mark 6:3: "Is this not the carpenter, the Son of Mary, and brother of James, Joses, Judas, and Simon?"

It will be important for us later on to recognize here that those among the 12 apostles named James, Judas, Simon (Peter), and Simon the Zealot were different people; they were not from Jesus' own family. Later on, however, we find that one named "James" becomes the leader of the Jerusalem church. This is not the original apostle James, but James the brother of Jesus, who also writes the Epistle of James.

The leadership of the initial nucleus of believers was brought once again up to 12 apostles when Matthias was chosen to replace Judas. Some, for a variety of reasons, feel that this could have been a precipitous decision taken under the pressure of one of Peter's well-known impulses. But it seems to me that if their 10 days of praise, worship, prayer and supplication were all they appear to be, the disciples would have been closely enough in touch with the Father to have known His will for Matthias.

More than anything else, however, it was the dramatic answer to prayer, which we see in the next chapter, that qualifies this as "history's most powerful prayer meeting."

REFLECTION QUESTIONS

1. Do you think it makes sense to say that theology emerges from ministry and not the other way around? Why?
2. Discuss the concept that Jesus ministered on Earth through His human nature by the power of the Holy Spirit. Does that mean He was not God during His incarnation?
3. Can you name others who have shifted their paradigms toward accepting supernatural signs and wonders in ways similar to Charles Kraft or Jack Deere or Peter Wagner?
4. Do you share the concern that some Christians tend to be "professional tarriers" and spend a disproportionate amount of their time and energy enjoying their personal relationship to God while scarcely getting around to moving out and sharing God's love with others?
5. What is your personal view of the "baptism of the Holy Spirit"? How does this relate to being "filled with the Holy Spirit"?

4

THE SPIRITUAL EXPLOSION AT PENTECOST

ACTS 2
The Holy Spirit Comes in Power

[1] *Now when the Day of Pentecost had fully come, they were all with one accord in one place.* [2] *And suddenly there came a sound from heaven, as of a rushing mighty wind, and it filled the whole house where they were sitting.* [3] *Then there appeared to them divided tongues, as of fire, and one sat upon each of them.*
[4] *And they were all filled with the Holy Spirit and began to speak with other tongues, as the Spirit gave them utterance.*

PENTECOST—THE HARVEST FESTIVAL

[1] *Now when the Day of Pentecost had fully come.*

"Pentecost" is the Greek word for "fiftieth." It marked the annual Jewish festival scheduled for 50 days after the Passover. It was called the Feast of Weeks, but also the Feast of Harvest, because on that day Jewish people presented to the Lord the firstfruits of the annual wheat harvest (see Exod. 34:22).

Was it a coincidence that the Holy Spirit would bring the power the disciples needed for being witnesses to Jesus in Jerusalem, Judea, Samaria and to the uttermost parts of the earth precisely on the day designated for Jews to lift their thanks to Jehovah God for the harvest? Possibly so, possibly a divine coincidence.

The disciples were about to begin reaping a harvest of souls that has continued now for almost 2,000 years. Jesus had said to His disciples, "Behold, I say to you, lift up your eyes and look at the fields, for they are already white for harvest! And he who reaps receives wages, and gathers fruit for eternal life" (John 4:35-36). Jesus had also said, "The harvest truly is plentiful, but the laborers are few. Therefore pray the Lord of the harvest to send out laborers into His harvest" (Matt. 9:37-38).

What is it that the disciples were praying for "with one accord in one place"? They were praying for the Holy Spirit to come upon them and impart to them the power needed for carrying the gospel of the kingdom across all conceivable barriers. They were praying that God would send them forth as laborers into the harvest fields of the day.

It is good missionary strategy to develop what Donald McGavran calls "a theology of harvest." McGavran is impatient with missionaries and evangelists who are satisfied with *searching* for the lost with little or no regard for how many are ultimately *found*. Too many Christian workers have seen such little fruit for their labors that, McGavran says, they "had to find a rationale for existence and continuance that did not depend on numbers or converts." They would say, "Results should not be used to evaluate success or failure."[1]

Fortunately, the disciples in the Upper Room knew nothing of such a "search theology." They were praying for something much more positive. They knew that Jesus had come to save the lost, and they knew that God's intent was, as McGavran so forcefully puts it, "to marshal, discipline, strengthen, and multiply His churches until all people on earth have had the chance to hear the gospel from their own kindred, who speak their own language and whose word is unobstructed by cultural barriers."[2] This is a theology of harvest that was as valid then as it is now.

VISIBLE SIGNS OF THE INVISIBLE SPIRIT

Presumably, all 120 were together in some house when their prayers were finally answered and the Holy Spirit came. We are not sure whether the house was the Upper Room or perhaps some other facility in the Temple grounds, because they were spending time daily in each place. Because of the large space that would have been needed to accommodate the crowd that gathered, it was most likely a structure connected with the Temple.

Again, "they were all with one accord"—a significant phrase, in my opinion, repeated from Acts 1:14 to remind us of the need for spiritual agreement in prayer as a prerequisite for receiving optimum spiritual power.

When the Holy Spirit came, there was no room for doubt that it was a unique occasion. Nothing like this had happened when Jesus, the Second Person of the Trinity, was on Earth with His disciples. God showed them clearly what He meant when He said that it would be to their *advantage* to have the Holy Spirit with them instead of the Son. Three tangible signs indicated that the Holy Spirit had come:

[2] ***And suddenly there came a sound from heaven, as of a rushing mighty wind . . .***

The sound must have been tremendous. Those who live in areas that do not experience windstorms or tornadoes or hurricanes may not appreciate the volume of sound that comes from strong winds. There was no indication that an unusual meteorological wind was actually blowing at the time. But we should not miss the possible significance of wind (even if only its sound) being used as an analogy for the Holy Spirit, as in John 3:8: "The wind blows where it wishes, . . . So is everyone who is born of the Spirit." The sound apparently was public and external, not just some inner phenomenon of group psychology that only the believers experienced. It was loud enough, unusual enough and probably terrifying enough so that people who were in the Temple area of Jerusalem, or from other parts of the city as well, were drawn toward it to see what strange thing might be happening (see Acts 2:6). In our day, it would have made the 6:00 P.M. news.

[3] ***. . . there appeared to them divided tongues, as of fire, and one sat upon each of them.***

The first tangible sign was audible; the second was visual. At presumably the same time they heard the sound of wind, the disciples actually saw 120 separate fires shaped like tongues resting on each of them. At that moment, few would have had to be reminded of John the Baptist's prophecy concerning Jesus: "He will baptize you with the Holy Spirit and with fire" (Luke 3:16).

Those who were familiar with the Old Testament knew well how fire was often used by God to give tangible evidence of His power, His presence and His holiness. The climax of the great power encounter between Elijah and the priests of Baal was fire: "The fire of the Lord fell and consumed the burnt sacrifice, and the wood and the stones and the dust, and it licked up the water that was in the trench" (1 Kings 18:38). Moses experienced God's presence in the burning bush (see Exod. 3:2), and Isaiah's lips were touched with a burning coal of holiness from the altar (see Isa. 6:6-7). Nothing could be more indicative of the need for each person who is to be used by God for world evangelization to experience His power, live in His presence and be characterized by His holiness. These were all included in "the Promise of the Father" (Acts: 1:4).

[4] *And they . . . began to speak with other tongues . . .*

The third tangible sign was oral. Few things could be more surprising to human beings than suddenly speaking in a language they had not learned. When the Holy Spirit came, the disciples immediately experienced the first fulfillment of Jesus' prophetic word to them: "Most assuredly, I say to you, he who believes in Me, the works that I do he will do also; and greater works than these he will do, because I go to My Father" (John 14:12).

Some have trouble with the "greater works" part of this promise. They ask how anyone could do greater works than Jesus Christ. The answer lies in the fact, as I have previously explained, that the power by which Jesus did His works was the Holy Spirit, and that the power through which Jesus' disciples did their works is the same Holy Spirit, who is God Himself and who can do works of any magnitude at any time He wishes. If we relied on human power to do our works, none of us could even approach any of Jesus' works. But our works can be done with superhuman power, provided by God Himself.

To me it is notable that the first miracle recorded after Jesus' ascension is a work that, as far as we know, the Holy Spirit never did through Jesus. Jesus never spoke in a language He didn't learn. But the disciples did. In fact, among them, they spoke in at least 15 other tongues and were understood by those who spoke them as their native languages. Whether this is a *greater* work can be debated. But at the very least, it was vastly *different* from anything that had happened before.

In my international travels, I hear from time to time how this miracle is occurring today. For some time, I recorded the instances of missionaries supernaturally receiving the vernacular language that were reported to me by credible witnesses, but I no longer do that. Not that this miraculous gift of language has become routine (I did not receive it when I went to Bolivia as a missionary!), but it is frequent enough to no longer be particularly surprising. I did spend some personal time with American missionaries to Argentina, James and Jaime Thomas, who themselves instantly received the Spanish language, including an Argentine accent, while in the city of Cordoba. Several other instances are documented in my book *How to Have a Healing Ministry in Any Church* (pp. 157-160).

THE AMAZED UNBELIEVERS

> [5] *Now there were dwelling in Jerusalem Jews, devout men, from every nation under heaven.* [6] *And when this sound occurred, the multitude came together, and were confused, because everyone heard them speak in his own language.* [7] *Then they were all amazed and marveled, saying to one another, "Look, are not all these who speak Galileans?* [8] *And how is it that we hear, each in our own language in which we were born?"* [13] *Others mocking said, "They are full of new wine."*

Who were these Jews dwelling in Jerusalem?

Coming "from every nation under heaven" (an obvious literary exaggeration, because none had come from Japan or Aborigine Australia or Tibet) refers to the nations of the first-century Jewish dispersion. These Jews, who lived with their families in Jewish communities outside of the Holy Land, ordinarily anchored by a local synagogue, were known as Hellenistic Jews. In the society of that day, they were clearly distinguished from the *Hebrew* Jews who did live in the Holy Land. For most, their heart language would have been the vernacular of the city or province or nation where they were born and reared and where they did most of their business. A large number would also know Greek, the trade language of the Roman Empire in those days. In fact, the word "Hellenistic" means that they were molded to some degree by Greek culture, including the Greek language.

Missiologically speaking, the Hellenists would ordinarily be regarded as a people group distinct from the Hebrews, and therefore, reaching them would require E-2 evangelism on the part of the Hebrew believers. To complicate matters further, their various identities with certain Roman provinces or cities or republics or nations outside Roman jurisdiction, such as Iran (Parthians) or Iraq (Mesopotamia), as well as their own particular heart languages, would divide them into many other significant subgroups.

Luke lists 15 language groups in Acts 2:9-11, but there is no reason to assume that this is a complete list as opposed to a representative list. It seems strange, for example, that none are mentioned from Greece or Syria. The Jewish Talmud reported that there were 70 nations in the Jewish dispersion, and because Luke says they had come "from every nation under heaven," it could well be that many more than 15 language groups were actually represented.

Although most of them would be *Hellenistic Jews*, a number of them were also "proselytes," according to verse 10. The proselytes were Gentiles by birth, but they had decided to convert to Judaism and had gone through the prescribed rituals that included baptism and circumcision for the males.

WHY WERE THERE SO MANY IN JERUSALEM?

It is not known exactly how many inhabitants Jerusalem had during the time of Jesus. Joachim Jeremias, a specialist on the social conditions of Jerusalem in the first century, estimates the population to be somewhere around 25,000 or 30,000. But then he says, "There can be no doubt that the influx of pilgrims at Passover time from all over the world was immense, and amounted to several times the population of Jerusalem."[3] Passover, however, was only one of three major Jewish festivals that annually attracted large numbers of pilgrims. Passover was held in early spring, Pentecost came 50 days later, then the Feast of the Tabernacles took place each fall. Of the three, Pentecost had the advantage of occurring during the most ideal weather period in the eastern Mediterranean region, and it may well have been the annual festival that attracted the most visitors.

On the Day of Pentecost, when the Holy Spirit came, 100,000 Hellenists would have been visiting Jerusalem, possibly even 200,000.

THE FIRST ATTEMPT AT E-2 EVANGELISM

[8] ***And how is it that we hear, each in our own language in which we were born?***

From the time Jesus was baptized, and to this point, virtually all the evangelism recorded in the Bible was monocultural, or E-1 evangelism. This is an extremely significant passage because it is the first time in the New Testament record that the disciples took the gospel across a discernable cultural barrier and engaged in cross-cultural, or E-2, evangelism.

Even if the Holy Spirit had come upon the disciples with fire in the Upper Room, by now they must have been located in the Temple area because of the "multitude" that gathered. This first public evangelistic service could have attracted tens of thousands of people, as do many such services today.

Although they were all Jews, the gap between the Hebrews and the Hellenists was more formidable than some might think. For example, only in rare exceptions, such as business associates, would they even spend a social evening together any more than Indonesian Muslims today would normally socialize with Saudi Arabian or Turkish Muslims in the Ramadan pilgrimage to Mecca. The Elamites who were there in Jerusalem, for example, were from families that never returned to Palestine from the Babylonian captivity but, rather, had settled in the area north of the Persian Gulf, part of the Persian empire, but with their own vernacular language as well. They, like the Hebrew Jews, might have been descendants of Abraham, but they would have very little in common with each other except to mingle impersonally in crowds, such as the crowd that gathered at the Temple when the sound of rushing mighty wind drew many people there.

To further highlight the drama of this event, I will repeat that not only were virtually all of the believers up to this time *Hebrew Jews* as opposed to *Hellenistic Jews*, but also the vast majority, including all the leadership, were *Galilean* Hebrews as opposed to *Judean* Hebrews. The Galileans were the hillbillies of the day, regarded as culturally backward by many Judeans and undoubtedly by the Hellenists as well. But the Galileans were the aggressive evangelists, the instruments chosen by God to take the good news that the Messiah had come to Hellenists from all over the world. To draw a present-day parallel among white European-Americans, it would be roughly equivalent to West Virginia coal miners attempting to evangelize the Massachusetts Institute of Technology (MIT) alumni association. One of the first things that would predictably turn off the MIT graduates would be what they would consider the evangelists' unsophisticated Appalachian accent.

CONTEXTUALIZING THE GOSPEL

The apostles could have preached to the crowd in the Temple in Aramaic and they would have communicated fairly well. Those among them who might have known Greek could have done the same. But God had other plans to cross what we now see as a formidable cultural barrier. He did something that is now established as a missiological principle. God took steps to contextualize the gospel, thereby showing that He respects the culture and language of each of the multiple groups gathered there. The method He used was to perform a miracle of language and allow the disciples to speak in languages they had never learned.

The first principle of cross-cultural evangelism is to present the message of Christ in cultural forms appropriate to the new people group. Today's missionaries would not feel adequately equipped if they were not steeped in cultural anthropology and did not have the tools to distinguish what is a nonnegotiable part of the Christian faith from cultural baggage they might unconsciously carry along with them as foreigners. Early missionaries to Africa, for example, in many cases retarded the spread of the gospel due to some culturally biased decisions concerning polygamy. In parts of Asia, missionary rules relating to ancestor worship often went beyond what true biblical requirements would be. But these are some of the advanced issues in contextualization. More basic would be the common agreement that if people of other cultures are going to be evangelized effectively, the gospel must be preached in their heart language, and the Bible must be translated into their vernacular.

RESISTANCE AND RECEPTIVITY

[12] *So they were all amazed....* [13] *Others mocking said, "They are full of new wine."*

Ordinarily, when the gospel is preached to unbelievers, some accept it and some reject it. Some are receptive and some are resistant. To return to the harvest analogy, not all crops ripen at the same time. Even all of the same crop does not ripen at once, as we know from the annual United States wheat harvest in which the wheat in the southern states ripens before the wheat in the northern states. Where do the harvesters go? They naturally go where the harvest is ripe, not where it is still green.

The disciples at Pentecost knew this because Jesus had previously demonstrated it for them. When He first sent them out on their own to the "lost sheep of the house of Israel" (Matt. 10:6), He told them to research each city to find "who in it is worthy, and stay there till you go out" (Matt. 10:11). These are the receptive, the whitened harvest. And the resistant? "Whoever will not receive you nor hear your words, when you depart from that house or city, shake off the dust from your feet" (Matt. 10:14).

We see both kinds at Pentecost. Those who were receptive recognized the extraordinary miracle of languages. They said, "Aren't these people those hillbilly Galileans?" (see Acts 2:7). They knew that in no human way could such uneducated people speak in Egyptian or Arabic or Persian, but that was exactly what they were doing! They knew it could only have been done by supernatural power, and they sincerely wanted to know more about it. They said, "Whatever could this mean?" (2:12).

But the resistant were also there. Although they were personally witnessing the same miraculous power of God, they refused to acknowledge it as such. They accused the apostles of being drunk, even though they must have known that one of the recognized phenomena of drunkenness is not beginning to speak in languages one has never learned. Even though the noise of the wind and speaking in unknown tongues should have impressed them, because, as Paul says, "For Jews request a sign" (1 Cor. 1:22), they remained indifferent. They are a prime example of the god of this age successfully blinding the minds of those who do not believe (see 2 Cor. 4:4).

SPEAKING IN TONGUES

Speaking in tongues will surface several times again as we move through Acts, so it may be helpful to discuss the issues involved in some detail at this point and simply refer back to them later.

Although the phenomenon of speaking in tongues can be found from time to time in the history of the Christian Church, it had never mainstreamed throughout the universal Body of Christ as it did in the twentieth century. The event that seemed to spark the modern tongues movement occurred during a New Year's Eve service in Topeka, Kansas, beginning on December 31, 1900, and ending on January 1, 1901, precisely the first day of the twentieth century. The prophetic symbolism of the day itself has not been lost to historians who have traced the subsequent tongues movement and observed its virtual universality 100 years later.

But this did not come without opposition. The Pentecostal movement that emerged from Topeka, and later the Azusa Street revival in Los Angeles, was resisted as well as scorned by more traditional Christians. Pentecostals were listed by some theologians as a false cult, along with Jehovah's Witnesses and Christian Scientists. The German Lutheran Church issued a "Berlin Declaration," stating that the power exhibited by Pentecostals was from below, not from above. Because many of them were from a social class similar to first-century Galileans, the tongues speakers were scorned as

"Holy Rollers" or as practicing the "hillbilly religion."

After the middle of the century, however, diplomatic Pentecostal leaders, such as David du Plessis and Thomas Zimmerman, guided the tongues-speaking movement into fellowship with more mainstream evangelicalism, with the World Council of Churches, as well as with the Vatican. The process gained momentum through the appearance of the charismatic renewal and then the Third Wave. Now, the most rapidly growing segment of Christianity worldwide, known by many as The New Apostolic Reformation, regards speaking in tongues as a common, but not a necessary, part of Christian life. Some new apostolic churches use tongues extensively, others tend to discourage it (although few would oppose it) and most are in between. To none is speaking in tongues any longer a serious or divisive issue.

The Gift of Tongues

Except for a diminishing number of Christians who are holding out for a cessationist theology (supposing that the more dramatic miraculous gifts of the Spirit ceased with the close of the Apostolic Age), there is widespread agreement that speaking in tongues is a bona fide gift of the Holy Spirit found among believers today. "Different kinds of tongues" as well as "interpretation of tongues" are listed as spiritual gifts in 1 Corinthians 12:10. In my book *Your Spiritual Gifts Can Help Your Church Grow*, I define it as follows:

> The gift of tongues is the special ability that God gives to certain members of the Body of Christ (1) to speak to God in a language they have never learned and/or (2) to receive and communicate an immediate message of God to His people through a divinely anointed utterance in a language they have never learned.[4]

Notice that tongues can either be private, between the individual and God, or public, directed to the congregation as a whole. Private tongues are described by the apostle Paul in these words: "He who speaks in a tongue does not speak to men but to God, for no one understands him" (1 Cor. 14:2). Paul places no restrictions on the use of private tongues, but he does on public tongues. They must be used only when accompanied by interpretation, otherwise "you will be speaking into the air" (1 Cor. 14:9). He adds, "Therefore let him who speaks in a tongue pray that he may interpret"

(1 Cor. 14:13). Public tongues plus interpretation are regarded as the equivalent of prophecy, although Paul prefers prophecy (see 1 Cor. 14:5,39).

A Miracle of Languages

Were the tongues spoken on Pentecost the gift of tongues or something else? I agree with Simon Kistemaker who says, "We cannot equate the Pentecost event with tongue speaking in the Corinthian church. . . . Whereas in the Corinthian church ecstatic speech has to be interpreted, at Pentecost the hearers do not need interpreters because they hear and are able to understand in their own languages."[5] I think that what happened at Pentecost was more of a "miracle of languages" than a "gift of tongues."

This is not to imply that the spiritual gift of tongues is never a true human language that at the time neither the speaker nor the hearers can identify. Sometimes it is. On a recent visit to England, for example, I learned of an incident where a monolingual British pastor was ministering to a multilingual Arab who happened to be serving as the principal translator in England for the OPEC oil cartel. The pastor sensed that God wanted him to pray about a certain physical ailment the Muslim was suffering, and as he did so, he prayed some in tongues, as was his custom. The Arab was amazed, just as were the unbelievers on Pentecost. The pastor had first prayed in fluent Iranian, then later in fluent Ugaritic, an obsolete language! The meaning of the prayers in the two different languages was identical. In this case, the Arab acknowledged it as a miracle of God, was born again, and is now a strong witness among fellow Muslims.

On the other hand, some social scientists, fascinated with the phenomenon of *glossalalia*, to use the Greek term, have tape-recorded tongue speaking and submitted it to analysis of professional linguists. Their conclusion is that the speech they examined follows no known human language structure, ancient or modern. The difference between these two instances might be what Paul referred to when he said, "Though I speak with the tongues of men and of angels" (1 Cor. 13:1). Some apparently are human languages; some are not.

Tongues and the Pentecost Event

I use the term "Pentecost event," because I believe these initial stages of world evangelization were so crucial that two other occasions also recorded in Acts should join the outpouring of the Holy Spirit on the Day of Pentecost as equal parts of a total "Pentecost event." All three were milestones:

- Breaking the barrier between Hebrew Jews and Hellenistic Jews in Jerusalem on the day of Pentecost (see Acts 2)
- Breaking the barrier between Jews and Samaritans through Philip in Samaria (see Acts 8:5-25)
- Breaking the barrier between Jews and Gentiles through Peter in the house of Cornelius (see Acts 10)

Through this three-part event, the groundwork was laid for the spread of the gospel to Jerusalem, Judea, Samaria and to the uttermost parts of the earth, as Jesus commanded in Acts 1:8.

In each of the three cases, the Holy Spirit came in power, indicating once again that the gospel would be spread only through the combination of supernatural intervention and human obedience to God. Two were accompanied with the phenomenon of tongues, and one was not:

- "At Pentecost, . . . they were all filled with the Holy Spirit and began to speak with other tongues, as the Spirit gave them utterance" (Acts 2:4).
- "In Samaria, . . . they laid hands on them, and they received the Holy Spirit" (Acts 8:17). No mention is made of tongues.
- "In Cornelius's house, . . . the Holy Spirit fell upon all those who heard the word. For they heard them speak with tongues and magnify God" (Acts 10:44,46).

Some Christian leaders, who have a more universal view of tongues in the Body of Christ than I, will assume that, although tongues was not mentioned concerning Samaria, the believers must have spoken in tongues because they did so at Pentecost and in Cornelius's house. One of these is Pentecostal scholar Stanley Horton, who says, "The fact that Luke does not mention speaking in tongues here is not significant," and then goes on to affirm that the thing that must have caught the attention of Simon the sorcerer in Samaria must have been the Samaritans speaking in tongues.[6] Horton could be right, but we must keep in mind that an argument from silence on one side tends to neutralize an argument from silence on the other. I personally do not think it makes much difference whether they spoke in tongues in Samaria or not. The principal issue, in my mind, is that the Holy Spirit came with power, and the barrier between Jews and Samaritans was broken down.

PETER'S ANOINTED SERMON

[14] *But Peter, standing up with the eleven, raised his voice and said to them, "Men of Judea and all who dwell in Jerusalem, let this be known to you, and heed my words.* [36] *Therefore let all the house of Israel know assuredly that God has made this Jesus, whom you crucified, both Lord and Christ."*

After the sound, the fire and hearing the gospel in their own languages from the mouths of a motley group of Galileans, many were ready to learn what all this was about. They had asked, "Whatever could this mean?" (Acts 2:12), and now they were about to know. Peter takes leadership here; the other 11 are near him and add their encouragement and approval. Peter also had taken leadership in the Upper Room when they appointed Matthias as the twelfth apostle. Peter is the central character in the book of Acts through chapter 8; he appears several times more through chapter 12; then Paul becomes Luke's central figure for the rest of the book. Meanwhile, James, the natural brother of Jesus, and not the James of the original 12, replaces Peter as the leader of the Jerusalem church by the time of the Jerusalem Council in chapter 15.

What language did Peter use to address the multitude? He came from Bethsaida (see John 1:44), which means "Fisherman's City," right on the border of Gentile territory. He would probably have been familiar with Greek as a trade language, but likely with a fluency similar to that of English fluency of many Mexicans who live near the United States border. Just as most such Mexicans would be more comfortable speaking Spanish, so Peter would undoubtedly have been more comfortable in his native Aramaic, a first cousin of the Hebrew language which by then was no longer in widespread use.

The reason I refer to Peter's message as "anointed" is not just because of its unusual results, but also because of the Greek word used for the English "said to them" in Acts 2:14. Our English versions hide this, but the word derives from *apophthengesthai*, which means "to address someone enthusiastically," according to *The New International Dictionary of New Testament Theology*.[7] This is the same word previously used in 2:4 when the disciples began to speak in tongues and the Holy Spirit "gave them utterance." This message of Peter's, like the speaking in tongues, was not something to be explained by skills of human rhetoric or oratory, but only by divine anointing.

WHAT DID PENTECOST MEAN?

[15] *For these are not drunk, as you suppose...* [16] *But this is what was spoken by the prophet Joel.*

Peter launches his sermon by using two points of contact with his audience. The first is the stupid accusation that the disciples were drunk. His sarcastic retort is, as *The Living Bible* puts it, "Some of you are saying these men are drunk! It isn't true! It's much too early for that! People don't get drunk by 9 A.M.!" The second point of contact was a reference to the prophet Joel, a spiritual authority recognized by everyone in his audience, whether Hebrew or Hellenist.

Informed Jews would have known from Joel that the "last days" would be marked by some kind of outpouring of God's Spirit, but until seeing the things that had happened that day and hearing Peter's application, they would have had no idea that it had actually begun. The "last days" means that period of time between Jesus' first coming and His second coming. It is the period of time in which we live today. No one knows when Jesus' second coming will take place, but we do know for sure that it is almost 2,000 years nearer than it was on the Day of Pentecost. We also know that the Great Commission, for the first time since Pentecost, could possibly be completed in our generation.

This, I believe, is why the spiritual warfare directly related to spreading the gospel of the Kingdom has been escalating so rapidly and has become more intense than it ever has been in the past. The book of Revelation says, "For the devil has come down to you, having great wrath, because he knows that he has a short time" (Rev. 12:12). I would not be surprised if this prophecy were being fulfilled before our very eyes. The "last days" are not forever. They are on a timeline, and it might well be that we are nearing the end, although I am not about to set any dates for the Second Coming. Everyone who has tried it so far has been wrong!

What I desire to stress are the stated characteristics of these "last days":

- the outpouring of the Holy Spirit
- prophecy
- visions and dreams
- signs and wonders
- salvation to those who believe
- retaking the dominion over creation that Adam lost to Satan

This is what Pentecost meant then, and it is what larger and larger segments of the Body of Christ are discovering and applying to our evangelistic task today. Power ministries are helping open people's minds in China, in Indonesia, in Nigeria, in India, in Brazil and in many other nations of the world today. The "last days" are continuing, and Joel's prophecy is continuing to be fulfilled.

THE HEART OF THE GOSPEL

Signs and wonders do not save people. Neither do prophecy or visions and dreams. Only the gospel of Christ "is the power of God to salvation for everyone who believes" (Rom. 1:16). That is why Peter, in his message, carefully outlines the story of Jesus of Nazareth in the following Acts references:

- Jesus' life and ministry on earth (see 2:22)
- Jesus' crucifixion (see 2:23)
- Jesus' resurrection from the dead (see 2:24-32)
- Jesus' exaltation at the right hand of God (see 2:33-35)
- Jesus, the Christ or the Jewish Messiah (see 2:36)

Ministry in the miraculous power of the Holy Spirit is not primarily an end in itself but only a means toward the end of making disciples. Disciples are made only through a personal relationship to Jesus Christ as Lord and Savior.

Peter drove his words home by accusing his listeners of making a huge mistake when they crucified the very person whom God had sent as their Messiah to save them. It must have taken incredible courage to make such a direct application to that crowd of Jews, but under the anointing of God, it turned out to be appropriate. Many in the audience were, indeed, ready to confess that they had taken Jesus "by lawless hands" (2:23) and crucified Him (see 2:36), even though they might not have been personally present when Herod asked them to choose between Barabas and Jesus.

THE PEOPLE RESPOND WITH OPEN HEARTS

[37] . . . *"Men and brethren, what shall we do?"*

The convicting power of the Holy Spirit had come upon them and hearts were opened. Peter responded by giving them two action steps:

Repentance. Repentance means turning away from sin, changing the mind and turning toward God. This is what is needed to become a disciple of Jesus. It is establishing a personal relationship with Jesus through faith.

It is notable that Peter did not pile upon his listeners a list of ethical demands to which they had to agree before they could be saved. Some today have the tendency to superimpose their own ethical agendas on the gospel, thereby hindering its spread. Repentance should come at the point of guilt of which the Holy Spirit is revealing at the moment, such as crucifying Jesus, in this particular case. It would be unwise to include that point in a message to Jews today, and irrelevant in a message to Gentiles. Anointed preaching will reveal the points at which the Holy Spirit Himself is doing the convicting, and this brings positive response.

The technical term for this initial step of repentance and faith in Jesus Christ is "discipling." The subsequent lifetime road of discipleship, beginning then and producing the ethical changes that mold disciples into Christ-likeness, is called "perfecting." As missiologist Donald McGavran says, "Antigrowth concepts arise from confusing perfecting with discipling."[8] Peter did not make that mistake.

Baptism. Baptism is the primary outward, visible action that validates the inward decision to follow Jesus Christ as Lord and Savior. For most segments of Christianity, baptism is the principal initiatory rite that identifies believers with the Body of Christ, the Church. Peter did not suggest postponing baptism until a certain stage of perfection had been reached. His word was that if they were serious about receiving remission of their sins, they should prove it by being baptized immediately.

THE RESULTS OF A GREAT DAY FOR GOD'S KINGDOM

[41] *Then those who gladly received his word were baptized; and that day about three thousand souls were added to them.*

The results of Pentecost included both *quantitative* church growth and *qualitative* church growth. The two should never be thought of as separate. Healthy churches usually grow. Unhealthy churches tend not to grow.

Putting together a scenario in which 3,000 were baptized in one day, beginning around noon, is an interesting challenge. If only the 12 were doing the baptizing, it would mean 42 an hour for each of the apostles. It could be done. I recently received a newspaper report from South Africa describing a baptism of 70,000 in one day performed by 1 archbishop and 21 bishops. This would have been 23.3 times the number baptized on Pentecost. The quantitative growth begun at Pentecost is not only continuing today, but it is also increasing.

Of all the descriptions of Christian churches in the New Testament, this first church planted in Jerusalem on the Day of Pentecost is the one a great many today would choose to imitate if they could. It was not only a megachurch, but it was also one of high quality.

[42] *And they continued steadfastly in the apostles' doctrine and fellowship, in the breaking of bread, and in prayers.* [43] *Then fear came upon every soul, and many wonders and signs were done through the apostles.* [44] *Now all who believed were together, and had all things in common,* [45] *and sold their possessions and goods, and divided them among all, as anyone had need.* [46] *So continuing daily with one accord in the temple, and breaking bread from house to house, they ate their food with gladness and simplicity of heart,* [47] *praising God and having favor with all the people. . . .*

Luke records six distinct areas reflecting the spiritual quality of this young church. Apostolic leadership was undoubtedly a major contributing factor to new converts maturing in Christ so rapidly. Another factor would have been the relatively low threshold for devout Jews to decide to cross over and follow Jesus as their Messiah. They still worshiped on the Sabbath in the Temple, they kept the law and they maintained their existing social and family ties. The threshold would be much higher for Gentiles later on in Acts.

The Six Spiritual Qualities

Learning more about God. The phrase "apostles' doctrine" means teaching in general, not just theology per se. The believers submitted to the spiritual authority of the apostles and followed their leadership. Because the apostles had just received 40 days of Jesus' teaching "things pertaining to the kingdom of God" (1:3), it is easy to imagine that much of what the apostles taught through deed and word would have been this. The Jews' belief in

Jehovah God was solid, but the new believers had to adjust to being in "the last days" (2:17) according to the fulfillment of Joel's prophecy, particularly to move daily in the power of the Holy Spirit, which had never previously been possible for the Jewish rank and file.

Fellowship with one another. While they were growing in their vertical relationship to God, the new believers were also growing in their horizontal relationship to each other in Christian fellowship. This relationship is stressed heavily here, mentioned in four of the six verses in the passage. One of the key factors of church health is to design ways and means for fellowship to be an integral part of church life week in and week out. If it is absent, the church will tend to plateau or decline. New members must be absorbed fairly rapidly. This is one of the reasons the cell church movement is having an increasing impact in virtually every part of the world.

In Jerusalem, eating together was important. Many scholars feel that "the breaking of bread" in 2:42 can mean the Lord's Supper, but that "breaking bread from house to house" in 2:46 means sharing meals with other believers at home. Both are important in building strong foundations for a growing church.

These believers were also more radical in their giving to the church and sharing material possessions than many of us are today. Their relationships with each other were so strong that they could not tolerate anyone in the church living with material need while others enjoyed relative prosperity. As family members will frequently do for each other, they "sold their possessions and goods" so they would have resources to care for the needy. They apparently were going far beyond the tithe, which they would have done in any case as part of their Jewish law.

Churches in which members do not at least tithe their income, that is, give at least 10 percent to the Lord's work and presumably to the local church, are obviously not high-quality churches. Jesus taught that this is an important outward sign of inward commitment to God when He said, "For where your treasure is, there your heart will be also" (Luke 12:34). Pastors who desire to measure the commitment of their members should begin by looking at their giving records. In Jerusalem, the believers would not have been embarrassed by this as would the members of many of today's churches.

Worshiping God. The believers customarily went to the Temple daily, and there they would worship God and thank Him for sending His Messiah.

Worship in our day is becoming an increasingly high-profile activity in many churches than it has been in past generations.

In fact, a worldwide phenomenon has been emerging centered around a relatively new form of worship. It could well be that the most powerful unifying factor among the new apostolic churches, exploding in growth on every continent, is long periods of praise and worship based on contemporary spiritual songs composed month after month by members of the local congregation or of the particular apostolic network in which it participates. This style of worship allows great latitude for body language, and is typically peppered with enthusiastic applause directed toward God Himself. Increasing numbers of more traditional churches are now moving from pipe organs, pianos and choirs toward contemporary worship.

Prayer. Prayer, presumably both corporate and individual, characterized the Jerusalem church. This has been a severely neglected area of our Christian life in many of our churches today. Prayer is ordinarily talked about much and practiced little. But things are changing. Since about 1970, a great worldwide prayer movement has been sweeping across churches, more strongly in some areas than others. Previous to 1970, the churches of all denominations in Korea had been setting an example for the world. They have been accustomed to practicing prayer as much as talking about it, and the quantitative and qualitative growth of Korean churches has led the whole through several decades. Korean pastors are the first to stress prayer in both deed and word. Early morning prayer meetings year around, all-night prayer on Friday nights and fasting and prayer retreats on multiple prayer mountains have been as characteristic of Korean churches as preaching sermons or taking up offerings.

Power ministries. When we read that "fear came upon every soul," the meaning is not that the believers were scared of something, but that they were in awe of the power of God that was constantly being manifested around them. The apostles were modeling the continuance of the signs and wonders characteristic of the days when they were with Jesus. Healings and deliverances from demons would be commonplace in the life of the Jerusalem church, just as they are in many churches today. For example, in Argentina, where a notable revival has been recorded, most churches practice power ministries as they did in Jerusalem. In fact, one of the churches in Buenos Aires has a staff member who has the title "minister of miracles," and part of the job description is to collect the medical and legal evidence necessary to verify some of the unusual miracles, such as teeth being filled, obese people instantly losing weight and new hair growth on bald heads. When things such as this happen, naturally, both believers and unbelievers are in awe before the amazing power of God.

Outreach. Reaching the lost was a priority for this church from the beginning. They had "favor with all the people," meaning that those who had not yet accepted Jesus as their Messiah and been baptized into the Church. Such fellowship, worship and miraculous power of God would have made it easy for the believers to turn inward, to say that they needed to learn more about Jesus and to relate more intimately with Him, neglecting the spiritually lost people in their community. But they did not yield to this temptation, as we know from the concluding sentence of Acts 2:

> [47] ***And the Lord added to the church daily those who were being saved.***

What a church!

REFLECTION QUESTIONS

1. Review and discuss the three visible signs of the invisible Spirit: audible, visual and oral. Have you ever heard of or experienced anything like that today?
2. This chapter contends that Pentecost was a truly *cross-cultural* missionary incident even though Jews were preaching to Jews. How do you explain this?
3. Do you think that every Christian should speak in tongues at some time or other? How does your answer relate to the "gift of tongues"?
4. Name the three phases of the "Pentecost event" and relate each one to breaking a missiological barrier.
5. The church that started in Jerusalem at Pentecost was in many ways an ideal church. What were some of its characteristics that our churches today would do well to imitate?

5

ONE HUNDRED THIRTY CONVERTS A DAY CAN SHAKE A CITY

ACTS 3 AND 4

Once the Day of Pentecost and the Feast of Harvest had ended, and the tens of thousands of pilgrims who had come to Jerusalem for the festival had gone home, the city almost returned to normal. But not quite. Things would never be the same, as we see from Peter and John's rather casual and routine visit to the Temple about three months later.

A MIRACLE IN PLAIN SIGHT: ACTS 3

[1] ***Now Peter and John went up together to the temple at the hour of prayer, the ninth hour.*** [2] ***And a certain man lame from his mother's womb was carried, whom they laid daily at the gate of the temple which is called Beautiful, to ask alms from those who entered the temple;*** [3] ***who, seeing Peter and John about to go into the temple, asked for alms.***

Peter and John had grown up together in the fishing community of Bethsaida in Galilee. Along with James, they had been given the privilege of forming the inner circle of three who were personally the closest to Jesus. They were the only disciples who had been eyewitnesses of Jesus' transfiguration (see Matt. 17:1), and they were the three whom Jesus called apart from the other eight when He went to His prayer vigil in Gethsemane (see Mark 14:33).

MESSIANIC JEWS

For Peter and John and the other disciples, going to the Temple at three o' clock in the afternoon for the daily prayer meeting was routine. When they could, they also, undoubtedly, attended the other two daily prayer meetings that were held mornings and evenings. We sometimes forget that, at this point in time, none of the believers was a "Christian" in the proper sense of the word. They were known as "disciples of Jesus the Messiah," or as "the brethren," or as "followers of The Way," or as "believers," but they were all Jews. Believers were not called "Christians" until almost 15 years later when Gentile churches began to be planted in Antioch.

Many of those who participate in the growing messianic Jewish movement today prefer to be called "messianic Jews" rather than "Christians." They often remind us that, whereas in biblical times many Jewish followers of Jesus had to be reprimanded for attempting to "Judaize" the Gentiles and, thereby, block them from accepting Christ, so today many Gentile believers insist on "Gentilizing" the Jews, and they should likewise be reprimanded. Both of these errors violate the missiological principle of contextualization that I have mentioned previously, and they can prevent the gospel from effectively being carried across cultural barriers. They cast the act of accepting Christ into a *cultural* mold rather than allowing it to become an essentially *religious* decision. This, predictably, becomes a retarding factor in world evangelization.

Peter and John, as well as all the other disciples of the day, looked like Jews, talked like Jews, behaved like Jews, regarded themselves as Jews and were seen by the unbelievers as Jews, although perhaps of a rather odd variety. As a missiologist, unlike many previous commentators, I am personally so sensitized to this that, as I write this book, I find myself having a hard time using the term "Christian" to refer to the believers until we come to Acts 11:26, where we read, "And the disciples were first called Christians in Antioch." They were not called Christians in Jerusalem. Peter, the apostle to the circumcision (Jews), much later accepted the term, but I would imagine somewhat reluctantly. He writes, "Yet if anyone suffers as a Christian" (1 Pet. 4:16). Actually, other than these two appearances, the word "Christian" is used only once more in the Bible, where Agrippa, a Gentile, says to Paul, the apostle to the Gentiles, "You almost persuade me to become a Christian" (Acts 26:28). Ralph Winter suggests that Agrippa was using the term derisively, meaning something like "Messiah-nut."[1]

THE LAME BEGGAR

Those who are familiar with societies that have a widespread presence of beggars come to take them for granted. Beggars are a familiar daily sight in cities. They attract no more special attention than do people who might be buying a hot dog, or a crowd waiting for a theater to open or passengers getting off a bus. They are part of the way of life and, as far as the average citizen is concerned, the way it always has been and always will be.

Furthermore, individual beggars, particularly the immobile ones, have often acquired personal jurisdiction over a certain physical turf they have staked out, usually on a busy sidewalk. They are in the same place every day, seven days a week. In some Latin American cities beggars have gone as far as to organize beggars' unions. My friend Sam Wilson once told me that one time when he was in Cuzco, Peru, the beggars went on strike until the merchants agreed to double their daily handouts!

When Doris and I were raising our family in Cochabamba, Bolivia, we would always have the children give some money to the "shaky man" who was on the sidewalk near the door to our church. If he wasn't there on a Sunday, we would assume that he must be sick and we would be concerned about him, even though he couldn't talk and we never knew his name. Many of these beggars make a reasonable living, although they would not appear to do so to judge by their dress and lifestyle. From time to time, however, newspapers report stories about beggars who have died and left considerable sums of money behind in their living quarters.

This, I think, could fairly well describe the scenario that faced Peter and John as they went into the Temple. They must have seen that same lame man a hundred times and may well have occasionally dropped coins into his tin cup. In fact, Jesus, who also was a Jew and frequented the Temple while in Jerusalem, must have passed him many times as well. Everyone, including Peter, John, Jesus and hundreds who saw him every day, knew that he couldn't walk, due to a birth defect, and had to be carried by others to his place. If his picture had appeared in a newspaper, a large percentage of Jerusalem residents would have said, "Oh, yes, I recognize that man. He sits at the Beautiful Gate."

It was a perfect setup for a public miracle to be done in plain sight.

Instant Healing

[4] *And fixing his eyes on him, with John, Peter said, "Look at us."*
[5] *So he gave them his attention, expecting to receive something from them.*
[6] *Then Peter said, "Silver and gold I do not have, but what I do have*

I give you: In the name of Jesus Christ of Nazareth, rise up and walk."
[7] *And he took him by the right hand and lifted him up, and immediately*
his feet and ankle bones received strength.

Saying to a beggar, "look at us," was definitely out of the ordinary. Part of the expected behavior pattern in a beggar society is not to make eye contact. The beggar would have instantly understood that Peter was establishing a social relationship, brief as it might have been. Because the beggar was asking for alms, he expected a handout. Peter's statement that they had no money would have been both unexpected and unwelcome, because receiving money was the highest agenda item on the beggar's mind. Peter's words did not imply that the disciples were poverty-stricken, but more likely that they were not carrying any money with them at the time. But he was about to offer the beggar something that money couldn't buy.

I would surmise that because the beggar was lame from birth, the possibility that he would ever walk had never entered his mind, any more than a person born with blue eyes would ever expect them to turn brown. Peter didn't stop to interview the man or to prepare him emotionally for what was about to happen. He spoke to the man in Jesus' name and commanded him to "rise up and walk." The man was instantly healed in plain sight of everyone else visiting the Temple that afternoon!

This was not the first miracle done by the apostles after Jesus' ascension. We have already seen that "many wonders and signs were done through the apostles" (Acts 2:43). But other than the miracle of languages on the Day of Pentecost, this is the first one described in detail. Because this is all part of Luke's literary way of preparing the kickoff for at least 2,000 years of subsequent world evangelization, such an initial mighty work of God needs some analysis. Luke highlights at least four important points here.

The Medical Report

Luke, a physician, gives details—such as the bones of the feet and ankles receiving strength, Peter grasping him by the *right* hand, and the fact that it was a birth defect—that other reporters without his medical training might not have mentioned. Furthermore, long, drawn-out physical therapy did not seem to be called for, as it comes after much orthopedic surgery today. But in moments, the invalid was leaping and running around. He didn't even have to teach himself to walk, which is surprising, given the fact that he had never previously learned how. This healing could only be regarded as being caused by miraculous supernatural power, not explained away as a faulty medical diagnosis, the only respectable explanation that some physicians choose to give for similar miracles today.

Luke, of course, was not a personal eyewitness of this event. Yet, he reports it as a straightforward fact. The issue of how miracles are verified and how the true is distinguished from the false is an important one, which I will deal with again when we later come to some other dramatic events, such as raising the dead. Meanwhile, at least for Luke, who was a physician, the secondhand accounts of credible witnesses apparently were sufficient evidence for him to report the miracle in some detail to his friend Theophilus. In all probability, no physician at all was involved with the incident, and, therefore, medical reports were not available to consult. If Peter and John said it happened, that would have been proof enough for Luke.

The Authority to Heal

Peter was no novice at divine healing. He had healed many, both before and after the resurrection of Jesus. We can assume, therefore, that he chose his words carefully when he said, "What I do have I give you."

What is it that Peter had, and where did he get it?

First of all, we must observe that Peter apparently had something in his personal possession that he could use at will, parallel to money, which he didn't have at the moment but which he could have spent as he desired. The thing that Peter had and could give away was healing power. It had been included in Jesus' promise that "you shall receive power when the Holy Spirit has come upon you" (Acts 1:8). Jesus told Peter and the others that they could expect to do the works He did, explaining that the power of the Holy Spirit they would receive was the same power by which He did His healing miracles.

Later, Paul explains that the Holy Spirit gives "gifts of healings" to some members of the Body of Christ (see 1 Cor. 12:9) in the same way that others demonstrate spiritual gifts of teaching or administration or helps or prophecy. Would Peter have been given a gift of healing? I believe that he probably had the gift, knowing a good deal about Peter's subsequent career. But for a healing such as the lame man's at the Temple gate, a gift of healing is not always a necessary prerequisite. For example, all Christians have a *role* of witnessing for Jesus, even if they do not have the *gift* of evangelist. I believe that all Christians also have a *role* of praying for the sick. Even by simply using a role, a healing like this could have taken place.

Those who do have the gift of healing fully realize that the power to heal is not innate in them, except to the extent that the Holy Spirit dwells within them. That is why Peter, using a frequent pattern for healing ministries, said, "In the name of Jesus Christ of Nazareth." This was a statement of authority, again not of Peter's intrinsic authority, but authority delegated to him by Jesus.

When Jesus first sent Peter and the others out to heal the sick, He gave them the necessary power to do it (see Matt. 10:1). The Greek word for this power is *exousia*, which carries with it the meaning that the power is not inherent but delegated by a higher authority. It is similar to the power an ambassador has been given by the president. For example, U.S. ambassadors would get nowhere in foreign countries by presenting themselves in their own name. Rather, they say, "I come in the name of the President of the United States." That is exactly why Peter said he had come "In the name of Jesus Christ of Nazareth."

Some may observe that in Acts 1:8, when Jesus says, "You shall receive power," He uses another common Greek word, *dunamis*. This word does imply "strength based on inherent physical, spiritual, or natural powers" according to *The New International Dictionary of New Testament Theology*.[2] It implies that the disciples from then on would have the indwelling *dunamis* power of the Holy Spirit, but that this spiritual power could only be used by the *authority* given by Jesus. Invoking the name of Jesus is a declaration of the authority to heal.

Faith in Healing

It is obvious that the faith of this beggar, either in Jesus Christ or in divine healing, had nothing to do with the miracle. As I have read other commentaries on this passage, I have been surprised that this seems to bother some. Without mentioning names, I will say that one excellent commentator affirms that in the New Testament, miracles are connected with faith, with which I agree. But from that he deduces that this crippled man could only walk if he had first put his faith in Jesus as his personal savior. Another says that we can *assume* that he became a believer. I don't think either one of these will satisfy closer scrutiny.

The New Testament has examples of three different possible agents of the faith necessary for divine healing to take place, the sick person being only one of the possible agents.

When two blind men came to Jesus (see Matt. 9:27-31), He said, "Do you believe that I am able to do this?" When they affirmed that they did believe, Jesus said, "According to your faith let it be to you" (v. 29). They were both healed, and their personal faith played an important role. The sick person in that case was the agent of faith for healing. But this is not the only way it happens.

Another agent of faith is an intermediary. A Roman centurion once asked Jesus for healing on behalf of his servant who was paralyzed, perhaps much like the lame man at the Temple gate. In this case, Jesus congratulated the centurion and said, "I have not found such great *faith*, not even in Israel!" (Matt. 8:10). Not only did the ailing servant have no faith, but he probably had no idea even who Jesus was or that his master was asking for healing. Nevertheless, he was miraculously healed through the faith of an intermediary.

The third agent of faith is the person who does the healing. Unless we read things into the text that are not there, the most reasonable conclusion is that the agents of faith for the healing of the lame beggar were Peter and John.

We might hope that the beggar was saved, but if he wasn't, he would not be the first to experience miraculous healing without a subsequent commitment to Christian discipleship. John 6, for example, begins with many people following Jesus "because they saw His signs which He performed on those who were diseased" (John 6:2). But before the chapter ends, Jesus has to say, "There are some of you who do not believe" (John 6:64). And, "From that time many of His disciples went back and walked with Him no more" (John 6:66). The fact that the beggar "praised God" proves no more than that he was doing what all Jews are supposed to do when they go into the Temple, and that he acknowledged his healing came from Jehovah.

As I have pointed out previously, healing by itself does not save. Healing can open people's minds to consider the gospel, but only a response to the gospel and personal faith in Jesus Christ as Savior and Lord can save. Whether the beggar did this we do not know.

The Timing

If Jesus Himself had passed this lame man numerous times when going in and out of the Temple, and if Peter and John had seen him there day after day, why had no one healed him previously?

A key to ministering with divine healing is to be sensitive to God's timing. Jesus said, "The Son can do nothing of Himself, but what He sees the Father do" (John 5:19). Jesus' miraculous works were done according to the Father's timing. Peter was obviously following this lead. On this particular trip to the Temple, Peter had extraordinary compassion on the lame man and a great desire to see him healed. Where did this desire come from? Presumably from the Father, "For it is God who works in you both to will and to do for His good pleasure" (Phil. 2:13). Why the Father chose this particular time, and not another, we may never know.

Because Peter was so sure of the timing of the Father, he chose not to pray a prayer of petition, asking God to heal the lame man, which is the most common form of healing prayer. He spoke directly to the lame man and commanded him to stand up!

AN EXUBERANT TESTIMONY

[8] *So he, leaping up, stood and walked and entered the temple with them—walking, leaping, and praising God.* [9] *And all the people saw him walking and praising God.* [11] *Now as the lame man who was healed held on to Peter and John, all the people ran together to them in the porch which is called Solomon's, greatly amazed.*

The healed man let everybody know that he was healed. An impossible dream had come true! He testified by deed: walking and jumping! He testified by word: praising God! He recognized that it was God who had healed him. Peter did not seek or receive any credit. He didn't pass the offering plate and take a collection for his ministry. The focus and the glory were on God.

The people in the Temple who saw it could neither ignore nor doubt the power behind Peter's use of the name of Jesus Christ of Nazareth. They all had known this lame man and now they saw him whole. They were as surprised and amazed as the others had been three months earlier when they heard the tongues spoken on the Day of Pentecost. And they were just as ready as the others to listen to Peter's explanation.

PETER'S INTERPRETATION OF THE MIRACLE

[12] *So when Peter saw it, he responded to the people: "Men of Israel, why do you marvel at this? Or why look so intently at us, as though by our own power or godliness we had made this man walk?* [13] *The God of Abraham, Isaac, and Jacob, the God of our fathers, glorified His Servant*

Jesus. . . . [16] *And His name, through faith in His name, has made this man strong, whom you see and know. Yes, the faith which comes through Him has given him this perfect soundness in the presence of you all.*

As he addressed this second group in the Temple, Peter took wise precautions to assure them that he was still a bona fide Jew. Phrases such as "men of Israel"; "the God of Abraham, Isaac and Jacob"; "the God of our fathers" knit him with the audience and helped them ignore the fact that he was speaking with an unsophisticated Galilean accent. His biblical text was from Moses, and he mentioned Samuel and the prophets. What had been happening over the past three months was the introduction to a new era in the total history of salvation, nothing less than a new covenant. But as a good communicator, Peter began with the old covenant, which was known, and then moved to the new covenant, which, for the Jews, was as yet unknown.

However, they liked what they heard about this new covenant very much because Peter helped them understand the true power behind the miracle. He explains that it was not some power inherent in Peter or John, and Peter appropriately uses the word *dunamis* here (v. 12). Peter does not mention the power of the Holy Spirit at this point because it would have confused them. Some of them would have heard Peter say, "In the name of Jesus Christ of Nazareth," and they knew who Jesus was well enough to cringe when Peter reminded them, as he also did on Pentecost, that they were corporately guilty of crucifying the true Servant of God. He told them that Jesus had been raised from the dead, and that they should receive and respect Him now if they had not done so previously.

Many of them wanted to get in touch with the power of Jesus that they had seen with their own eyes. Peter, therefore, took the opportunity to make three demands:

1. Repent

[19] *Repent therefore and be converted . . .* [26] *. . . in turning away every one of you from your iniquities.*

This is the same thing Peter said on the Day of Pentecost. They had to repent of killing the Messiah even though they may have been ignorant of what they were doing at the time (see 3:17). Ignorance of sin does not excuse it and erase guilt, particularly when the sin has done damage to others. It needs to be confessed.

Acts 3:19 is one of the principal places in the New Testament where we run across the concept of identificational repentance. Identificational repentance means confessing and remitting sins that we may not have committed personally, but with which we are identified for one reason or another. It is what Daniel did when he said he was "speaking, praying, and confessing my sin and *the sin of my people Israel*" (Dan. 9:20), and what Nehemiah meant when he confessed to God, "Both *my father's house* and I have sinned" (Neh. 1:6).

Obviously, very few of the Jews here at the Temple, or among the Hellenists who were visiting Jerusalem on the Day of Pentecost, would personally have been in the crowd who shouted to Pilate, "Crucify Him, crucify Him!" (Luke 23:21). None of them would have been among the Roman authorities who actually passed the sentence, or among the soldiers who nailed Him to the cross. Nevertheless, Peter demanded that they repent of crucifying Jesus, and many of them did.

As we advance in our knowledge of strategic-level spiritual warfare, the principles and practice of identificational repentance are assuming more and more of a central role. Books by John Dawson, such as *Taking Our Cities for God* and *Healing America's Wounds*, and by Cindy Jacobs, such as *Possessing the Gates of the Enemy*, have been helpful in understanding how to do identificational repentance. I have also written about it in *Praying with Power*. A major public example of identificational repentance was carried out by hundreds of dedicated Christians between 1996 and 1999, for the 900-year anniversary of the First Crusade. Called the "Reconciliation Walk," they carefully mapped out and walked all the known routes of the First Crusade between Cologne, Germany, and Jerusalem, repenting for the sins of our forefathers against Muslims and Jews.

2. Receive Forgiveness

[19] . . . ***that your sins may be blotted out, so that times of refreshing may come from the presence of the Lord.***

Repenting and placing faith in Jesus Christ will allow God not only to forgive sins, but also to *obliterate* them. We ourselves may remember them later, but God refuses to. Peter was saying that God would not only forgive the people for crucifying Jesus, but that all the rest of their sins would be forgiven as well.

They could hardly have comprehended fully that this would mean, for example, that there would be no more need to observe an annual day of atonement, but they could at least begin to understand it somewhat. The more they understood it, the more spiritual *refreshing* they would experience. Many of them received this as "good news," another term for the "gospel."

3. Join Forces for World Evangelization

[25] *You are the sons of the prophets, and of the covenant which God made with our fathers, saying to Abraham, "And in your seed all the families of the earth shall be blessed."*

This quote from Genesis 12:3 is the Great Commission in its Old Testament version. The "families" of the earth is a synonym for "nations" or "peoples." This was such a radical suggestion to the ethnic Jews (mostly Hebrews in this case) whom Peter was addressing, that I would imagine very few, if any, would have picked up the significance of Peter's challenge. There was not much love in their hearts for the *goyim*, or Gentiles, and some, to be honest, would have preferred that God *not* bless them. But Peter would not have forgotten that God gave him and the others the power of the Holy Spirit, not just to heal lame beggars, but also to be effective witnesses in Jerusalem, Judea, Samaria and the uttermost parts of the earth.

GOING TO JAIL FOR DOING GOOD: ACTS 4

[1] *Now as they spoke to the people, the priests, the captain of the temple, and the Sadducees came upon them,* [2] *being greatly disturbed that they taught the people and preached in Jesus the resurrection from the dead.* [3] *And they laid hands on them, and put them in custody until the next day, for it was already evening.*

The word about what was happening in a certain section of the Temple grounds that afternoon quickly spread throughout the rest of the Temple. The beggar was healed before 3:00 P.M., but the Temple officers didn't show up until later, when the gates of the Temple were to have been closed. By then, it must have been clear to some leaders that the reaction to this unexpected event could be escalating to the point where it could threaten Jerusalem's status quo. In any case, it had apparently upset the peace and quiet of the daily Temple routine and rituals. So a group of authorities decided to put a stop to it.

Some priests who happened to be on duty in the Temple came with the others. Priests and Levites administered the daily sacrifices.

The captain of the temple was the chief of the Temple police. He was second in command to the high priest himself, and his presence signaled that the disturbance, as they regarded it, was being taken very seriously by Temple leaders. He undoubtedly would have brought several Temple police officers with him.

The appearance of the Sadducees has more than a passing significance. They were not a large group in Jerusalem, but they had gained disproportionate political power. The Romans largely left the internal affairs of Jerusalem in the hands of a Jewish aristocracy, and as Richard Rackham says, "This hierarchical aristocracy was Sadducean in theology. In fact the high priest and they that were with him practically formed the sect of the Sadducees."[3]

The Sadducees did not pay much attention to Jesus in the early part of His ministry, but toward the end, when it became evident that political implications might be involved, they actively began to oppose Him. Why? They were part of the Jewish aristocracy and, as Donald Hagner points out, they were, therefore, very much interested in maintaining the status quo. "It follows," says Hagner, "that they pursued policies designed to appease the governing authorities of Rome."[4] Thus, for a *political* reason they did not like the looks of the disturbance in the Temple.

But some important *spiritual* reasons were present as well. Peter had openly proclaimed "in Jesus the resurrection from the dead," but the Sadducees believed "that there is no resurrection of the dead, nor any future life whether of bliss or sorrow."[5] For this reason the Pharisees, who included such biblical notables as Nicodemus, Gamaliel and Saul of Tarsus, seem to be less opposed than the Sadducees to Jesus' movement as it was developing under the apostles. In fact, Rackham suggests that many of the Pharisees "were secretly delighted to have the aid of the new teachers in vigorously asserting the doctrine of the resurrection as against the Sadducees."[6]

The Pharisees, along with the apostles of Jesus, had a further problem with the Sadducees who, as Hagner says, "appear to have rejected the belief in angels and demons."[7] No wonder Jesus said to the Sadducees in disgust, "You do not know the Scriptures nor the power of God" (Mark 12:24). Not knowing the power of God would make it very difficult, if not impossible, for the Sadducees to gain any realistic understanding of the explosive spread of the gospel, with the miraculous events accompanying it both at that time and in the future.

A CHURCH GROWTH REPORT

[4] ***However, many of those who heard the word believed; and the number of the men came to be about five thousand.***

No particular literary reason exists for this statement to be inserted into a narrative that begins with the arrest of the apostles and continues in the very next verse with the trial before the Sanhedrin the following morning. Why, then, is it here? Apparently, Luke wants to remind us of what the ultimate objective of activities, such as healing lame people, preaching to crowds in the Temple, and suffering persecution continues to be, namely, making disciples of all nations—including Jerusalem, Judea, Samaria and the uttermost parts of the earth.

The report that the apostles are put into jail for doing the good deed of healing a lame man could be discouraging for many readers of Acts. So Luke, as he does from time to time, pauses ever so briefly to give us a progress report on the spread of the gospel. It seems that Luke was quite pragmatic, in the good sense of the word. He clearly understood what the goals were and measured success or failure against the goals. Ernst Haenchen says, "Luke loves the multitudes of converts, the mass-successes. Not that he was unduly impressed by sheer numbers. But the crowds streaming into the fold of Christ are for him the visible expression of the divine blessing resting on the Church."[8]

The number "5,000" is impressive, purposely so if Luke inserted this report in order to encourage believers in the midst of an account of persecution. If the 5,000 consisted of the believers in Jerusalem, the Church would have grown from 3,000 on Pentecost to 5,000 three months later, or by 20 converts a day. However, the calculations appear to be somewhat more complex than that.

For one thing, if the picture we have of the crowd at Pentecost is correct, many of the 3,000 converts on that day would have been Hellenistic Jews who had come as pilgrims to the Feast of Harvest in Jerusalem. But then they would have returned to any number of other cities and provinces in the Roman

Empire. The fact that the gospel was preached in at least 16 languages that day causes us to suppose that they had scattered back to at least 16 language areas, probably many more. We are not told how many of the 3,000 were Hebrews who would have stayed in Jerusalem or other parts of Palestine and how many were visiting Hellenists.

In any case, the 3,000 on Pentecost is probably not a figure exclusively for believers who had permanent residence in Jerusalem. Perhaps the 5,000 should not be taken as such a figure either. It could mean those in Jerusalem only, or it could mean the city and the surrounding countryside in Judea or the number of messianic Jews, wherever they might live.

Whatever the scope, the total of believers would be more than 5,000 because the 5,000 are said to be men only. Here the gender-specific word *aner* is used, meaning men as opposed to women, rather than the Greek *anthropos,* which includes both men and women. Men would be regarded as heads of nuclear families, and the ordinary pattern of conversion in that culture would have been that when the head of the household makes a decision of such a magnitude, it becomes a decision for the rest of the family as well. A conservative estimate of one woman and one child for each man would put the figure at 15,000 believers. It could be considerably higher because many Jewish households would have included more than just the nuclear family. And parents having just one child was not the ordinary pattern.

If the number of believers was 15,000 or more, the figure would then be disproportionate to Joachim Jeremias's estimate of 25,000 or 30,000, mentioned in my last chapter, as the total population of Jerusalem. One explanation of this is that Jeremias's figure may be too low. Howard Marshall says, "Estimates of the total population of Jerusalem range from 25,000 to about ten times that figure."[9] The probability is that, in the absence of Bureaus of the Census, no one really knows and, therefore, no one can pinpoint the exact scope of Luke's number.

Whether it was for Jerusalem specifically or for the believing community in general, the church growth from 3,000 to 15,000 in three months calculates to 130 new converts a day. This kind of momentum, which at least would have included the city of Jerusalem, would be enough to concern the Sadducees and other groups in power. It would also cause them to act as decisively as they could when a public incident, such as the healing of the lame man in the Temple, would provide a plausible excuse.

EXPLAINING SPIRITUAL POWER TO THE ESTABLISHMENT

[5] *And it came to pass, on the next day, that their rulers, elders, and scribes,*
[6] *as well as Annas the high priest, Caiaphas, John, and Alexander, and as many as were of the family of the high priest, were gathered together at Jerusalem.*

Although he doesn't use the word as such, Luke here describes a meeting of the Sanhedrin, referred to as the council later in verse 15. This was no insignificant group. F. F. Bruce says that the Sanhedrin was "the senate and supreme court of the Jewish nation."[10] The situation must have been considered extremely serious for such an array of dignitaries to make room on their calendars for this impromptu meeting.

The Sanhedrin consisted of 70 members plus the high priest, who served as president. Bruce says, "The Sanhedrin at this time included a majority of members from the Sadducean party, supporting the chief-priestly interests, and a powerful minority from the Pharisaic party, to whom most of the scribes or professional exponents of the Law belonged."[11] They are referred to here as "rulers, elders, and scribes." They were basically in charge of the affairs of the Jewish nation, so Peter and John had been taken right to the top.

[7] *And when they had set them in the midst, they asked, "By what power or by what name have you done this?"*

These people, who were sitting as judges over Peter and John, were the same ones who, only a few months earlier, had met for the trial of Jesus. At that time they must have felt that they had put a definitive stop to any potential uprising by having the Roman government crucify Him. But now the *name* of Jesus surfaces in a dramatic way once again, and they are visibly concerned. Killing Jesus, apparently, hadn't stopped the movement! When they ask "by what name," they are clearly raising the question of authority, as I have mentioned previously. They are anxious to protect their own authority, and predictably nervous about anyone who had claimed to be King of the Jews. They must have known that by then perhaps 10 percent or 20 percent of their city was following Jesus, or at least were favorable toward the new movement.

It is significant that they do not raise the question of the validity of the miracle, as such tribunals might do in today's rationalistic and scientific age. They held the same basic worldview as the apostles and, therefore, were not disposed to question the supernatural power that seemed to dwell in Peter and John. Their question was much more insidious. Simon Kistemaker says that by emphasizing the pronoun "you," "The apostles are addressed as if they, with the beggar as their accomplice, have perpetrated a crime."[12]

But the Sanhedrin's question, as we know from the record in Acts, was a setup for Peter's chance to testify to them about the power of Jesus. Peter remembered well that Jesus had said, "They will lay their hands on you and persecute you, . . . and you will be brought before kings and rulers for My name's sake. But it will turn out for you as an occasion for testimony" (Luke 21:12-13).

[8] *Then Peter, filled with the Holy Spirit, said to them, "Rulers of the people and elders of Israel:* [9] *If we this day are judged for a good deed done to the helpless man, by what means he has been made well,* [10] *let it be known to you all, and to all the people of Israel, that by the name of Jesus Christ of Nazareth, whom you crucified, whom God raised from the dead, by Him this man stands before you whole.*

Although it was not true of everything Peter ever did or said, on this occasion, as on the Day of Pentecost, he was filled with the Holy Spirit. This is not a mere reiteration of the theological fact that all true Christian believers are indwelt by the Holy Spirit. At conversion, we are all "made to drink into one Spirit" (1 Cor. 12:13). Paul also says, "The Spirit of Him who raised Jesus from the dead dwells in you" (Rom. 8:11). However, being "filled with the Spirit" is a special empowering of the Holy Spirit over and above the ordinary, something that God desires and that we as individuals are actively to pursue. I make a daily habit of asking God to fill me with His Holy Spirit, and I believe He does, because Jesus said that just as a good father will not give a scorpion to a son who asks for an egg, "How much more will your heavenly Father give the Holy Spirit to those who ask Him!" (Luke 11:13).

For special needs, God gives the Holy Spirit in a special measure. Thus, under a special anointing of the Holy Spirit, Peter answers the Sanhedrin both defensively and offensively.

By way of defense, Peter explains how the miracle happened. He affirms what the Sadducees in the room did not want to hear, namely, that the man they had crucified had been raised from the dead, and that it was by God's power and through the authority of His name that the beggar was healed.

Peter could have elaborated a bit and stopped there. He had answered their question. But the Holy Spirit, who had filled Peter, moved him forward to turn the tables. They had implied that Peter was guilty of a crime, but now Peter becomes the accuser: "You crucified Him!" They had sinned against God because (1) God had raised Jesus from the dead to prove His authenticity, and (2) Jewish Scripture had predicted it in Psalm 118:22: "The stone which the builders rejected has become the chief cornerstone." Peter then sums it up by saying:

[12] *Nor is there salvation in any other, for there is no other name under heaven given among men by which we must be saved.*

Few, if any, of the priests or leaders responded positively and accepted Jesus as their Messiah at this stage. Later on, many of them did, but at this time they still hadn't come to terms with the fact that Jesus' kingdom was not of this world, and their personal and most immediate desire was to protect the political status quo in Jerusalem.

A THREAT WITH NO SUBSTANCE

[15] *But when they had commanded them to go aside out of the council, they conferred among themselves,* [16] *saying, "What shall we do to these men? For, indeed, that a notable miracle has been done through them is evident to all who dwell in Jerusalem, and we cannot deny it.* [17] *But so that it spreads no further among the people, let us severely threaten them, that from now on they speak to no man in this name."*

The members of the Sanhedrin were astonished at hearing such things from these Galileans whom they considered "uneducated and untrained" (4:13). If taken literally, the word for "uneducated," *agrammatoi*, could mean "illiterate"—literally, "without letters," that is, not knowing the ABCs. But whether Peter and John were or were not literate, there was no question, even in the minds of the sophisticated leaders of Jerusalem, that Peter and John had been with Jesus. The Jews had likewise marveled at Jesus, saying, "How does this Man know letters, having never studied?" (John 7:15).

The members of the Sanhedrin then went into a closed-door session and made two decisions. One was to accept the validity of the miracle because, by then, virtually everyone in Jerusalem had heard of it. The word had spread as quickly as it would today, having made the 6:00 P.M. news. The second decision was to intimidate the apostles so their movement would spread no further.

If this was a closed-door session, how would Luke have known what they discussed? It could have been that Saul, later the apostle Paul, had been present because he had been a member of the Sanhedrin. He might later have told the story to His companion Luke.

But a further question arises: Why didn't they attempt to refute the apostles' major claim—that Jesus had been raised from the dead? If they did, that could have stopped the new movement without having to make an empty threat to Peter and John. For one thing, they had already debated it and bribed soldiers to lie about it, and that hadn't worked. It was a fact that Jesus had risen again. And for another thing, as we have seen, the Sadducees and Pharisees disagreed on the doctrine of the resurrection in general, and they both knew that raising the issue in the Sanhedrin would have disrupted the meeting.

THE SHOWDOWN

[18] *And they called them and commanded them not to speak at all nor teach in the name of Jesus.* [19] *But Peter and John answered and said to them, "Whether it is right in the sight of God to listen to you more than to God, you judge.* [20] *For we cannot but speak the things which we have seen and heard."* [21] *So . . . they let them go, finding no way of punishing them . . .*

Think of the scenario. Here was the Israeli Supreme Court—71 learned, bearded, cold-eyed, scowling rabbis interrogating two hillbilly fishermen. No oddsmaker would have given the apostles the slightest chance of winning this showdown. The verdict was gravely announced with appropriate courtroom pomp and circumstance: No more preaching! Surprisingly, the apostles defied the Sanhedrin, perhaps realizing through the Holy Spirit that by now they had strong public opinion on their side. Their response might even have bordered on civil disobedience, but their priorities in desiring to serve God, no matter what, were straight. Realizing that their bluff had been called, the authorities freed the apostles.

This episode, in my opinion, was the most significant event to date for the spread of the gospel among the Jews since Jesus had left the earth. Pentecost may well have been more theologically significant, but probably not more strategically significant. This public test case involving the highest spiritual and religious authorities in first-century Judaism functionally cleared the way for the gospel to continue to spread through the Jewish community, both to Hebrew and Hellenist, which it rapidly proceeded to do.

WHAT HAPPENED TO THE CHURCH?

[23] *And being let go, they went to their own companions and reported all that the chief priests and elders had said to them.* [24] *So when they heard that, they raised their voice to God with one accord and said: "Lord, You are God, who made heaven and earth and the sea, and all that is in them, . . .* [29] *Now, Lord, look on their threats, and grant to Your servants that with all boldness they may speak Your word,* [30] *by stretching out Your hand to heal, and that signs and wonders may be done through the name of Your holy Servant Jesus."*

We do not know how many would have been in the group of "companions" to whom Peter and John reported. This could well have been what we call today their "support group," made up most likely of some of those who were in the Upper Room on the Day of Pentecost. They, undoubtedly, had been praying through the trial, and when they heard the outcome, their immediate response was to lift their voices in corporate praise to the Lord of lords. They acknowledged the sovereignty of God who had prepared the way for Peter and John so that the Sanhedrin would "do whatever Your hand and Your purpose determined before to be done" (4:28). They prayed for the two major emphases of the whole book of Acts:

- boldness to spread the gospel of the kingdom in Jerusalem, Judea, Samaria and to the uttermost parts of the earth
- supernatural power in signs and wonders to accompany their ministry of evangelization

God answered their prayer immediately, and visibly, because they obviously were praying according to His will:

[31] *And when they had prayed, the place where they were assembled together was shaken; and they were all filled with the Holy Spirit, and they spoke the word of God with boldness.*

REFLECTION QUESTIONS

1. How do we explain that it is not exactly accurate to refer to the early believers in Jerusalem as "Christians"? What are more accurate terms?
2. The blind beggar received healing even though he didn't have faith. What are different ways that faith enters the healing process?
3. Why would the Sadducees—even more than the Pharisees—be so upset over what was happening in Jerusalem?
4. The Jerusalem church grew from 3,000 to 15,000 in three months. What would your community look like if the church increased fivefold in a short time?
5. The Sanhedrin ordered the apostles to stop preaching, but they ignored the order. Is this civil disobedience? Can such a thing be justified?

6

FOLLOW THESE SIGNS TO SALVATION

ACTS 4 AND 5

These were exciting days for those who had committed their lives to follow Jesus. By this time, the church leaders were beginning to feel that the kingdom of God was not going to be seriously restrained by worldly religious and political powers such as the Sanhedrin. The gates of Hades, as Jesus had said, were not going to stand in the way of the gospel. God had once again manifested Himself physically by shaking the room where the believers were praying (see Acts 4:31). Many newer believers were there this time who had not been present on the Day of Pentecost, but they saw and felt a very similar incident. Once again, they "were all filled with the Holy Spirit" (Acts 4:31).

After describing this remarkable event, Luke changes the pace and pauses, as he frequently does, to scan the broader picture. Here, Luke looks at the general behavior of this newborn first-century church and shows us how their lifestyle reflected the values of the kingdom of God. Their lives displayed what many would call the "signs of the kingdom."

THE SIGNS OF THE KINGDOM AND THE BLESSING OF GOD: ACTS 4

[32] *Now the multitude of those who believed were of one heart and one soul; neither did anyone say that any of the things he possessed was his own, but they had all things in common.* [33] *And with great power the apostles gave witness to the resurrection of the Lord Jesus. And great grace was upon them all.*

Right from the start, the believers had built two important things into their lifestyle: (1) they generously shared their material goods with one another, and (2) they witnessed with power. As a result, "great grace was upon them all." God was responding to their service to Him by pouring out His blessing.

Both of these characteristics of the Jerusalem church are *signs that the* kingdom of God was present in their midst. They, of course, are not the only signs of the Kingdom, but they are important enough examples for Luke to occupy the rest of Acts 4 and all of chapter 5 in detailing how they were being implemented.

WHAT ARE THE "SIGNS OF THE KINGDOM"?

Jesus said to His disciples, "And this gospel of the kingdom will be preached in all the world as a witness to all the nations, and then the end will come" (Matt. 24:14). The heart of the Christian message is the kingdom of God. In the Lord's Prayer itself, Jesus asked His followers to pray: "Your kingdom come. Your will be done on earth as it is in heaven" (Matt. 6:10).

If this is what we preach about and pray about, how do we know if, and when, our prayers are being answered? We know by observing tangible signs of the Kingdom.

As we have seen on many occasions up to this point, the kingdom of God is not a sociopolitical kingdom. We are not aiming for a theocracy. It is easy to fall into this kind of erroneous thinking, as we see from the disciples themselves. Even though, while He was on Earth, Jesus took great pains to explain to His disciples and others that "My kingdom is not of this world" (John 18:36), they did not fully understand it until long after He had left. As we saw in Acts 1, they were still saying, "Lord, will You at this time restore the kingdom to Israel?" (Acts 1:6). They were hoping that Jesus would liberate them from the political yoke of the Romans. In fact, this idea had contributed greatly to the strong opposition of the Sadducees who had been doing very well under the Romans and who wished to preserve the status quo.

Unfortunately, this idea has not disappeared over 20 centuries. Many good-hearted Christians are still hoping wistfully that secular government will legislate the Ten Commandments and the Sermon on the Mount. They are saying, "Jesus, will you restore Your kingdom to our nation?" The desire that God's kingdom will come is commendable. A chief reason for Jesus' death on the cross as the Second Adam was to empower His people to regain the dominion over creation that was offered to the First Adam. But the weapons of our warfare are spiritual, not carnal.

The kingdom of God does not have geographical or political boundaries. It is present in the world through communities of believers who recognize Jesus Christ as the Lord of their lives and who encourage the signs of the kingdom to characterize their behavior both individually and collectively. This is exactly what the members of the Jerusalem church were doing in those early days.

When Jesus first began His public ministry, Matthew says that He preached, saying, "Repent, for the kingdom of heaven is at hand" (Matt. 4:17). One of the first places Jesus went was to His hometown of Nazareth where He used the synagogue as His platform to make the first public announcement of His ministry agenda. As Luke adds details to this story (see Luke 4:16-19), he does not explicitly state that Jesus' agenda items are "signs of the kingdom," but it is not at all out of line to surmise that they are exactly that. Here are these signs that, incidentally, were taken directly from the Old Testament in Isaiah 61:

1. Preaching the gospel to the poor
2. Healing the brokenhearted
3. Preaching deliverance to captives
4. Restoring sight to the blind
5. Liberating the oppressed
6. Instituting the acceptable year of the Lord

Through the years, as would be expected, these signs have been interpreted in a variety of ways. Some take them quite literally, while others strive to extract deeper spiritual meanings or see them as metaphors. My purpose at this point is not to discuss varieties of interpretations but simply to point out that whatever one's understanding of them, when these ministries characterize the behavior of Christians, God's kingdom is present.

But the list is longer. At one point, John the Baptist was downhearted and discouraged. He had also preached, "Repent, for the kingdom of heaven is at hand" (Matt. 3:2), but he wasn't seeing God's kingdom coming quite as rapidly and widely as he thought it should. Even as great a man as John the Baptist wondered about the shape of the new kingdom when confronted with his own death while Jesus was in full swing with His own ministry. John's message to Jesus, "Are You the Coming One?" was a plaintive cry. Jesus' answer was kind and profound. He simply responded by listing more of the tangible signs of the Kingdom that had been publicly visible through His ministry, and by demonstrating them right before the eyes of John the Baptist's messengers (see Luke 7:20-23). Without repeating any of the signs already listed above, here are the additional ones:

7. Healing the sick
8. Casting out evil spirits
9. Making lame people walk
10. Cleansing lepers
11. Restoring hearing to the deaf
12. Raising the dead

When Jesus sent out His disciples to preach the gospel in all the world, He said that they would expect the signs of the Kingdom to follow them as they went (see Mark 16:15-18). Although some biblical scholars debate whether the original Greek text of Mark actually included this passage, most agree that the signs listed were, in fact, characteristic of the lifestyle of those who were preaching the gospel of the Kingdom in those days. We can therefore add:

13. Speaking in new tongues
14. Safely picking up serpents (see Acts 28:3-5)
15. Immunity to poison

These 15 signs of the Kingdom are by no means exhaustive. The New Testament is peppered with other significant characteristics of the lifestyle of Christians that just as clearly reflect the presence of the kingdom of God as do these. However, these 15 signs do give us a broad picture in which to understand Luke's description of how the believers in Jerusalem were working out some of them in their daily life both in the church and in the workplace.

ONE OF THE SIGNS: SHARING MATERIAL GOODS (ACTS 4:34–5:11)

The last time Luke paused to describe the church was after the Day of Pentecost. There he mentioned, almost in passing, sharing material goods (see Acts 2:44-45). Now he again describes the church after the events surrounding the healing of the lame man, which, I postulated in the last chapter, possibly would rank alongside of Pentecost in significance for advancing the Kingdom. Luke also discloses in more detail how they were sharing material goods.

Sharing material goods is one of those signs of the Kingdom outside the 15 already listed. It characterizes those who have been "filled with the Holy Spirit" (Acts 4:31), as these believers were, because one of the fruits of the Holy Spirit is "goodness" (see Gal. 5:22). A clear Kingdom principle that Jesus often taught was to regard material possessions as secondary. He said, "Do not lay up for yourselves treasures on earth, where moth and rust destroy and where thieves break in and steal" (Matt. 6:19). He also taught, "You shall love your neighbor as yourself" (Matt. 22:39).

Put these things together, and it is understandable why the believers in Jerusalem "did [not] say that any of the things [they] possessed was [their] own, but they had all things in common" (Acts 4:32).

The Kingdom principle is not that we are to do without material goods. We must constantly guard ourselves against the influence of the evil spirit of poverty that would plant the idea in our minds that poverty somehow promotes piety. No, the principle here is that we should not *prioritize* material goods. We should prioritize unselfishly loving our fellow believers and also our wider circle of neighbors whether they are Christians or not. This is what Jesus meant when He said, "Seek first the kingdom of God and His righteousness, and all these things shall be added to you" (Matt. 6:33). Here is another statement of priorities. If we prioritize the Kingdom and its values, we will not lack "all these things," which refers to material goods. In the Lord's Prayer, we first pray, "Your kingdom come," and then, "Give us this day our daily bread." The order is very important because it indicates the proper priorities. If we follow God's priorities, He will see that we are taken care of materially and that we prosper.

Putting the Principle into Practice

[34] ***Nor was there anyone among them who lacked; for all who were possessors of lands or houses sold them, and brought the proceeds of the things that were sold,*** [35] ***and laid them at the apostles' feet; and they distributed to each as anyone had need.***

The believers in Jerusalem decided to implement the principle of sharing material goods by selling real estate. Some modern readers stumble slightly at this passage because it seems to go against private ownership of land. But this thinking confuses the *principle* with the *practice*. The principle does not address private ownership of land, but prioritizing the values of the kingdom of God. To these believers, material goods were secondary, as they should have been. Money should never be seen as an end in itself but rather as a means to accomplish a higher end.

We need not conclude that *everyone* in the church sold *every* house or lot they possessed. Our translation, "all who were possessors of lands or houses sold them," may not be the best way of understanding the underlying Greek text. Bible scholars generally agree that this is not some sort of appeal for a type of Christian communism, because private ownership of property is affirmed both in the Old Testament and in the New Testament. For example, Mary the mother of Mark obviously kept her private house (see Acts 12:12).

Even so, the principle is a radical one. I like the way John Stott puts it: "Although in fact and in law they continued to own their goods, yet in heart and mind they cultivated an attitude so radical that they thought of their possessions as being available to help needy sisters and brothers."[1] The amazing result was that no poverty existed in the Church: "Nor was there anyone among them who lacked."

Christians Should Not Be Poor

As I understand God's kingdom economy, nothing is wrong with having rich people in the church, but something is wrong about having poor people in the church. The Old Testament principle in Deuteronomy 15:4 states that there should be "no poor among you." The New Testament principle states that the gospel, or the "good news," should be preached to the poor (see Luke 4:18). When the people of God are "of one heart and one soul" (Acts 4:32), as they were in Jerusalem, implementing the principle of providing for the poor requires neither argument nor planning. It happens as naturally as a mother providing food for her baby.

I am appalled when I read the annual reports of the levels of giving in our American churches. No wonder we are not able to take care of our poor, even among our own church members. As I have mentioned before, the bare minimum of giving, for a Christian who desires a Kingdom lifestyle, is 10 percent of income. In most American churches, however, the median giving is less than 3 percent.

Few of us may be ready to sell real estate in order to give tangible evidence that the Kingdom has come and that we have our priorities straight. Actually, over the span of 2,000 years of the spread of Christianity, such a practice has rarely been implemented except in case of emergency. However, if we simply started with a tithe, many of our church financial problems would be over, and we would be able to provide for the poor better than we have been. Another step in which I believe, and which my wife and I have practiced for more than 20 years, is the "graduated tithe," which means increasing the *percentage* of giving each year that God blesses with an increase of annual income. Ten percent has been left far behind and, so far, we are not lacking.

If we more diligently put the principle of sharing material possessions into practice, someone might be able to say about our church, "And great grace was upon them all" (Acts 4:33). What a blessing that would be!

AN EXAMPLE: BARNABAS

[36] ***And Joses, who was also named Barnabas by the apostles (which is translated Son of Encouragement), a Levite of the country of Cyprus,*** **[37]** ***having land, sold it, and brought the money and laid it at the apostles' feet.***

This is the first mention of Barnabas, who becomes a major character in the book of Acts and whom Luke mentions more than 20 times. In this story of how the signs of the Kingdom were being manifested in the Jerusalem church, Luke carefully selects Barnabas as a model of an ideal believer. Barnabas provides us a concrete example of how the principle of sharing material goods was being implemented; and later, Ananias and Sapphira show how the same principle was violated. Luke characterizes Barnabas as "a good man, full of the Holy Spirit and of faith" (Acts 11:24). Here Luke lists three specific things about this remarkable man:

Barnabas was a Levite. This is of passing interest because, as some may recall, the Old Testament Levites were not supposed to own property (see Deut. 18:2), and they were given no territory in the Promised Land (see Josh. 13:14). However, as Everett Harrison points out, "Even by the time of Jeremiah this was not strictly maintained (Jer. 1:1; 32:6-15)."[2] This also serves to remind us that up to this point all the believers were still Jews, and among Jews, being a Levite was important enough to note even in a brief biographical sketch.

Barnabas was a Hellenistic Jew. I pointed out in chapter 2 that all 12 of Jesus' inner circle were *Hebrew* Jews. We do not know whether there were any exceptions to this among the 120 in the Upper Room on Pentecost, although Joseph Barsabas is thought by some to be a Cyprian, as was Barnabas. In any case, Barnabas is the first clearly *Hellenistic* Jew mentioned in Acts. These, as has been said, were born and raised outside of Palestine and were much more influenced by the prevailing Greek culture than were the Hebrews. Therefore, they were called "Hellenists," a term that means "like the Greeks." It is important to keep in mind that Barnabas was not a Gentile, but a Jew by race who also spoke Greek and, culturally, was somewhat different from the Hebraic Jews.

This difference becomes crucial when a conflict between the Hebrews and Hellenists erupts in Acts 6. In terms of selling private property, it is likely that the Hellenists would have been more affluent and thus would have owned more property than the Hebrew Jewish believers. (More on this in the next chapter.)

Barnabas was an encourager. The apostles thought so highly of this man, whose original name was Joses, that they gave him a nickname, Barnabas, meaning Son of Encouragement. William LaSor says, "Barnabas was good at exhorting, encouraging, comforting. He must have been a wonderful man to have been given such a wonderful name!"[3] It seems that Barnabas had a pastor's heart and was a phlegmatic personality type; quite a contrast from Paul, with whom a significant conflict arises almost 20 years later.

AN EXCEPTION: ANANIAS AND SAPPHIRA: ACTS 5

[1] *But a certain man named Ananias, with Sapphira his wife, sold a pos-*
session. [2] *And he kept back part of the proceeds, his wife also being*
aware of it, and brought a certain part and laid it at the apostles' feet.
[3] *But Peter said, "Ananias, why has Satan filled your heart to lie to the*
Holy Spirit and keep back part of the price of the land for yourself?
[4] *While it remained, was it not your own? And after it was sold, was it*
not in your own control? Why have you conceived this thing in your
heart? You have not lied to men but to God." [5] *Then Ananias, hearing*
these words, fell down and breathed his last. So great fear came upon all
those who heard these things. [6] *And the young men arose and wrapped*
him up, carried him out, and buried him. [7] *Now it was about three*
hours later when his wife came in, not knowing what had happened.
[8] *And Peter answered her, "Tell me whether you sold the land for so*
much?" And she said, "Yes, for so much." [9] *Then Peter said to her,*

"How is it that you have agreed together to test the Spirit of the Lord? Look, the feet of those who have buried your husband are at the door, and they will carry you out." [10] *Then immediately she fell down at his feet and breathed her last. And the young men came in and found her dead, and carrying her out, buried her by her husband.* [11] *So great fear came upon all the church and upon all who heard these things.*

Barnabas was the example of those who used the practice of selling property for God's glory, while Ananias and Sapphira are examples of those who attempted to use it to enhance their own reputation.

What was Ananias's and Sapphira's sin? A cursory reading might lead to the notion that their sin was withholding money and not giving enough to the church. But Peter clearly points out that Ananias had two other options he did not elect to take.

First, Ananias could have decided not to sell the property at all, but keep it for himself. "While it remained, was it not your own?" This is another indication that the Jerusalem church was not practicing a form of Christian communism, because selling private property was regarded as a personal decision, not a requirement legislated by the church and imposed on its membership. Had Ananias and Sapphira chosen this option, they certainly would not have received God's death penalty.

Second, Ananias could have sold the property and made a partial donation to the church. "And after it was sold, was it not in your own control?" If he had made an aboveboard partial donation, presumably he would not have been rebuked.

Instead, Ananias and Sapphira made the decision to lie to the church about how much they had sold the property for in order to make themselves appear as committed to God's kingdom and its priorities as Barnabas and others were. Big mistake! Stinginess could have been tolerated, but not pride-fueled hypocrisy. Ananias's intentional, premeditated deception was seen as a more serious sin than usual: "You have not lied to men but to God."

"The Devil Made Me Do It!"

What caused Ananias and Sapphira to do this? Obviously, Satan had something to do with it, because Peter says, "Why has Satan filled your heart?" At this point, Peter was talking from personal experience. When Peter had rebuked Jesus on one occasion, Jesus had said, "Get behind me, Satan" (Matt. 16:23).

Peter had learned from personal experience that he could not excuse his own moral lapses before God by saying, "The devil made me do it." Although Satan certainly was behind Ananias's deception, Ananias couldn't blame his misbehavior on Satan. He himself was the one who, giving in to Satan, had plunged into an outright, blatant lie to the Holy Spirit, and he was the one who subsequently received the judgment of God.

Ananias could have resisted Satan's temptation, as can any believer in such a situation. James says, "Resist the devil and he will flee from you" (Jas. 4:7). Paul asserts that God provides ways of escape with each temptation, and that the choice to take the way of escape, or not, is ours (see 1 Cor. 10:13).

This is not to ignore the fact that Satan has gained more control over some believers than others. Although it is not theologically sound to suppose that a Christian can be demon *possessed*, it is clear that demonization can occur at least to the extent of Satan "filling the heart," as in the case of Ananias. Some are more comfortable with the terms "demonic oppression" or "demonic affliction" or "demonic influence," while others transliterate the Greek and use "demonization." All are attempts to acknowledge that Satan goes about like a roaring lion, seeking whom he may devour (see 1 Pet. 5:8), and that at times he succeeds.

Even in cases of severe demonization, more frequently than not the afflicted believer has given Satan a legal ground, or a stronghold, from which to operate. Peter's question to Ananias, "Why has Satan filled your heart?" carries the clear implication that Ananias somehow had allowed the enemy to do it. Now he was paying the consequences, and his wife, who had joined him in the plot, would soon follow suit.

Some may be asking how curses relate to this. It is true that believers can be victimized through satanic attack with no fault of their own, as was Job. But although powers of darkness can influence health, loved ones, material possessions and peace, *moral decisions* are strictly the responsibility of the individual. Satan can deceive us, but he cannot make our moral choices for us. Although Job was a victim of almost every conceivable direct attack of Satan, in moral issues he maintained his uprightness and did not sin (see Job 1:22; 2:3,10). Ananias could have done the same but he chose not to.

Hearing from God

How did Peter know that Ananias was lying? As I study the commentaries on this passage, I am rather fascinated at how few commentators raise this question. Of course, there could have been some natural explanations. Ananias may have been one of those poor liars who can't help but give it away. Or Peter may have received some insider information about the real estate deal before Ananias showed up. As I read it, however, the whole tone of the passage seems to indicate that something much more supernatural is behind this event.

Although I cannot prove it directly from the text, I have a hunch that if someone had asked Peter how he knew, he would have said, "God told me." It is not out of line to suppose that we have here an example of New Testament prophecy (see 1 Cor. 14:24-25). Peter, filled with the Holy Spirit, had his ear carefully tuned to receiving revelation from God that was directly applicable to the situation. Stanley Horton agrees when he says, "Perhaps this was revealed to him through one of the gifts of revelation."[4]

This is how Peter would also have known that God was going to apply capital punishment. The sentence of death was not from Peter; it was from God. Although Luke does not record that Peter spoke the sentence to Ananias, it is clearly recorded that he did speak it to his wife, Sapphira (see Acts 5:9).

I believe that one of the main lessons of this dramatic passage is that the Holy Spirit is a real person and He is directly in touch with the Church and with every individual member.

Speaking of the Church, Luke ends this story by saying, *So great fear came upon all the church.* This is the first use of the technical term "church" from the Greek *ekklesia* in the book of Acts, but it is subsequently used 22 more times. Some may say, How about Acts 2:47, where we read, "And the Lord added to the *church* daily those who were being saved"? The Greek term *ekklesia* does not appear in this verse, and many modern translations reflect this by saying, "the Lord added to *their number*" rather than to "*the church.*"

ANOTHER SIGN OF THE KINGDOM: POWER MINISTRY (ACTS 5:12-42)

The theme of this chapter is to highlight the signs of the kingdom of God, which, as all true signs do, point to a certain destination. For the book of Acts, that destination is the blessings of God's kingdom spreading from Jerusalem to Judea, Samaria and the ends of the earth. Although the church and the kingdom of God are not one and the same, churches that do display the signs of the Kingdom bring the two together here on Earth.

We have seen that one of the signs of the Kingdom clearly displayed in the church in Jerusalem was a willingness to share their material goods, particularly with the poor. Another sign was their active involvement in what we call today "power ministries." For example, when Jesus healed a blind and mute man by casting out a demon, He explained, "But if I cast out demons by the Spirit of God, surely the kingdom of God has come upon you" (Matt. 12:28). How do we know that the kingdom of God is authentically among us? One way is to see healings and demonic deliverances as part of the ongoing ministry of the Church.

Quantity and Quality

Church growth needs to take place both in quantity and in quality. Luke seems to realize this as he weaves them together in these first few chapters of Acts:

- *Quality* in Acts 1. Here we observe the believers in prayer and in organizing themselves by appointing Matthias as Judas's replacement.
- *Quantity* in Acts 2:1-41. The Day of Pentecost sees 3,000 come to Christ.
- *Quality* in Acts 2:42-47. The church continues steadfast and shares their material goods.
- *Quantity* in Acts 3:1–4:22. The lame man is healed and the church grows to 15,000.
- *Quality* in Acts 4:23–5:11. Believers pray and share their material possessions.
- *Quantity* in Acts 5:12-42. Signs and wonders point the way to salvation for many.
- *Quality* in Acts 6:1-6. Reorganization of the church.
- *Quantity* in Acts 6:7. Many priests are converted.

Sharing material goods can be seen as a sign of the Kingdom that contributes to internal growth or to the *quality* of the church. In contrast, the signs and wonders and power ministry seem to point more toward the outward ministry to the world and, therefore, to *quantitative* church growth. Both are needed.

THE MIRACLES AND WONDERS

[12] ***And through the hands of the apostles many signs and wonders were done among the people. And they were all with one accord in***

Solomon's Porch. [13] *Yet none of the rest dared join them, but the people esteemed them highly.* [14] *And believers were increasingly added to the Lord, multitudes of both men and women,* [15] *so that they brought the sick out into the streets and laid them on beds and couches, that at least the shadow of Peter passing by might fall on some of them.* [16] *Also a multitude gathered from the surrounding cities to Jerusalem, bringing sick people and those who were tormented by unclean spirits, and they were all healed.*

The parallel with Acts 2 continues. There, "they were all filled with the Holy Spirit" (2:4) and here, "they were all filled with the Holy Spirit" (4:31). There, God sent a tangible "sound from heaven, as of a rushing mighty wind" (2:2), and here, "the place where they were assembled together was shaken" (4:31). There, they "sold their possessions and goods, and divided them among all" (2:45), and here, they sold their possessions and "had all things in common" (4:32). There, "many wonders and signs were done through the apostles" (2:43), and here, "through the hands of the apostles many signs and wonders were done among the people" (Acts 5:12).

Luke is also anxious to remind us once again that the purpose for all this was the spread of the kingdom and the salvation of souls. There, "the Lord added to the church daily those who were being saved" (2:47), and here, "believers were increasingly added to the Lord, multitudes of both men and women" (5:14). Notice that the word "multitudes" indicates substantial acceleration in growth.

The title of this chapter, "Follow These Signs to Salvation," is meant to point out that the signs of the kingdom of God have as their major purpose to bring glory to God through the salvation of the lost. At this point, we are dealing with "many signs and wonders." These signs and wonders are to be seen as one of the manifestations of receiving "power when the Holy Spirit has come upon you," to repeat the last words of Jesus spoken in Acts 1:8. Because Acts 1:8 is the acknowledged table of contents for the book of Acts, the working of the Holy Spirit through power ministries needs to be understood as thoroughly as possible.

PARADIGM SHIFTS

Many Christians today, particularly those of us not rooted in Pentecostal or charismatic traditions, have had to make major adjustments to the restoration of ministries of the miraculous spreading throughout the whole Body of

Christ beginning in the 1980s. Most of us, including myself, have had to go through paradigm shifts in order to adjust our thinking, our attitudes and our ministry to what for us is a new spiritual reality. Although we previously read and believed the Acts of the Apostles, the stories of signs and wonders we found there seemed rather misty, relegated to something that might have occurred in the distant past, or something that might yet be occurring on a far-off mission field but with little relevance to mainstream United States Christianity. Some of us might even have thought that our superior version of Christianity was mature enough and sophisticated enough that these rather primitive manifestations were no longer needed.

A major factor in stimulating traditional evangelical paradigm shifts was the leadership of John Wimber, who began his own paradigm shift around 1978. Wimber systematized his theories by joining me to teach the much-publicized Fuller Seminary course "MC510: Signs, Wonders and Church Growth" for several years. He had developed the practice through founding the Vineyard Christian Fellowship of Anaheim, California, which rapidly became one of America's most outstanding megachurches, eventually spawning a whole new denomination.

A corresponding body of literature sprang up. Wimber's ideas are summarized in his books *Power Evangelism* and *Power Healing*. At the time he was teaching at Fuller, two School of World Mission faculty members became Wimber disciples, went through their personal paradigm shifts, and wrote books of their own. Charles Kraft, from the Evangelical Covenant Church, wrote *Christianity with Power*, and I, from the Congregational Church, wrote *How to Have a Healing Ministry in Any Church*. Many other books, also written by those outside the Pentecostal and charismatic traditions, have been added. In order to label this new phenomenon, some used the term "Third Wave."

This dynamic, contemporary movement helped us understand the book of Acts in ways not reflected in the standard commentaries published before the emergence of the Third Wave, a notable exception being the Assemblies of God scholar Stanley Horton.

THE FACTS ABOUT SIGNS AND WONDERS

In order to understand this phenomenon of ministries in the miraculous, which will continue through the book of Acts, I am going to set forth some facts, then move on to interpretation.

First, power ministry was common. "And through the hands of the apostles many signs and wonders were done among the people" (5:12). The signs and wonders, of course, didn't start at this point. The lame man at the Temple gate had previously been healed. Signs and wonders are mentioned in Acts 2. And many, of course, had been healing the sick and casting out demons while Jesus was still on Earth (see Mark 9:38-39; Luke 9:49-50; 10:1,9).

Second, sick people from surrounding areas were brought into Jerusalem for the specific purpose of receiving divine healing and deliverance from demonic spirits (see 5:16). This seems to be significant from the evangelistic point of view. Presumably, those who had been healed by the power of God later returned to their homes and testified of their healing and of Jesus as Messiah. Because it is likely that they came from many parts of Judea, they probably would have become the major carriers of the gospel from "Jerusalem to Judea" as Jesus had mandated in Acts 1:8. Previously, from what we know, the gospel at that particular time would have been limited largely to Jerusalem and Galilee, the province to the north where most of Jesus' earthly ministry took place.

How the gospel spread through the testimony of these simple believers, without prestigious apostles and other leaders accompanying them, can be clearly understood by observing the rapid spread of Christianity throughout mainland China today. My friend David Wang of Asian Outreach helped me through my paradigm shift in the early 1980s by bringing me firsthand reports of multitudes of simple Chinese people coming to Christ through signs and wonders.

Wang told, for example, of a commune of more than 30,000, all of whom were Christian. The commune had become known as "Yesu Mountain." The Christian church there for years had been small and struggling, virtually throttled by an aggressive communist party leader from Beijing. Then the communist official developed advanced cancer in his nose that was beyond the scope of medical science. In desperation and in fear of losing his life, he swallowed his pride and asked the Christian leader he had been persecuting to pray to God for healing. The cancer was totally cured, the man became a believer and the way was opened for a people movement that swept the whole commune. The officer was subsequently jailed, but he rejoiced for the privilege of suffering for Christ, as did many in the book of Acts (see Acts 5:41).

Throughout China today, such stories are almost as common as chopsticks.

Since we know that in China, 1.5 million believers grew to more than 100 million in 30 years, we can say without any possible contradiction that continuing equivalent growth of the Christian community at this writing would be 20,000 to 35,000 per day! In sheer magnitude, it dwarfs anything that Luke could have possibly imagined.

Third, "They brought the sick out into the streets . . . that at least the shadow of Peter passing by might fall on some of them" (5:15). Apparently Peter, at the time, was ministering in the role of what some would call a "faith healer" today. Others were doing miracles as well, but it seems that Peter had a special anointing. In fact, it was so powerful that some were healed simply through being near him, even though they received no personal ministry or prayer. Although it is unusual both yesterday and today, nevertheless, similar things are being reported in our time. Personal friends of mine, such as Cindy Jacobs, Reinhard Bonnke and the late John Wimber, have experienced anointings seemingly as powerful as Peter's.

INTERPRETING THE FACTS

My intention in this section is not to repeat the material on signs and wonders covered in books such as those referenced previously, but rather in a limited space to help those readers who may be considering a paradigm shift. Such a shift will greatly enhance our ability to apply what we learn from the book of Acts to Christian life and ministry today.

At the same time, I realize that others keenly feel differently about such a paradigm shift.

For example, one of the commentators I have been using says, after describing some biblical miracles, "We should not, therefore, expect to do these things ourselves today. . . . Even the healing miracles of the Gospels and Acts had features which are seldom manifested even in the signs and wonders movement today." My information leads me to a different conclusion. Evidence from many parts of the world points to the literal fulfillment of Jesus' words: "He who believes in Me, the works that I do he will do also; and greater works than these he will do, because I go to my Father" (John 14:12).

WHAT IS THE PURPOSE OF MIRACLES?

It is important to understand, first of all, what miracles *are not.* Miracles *are not:*

- for public display or curiosity, like a circus act, to arouse astonishment;
- to bring personal status or gain to the "faith healer" or to other Christians whom God uses to heal the sick;
- a form of Christian magic by which we manipulate the supernatural;
- exclusively psychosomatic in their operation.

On the other hand, miracles *are*:

- signs of the presence of the kingdom of God, as I have extensively argued;
- expressions of God's compassion to alleviate those who are sick, in pain or demonized;
- signs pointing to the power of Jesus Christ and His cross to save unbelievers, as Luke reports in Acts 5:14.

How Many for Whom We Pray Are Actually Healed?

Luke reports that the multitude of people who came into Jerusalem were all healed (see 5:16). For those of us who are attempting to practice power ministries today, this is extraordinary. Hermeneutically speaking, the word "all" does not always have to mean "every single one without exception." But I know of no good reason to doubt that in this case every single one was, in fact, healed. For one thing, it would mean that Peter's shadow itself was one of the effective instruments of healing. This was certainly a notable occurrence.

In most cases we know of today, not everyone is healed. I have heard of exceptions to this, but they clearly appear to be exceptions, not the rule. When I began my healing ministry, I supplied report forms to each person I prayed for over a five-year period. Generally speaking, 25 percent to 30 percent were completely healed, 50 percent to 60 percent reported some degree of healing and around 20 percent sensed no improvement. I have compared these findings with other healing ministries and found comparable outcomes. I believe that we should aim for the 100 percent healing we find in Acts 5:16, but I also believe that, meanwhile, we should glorify God for the healing that does take place through prayer and the power of the Holy Spirit, even if all are not healed.

We can take some comfort in the fact that Jesus Himself did not heal every sick or demonized person He met. When Jesus returned to His hometown of Nazareth, "He did not do many mighty works there because of their unbelief"

(Matt. 13:58). At the pool of Bethesda, Jesus found a great multitude of sick people but healed only one of them (see John 5:1-9). And as I mentioned previously, Jesus must have passed by the lame beggar at the Temple gate many times, but the healing came later through Peter and John (see Acts 3:1-11).

How Long Did Those Who Were Healed Stay Well?

We have no report of the answer to the question of how long those who were healed stayed well, but one thing we do know—they all eventually died. It is good to keep in mind that healing is extremely valuable, but it is only temporal. That is why Jesus reminded His disciples, after a powerful healing campaign, that more important than the healing is to have one's name written in heaven (see Luke 10:20). Ministries in the miraculous, as I like to say, are only the *signs* pointing to the *Son*. The most important thing is salvation, and that is why Luke constantly reiterates that lost people were being saved.

Did Only the Apostles Have Healing Power?

In Acts 2:43 we read, "And many wonders and signs were done through the apostles." Then, in Acts 4:33, "With great power the apostles gave witness." And, here in Acts 5:12, "And through the hands of the apostles many signs and wonders were done among the people." In light of this, one unnamed commentator concludes that such healings "were never intended for the church at large."

It is true that in the book of Acts, Luke has a great deal to say about the apostles' healing ministry. But as I read the New Testament, there is no intention to confine healing to the 12. Jesus demonstrated this by sending out 70 on ministries of healing and casting out demons, recorded in Luke 10. In Acts itself, Stephen, who was not an apostle, "did great wonders and signs among the people" (Acts 6:8). Also, multitudes listened to Philip's preaching, "seeing the miracles which he did" (Acts 8:6). Jesus expected that those who believe will "lay hands on the sick, and they will recover" (Mark 16:18). Later, the apostle Paul lists "gifts of healings" among the spiritual gifts God distributes throughout the Body of Christ (see 1 Cor. 12:9).

THE UPSHOT? BACK TO JAIL! (ACTS 5:17-32)

[17] ***Then the high priest rose up, and all those who were with him (which is the sect of the Sadducees), and they were filled with indignation,*** [18] ***and laid their hands on the apostles and put them in the common prison.***

The Sadducees once again led the persecution. One of the reasons was that larger crowds were now listening to the apostles' giving "witness to the resurrection of the Lord Jesus" (Acts 4:33), contradicting the Sadducees' teaching that there was no possibility of resurrection. Furthermore, they feared major social disruption emerging from the growing messianic Jewish movement in Jerusalem. It is interesting that the rival sect of Pharisees did not share the depth of feeling with the Sadducees on either of these issues.

Apparently, several apostles, perhaps all 12, were arrested this time, not just Peter and John.

[19] *But at night an angel of the Lord opened the prison doors and brought them out, and said,* [20] *"Go, stand in the temple and speak to the people all the words of this life."* [21] *And when they heard that, they entered the temple early in the morning and taught. . . .*

Some commentators find this story of an angelic visit a bit far-fetched and affirm that it must have been a human messenger. I like Everett Harrison's reply: "While it is true that the word for 'angel' can also mean 'messenger' and indicate a human being, this is rare; it is wholly unlikely in the present instance, where the full description 'angel of the Lord' emphasizes celestial origin and dignity."[5]

Miracles are not always done by human agents, although this is the most common pattern in the New Testament. They are also done by angels, as in this case, and by direct, divine intervention, as Saul of Tarsus later experienced on the Damascus road.

The angel commanded the apostles to disobey the Sanhedrin and to preach the gospel in the Temple. In a case such as this, whom do we obey? Is civil disobedience ever justified? We will focus on more of this shortly.

Arrested Once More!

[24] *Now when the high priest, the captain of the temple, and the chief priests heard these things, they wondered what the outcome would be.* [25] *Then one came and told them, saying, "Look, the men whom you put in prison are standing in the temple and teaching the people!"* [26] *Then the captain went with the officers and brought them without violence, for they feared the people, lest they should be stoned.*

It is well to remember that the Sanhedrin was the supreme court of Israel. This must have been an extremely embarrassing moment for them—not a good day! The same authorities who arrested Peter and John came again for the 12. This time, Luke takes pains to mention that they did not use force in the arrest. Why? By now, large numbers of people were getting healed, and, therefore, they loved, and owed a great deal to, the apostles. The authorities were afraid of being stoned, a fear that we can well appreciate through frequent television news reports of disturbances in the Middle East today.

[27] . . . *And the high priest asked them,* [28] *saying, "Did we not strictly command you not to teach in this name? And look, you have filled Jerusalem with your doctrine, and intend to bring this Man's blood on us!"*

The issue of civil disobedience is now coming to a head. And a new underlying fear is surfacing—what would happen if the people of Jerusalem blamed the Sanhedrin for the death of Jesus? Even if Luke hadn't told us directly about the rapid growth of the church in Jerusalem during these days, the statement of the high priest about filling "Jerusalem with [the apostles'] doctrine" would suffice as a word of encouragement for Christian readers.

[29] *Then Peter and the other apostles answered and said: "We ought to obey God rather than men.* [30] *The God of our fathers raised up Jesus whom you murdered by hanging on a tree.* [31] *Him God has exalted to His right hand to be Prince and Savior, to give repentance to Israel and forgiveness of sins.* [32] *And we are His witnesses to these things . . ."*

I know of Christian leaders today who are very critical of government officials, until they get invited to meet them personally. Then they change their tune. Not Peter! He directly accused them of murdering Jesus, reaffirmed the Resurrection and announced that he would engage in civil disobedience and obey God rather than the Sanhedrin. With this direct challenge to their authority, it is perfectly understandable why they wanted to kill the apostles.

The Verdict

[33] When they heard this, they were furious and took counsel to kill them. [34] Then one in the council stood up, a Pharisee named Gamaliel, a teacher of the law held in respect by all the people . . . [35] And he said to them: "Men of Israel, take heed to yourselves what you intend to do regarding these men. [38] And now I say to you, keep away from these men and let them alone; for if this plan or this work is of men, it will come to nothing; [39] but if it is of God, you cannot overthrow it—lest you even be found to fight against God."

Luke seems to make the point that God's wisdom was given to the Sanhedrin through a Pharisee who was unafraid to confront the majority Sadducees. Gamaliel was a man of great respect, the chief mentor of Saul of Tarsus before he became the apostle Paul (see Acts 22:3). Gamaliel's wise counsel became crucial to maintaining the momentum of the early Christian movement.

[40] And they agreed with him, and when they had called for the apostles and beaten them, they commanded that they should not speak in the name of Jesus, and let them go.

Unfortunately for the apostles, the Sanhedrin took only part of Gamaliel's advice. Instead of leaving them completely alone, they had them beaten. This would ordinarily have been a severe physical punishment, but given the mood of the general public in Jerusalem at the time, one wonders whether the beating might have been more of the token variety. In more severe cases, their friends would have had to come and carry them away.

[41] So they departed from the presence of the council, rejoicing that they were counted worthy to suffer shame for His name. [42] And daily in the temple, and in every house, they did not cease teaching and preaching Jesus as the Christ.

Whatever the punishment, the apostles' reaction was joy. The crucial event was over. The supreme court had caused the apostles to pay their debt to society for their perceived criminal actions. And now, much to the consternation of the Sadducees in particular, the apostles disobeyed their command not to preach and continued to spread the word about Jesus with relative impunity. The gospel of Christ had now become firmly planted in the social soil of the city of Jerusalem, and it would continue to bear much fruit for nearly 40 more years.

REFLECTION QUESTIONS

1. Look over the list of the 15 different signs of the kingdom of God. Which of the signs are evident in your church? Would you desire that the others become evident as well?
2. Very few Christians today go as far as to sell their real estate and give the proceeds to the church. Are there other ways that the same kind of dedication can be and is being shown?
3. Ananias committed a sin that cost his life. Satan had filled his heart. Why couldn't he blame his own failure on Satan?
4. The Church should grow both in quantity and quality. Review some of the ways we have seen both of them happen so far in Acts.
5. Supernatural signs and wonders were a vital part of the ministry of the apostles. Why do you think some would say that we shouldn't expect them today?

7

SHOULD FOREIGNERS RUN THE CHURCH?

ACTS 6

A great deal happens in the first seven verses of Acts 6 that has important implications for the subsequent expansion of the entire Christian movement.

Back in chapter 2, I pointed out how the "people approach to world evangelization" has now been adopted by missiologists all over the world. This is a rediscovered insight that has been in the Bible all along. But for Americans especially, who have all but forgotten their own ties to ethnic backgrounds, this concept vaults them beyond the exclusive focus on individual evangelism. It helps them move toward strategic thinking with a focus on whole groups of people and their social characteristics. Acts 6 gives us insight into this by letting us know for the first time that not one but two people groups had been mixed together in the local church in Jerusalem. What began as a monocultural church had suddenly become a bicultural church.

How the Holy Spirit led the apostles to handle this phenomenon is a valuable lesson in dealing with multicultural situations wherever and whenever they occur in the Church or in missions. The practical application from these seven verses is definitely missiological in nature. As a reminder, my highest priority in publishing this modern commentary on the book of Acts is not to replace the standard commentaries, but rather to supplement them in the areas of our contemporary knowledge of power ministries and missiology. The previous chapter emphasized power ministries, while this one will emphasize missiology or key principles to be applied to cross-cultural ministries.

RESTRUCTURING THE CHURCH

The more bicultural the church at Jerusalem became, the more obvious it was that some radical changes in its structure needed to be considered.

As Luke steps back, so to speak, to take another broad look at the church, he stresses two things: the numbers, as he usually does, but also the ethnic or cultural composition of the church.

WHO'S COUNTING?

[1] ***Now in those days, when the number of the disciples was multiplying...***

Luke uses a different word to describe the growth of the church here, quite possibly reflecting an increasing *rate* of growth. Although the literal meaning of the Greek words cannot be pushed too far in this direction, nevertheless, the English words in our *New King James Version* say it clearly. In Acts 2:47 and 5:14, the Lord *added* those who were being saved, and here the number *was multiplying*. Growth by addition apparently had become growth by multiplication. It was like compounding interest; the increasing numbers of disciples were aggressively moving out in witness, presumably accompanied by power evangelism.

How many believers were there by this time?

This is the fifth church-growth report given so far by Luke. The first, in Acts 2:41, gave us the number of 3,000. The second, in Acts 2:47, says more were added, without mentioning a specific number. The third, in Acts 4:4, mentions 5,000 men, and at that point, I suggested that a very conservative estimate might be a total of 15,000. The fourth, in Acts 5:14, still uses the word "added" to indicate that large numbers of both men and women became believers. Acts 6:1 is the fifth report. R. C. H. Lenski says, "It has been conservatively estimated that at this time the total number of the disciples was between twenty and twenty-five thousand."[1] As I have mentioned, it is not necessary to imagine that 25,000 were all in the city of Jerusalem itself, although they might have been, and therefore many more would have been in other places.

In my opinion, it is important to notice once again that Luke regularly reports church growth. I say that because some Christian leaders today tend to scorn the use of numbers. Some label reporting growth as "triumphalism." Others say, "We're not interested in the numbers game." A common cliché goes: "We strive for quality, not quantity." I have even heard the use of numbers called "numerolatry," a particularly serious accusation because it implies a form of idolatry. Should Luke be charged with "numerolatry" because he shows such a persistent interest in numbers?

I think it is safe to assume that Luke was not committing idolatry nor engaging in triumphalism by his frequent reporting of church growth, often with specific numbers. Although I would agree that some do abuse numbers these days, most leaders whom I know do not. David gives us an example of abusing numbers. In 1 Chronicles 21:1, we read, "Now Satan stood up against Israel, and moved David to number Israel." David did this for his own glory and soon found it was a major mistake. "I have done very foolishly," he later admitted (1 Chron. 21:8). But, on the other hand, God, not Satan, said to Moses, "Take a census of all the congregation of the children of Israel" (Num. 1:2). So counting numbers of people, in and of itself, is obviously not contrary to God's nature.

Church-growth expert Donald McGavran says, "The numerical approach is essential to understanding church growth. The church is made up of countable people and there is nothing particularly spiritual in not counting them."[2] I agree, and find it particularly encouraging that Luke apparently does also.

A BICULTURAL CHURCH

[1] . . . *there arose a murmuring against the Hebrews by the Hellenists* . . .

Keep in mind that all the believers at this point were still Jews. No Samaritans or Gentiles had yet been brought into the fold. Whereas this will soon change, the apostles were still following the direction Jesus gave them: "Do not go into the way of the Gentiles, and do not enter a city of the Samaritans, but go rather to the lost sheep of the house of Israel" (Matt. 10:5-6). They must occasionally have sensed deep down that eventually they would be making disciples of *all nations* (see Matt. 28:19), and that the gospel would move from Jerusalem to Judea out to Samaria and to the ends of the earth as Jesus had told them (see Acts 1:8), but the time for that had not yet come.

One reason it had not come, I believe, is that the original apostles, who were all Hebrew Jews, had not as yet even learned how to relate properly to a culture quite akin to their own, namely, Jews who were culturally half-Greek, that is Hellenistic Jews. If they could not relate that well to the Hellenists, how could they possibly relate to the much despised Samaritans or, worse yet, the Gentiles?

A problem had surfaced regarding widows, which I will describe in more detail later on. But here we must realize that the widow problem was only on the surface. I agree with Howard Marshall who says, "The complaint about the poor relief was but a symptom of a *deeper problem*, namely, that the Aramaic-speaking [believers] [i.e., Hebrews] and the Greek-speaking [believers] [i.e., Hellenists] were dividing into two separate groups"[3] (emphasis mine).

As one small indicator that something very significant is at stake here, Luke not only tells us that disciples were multiplying at the beginning of the incident, but only six verses later, after it is resolved, he repeats this information even more enthusiastically (see Acts 6:7).

In order to understand what was really going on in the church, we first need to understand the characteristics of each of these two ethnic groups.

The Hebrews

To refresh what I pointed out earlier, all the original followers of Jesus were Hebrew Jews and were likely never called "Christians." In fact, up to the Day of Pentecost they were, with few possible exceptions, all *Galilean* Hebrews as opposed to *Judean* Hebrews (Judas being the possible exception). Remember that the Galileans were regarded by the Judeans as the first-century equivalent of hillbillies. On the Day of Pentecost, the more sophisticated Judeans in their own city of Jerusalem exclaimed with no little astonishment, mixed with a measure of disdain, "Look, are not all these who speak Galileans?" (Acts 2:7).

However, by the time we arrive at this passage in Acts 6, many of the believers were Judeans as well. Particularly in the great healing campaign where even Peter's shadow was healing the sick, a considerable number had come into Jerusalem from surrounding towns in Judea and had been healed and saved (see Acts 5:15-16). We can safely presume, therefore, that by this time the majority of the Hebrew believers in Jerusalem would likely have been Judeans. At the same time, many other groups of Galileans had undoubtedly also become followers of Jesus up north in their own province of Galilee.

The Hebrews spoke Aramaic as their mother tongue, a language closely related to Hebrew. Some of the better-educated ones would also speak Greek, which was the trade language of the entire eastern segment of the Roman Empire, and even farther east beyond the boundaries of that empire. They read their Old Testament in the original Hebrew. They worshiped regularly in the Temple. Some of them were no doubt Levites and thus were routinely involved in Temple rituals.

It is easy to understand, therefore, how the Hebrews would, and did, think of themselves as spiritually superior to the Hellenists. Even in the church, this attitude could have carried over and contributed to the friction that had developed between the two groups.

The Hellenists

The Hellenists were Greek-speaking Jews. The Greeks' own word for their native land of Greece is *Hellas*, a word derived from a Greek deity named Hellen, a son of Zeus. So "Hellenists," as applied to Jews, would mean "like the Greeks." They belonged to what is known as the "Jewish dispersion," meaning the migration of Jewish families from their original homeland in Palestine to various other nations of the ancient world. Most large cities of the Roman Empire would have a Jewish community, and it would not be uncommon to find a synagogue among them. Even secular scholars today admit that 10 percent of the Roman Empire was Jewish, an even higher percentage in the Eastern portion, with a million Jews in Alexandria alone.

Although they spoke Greek as a trade language, their mother tongue would more likely have been the regional vernacular of the city or area where they and their families lived, much as the Italian community in Philadelphia today speaks English as their mother tongue, although many can communicate in Italian as well. However, the important thing to keep in mind is that the Hellenists could not typically speak fluent Aramaic unless they had lived in Jerusalem for some time. They did not read their Old Testament in Hebrew but in the Greek translation called the Septuagint.

Up to the Day of Pentecost, few Hellenists, even though they were full-blooded Jews, had become followers of Jesus as their Messiah. There may have been an exception or two, such as Joseph Barsabas who was among the 120 in the Upper Room and who also became a candidate for the twelfth apostle (see Acts 1:23), but these were few and far between. Therefore, when we get to Acts 6, we can understand that because virtually none of the Hellenists would have had a personal memory of Jesus Himself, as did many Hebrews, they might easily succumb to a spiritual inferiority complex when they were around the Hebrews. This caused a problem.

Why were so many Hellenists in Jerusalem? Enormous numbers of them visited regularly for special feast occasions such as Pentecost. But why would some move there to live and, therefore, be considered a part of the church of the city?

Simon Kistemaker suggests that "many of these devout Jews were elderly people who wanted to spend the rest of their lives in the holy city."[4] If this is true, it would follow that of the millions of Jews throughout the dispersion, only the most affluent among them would be able to realize their dreams of finishing their days and being buried in Jerusalem. Therefore, the Hellenists in the Jerusalem church would likely be better off financially, on the average, than the Hebrews. In fact, all those actually mentioned by name as selling property to distribute to the poor happened to be Hellenists, such as Barnabas, who was from Cyprus (see Acts 4:36-37). Jerusalem must have been the Miami Beach of the first century, the place where many wealthy Jews go to retire and live out their days.

The Hellenistic Jews also went to Jerusalem for a theological reason. Messianic hopes for centuries, in Israel, projected the Messiah's arrival in the holy city of Jerusalem. Even today you can see the many burial grounds just outside the walls. Lively belief in resurrection yielded the confident hope of being on hand when Messiah would come.

Varieties of Hellenists

Even more significant for understanding Acts 6 is that when a considerable number of Hellenistic Jews in Jerusalem came from one particular region of the Roman Empire and spoke a common vernacular, these families would naturally form their primary social groups with each other, not with those Hellenists who spoke other dialects, much less with Aramaic-speaking Hebrews. In recent years, for example, many Russian Jews have moved to Los Angeles, and they prefer to socialize more with themselves than with other Jews who have been in America for generations. In fact, Kistemaker says, "Each group had its own synagogue before these people became Christians," and he points out that they maintained these language-based assemblies even after they had become disciples of Jesus.[5]

In modern categories, it could be helpful to think of the Hellenistic Jews in Jerusalem as hyphenated ethnics. Let me explain. Whereas, for example, we have many Chinese in the United States, all Chinese do not regard themselves as belonging to the same *primary* group. They will easily mix together in public gatherings on Chinese New Year or to support favorable political causes, but these, similar to the Jews worshiping in the Temple in Jerusalem, are *secondary* groups, sociologically speaking. When it comes to *primary* groups, Taiwanese-Chinese, Mainland-Chinese, Hong Kong-Chinese and

Malaysian-Chinese, to cite obvious examples, tend not to associate too much with each other, even though they might reside in the same American neighborhood. Most of them can speak some English, but Taiwanese or Cantonese or Mandarin is the preferred language for their more intimate socializing.

Being good Jews, the Hellenists would commonly attend the Temple, which should be seen as a mixed and *secondary* group. But their *primary* group remained the synagogue. According to the Talmud, Jerusalem had 480 synagogues at the time. Some of these are named later in Acts 6:9 as "the Synagogue of the Freedmen (Cyrenians, Alexandrians, and those from Cilicia and Asia)." To flash back to the Hellenistic groups mentioned in Acts 2, it is conceivable that Parthian-Hellenists, Egyptian-Hellenists, Mesopotamian-Hellenists, Arab-Hellenists and many others would prefer the close fellowship of their own ethnic-oriented synagogues.

We are not sure, but it could even be that by this time the born-again Hellenists actually outnumbered the Hebrew followers of Jesus in the Jerusalem church.

WHO IS RUNNING THE CHURCH?

The result was understandably a phenomenon very common in cross-cultural ministries today, not only in foreign lands, but in many American cities as well. The church is bicultural, Hebrews and Hellenists, but only one of the groups, the Hebrews, is providing the top directive leadership. The apostles were all Hebrews. Like many foreign missionaries today, who have fallen into the error of personally assuming the leadership of churches in the new cultures to which they have been sent, the apostles quite possibly assumed that Aramaic should be the acceptable language of worship. But in any case, on other occasions they were probably accustomed to talking behind the Hellenist believers' backs in Aramaic, a language the Hellenists could not understand. No wonder friction developed!

Some may question why such a conflict would occur, considering that the Hebrews were natives of Palestine. They were not foreign missionaries. This raises the extremely crucial missiological issue of the distinction between *cultural* differences and *geographical* differences among people groups. Cross-cultural (E-2 and E-3) evangelistic challenges can frequently be found in the same city and even in the same neighborhood. Often those who are born in one country and who live in close proximity to unreached people groups in their same country are not the best choices to evangelize them. A rather sad case in point is that Anglo-Americans are not a very likely force for evangelism to unreached American Indian tribes even though the members of both groups are natives of the United States. Thus, the relationship of Hebrews to Hellenists must be interpreted as a missiological issue even though the Hebrews did not have to travel outside their native land to become involved.

This clearly illustrates the crying need in our home churches for a grasp of the missiological basics. This event alone can allow U.S. believers to understand both the typical mission field situation as well as the parallel dynamics in U.S. cities today.

CHOOSING THE RIGHT LEADERS

One of the most crucial issues in cross-cultural ministry is leadership selection and training. We are soon going to see that when the apostle Paul planted new churches among the Gentiles, he almost immediately ordained leaders in the churches—leaders who understood the language, ate the same food, shared common values and handled money in mutually acceptable ways.

However, here in Jerusalem, the way the Hebrews were handling the money in the Jerusalem church apparently was not acceptable to their Hellenist brothers and sisters, and a serious dispute arose as a result.

THE WIDOW PROBLEM (ACTS 6:1)

> [1] . . . *there arose a murmuring against the Hebrews by the Hellenists, because their widows were neglected in the daily distribution.*

As I have mentioned, the problem concerning widows was only a symptom of a much deeper issue revolving around cultural dissonance. Multiethnic situations, where people programmed with different sets of cultural values and behavior patterns are forced to live in close proximity to each other, are inherently loaded with potential areas of misunderstanding and conflict. As we well know in our modern multicultural United States society, these areas most frequently involve perceived issues of injustice, discrimination, unfairness, racism, prejudice and oppression. Usually the minority group realizes what is happening long before the majority group.

At this point, the numerical majority of the Jerusalem church could well have been Hellenists. But in issues of social justice, the determining factor for potential social conflict is not necessarily numbers, but *power*, as black South Africans, who are the vast numerical majority in their nation, long realized, while white South Africans lived in denial for centuries and enforced apartheid. In Jerusalem, the church leaders were Hebrews, and they undoubtedly felt that it was only proper for them to exercise authority, being the real Hebrews! This put the Hellenists in a "minority" position despite their superior numbers. It is always problematic when a majority is ruled by a minority.

WHY THE HELLENISTS WERE UPSET

Why, then, would the care of widows become an issue of justice in the eyes of the Hellenists? Let's look at it.

First of all, most of the widows who needed help were undoubtedly Hellenists, not Hebrews. For a starter, the Hellenists would have had a much higher age profile than the Hebrews because the more elderly, retired Hellenists from all over the Jewish dispersion were the ones most likely to move back to Jerusalem to live out their days in the holy city. For many, this move would involve a physical separation from their extended families who still lived in Asia or Rome or Alexandria or wherever. Jews ordinarily have tight family ties. When a Hebrew father died, his widow would more than likely be cared for by her grown children who lived in Jerusalem or nearby. But not the Hellenistic widow, because her grown children would not live in Jerusalem. Such a problem no doubt existed before Pentecost and they simply tolerated it. Now, however, with Spirit-refreshed consciences, they wanted to be sure that all widows were cared for.

Second, it would be reasonable to suspect that most of the money in the Jerusalem church benevolence fund would be Hellenistic money. Because they were rich enough to retire in Jerusalem, most Hellenists would probably be upper-middle to upper class. It could well be that the Hebrews would tend to be drawn from the middle to lower-middle classes in Jerusalem. In fact, after the Hellenists left Jerusalem later on, the Jerusalem church became known for its poverty (see Rom. 15:26). If this is true, a good bit of the property that had been sold and donated to the church would presumably have been Hellenists' property.

Third, the major complication has to do with the leadership. If my assumptions are valid, although most widows would have been Hellenists and most of the available money was Hellenist money, the leadership who had the power to determine how the money was spent was Hebrew, namely, the 12 apostles. This, understandably, would have disturbed the Hellenistic believers.

None of this is to imply that the apostles were not wonderful people, filled with the Holy Spirit, exhibiting the fruit of the Spirit in their daily lives and sincerely supposing that they were treating the Hellenists with fairness and deep Christian compassion. Their character was not the issue. The problem was that they were monocultural and they were just beginning to learn how to relate to brothers and sisters in Christ from a different culture. Their *spirituality* was not deficient; their *missiological sensitivities* were.

One of the most difficult lessons for cross-cultural missionaries to learn is that when they plant a church in a culture different from their own, the leadership of the new church must come from those rooted in the second culture or else the new church will not grow and develop as it should. Missionaries may understandably assume that because they have been Christians longer and know the Bible better and pray harder and adhere more rigidly to norms of Christian behavior than do their new converts, they can and should assume leadership of the new church. They do so, however, to their own detriment and they inadvertently hinder the spread of the gospel over the long haul. I say long haul because naturally some leadership must be given by the missionaries to the initial nucleus of babes in Christ who still need the milk of the Word. But the sooner this can be turned over to the nationals the better.

Many missiologists have now adopted a four-stage concept of missionary work first suggested by Harold Fuller: *pioneer, paternal, partnership* and *participation.* Note that *paternal* must give way early to *partnership,* but that even *partnership* can be wearing on national leaders. They need the kind of true freedom of leadership that can only come after missionaries have laid a good foundation and moved from full-fledged *partners* to clearly subordinate *participation* in the national church. At this point, missionaries may well give most of their time assisting a national church movement with its own missionary outreach to other peoples, rather than, as expatriates, being pastors or church leaders or even evangelists.

This is the missiological lesson that God was teaching the apostles in Jerusalem through what was, undoubtedly, for them a painful experience.

They assumed, as do many missionaries, that those from the second culture could become part of their church and peacefully accept their leadership. Such things do happen, but they are the exceptions, not the rule. A familiar example of an exception to the rule would be slaves in the Deep South in the days of Uncle Tom, many of whom became faithful Christians, but who were forced to join churches led by whites and often made to sit together in the balcony. Such an arrangement is not the ideal pattern on a long-term basis when attempting to win the lost in a multicultural society.

THE CONFLICT ERUPTS!

Similar to the nature of a volcano, this problem involving a social injustice toward a minority in the church may have appeared dormant for a time, but eventually the top blew off and it erupted. The Hellenists became so irritated that they rose up. In such situations today, they might have cried, as many have done, "Missionary, go home!" In many ways, the Hellenists' "murmuring against the Hebrews" was a functional equivalent.

So the Hellenists complained. Somehow their grievances, which presumably up to that time had been talked of only behind closed doors in their messianic synagogues and home groups, came to the surface. As is often the case, the Hebrew apostles might well have been among the last to know that they had a severe problem on their hands. They had been very busy in giving leadership to the rapidly growing church. They were elated at continual reports of healings and miracles and they thought everything was all right. But, obviously, some things were going wrong, so they knew that they had to take some action.

CONFLICT RESOLUTION

[2] ***Then the twelve summoned the multitude of the disciples . . .***

To begin the process of conflict resolution, the apostles wisely called a congregational meeting. This action in itself indicates that by then they had realized that the problem was serious. Such a meeting of "the multitude of disciples" would never be called again, to our knowledge. When another conflict arose later on in Acts 15, it would be resolved apostolically by a council of leaders instead of the congregation.

We have no reason to imagine that all 25,000 believers would attend this meeting, if indeed that many were in Jerusalem at the time. If our contemporary experience is any indication, most church members are not particularly anxious to go to a business meeting. I would imagine that those who were motivated to attend would largely be Hellenists because they were the ones who had initiated the grievance. So the nature of the gathering would most likely be the Hebrew apostles meeting with a number of the Hellenist disciples to listen to their point of view and to gather the facts necessary to make a wise decision.

We also need to realize that this meeting would not have been organized and run under Roberts' Rules of Order, as a typical United States congregational meeting might be conducted today. Church government, in those days, was not based on taking votes, with the majority winning. God had given the spiritual authority to the 12 apostles, and the final decision was theirs. However, they desired to base their decision on accurate information and an accurate reading of the emotional state of affairs of the believers. I can imagine that a meeting of this nature would not have been dull or boring.

THE APOSTLES' POSITION

[2] ***Then the twelve summoned the multitude of the disciples and said, "It is not desirable that we should leave the word of God and serve tables. . . .*** [4] ***but we will give ourselves continually to prayer and to the ministry of the word."***

After carefully considering the matter, the apostles were ready to announce their decision. First they wanted to make their own position clear to the church. They had decided that from then on they would give their full time to the *spiritual* leadership of the church and leave *administrative* matters to others.

Among other things, the apostles by then were probably beginning to come to terms with their spiritual gifts. It takes time to know with reasonable assurance what our spiritual gifts are, but when we do know, God expects us to build our ministry schedules around them. The apostles, all Hebrews, were learning that they did not have the ability or the spiritual gifts to manage a multicultural church and competently handle the problems of the Hellenists. I would imagine that, as frequently happens on the mission field today, a number of serious issues were hidden under the surface, and the widow problem was simply the one, among many others, that first became public.

EVEN APOSTLES CAN BE ETHNOCENTRIC

I realize that many do not like to imagine that great spiritual leaders such as the 12 apostles could have been unable to rise above cultural limitations. Therefore, they like to think of this incident as simply a matter of efficient church administration rather than as an ethnic clash. But if any would doubt that the apostles were still ethnocentric, the doubts will go away when we later see how they reacted to Peter when he came back from the house of Cornelius in Acts 10, and to Paul when he finished his first term of missionary service among Gentiles in Acts 15.

Fortunately, the apostles were flexible. They were learning how to relate to those of a different culture. By this time, it had become clear to them that the Hellenist segment of the church needed Hellenistic, or indigenous, leadership. Although they might well have been in a state of denial previously, reality was dawning on them. As Howard Marshall says, "the Aramaic-Speaking Christians and the Greek-Speaking Christians were dividing into two separate groups."[6]

This division was not a small one or a temporary one. The great persecution that followed Stephen's ministry drove out from Jerusalem the *Hellenists* but not the *Hebrews,* as we will see in Acts 8:1. Of that event, Ernst Haenchen says, "At the moment of the persecution the primitive community embodied two groups which were already so clearly distinct even to outsiders that the one was persecuted, the other left unharmed."[7]

SELECTING THE NEW LEADERS

[3] *Therefore, brethren, seek out from among you seven men of good reputation, full of the Holy Spirit and wisdom, whom we may appoint over this business;* [5] *And the saying pleased the whole multitude. . . .*

The verb for leadership selection, "seek out," is translated in other versions as "choose" or "select," or words to that effect. Many of us have a tendency to read our own culture into the text and imagine that they must have held some kind of election. I do not believe this was the case. The seven did not become leaders as a result of either an election or the apostles' whim. They had already emerged as leaders and had been so recognized among their own people group long before this time.

We do not create leaders in the church by choosing them. God has already created them and chosen them and given them appropriate gifts, and they are then recognized as leaders when the church is healthy. Elections, campaigning and rivalry among candidates for leadership, either spoken or unspoken, have no place in the church. Acts mentions no church elections after the coming of the Spirit on the Day of Pentecost!

The Best Leaders Are Indigenous

These leaders were to be chosen "from among you." Among whom? A corollary of the cultural distinctions within the Jerusalem church, which I have been detailing, would be that they would be recognized by the Hellenists from among the Hellenists. Missiologists call this "indigenizing the church." The indigenous church is a church that governs itself, finances itself and propagates itself. The essential first step toward making this happen is to choose leaders from among those who are culturally compatible and who will be intuitively sensitive to special needs of the church members, such as caring for widows in this case.

Although the cultural match is a beginning, the leaders must also be "of good reputation." Presumably, they will be high-visibility individuals whose lives have been openly scrutinized by believers and nonbelievers alike. They need to be people of high moral and ethical standards and respected as such by the community. Character counts!

The Filling of the Holy Spirit

Only those "full of the Holy Spirit" should be considered for top church leadership. This is an interesting qualification because it clearly implies that not all Christians are, in fact, full of the Holy Spirit. This, obviously, is not a statement dealing with the *presence* of the Holy Spirit in the believer, because He is present in all. Paul says, "Do you not know that your body is the temple of the Holy Spirit who is in you?" (1 Cor. 6:19). So if the people were to choose only those "full of the Holy Spirit," how could they tell which ones were?

For one thing, they could look for those who had exhibited in their lives the *fruit* of the Holy Spirit: "love, joy, peace, longsuffering, kindness, goodness, faithfulness, gentleness, self-control," according to Galatians 5:22-23. These qualities would also have contributed to making them people "of good reputation."

For another thing, they could have observed the ones through whom the miraculous work of the Holy Spirit was already being done in power ministries, and it appears they did so. Later, we are told that Stephen "did great wonders and signs among the people" (Acts 6:8), and that Philip also did many miracles (see Acts 8:6-7).

The new leaders should be those "full of wisdom." They were to be mature, practical people who could make good decisions.

Servant Leadership

The apostles themselves modeled the kind of wisdom and good decision-making they recommended to others. Therefore, "the saying pleased the whole multitude." When apostolic leadership is anointed by God, the apostles' decisions are readily accepted by the people. The vision and initiative will originate from the apostles, but the decision meets the needs of the group and is thereby pleasing to all. This is what is implied in the biblical concept of "servant leadership." People gladly follow servant leaders because they are confident that the decisions made will be decisions for the benefit of the followers. Good leaders have a reputation of not making decisions for personal benefit. In this case, the apostles were relinquishing a great deal of power to the Hellenists for the benefit of the church as a whole. Not only would they end up with fewer people under their direct authority, but they also were giving up control of considerable financial resources that, in themselves, were a significant source of power.

WHO WERE THE NEW LEADERS?

[5] . . . *And they chose Stephen, a man full of faith and the Holy Spirit, and Philip, Prochorus, Nicanor, Timon, Parmenas, and Nicolas, a proselyte from Antioch,* [6] *whom they set before the apostles; and when they had prayed, they laid hands on them.*

Knowing what we now know, it comes as no surprise that the seven leaders chosen by the Hellenists were all themselves Hellenists. How do we know they were? We know by the names, all being Greek names. Some Bible scholars who have decided ahead of time that it would not have been politically correct for the Jerusalem church to select all Hellenists argue that in those days there was no prohibition on Hebrews taking Greek names. However, I agree with Hans Conzelmann, who says, "It is true that even in Palestine, Greek names are common (cf. Andrew and Philip from the circle of the Twelve), but still it is remarkable that in an entire group not a single non-Greek appears."[8] In his more recent commentary, Simon Kistemaker reports the consensus that "scholars favor the explanation that all seven were Hellenistic Jews whose native tongue was Greek."[9]

Three of them, Nicanor, Timon and Parmenas are relatively unknown. Nicolas is the only one of the seven not born an ethnic Jew. He was a proselyte, which means he was born a Gentile and later chose to convert to Judaism. So he was a Jew by adoption, not by birth, so to speak. Prochorus later becomes a bishop, according to history. The two most prominent among the seven, however, were Philip and Stephen.

PHILIP AND STEPHEN

Philip is not to be confused with the apostle Philip of Bethsaida whom Jesus early on called by saying, "Follow Me," and who then brought Nathanael to Jesus, both becoming part of the original 12 disciples (see John 1:43-45). That Philip was a Galilean Aramaic-speaking Hebrew, a member of Jesus' own ethnic group. This Philip, a Greek-speaking Hellenistic Jew, later became known as "Philip the evangelist" (Acts 21:8), and he is the pioneer missionary to the Samaritans in Acts 8.

Stephen is clearly the most prominent member of the seven. In fact, Luke takes pains to pause right in the middle of the roll call of the new leaders to record that Stephen was "a man full of faith and the Holy Spirit." This is quite a compliment, which Luke subsequently uses only once again in Acts to describe Barnabas in Acts 11:24. The faith that characterized Stephen, apparently, was more than the normal saving faith that each Christian must have, and more than the faith that is the expected fruit of the Spirit. It probably was the spiritual gift of faith mentioned in 1 Corinthians 12:9. This is the faith to "remove mountains," as Paul says in 1 Corinthians 13:2. The rest of Acts 6 and all of Acts 7 tell the glorious, and yet sad, story of how Stephen became Christianity's most famous martyr.

WERE THE SEVEN HELLENISTS "DEACONS"?

Many sermons I have heard on Acts 6 regard the seven as the first local church board of deacons, and some preachers make an application of this passage to the office of deacon that has been established in many of today's churches. One reason they do this is because most of the classical commentaries that preachers would likely consult suggest this interpretation. The assumption of many commentators is that the 12 apostles delegated their day-to-day administrative chores to these seven, assigning these supposed "deacons" to distribute food while the apostles did the important things, such as praying and teaching the Word. Their main function, in this view, was to relieve the top leadership of busywork. *The New Testament in Modern English,* by Philips, has a subtitle over this passage: "The first deacons are chosen."

My own view, as I have been explaining, is quite different. I agree with Derek Tidball who points out that the seven "are not subsequently seen as table-waiters but as preachers and missionaries. Some scholars have therefore concluded that they did not form a group beneath the apostles, but alongside of them—a distinct ethnic leadership group."[10] Although Luke is gentle in the way he records this historical event, its significance for missiology and for the advance of the Kingdom into Samaria and to the ends of the earth is enormous. These are definitely more than your run-of-the-mill "deacons."

The Greek word behind "deacon" is *diakonia,* which in today's English means ministry or service. Here is how John Stott explains it: "*Diakonia* is a generic word for service; it lacks specificity until a descriptive adjective is added, whether 'pastoral,' 'social,' 'political,' 'medical,' or another. All Christians without exception . . . are themselves called to ministry."[11] In this sense, therefore, it would not be inaccurate to say the seven were "deacons," although the word itself, *diakonos*, is not used at all in the passage.

However, this leads us nowhere, because other forms related to the word *diakonos* are used here both for the ministry to "serve tables" (6:2), commonly attributed to the seven, and also "ministry of the word" (6:4), commonly attributed to the 12. If the 7 were "deacons," then the 12 apostles were "deacons" also, as far as the Greek text is concerned.

If the seven were nothing but deacons appointed to do social work among the entire conglomerate Jerusalem church, it would then make little sense for them all to be Hellenists. That is why, as I mentioned before, several commentators attempt to argue that the seven most probably would have included some Hebrews who used Greek names.

Why would some take pains to argue that the seven were essentially table-servers when the facts seem to point in such a different direction? Unless I am mistaken, it is primarily because these commentators are extremely uncomfortable with the thought that two ethnic groups in the same church could not get along well with each other. It would not seem politically correct to them when sociologist Derek Tidball says, "The strong coherence of the small band of Jesus' disciples was therefore now broken."[12] However, it is a fact that must be recognized, and a further indication that, as Hans Conzelmann says, the seven "do not stand *beneath* the Twelve, but *alongside* them."[13] In my opinion, this is an extremely important observation.

THE POSITIVE OUTCOME OF CHURCH DIVISION

Although the term "church split" is harsher than Luke would use, this passage is an account of the first major church split. We often think of church splits in a negative light because so many that we have seen or heard of are ugly, carnal affairs. They need not be that way, however, as we learn from the Jerusalem church. This split came about by the leading of the Holy Spirit for the best of both parties and for the glory of God. What happened as a result of this significant division?

[7] ***And the word of God spread, and the number of the disciples multiplied greatly in Jerusalem, and a great many of the priests were obedient to the faith.***

Whenever Luke gives such an upbeat report of church growth in Acts, it is because the outcome of what has just happened, even if it is something like the apostles' being physically beaten by the Sanhedrin (see Acts 5:40-42), has a positive outcome for the kingdom of God. The outcome of this case of church division was no exception.

The Hellenist believers immediately became more content and they stopped their murmuring. They were no longer under the leadership of Aramaic-speaking Hebrews who had hillbilly roots in Galilee. Their new leaders were, from their perspective, cosmopolitan, well-educated, affluent and spiritual Christians who could easily understand their problem not only with widows but also with anything else that would arise. They now felt liberated and, therefore, they could be more enthusiastic about serving God and extending His kingdom. Things always go better when people are happy.

EVANGELIZING PRIESTS

For the first time in this rapid spread of the gospel, "a great many of the priests were obedient to the faith." This raises the interesting question: Why did the movement of the gospel among the priests begin only after the Jerusalem church had undergone its ethnic division? Let's look at it.

These priests are not to be confused with the high priests who joined the Sadducees in persecuting the apostles (see Acts 4:1 and 5:17). Joachim Jeremias calculates, rather laboriously, the number of priests in Jerusalem at the time to be approximately 8,000 along with some 10,000 Levites.[14] Ernst Haenchen affirms that, "The eight thousand or so priests had livings so exiguous that they were obliged to follow a trade during the ten or eleven months [of the year] in which their service of the Temple left them free to do so."[15] Richard Rackham adds, "There was a great gulf between the ordinary priests and the class of ruling and wealthy 'high priests.' "[16]

These priests who were being saved were poor, while the high priests and the Sadducees were rich and would have had a great deal to lose from the change in the political status quo that the Jesus movement was threatening. But the ordinary priests would have had nothing to lose and everything to gain by following Jesus as Messiah. There is some evidence, in fact, that they were being exploited by the high priests. Because of this, Rackham's conclusion sounds very plausible: "So when a large body of the priests joined the apostles, it would have the effect, politically, of a very practical protest against their Sadducean rulers."[17]

If this is correct, why would the priests have waited so long to commit themselves to the new faith? My hypothesis, and it is only that, is that the priests would have been extremely ethnocentric Hebrews. As long as the church was perceived by them, as outsiders, to be a random mixture of Hebrews and Hellenists, the priests would not want to consider responding to the gospel they were preaching. But when the Hellenists became indigenized and moved ahead under their own leadership, the priests now could become a part of a more purely Hebrew messianic community without compromising their own integrity. This was still a messianic Jewish (not a "Christian") group, and the priests would naturally have continued performing their Temple duties as always, but now as part of a significant movement that was defying the rule of the Sadducees.

The principle is that the multiplication of many different kinds of churches, including those formed along ethnic lines, provides more options for unbelievers who are looking for a church in which they think they can feel comfortable. When this opportunity is available, their decision for Christ is properly a religious, rather than a social or cultural, decision. The result is, as Luke indicates, that the disciples multiplied greatly and churches grew.

POSITIONING FOR THE FUTURE

The most important outcome of this landmark event, in my opinion, was the learning experience it provided for the leaders of the Jerusalem church, which they would later apply to taking the gospel of Christ past Jerusalem and Judea out to Samaria and to the ends of the earth. Through it, the 12 apostles received a crash course in missiology. Although they did not all become cross-cultural missionaries, they were finally positioned to provide what leadership they could to a new era of international evangelism. The first major step in that direction would be taken by Stephen, one of the Hellenist leaders they had just laid hands on and blessed.

REFLECTION QUESTIONS

1. The chief players in the unfolding of Acts 6 are Hebrew Jews as opposed to Hellenistic Jews. Discuss the differing characteristics of each group.
2. When two strong ethnic groups are in the same church, conflict frequently surfaces. In this case, the problem centered on widows. What was it about widows that upset the Hellenists?
3. When missionaries plant a church and then insist on retaining the leadership for too long a time, they frequently run into serious trouble. Did the Hebrew apostles in Jerusalem make a similar mistake?

4. It is common to regard the seven individuals whom the apostles chose as "deacons." Were they deacons as we understand the word today, or were they something else?
5. Can anything good come out of a church split? Explain your response.

8

SAMARIA: PREACHING ON THE OTHER SIDE OF THE TRACKS

ACTS 6, 7 AND 8

Up to this point, we have been dealing with E-1 and E-2 evangelism. As a reminder, E-1 is monocultural evangelism, reaching people from the same culture. Our example was Hebrew Jews evangelizing Hebrew Jews whether they happened to be Galilean Hebrews or Judean Hebrews. E-2 is cross-cultural evangelism, but across a relatively narrow cultural barrier, such as Hebrew Jews evangelizing Hellenistic Jews.

Now we move on to E-3 evangelism, taking the gospel to Samaria. The cross-cultural barrier here is considerably higher. As we saw in the last chapter, Hebrews and Hellenists had enough of a challenge in attempting to get along with each other, but that was minor compared to the challenge of reaching the much-despised Samaritans for Christ.

Jesus' Great Commission in Acts 1:8 was: "You shall receive power when the Holy Spirit has come upon you; and you shall be witnesses to Me in Jerusalem, and in all Judea and Samaria, and to the end of the earth." The top leader for advancing the Kingdom in Jerusalem and Judea was Peter. The two leaders for moving into Samaria are now Stephen and Philip, and the leader for the Gentiles will be Paul. These are, in fact, the four chief figures in the whole book of Acts.

Many get so caught up with the drama of Stephen's execution that they fail to see clearly how Stephen's ministry prepared the way for Philip's evangelistic mission in Samaria. Actually, as I will explain in considerable detail, Stephen was the *theoretician* for this first bold E-3 initiative, while Philip was the *practitioner* who implemented the theory.

When I say "bold" initiative, the implications of Jews showing love to non-Jews and sharing their faith with them was so radical in the eyes of unbelieving Jews that not only did they execute Stephen for suggesting such a thing, but they also drove most of Stephen's fellow Hellenistic disciples out of the city of Jerusalem.

WHY WAS STEVEN EXECUTED?

The crucial question we will first deal with is: Why was Stephen executed? Understanding this will clear up a number of other questions we might naturally have about the basic mechanisms underlying cross-cultural (E-2 and E-3) missions in general.

STEPHEN AND HIS MINISTRY: ACTS 6

[8] ***And Stephen, full of faith and power, did great wonders and signs among the people.*** [10] ***And they were not able to resist the wisdom and the Spirit by which he spoke.***

As we detailed in the last chapter, Stephen was much more than a "deacon" or some social worker running errands for the 12 apostles. He had become a strong leader in his own right and he had earned his leadership status among the Hellenistic believers long before the apostles laid hands on him. Despite the brevity of his ministry, Stephen is unquestionably one of the most important figures in the whole history of the Christian movement.

Among other things, Stephen "did great wonders and signs among the people." This is of more than passing interest because it is the first time in the book of Acts that Luke attributes ministry in the miraculous to anyone but the 12 apostles. This is another way of Luke's informing us that Stephen, and by implication the other six Hellenistic leaders, ranked not *under* the apostles, but *alongside* them. These signs and wonders drew widespread attention to Stephen's message of salvation, and large numbers were responding.

THE ISSUE OF CESSATIONISM

At this point, some might raise the question as to whether believers in general should expect to participate in power ministries such as healing the sick and casting out demons, or whether such ministry is restricted to the apostles and those upon whom the apostles personally laid hands, like Stephen. Some theologians, such as the renowned Benjamin Breckinridge Warfield of Princeton Theological Seminary in the early years of our century, have made a doctrinal position out of this issue called "cessationism," from the word "cease." They energetically argue that miraculous works, like healings and miracles and prophecy, ceased when the generation represented by Stephen passed from the scene and works of supernatural power ceased and were no longer a part of the normal ministry of the Church from then on.

Fortunately, this position is steadily becoming extinct. Jack Deere's definitive book, *Surprised by the Power of the Spirit*, has discredited cessationism almost to the point of a coup de grâce. Nevertheless, you will still find some standard commentaries on Acts affirming that we must not imagine that Stephen ministered in areas of power and the miraculous before the apostles laid hands on him. If he had, it would tend to discredit their cessationist theory, which teaches that only the apostles and those on whom they laid hands operated in power ministries.

I agree with F. F. Bruce, who says, "Since at that time [Stephen] was already 'full of faith and the Holy Spirit' (v. 5), it is reasonable to conclude that this fullness was accompanied by the 'grace and power' which enabled him to perform ['great signs and wonders']."[1] When we think of it, in the environment of what we know of the Jerusalem church, quite possibly no one would have been considered for top leadership among the Hebrews or the Hellenists who was not already being used by God in power ministries. That is why the apostles set forth as one of the leadership qualifications "full of the Holy Spirit" (Acts 6:3).

Although I believe and teach that all committed disciples of Jesus Christ should expect to heal the sick and cast out demons by the power of the Holy Spirit (see John 14:12), I also realize that not all will minister with the same degree of power. Stephen was one of those who saw more dramatic results from his ministry than others. It is not Luke's ongoing custom to use adjectives to describe the quality of signs and wonders, but here is an exception. He says that Stephen's were "great"!

Luke also mentions that Stephen's opponents "were not able to resist the wisdom and the Spirit by which he spoke." Stephen ministered in word and deed. His deeds were the miracles, and his word was the spoken message of the death and resurrection of Jesus Christ. Stephen's message was so reasonable, and he could defend it so well, that he won all the arguments. Because his enemies found they could not silence him intellectually, they decided to take their only viable recourse and silence him physically.

What happened?

THE FALSE ACCUSATION

[9] *Then there arose some from what is called the Synagogue of the Freedmen . . . disputing with Stephen.* [11] *Then they secretly induced men to say, "We have heard him speak blasphemous words against Moses and God."* [12] *And they stirred up the people, the elders, and the scribes; and they came upon him, seized him, and brought him to the council.* [13] *They also set up false witnesses who said, "This man does not cease to speak blasphemous words against this holy place and the law;* [14] *for we have heard him say that this Jesus of Nazareth will destroy this place and change the customs which Moses delivered to us."*

Somewhat predictably, the enemies of Stephen, who was a Hellenist, would emerge from among the unbelieving Hellenistic Jews who worshiped in the various synagogues in Jerusalem, such as "the Synagogue of the Freedmen." Once the Hellenistic church had been indigenized and secured its own leadership, it began growing even more rapidly and, therefore, it posed an increasingly serious threat to the status quo of the Hellenistic community in general. The previous opposition, when only the Hebrew apostles were leading, came principally from the Hebrew Sadducees. Of course, even in this case, it eventually got back "to the council," which was the Sanhedrin with its majority of Sadducees, but that is not where it began.

Why would the Hellenists, who did not seem to be as rigid in applying the strict Jewish lifestyle as did the Hebrews, become so upset over Stephen? There might be two reasons: one social and one theological.

As is frequently the case, the social reason precedes the theological reason. First-century Jerusalem, as I have said, was similar to Miami Beach, a wonderful place for Jews to retire and live out their days. A high value in retirement communities is peace and predictability. The Hellenists, as a group, would have invested a considerable amount of money in Jerusalem with the goal of creating and maintaining a high quality of life. They were very proud of their city the way it was, and threats to its social stability were not readily welcomed.

A MAJOR SOCIAL DISRUPTION

If the picture we have of the explosion of the messianic Jewish movement throughout the city of Jerusalem is anywhere near accurate, a major social disruption was going on. The lame were walking, the blind were seeing, the dead were being raised and people were speaking in languages they had never learned. It was bad enough when this movement was being led by motley, hillbilly-like Galileans, but it was much worse when it was being led by sophisticated Hellenists such as Stephen. Leisure World in Zion was experiencing a social earthquake, and collective emotions were definitely on edge. Something had to be done to stop it! The basic well-being of the Hellenists was being severely threatened!

LOOKING FOR THEOLOGICAL FLAWS

The Hellenistic Jews knew that they could not build a strong enough case against Stephen on social or emotional grounds alone. So they began to search Stephen's teaching for possible theological flaws, particularly because blasphemy was at that time a felony in Jerusalem. Their accusation of Stephen, false as it was, took on two parts: (1) "We have heard him speak blasphemous words against Moses," and (2) "This man does not cease to speak blasphemous words against this holy place," meaning the Temple.

These were very serious accusations, and in each they attempted to implicate *both* Stephen and Jesus of Nazareth. Here are their accusations:

- Stephen speaks against Moses and the law (6:11,13), and Jesus wants to change the customs of Moses (6:14).
- Stephen speaks against God and His Temple (6:11,13), and Jesus wants to destroy the Temple (6:14).

THE REAL ISSUE

Because neither of the above charges was true, we can assume that there must be a more fundamental underlying problem. What could it have been? Let's first attempt to understand the *Jewish* point of view, then move on to *Stephen's* point of view.

The Jewish Faith Perverted as a National Religion

The Jews tended to think that God is a tribal God, the God of Israel, and they were exclusively His chosen people. Other people groups may have their gods as well, but the God of Israel is the one true God. And Jehovah was the God *only* of Israel, and not the God of other peoples. This was not only a *religious* concept, but also a *patriotic* one. The whole internal fabric of the nation of Israel would stand or fall on that narrow doctrine of God.

From this nationalistic point of view, then, access to God could only be attained through the priests in Jerusalem and the sacrifices in the Jewish Temple. Multiple synagogues in different places were not *substitutes* for the Temple, only *reflections* of it. Because the actual Temple was so crucial, hundreds of thousands of Jews from the dispersion would return to Jerusalem for the various feast days each year to gain access to God. In no other place could He be found in that way.

God would welcome non-Jews from other peoples of the world. But they could not access God in their own people groups because Jehovah was only the God of Israel, not of their particular ethnic group. If they wanted to worship Jehovah God, they would first need to repudiate their native cultural ties and consent to become Jewish through prescribed rites such as baptism and circumcision for the males. Accordingly, the Jews were sending out proselytizing bands to evangelize other people groups and encourage Gentiles to become Jews and, thus, to find God. Once they did, the mutual understanding was that they were no longer Gentiles, but Jews. One of the seven new Hellenistic leaders, Nicolas for example, was a former Gentile who had done this (see Acts 6:5), and these converts were called Jewish proselytes.

Stephen's Biblical Point of View

Through revelation from the Holy Spirit, Stephen had realized that Jehovah God was not a tribal God, but that He was sovereign over the whole universe. He was the God not only of Israel, but also of every nation on Earth. Stephen might have remembered the psalm that says, "The Lord is great in Zion, and He is high above *all the peoples*" (Ps. 99:2, emphasis added).

The Jewish symbols of God's presence–the Temple and the law of Moses–were true and valid. Stephen would never have spoken against the Jews' obeying the law and accessing God in the Temple. He himself obeyed the law, and he regularly worshiped in the Temple. The accusations were so absurd that Stephen's enemies had to find false witnesses.

Stephen also knew that although the Temple and the law were *valid*, they were not *exclusive* means of finding God. Here is his main difference with the unbelieving Jews: Stephen was implying that people do not have to become Jews in order to get to God! Stephen at some time may have quoted Jesus' words to the Samaritan woman: "The hour is coming when you will neither on this mountain, nor in Jerusalem, worship the Father. . . . God is Spirit, and those who worship Him must worship in spirit and truth" (John 4:21,24).

Although the gospel was being preached in Jerusalem and Judea, up to this point it was being preached to Jews only, so what we're dealing with had not yet become an issue. Stephen has now gone down in history as one of Christianity's greatest leaders because he was the first one who began to prepare the way for the gospel to move out of the Jewish sphere and to the Samaritans and the Gentiles. The gospel was for *panta ta ethne*, *all* the peoples, and not just the Jews (see Acts 7:48-50). As we will see, this was Stephen's point of view and this is what severely threatened his enemies and made them angry. In a word, they were not willing to share their God!

STEPHEN'S LANDMARK SPEECH

Stephen's response to these false accusations is the longest speech recorded in the book of Acts. Why? Unquestionably, it is Scripture's most important missiological statement other than the findings of the Council of Jerusalem in Acts 15. It is not a mere coincidence that they both deal with the same issue. What is the issue? Simply put: *It is not necessary to give up your own culture and to become a Jew (or anything else for that matter) in order to be saved.*

Stephen had a special anointing of God for delivering this speech:

[15] *And all who sat in the council, looking steadfastly at him, saw his face as the face of an angel.*

This anointing enabled Stephen to do two things that someone in his position ordinarily would not be expected to do. First, he did not deal with negatives by accusing his opponents of giving false testimony. He dealt only with positives. Second, he did accuse the leaders so forcefully of murdering Jesus that they wouldn't let him finish his discourse.

How God Spoke to His People: Acts 7

[2] *And he said, "Men and brethren and fathers, listen: The God of glory appeared to our father Abraham when he was in Mesopotamia . . .* [9] *And the patriarchs, becoming envious, sold Joseph into Egypt. But God was with him. . . .* [30] *And when forty years had passed,*

an Angel of the Lord appeared to him [Moses] in a flame of fire in a bush, in the wilderness of Mount Sinai. [44] *Our fathers had the tabernacle of witness in the wilderness . . ."*

In order to make his point, Stephen chooses three of the outstanding heroes of the Jewish faith: Abraham, Joseph and Moses. No Jew would doubt that God had spoken to each of them personally. But interestingly enough, He spoke to all of them *outside* of the Holy Land. He spoke to Abram (Abraham) in Mesopotamia, to Joseph in Egypt and to Moses on Mount Sinai. The clear implication: None of these patriarchs needed to come to the Temple in Jerusalem to hear from God!

Then Stephen refers to the portable tabernacle in the wilderness, which also was outside the Holy Land, that could be used any place to bring people into contact with God. He contrasted this to the Temple:

[47] *But Solomon built Him a house.* [48] *However, the Most High does not dwell in temples made with hands* . . .

In all probability, not one of the 12 original apostles, at this point, could have so clearly expounded the doctrine that the gospel of the Kingdom is much broader than Judaism with its symbols and rituals. Being a Hellenist would have helped Stephen immensely to comprehend this insight and draw out its missiological implications. Most of the Hebrew believers had not yet really accepted it. We realize that when Peter later went to the house of Cornelius (see Acts 10), and when the Jerusalem Council was convened almost 20 years later (see Acts 15). Some, in fact, never did catch on.

Applying the Principle to Samaria

The general principle behind Stephen's speech is that God's people *must* move out in mission. They must become "missionary people," to use the title of Charles Van Engen's excellent book *God's Missionary People.* Van Engen says, "As local congregations are built up to reach out, they will emerge from their sapling stage to be their true nature, bearing fruit as missionary people."[2]

It may be that even as he was speaking to the Sanhedrin, Stephen knew that the time had come to preach in Samaria. Scholars point to two indirect references to Samaria in his speech that could have been intentional but that the average reader might not notice. Stephen speaks of the tomb in Shechem "that Abraham bought" (7:16). That tomb was located in Samaria. Also, from Deuteronomy, he cites the promise of a prophet to come (see Acts 7:37), which was the only messianic prophecy in the reduced portion of the Old Testament Scriptures that the Samaritans had accepted. How would Stephen have known? It may well have been a prophetic word from God, because he was filled with the Holy Spirit.

WHO WERE THESE SAMARITANS?

After the time of King Solomon, the northern Israelite kingdom, called "Israel," separated from the southern Israelite kingdom, called "Judah." The capital city of the northern kingdom was Samaria, and sometimes, therefore, the whole northern kingdom is referred to as "Samaria," after the city. In 721 B.C., the neighboring Assyrians captured Samaria and forced the Israelites there to intermarry with them, creating a mixed Israelite-Assyrian race. From that time on, they were considered impure and non-Jewish by the pure-blooded Jews. The Samaritans offered to help build the Temple in Jerusalem, but were turned down, so they built their own temple at Mount Gerazim, which the Jews later proceeded to destroy. Samaritans and Jews disliked each other immensely. The woman at the well reflected this when she casually said to Jesus, "How is that You, being a Jew, ask a drink from me, a Samaritan woman?" (John 4:9).

Stephen knew this, of course, and he knew that the Samaritans would never accept worship at the Jewish Temple in Jerusalem as a precondition for salvation through Jesus as Messiah. Therefore, in order to contextualize the gospel for Samaritans, Stephen had to de-absolutize Jewish Temple worship as the one and only way to come to Jehovah God. Nothing was wrong with the Temple—Stephen himself worshiped there—but cross-culturally it was excess baggage if loaded on the simple gospel of repentance for sin and faith in Jesus Christ. To the Sanhedrin, however, such a thing would sound like blasphemy.

As if these things weren't bad enough, Stephen went on to accuse his accusers, not of giving false testimony, but more ominously of murdering their Messiah:

> [51] *You stiff-necked and uncircumcised in heart and ears! You always resist the Holy Spirit; as your fathers did, so do you.* [52] *Which of the prophets did your fathers not persecute? And they killed those who*

foretold the coming of the Just One, of whom you now have become the betrayers and murderers.

They had heard enough! The Sanhedrin, showing an enormous surge of emotion, decided that the best way to deal with this troublemaker would be to execute him.

THE EXECUTION

[54] *When they heard these things they were cut to the heart, . . .* [55] *But he, being full of the Holy Spirit, . . .* [56] *and said, "Look! I see the heavens opened and the Son of Man standing at the right hand of God!"* [58] *and they cast him out of the city and stoned him. . . .*

For all the difference it makes, this was an illegal execution. As in the case of Jesus, they would legally have been required to go to the Roman officers before taking such action, for only the Romans could serve the death penalty. Thus, it would not be inaccurate to label this precipitous action as murder. It had no more legal backing than a Ku Klux Klan lynching.

The trigger for violence was not Stephen's rebuke or even calling them stiff-necked and uncircumcised in heart and ears! It was Stephen saying, "Look! I see the heavens opened and the Son of Man standing at the right hand of God!" As Ernst Haenchen says, "If Jesus stands on the right hand of God, this must show that the Christians are right in the sight of God and that the High Council is virtually God's enemy."[3] From this point on, there was no stopping them.

Stephen died for his Lord with words similar to his Master's on his lips:

[60] . . . *"Lord, do not charge them with this sin."*

WHY WAS STEPHEN MURDERED?

Because this event is such a crucial turning point in the history of Christianity, let me concisely summarize what happened. Stephen had established that there was a fundamental, not just a superficial, difference between the old order, that of Jewish Temple worship, and the new order, later called Christianity. No compromise was possible. All people groups, not just the Jews, could now have direct access to God through Jesus the Messiah. Gentiles could now be saved and remain Gentiles. This principle is the indispensable premise of all cross-cultural missionary work. It was, and still is, very difficult for many devout Jews to accept.

Stephen had made explicit what had always been implicit, and by doing it he had polarized the opinions. From that point on, high-level persecution was inevitable.

LUKE INTRODUCES SAUL

[58] . . . *And the witnesses laid down their clothes at the feet of a young man named Saul.* [8:1] *Now Saul was consenting to his death.* [3] *As for Saul, he made havoc of the church, entering every house, and dragging off men and women, committing them to prison.*

No church leader at this point could possibly have believed that Saul of Tarsus, undoubtedly called by some "Saul the Terrible," would later be transformed by the power of the Holy Spirit and, as the famous apostle Paul, lead the advance of the kingdom of God into the Gentile world. It sounds very much as if, at that time, Saul could have been the actual ringleader of the fierce persecution that began with Stephen's death.

GETTING RID OF THE HELLENISTIC BELIEVERS: ACTS 8

[1] . . . *At that time a great persecution arose against the church which was at Jerusalem; and they were all scattered throughout the regions of Judea and Samaria, except the apostles.* [4] *Therefore those who were scattered went everywhere preaching the word.*

A chain reaction occurred. The more the Jews thought about the implications of Stephen's message, the more threatened they became. Previously, the persecutions had been directed specifically against certain leaders such as Peter and John (see Acts 4:3), the 12 apostles (see Acts 5:18) or Stephen. Now, the fury of the enemies of the gospel is loosed against the believers in general for the first time.

In order to get an accurate picture, we should not interpret the phrase "they were all scattered" too literally. Everett Harrison warns us, "This can hardly be taken strictly, since many were detained and imprisoned. This is an example of hyperbole which is not uncommon in Scripture when emphasis is desired."[4] As an obvious example, Harrison points to Mark 1:5, which says that when John the Baptist came, "all the land of Judea" went out to him and "all" were baptized. Or when we commonly say, "Everybody in town was at the football game!"

The three words "except the apostles" have more significance than many realize. The apostles, as far as we know, were not personally involved in the incident with Stephen. They likely regarded it as a situation brought on by the Hellenistic group, which they had blessed by laying hands on the seven leaders, but for which they no longer felt a paternal responsibility. This is a common attitude of missionaries today who release the national church to their indigenous leadership, then distance themselves when the nationals make choices that may seem misguided to the missionaries. F. F. Bruce says, "We may conclude that it was the Hellenists in the church (the group in which Stephen had been a leader) who formed the main target of attack, and that it was they for the most part who were compelled to leave Jerusalem."[5] Then Bruce adds, "From this time onward the Jerusalem church appears to have been a predominantly 'Hebrew' body."[6] Not that there were no exceptions, or that things would never change as time went on. We know, for example, that the person the Jerusalem church chose to make a fact-finding visit to Antioch about 15 years later was Barnabas, a Hellenistic disciple (see Acts 11:22).

The upshot of all of this?

[4] ***Therefore those who were scattered went everywhere preaching the word.***

As frequently happens, what would seem to be a setback for the church is used by God for His glory and the spread of His kingdom.

PREACHING CHRIST IN SAMARIA

Stephen and Philip were the two highest-profile individuals among the seven chosen to lead the Hellenistic segment of the Jerusalem church. Because Stephen had been executed, it is a safe assumption that some of the other six might have been included among those who were killed in the "great persecution" in which "they were all scattered throughout the regions of Judea and Samaria." Philip was one of those who went from Jerusalem to Samaria.

The late Stephen, as I have mentioned, seems to have been the theoretician who developed the missiological and theological rationale for the possibility of church planting among the non-Jewish Samaritans. He had cleared the way for the notion of such a thing, as an authentic *Samaritan* disciple of Jesus, when previously there had only been *Jewish* disciples of Jesus. This sounds obvious to us today. But we have to be reminded that when Philip went to Samaria, probably the majority of Jewish believers, if approached in an opinion poll, would have said that Samaritans should only be allowed to become disciples of Jesus if they first agreed to become Jewish proselytes.

[5] ***Then Philip went down to the city of Samaria and preached Christ to them.*** [6] ***And the multitudes with one accord heeded the things spoken by Philip, hearing and seeing the miracles which he did.*** [7] ***For unclean spirits, crying with a loud voice, came out of many who were possessed; and many who were paralyzed and lame were healed.***

PHILIP: EVANGELIST AND MISSIONARY

There are two important Philips in the New Testament. One was numbered among the original 12. He was a Hebrew who remained in Jerusalem. The other, a Hellenist, became Christianity's first recognized cross-cultural missionary, called of God to evangelize Samaria.

Today we hear a good deal about evangelists such as Billy Graham or Luis Palau or Reinhard Bonnke, as well as many others. In light of that, it is interesting that the only example we have in the New Testament of a person who was specifically recognized as an evangelist was Philip. Much later in the book of Acts, he is referred to as "Philip the evangelist, and he had four virgin daughters who prophesied" (Acts 21:8-9).

Philip, presumably, had at least two dominant spiritual gifts, that of evangelist and that of missionary. We do not know whether his colleague Stephen had either of these gifts, but Stephen obviously had the gift of wisdom (see Acts 6:10) and of faith (see Acts 6:5). My definitions of Philip's gifts are as follows:

> The gift of *evangelist* is the special ability that God gives to certain members of the Body of Christ to share the gospel with unbelievers in such a way that men and women become Jesus' disciples and responsible members of the Body of Christ.[7]

> The gift of *missionary* is the special ability that God gives to certain members of the Body of Christ to minister whatever other spiritual gifts they have in a second culture.[8]

Most of the evangelists we know are monocultural evangelists, but Philip is the prototype of subsequent cross-cultural evangelists, whom we often refer to as "missionaries." His target was Samaria, although we do not know whether this meant the city of Samaria itself or the region of Samaria. Some speculate that the city in Samaria, where he first preached, might actually have been Gitta, the hometown of Simon the sorcerer, who appears later.

EVANGELIZING BY WORD AND DEED

Philip's ministry had two parallel and closely related elements: word and deed. We read of "the things spoken by Philip" and also of "the miracles which he did." This follows what would have been expected from Jesus' words in Acts 1:8, where He spoke of receiving the power of the Holy Spirit and also of being cross-cultural witnesses. Philip was practicing New Testament "power evangelism," to borrow the title of John Wimber's seminal book on the subject.[9] Because this is the only biblical description we have of the ministry of a person specifically designated as an "evangelist" in the New Testament, one wonders why more evangelists today would not seek to combine miraculous deeds with their words, as did Philip. If they did, we might also see similar "multitudes with one accord" responding to such a holistic gospel. Fortunately, the number of evangelists who are now combining the two is increasing dramatically around the world, and the kingdom of God has never spread more rapidly. We are fortunate to have scholarly confirmation of this through Philip Jenkins' books *The New Christendom* and *The New Faces of Christianity*.

Philip's ministry in word was "[preaching] Christ to them." This means that he was presenting Jesus as Messiah, a synonym of "Christ." This message made sense to the Samaritans, as we know from the Samaritan woman whom Jesus met at the well. She said, "I know that Messiah is coming" (who is called Christ). "When He comes, He will tell us all things" (John 4:25). Philip's goal was to see large numbers of "messianic Samaritans," and from what we read here he was accomplishing it well.

The major reason that people in Samaria would listen to his claims that Jesus was the long-awaited Messiah was the power ministry seen through *miracles, healings and deliverance from evil spirits*. I would imagine that Philip also had the spiritual gifts of healing, miracles and deliverance to accompany his gifts of evangelist and missionary.

It is notable that Luke would mention that the Samaritan multitudes were "hearing and seeing the miracles which he did." The phrase "hearing" miracles seems strange until Luke goes on to say: "For unclean spirits, crying with a loud voice, came out of many." These evangelistic meetings, apparently, were noisy, rather boisterous and probably messy events. Incorporating mass deliverance into evangelistic crusades is not part of the usual experience of most American Christians, but it is as common in many Third World settings today as it was in Samaria then.

Argentine evangelist Carlos Annacondia, a personal friend of mine, can hardly conceive of public evangelism apart from demonic deliverance. I have been among the thousands standing in the open air in his meetings when he forcefully rebukes, even taunts, the demonic spirits in the audience. Scores, sometimes hundreds, fall to the ground under demonic manifestations with many of the demons "crying with a loud voice." Well-trained teams of "stretcher bearers" circulate through the crowd, escorting or physically carrying the demonized to a huge tent behind the platform called the "spiritual intensive care unit." There, skilled deliverance teams minister one by one, sometimes through the night, until all have been freed from the dark angels who had been oppressing them.[10]

I mention this to keep us from thinking that such noisy and messy, but at the same time powerful, works of the Holy Spirit are simply relics of the past. They are also happening today wherever the kingdom of God is in rapid advance.

WHAT GOOD ARE MIRACLES AND SIGNS?

Ministries of the miraculous, where paralyzed people walk, deaf people hear and demonized people are freed, never save anyone. Healings bring glory to God, but even the most dramatic ones are at best temporal. They do not impart eternal life. The *deeds* only prepare the way for the *Word*.

But, make no mistake, they prepare the way well. Although modern Westernized commentators don't usually highlight the fact, nevertheless the whole Gospel of John is organized around seven miracles (changing water to wine, healing a boy, healing a cripple, feeding 5,000, walking on water, healing a blind man and raising a dead man), and as John says, "Jesus did many other signs" (John 20:30). John tells us that the seven signs he chose around which to structure his Gospel "are written that you may believe that Jesus is the Christ, the Son of God, and that believing you may have life in His name" (John 20:31). The miracles themselves draw attention, but they are only *signs* pointing to salvation through faith in Jesus as Messiah. This is what Philip was practicing.

RESULTS OF PHILIP'S POWER EVANGELISM

[8] *And there was great joy in that city.* [12] *But when they believed Philip as he preached the things concerning the kingdom of God and the name of Jesus Christ, both men and women were baptized.* [14] *Now when the apostles who were at Jerusalem heard that Samaria had received the word of God, they sent Peter and John to them,* . . . [25] *So when they had testified and preached the word of the Lord, they returned to Jerusalem, preaching the gospel in many villages of the Samaritans.*

There was great joy in the city of Samaria from the outset of Philip's ministry there. At this point, it was probably not as yet the joy of salvation, but the joy over being healed and seeing their loved ones healed. Whatever Philip had come to say was being seen as "good news," another term for the gospel.

Many Samaritans then believed. They believed the good news concerning the kingdom of God that Philip had been demonstrating before their very eyes. The Kingdom had come, and Samaritans were being accepted into it. They sealed their commitment through public baptism, and the Church of Jesus Christ was firmly planted in their midst.

When this news got back to the Hebrew believers who had remained in Jerusalem after the persecution of the Hellenists, it must have caused no small stir. They had not sent Philip as a missionary; he had been driven out by the Jews, most likely at the instigation of the notorious Saul of Tarsus. How much attention they had paid to Stephen's historic message we do not know, but, in any case, the phenomenon of large numbers of messianic Samaritans must have caused the Hebrew believers an uncomfortable mixture of joy and consternation.

The fact that they immediately sent their two top leaders, Peter and John, to investigate, indicates that the issues must have been seen as extraordinarily significant. These Samaritans were being baptized in the name of Jesus. Were they really brothers and sisters in Christ? Peter and John had been with Jesus at Sychar in Samaria when "many of the Samaritans of that city believed in Him," hearing the testimony of the woman at the well (see John 4:39-42). They had been prepared. Peter also had been the representative of the 12 for receiving the keys of the kingdom of heaven (see Matt. 16:18-19), and, as such, he was present when the Kingdom opened wide to the Jews on Pentecost (see Acts 2), he was there when it opened to the Samaritans, and later he was there when it opened to the Gentiles in the house of Cornelius (see Acts 10).

THE SAMARITANS RECEIVED THE HOLY SPIRIT

[14] . . . *they sent Peter and John to them,* [15] *who, when they had come down, prayed for them that they might receive the Holy Spirit.* [16] *For as yet He had fallen upon none of them. They had only been baptized in the name of the Lord Jesus.* [17] *Then they laid hands on them, and they received the Holy Spirit.*

Acts 8:14-17 is a favorite text for those who teach that the baptism in the Holy Spirit is a second work of God's grace subsequent to salvation. The Samaritans had been saved and baptized in water but had not as yet received the Holy Spirit. Through prayer and the laying on of hands, the Holy Spirit came upon them.

Others disagree. The reason this has become a continuing point of debate among committed Christians is that the Bible itself is not entirely clear. Passages such as this one encourage one point of view. Passages such as 1 Corinthians 12:13, "For by one Spirit we were all baptized into one body . . . and have all been made to drink into one Spirit," encourage the point of view that the baptism of the Holy Spirit occurs at conversion. Subsequent to conversion, many fillings with the Holy Spirit, or special anointings, or whatever we call them, can and should occur. I have my personal point of view, but I am not interested here to attempt to prove that I am right and that others are wrong. Fortunately, we are all seeking the same thing, namely, the powerful energizing of the Holy Spirit for ministry.

I will, however, reiterate what I mentioned in chapter 4 about the three phases of the Pentecost event. I believe that Pentecost, or the coming of the Holy Spirit, was a one-time historical incident, as were the death and resurrection of Jesus. This unique first-century event had three parts, or phases. Phase one happened on the Day of Pentecost itself in Acts 2; phase two happened here in Acts 8; and phase three happened later in the house of Cornelius in Acts 10. My point is that if the Pentecost event in three parts was a unique historical occurrence, there is no intrinsic need to suppose that the sequence of first being saved, then later receiving the Holy Spirit, would necessarily carry on in the church through the centuries.

IS SPEAKING IN TONGUES THE ONLY VALIDATION?

It seems strange that Luke mentions speaking in tongues in phases one and three, but not here in phase two. Still, the apostles must have had some tangible way of knowing that when "they laid hands on them . . . they received the Holy Spirit." There is no denying that speaking in tongues is one of the biblical evidences of being filled with the Holy Spirit, but I do not agree that it should be seen as the one and only validating physical evidence.

A milestone in this century-long debate was the publication of *The Beauty of Spiritual Language* by Jack Hayford, one of the most impeccably credentialed, classical Pentecostal leaders of our times. Classical Pentecostals have formed the largest bloc of those who have historically argued for the "initial evidence" doctrine that all who receive the baptism of the Holy Spirit validate that experience physically by speaking in tongues at least once.

In his book, which predictably encourages the gift of tongues for all Christians, Hayford nevertheless says, "As readily as I want to honor my Pentecostal forebears for preserving the testimony of tongues and for generating a passion for Spirit-fullness among millions, at the same time I confess that I believe an unintentional but nonetheless restrictive barrier was built," referring specifically to the initial-evidence requirement.[11]

Although speaking in tongues can be an evidence, and quite possibly was in Samaria (even though it isn't mentioned), other evidences can be new intimacy with the Father, the joy of the Holy Spirit, falling in the power of God, power to heal the sick and cast out demons, prophecy, a driving passion for winning the lost, and many others.

THE APOSTLES' VERDICT

The missiological question remains: How well did the Hebrew apostles, Peter and John, like what they saw in Samaria? Could they accept the radical shift involved in affirming the validity of "messianic Samaritans"? Could Samaritans become part of the family of Jehovah God without first becoming Jews? Apparently they were convinced, because:

[25] . . . *they returned to Jerusalem, preaching the gospel in many villages of the Samaritans.*

Peter and John were now themselves evangelizing Samaritans! They were planting churches in Samaritan villages and not requiring them to switch their place of contact with God from Mount Gerazim to Jerusalem. This would have been a difficult adjustment for strict Jews to make, but the Samaritans were at least half Jews. Considerably more difficult would be the adjustment the apostles would have to make in the future when they would cross the barrier to outright Gentiles.

SIMON THE SORCERER AND SPIRITUAL WARFARE

A very important incident occurs when Philip is in Samaria, which has implications far beyond cross-cultural church planting in Samaria itself. Almost half of the Samaria passage explains Philip's ministry to just one individual, Simon the Sorcerer, and the help he then received from Peter. I say it has wider implications because it is the first time Luke discusses an event involving occult-level spiritual warfare.

Three levels of spiritual warfare may be fairly well discerned, all of them relating to each other through the intricate workings of the kingdom of darkness: (1) ground-level spiritual warfare that is casting ordinary demons out of people; (2) occult-level spiritual warfare involving the satanic power of magicians, sorcerers, witches, New Age channelers, shamans and the like; and (3) strategic-level spiritual warfare dealing with principalities, powers and territorial spirits.

The intrusion of the kingdom of God into previously unchallenged areas dominated by the kingdom of Satan is an underlying theme throughout Acts, although Luke surfaces it only from time to time. Yale University biblical scholar Susan Garrett has recently produced what I would imagine to be the definitive study of magic and the demonic in Luke's writings. In her book *The Demise of the Devil*, she says, "The remarks about Satan in Luke's Gospel and Acts are, if small in quantity, mammoth in significance. When taken seriously, the traces and clues that Luke has dropped along the way suggest that one can scarcely overestimate Satan's importance in the history of Salvation told by Luke."[12]

Just to anticipate some of these "traces and clues," ground-level spiritual warfare is described frequently throughout Acts. Another example of occult-level spiritual warfare comes with the seven sons of Sceva in Acts 19. Strategic-level spiritual warfare surfaces with Bar-Jesus or Elymas in Acts 13 and with the Python spirit in Acts 16, and all three are tied in with Paul's ministry in Ephesus in Acts 19.

Here in Samaria the statement that "unclean spirits, crying with a loud voice, came out of many who were possessed" (8:7) displays ground-level spiritual warfare. The occult-level warfare involves Simon the Sorcerer:

> [9] *But there was a certain man called Simon, who previously practiced sorcery in the city and astonished the people of Samaria, claiming that he was someone great,* [10] *to whom they all gave heed, from the least to the greatest, saying, "This man is the great power of God."* [11] *And they heeded him because he had astonished them with his sorceries for a long time.* [13] *Then Simon himself also believed; and when he was baptized he continued with Philip, and was amazed, seeing the miracles and signs which were done.*
>
> [18] *Now when Simon saw that through the laying on of the apostles' hands the Holy Spirit was given, he offered them money,* [19] *saying, "Give me this power also, that anyone on whom I lay hands may receive the Holy Spirit."* [20] *But Peter said to him, "Your money perish with you, because you thought that the gift of God could be purchased with money!* [21] *You have neither part nor portion in this matter, for your heart is not right in the sight of God.* [22] *Repent therefore of this your wickedness, and pray God if perhaps the thought of your heart may be forgiven you.* [23] *For I see that you are poisoned by bitterness and bound by iniquity."*

[24] *Then Simon answered and said, "Pray to the Lord for me, that none of the things which you have spoken may come upon me."*

This story contains many unknowns. Was Simon's original profession of faith and baptism valid or just a sham? After Peter later rebuked him, did he repent? As far as Simon the Sorcerer is concerned, does the story have a happy ending or a sad ending? Although I have no way of proving it, I would like to believe that Simon was really saved through Philip's preaching, that he subsequently made a huge mistake as a new babe in Christ, that the Holy Spirit used Peter's rebuke to straighten him out, and that he repented and lived happily ever after. Whether this is the actual case or not, what do we learn from this incident?

WHAT CAN WE LEARN?

Simon the Sorcerer's power in the city was enormous. The citizens "all gave heed" to this man "from the least to the greatest," and they regarded him as God, "saying, 'This man is the great power of God.' " It could well be that the territorial spirit assigned to keep this city in darkness had attached itself to the Sorcerer. Underneath the whole thing we should recognize, as Susan Garrett says, that these "narrated encounters are not merely skirmishes between prophets or wonder-workers, but confrontations between Satan and the Spirit of God."[13] In order to gain this power over the city, Simon's magical power must have been real. "Simon is no mere con artist, or cheap charlatan," says Garrett, "but someone far more sinister, endowed with the power of Satan and disguising himself as the 'great power of God.' "[14]

Philip came into that city, which was under a fascination of power, with most Samaritans probably not even realizing that the power to which they were subject was the power of Satan. The only kind of message that could possibly have impressed these people was a message involving not only a word, but also a demonstration of power. Missiologists call it a "power encounter." Missiologist Paul Pierson says, "The message was authenticated by clashes between the healing power of God and the destructive forces of evil. . . . Such 'power encounters' would often accompany new breakthroughs in the book of Acts and all through Christian history."[15] Philip's miracles and signs, done under the authentic power of God, were clearly recognized as superior to the counterfeit power of the devil. Even Simon the Sorcerer was amazed, "seeing the miracles and signs which were done."

Luke is showing us here that Philip's message was an early reflection of Jesus' later assignment to the apostle Paul. Paul was to go to the nations "to open their eyes and to turn them from darkness to light, and from the power of Satan to God" (Acts 26:18). Susan Garrett says, "Philip's dramatic exorcisms and healings of the possessed, paralyzed, and lame gave incontrovertible proof of Satan's subjugation, and hence of the certainty of the Kingdom of God with Christ as Lord."[16]

Philip's power ministry was the beachhead in this intense episode of spiritual warfare. The decisive victory, as far as the city was concerned, was Peter's rebuke to the powers of darkness operating through Simon the Sorcerer. Satan's last stand was to tempt Simon to offer money to buy God's power. This would have been normal behavior among professional magicians and sorcerers, so it was an easy temptation for Simon to yield to. Although Peter doesn't address Satan or the spirits directly, his rebuke to Simon is a public announcement that God's power is demonstrably greater than Satan's. The "bitterness and iniquity" that had poisoned Simon was clearly from the prince of evil.

Susan Garrett brilliantly expresses the essence of this historic power encounter: "Satan does still have some power, but he is handily subjugated when confronted by the vastly greater divine authority that Christians wield. Peter's righteous rebuke reduces Simon from a famous magician, impiously acclaimed by all the people of Samaria as 'the great power of God,' to a meek man who fears for his own destruction and so asks the servant of the Lord to intercede for him."[17]

SOUTH TO ETHIOPIA AND NORTH TO CAESAREA

As a further demonstration of the extraordinary power of God on Philip for cross-cultural evangelism, no less than an angel comes to Philip and instructs him to go to the Gaza Strip. Afterward, an even more remarkable miracle occurs when Philip is bodily transported by the Holy Spirit from there to Azotus (or Ashdod [8:39-40]).

> [26] *Now an angel of the Lord spoke to Philip, saying, "Arise and go toward the south along the road which goes down from Jerusalem to Gaza."* . . . [27] *So he arose and went. And behold, a man of Ethiopia, a eunuch of great authority under Candace the queen of the Ethiopians,*

who had charge of all her treasury, and had come to Jerusalem to worship, [28] *was returning. . . .* [35] *Then Philip opened his mouth, and beginning at this Scripture, preached Jesus to him.* [37] *. . . And [the eunuch] answered and said, "I believe that Jesus Christ is the Son of God."* [38] *. . . And both Philip and the eunuch went down into the water, and he baptized him.*

Although Luke does not tell us for sure, there is a strong possibility that this Ethiopian was a Gentile God-fearer like Cornelius. Such God-fearers were born Gentiles. They worshiped Jehovah God, but they had not taken the more radical step of becoming Jewish proselytes. If so, this is the first instance we have of a Gentile conversion, but because Luke leaves it rather ambiguous and makes nothing more of it, we will also postpone the discussion of E-3 Gentile evangelism until we come to Acts 10, where Peter visits the house of Cornelius.

From there, Philip preaches the gospel up the eastern coast of the Mediterranean, and the story of how the gospel first moved from Jerusalem and Judea to Samaria ends. Next, the kingdom of God pushes on through many of the gates of Hades, which try to hinder it, to the Gentiles, whom Jesus termed "the end of the earth" (Acts 1:8).

REFLECTION QUESTIONS

1. Name some actual examples of E-1 and E-2 and E-3 evangelism in your own city or nation. What are the major differences in the planning and execution of each?
2. Something that Stephen said must have been extremely upsetting to his hearers, causing them to murder him. What exactly was it?
3. Who were the Samaritans? Why was evangelizing them not a normal thing to expect from Jews?
4. Do you think the Samaritans spoke in tongues when they received the Holy Spirit? Why?
5. Describe the differences between ground-level, occult-level and strategic-level spiritual warfare. Where does Simon the Sorcerer fit into the picture?

9

MEET PAUL—THE GREATEST MISSIONARY OF ALL TIME

ACTS 9

Our story of the amazing spread of the gospel through the mighty power of God continues with this shocking description of one of the sworn enemies of Jesus and His followers:

> [1] ***Then Saul, still breathing threats and murder against the disciples of the Lord, went to the high priest*** [2] ***and asked letters from him to the synagogues of Damascus, so that if he found any who were of the Way, whether men or women, he might bring them bound to Jerusalem.***

Who was this Saul? It is not farfetched to consider Saul, whose name was later changed to Paul, as the second most significant figure in the history of Christianity next to Jesus Himself. Paul wrote one-fourth of the New Testament. Two-thirds of the book of Acts tells Paul's story. His conversion was so important that it is related three different times in Acts. Paul was the principal "bridge of God" from the Jews to the Gentiles, to paraphrase the title of missiologist Donald McGavran's landmark book *The Bridges of God*. Later we will see that Paul was not the very first missionary to the Gentiles, but he was certainly the most prominent, and he became the prototype of all subsequent cross-cultural missionaries. Few would consider it an exaggeration to label Paul "the greatest missionary of all time."

FROM A LION TO A LAMB

Before he met Jesus, Paul was a terror. John Stott said it vividly when he wrote, "Some of the language Luke uses to describe Paul in his pre-conversion state seems deliberately to portray him as 'a wild and ferocious beast.' "[1] Stott examines the Greek words and cites several scholars who conclude that the language reflects "the ravaging of a body of wild beasts," or "the panting and snorting of wild beasts," and what Paul did to the church was similar to the "mangling by wild beasts, e.g. lions." The lion, by the grace of God, later became a lamb.

Paul was born in Tarsus, a city in what then was Cilicia and what today is Turkey, on the northeast corner of the Mediterranean Sea. Tarsus was a Greek-speaking city, but from this we should not automatically conclude that Paul was a typical Hellenistic Jew. Richard Longenecker says, "It was possible for a thoroughly Hebraic Jew to be born and reared in the Diaspora."[2] The evidence we have points to the more likely conclusion that Paul's principal self-identity was that of a Hebrew as opposed to a Hellenist. He undoubtedly knew Greek, but as a second language, spoken with what we might call today a Yiddish accent. He calls himself a Hebrew born of Hebrews (see Phil. 3:5). Aramaic was his mother tongue, as suggested in the language of Jesus speaking to him on the Damascus road.

Many of the Jews residing in Tarsus, perhaps the majority, would indeed have been Hellenists. They would have been using the *Septuagint*, the Greek translation of the Old Testament, as their Bible and holding their synagogue services in Greek. But, as F. F. Bruce says, "Paul would have been given little opportunity of imbibing the culture of Tarsus during his boyhood: indeed, his parents made sure of an orthodox upbringing for him by arranging for him to spend his formative years in Jerusalem."[3] A modern parallel might be Hasidic Jews in New York City. Although they are citizens of New York City and of the United States of America, they, nevertheless, find their primary social and cultural self-identity as Orthodox Jews. At the same time, the majority of other Jews in New York City are much more Americanized, just as the majority in first-century Tarsus would likely have been Hellenized.

Paul, therefore, was probably raised in a Jewish ghetto. The word "ghetto" is more broadly used in our day, but through the centuries it usually meant the place where the Jewish community, largely unassimilated, lived in European cities. This fits in with the way Luke reports Paul's public self-description:

> [22:3] ***I am indeed a Jew, born in Tarsus of Cilicia,***
> ***but brought up in this city at the feet of Gamaliel,***
> ***taught according to the strictness of our fathers' law,***
> ***and was zealous toward God.***

As we saw in Acts 5 when the apostles were brought before the Sanhedrin, Gamaliel was the chief leader of the Pharisees in Jerusalem. Paul greatly values his time studying with Gamaliel, and says later to King Agrippa:

> [26:4] *My manner of life from my youth, which was spent from the beginning among my own nation at Jerusalem, all the Jews know. . . .*
> [5] *that according to the strictest sect of our religion I lived a Pharisee.*

At another point Paul added, "I am a Pharisee, the son of a Pharisee" (23:6).

Paul was a full-blooded Jew. He says that he was "circumcised the eighth day, of the stock of Israel, of the tribe of Benjamin" (Phil. 3:5). Not all full-blooded Jews back in those days, just as in these days, were devout practitioners of their faith. Some Jews today, in fact, are self-declared atheists or agnostics. Paul, however, was what we could call a "fanatic Jew." He says, "I advanced in Judaism beyond many of my contemporaries in my own nation, being more exceedingly zealous for the traditions of my fathers" (Gal. 1:14).

I have gone into a good bit of detail on Paul's early background for two reasons. One, it helps us understand why he might act like such a "wild beast" in persecuting the believers. Two, since the essence of missiology is cross-cultural ministry, it is important to know as clearly as possible what the *cultural* dimensions of Paul's career of taking the gospel to the Gentiles realistically involved.

Some may have noticed that I am citing passages from Acts 22 and Acts 26 along with those from Acts 9. By way of explanation, Paul's conversion story appears in all three places, and in my opinion it will be more helpful if we collate all three in this chapter instead of postponing the mention of significant bits and pieces until we come to them later and in a different context.

THE ROARING LION

We are told in the Bible, "Your adversary the devil walks about like a roaring lion, seeking whom he may devour" (1 Pet. 5:8). What could better describe Paul, then named Saul, as he walked to Damascus "breathing threats and murder against the disciples of the Lord" (Acts 9:1)?

To understand why Paul was going to Damascus, we must flash back briefly to the story of Stephen in Acts 7 and 8. Stephen, as we have seen, was the first theologian of cross-cultural missions. He was an ethnic Jew, but a Hellenist, as opposed to a Hebrew as Paul was. Stephen clearly saw that although the gospel was for Jews, it was also for non-Jews. He saw that salvation through Jesus was not restricted to those who kept the Jewish law and who worshiped in the Jerusalem Temple. This naturally irritated the Jewish traditionalists and they recruited false witnesses who said, "This man does not cease to speak blasphemous words against this holy place and the law" (6:13). Stephen's subsequent explanation in Acts 7 fanned the flames of their unbelief rather than quenched them, and they reacted by murdering Stephen. Luke makes a point of mentioning that Paul was there in person: "And the witnesses laid down their clothes at the feet of a young man named Saul" (7:58).

Paul was diametrically opposed to Stephen's theology of mission at that time. Paul firmly believed that no one could be acceptable to God without becoming a Jew and obeying the law. And because he was a fanatic, as we have seen, he took action:

> [8:1] *Now Saul was consenting to his death. . . .* [3] *. . . he made havoc of the church, entering every house, and dragging off men and women, committing them to prison.*

It is not difficult to feel the emotion here. We are looking at a man obviously under the power of the enemy who has come to steal, to kill and to destroy. His misdirected zeal has overshadowed any sense of human compassion. This sets the stage for the irony that such a wild beast could later become, of all things, a missionary to the Gentiles, explicitly inviting them to follow Christ without submitting to the Jewish law. Some years later, Paul himself describes this irony to a crowd of Jews in Jerusalem:

> [22:19] *So I said, "Lord, they know that in every synagogue I imprisoned and beat those who believe on You.* [20] *And when the blood of Your martyr Stephen was shed, I also was standing by consenting to his death, and guarding the clothes of those who were killing him."* [21] *Then He said to me, "Depart, for I will send you far from here to the Gentiles."*

The reaction of the Jewish crowd? They had no liking for what they heard:

> [22:22] *And they listened to him until this word, and then they raised their voices and said, "Away with such a fellow from the earth, for he is not fit to live!"*

The crowd's desire to kill Paul was exactly how Paul had previously perceived Stephen and the others who had believed in Jesus as their Messiah! He understood exactly what they were saying.

HEADING FOR DAMASCUS

Paul had become a full-time persecutor of the messianic Jews. He had done his best to wipe them out in Judea and Samaria, and perhaps some of the believers from there had escaped to Damascus when that persecution came. Apparently Paul was not seeking believers who were natives of Damascus itself, but only those who had gone there from Jerusalem. His purpose was to arrest them and "bring them bound to Jerusalem" (9:2), where the Sanhedrin had jurisdiction and where they could then be punished.

Paul took with him "letters . . . to the synagogues of Damascus" (9:2). Keep in mind that believers were still Jews in those days and they kept the Jewish law and attended their synagogues. No one was yet called a "Christian," and no one would be called a Christian until the first Gentile churches were firmly established in Antioch. Unfortunately, at least one modern version of the Bible translates the word "disciple" in Acts 9:10 as "Christian," and is, therefore, somewhat misleading.

Rather than "Christian," they are called here those "who were of the Way" (9:2). This is one of the more common terms for first-century believers. For example, in Ephesus, later on "there arose a great commotion about the Way" (19:23), and when Paul is defending himself before Felix, he explains that he worships God "according to the Way" (24:14).

The issue was not whether they were Jews or not. The issue was whether these messianic Jews in Damascus were perceived to be blaspheming God as Stephen had been accused of doing. Paul, with his extremely Jewish ethnocentric point of view, thought they were, and they needed to be punished for it.

THE VISION ON THE ROAD

[9:3] *And as he journeyed he came near Damascus, and suddenly a light shone around him from heaven.* [4] *Then he fell to the ground, and heard a voice saying to him, "Saul, Saul, why are you persecuting Me?"* [5] *And he said, "Who are You, Lord?" And the Lord said, "I am Jesus, whom you are persecuting. It is hard for you to kick against the goads."*

[22:6] *Now it happened, as I journeyed and came near Damascus at about noon, suddenly a great light from heaven shone around me.* [7] *And I fell to the ground and heard a voice saying to me, "Saul, Saul . . ."*

[26:13] *At midday . . . along the road I saw a light from heaven, brighter than the sun, shining around me and those who journeyed with me.* [14] *And when we had all fallen to the ground, I heard a voice speaking to me and saying in the Hebrew language, "Saul, Saul . . ."*

Paul's conversion, related no less than three different times in the book of Acts, is one of the more awesome displays of the power of God in human affairs that we find in Scripture. It included a supernatural light, a vision, a falling under the power of the Spirit, hearing the voice of God and a new birth "not of blood, nor of the will of the flesh, nor of the will of man, but of God" (John 1:13).

It is hard to imagine being in the Middle East under the noonday sun, and then being enveloped in yet a brighter light. We don't know how many others were with Paul on this trip, but all of them saw the light. I have not personally experienced such a phenomenon, but several of my friends testify to experiences similar to Paul's. The light here, as in more recent counterparts, is presumably a visible manifestation of the glory of a holy God. In the transfiguration, it is said that Jesus' "face shone like the sun, and His clothes became as white as the light" (Matt. 17:2).

My friend Jack Hayford is one who has experienced seeing the tangible light of God. In the early days of his pastorate in The Church On The Way in Van Nuys, California, he had been struggling with a lethargic congregation and a plateaued membership of about 100 people. Then one Saturday, Jack went into the sanctuary alone and saw it filled with a silvery mist. He says, "No earthly dust had the glowing quality that this mist possessed as it filled the whole room, even where the sunlight was not shining."[4] After God filled the sanctuary with His glory, a church growth phenomenon began that approached 15,000 congregants before Jack's retirement years later.

Light dispels darkness. Paul will later write to the Corinthians about "the light of the gospel of the glory of Christ" (2 Cor. 4:4), and affirm that "it is the God who commanded light to shine out of darkness who has shone in our hearts to give the light of the knowledge of the glory of God in the face of Jesus Christ" (4:6). From the time Paul saw the light on the Damascus road, his burning desire was to share that light with those who were still in darkness, as he had been for so many years.

SEEING THE RISEN CHRIST

All three accounts of Paul's conversion affirm that he heard a voice, but none of the three states expressly that he saw Jesus. Three days later in Damascus, however, Ananias, speaking prophetically, says, "Brother Saul, the Lord Jesus, *who appeared to you* on the road as you came . . ." (Acts 9:17, emphasis added). We could presume that if Jesus had appeared, Paul would have seen Him, although it could also have been just the light and the voice. A clearer indication that he actually saw Jesus, however, comes when Paul goes to Jerusalem three years later and declares to the apostles "how he had *seen the Lord* on the road" (v. 27, emphasis added).

Further confirmations come from Paul as he later writes his letter to the Corinthians. There, he defends his apostolic authority with the rhetorical question, "Have I not seen Jesus Christ our Lord?" (1 Cor. 9:1). And he defends it again when speaking of Jesus' resurrection, "Then last of all He was seen by me also, as by one born out of due time" (15:8).

It is easy to assume that after Jesus appeared to Paul on the Damascus road, He has not made, nor does He make, such visible appearances. Some theologians say as much when they discuss Paul's apostolic credentials. But, as a matter of fact, appearances of Jesus Himself, like the light of God's glory, are being reported with some regularity today, particularly in the two-thirds world. It may be that we in the Western world are visited by Jesus less frequently or that our cultural presuppositions, including those in Christian circles, are such that we are not prepared to lend credibility to such reports and, therefore, those who may see Jesus would be reluctant to tell others.

But after seeing Jesus on the Damascus road, Paul had other similar experiences. For example, when he went back to the Temple in Jerusalem as a believer, Jesus appeared to him again. Paul says, "Then it happened, when I returned to Jerusalem and was praying in the temple, that I was in a trance, and saw Him saying to me . . ." (Acts 22:17-18). Years later Luke records, "the following night the Lord stood by him [Paul] and said . . ." (23:11). Paul probably saw Jesus many times.

WHO WAS THE "DOCTOR"?

Because Jesus is the same yesterday, today and forever, I believe that we should not consider it particularly strange if we hear similar accounts today. *Christianity Today*, for example, published a story that seems to be authentic. In a certain province in China, where the gospel has been spreading like wildfire through many displays of power ministries reminiscent of the book of Acts, a woman who had never been in contact with Christians was suffering from an inoperable brain tumor. Jesus came to her as a total stranger, ministered to her and healed the brain tumor. Then He told her to travel to a certain nearby village where she would learn who He was. She obeyed, contacted a group of house church believers, learned that her "doctor's" name was Jesus Christ, and became a faithful Christian.[5]

Whether the risen Christ had been bodily present with this Chinese woman or whether she had seen Him in a vision is not clear. At the end of the day, it really matters very little. A recent report from my friend Wolfgang Simson tells of Jesus using a dream to appear to a Muslim man in Egypt. This man had been Minister of Religious Affairs under former President Sadat. He had sent his 12-year-old daughter to London for treatment for polio. While in the hospital, two Christian women prayed for her, she was instantly healed and she jumped out of bed.

Simson reports, "Just the night before, her Muslim father saw in a dream how Isa (Jesus) was standing next to the bed of his daughter. He saw Him putting His hand on her and healing her.

"The next day, he received a phone call from his daughter. Before she could tell her story, he said, 'Don't tell me what has happened because I already know. Jesus has healed you!' "[6]

CALLED THROUGH VISIONS AND DREAMS

Relatively few Christian workers in Western nations have been called into ministry through visions or dreams, as was the apostle Paul. I personally was not called that way. Nonetheless, our call is no less authentic. But elsewhere things are different.

For example, Edward Murphy reports that a survey of West African Bible school students shows that dreams or visions were the most common way God had called them into ministry. The group surveyed was remarkable in that they represented an African church established by Western missionaries serving with a mission that was overtly noncharismatic and did not encourage power ministries. The missionaries there would not have been called through visions or dreams. Summing it up, Murphy says, "While this means of divine communication may not be as relevant in Western society, it is apparently very relevant in West African society . . . God accommodates Himself to human cultures as He seeks to communicate Himself to them."[7]

FALLING TO THE GROUND

We know that all of those in Paul's traveling party saw the light. We also know that they heard a conversation going on. However, they did not see Jesus, nor were they able to pick up the words of the dialogue as Paul did. Acts 9 says, "the men who journeyed with him stood speechless, hearing a voice, but seeing no one" (9:7), while Acts 22 adds, "those who were with me . . . did not hear the voice of Him who spoke to me" (v. 9).

The phenomenon of people falling to the ground under the immediate manifestation of the power of God seems to be on the increase in Christian circles. Sometimes called "resting in the Spirit" or "slaying in the Spirit" or "falling under the power," it was common in the camp meetings and the brush arbor meetings of the early holiness movement of the nineteenth century, and it carried through the twentieth century by the Pentecostal and charismatic movements. In our day, it is being seen with growing frequency, including in some of the more traditional evangelical churches.

Two prominent figures identified with the traditional evangelical camp, who have recently studied this phenomenon and written about it, are Jack Deere and John White. Deere finds instances of falling in the power of the Spirit in the ministry of John Wesley and in the American Great Awakening, mentioned frequently by Jonathan Edwards.[8] John White tells of instances he has witnessed in Argentina and in the United States, in some cases, of many people falling at the same time, as they did on the Damascus road.

Although Deere and White both warn of carnal abuses and possible satanic counterfeits, they interpret this activity generally as a work of the Holy Spirit. John White describes a personal experience of being slain in the Spirit in these words: "I lay on my face, a quivering mass of adoring jelly. I, therefore, am unable to dismiss what I see of certain phenomena in the present, or what I read about in the past."[9]

HEARING THE VOICE OF GOD

[9:4] *Then he fell to the ground, and heard a voice saying to him, "Saul, Saul . . ."*

[22:7] *And I fell to the ground and heard a voice saying to me, "Saul, Saul . . ."*

[26:14] *I heard a voice speaking to me and saying in the Hebrew language, "Saul, Saul . . ."*

The voice Paul heard on the Damascus road was so clear that he could quote it verbatim; it was in his native language. Paul received a revelation from God Himself. Later on, if someone had asked Paul, "Why did you become a missionary to the Gentiles?" Paul might well have answered, "Because God told me to."

GOD SPEAKS TODAY

Because power ministries are increasing so rapidly today, it is becoming more common to hear Christian leaders justify decisions or actions by saying, "God told me to." The obvious potential of abusing this *modus operandi* is so great that many are questioning whether it has any place at all as a part of respectable Christian behavior. Some refer to it as "extra-biblical revelation" and argue that all of God's revelation is contained in the canon of Scripture and that God does not engage in "present-day revelatory activity." This is why, according to this point of view, Paul and others living before the biblical canon was closed needed to hear directly from God more than we do today.

Recognizing that claiming to hear from God can be, and at times is, abused, we should nevertheless agree that it has substantial biblical precedence in both the Old Testament and the New Testament. Pastor Jack Hayford has described it vividly: "As I say, 'God spoke to me,' I am being even more specific than referring to general revelation or to private inner impressions. I reserve these words intentionally for the rare, special occasions when, in my spirit, I have had the Lord speak directly to me. I do not mean, 'I felt impressed' or 'I sensed somehow.' Instead, I mean that at a given moment, almost always when I least expected it, the Lord spoke *words* to me. Those words have been so distinct that I am virtually able to say, 'And I quote.' "[10]

Jack Hayford has gained such wide respect in Christian circles that few would see him as irresponsible or abusive in the use of the phrase "God told me to." At no time would Hayford, or any other responsible Christian, equate the words they hear from the Lord with Scripture. The incident in Acts 9, where Paul heard God's voice, was later inscripturated by Luke, but this carries no implication that God has limited His direct communication to people or events recorded in the Bible. The Bible simply gives us examples of how God's nature is displayed through His actions.

DISTINGUISHING TRUE FROM FALSE

How can we tell whether a person's affirmation that he or she has heard God's voice is correct or incorrect? It is good to keep in mind that the church functions as the Body of Christ and that each individual member is a part of the whole. When the Body of Christ is functioning well and when the fruit of the Spirit is as normative as it should be, people who believe they have heard God's voice will seek confirmation from others before they make it public.

Churches and Christian groups would do well to use the following three-stage filtering process in arriving at a consensus:

1. Was it a true word? Did the person hearing from God confuse a personal inner thought with the voice of God? Was more emotion than revelation involved? Each one should be humble enough to admit that these are always possibilities.

2. Was the interpretation accurate? Even if the words were correctly heard, care needs to be taken in extracting the meaning,

especially when the word is in poetic or parabolic form or if it comes as a dream.

3. How is it to be applied? Should all, or any, of what God has said be communicated to others? If so, to whom? What is God's timing for the application?

A consensus on such questions will help the Body of Christ receive the most benefit from divine communication.

PAUL CONTINUES TO DAMASCUS

[9:6] *So he, trembling and astonished, said, "Lord, what do You want me to do?" Then the Lord said to him, "Arise and go into the city, and you will be told what you must do."* [8] *Then Saul arose from the ground, and when his eyes were opened he saw no one. But they led him by the hand and brought him into Damascus.* [9] *And he was three days without sight, and neither ate nor drank.*

[22:10] *So I said, "What shall I do, Lord?" And the Lord said to me, "Arise and go into Damascus, and there you will be told all things which are appointed for you to do."* [11] *And since I could not see for the glory of that light, being led by the hand of those who were with me, I came into Damascus.*

The tangle of thoughts and feelings running through Paul at this point in time must have been enormously confusing. Who knows if his mind didn't flash back to Stephen's death and the martyr's gracious words, "Lord, do not charge them with this sin" (7:60)? The Jesus whom Paul hated was now supernaturally drawing Paul into a loving, personal relationship. It would take Paul a while to sort all of this out.

Simon Kistemaker says it as well as any: "What a reversal of events! Paul, who desired to dash the believers to the ground, is lying face down on the ground. He, who wished to bring prisoners bound from Damascus to Jerusalem, now is led as a prisoner of blindness into Damascus. . . . He, who came to triumph over the Christian faith, now submits to the Captain of this faith."[11]

Paul's three-day blindness, which he attributes to the effects of the brilliant light he saw, would forever seal in his mind the stark contrast between light and darkness, a common theme in his later Epistles. His companions must not have seen the light so intensely, just as they did not hear the words as clearly, because they were not blinded. The significance of this blindness for Paul's conversion is pinpointed by Richard Rackham: "[Paul] is crucified with Christ, and the three days of darkness are like the three days in the tomb."[12] Paul would later write, "I have been crucified with Christ; it is no longer I who live, but Christ lives in me" (Gal. 2:20).

PAUL'S COMMITMENT TO THE BODY OF CHRIST

Church growth leaders insist that the most complete understanding of what evangelism really is involves a twofold commitment: (1) commitment to Jesus Christ as Lord and Savior, and (2) commitment to the Body of Christ. Definitions of evangelism that see it as preaching only, or as simply registering decisions for salvation through Christ, are inadequate. Both preaching and decisions for Christ are essential, of course, but the process is not concluded until unbelievers become disciples of Jesus Christ and responsible members of His Church.

Paul's conversion was twofold. He committed himself to Jesus on the Damascus road, immediately referring to Jesus as "Lord." He committed himself to the Body of Christ in the city of Damascus, and to the representative of the Church whom God had selected, whose name was Ananias.

Who was Ananias? He was not the husband of Sapphira—the couple whose conspiracy of greed resulted in their premature death (see Acts 5:1-11)—but another man having the same name. He is one of the more notable figures in the New Testament, yet we know nothing else about him other than his participation in Paul's conversion experience. He was significant in Paul's life, yet Paul never mentions him in his later Epistles. We know that he was a believer in Christ (see 9:10) and that he was a devout Jew, highly respected by his fellow Jews (see 22:12).

At that time, most believers (the exceptions would be the messianic Samaritans) did not regard themselves, and were not regarded by the general public, as anything other than Jews or perhaps messianic Jews. It is notable that God would not choose an apostle or high-profile church leader, but someone we would probably regard today as a workplace leader to baptize and provide foundational spiritual instruction to the future Christian apostle who would be second only to Jesus Christ.

> [9:10] *Now there was a certain disciple at Damascus named Ananias; and to him the Lord said in a vision, "Ananias." And he said, "Here I am, Lord."* [11] *So the Lord said to him, "Arise and go to the street called Straight, and inquire at the house of Judas for one called Saul of Tarsus, for behold he is praying.* [12] *And in a vision he has seen a man named Ananias coming in and putting his hand on him, so that he might receive his sight."* [13] *Then Ananias answered, "Lord, I have heard from many about this man, how much harm he has done to Your saints in Jerusalem.* [14] *And here he has authority from the chief priests to bind all who call on Your name."* [15] *But the Lord said to him, "Go . . ."* [17] *And Ananias went his way and entered the house; and laying his hands on him he said, "Brother Saul, the Lord Jesus, who appeared to you on the road as you came, has sent me that you may receive your sight and be filled with the Holy Spirit."* [18] *Immediately there fell from his eyes something like scales, and he received his sight at once; and he arose and was baptized.*

> [22:12] *Then a certain Ananias, a devout man according to the law, having a good testimony with all the Jews who dwelt there,* [13] *came to me; and he stood and said to me, "Brother Saul, receive your sight." And at that same hour I looked up at him.* [14] *Then he said . . .* [16] *"And now why are you waiting? Arise and be baptized, and wash away your sins, calling on the name of the Lord."*

ANANIAS'S REMARKABLE VISION

We cannot say for sure, but it appears that, until this vision, Ananias was unaware that Saul the Terrible, as he must have been regarded by the disciples who followed the Way, had actually arrived in Damascus. However, Ananias did know Saul's reputation and that he was bringing subpoenas from the high priests in Jerusalem. Here is the second time in three days that Jesus actually appeared to a person and spoke words so clearly that they could later be quoted.

The detail in this prophetic vision is remarkable. God told Ananias specifically who the person was to whom he should minister (Saul of Tarsus), exactly where he was located (Judas's house on Straight Street), what he was doing at the moment (praying), his new condition (God's chosen vessel), and what Ananias was supposed to do (lay on hands and heal the blindness). He also told Ananias that Saul would be expecting him because Saul had experienced a similar specific vision of "a man named Ananias coming in and putting his hand on him" (9:12).

HEAVY ON KNOWLEDGE BUT LIGHT ON POWER

In the earlier years of my Christian experience, and later as an ordained minister and missionary, I had no expectation whatsoever that God would desire to communicate important information to His people in this way. I did not doubt in the least that He had done it to Ananias, but the Christianity I had been taught, and was practicing, was heavy on knowledge and light on supernatural power. When I would hear of such things purportedly happening, I would usually relegate those who claimed to be experiencing them to the lunatic fringe and pay no more attention to them.

In recent years, however, as I have dedicated myself to researching the spiritual aspects of church growth and missiology, I have discovered that such specific prophecies are not at all uncommon today. My files contain documentation on many of them.

For example, I recall a young man who came to one of my classes at Fuller Seminary some years ago. I asked him why he chose Fuller. He said that he had been studying in another nationally known seminary. But he, and his faith, seemed to be drying up. He began doubting whether he had really been called to the ministry and was considering leaving seminary and moving into another career. However, in prayer, he heard the voice of God telling him specifically to go to Fuller. The unusual thing about this was that at the time he knew nothing about Fuller. He didn't even know that a seminary by that name existed. The word was so specific, however, that he began inquiring and eventually learned that Fuller was indeed a seminary, far across the country on the West Coast. He obeyed the Lord, took the risk, came to Fuller and blossomed into a fruitful pastor and servant of God.

My friend could accurately have said, "I came to Fuller because God told me to." In a similar but more dramatic situation in the late 1980s, my friend John Wimber received a telephone call from a man highly regarded for his gift of prophecy. He informed John that he was going to visit California soon because God had told him to. Furthermore, so that John would know that it was truly God who was sending him, an earthquake would strike under Fuller Seminary the day he arrived. The prophet came, and on that very day a powerful earthquake shook Pasadena. Its epicenter was not exactly under Fuller Seminary, but rather it was under city hall, one block away. Close enough! I spent the next three days picking up books and putting them back on my shelves.

As I have said, accounts of such incidents are multiple. I mention them here simply to keep reminding us that I consider the book of Acts to be a training manual for modern Christians. Rather than some relic of the past, I see Acts as a contemporary guidebook for how the Christian faith most naturally spreads across cultures and around the world. Rather than reading Acts as a fascinating account of yesteryear, I like to read it with the expectation that God will continue to do the sort of things we read there, as His kingdom advances in our own day.

I have heard some say that although it might be possible that God speaks specifically to people today as He did in Acts, such a revelation should be limited to the individual person. They argue that it is excessively arrogant to expect God to say something through a person that might be directional for the whole Church. Paul's experience, however, was much broader than his simply becoming a believer and receiving his sight after three days. It profoundly set the course for Christianity as a whole through the centuries. Let's look at this part of God's word to Paul.

PAUL'S COMMISSION TO THE NATIONS

I've already mentioned that Paul could have said he became a missionary because "God told me to." This word came to him not only directly from God (see Acts 22:15-18), but also through a prophecy given by a layperson, Ananias (see 9:15-16; 22:14-15).

[9:15] . . . *he is a chosen vessel of Mine to bear My name before Gentiles, kings, and the children of Israel.* [16] *For I will show him how many things he must suffer for My name's sake.*

[22:14] . . . *The God of our fathers has chosen you that you should know His will, and see the Just One, and hear the voice of His mouth.* [15] *For you will be His witness to all men of what you have seen and heard.*

> [26:16] . . . *I have appeared to you for this purpose, to make you a minister and a witness both of the things which you have seen and of the things which I will reveal to you.* [17] *I will deliver you from the Jewish people, as well as from the Gentiles, to whom I now send you,* [18] *to open their eyes and to turn them from darkness to light, and from the power of Satan to God, that they may receive forgiveness of sins and an inheritance among those who are sanctified by faith in Me.*

When he stood before King Agrippa years later, Paul called this his "heavenly vision" (26:19) and he could assure the king that he had been obedient to it throughout his entire ministry.

It is unclear whether the words spoken by Jesus to Paul in Acts 22 were actually the direct words he heard on the road before arriving in Damascus, or whether, as he was repeating them to King Agrippa, Paul had simply telescoped them into a briefer summary. In this passage, Paul does not mention either Ananias or his three days of blindness. I see little value in laboring the point because the effect is the same either way. Words from Jesus spoken through legitimate personal prophetic utterances are no less valid than those spoken by Jesus Himself to the person, whether by a physical appearance, vision or dream.

It becomes highly important, however, that Paul's commission was given to him by Jesus, whether through Ananias or otherwise. Paul makes an issue of this when he later writes his letter to the Galatians. He introduces himself by saying, "Paul, an apostle (not from men nor through man, but through Jesus Christ and God the Father who raised Him from the dead)" (Gal. 1:1). Although Ananias spoke them, the words "he is a chosen vessel of Mine to bear My name before Gentiles, kings, and the children of Israel" (Acts 9:15) are commissioning words from Jesus to Paul. As F. F. Bruce says, Ananias was at this moment "[Christ's] mouthpiece," and "certainly a duly authorized prophet," and therefore, "it was Christ himself who commissioned Saul to be his ambassador."[13]

I myself can testify that receiving such commissioning words as these, directly from Jesus, brings powerful spiritual sustenance later on, especially when difficult times arise. Jesus told Paul "how many things he must suffer for My name's sake" (9:16). In 1989, at the massive Lausanne II Congress on World Evangelization in Manila, Philippines, God spoke to me in as clear, although less dramatic, a way as He spoke to Paul. He said, "I want you to take international leadership in the field of territorial spirits." At that time, issues surrounding territorial spirits, or what we now call "strategic-level spiritual warfare," were not common topics of conversation. The Congress itself, however, represented a breakthrough among its largely traditional evangelical constituency because no less than five workshops dealing with territorial spirits were offered there.

THE HEAVENLY VISION CAN BE COSTLY

This was a kind of heavenly vision to me. After that, I became international coordinator of the Spiritual Warfare Network (later Strategic Prayer Network and then Global Apostolic Prayer Network). For years I taught courses on strategic-level spiritual warfare at Fuller Seminary, and I have published seven books on the subject. Much of what I have learned is reflected in parts of this commentary on Acts. But at the same time, I have been severely criticized and I have suffered attacks of the enemy on myself and on my family.

At times, I read Paul's accounts of his own sufferings, his tribulations, imprisonments, stripes, times of sleeplessness, stonings, shipwrecks and many other difficulties in serving the Lord. Then I ask what it was that sustained him through all of those difficulties. Clearly it was his heavenly vision. He was sure that he was doing God's will because his commission had come directly from God. When I am down, personally, I also take heart because my assignment, at least for this particular phase of my ministry, came directly from God. Seen in this light, I have no question in my mind about obeying the heavenly vision regardless of the cost. I must do it.

THE APOSTLE TO THE UNCIRCUMCISED

The Lord's commission to Paul combines the two major themes of the Acts of the Apostles: missiology and power ministries. Jesus said, "I now send you, [to the Gentiles; e.g., missiology] . . . to turn them . . . from the power of Satan to God" (e.g., power ministries) (26:17-18).

For those of us who are committed to world evangelization, this is the most important part of Paul's conversion experience. Paul was a highly unlikely candidate to be a missionary to the Gentiles. I am not exactly surprised that some of the commentators I am reading tend to take the opposite view and say that Paul's upbringing in Tarsus, a Gentile city, uniquely prepared him to minister to Gentiles.

One commentator, as I recall, speculates that Paul might have been an alumnus of the "University of Tarsus," reflecting the common knowledge that Tarsus, along with Alexandria and Athens, was a recognized center of what we today would call higher education. Anticipating this, I made a special point at the beginning of this chapter to explain that Paul was, at his core, a *Hebrew* Jew as opposed to a *Hellenistic* Jew, that he was raised in a Jewish ghetto in Tarsus, and that at an early age his parents sent him to Jerusalem to be trained in rabbinic schools rather than in a Gentile-oriented educational system in Tarsus (see 22:3; 26:4).

In the true sense of the word then, Paul was called to be an E-3 missionary. As I have explained previously, E-3 (i.e., evangelism three) is a technical term used in missiology to describe a radical cross-cultural gap. E-1 is monocultural evangelism and E-2 is cross-cultural, but the cultural gap between the missionary's home culture and that of the people to be evangelized is more moderate than for the E-3 missionary. God did not hesitate to recruit Paul for the most difficult of all missionary work. And the nature of some of the difficulties became clear when the apostles in Jerusalem, who were, by and large, monoculturally oriented, had to come to terms with the nature of Paul's E-3 ministry, in the Jerusalem Council more than 15 years later. It was not easy for them to do so.

The Greek word for "Gentile" translated here is *ethnos,* which also means nations—not nations in the *geopolitical* sense, but nations in the *cultural* sense. Our English word "ethnic" derives from *ethnos* as well. In modern missiology, we refer to these nations as "people groups." Jews are included among the world's people groups today, but when Paul was commissioned, *ethnos* meant specifically non-Jewish people groups in general. It is the same word Jesus used when He commissioned His disciples to "Go . . . and make disciples of all the *nations*" (Matt. 28:19, emphasis added).

Paul was also to witness to his own Jewish people. Jesus said he was "to bear My name before Gentiles [*ethne*], kings, and the children of Israel" (Acts 9:15). But Paul's *primary* calling was as an apostle to the Gentiles, the uncircumcision. In contrast, Peter's chief task was to be an apostle to the Jews, the circumcision. Paul later clearly writes about this when he says, "[God] who worked effectively in Peter for the apostleship to the circumcised also worked effectively in me toward the Gentiles" (Gal. 2:8). As events continue to unfold, Peter did some work among Gentiles and Paul did some work among Jews, but essentially Paul was an E-3 missionary while Peter was an E-1 evangelist.

FROM THE POWER OF SATAN TO GOD

Jesus not only commissioned Paul to evangelize the nations, but He also outlined his job description. He told Paul that when he entered a given people group he would find them under an awesome power, the power of Satan. His job would be "to open their eyes and to turn them from darkness to light, and from the power of Satan to God" (Acts 26:18).

This was no small task. Satan is none other than "the god of this age" (2 Cor. 4:4) and "the prince of the power of the air" (Eph. 2:2). The nations to which Paul was to take the message were all under the power of Satan and they had been under his control for millennia. Satan fully intended to keep these nations under his dominion, and he was not willing to let any of them go without a fight. The fight would consist of what we call today "spiritual warfare." By the time Paul wrote Ephesians nearly 30 years after he began his ministry, he had learned a great deal about spiritual warfare, saying, "We do not wrestle against flesh and blood, but against principalities, against powers, against the rulers of the darkness of this age, against spiritual hosts of wickedness in the heavenly places" (Eph. 6:12).

Paul would also write, "For the weapons of our warfare are not carnal but mighty in God for pulling down strongholds" (2 Cor. 10:4). Biblical scholar Clinton Arnold examines all the weaponry mentioned in the writings of Paul and concludes, "If Paul were to summarize the primary way of gaining access to the power of God for waging successful spiritual warfare, he would unwaveringly affirm that it is through prayer."[14] Effective prayer is extremely important for breaking into unreached people groups.

Paul had no option regarding whether or not he would engage in spiritual warfare as a part of his apostolic ministry to the nations. For the most part he did it well. Athens, as we shall see, was an exception. And Paul paid the price with the afflictions and tribulations he later describes, but he is very clear on who ultimately wins this war. As he says to the Colossians, Jesus on the cross "disarmed principalities and powers, He made a public spectacle of them" (Col. 2:15).

As a result, many people, indeed, were taken from the power of Satan to God under the ministry of Paul, and multitudes have come from darkness to light through the spread of the gospel in subsequent centuries.

PAUL IN DAMASCUS

Several other things happened to Paul in this memorable visit to Damascus.

> [9:17] *And Ananias went his way and entered the house; and laying his hands on him he said, "Brother Saul, the Lord Jesus, who appeared to you on the road as you came, has sent me that you may receive your sight and be filled with the Holy Spirit."* [18] *Immediately there fell from his eyes something like scales, and he received his sight at once; and he arose and was baptized.* [19] *So when he had received food, he was strengthened. . . .*

Paul was not only healed spiritually, but he also experienced physical healing, ending three days of blindness. This came with the laying on of Ananias's hands. Laying on of hands is not a requirement for physical healing, but God often chooses to release His power through such a healing touch. Jesus said that as one of the signs that would follow His disciples "they will lay hands on the sick, and they will recover" (Mark 16:18).

Paul was well prepared to receive Ananias's power ministry. He had been fasting for three days, and he was engaged in a time of prayer when Ananias arrived. Fasting, like the laying on of hands, is not a prerequisite for receiving the power of God, but fasting is a significant spiritual exercise that God highly honors.

In Paul's case, the healing was a bit more dramatic than it frequently is. As a physician, Luke would naturally be interested in recording what physiological changes might have taken place, and he tells us that something like scales fell from Paul's eyes. This brings to mind an occasion in Argentina when the late Omar Cabrera prayed for a woman who had cataracts, and the physical cataracts literally fell from her eyes into her hands.

Without delay, Paul makes his profession of faith and his commitment to the Body of Christ public through baptism. Although the details are not recorded here, we may safely assume that Ananias did the baptizing. We can also assume that Paul was filled with the Holy Spirit because Ananias said he had been sent to him "that you may receive your sight and be filled with the

Holy Spirit" (9:17). We have no further details, however, regarding how or when this happened or if any initial physical evidence was connected with the event.

THE LIFE OF A NEW BELIEVER

[19] . . . Then Saul spent some days with the disciples at Damascus. [20] Immediately he preached the Christ in the synagogues, that He is the Son of God. [21] Then all who heard were amazed, and said, "Is this not he who destroyed those who called on this name in Jerusalem, and has come here for that purpose, so that he might bring them bound to the chief priests?" [22] But Saul increased all the more in strength, and confounded the Jews who dwelt in Damascus, proving that this Jesus is the Christ.

Paul spent time "with the disciples." Imagine the joy of the believers when Saul the Terrible, instead of persecuting them, was baptized and decided to become one of them! Although Damascus was a Hellenized city, it also had a sizable resident Jewish community. It seems probable that before the Hellenistic Jewish believers had been ousted from Jerusalem following Stephen's death, some of the Damascus Jews had formed their own messianic community and were worshiping Jesus. They still would have attended the synagogues because they continued to be Jews. Actually, the only ones who would have had reason to fear Saul's persecution would have been the recent arrivals from Jerusalem. Nevertheless, the whole Body of Christ probably prayed fervently for protection, and together they rejoiced when their prayers were answered to a degree much greater than they might have had faith to believe.

The reason the believers accepted their former enemy so readily was undoubtedly due to the bridges built by Ananias. Not only did they respect Ananias as a person, but the powerful and detailed prophecies he had received also produced a great deal of confidence in the group that what was happening was clearly of God.

Paul also spent time "in the synagogues" (9:20) with the unbelieving Jews. Although the number is not known exactly, 40 to 50 Jewish synagogues could have been established in Damascus at that time. (In Jewish practice, only 10 adult males were needed to establish a new synagogue.) Imagine the surprise of the Jews when the most notorious enemy of the Way came into their synagogues preaching that Jesus is indeed the way, the truth and the life! "All who heard were amazed" (9:21). They were caught off guard. Paul was "proving that this Jesus is the Christ" (9:22). The Greek word here denotes logical proofs, and Paul was probably applying some messianic passages from the Jewish Old Testament.

How is it that this new believer so rapidly "increased all the more in strength, and confounded the Jews" (9:22)? Certainly Paul was above average in intellect. As an opponent of messianic Judaism, he had previously thought through the central issues, although now he began taking the opposite side. But much more than that, he later reveals that "the gospel which was preached by me is not according to man. For I neither received it from man, nor was I taught it, but it came through the revelation of Jesus Christ" (Gal. 1:11-12). Jesus Christ was Paul's mentor, and Paul had established such an intimacy with God that the kind of dialogue recorded on the Damascus road undoubtedly continued on a regular basis. Just the fact that Paul was winning debates with Jewish rabbis shortly after his conversion testifies to the extraordinary supernatural power accompanying his divine crash course.

A SPIRITUAL RETREAT IN ARABIA

How long did it actually take Paul to learn the theology he used to confound the rabbis? Luke does not make this clear for us. We read about "some days" in Acts 9:19 and "after many days were past" in 9:23. But later, when Paul tells his own story in the book of Galatians, he says that from the time of his conversion to the time Luke tells us he goes to Jerusalem in Acts 9:26, three years had passed (see Gal. 1:18). Some of these three years were spent in Damascus and some in Arabia. In Galatians Paul says, "I went to Arabia, and returned again to Damascus" (1:17).

The fact that Paul left Damascus to escape a plot to kill him indicates that he probably didn't go back right away. So the most likely sequence seems to be that fairly soon after his conversion, he spent time in Arabia, a desert area east of Damascus, then he went back for the ministry in the Damascus synagogues where the rabbis were amazed.

What was Paul doing in Arabia?

Because we have no specific details, the best we can do is speculate from other bits and pieces of information we do have. I would imagine that a good bit of his time in Arabia was spent working out the implications of the radical paradigm shift Paul had just experienced. Jesus, the Son of God, had now become the center of Paul's readjusted worldview. Because his center had changed, all of his thinking was up for revision.

As I have mentioned, Paul was receiving revelation directly from Jesus Christ, not from human teachers. Much of this has come down to us in the large section of the New Testament that Paul later wrote. Today, new converts also can expect to hear from Jesus, but He speaks to us primarily (not exclusively) through the written Word, which Paul did not have. Undoubtedly, Paul was working out the proofs that Jesus was the Messiah, proofs we read about in Acts 9:22.

PREACHING TO THE ARABS?

Only a few of the commentaries I have seen surmise that Paul was also preaching to the Arabs. For example, F. F. Bruce says, "It certainly appears from a piece of evidence elsewhere in his correspondence that it was not simply a quiet retreat that Paul sought in Arabia."[15] Something Bruce does not mention is in Galatians 1, where Paul talks about his three years in Arabia and Damascus; Paul speaks of God's call to "preach Him [Christ] among the Gentiles" (Gal. 1:16).

More important, however, is what Paul later writes to the Corinthians: "In Damascus the governor, under Aretas the king, was guarding the city of the Damascenes with a garrison, desiring to apprehend me; but I was let down in a basket through a window in the wall, and escaped from his hands" (2 Cor. 11:32-33).

Aretas was, at that time, the king of Arabia (more technically, the Nabataean kingdom). This extended almost up to the very walls of Damascus, and the Arab soldiers were apparently waiting by the city gates to capture Paul if he should come out of the city.

But meanwhile opposition rose up on a second front *within* the city:

[23] *Now after many days were past, the Jews plotted to kill him.*
[24] *But their plot became known to Saul. And they watched the gates day and night, to kill him.* [25] *Then the disciples took him by night and let him down through the wall in a large basket.*

It is obvious enough from what we have already seen why the Jews in Damascus would be going after Paul. The rabbis were extremely unhappy with Paul's convincing arguments that Jesus was the true Messiah, as many rabbis also are today.

But why would the Arabs outside Damascus also be upset?

This is the evidence we have that points to the possibility that Paul had spent some of his time in Arabia actively evangelizing. F. F. Bruce suggests, "The hostile interest which the Nabataean authorities took in him implies that he had done something to annoy them—something more than to withdraw to the desert for solitary contemplation."[16] He was, undoubtedly, also preaching the gospel.

So in all probability, during his time in Arabia, Paul was not only receiving his theology by revelation from Jesus Christ, but he was also beginning to apply what he was learning by witnessing to the Gentiles, as he had been commissioned to do on the Damascus road. We have no idea whether or not conversions occurred in Arabia, but we do know that, not surprisingly, Paul stirred up so much opposition that the government had to step in.

Apparently, this was the beginning of Paul's cross-cultural ministry. Instead of assuming that Paul's later ministry in Antioch was his first E-3 missionary experience, we have good reason to believe it could have begun in Arabia.

BACK TO JERUSALEM

After his ignominious escape in a basket lowered at night over the city wall of Damascus, Paul decided to go back to Jerusalem.

> [26] *And when Saul had come to Jerusalem, he tried to join the disciples; but they were all afraid of him, and did not believe that he was a disciple.* [27] *But Barnabas took him and brought him to the apostles. And he declared to them how he had seen the Lord on the road, and that He had spoken to him, and how he had preached boldly at Damascus in the name of Jesus.* [28] *So he was with them in Jerusalem, coming in and going out.*

After three years, Paul was still between a rock and a hard place. The Jews considered him a traitor and an apostate—worse than Stephen—and some of them were trying to help him join Stephen as a martyr. On the other hand, the messianic believers in Jerusalem couldn't trust him either. He had been the disciples' public enemy number one.

Just as Ananias built the bridge between Paul and the disciples in Damascus, Barnabas, a respected pillar of the church in Jerusalem, builds the bridge here. Barnabas was living up to his name "Son of Encouragement," which we read in Acts 4:36. Barnabas trusted Paul's credibility and took him to the apostles.

At first it might sound as though all 12 of the apostles were in Jerusalem, but this was not the case. Most of the apostles were by then out on the road, multiplying churches and training leadership for them. When Paul later writes about this visit, he says, "I went up to Jerusalem to see Peter, and remained with him fifteen days. But I saw none of the other apostles except James, the Lord's brother" (Gal. 1:18-19).

James was by then recognized as an apostle, but he was not one of the two named "James" belonging to the original 12. Among the original 12 were (1) James the son of Zebedee, also the brother of John, and (2) James the son of Alphaeus. The James whom Paul met was neither of them, but rather James the son of Joseph and Mary. He was, therefore, Jesus' natural brother. This is the one who later wrote the book of James. He became Peter's successor as the leader of the Jerusalem church and later played a prominent role in the Council of Jerusalem, which takes place about 15 years from this point, in A.D. 49.

When Paul wasn't talking with Peter and James, he was out preaching, especially to the Hellenists, the Greek-speaking Jews. They are the same ones who had Paul hold their coats while they were murdering Stephen, and then they later tried to kill Paul as well.

[29] ***And he spoke boldly in the name of the Lord Jesus and disputed against the Hellenists, but they attempted to kill him.*** [30] ***When the brethren found out, they brought him down to Caesarea and sent him out to Tarsus.***

The believers decided to send Paul away primarily because they wanted to save his life, but it is probable they also thought he was stirring up too much trouble. Like many new Christians, Paul's enthusiasm may have been outweighing his wisdom at the time.

But more important were Jesus' own words to Paul, which Paul relates in Acts 22:

[17] *Now it happened, when I returned to Jerusalem and was praying in the temple, that I was in a trance* [18] *and saw Him saying to me, "Make haste and get out of Jerusalem quickly, for they will not receive your testimony concerning Me."* [19] *So I said, "Lord, they know that in every synagogue I imprisoned and beat those who believe on You.* [20] *And when the blood of Your martyr Stephen was shed, I also was standing by consenting to his death, and guarding the clothes of those who were killing him."* [21] *Then He said to me, "Depart, for I will send you far from here to the Gentiles."*

Paul recognized that the gospel was "for the Jew first" (Rom. 1:16), but he never did particularly well in evangelizing Jews. He was called as an apostle to the uncircumcision, and this word of Jesus in the Temple was a further confirmation of that call.

In missiological theory we talk of the "harvest force" and the "harvest field." A given field might be ripe enough, but if the wrong harvester goes in, little fruit will be reaped. At this point in time, unbelieving Hellenistic Jews were generally very receptive to the gospel, but Paul was not an anointed harvest force for them. His anointing was to the Gentiles, so off he went to his hometown of Tarsus.

At this point, Paul drops out of the New Testament narrative for 10 years. It could be that he was ministering to the Gentiles in Syria and Cilicia, the area around Tarsus, but we do not know for sure. He comes back into the picture when his friend Barnabas invites him to join the missionary team that was ministering to the new Gentile churches in Antioch in Acts 11.

THE CHURCHES WERE GROWING

Paul had stirred up so much trouble in Jerusalem that his departure made a big difference:

[9:31] *Then the churches throughout all Judea, Galilee, and Samaria had peace and were edified. And walking in the fear of the Lord and in the comfort of the Holy Spirit, they were multiplied.*

REFLECTION QUESTIONS

1. Paul's dramatic conversion was not the only time a life has been radically changed by Jesus. Name some others you have known or heard about who had similar conversions.
2. Review and discuss the differences between Stephen's theology of mission and that of Paul (or Saul) before his conversion. This remains a central issue in our understanding of the book of Acts.
3. The possibility of God speaking directly to us one on one is rejected by some as "extrabiblical revelation." What are your thoughts on this phenomenon?
4. Try to describe in your own words what is meant by referring to Paul as an E-3 missionary. Why wasn't he an E-1 or E-2?
5. It seems that the Jerusalem church was better off not having Paul there than having him there on this early visit. Why would that be?

10

PETER BLAZES THE TRAIL TO THE GENTILES

ACTS 9, 10 AND 11

The message of the Way was spreading rapidly through Jerusalem, Judea, Samaria and nearby lands. Whereas Luke reported that "the word of God spread, and the number of disciples multiplied greatly" (Acts 6:7), now "the *churches* throughout all Judea, Galilee, and Samaria . . . were multiplied" (9:31, emphasis added). From the multiplication of *disciples* (Acts 6) we now move to the multiplication of *churches* (Acts 9). This is exponential increase.

THE MOST EFFECTIVE EVANGELISM

Nothing is more important in developing a strategy for evangelizing a given geographical area than multiplying new churches. I continue to affirm what I have said and written on many occasions: "The single most effective evangelistic methodology under heaven is planting new churches."[1] This axiom not only applies to areas where Christian churches have not previously existed, but it also applies to areas, like France for example, where Christianity may have been present for centuries.

In the same way the gospel spreads throughout the book of Acts, in our day it also spreads through multiplying churches. No other way is possible. The definition of exactly what a true church is will vary among theologians and Christian leaders. I believe that a church exists wherever a group of believers meets together on a regular basis to celebrate their mutual faith in Jesus Christ as Savior and Lord, where they lift their voices together in worship and praise to God Almighty, where they are committed to each other in ministry and loving care, and where they agree to obey God to the best of their abilities. A church can take many forms—from a group meeting under a tree in Indonesia, to a weekly meeting of Christian university students in a dorm, to believers congregating in a hotel conference room in Argentina, to worshipers gathering in a cathedral in England, to disciples huddled in a house in China with the doors closed, or to the customary local church in your neighborhood.

Evangelism is most effective when it demands the kind of dual commitment Paul made in Acts 9: a commitment to Jesus Christ as Lord, and a commitment to the Body of Christ. When seen in this light, evangelism intrinsically requires multiplying churches.

Sometimes the church planting is monocultural. In practice, the vast majority of church plants anywhere in the world are monocultural. From the viewpoint of worldwide evangelistic strategy, however, the most significant church planting is done by those called of God to break across cultural boundaries and to establish the first vital outposts of Christianity in a previously unreached people group. When this is done well, monocultural (E-1) church planting then takes over for the long haul, but it cannot begin without initial cross-cultural (E-2 or E-3) church planting.

WHY PETER?

People could readily imagine Paul, after growing up in a Greek city, being "soft on Gentiles." But God wanted to use a completed Hebrew Jew like Peter to recognize the radical possibility of Gentiles truly being born again and accepted by God as equals in the Kingdom. As a consequence, Peter, not Paul, was the person called by God to blaze the trail for church planting among the Gentiles. I say "blaze the trail" because that's about all he did. Peter has gone down in history primarily as an apostle to the circumcision, to his own people group—the Jews. Paul is the one who later becomes the most prominent church planter among Gentiles. But God had specific and significant reasons for selecting Peter to minister in the house of the Gentile Cornelius and to baptize him and his family. Peter, in this particular role, was to Paul what John the Baptist was to Jesus. He was preparing the way.

Peter at this time was regarded as the leader of the establishment apostles. Along with James and John, he was characterized as a "pillar of the church" (see Gal. 2:9). When the issue of Gentile conversion comes to a head later in Acts 15, it is Peter's theology, forged initially in the house of Cornelius, that sets the tone for the final decision. Because theology in general tends to emerge from ministry (and usually not vice versa), an essential part of God's plan for subsequent world evangelization was to compel Peter to engage in a relatively brief time of cross-cultural ministry.

I say "compel" because Peter likely would not have chosen to evangelize Gentiles. God, as we will see, resorted to some extraordinary manifestations of supernatural power in this case to persuade Peter to go into Cornelius's house. Why would Peter be reluctant? He simply did not have the missionary gift. Cross-cultural ministry was uncomfortable for him.

THE MISSIONARY GIFT

What is the missionary gift? In my book *Your Spiritual Gifts Can Help Your Church Grow*, I define the missionary gift as follows: "The gift of missionary is the special ability that God gives to certain members of the Body of Christ to minister whatever other spiritual gifts they have in a second culture."[2] To say that Peter did not have the missionary gift is far from considering him a second-class citizen—my best estimate is that something like only 1 percent of all Christians actually have the missionary gift.

However, it is regrettable that some confuse the missionary gift with the gift of apostle. At least one version of the Bible unwisely, in my opinion, translates the Greek *apostolos* (apostle) as "missionary." Peter was an example of one who had the gift of *apostle* but not the gift of *missionary*. Paul, on the other hand, had both the gift of *apostle* and the gift of *missionary*. This will become evident when later we look at some friction between the two, which Paul writes about in Galatians.

Although he did not have a missionary gift, Peter was nevertheless God's icebreaker not only with the Gentiles in Cornelius's house, but also, as we have previously seen, with the Samaritans, moving into Samaria as Philip was leading a great movement toward God. Before we get to Peter's ministry to the Gentiles, we will first look at some of his more usual monocultural ministry in Judea.

THE HARVEST IN LYDDA AND SHARON: ACTS 9

[32] *Now it came to pass, as Peter went through all parts of the country, that he also came down to the saints who dwelt at Lydda.* [33] *There he found a certain man named Aeneas, who had been bedridden eight years and was paralyzed.* [34] *And Peter said to him, "Aeneas, Jesus the Christ*

heals you. Arise and make your bed." Then he arose immediately.
[35] *So all who dwelt at Lydda and Sharon saw him and turned to the Lord.*

Peter spent some of his time in itinerant ministry, planting churches, encouraging believers and training leaders. It says here that he "went through all parts of the country." In all probability, all of the other 12 apostles were doing similar things. We recall that when Paul arrived in Jerusalem from Damascus, only one of them, Peter, happened to be there.

A church had already been planted in the city of Lydda, located in the plain of Sharon in western Judea. How the church was started we do not know for sure, but there is a possibility that Philip could have evangelized in Lydda after he baptized the Ethiopian eunuch and was caught away by the Holy Spirit. We are told that Philip then "preached in all the cities till he came to Caesarea" (8:40). Lydda happened to be in that region.

PARALYZED EIGHT YEARS AND HEALED

I would imagine that many dramatic things took place in Lydda through the ministry of the Holy Spirit, but undoubtedly the most notable was the miraculous healing of Aeneas who had been paralyzed for eight years. Aeneas might have been a believer when Peter first met him, but more likely he was an unbeliever—as was the lame man at the gate of the Temple who was also healed by Peter, accompanied by John in Acts 3.

Healing or Miracle?

The technical line between a healing and a miracle may be difficult to draw because of the wide areas of overlap. However, there does seem to be some distinction, because in the list of spiritual gifts in 1 Corinthians 12, both "gifts of healings" (v. 9) and "the working of miracles" (v. 10) appear as separate items. It would seem to me that a man who had been paralyzed for eight years and who instantly started to walk would fall more into the miracle category. In the healing ministry that I personally have done over the past few years, I have seen literally hundreds of people healed from chronic back pain, but I have yet to see a paralyzed person who has come to me in a wheelchair get out of the wheelchair and walk. I know that God does this through others today just as He did in Lydda, but He has not as yet done that through me. That is why I am willing to affirm that I have the spiritual gift of healing, but I do not think I have the gift of miracles.

One of the most remarkable things about the healing of Aeneas was that Peter did not pray for him, as far as we are told. He simply made a declaration: "Aeneas, Jesus the Christ heals you. Arise and make your bed" (9:34).

Healing stories that we read about in the New Testament often seem a good bit simpler than the healing ministries in some of our churches today. Whether the power of God was more immediate and easier to get in touch with in those days I do not know. True, when we conscientiously develop divine healing ministries over some years, it is not unusual from time to time to see miraculous healings equal to, or possibly surpassing, the drama accompanying the events we read about in the Gospels and Acts. Such things seem to be more common today in parts of the Global South rather than here in America.

Highlighting the Successes

Could a possible explanation be that the pattern of Matthew, Mark, Luke and John was to single out such exceptions and highlight them in their gospels? We do know that John carefully selected seven outstanding miracles around which to structure the whole Gospel of John. If this were the pattern of the biblical writers, it would be a considerable consolation to those of us who struggle from day to day and from week to week with what seems to be rather limited access to the power of God.

Because of this, the people I know who have a healing ministry rarely make the kind of declaration that Peter made in Lydda. I teach my students to take a more cautious approach and to be a bit more tentative in their conclusions about what might have happened. The exception to this comes on the rare occasions when we get a strong word from the Lord during prayer, that this time the healing will be instant and complete. Something like this must have happened to Peter because "[Aeneas] arose immediately" (9:34).

A "Lyddic" People Movement

The evangelistic results of Aeneas's dramatic healing were awesome. "All who dwelt at Lydda and Sharon saw him and turned to the Lord" (9:35). Although this admittedly may be a case where the biblical "all" should be taken figuratively instead of literally, at the very least a large segment of the population of the city of Lydda and the surrounding plain of Sharon became disciples of Jesus. The description is that of a classic people movement, so much so that missiologist Donald McGavran, one of the chief theoreticians of the field, labels one of his five types of people movements "Lyddic movements." In a Lyddic movement, McGavran says, "The entire community becomes Christian."[3]

Such a thing actually has happened on occasion in modern days, and one of our hopes is that the frequency will increase considerably as we move forward in world evangelization. In some nations, entire Muslim villages have declared themselves Christian overnight. In the Beoga Valley of Irian Jaya, the entire Uhunduni people group of 4,500 made a joint decision to become Christian and publicly burned their fetishes. A large commune in mainland China declared itself Christian and the commune became known as "Jesus Mountain." Whole Aymara townships in the Bolivian Andes have decided to turn to the gospel from one day to the next. Reports have recently begun to filter out of the Himalaya Mountains, telling of former "lama villages" that are now "Jesus villages." These are just a few of the contemporary examples.

Honoring Group Decisions

A people movement, McGavran says, is "a multi-individual, mutually-interdependent conversion."[4] This is important in missiology, because in most non-Western parts of the world all-important decisions are *group*, as opposed to *individual*, decisions. This may sound strange to us Westerners who have been taught to hold rugged individualism as a high cultural value. But our way of expecting each person to step out from the group and make a personal decision to follow Jesus Christ makes little sense to many peoples of our world today. To many peoples, it appears that if choosing to follow Christ is left up to each person, then accepting Christ must not be a very important decision because, in their minds, all of life's *important* decisions are made by the group, never by individual people violating their commitment to each other and stepping out on their own.

It would be reasonable to expect that something like this would have happened in Lydda. It is doubtful that Peter would have preached a sermon, invited inquirers to come forward and had a team of counselors to interview each person and pray with each one to receive Jesus as Savior and Lord. Rather, the leaders and opinion makers of Lydda would have carefully observed the public testimony of the small group of disciples that was already in their city, examined the evidence presented by Peter in both word and deed, and over a period of time come to a community consensus that Jesus was truly the Messiah they had been waiting for through the centuries.

Relationships Remain Intact

As is characteristic of all types of people movements, this decision would not have involved crossing unfamiliar racial, linguistic or cultural barriers. They were not asked to join up with Gentiles or Samaritans. Their established relationships with their families, their friends and their synagogues would have remained intact. It was a religious or spiritual decision they were willing to make on its own merits, which they did. "All . . . Lydda and Sharon saw him and turned to the Lord" (9:35).

The thing that triggered the people movement in Lydda was that they "saw him," referring to Aeneas who had been paralyzed for eight years and was now walking. This public display of the power of God was the "deed" part of Peter's ministry. Luke seems to highlight this frequently in Acts. He speaks of Jesus attested by "miracles, wonders, and signs" (Acts 2:22), of the apostles in Jerusalem doing "many wonders and signs" (2:43), of Stephen doing "great wonders and signs among the people" (6:8), of "the miracles which [Philip] did" (8:6), and of "signs and wonders to be done by [Paul and Barnabas's] hands" (14:3). In fact, in people movements today, such a form of power ministry is often (although not always) the catalyst that serves as the principal "sign" to point people to the Savior.

A vivid illustration comes out of mainland China, where a 70-year-old woman was the leader of a secret house church, the only person who knew where the Bibles were hidden or who could be trusted. When she suddenly died of a heart attack, her family was shocked and they prayed to God that she would come back to life. Carl Lawrence tells it this way: "After being dead two days, she came back to life. She scolded her family for calling her back. They reasoned with her. They at least needed to know the location of the Bibles! They said they would pray that in two days she could return to the Lord. It would take that much time to set the matters straight."[5] Sure enough, after two days of caring for family administrative affairs, she told her family she was seeing angels coming to her and she went once again to be with the Lord.

The result? The entire Chinese village, like Lydda, turned to the Lord.

Raising the Dead

Such a story as this one out of China raises questions in many minds. It may seem too farfetched to some. Does God *really* raise people from the dead? While he was still in Lydda, a call came to Peter that will allow us to examine this matter of the dead being raised in some detail.

> [36] *At Joppa there was a certain disciple named Tabitha, which is translated Dorcas. This woman was full of good works and charitable deeds which she did.* [37] *But it happened in those days that she became sick and died. When they had washed her, they laid her in an upper room.* [38] *And since Lydda was near Joppa, and the disciples heard that Peter was there, they sent two men to him, imploring him not to delay in coming to them.*

Peter received an urgent, unexpected call from Joppa, brought by two brothers from the church there. This was another church, in all probability, first planted by Philip (see 8:40). Joppa, a harbor on the Mediterranean Sea, was about a three-hour trip from Lydda. One of the highly respected women of the church, Dorcas, had suddenly died. She was respected because of her many good deeds done through her obvious spiritual gifts of mercy and service. Undoubtedly she was an affluent woman.

Word had come to the believers in Joppa that Peter was in nearby Lydda. They probably had received word of the wonderful healings and miracles going on there, Aeneas being one of the outstanding examples. Peter's gift of healing would have by then been well known among the messianic Jews in Joppa. It may have been that some of them, or their relatives, would have been among those who took the sick to Jerusalem where the power of God was so strong that even Peter's shadow was healing the sick (see 5:15-16).

Although we have no direct evidence to affirm that raising the dead had been taking place as a regular, ongoing part of the ministry of the apostles and others in those days, we have no reason to deny it either. It would seem likely that it was, considering that the first time Jesus sent out Peter and the other disciples to preach the message of the kingdom of God, He commanded them to "heal the sick, cleanse the lepers, *raise the dead*, cast out demons" (Matt. 10:8, emphasis added). If that were the case, then calling on Peter to minister to Dorcas might not seem to be a totally unreasonable request on the part of the church at Joppa.

Dorcas was really dead. Her expiration had been reported by Luke, a recognized physician. I point this out because as I have researched the phenomena connected with signs and wonders in the world today, I have found that some, who prefer not to believe that miracles of the magnitude of raising the dead could be occurring, argue their point by casting doubt on whether the subject was really dead at all. Muslims do this, for example. For a starter, they refuse to believe that Jesus was raised from the dead, so they explain the obvious historical facts by denying that He actually died on the cross.

One American professor refused to believe that the dead were being raised, as reported in the great Indonesia revival of 1965-1970, because after field research he concluded that the Indonesian concept of death was different from ours. I find this somewhat ludicrous, however, because Indonesians, just like Americans, bury only dead people who are really dead. In fact, day by day, the average Indonesian would have much more direct contact with death than the average American.

"Tabitha, Arise"

[39] ***Then Peter arose and went with them. When he had come, they brought him to the upper room. . . .*** [40] ***But Peter put them all out, and knelt down and prayed. And turning to the body he said, "Tabitha, arise." And she opened her eyes, and when she saw Peter she sat up.*** [41] ***Then he gave her his hand and lifted her up; and when he had called the saints and widows, he presented her alive.***

Just to ask Peter to walk for three hours in order to minister to Dorcas was in itself evidence that the believers in Joppa had an extraordinarily high level of faith. It would be reasonable to expect that much prayer and intercession had already been in progress there. They probably had high expectations that Dorcas would indeed be healed. Unlike some dramatic instances of power ministries, such as the healing of the lame man at the Temple gate (see Acts 3), this one was fully premeditated.

"They brought him to the upper room. . . . But Peter put them all out." Why? From what has just been said, I do not think they were put out of the room because of their supposed unbelief. Peter could have been trying to avoid embarrassment in case nothing happened, but I doubt that as well. A more likely possibility is that he was following the pattern he himself had observed when Jesus raised Jairus's daughter from the dead. On that occasion, Jesus permitted no one to follow Him except Peter, James and John and the parents of the girl (see Mark 5:37,40).

Although techniques should not be seen as a determining factor in divine healing or miracles, it is a fact that many who engage in power ministries tend to mirror the behavior of their mentors. If their mentors' hands tremble while praying for the sick, the disciples' hands may tremble also. Using oil, singing certain worship songs, praying in a distinct tone of voice, reciting liturgical prayers and many other behavioral patterns seem to be transmitted through a kind of spiritual impartation. Peter provides us an example of this by sending the mourners out of the room, as his mentor, Jesus, had done.

We are not told if Peter prayed when he healed Aeneas. But in this case, after the others had left, "Peter . . . knelt down and prayed" (Acts 9:40). What did he pray? I would think Peter would have been asking God to make clear to him what His will was in this particular case. The more difficult a power ministry assignment, the more necessary it is to be as sure as possible of God's will in each particular case. Raising the dead is obviously near the apex of difficulty, at least from a human perspective. On a few occasions, I have approached the Lord to seek His will about praying that the dead would be raised, but I have received a negative response each time. By the time Peter finished praying, however, he knew that this was God's will and God's time.

This is why Peter could take the direct approach, as he had done with Aeneas. He used a specific command: "Tabitha [Dorcas], arise." God apparently had already restored life to the dead body while Peter had been praying. How much of Peter's prayer had also included petition we do not know. But he might have said something like, "Father, I bring this dear saint of God before You and ask that You honor the prayers of the church and restore life to her." In any case, before he finished praying, Peter knew that God had said yes.

Dorcas sat up, and the church rejoiced to see her alive!

Evangelistic Results

Although healings and miracles have intrinsic value, such as relieving pain or allowing lame people to walk or blessing the congregation at Joppa with the renewed presence of Dorcas whom they loved so much, more important, they are "signs" of the kingdom of God. They are signs that point to Jesus Christ as the Lord of lords. God desires to use these signs to bring unbelievers to salvation.

God used this miracle in Joppa for that purpose:

[42] ***And it became known throughout all Joppa, and many believed on the Lord.***

The faith of the believers in Joppa at that moment must have been about as high as it can possibly go. Everyone in the city soon heard about Dorcas, and great power occurred in witnessing.

However, it is notable that although "all who dwelt at Lydda and Sharon . . . turned to the Lord" (9:35), in Joppa, all heard about it, but Luke merely says that "many believed on the Lord" (v. 42). The results were good, but not as good as they were in Lydda. Why?

The first part of the answer to this puzzle is that many factors influence the growth and nongrowth of churches besides the effects of miracles and power encounters. Any number of differences, of which we are totally unaware, could have explained why a virtual "clean sweep" occurred in Lydda, but something short of that apparently occurred in Joppa. Actually, the magnitude of the miracle was greater in Joppa, but not the total evangelistic outcome.

If the hypotheses we have been developing concerning strategic-level spiritual warfare have validity, they could provide a possible explanation. Although Luke doesn't furnish the specific details for us, it might well have been that related to the healing of Aeneas in Lydda, the territorial spirits or strongmen over the city had been bound and they, therefore, had loosed their grip on the unsaved people there. For some reason, a similar thing might not have happened in Joppa when Dorcas was raised from the dead. It could have been that the principality over Lydda was attached to Aeneas himself, just as the principality over western Cyprus was apparently dominating the sorcerer Bar-Jesus, or Elymas, according to the interpretation I will later suggest in Acts 13. If so, the phenomenon of a clean sweep in Lydda is more understandable.

WHAT DO WE LEARN FROM SEEING THE DEAD RAISED?

Here we have the first, but not the last, case of a dead person being raised in the book of Acts. Another case will come when Paul ministers in Lystra (see

Acts 14). In the biblical narrative, we first see Jesus, the Second Person of the Trinity, raising dead people, such as Jairus's daughter and Lazarus, and then being raised from the dead Himself. Now we're switching from the Gospels to Acts where a human being, Peter, also serves as God's instrument to raise the dead. What do we learn from this?

1. *Raising the dead is a Christian ministry.* It obviously may not be part of the normal ministry of an average church, but it is something that pleases God to do through His people from time to time. As I have mentioned, it was part of the commission Jesus gave His disciples when He first sent them out on their own. Among other things, He told the 12 to "raise the dead" (Matt. 10:8). I recall chatting with an evangelist in Nigeria who said he had seen the dead raised in his ministry. When I asked him how many, his surprisingly nonchalant answer was, "I can't remember!"

2. *Raising the dead represents only a partial victory over death.* For one thing, all those who were raised from the dead, with the exception of Jesus Himself, eventually died again. Second, death remains a tragic human phenomenon. No one lives forever physically.

3. *The ultimate cause of death is Satan.* Satan made it happen first in the Garden of Eden, and since then, all human beings must pay the price for the imputed sin of Adam and Eve. "The wages of sin is death" (Rom. 6:23). We all must die.

4. *Death is not God's original intention for humans, nor is death a feature of the full kingdom of God.* Death will one day be cast into the lake of fire (see Rev. 20:14). Paul calls death the "last enemy" (1 Cor. 15:26). In the New Jerusalem, "God will wipe away every tear from their eyes; there shall be no more death" (Rev. 21:4).

5. *In light of this, raising the dead is a sign of the kingdom of God.* When Jesus once listed the signs of the Kingdom to reassure John the Baptist that He was the true Messiah, He included the fact that "the dead are raised" (Luke 7:22). This, among many other things, proves that the kingdom of God is among us, although

not yet in its fullness. Every dead person raised is a direct insult to Satan. It is a foretaste of the final victory over the "last enemy." Death may still be with us, but it is on the way out. Meanwhile, the effects of physical death are nullified by eternal life for those who believe in Jesus Christ.

6. *The underlying purpose of raising the dead, I repeat, is to display a sign of the power of God so that people will be saved:* "And it became known throughout all Joppa, and many believed on the Lord" (Acts 9:42).

THE BREAKTHROUGH TO THE GENTILES: ACTS 10

The account of Peter going to the house of the Gentile Cornelius is the longest story told by Luke in the whole book of Acts. The three stories that take up the most space are:

- Peter and Cornelius (Acts 10–11)—77 verses
- Stephen's speech and death (Acts 6–7)—67 verses
- Paul's conversion (Acts 9, 22 and 26)—61 verses

What do all three stories have in common? They are all crucial incidents related to breaking cultural barriers in order for the gospel to move from Jews to non-Jews. This is another indication that Acts should be read and understood as essentially a missiological document if we are to receive its maximum value for our lives and our ministries. Let's once again refresh our memories about Luke's central theme in the book of Acts:

> But you shall receive power when the Holy Spirit has come upon you; and you shall be witnesses to Me in Jerusalem, and in all Judea and Samaria, and to the end of the earth (1:8).

God Speaks to Cornelius

The story begins with God speaking a word directly to Cornelius:

> **[10:1]** ***There was a certain man in Caesarea called Cornelius, a centurion of what was called the Italian Regiment,*** **[2]** ***a devout man and one who***

feared God with all his household, who gave alms generously to the people, and prayed to God always.

Caesarea was a Gentile city, 30 miles north of Joppa, where Peter had been ministering after raising Dorcas from the dead. Although Caesarea was predominantly Gentile, many Jews also resided there, and they attended several different synagogues.

As a centurion, Cornelius would have been a captain of the Roman army in charge of 100 soldiers. Each Roman legion comprised 3,000 to 6,000 men divided into 10 cohorts (300 to 600 each) and 60 centuries (100 each when at full strength).

It is significant that Cornelius was "one who feared God with all his household." At that time, by far the most receptive Gentiles to the gospel of Christ were these "God-fearers" such as Cornelius. As I mentioned a while back, the Ethiopian eunuch who was led to Christ by Philip in the Gaza Strip was not only the first Gentile convert of whom we have record, but was also in all probability another God-fearer.

Who Were the "God-Fearers"?

Some of the first-century Jews, unlike most Jews today, were aggressively evangelistic. Back then it was customary for Jews to send out proselytizing bands into Gentile regions to seek converts, called "proselytes." Recall that the Jewish theology of the day taught that the only way a human being could be reconciled to Jehovah God was by first becoming a Jew. Outside of Judaism, salvation was not possible in their minds.

Therefore, the evangelistic message was, "Find God—be a Jew!" And this message received considerable response. Proselytes were those who responded by going all the way; others, commonly called "God-fearers" or "devout persons," did not quite make all the steps. Society in many parts of the Roman Empire had become so corrupt, and life for many had become so hopeless, that numbers of Gentiles were looking for serious answers to their questions about the meaning of life. Some were strongly attracted to the monotheism and high moral and ethical standards of the Jewish faith. They were impressed by the lifestyle of the Jewish community and desired to become a part of it and to worship Jehovah.

For people to become a part of the Jewish faith, the process involved a threefold rite, according to F. F. Bruce:

1. "Circumcision (for male proselytes),
2. "A purificatory self-baptism in the presence of witnesses, and
3. "The offering of a sacrifice (while the Jerusalem temple stood)."[6]

These obviously were very demanding requirements, but some non-Jews were willing to accept them, and Jewish proselytes who once were Gentiles were to be found in many of the synagogues throughout the Roman Empire. It is important to understand that when Gentiles became proselytes, they were no longer Gentiles. They, their families and the Jews themselves considered them from that day on to be Jews and not Gentiles.

Understandably, many Gentiles would be attracted to the monotheism and the high ethical standards of the Jews, but they were not prepared to take the radical step of becoming proselytes and making a total break with their Gentile roots. Recognizing this, the Jews of the day had created a special place for such people in their synagogue communities as so-called "God-fearers." They enjoyed a recognized affiliation with the synagogue, worshiped the God of the Jews and agreed to adhere to the Jewish law to the best of their abilities, observing the Sabbath and the dietary laws as strictly as they thought they could.

When they went to synagogue meetings, however, the God-fearers had to congregate in a separate designated place. They could not enter the worship area of the synagogue itself because they were still *Gentiles*, and as such were regarded by Jews as unclean. We need to understand this thoroughly in order to give us the right backdrop for comprehending the magnitude of Peter's ministry to Cornelius, one of these God-fearers. John Stott says, "It is difficult for us to grasp the impassable gulf which yawned in those days between the Jews on the one hand and the Gentiles (including even the 'God-fearers') on the other. . . . No orthodox Jew would ever enter the home of a Gentile, even a God-fearer, or invite such into his home."[7]

For reasons that will become clearer as we move on, the God-fearers, more than any other category of Gentiles, were open to hearing the gospel and receiving Jesus as their Messiah. It could well be that the absence of any evangelistic fruit from Paul's ministry in Arabia, at least any that was worthy of mention by Luke, may have been due to the absence of God-fearers. Paul may have learned by trial and error that ordinary Gentiles (such as Arabs) at that time were not a particularly ripened harvest field, but he later discovered that the God-fearing Gentiles were definitely ready to hear about Jesus.

God Had Prepared Cornelius

Two special qualities seem to make Cornelius stand out from the average God-fearer. First, Cornelius "gave alms generously to the people" (10:2). He was practicing what Jesus called the second commandment, in loving his neighbor as himself. This did not save him, but it evidenced the advanced work of grace in his life and helped prepare him for an additional step of faith.

Second, Cornelius "prayed to God always" (10:2). Cornelius had come into a relationship with God to the extent that God knew and used his name, as we shall see. God chose to contact Cornelius in the "ninth hour," or 3:00 P.M., which was a normal Jewish hour of prayer.

An Angel Visits Caesarea

> [3] *About the ninth hour of the day he saw clearly in a vision an angel of God coming in and saying to him, "Cornelius!"* [4] *And when he observed him, he was afraid, and said, "What is it, lord?" So he said to him, "Your prayers and your alms have come up for a memorial before God."*

When Cornelius tells the story later, he adds:

> [30] *Four days ago I was fasting until this hour; and at the ninth hour I prayed in my house, and behold, a man stood before me in bright clothing,* [31] *and said, "Cornelius, your prayer has been heard, and your alms are remembered in the sight of God."*

As Luke describes it, the angel came in a vision, and when Cornelius tells it later, he does not mention a vision but speaks of the angel himself. Angels do appear in bodily form and they also appear in visions. The important thing for Cornelius was that somehow he saw a man in the room dressed in bright clothing and he recognized that man to be an angel.

If the angel came as an answer to prayer, what could Cornelius's prayer have been? Not only had he been praying that day, but he had been fasting as well. Realizing that what was about to happen came as a direct answer to Cornelius's prayer, his prayer would undoubtedly have been a cry of his heart to know God personally. Cornelius's affiliation with the synagogue would have allowed him to recognize God theologically as the Creator of heaven and Earth, but he now desired a personal relationship. In a word, he needed to be saved, to be released from an earnest but legalistic faith.

The angel's instructions were simple:

[5] *Now send men to Joppa, and send for Simon whose surname is Peter.*
[6] *He is lodging with Simon, a tanner, whose house is by the sea.*
He will tell you what you must do.

We later learn more of what the angel meant:

> [Peter] will tell you words by which you and all your household will be saved (Acts 11:14).

I find the detail of this remarkable. This story leaves little room to doubt that it is part of the very nature of God to communicate specifically to human beings. The angel knew Cornelius's name, Peter's two names, Peter's address and, of course, the content of Cornelius's petition. Such words from God bring forth an immediate desire to obey, which Cornelius did:

[7] *And when the angel who spoke to him had departed,*
Cornelius called two of his household servants and a devout soldier from
among those who waited on him continually. [8] *So when he had*
explained all these things to them, he sent them to Joppa.

Reflecting back to the last chapter, Cornelius could have honestly said that he sent the three people to Joppa "because God told me to."

Peter's Famous Vision: Animals in a Sheet

[9] *The next day, as they went on their journey and drew near the city,*
Peter went up on the housetop to pray, about the sixth hour.
[10] *Then he became very hungry and wanted to eat; but while*
they made ready, he fell into a trance.

As with Cornelius, God chose to communicate directly to Peter while he was setting aside a specific, probably a routine, time to pray. This time God spoke not through an angel, but directly by the Holy Spirit (see 10:19). Sometimes we resist establishing and following a rigid, predetermined daily schedule for prayer. We say that we want to avoid "legalism" or we don't want to "get into a rut." We should note, however, that at this particular hinge point in history, God chose to honor the routine prayer times of both Cornelius and Peter, speaking to them clear and directive words precisely then. Something about such seemingly routine habits of prayer apparently pleases God.

[11] *And [Peter] saw heaven opened and an object like a great sheet bound at the four corners, descending to him and let down to the earth.* [12] *In it were all kinds of four-footed animals of the earth, wild beasts, creeping things, and birds of the air.* [13] *And a voice came to him, "Rise, Peter; kill and eat."* [14] *But Peter said, "Not so, Lord! For I have never eaten anything common or unclean."* [15] *And a voice spoke to him again the second time, "What God has cleansed you must not call common."* [16] *This was done three times. And the object was taken up into heaven again.*

We need to be reminded that Peter was not a Christian. He did not even know the word "Christian" at this point in time. He was a Jew, albeit a messianic Jew. He was born again but he still behaved according to the rules that his mother and father had taught him. He faithfully kept the Jewish law. One thing Peter's mother had taught him was never to enter a Gentile house, and he probably had never previously violated this rule.

When Peter was with Jesus, he saw the Master minister to a Gentile Syro-Phoenician woman's daughter (see Mark 7:24-30) and a Roman centurion's servant (see Matt. 8:5-13). Neither of these events, however, changed the inbred behavior of Peter or of any of the other apostles for that matter. Peter had visited the great ingathering of Samaritans initiated by Philip, and he had approved of the legitimacy of "messianic Samaritans." That was indeed a significant milestone, but in doing this he had not violated any part of the Jewish law.

It is hard for us today to understand just how revolting to Peter, or to any Orthodox Jew of that day, would be the thought of entering a Gentile home, particularly risking contact with unclean food. Someone has said that a social situation that approaches it today might be the prejudice that high-caste Hindus have against low-caste Hindus or untouchables. For Peter even to consider such a thing would be for him an enormously difficult decision.

To make it worse, none of the other apostles to whom Peter was accountable were there with him. If Peter could have consulted with someone such as John or James and had at least one other agree with him, it would have been much safer. But deciding on his own would entail a great risk. If the others didn't agree when they later found out, irreparable damage could be done to the young church.

In light of this, God knew that ordinary communication processes would not be adequate to move Peter in the radical direction He wanted him to go. So God did an extraordinary thing and gave Peter the famous vision of the unclean food in the sheet. Peter's background had personally prepared him to receive visions. For one thing, it would fit his worldview. Unlike many today, Peter believed that one of God's normal ways of communicating from time to time was through visions and dreams. He was praying at the time, so his heart was open to God. He may have been fasting, too. Luke doesn't say he was, but we read that Peter "became very hungry" (Acts 10:10). Prayer along with fasting removes obstacles to hearing the voice of God.

Why would God choose Peter for this task and not Paul? Paul was the one who would be the career E-3 missionary to the Gentiles, not Peter, who later goes down in history as the apostle to the circumcision. The answer, I think, is straightforward: To establish unequivocally the bedrock theological principle that the gospel was for the Gentiles as well as for the Jews, no less than one of the original 12 apostles needed to receive the revelation from God and the accompanying personal experience. God was preparing Peter, not to be a career missionary to the Gentiles, but rather, to give the right word at the right time in the Council of Jerusalem many years later. Furthermore, of all the 12 apostles, Peter was probably the greatest risk taker.

Unclean Food

Leviticus 11 lists "the animals which you may eat" (Lev. 11:2) and those "you shall not eat" (Lev. 11:4). Every Jew had been trained in this list from infancy. The language of the law is strong. For example, it says, "You shall not make yourselves abominable with any creeping thing that creeps; nor shall you make yourselves unclean with them, lest you be defiled by them" (Lev. 11:43). No Jew went around fighting the temptation to eat a ham sandwich or rabbit stew or steamed clams—the very thought of eating such things was nauseating. As a part of my missionary lifestyle, I eat just about anything. But I must admit, I think I would have a hard time among the Masai in Kenya if they offered me one of their delicacies: milk mixed with cow's blood. The Jews probably thought the same about eating a filthy pig.

The Jews weren't allowed even to *touch* unclean food. They could drink milk, but not if it had been milked from the cow by a Gentile. They couldn't eat sheep if the animal had not been slaughtered by a rabbi and certified as kosher food.

The sheet that God lowered in front of Peter was filled with all this unclean food and much more. When God said, "Rise, Peter; kill and eat" (Acts 10:13), these must have been the most shocking words Peter had heard since Jesus told him years ago that He would die and Peter would betray Him. Peter's knee-jerk reaction this time was the same as then: "Not so, Lord!" (10:14). Just to make sure no miscommunication had occurred, God then added, "What God has cleansed you must not call common" (10:15) and repeated the vision twice more.

Understandably, Peter did not instantly comprehend the meaning and the implications of the vision he had seen.

Cornelius's Party Arrives

[17] . . . *the men who had been sent from Cornelius had made inquiry for Simon's house, and stood before the gate.* [18] *And they called and asked whether Simon, whose surname was Peter, was lodging there.*

Meanwhile, Peter was still alone, processing what he had seen and heard. Events were moving rapidly. Again, to minimize any possibility that Peter would respond incorrectly, the Holy Spirit spoke directly to Peter a second time:

[19] *While Peter thought about the vision, the Spirit said to him, "Behold, three men are seeking you.* [20] *Arise therefore, go down and go with them, doubting nothing; for I have sent them."*

God was moving Peter one step farther. Not only did He want to adjust Peter's aversion to unclean food, but now God also wanted Peter to realize that he was to associate with unclean *people*. The three at the gate were three Gentiles!

[21] Then Peter went down to the men who had been sent to him from Cornelius, and said, "Yes, I am he whom you seek. For what reason have you come?" [22] And they said, "Cornelius the centurion, a just man, one who fears God and has a good reputation among all the nation of the Jews, was divinely instructed by a holy angel to summon you to his house, and to hear words from you."

Because of the power of the vision Peter had received and the incredible divine synchronization of the timing of these interlocked events, Peter was thoroughly prepared to begin moving in the direction he now understood God was taking him. In light of this, the next phrase is highly significant: "Then he invited them in and lodged them" (v. 23).

No self-respecting Orthodox Jews would, on the spur of the moment, invite three uncircumcised Gentile strangers into their houses, particularly at mealtime. But Peter invited them for one reason: God had told him to. The Romans would have had no problem eating the kosher food served in Simon the tanner's house, but it was in all probability the first time they themselves had been invited into a Jewish house, and perhaps their first authentic kosher meal. They stayed overnight as well.

The problem would have been all on the Jewish side. In taking this risk, Peter was making the first small move into what would be a major turning point in the history of Christianity. The bigger risk was yet to come, for entertaining the Gentiles, as F. F. Bruce says, "did not expose him to such a risk of defilement as would a Jew's acceptance of hospitality in a Gentile's house."[8]

Peter Steps over the Line

[23] . . . *On the next day Peter went away with them, and some brethren from Joppa accompanied him.* [11:12] . . . *Moreover these six brethren accompanied me . . .*

Peter took a team of six other believers with him so that whatever happened would be attested by reliable witnesses. Furthermore, the others, particularly if intercessors were among them, would provide welcome onsite prayer support for the extraordinary ministry to which God had called Peter.

[10:24] *And the following day they entered Caesarea. Now Cornelius was waiting for them, and had called together his relatives and close friends.* [25] *As Peter was coming in, Cornelius met him and fell down at his feet and worshiped him.* [26] *But Peter lifted him up, saying, "Stand up; I myself am also a man."*

Cornelius displayed his theological ignorance by attempting to worship Peter. But at the same time, he displayed his openness to whatever Peter had for him, because by then he was sure it would come from God.

Undoubtedly, many people had gathered in Cornelius's home. While the others were listening, Peter and Cornelius debriefed each other on their divinely synchronized visions, and the ice was broken.

The 10 verses Luke provides here are probably only a brief summary of all that Peter said to the group gathered in Cornelius's home.

[34] *Then Peter opened his mouth and said: "In truth I perceive that God shows no partiality.* [35] *But in every nation whoever fears Him and works righteousness is accepted by Him.* [36] *The word which God sent to the children of Israel, preaching peace through Jesus Christ—He is Lord of all—*[37] *that word you know, which was proclaimed throughout all Judea, and began from Galilee after the baptism which John preached:* [38] *how God anointed Jesus of Nazareth with the Holy Spirit and with power, who went about doing good and healing all who were oppressed by the devil, for God was with Him.* [39] *And we are witnesses of all things which He did both in the land of the Jews and in Jerusalem, whom they killed by hanging on a tree.* [40] *Him God raised up on the third day, and showed Him openly,* [41] *not to all the people, but to witnesses chosen before by God, even to us who ate and drank with Him after He arose from the dead.* [42] *And He commanded us to preach to the people, and to testify that it is He who was ordained by God to be Judge of the living and the dead.* [43] *To Him all the prophets witness that, through His name, whoever believes in Him will receive remission of sins.*

Peter's introductory words say it all: "God shows no partiality." Cornelius and the rest of the people in his house were ready to believe that God was going to save them. Peter summarized the chief elements of the gospel in his message, but at one point he targeted it specifically to the Gentiles:

"whom they killed by hanging on a tree." This focuses on the action of nailing Jesus to the cross, which Roman soldiers such as those under Cornelius's command, had performed. When Peter preached to Jews, he did not stress the act of *nailing* Jesus to the cross, but rather the *accusations* against Jesus that ultimately led to crucifixion (see Acts 2:23). In short, we all, both Jews and Gentiles, share the blame for Jesus' death and, therefore, we need to repent.

This is a somewhat elementary but nevertheless real example of what missiologists call "contextualizing" the gospel. It doesn't change the gospel message, but it does change the way it is tailored to a variety of audiences who have a wide array of felt needs. We will see much more radical examples of this when we study the missionary experiences of the apostle Paul.

Pentecost—Phase III

In my comments on Acts 2, I suggested that we do well to regard Pentecost, or the coming of the Holy Spirit in power, as a three-phase event. Each phase marks a significant cross-cultural advance of the gospel. Phase I is in Acts 2 where the gospel crossed the barrier between Hebrew Jews and Hellenistic Jews. Phase II is in Acts 8 where the barrier was broken between Jews and Samaritans. And this is Phase III, where the gospel moves across the cultural chasm between Jews and Gentiles.

Note that Peter was involved personally in all three of these phases. In Matthew 16:19, Jesus tells Peter that as a spokesperson for the rest, He would give him the keys of the kingdom of heaven in order to build His Church. It could be that what we see here are three high-profile uses of those keys.

The ministry of the power of the Holy Spirit in Cornelius's house was awesome. Peter never had a chance to finish his message:

> [44] ***While Peter was still speaking these words, the Holy Spirit fell upon all those who heard the word.***

From Luke's report, it seems as though Peter experienced a clean evangelistic sweep. All the unbelievers present were apparently saved. Luke does not list all of the visible manifestations of the Holy Spirit in that meeting, but he stresses the one that attracted the most attention:

> [45] ***And those of the circumcision who believed were astonished, as many as came with Peter, because the gift of the Holy Spirit had been poured***

out on the Gentiles also. [46] *For they heard them speak with tongues and magnify God. . . .*

While the gift of tongues in Pentecost Phase I (Acts 2) was specifically intended for the proclamation of the gospel to representatives of the many ethnic groups present in Jerusalem at that time, the gift of tongues here in Cornelius's house seems more intended to be a confirmation of the validity of these initial Gentile conversions. Speaking in tongues, in this particular case the initial physical evidence of the filling of the Holy Spirit, was sufficient for Peter to order baptism immediately:

[47] *"Can anyone forbid water, that these should not be baptized who have received the Holy Spirit just as we have?"* [48] *And he commanded them to be baptized in the name of the Lord. . . .*

Although Luke doesn't mention it, it is important to note that the matter of circumcision does not surface here. As we will see when we move ahead toward the Jerusalem Council, circumcision becomes an enormously significant issue, the key point in affirming the validity of cross-cultural missionary work to the Gentiles.

PETER IS IN BIG TROUBLE: ACTS 11

As he would have anticipated, Peter's most formidable challenge was just ahead. How would he report what he had just done to his Jewish apostolic colleagues who had not seen the vision of the animals in the sheet and who had not been in Cornelius's house when the Holy Spirit fell with power?

[2] *And when Peter came up to Jerusalem, those of the circumcision contended with him,* [3] *saying, "You went in to uncircumcised men and ate with them!"*

The leaders of the Jerusalem church were furious. They were not particularly ready to hear Peter say words to the effect, "I went to Cornelius's house and ate with Gentiles because God told me to." Much as they believed that God does speak directive words to individual people, they needed more than that to assimilate this one. They were shocked!

Who are "those of the circumcision"? Biblical scholars do not agree whether a conservative group of messianic Jews who continued to insist that Gentiles be circumcised as a prerequisite for being a disciple of Jesus Christ had begun to form in Jerusalem this early. By Acts 15, however, the conservative messianic Jews were in full operation, teaching, "Unless you are circumcised according to the custom of Moses, you cannot be saved" (Acts 15:1). But here, perhaps, "those of the circumcision" only means Jewish believers in general. Whatever the precise meaning, they were extremely upset with Peter.

Peter defended his activities by describing his ministry experience rather than arguing theology. Chances are that at this time he wouldn't have yet worked out a cogent theology to explain what he had just seen firsthand. Once again I will point out that, as we see in most of the subsequent history of Christianity, theology emerges from ministry, not vice versa.

Peter's most convincing point was that the new Gentile believers in Caesarea had spoken in tongues. He says:

> [17] ***If therefore God gave them the same gift as He gave us when we believed on the Lord Jesus Christ, who was I that I could withstand God?***

The power of the Holy Spirit must have fallen strongly on the group in Jerusalem who had at first criticized Peter so severely, because in response to his simple testimony their anger turned to silence and then to approval.

> [18] ***When they heard these things they became silent; and they glorified God, saying, "Then God has also granted to the Gentiles repentance to life."***

PETER'S TREMENDOUS VICTORY

To summarize, Peter concluded a relatively short assignment to cross-cultural ministry by experiencing a tremendous victory. Although he did not have the ongoing spiritual gift of missionary, he nevertheless served God from his role as an obedient servant. We ourselves do many things from our roles as faithful Christians although we might not have the gift for a more permanent ministry in those roles. For example, I have led people to Christ although I don't have the gift of evangelist; I have cast out demons although

I don't have the gift of deliverance; I have prophesied although I don't have the gift of prophecy. On the other hand, I teach and I write books, not out of a role, but because God has given me the spiritual *gift* of teaching.

Paul is the one who emerges later as having a strong gift of missionary. As we will soon see in more detail, Peter makes some serious mistakes when he attempts to minister to the first Gentile *church* in Antioch. God had anointed Peter as an ongoing apostle to the circumcision, but when called upon at a special time to break the Gentile barrier in the house of Cornelius, he rose to the occasion, ministered to the uncircumcision and turned a key to the Kingdom that has seen multiplied benefits through the centuries.

REFLECTION QUESTIONS

1. The concept of "people movements," involving the members of a whole group making a decision to accept Christ all at once, is foreign to most of us. Do you think it is valid? What would be some of its dangers?
2. How could it be that some committed Christians who believe Peter raised Dorcas from the dead doubt that the dead are being raised today?
3. Proselytes and God-fearers were both born Gentiles. How did they differ from each other? What difference would it make in their receptivity to the gospel?
4. Obviously, God's choice of Cornelius to lead the first notable conversion of Gentiles was a deliberate choice. What were the two or three principal reasons God would have chosen Cornelius as opposed to any one of hundreds of other Gentiles?
5. Of all the things that persuaded Peter that he should violate traditional Jewish law and actually enter the house of a Gentile such as Cornelius, which do you think could have been the most important?

11

PLANTING THE FIRST GENTILE CHURCH

ACTS 11

Peter blazed the trail, and by baptizing Cornelius, and Cornelius's family and friends, he laid the foundation for all future ministry among the Gentiles of the world. As soon as Luke finishes his account of this event, which turns out to be the longest story in the book of Acts, he immediately tells us how the first Gentile church was planted. It was not to be planted in Cornelius's city of Caesarea, but rather in Antioch of Syria.

THE BIG PICTURE

As we frequently do, let's once again take a look at the big picture of the book of Acts. Our guiding light, as always, is Acts 1:8:

> But you shall receive power when the Holy Spirit has come upon you; and you shall be witnesses to Me in Jerusalem, and in all Judea and Samaria, and to the end of the earth.

My rationale for writing this commentary on Acts is to expand on the two themes of this verse—missiology and power ministry—more than other commentaries have done.

Missiologically, three broad cultural groups are highlighted in Acts 1:8: Jews, Samaritans and Gentiles. From this perspective, the entire book of Acts can be outlined around the three groups:

- Part I deals with church growth in Jerusalem and Judea. Evangelism is directed mostly at the Jews, and Peter is the central figure. This covers Acts 1-6.

- Part II deals with church growth in Samaria. Stephen and Philip are the central figures, Stephen being the theoretician and Philip the practitioner. This covers Acts 6–8.

- Part III deals with church growth among the Gentiles. Paul becomes the central figure, and this is by far Luke's largest emphasis, covering Acts 9–28, or more than two-thirds of the book. To lead in, Luke introduces Paul (Acts 9), tells how Peter blazed the trail to Cornelius's house (Acts 9–11), transitions from Peter to Paul (Acts 11–12) and then spotlights Paul's ministry for the rest of the book (Acts 13–28).

As indicated in Acts 1:8, this cross-cultural advance of the kingdom of God would be characterized by the supernatural power of the Holy Spirit working through the disciples. Luke highlights this in Part I by the miracle of tongues or languages in Acts 2:4, and "many signs and wonders" in 2:43, 4:30 and 5:12.

In Part II, Stephen "did great wonders and signs among the people" (6:8) and "multitudes with one accord heeded the things spoken by Philip, hearing and seeing the miracles which he did" (8:6).

Now, as we move into Part III, we have already seen Peter healing Aeneas and raising Dorcas from the dead. Such power ministries will continue with Paul and Barnabas later "declaring how many miracles and wonders God had worked through them among the Gentiles" (15:12).

BELIEVERS WERE PERSECUTED, BUT THEY EVANGELIZED

[11:19] ***Now those who were scattered after the persecution that arose over Stephen . . .***

To refresh our memories, Stephen had delivered a powerful message to the Sanhedrin, suggesting that God could save people apart from the Temple in Jerusalem and apart from the Jewish law. It cost him his life. None other than Paul, then called Saul, took leadership of the explosive persecution that followed this event, and the believers were scattered. To review Acts 8:3-4:

> As for Saul, he made havoc of the church, entering every house, and dragging off men and women, committing them to prison. Therefore those who were scattered went everywhere preaching the word.

The same passage states:

> . . . they were all scattered throughout the regions of Judea and Samaria, except the apostles (v. 1).

The phrase "except the apostles" strongly implies that it was not the *Hebrew* Jewish believers, but the *Hellenistic* Jewish believers who had been driven out of Jerusalem. The initial church split between the two groups was described in Acts 6 where the apostles decided to appoint the seven leaders of the Hellenistic church.

We need to keep in mind that when these Hellenistic believers traveled through the region witnessing and planting churches, the churches they planted did not take the form we are accustomed to today. The believers had no separate Christian church buildings where they met. They had no large congregations with a pastor and staff. They were Jews and therefore they continued worshiping God on Saturdays in their synagogues. When they met with other believers or messianic Jews for fellowship, prayer, worship or the Lord's Supper, it was in their homes. The Greek word for church, *ekklesia*, simply means "assembly," "gathering" or "the people of God." It did not mean a church building nor did it carry many of the other institutional implications the word "church" does today. Nor did it mean the synagogue. It is notable that the early Jewish believers tended to avoid using the word "synagogue" for their assemblies.

Church planting, then, meant to proclaim the gospel in word and deed, and to gather those who believed into fellowship groups, meeting in any number of homes. Those in a given city who were called followers of Jesus Christ were the church in that particular city.

When, beginning in Antioch, churches that were essentially composed of Gentiles came into being, a new dimension of the church began. These Gentile believers, by and large, had no reason to worship in the synagogue on the Sabbath. But this development comes later. As the Hellenistic Jews went out from Jerusalem, they did not preach to Gentiles, but to Jews only, as the second part of Acts 11:19 says:

> [11:19] ***Now those who were scattered after the persecution that arose over Stephen traveled as far as Phoenicia, Cyprus, and Antioch, preaching the word to no one but the Jews only.***

Geographically, the persecuted believers headed west from Jerusalem and turned right at the Mediterranean Sea. Luke mentions three places in particular, but we have no reason to doubt that they might have evangelized Jews living in other places as well. In fact, some might have turned left and gone toward Alexandria. However, the three places specifically mentioned are:

1. *Phoenicia*. Phoenicia was a province beginning just north of Galilee, having three principal cities in the Mediterranean: Ptolemais, Tyre and Sidon. In Acts 21, we are later told that the disciples were at Tyre (see vv. 3-4) and Ptolemais (see v. 7). We would be safe to assume that some disciples had gone to Sidon also, and that all three of these churches were planted by the fleeing Hellenists.

2. *Cyprus*. Cyprus was a large island a little more than 100 miles from the mainland. Some believers might have gone there from Sidon by sea. Two major cities were located in Cyprus: Salamis in the east and Paphos in the west. The church, or churches, on Cyprus fairly rapidly became missionary-sending churches because we read in Acts 11:20 that missionaries went from Cyprus to Antioch.

3. *Antioch*. Antioch was the capital of Syria. In the Roman Empire, only Rome and Alexandria were larger cities, so Antioch was a highly important and strategic center. The population of Antioch at that time is estimated by some to be 500,000. It was not on the coast, but about 20 miles inland on the Orontes River. Antioch is now in Turkey and carries the name Antakya. When Rome conquered Syria in 64 B.C., Pompey designated Antioch as a free city and made it the capital of western Asia. The city was favored with majestic architecture and beautifully paved streets. It was an important commercial center through which the goods and produce of the regions to the east found their way to the shipping routes of the Mediterranean.

Antioch had an exceptionally large Jewish population. F. F. Bruce says, "Jewish colonization in Antioch began practically from the city's foundation."[1]

That means Jews had been living there for some 300 years. Some have estimated Antioch's Jewish population to be 25,000 at the time of the events in the book of Acts. As was customary, the Jews would have resided in a special section of the city called "the Jewish quarter." The Jews in Antioch are said to have been more aggressive and more successful in proselytizing Gentiles than most. When the seven Hellenistic leaders were appointed by the apostles in Acts 6, one was "Nicolas, a proselyte from Antioch" (v. 5).

The Gentile part of Antioch had fallen into moral degradation. Simon Kistemaker says, "Antioch was known not for its virtues but for its vices: it was a city of moral depravity."[2] This would have been, to a large extent, because of the spiritual captivity of many in the city to the demonic principalities of Artemis (Diana of the Ephesians) and Apollo. Their center of worship was located in the nearby suburb of Daphene, where ritual prostitution drew its crowds. W. J. Conybeare and J. S. Howson describe Daphene as "a sanctuary for a perpetual festival of vice."[3]

I have spent some time in describing the city of Antioch because from this point it begins to rise in importance parallel to Jerusalem for the Jews. It is the place where the first Gentile church, in the proper sense of the word, was to be established.

THE MISSION TO ANTIOCH'S JEWS

Meanwhile, the Hellenists who left Jerusalem under the persecution had planted the first church in Antioch. But it was a church planted among Jews, not among Gentiles. This is an example of what we have been calling E-1, or monocultural, evangelism. From the missiological perspective, the geographical distance covered in an evangelistic effort is secondary compared to the cultural distance. I recall missiologist Ralph Winter once saying that the first thousand miles are insignificant when compared to the last three feet!

In this case, the Hellenistic believers would have traveled 300 miles or so from Jerusalem to Antioch, a considerable distance in those days. But when they arrived in Antioch, they would have taken up residence in the Jewish quarter of the city and they would have established their primary social relationships among the Jewish citizens. They would inevitably have had some social contact with Gentiles in such a cosmopolitan city, but such contacts would be secondary as far as personal relationships were concerned. They would not have eaten with Gentiles, they would not have invited them into their Jewish homes nor would they have gone out of their way to share the gospel of Jesus Christ with them. This is why Luke specifically says they were "preaching the word to no one but the Jews only" (11:19).

If some may have difficulty imagining this, a modern parallel would be the evangelization of the Korean immigrant population in Los Angeles in the 1980s and 1990s. So many Koreans came that a section of Los Angeles was designated "Koreatown," similar to the Jewish quarter in Antioch, except that many more Koreans reside in Los Angeles than Jews did in Antioch. Pastors and evangelists came to Los Angeles from Korea in considerable numbers to evangelize the Koreans, and they had outstanding success. In Korea itself, some 20 percent of the population is Christian, but in Los Angeles the number of Christians among first-generation Korean-Americans is reported at nearly 70 percent!

Most of this evangelism in Los Angeles was successful because it was also E-1 evangelism. When the Korean pastors arrived in Los Angeles, they found people who spoke the same language, ate the same food, harbored the same prejudices, married the same kind of people, honored their ancestors in the same way and shared many other common interests. We might say that these pastors and evangelists from Korea "preached the word to none but Koreans only."

It could be pointed out with a good deal of validity that Los Angeles Korean-Americans are somewhat different from Korean-Koreans. The same would have been true of Hellenistic Jews in Antioch as compared to Hellenistic Jews in Jerusalem. It could be argued that they should be seen as distinct people groups, and in that case the evangelism could be E-2 rather than E-1. This might be true, but it simply illustrates that a bit of subjectivity is involved in discerning boundaries between some people groups. This is why, at the present time, some missiologists will say that 3,000 people groups are still unreached in the world while others will say the number is 8,000. The issue is not right or wrong but a matter of subjective personal judgment as to where to draw the lines.

The major point here in Acts 11, however, is that these Hellenists from Jerusalem did not preach to the *Gentiles* in Antioch any more than the Korean evangelists in Los Angeles would have preached to the non-Korean Anglo-Americans, African-Americans or Hispanic-Americans. Add to this the Japanese-Americans toward whom modern-day Koreans harbor feelings similar to the feelings of Jews toward Gentiles in the first century.

Two Missions to Antioch, Not One

[20] *But some of them were men from Cyprus and Cyrene, who, when they had come to Antioch, spoke to the Hellenists [Gentiles], preaching the Lord Jesus.* [21] *And the hand of the Lord was with them, and a great number believed and turned to the Lord.*

Were there in fact *two* mission advances into the city of Antioch instead of *one*? Was the first mission undertaken by the Hellenistic Jewish sisters and brothers who left Jerusalem after Stephen's death, and the second by a group of unrelated missionaries? Did one target the Jewish population of Antioch and the other the Gentile population? Were there several years between the first arrival of each group?

This is a particularly important question for missiologists, especially for those who have a high view of culture and believe that the people approach to world evangelization has been, and still is, the most viable strategy for planning and executing cross-cultural evangelism. Because I am one who tends to interpret missionary work from such a perspective, my conclusion is that to most accurately understand the information that Luke provides in Acts 11, a two-mission hypothesis is most useful.

I am well aware of the risk I am taking in suggesting this. Why a risk? Because none of the respected commentators whom I have been consulting throughout my study of Acts proposes that two separate missions occurred. At the same time, none of them rejects the idea, apparently because such a hypothesis has not yet been raised as a point of discussion among traditional biblical scholars.

Almost all of the commentators, however, pause with no small frustration at this point, trying to make a coherent whole out of the bits and pieces of information that Luke provides. Howard Marshall says, "There can be no doubt that a successful period of evangelism among Gentiles was initiated. . . . What we do not know is how the church was led to take this step."[4] Simon Kistemaker says, "We are unable to explain why Jewish people from Cyrene in North Africa came to Antioch."[5] F. F. Bruce says, "But in Antioch some daring spirits among them, men of Cyprus and Cyrene, took a momentous step forward. If the gospel was so good for the Jews, might it not be good for the Gentiles also?"[6]

Although they do not wrestle specifically with the two-mission hypothesis, the biblical scholars do discuss extensively two other important items in this passage. One is whether it makes the best sense to conclude that planting the church among the Gentiles in Antioch came *before* the conversion of Cornelius or *after*. In my opinion, and that of most of the commentators I am using, there are no convincing reasons to change the order Luke uses in the Acts of the Apostles. Cornelius came first, then the Gentiles in Antioch.

WHO ARE THE "HELLENISTS"?

A much more crucial issue from the viewpoint of missiology is who these people called "Hellenists" in the *New King James Version*, the version I am using, really are. Some of the ancient Greek texts use *Hellenas* or "Greeks," while others use *Hellenistas* or "Hellenists." Simon Kistemaker sums it up well: "[Luke] intimates that the Jewish Christian missionaries addressed not the Greek-speaking Jews, whom he elsewhere calls *Hellenists*, but the non-Jewish Greeks, whom he repeatedly classifies as *Hellenas*. The internal evidence, therefore, seems to favor the reading *Greeks*."[7]

When I quoted Acts 11:20 on a previous page, I inserted the word "Gentiles," i.e., "they . . . spoke to the Hellenists [Gentiles]." Who were these Gentiles? This is a secondary issue but an interesting one. R. C. H. Lenski points out that "Luke omits any further characterization such as used in connection with Cornelius in 10:2, to the effect that they were 'fearing God.'"[8] An argument from silence proves nothing for sure but it does indicate that we cannot be certain whether these Gentiles were, in fact, God-fearers or whether they were other Gentiles who had no personal connection with the Jewish synagogues whatsoever. There could have been some of each for all we know.

THE CCM (CYPRUS AND CYRENE MISSION)

My personal reconstruction of historical events has the Hellenistic believers leaving Jerusalem after Stephen's death and planting solid, growing churches in both Cyprus and Cyrene as well as many other places. Luke explicitly tells us they went to Cyprus (see 11:19), although he does not mention Cyrene. We have no reason, however, to doubt that they went to Cyrene as well. In another place Luke says, "those who were scattered went everywhere preaching the word" (8:4), so "everywhere" could well have included Cyrene. Cyrene was a city in North Africa, now Libya.

Let's assume, then, that the churches that were planted in Cyrene and Cyprus developed satisfactorily over the years, and that they eventually became missionary-sending churches, as healthy churches should. Charles Van Engen argues that by their very nature, true disciples of Jesus are "God's missionary people,"[9] and I do not think it is unreasonable to expect that these first-century believers would have been anything different.

Because these believers were still Jews, and had been Jews all their lives, they would have been familiar with what we have mentioned previously as the Jewish proselytizing bands. Jesus referred to these bands in passing when He said of the Pharisees: "For you travel land and sea to win one proselyte" (Matt. 23:15). The proselytizing bands functioned apart from the local synagogues as what some missiologists call "sodalities," roughly equivalent to what we know as "parachurch organizations" today.

It is altogether possible that believers from both Cyprus and Cyrene who had the spiritual gift of missionary had joined forces to establish what would be to us a parachurch missionary agency. This is exactly what we will see Paul, Barnabas and some others doing when we come to Acts 13. There is no need to think that Paul and Barnabas were the first ones to do it; they are just the ones about whom we know the most. When we come to Acts 13, I will explain the so-called "modality-sodality theory" in more detail.

If these proselytizing bands did do church planting, let's call this group the "Cyprus and Cyrene Mission," or the "CCM," just to coin a term for communication purposes.

When Did the CCM Arrive in Antioch?

Biblical scholars do not agree on how the chronology of Acts falls into place at several points. It is, for sure, a complex matter, and the arguments on all sides are readily available to any who desire to consult the classical commentaries. In the first chapter of this commentary, I discuss the chronology and set out my own conclusions in a timeline that seems to me to be the most reasonable way of interpreting all the facts we have. For this discussion about when the CCM might have arrived in Antioch and begun to plant Gentile churches, I am following that timeline chronology.

As we will see later in Acts 11, Paul was called to Antioch in A.D. 46, fairly soon after the Gentile churches had been planted there. It is a judgment call, but I would think this would be three or four years, at the most, after the CCM missionaries first arrived. This would put the arrival of the CCM at A.D. 42 or 43, possibly a little later.

That was Mission Number 2, but how about Mission Number 1? Stephen's death and the persecution that scattered the Hellenistic believers occurred in A.D. 32, the year before Saul's conversion in A.D. 33. We do not know how long it took these Hellenistic Jewish missionaries to begin to plant churches in the Jewish ghetto of Antioch, but it was probably not more than a year or two at the most. So those first churches might have started around A.D. 34.

One more thing. Soon after Paul arrived and began to minister in Antioch, the believers there took up an offering and sent it to the church in Jerusalem, which at the time was suffering from a famine (see 11:27-30). In Galatians, Paul says that he and Barnabas took that offering 14 years after he made the short visit from Damascus to Jerusalem following his conversion (see Gal. 2:1). How the 14 years might exactly fit the sequence of events is part of the ongoing scholarly discussion on chronology, but it is not particularly relevant to my point here.

My point is that, based on these facts, *several years would have elapsed, perhaps 8 or 10 years, between the time of the first mission targeting the Jews of Antioch and the second mission targeting the Gentiles of Antioch.*

What Did the CCM Do?

Let's try to reconstruct the scenario in Antioch as a missiologist might see it. Here is Antioch, a cosmopolitan city of 500,000. William LaSor says, "The city was divided into 'quarters,' and had a large Jewish population, as well as Syrian, Greek, and Roman communities."[10] From this, we know that it comprised at least four people groups, undoubtedly many more. But working from the information we have at hand, we can meaningfully discuss only the two broader people groups, the Jews and the Gentiles.

The Jewish population, as we have previously mentioned, consisted of 25,000 people. This is a large number of Jews, as LaSor says, but it is only 5 percent of the total population of Antioch. Antioch also had 475,000 Gentiles when the CCM arrived to evangelize them.

When the CCM missionaries got to Antioch they found a well-established church, about 10 years old, in the Jewish quarter. The believers there were seen by themselves, and by the other residents of Antioch, as minority Jews who worshiped in the synagogues, kept a kosher kitchen, considered uncircumcised Gentiles as unclean and followed Jesus Christ as their Messiah.

Luke has told us specifically that these people were "preaching the word to no one but the Jews only" (Acts 11:19). They were making no attempt that we are aware of to reach the 475,000 Gentiles in Antioch. Because of this, they were an unlikely force for evangelism to Antioch's unreached people groups.

Preaching to Gentiles Only

The CCM missionaries arrived in Antioch with a different perspective. We might surmise that their specific calling from God was "preaching the word to no one but the [Gentiles] only." They were intentionally cross-cultural. Unlike those in the Jewish quarter, they would likely have been given the missionary gift by the Holy Spirit. Although ethnically they were just as Jewish as those in the Jewish-quarter church, they were also significantly different from them. They came with an anointing of the Holy Spirit to communicate the gospel cross-culturally to the *Gentiles*. They were E-3 evangelists.

Methodologically, they would not have wanted to be strongly associated with the believers in the Jewish quarter. Why? Although in a city as large as Antioch, the vast majority of citizens would not have known about such things as disciples of Jesus Christ in the Jewish quarter; those who did know would have seen the Jewish believers as extremely ethnocentric, not to say racist. The messianic Jews would have been teaching that in order to worship God and enter their synagogues, Gentiles first would have to become Jews, be circumcised and agree to keep the Jewish law—at least the majority of them would have held that opinion. They would not as yet have absorbed the theological implications of Peter's visit to Cornelius's house. The theological principles behind the issue of Gentile circumcision continued to be poorly understood by Jewish believers in general, at least until the Council of Jerusalem, which came several years after the first Gentile church was established.

The CCM missionaries, on the other hand, had resolved the theological issue, at least to their satisfaction. They were prepared to evangelize the Gentiles on the Gentiles' own merits, not requiring them to become Jews in order to be saved. I can picture these missionaries not settling down in the Jewish quarter, but rather in the Syrian quarter or the Greek quarter or the Roman quarter in order to begin to multiply Gentile churches.

In a city so large and among people groups so distinct, I would not think that the social contact between the network of house churches in the Jewish quarter and the new churches of the Gentile quarters would have been extensive, if they had any direct contact at all. Furthermore, considering their theological differences, a modern analogy might be picturing Assemblies of God missionaries going to evangelize the lower castes of a large Indian city where the Lutherans had been established among middle castes for many years. They might acknowledge each other as part of the general Christian church of the city, but working contacts would be minimal or, most likely, nonexistent. The one thing that might have brought them closer together would be persecution, but we do not read of persecution arising in Antioch at that time.

The result would have been that a network of Syrian Gentile churches would have developed, and perhaps another network of Roman Gentile churches, and perhaps others, depending on how many of the specific Gentile people groups in Antioch the missionaries had targeted. These would undoubtedly have been as separate from each other as are the networks of Korean churches and Hispanic churches and African-American churches and messianic Jewish synagogues in Los Angeles today. In a broad theological sense, they are all truly "the Church of Jesus Christ in Los Angeles," but functionally they see themselves as significantly distinct from the others.

What meaningful social interaction the Gentile and the Jewish churches in Antioch might have had is unknown. But if what we know about intercultural communication applied then as it does now, whatever social interaction they might have had with each other, if any, would clearly have been a *secondary* social relationship. Their *primary* relationships would have been with fellow Jews or fellow Gentiles, as the case may be.

I realize that some will say such a reconstruction of the scenario in Antioch is not politically correct. They would prefer to postulate that Jewish believers and Gentile believers, whether Syrian, Greek, Roman or others, would all be worshiping together in the same assembly, eating together and intermarrying freely. I myself would also prefer this, because it would be a wonderful display of our oneness in Christ. I also would prefer that this be the case in Los Angeles or Calcutta or Mexico City or Kinchasa today. But such, unfortunately, is not usually so. It will happen in the New Jerusalem, and I can report that it is happening occasionally today where the values of the kingdom of God are strongly manifested. We should pray that it happens more often. But in the meantime, we need to be as realistic as possible and admit that through the centuries it has been the exception, not the rule.

Knowing what we know about the pre-Jerusalem Council generation of Jewish believers, it is extremely doubtful that Antioch was one of the exceptions to the rule. The multinational group mentioned in Acts 13:1 does not disprove my hypothesis, as we shall see later.

The Outcome

[21] ***And the hand of the Lord was with them, and a great number believed and turned to the Lord.***

Great church growth resulted from the church-planting initiative of the Cyprus and Cyrene Mission. These were the first known Gentile churches. The conversions of the Ethiopian eunuch and those in Cornelius's house were prototypes of household conversion, but they have not become examples of authentic Gentile church planting. Antioch was the prototype.

The great growth of the Gentile churches in Antioch was due primarily to the two strands we are following through the book of Acts: divine power and sound missiology. I have explained missiology in great detail, because this is a crucial hinge point in the history of Christianity. But how about the power? Some might observe that nothing is specifically mentioned here about healings or miracles or speaking in tongues.

Luke does say, however, that "the hand of the Lord was with them." Stanley Horton points out, "This expression is often used in the Bible to mean the power of the Lord or even the Spirit of the Lord."[11] Luke himself mentions "the hand of the Lord" on two other occasions in Acts, both describing displays of supernatural power. One was in a prayer meeting in Jerusalem where the believers prayed that God would act "by stretching out Your hand to heal, and that signs and wonders may be done through the name of Your holy Servant Jesus" (4:30). The other comes during a high-level power encounter between Paul and Elymas the sorcerer. Paul declares, "And now, indeed, the hand of the Lord is upon you, and you shall be blind, not seeing the sun for a time" (13:11).

True to form, then, we can reasonably understand that the CCM missionaries moved among the Gentiles in Antioch by using power ministries, all the more necessary because of the wicked influence of dark angels under such principalities as Diana and Apollo headquartered in nearby Daphene, which may well have been the seat of Satan for the region.

Barnabas Arrives to Speed Up the Growth

[22] Then news of these things came to the ears of the church in Jerusalem, and they sent out Barnabas to go as far as Antioch. [23] When he came and had seen the grace of God, he was glad, and encouraged them all that with purpose of heart they should continue with the Lord. [24] For he was a good man, full of the Holy Spirit and of faith. And a great many people were added to the Lord.

The news that attracted the attention of the leaders in Jerusalem was that Gentile *churches* were being multiplied in Antioch. They would have known about the Jewish-quarter churches there for some 10 years, so that wouldn't have been news. They might have been shocked at the notion of Gentile churches, except that Peter's experience in the house of Cornelius fortunately had broken the ice.

When they heard the news that Samaritans were coming to Christ through Philip, the church leaders at Jerusalem sent Peter and John to assess the situation and help as they could. They again followed the same pattern in Antioch, this time by sending Barnabas. Barnabas is later referred to as an apostle (see 14:4), but whether he was so regarded at this point we are not sure. In any case, he had become an outstanding leader in the Jerusalem church. He was one of those who had sold his land and given the money to the church (see 4:36), and he had taken Paul under his wing when he first visited Jerusalem as a new convert and was still subject to a great deal of suspicion among the believers (see 9:26-27).

When Barnabas was sent to Antioch, it was as a career missionary, not as a short-term missionary, as were Peter and John when they visited Samaria. Barnabas had the missionary gift, but neither Peter nor John did; they were both apostles to the Jews. Barnabas originally came from Cyprus, so he may have known some of the CCM missionaries from there. Even if he had not known them, at least they would have had much in common and they probably would have had many mutual friends. Barnabas was one of the Jewish believers, relatively few at that time, who could comfortably accept uncircumcised Gentiles into the church.

Somewhat uncharacteristically, Luke gives two church-growth reports in a row here. Before Barnabas arrived, "a great number believed and turned to the Lord" (11:21). When Barnabas had been there for a while, Luke says, three verses later, "and a great many people were added to the Lord." Apparently, good growth had become better growth. The *rate* of church growth had evidently increased as a result of Barnabas's ministry.

Why would this happen? One reason might be that Barnabas was an encourager and he brought with him an affirmation of apostolic approval from Jerusalem. He was an outstanding leader, and leadership is a proven principle of vigorous church growth.

Another reason would probably have been that Barnabas was said to be "full of the Holy Spirit and of faith" (11:24). This is Luke's way of affirming that Barnabas was operating under a strong anointing for power ministries. A similar thing had been said of Stephen, "a man full of faith and the Holy Spirit" (6:5), and then, "Stephen, full of faith and power, did great wonders and signs among the people" (v. 8). The faith Luke is referring to here is more than saving faith or sanctifying faith. It is the extraordinary faith that believes for the miraculous, the faith Paul refers to in 1 Corinthians 13 to "remove mountains" (v. 2). Barnabas would later report with Paul "how many miracles and wonders God had worked through them among the Gentiles" (Acts 15:12). If power ministries are seen not so much as ends in themselves but as signs pointing to the Savior, a frequent outcome is that "a great many people . . . [are] added to the Lord" (11:24).

PAUL ARRIVES TO TRAIN LEADERS

[25] ***Then Barnabas departed for Tarsus to seek Saul.*** **[26]** ***And when he had found him, he brought him to Antioch. So it was that for a whole year they assembled with the church and taught a great many people. . . .***

Why Barnabas invited Paul to join the large, rapidly growing Christian community in Antioch, Luke leaves largely to our imagination. I would think, however, that he had two principal reasons.

Paul Came for Leadership Training

First, as in any people movement, *training leaders is the major key to long-term success or failure.* Many of us are accustomed to hearing, at times, reports of enormous numbers of people registering decisions for Christ at citywide evangelistic crusades, but we find relatively few of them moving ahead as committed Christians a year later. Careful studies have shown that the major defect in strategy planning (not the only one, to be sure) has been the failure to select and train leaders. In the major growth spots of the world today, the desperate need is not for missionaries to come and evangelize—that is already happening in a remarkable way. The need is for missionaries who are principally church planters to come and train leaders. Without the concomitant multiplication of churches, evangelistic fruit will not be fruit that remains.

Luke does tell us that Paul "taught a great many people," so leadership training was evidently a part of Paul's job description.

But why Paul? He was not the only one who by that time could train leaders and church planters. Furthermore, Paul had practically disappeared from sight during the 10 years or so since he had been strongly encouraged by the apostles to get out of Jerusalem and go back home to Tarsus. It is also true that Barnabas had not forgotten Paul. Quite likely he had kept in touch with him during the 10-year period. It helps to remind ourselves that at that time Paul was not the famous Christian leader we now know. Barnabas had a much higher profile and much greater name recognition.

What had Paul been doing for those 10 years? He tells us in Galatians, "I went into the regions of Syria and Cilicia" (Gal. 1:21). Antioch was in this general territory, as well as Tarsus, although they were several days' journey apart. We later hear of churches in Syria and Cilicia (see Acts 15:23), but we do not know if they were planted by Paul or by others.

It is not certain to what extent Paul, who was a Hebrew of the Hebrews and of the strict sect of the Pharisees, had at this point absorbed the theology that Gentiles could be saved without being circumcised. Paul's theology of Jesus as the true Messiah was firm. He had known since his experience on the Damascus road that God was calling him to minister to Gentiles. But how well he was prepared for this ministry remains a question.

This leads me to what I believe is the second, and perhaps the most important, reason that Barnabas, under the leading of the Holy Spirit, invited Paul to come to Antioch from Tarsus.

Paul Came Not Only to Teach but Also to Learn

Second, *Paul came to Tarsus not only to teach but also to learn.* If the hypothesis that theology emerges from ministry is valid, a year's ministry experience in a growing network of Gentile churches would have been an invaluable theological crucible. Paul would have been in the midst of possibly thousands of Gentiles, who by then were born again and serving Christ in a variety of roles in the church and in the workplace without having been circumcised or without committing to follow the Jewish law.

I would not be surprised if the compelling reason that Barnabas set out to seek the relatively unknown Saul of Tarsus to recruit him for the missionary team in Antioch could be traced back to some revelatory word from God to the Antioch leaders. God's time had now come to fulfill the prophetic word to Paul through Ananias of Damascus that he would be sent to the Gentiles, "to turn them from darkness to light, and from the power of Satan to God" (26:18). Paul used the year in Antioch to grow in his experience of ministering cross-culturally to Gentiles and to mature his theological reflection about what would be involved in his future career.

THE WORLD'S FIRST "CHRISTIANS"

[26] . . . *And the disciples were first called Christians in Antioch.*

Previous to this, Christians had been called believers, disciples, followers of the Way, or brothers and sisters. It is only when large numbers of Gentiles accepted Christ that the label "Christians" was put on them. From where did the name derive? It is used only twice more in Scripture: once by King Agrippa to Paul (see 26:28) and the other time by Peter when he referred to people suffering because of the name (see 1 Pet. 4:14,16). I agree with Simon Kistemaker, who says, "We are inclined to think that the enemies of the faith ascribed this name to the Christians."[12]

It is not uncommon that a label, coined by outsiders sometimes in derision, becomes a permanent designation. Such a thing was true of Methodists and Quakers, to name just two examples. We are now so accustomed to being called "Christians," and proud of it, that it seems strange that people would first have used it to poke fun at born-again Gentiles.

A PROPHETIC WORD TO SHARE WITH THE POOR

[27] *And in these days prophets came from Jerusalem to Antioch.*
[28] *Then one of them, named Agabus, stood up and showed by the Spirit that there was going to be a great famine throughout all the world, which also happened in the days of Claudius Caesar.* [29] *Then the disciples,*

each according to his ability, determined to send relief to the brethren dwelling in Judea. [30] *This they also did, and sent it to the elders by the hands of Barnabas and Saul.*

This is the first time that prophets and the gift of prophecy are mentioned in Acts. Many other aspects of power ministry have been introduced, but now we see the Holy Spirit speaking specific words to the church by recognized prophets. Not that prophecy was unexpected. On the Day of Pentecost, Peter had announced that Joel's prophecy was now being fulfilled, part of which was, "I will pour out My Spirit in those days; and they shall prophesy" (2:18). I would imagine that prophecy had actually been an ongoing part of the normal life of this early church, although Luke postpones spotlighting it until now.

The spiritual gift of prophecy is mentioned in Romans 12:6 and 1 Corinthians 12:10, and the *office* of prophet, which is second only to apostle, is mentioned in Ephesians 4:11 and 1 Corinthians 12:28. An office means that a person's particular spiritual gift has been recognized by the church and that the person is authorized to engage in open ministry centered around that gift. Agabus and the others had both the gift and the office because they were recognized prophets.

The office of prophet is gaining more stature in Christian churches around the world these days than it has in the recent past. The churches of the New Apostolic Reformation, representing the fastest-growing segment of global Christianity, are giving new prominence to prophets, but they are not doing so exclusively.

New Testament prophecy includes both foretelling and forthtelling. In Agabus's prophecy that "there was going to be a great famine throughout all the world" (Acts 11:28), we have an example of *foretelling*. That God wanted the believers in Antioch to help the poor in Jerusalem was *forthtelling*. This can be seen as an exemplary model for the blend of charismatic vitality and social action.

The believers in Antioch did what they were expected to do when they received an authentic prophetic word from God—they obeyed. They gave generously and they sent the offering to Jerusalem with Barnabas and Paul.

Luke says they delivered the money "to the elders" (v. 30). Significantly, he doesn't say "apostles." This is an indication that the apostles were by then moving out from Jerusalem to spread the gospel, leaving the local church in the hands of the elders, or pastors, whom God had called and whom the apostles had trained for church leadership. Typically, apostles then, as now, are engaged primarily in trans-local ministry.

REFLECTION QUESTIONS

1. Reflect on the fact that in the time of the book of Acts, no church buildings, as such, were in existence. What implications might this have for our churches today?
2. Why might it be considered reasonable that the Hellenistic Jewish believers, when driven from Jerusalem, would not plant churches among Gentiles, even in predominantly Gentile cities?
3. The two-mission hypothesis suggested in this chapter is an important concept. Try to describe it in your own words. Explain how 8 to 10 years could have transpired before the second mission began.
4. When the so-called CCM missionaries arrived in Antioch to plant Gentile churches, the only brothers and sisters in Christ would have been found in the Jewish quarter. Why would the missionaries prefer to live in other parts of the city far from fellow believers?
5. How about the name "Christian"? Why would the believers in Antioch, but not in Jerusalem, be called Christians? How do you like the name "Christian" today?

12

THE POWER OF HEROD VERSUS THE POWER OF PRAYER

Acts 12

Luke is still in the process of making a transition from Peter as the first central figure in the Acts of the Apostles to Paul as the central figure. In the transition, he starts by telling of Paul's conversion, then he switches to how Peter evangelized the Gentiles in Cornelius's house, and then he tells about Paul going to Antioch and beginning to work with the first Gentile churches. At this point, Luke takes us back to Peter for the last time, except for his brief appearance a few years later at the Council of Jerusalem.

A FLASHBACK TO JERUSALEM

Actually, Acts 12 is a flashback. In Acts 11, Luke unfolded the story of church planting in Antioch, which took place over a period of 10 years or more. Acts 12 could really have started off, "Meanwhile, in Jerusalem . . ." This whole chapter is like a parenthesis. Barnabas and Paul are already on their way from Antioch to Jerusalem, carrying the offering that the believers in Antioch had collected to help the poor.

What happened in Jerusalem? Why did they need help? Were the elders surprised that the Gentile believers in Antioch would send the Jews a gift? Were they pleased with the amount of money they received? Were many poor people actually helped? Did this social service give impetus to the growth of the Jerusalem church? These and many other questions like them did not seem to be of much interest to Luke. He gives us no information about the ministry of Barnabas and Saul once they arrived in Jerusalem. Peter is once again the focus. When he finishes telling about Peter, Luke closes the parenthesis and simply tells us that Barnabas and Paul went back to Antioch.

The events that Luke records in Acts 12 are not such historical milestones as were, for example, Paul's conversion, Peter's visit to Cornelius's house or Gentile churches being planted in Antioch. However, they are extremely important for those of us who desire to be all that God wants us to be. The key lesson of the chapter is the power of prayer. I like the way Everett Harrison puts it: "The circumstances surrounding [Peter's] imprisonment are sketched in simple but dramatic fashion–the power of an earthly monarch pitted against the power of prayer to the Almighty."[1] We are looking at what many would call a power encounter.

HEROD'S HARASSMENT

[1] *Now about that time Herod the king stretched out his hand to harass some from the church.*

Who was Herod the king?

Herod was the surname of a family of rulers who served under the emperor of Rome. Three Herods are mentioned in the New Testament. Herod the Great is the one who had the babies killed soon after Jesus was born. Herod Antipas is the one who ordered the head of John the Baptist on a platter. This one is Herod Agrippa I, the grandson of Herod the Great. Then, to complete the picture, his son Herod Agrippa II is the one later called "King Agrippa" before whom Paul defends himself in Acts 25. He was not known as "Herod," as his father was, but as "Agrippa." It is not easy to keep track of all the Herods!

Persecution did not seem to be a severe problem for the church in Jerusalem after the death of Stephen and after the Hellenistic Jewish believers were run out of town. An atmosphere of peaceful coexistence seemed to hold between the Jews who believed that Jesus was the Messiah and the other more traditional Jews. The major theological issue apparently had not surfaced among them, namely, whether uncircumcised Gentiles could be saved without first becoming Jews. All Jerusalem males who had believed in Jesus up to that time had been circumcised, no problem. Even the Samaritans had accepted the Pentateuch, which taught that circumcision was the norm, so their conversion seemed to be tolerated.

Years later, when we come to the Council of Jerusalem, it is surprising to some to find that many of the believers in Jerusalem, perhaps the majority, still maintained their theological ethnocentricity: "But some of the sect of the Pharisees who believed rose up, saying, 'It is necessary to circumcise them [the Gentile believers], and to command them to keep the law of Moses'" (15:5). This point of view seemed to satisfy the unbelieving Jews enough to shrug off those of their number who had decided to become disciples of Jesus. As a result, "the churches throughout all Judea, Galilee, and Samaria had peace" (9:31).

But in the days of "Herod the king" something had changed. What was it?

Trouble Among the Jews!

Clearly, Peter's ministry in the house of Cornelius would have been the event that upset the peaceful status quo in Jerusalem. Peter, a Hebrew Jew who some thought should have known better, had actually entered a Gentile house in Caesarea, preached the gospel to a gathering of Gentiles there and, when they believed in Jesus Christ and were filled with the Holy Spirit, baptized them without requiring circumcision. The apostles in Jerusalem were predictably upset when they first heard about this, but when Peter returned from his trip, he succeeded in persuading them that it was valid for Gentiles to be saved and still remain Gentiles. This, however, was the beginning of serious trouble among other Jews in Jerusalem.

Meanwhile, the apostles had been training elders to take over the leadership of the Jerusalem church. When Barnabas and Paul carried the famine relief funds to Jerusalem, they delivered the money to the *elders*, not to the *apostles*. The apostles, who had come to agree with Peter that Gentile believers did not need to be circumcised, were by then out in a much wider itinerant ministry. It was then that Herod "stretched out his hand to harass some from the church" (12:1). Everett Harrison suggests, "James, the brother of John, and Peter may have been the only members of the twelve in Jerusalem at the time."[2] They were the ones that Herod put on his hit list.

James, the First Apostle to Die

[2] *Then he killed James the brother of John with the sword.*

Although James, along with Peter and John, was one of Jesus' inner circle, he doesn't seem to have assumed a particularly prominent role in the leadership of the Jerusalem church. The James who later becomes a high-profile church leader in Jerusalem is James the brother of Jesus, not James the brother of John, who was the son of Zebedee.

Why Herod singled out James is not altogether clear. Although he was an apostle, he was perhaps a safer target than Peter, the recognized leader of the whole messianic movement at the time. As an apostle, James would have been identified with the faction that was more tolerant of Gentile conversion. Although Luke does not furnish details, Herod in all probabiity would have worked with the Sanhedrin to indict James on some charge, perhaps one based on false accusations such as they did with Stephen, and then order his execution. James was killed "with the sword," or beheaded, rather than being stoned as Stephen was. Richard Rackham concludes, "The charge, then, was one of disloyalty rather than of breaking the law."[3]

Peter Imprisoned to Please the Jews

[3] ***And because he saw that it pleased the Jews, he proceeded further to seize Peter also. Now it was during the Days of Unleavened Bread.*** [4] ***So when he had arrested him, he put him in prison, and delivered him to four squads of soldiers to keep him, intending to bring him before the people after Passover.*** [6] ***And when Herod was about to bring him out, that night Peter was sleeping, bound with two chains between two soldiers; and the guards before the door were keeping the prison.***

Killing James turned out to be a good political move. Herod "saw that it pleased the Jews." He was on a roll. He held pleasing the Jews as a high value. Why? Because, strangely enough, according to Jewish law, he had no right to be king over the Jews!

The family and descendants of Herod the Great were Jewish proselytes, Gentiles who had converted to Judaism. Herod the Great had married a Jewish woman, Marianne, and he wanted to be regarded as a full Jew, so he went as far as to attempt to propagate a public lie through his court historian, Nicholas of Damascus. According to Joachim Jeremias, Nicholas "spread it around that [Herod] was descended from the first Jews who returned from exile in Babylon."[4]

Although Herod the Great never actually succeeded in this deceit, the effort was an astute political move because, although proselytes were regarded as legitimate Jews in many things, they also had some implicit limitations.

One of the most troublesome limitations was that, according to the official rabbinical interpretation of the law (see Deut. 17:15) at that time, only a full-blooded Jew could be king. Jeremias says, "According to the law, Herod was an illegitimate usurper."[5]

Herod the Great's grandson, this Herod Agrippa I who had just killed James, was under the same stigma. At one point, a rabbi named Simon had succeeded in stirring up a public demonstration against him, saying that Herod had no right to go into the Temple, because he was not a full-blooded Jew. Smarting from this, Herod had staged a showcase emotional appeal to win the sympathy of the general public.

According to custom, on a certain Jewish holiday the king should sit on a platform in the Temple and read the law to the people. Herod broke tradition and stood up instead of sitting down to grandstand his supposed humility and reverence for the law. Then Herod came to Deuteronomy 17:15: "You shall surely set a king over you whom the Lord your God chooses; one from among your brethren you shall set as a king over you; you may not set a foreigner over you, who is not your brother." When Herod read this, his voice cracked and he began weeping. Caught up in the emotion of the moment, the crowd of Jews cried out, "You are our brother! You are our brother!"[6]

As a good proselyte, Herod, of course, had been circumcised and he kept the Jewish law. He offered sacrifices in the Temple and observed the Passover. He had been accepted by his Jewish subjects, but he always recognized that his position was precarious. So whenever he could do something special to please the Jews and relieve his identity crisis, he gladly did it.

Upping the Ante

Now that Gentile circumcision had become an issue, killing the apostle James was one more way that Herod could try to please the Jews. It seemed to work so well that he decided he would up the ante and attempt the same with Peter.

Doesn't murder seem to be a drastic extreme to secure a higher rating in political opinion polls? To many it might, but not to the family of Herod. The demonic influence, especially the spirit of death, appeared to be extraordinarily strong through their bloodline. The patriarch, Herod the Great, killed all the male children under two years of age to try to eliminate the baby Jesus. When he discovered that a group of rabbis had questioned whether he should be king on the basis of what we have seen in Deuteronomy 17:15, he had the rabbis arrested and executed simply because their teaching did not please him. His son, Herod Antipas, ordered John the Baptist's head cut off and he proudly displayed it in front of his guests. For this current Herod, killing James and Peter, who were now regarded by some Jews as troublemakers, would have been a relatively small thing to him as long as it had good political results.

Demonic Principalities at Work

Jesus said, "The thief does not come except to steal, and to kill, and to destroy" (John 10:10). I would not doubt that the actions of these wicked Herods can be interpreted as more than ruthless politics. Obviously, spiritual forces of darkness are strong at work here, desiring to keep the kingdom of God from spreading throughout the world. It would be a severe setback for the budding Christian movement to lose its top leader and another apostle at this point. But note well that even more devastating for subsequent world evangelization would be propagating the doctrine that all people, whoever they might be, need to be circumcised and become Jews in order to be saved.

Herod may or may not have understood this. But the forces of Satan, possibly headed up in this case by the spirit of death, would certainly have understood it, and they were using their wicked power to attempt to make it happen. That is why, behind the scenes, a significant power encounter between the forces of darkness and the forces of light are shaping up.

Herod decided to arrest Peter "during the Days of Unleavened Bread" (Acts 12:3). Astute as he was, Herod may have chosen the Passover because Jews from all over would be visiting Jerusalem at that time, and obviously, more Jews would be able to witness what he was doing. The public festivities would also have allowed the word to get around more easily that Peter was being held for trial until after the Passover. At that time the execution would take place, and by now little could keep it from happening.

To avoid any possibility of his plans going awry, Herod took extraordinary security measures at the Jerusalem prison. He assigned "four squads of soldiers to keep him" (12:4). That would mean four soldiers at a time on six-hour shifts. Peter was "bound with two chains between two soldiers" (12:6), one soldier being chained to each of Peter's arms, and "the guards before the door were keeping the prison" (12:6). Maximum security!

Why would Herod take such unusual measures? Experience! Peter had been in the Jerusalem jail twice previously. The first time was with John for only one night, awaiting trial before the Sanhedrin the next day (see 4:3). The second time was with all of the apostles, and an angel had arrived during the night to free them without the guards outside knowing what had happened (see 5:17-23). This time Herod would not only post guards outside, but inside as well, chaining them to Peter so that presumably not even an angel could free him.

Prayer Can Save Lives

[5] ***Peter was therefore kept in prison, but constant prayer was offered to God for him by the church.***

This Scripture verse is fairly well known among biblical Christians, but it is not always well applied in our Christian communities today. I believe it is the single key verse to understanding Acts 12. The lesson is obvious: A cause-and-effect relationship was achieved between the prayer of the intercessors and Peter's release from prison. James was killed, and nothing is said about such a prayer meeting for him. Luke's silence does not mean, of course, that similar prayer for James *could* not have been offered. But whatever the case, we do know "that constant prayer was offered to God" on behalf of Peter and that the prayer was answered. Prayer was important enough to save Peter's life.

The phrase "constant prayer" is worth looking at for a moment. Other versions translate it as "earnestly praying" or "praying strenuously" or "praying unremittingly." This Greek word *ektenos* evidently is used to indicate a higher intensity of prayer than ordinary prayer. Luke uses it in another place to describe the intensity of Jesus' prayer in Gethsemane. There, Luke tells us that Jesus withdrew from the disciples "and He knelt down and prayed" (Luke 22:41). After a time an angel came and strengthened Him supernaturally. Following the angel's visit, Jesus went back to prayer and "He prayed more *earnestly* [*ektenos*]" (v. 44). This time when Jesus didn't pray in an ordinary way, but specifically prayed *earnestly*, "His sweat became like great drops of blood falling down to the ground" (v. 44). We recognize this as one of the most intense prayer times recorded in Scripture, but a similar level of prayer "was offered to God" (Acts 12:5) for Peter in Mary's house.

I personally became involved in the worldwide prayer movement some years ago. Since then, I have associated a great deal with those who have been called to a special ministry of prayer in our time, those who have the spiritual gift of intercession. I am not among those who have the gift of intercession, but I have been with groups of intercessors on many occasions when the intensity of prayer rises to a level roughly equivalent to Gethsemane. Even those of us who have only average levels of spiritual sensitivity can often literally feel the extraordinary spiritual power surging through such a group. The Holy Spirit comes in an unusual way, and time seems to stand still. It is a season of precious intimacy with the Father, and it brings a high degree of assurance that these prayers are being heard and acted upon in the heavenlies. A qualitative difference seems to occur between such "constant prayer" (*ektenos*) and the kind of prayer most of us are used to day in and day out.

THE GIFT OF INTERCESSION

Although any Christian can be caught up in such an intense level of prayer, and many could testify to that having happened on certain occasions, those who have the gift of intercession experience it more frequently. In my book *Your Spiritual Gifts Can Help Your Church Grow,* I define the gift of intercession as: "The special ability that God gives to certain members of the Body of Christ to pray for extended periods of time on a regular basis and see frequent and specific answers to their prayers, to a degree much greater than that which is expected of the average Christian."[7] After considerable research, my best estimate is that about 5 percent of the members of the Body of Christ have the gift of intercession.

By this I do not mean to imply that only a few Christians should intercede for others. All of us in the 95 percent category have a role to be good pray-ers and intercessors. The difference is similar to all of us having a role to witness for Christ, but only a relatively few having been given the gift of evangelist. We can't all be a Billy Graham any more than the whole body can be an eye. Nor do we all have the gift of intercession.

In my book *Prayer Shield*, I deal with the gift of intercession in considerable detail. My research has indicated that those who have the gift of intercession pray considerably longer than most. The minimum time period I found was one hour a day, but more usual for those who have the gift of intercession is between two and five hours each day. They enjoy prayer more, they see more frequent answers to their prayers, they hear from God more regularly and they pray more intensely.

Could it be that Mary, the mother of Mark, was one who had the gift of intercession? Although I can't prove it, I like to think that she did. The prayer meeting for Peter took place in her house (see Acts 12:12), so Mary's house could have been one of the first houses of prayer. Her son, John Mark, was a close colleague of Peter's, and it is fitting that Peter's very life was saved through intercession in Mary's house.

DOES PRAYER CHANGE GOD'S PLAN?

Some, I know, have difficulty believing that Herod, given the fact that a sovereign God has the whole world in His hands, could have taken Peter's life just because some believers might have neglected to pray. Can we really say that a cause-and-effect relationship is produced between our human prayers and what God Almighty does? Although I fully accept the doctrine of the sovereignty of God, I also believe prayer does change things.

One thing prayer does *not* change is the nature of God. Nor is prayer some way that we can manipulate God. This is what many of the defenders of God's sovereignty want to avoid, and I join them in this belief. However, the nature of God also includes involving human beings who have been reconciled to Him through Jesus Christ in His activities as members of His family.

As God's will unfolds, God, in His sovereignty, decides not to predetermine all that will happen among human beings, but to make a certain number of things contingent upon human participation. For example, God is not willing that any lost soul should perish (see 2 Pet. 3:9), yet He entrusts preaching the gospel to human beings. If humans choose to disobey, lost people will not be saved. The same thing happens with prayer (see Jas. 4:2b). Richard Foster says, "We are working with God to determine the future. Certain things will happen in history if we pray rightly."[8]

If, implicitly or explicitly, we doubt whether anything will be changed by our prayers, we have just made a declaration of unbelief or lack of faith. Yet, faith is a key to seeing prayers answered. Jesus said, "If you have faith as a mustard seed, you will say to this mountain, 'Move from here to there,' and it will move; and nothing will be impossible for you" (Matt. 17:20). Jesus also said, "And all things, whatever you ask in prayer, *believing*, you will receive" (21:22, emphasis added).

In my book *Churches That Pray*, I call prayer that works "action prayer." Many churches in which prayer has typically fallen more into the rhetorical category are now moving into action prayer. The major element feeding the growing excitement about prayer worldwide is seeing tangible answers to prayer. James says, "The effective, fervent prayer of a righteous man avails much" (Jas. 5:16). What does James mean by *effective* prayer? His illustration is of Elijah who prayed that it would not rain, and it didn't rain for three-and-a-half years. Then he prayed again and it started raining. Considering these illustrations both from the Bible and from contemporary experience, Walter Wink can say with confidence, "History belongs to the intercessors."[9] It helps us believe all the more that prayer did, in fact, save Peter's life.

Back to Mary, the mother of Mark. Could this intercessor have been an ongoing personal prayer partner for Peter? Again, we have no direct evidence that she was, but it is a provocative possibility.

PERSONAL PRAYER PARTNERS

Those who have the gift of intercession engage in four kinds of prayer ministries: general intercession, crisis intercession, personal intercession and warfare intercession. Some intercessors specialize in one, some in all four. Those to whom God gives a ministry of personal intercession pray a great deal for a particular leader or leaders. I believe that intercession for Christian leaders is the most underutilized source of spiritual power in our churches today. I think much greater effectiveness in ministry would be released and considerably fewer pastors would fall into sin and leave the ministry if personal intercession were more widely recognized and used across the Body of Christ. I wrote my book *Prayer Shield* to help realize that goal.

My wife, Doris, and I have an inner circle of 22 personal intercessors, and a wider circle of about 200. Whatever fruitfulness in ministry we enjoy, we attribute it primarily to the power of God released in our lives through the prayers of these faithful women and men. We have no hesitation in believing that Peter's life was saved through the prayers of Mary and her friends, because we are convinced that I would have been physically dead more than 10 years ago if it weren't for the "constant prayer" (Acts 12:5) (*ektenos*) of one of our intercessors. The powers of darkness attempted to kill me by causing me to fall off a ladder 12 feet high to land on the back of my head and neck on a cement floor on March 25, 1983. At exactly the same time, the Holy Spirit moved the intercessor, who was attending a concert in a church 15 miles away, to enter into one of those times of intense prayer similar to Jesus' prayer in Gethsemane. After 20 minutes of travail she was released, knowing the victory had been won. I was discharged from the hospital having nothing more serious than severe bruises.

Doris and I had no doubt that my life had been in danger, because the Holy Spirit had spoken to our intercessor during her intense prayer that the evil one had come to bring death and destruction. At the time, she was still relatively inexperienced in the ministry of intercession, but she had felt similar urges to pray for specific people on two other occasions during the preceding weeks. She did not yet know how to respond to those urges, however, and both of those people died! When my turn came, she responded and, thank God, she responded well!

Although we didn't know much about it at the time, the intercessor had obviously engaged in spiritual warfare. Satan and his forces of darkness lost that particular battle, because the power of God released through prayer was greater than any evil power he could muster in his attempt to kill me. A similar situation was taking place in Jerusalem here in Acts 12. Satan, in this case, was using a ruthless king instead of a fall from a ladder to do away with a Christian leader. The believers in Mary's house went into intense spiritual warfare, described as *constant prayer,* and they also won the victory.

Prayer is the chief weapon of spiritual warfare. Many other weapons are available to be sure, but prayer stands at the top of the list. While Peter was in jail during Passover, a high-level power encounter was taking place in the invisible world. I would love to be able to interview Mary, the mother of Mark, to learn the details of what was happening in that prayer session. Having interviewed many contemporary intercessors who have entered similar situations of *constant prayer,* I can well imagine some of the things that might have been going on in the heavenlies.

RELEASED BY AN ANGEL!

[7] *Now behold, an angel of the Lord stood by him, and a light shone in the prison; and he struck Peter on the side and raised him up, saying, "Arise quickly!" And his chains fell off his hands.* [8] *Then the angel said to him, "Gird yourself and tie on your sandals"; and so he did. And he said to him, "Put on your garment and follow me."* [9] *So he went out and followed him, and did not know that what was done by the angel was real, but thought he was seeing a vision.* [10] *When they were past the*

first and the second guard posts, they came to the iron gate that leads to the city, which opened to them of its own accord; and they went out and went down one street, and immediately the angel departed from him.

This is one of the clearest accounts we have of the visible and tangible activity of an angel in the New Testament. As a part of the spiritual drama of the power encounter that was taking place, let's go into some detail here. The title of this chapter suggests that we are dealing with "the power of Herod versus the power of prayer." How was the prayer of the Jerusalem believers answered?

John Stott says, "Our understanding of who this 'angel' was will depend largely on our presuppositions, and in particular whether we believe in the existence of angels and the possibility of the miraculous."[10] Certain ones who do not believe in the miraculous theorize that some sort of internal conspiracy within the prison guard could have taken place. But this is an unlikely explanation. Knowing what Luke has already written about angels in the Gospel of Luke, and earlier in Acts, we have no need to doubt that he is describing the authentic activity of a literal angel.

WHAT ARE ANGELS?

I like Gary Kinnaman's description of an angel. "Angels," he says, "are real. Angels are spiritual beings, godlike but not God. Nor are they human, or fleshy, although they may appear in human form. The precise 'substance' of their nature is unknown. They are immortal. They are not omnipresent—everywhere present at the same time—like God, but they are *immediately* present."[11] It was such a personal being who entered Peter's prison cell.

Why does God use angels? Why didn't the Holy Spirit Himself perform this miracle, as He apparently did when the "Spirit of the Lord caught Philip away" (8:39) from the Ethiopian eunuch and transported him bodily to Azotus, an equally notable miracle (see v. 40)? To me, the most satisfactory answer to this common question is not that God *has to* use angels at times to implement His will, but that He *wants to*. Sometimes He also uses human beings, and once in a while He uses demons, although against their will. On what basis God makes such choices we will probably never know in this life.

The Bible is clear from Genesis to Revelation, however, that God does use angels. Sometimes they are messengers, such as the one who told Mary she would give birth to the Messiah. Luke tells us that the angel's name was Gabriel (see Luke 1:26-38). At other times angels are delivery people, such as the one who took food and water to Elijah (see 1 Kings 19:5-8). We see angels bringing answers to prayer, providing protection and ministering to God's people. "Are they [angels] not all ministering spirits sent forth to minister for those who will inherit salvation?" (Heb. 1:14).

Most readers find it amazing that Peter, in the midst of what would usually be an emotionally charged situation, was peacefully sleeping in the prison between the two Roman guards. We might expect that he would be worrying or praying or worshiping, as Paul and Silas would do later in the prison in Philippi, but he was only sleeping. Then the angel appears.

WHAT DO ANGELS LOOK LIKE?

What does an angel really look like? Gary Kinnaman surveyed many people who had personally seen angels, in preparation for writing his book *Angels Dark and Light*. He reports "uncanny similarities" in the descriptions he received. "They are almost always very tall, usually around ten feet. They are bright, glowing white, often with a slight bluish tint. Their faces are indescribable, so their gender is unrecognizable. They are usually dressed in a full-length robe and frequently girded with a belt or sash of gold."[12] Most of those who have seen angels would know what Luke was talking about when he says "a light shone in the prison" (Acts 12:7).

Peter's release at the hands of the angel was so incredible that he himself didn't really believe it was happening. Removing the shackles with which he was chained to the guards without their knowing it (on a six-hour shift, professional military guards do not sleep), passing the two high-security guard stations outside, seeing the prison gate open as if it were on remote control, and finding himself in the streets of the city all alone was more than even an apostle of Jesus could assimilate quickly.

> [11] ***And when Peter had come to himself, he said, "Now I know for certain that the Lord has sent His angel, and has delivered me from the hand of Herod and from all the expectation of the Jewish people."***

How long it would have taken Peter to "come to himself" is left to our imagination. He first expected to wake up from a dream while still in prison, but when he realized that he had actually escaped from prison, he gave glory to God for the miracle. He soon headed directly for Mary's house where the all-night prayer meeting was still in progress.

[12] *So, when he had considered this, he came to the house of Mary, the mother of John whose surname was Mark, where many were gathered together praying.*

PRAYER AND SPIRITUAL WARFARE

Prayer saved Peter's life. From the information Luke has provided for us, it was not so much Peter's personal prayers that saved his life as it was the prayers of other members of the Body of Christ, the intercessors. By this I do not mean to discredit Peter's personal prayer life or his spirituality in the least. But in this particular incident, Luke emphasizes not the prayers of the apostle, but that "constant prayer was offered to God for him by the church" (12:5).

This is similar to Joshua's famous victory over the Amalekites in Rephidim. The battle in Rephidim was won by God's power released through intercession. But the intercession that day was not Joshua's. He was focused on fighting, not on praying. It was Moses' intercession, aided by Aaron and Hur, that moved the hand of God and gave Joshua the victory (see Exod. 17:8-14).

I think this is an excellent framework in which to understand the enormous spiritual power that can be released on behalf of Christian leaders, such as Joshua and Peter, through personal prayer partners. Not that intercession should ever be seen as a substitute for the leader's own prayer life, but we know from Scripture that it pleases God to respond to the prayers of intercessors and to release miraculous power that otherwise might have remained dormant. Details of how this is happening today can be found in my book *Prayer Shield.*

We should not lose sight of the magnitude of this power encounter. Whenever the human political authority over a population is involved, such as King Herod was, we can suspect that the spiritual battle is on the strategic or cosmic level (see Isa. 24:21 and Eph. 2:2). This power encounter was more than casting out a demon on the ground level or dealing with sorcery on the occult level. It undoubtedly involved the principalities and powers that Paul writes about in Ephesians 6:12.

STRATEGIC-LEVEL WARFARE

Peter's power encounter was similar to the spiritual battle in the heavenlies that we are allowed to glimpse briefly as a result of the prayers of Daniel the prophet. Daniel prayed that (1) God would forgive Israel for the terrible sins they had committed against Him, and that (2) the Babylonian captivity of the Jews would end. God answered Daniel's prayer immediately by sending an angel to him, much as an angel was sent to Peter in prison. But in Daniel's case, it took the angel 21 days to arrive. Why? Because he was delayed by the Prince of Persia and he needed the help of a stronger angel, Michael, to finally get through (see Dan. 10:1-14).

My point is that in both these cases we see human prayers answered by God through releasing powerful angels to implement His will. It is not always easy, either in the travail of human intercessors nor in the invisible spiritual realm, because simultaneously the forces of darkness are using whatever means they have at their disposal to counteract the ministry of good angels. In Daniel's case, the forces of darkness were able to cause some delay. This is what we call spiritual warfare, and the intensity of the battle rises the higher we move through human structures that have authority over the well-being of entire human populations.

When the spiritual warfare involved rulers such as King Cyrus of Persia or King Herod Agrippa I of Judea, we can be sure it was extremely intense. Prayer was the key to victory both times: Daniel's solitary prayer and fasting for 21 days and the intercessors in Mary's house representing the church, or the Body of Christ, in Jerusalem. Daniel didn't know the battle had been going on in the heavenlies until the angel finally arrived. And the intercessors in Mary's house certainly didn't know, because they could hardly believe it when Peter actually showed up.

GUARDIAN ANGELS?

[13] *And as Peter knocked at the door of the gate, a girl named Rhoda came to answer.* [14] *When she recognized Peter's voice, because of her gladness she did not open the gate, but ran in and announced that Peter stood before the gate.* [15] *But they said to her, "You are beside yourself!" Yet she kept insisting that it was so. So they said, "It is his angel."*

Predictably, the immediate aftermath of the miracle of Peter's release is causing no small amount of confusion. At first, the people in Mary's house thought Rhoda must have been kidding when she said Peter was there, and then they concluded, "It is his angel."

Why would the prayer participants have said this? Are there really such things as guardian angels? Do people have their own personal angels assigned to accompany them? Do people's angels resemble those whom they serve?

The idea that people, especially children, have guardian angels is so prevalent that many assume that it is something explicitly taught in the Bible. But such is not the case. The Bible teaches that angels do exist and that, among other things, they do guard people, but we don't have any clear teaching that God does assign individual angels to guard every person on a one-on-one relationship. The Jerusalem believers exclaiming "It is his angel" is about as close as any biblical passage comes. And notice that this is just reporting a human opinion—an opinion, incidentally, of the same people who had just been wrong when they said to Rhoda, "You are beside yourself!" All we do know from this is that the concept that Peter might have *his angel* was common then, as it is among many today.

[16] ***Now Peter continued knocking; and when they opened the door and saw him, they were astonished.*** [17] ***But motioning to them with his hand to keep silent, he declared to them how the Lord had brought him out of the prison. And he said, "Go tell these things to James and to the brethren." And he departed and went to another place.***

When Peter instructs them to "Go tell these things to James," he means James the brother of Jesus who had become the leader of the church in Jerusalem. This is the last we hear of Peter in Acts other than his appearance at the Council of Jerusalem in Acts 15. We do not know for sure where he went afterward nor do we know any details of his later ministry other than the little we can surmise from his two Epistles, which were written much later. Some think he eventually ministered in Rome.

KING HEROD: A DOUBLE LOSER

It is doubtful that Herod had any idea whatsoever that he was a chief combatant in a high-level, spiritual power encounter. It seems that demonic forces must have been controlling him, and their plan had been to use him to throw roadblocks into the pathway of the advance of the kingdom of God. To the extent possible, they would have kept the king ignorant of what they were doing. When Herod failed with Peter, the spirit world had little more use for the evil king.

[18] *Then, as soon as it was day, there was no small stir among the soldiers about what had become of Peter.* [19] *But when Herod had searched for him and not found him, he examined the guards and commanded that they should be put to death. . . .*

By failing to execute Peter, Herod lost big time. It is true that capital punishment was the norm for guards who let their prisoners escape in those days, but Herod could easily have waived it. He was in no lenient mood, however, because he had spread the word all over Jerusalem during the days of the Passover that the Jews would be invited to Peter's execution. Peter's escape was a public embarrassment and, consequently, the soldiers were killed. Herod had lost the spiritual power encounter and he had paid the price. However, God was not through with Herod. The worst was yet to come!

[20] *Now Herod had been very angry with the people of Tyre and Sidon . . .* [21] *So on a set day Herod, arrayed in royal apparel, sat on his throne and gave an oration to them.* [22] *And the people kept shouting, "The voice of a god and not of a man!"* [23] *Then immediately an angel of the Lord struck him, because he did not give glory to God. And he was eaten by worms and died.*

Herod had fallen deeper and deeper into perversity. Satanic forces apparently had gained free reign in his life until they brought him to make the same mistake that Lucifer made when he was originally thrown out of heaven. Lucifer said, "I will be like the Most High" (Isa. 14:14). Herod accepted the cry of the crowd, "The voice of a god and not of a man!" (Acts 12:22).

As a matter of fact, the crowd might well have been right. Herod might have been speaking with the voice of a god that had a small *g*–in other words, the voice of a demonic principality. This claim to supernatural power brought a tangible application of what Paul writes about in Romans: "God gave them up" (see Rom. 1:24). Herod had "served the creature rather than the Creator" (v. 25); God gave him up, and that was the end for him.

THE SPIRIT OF DEATH

The fact that Herod died a horrible death "eaten by worms" (Acts 12:23) might be an indication that it was evil spirits, perhaps led by the spirit of death, who actually killed him. "An angel of the Lord" (12:23) was involved as well. It would take a Frank Peretti to imagine what might be happening in the invisible world at the time. I am no Frank Peretti, but I have my personal suspicions. When I earlier described the monstrous wickedness and thirst for blood that had come through the generations of Herods, starting with Herod the Great, it appears that a spirit of death could have been passed from father to son. Some call such things "familial spirits."

As reports come in from spiritual-mapping efforts conducted in various parts of the world, the name "the spirit of death" seems to be emerging as one of the most powerful of all the ruling principalities of darkness. This may be connected with Paul's statement, "The last enemy that will be destroyed is death" (1 Cor. 15:26).

Resistencia, Argentina, was one of the first monitored and measured experiments in citywide spiritual mapping and strategic-level spiritual warfare focused on evangelism. It turned out that the most powerful of several spiritual principalities over the city was this very spirit of death. In Resistencia, the spirit of death also had a proper name, "*San La Muerte*," Spanish for "Saint Death." People fervently worshiped and served this spirit because he had promised them a good death if they did so. A high priestess directed the cult that boasted 13 shrines scattered throughout the city. Many people carried images of San La Muerte carved from human bone and surgically implanted under their skin so that San La Muerte would be with them always and that at the end of their lives he would give them a "good death."

These powers over the city of Resistencia had succeeded in keeping the gospel from spreading. The evangelical churches in Resistencia were weak and divided. They had been plateaued for more than 10 years. The three-year experiment was conducted under Harvest Evangelism, directed by my friend Ed Silvoso. My wife, Doris, and our friend Cindy Jacobs helped design and manage the strategic-level spiritual warfare phase of the project. The three years of ministry followed the guidelines found in Ed Silvoso's powerful book *That None Should Perish*. It was to culminate in a massive 11-day evangelistic crusade geared to reap the harvest that God had been ripening over the months.

When Doris and Cindy arrived in Argentina for the evangelistic crusade, they were met with some grisly news. One week previously, the high priestess of the cult of San La Muerte had been smoking in bed. Her bed caught fire and the flames consumed three things: the mattress, the woman and her idol of San La Muerte that was 10 feet away. Nothing else was burned! Satan's perverse irony was to promise her a "good death" and then finish her off in a most gruesome way. The devil does not play fair!

Our best assessment of the situation in Resistencia was that in all probability the high priestess's principal assignment from the devil at the time had been to prevent the evangelistic crusade from taking place. When she failed, the spirit world turned against her and killed her by fire. In Herod's case it was by worms. Either way, the fruit of the spirit of death is horrendous.

Acts 12 gives us the pattern. The battle lines had been set: the power of Herod versus the power of prayer. Because Christians were faithful in what some call "warfare prayer," the enemy was decisively defeated.

[24] *But the word of God grew and multiplied.*

When the demonic obstacles are cleared away, the church can grow. Unbelievers are no longer blinded by the god of this age, and they now can hear and respond to the gospel. Luke gives us an upbeat account of what a power encounter can do for evangelism.

When I reported the details of the Argentina experiment in my book *Warfare Prayer*, I said, "The evangelical population of Resistencia virtually doubled in the calendar year of 1990."[13] By the end of the two subsequent years, the increase had gone from 100 percent to 500 percent! In Resistencia "the word of God grew and multiplied." Even as I write this many years later, the kingdom of God continues to flourish in Resistencia and the surrounding area.

I like the way John Stott sums up Acts 12: "The chapter opens with James dead, Peter in prison, and Herod triumphing; it closes with Herod dead, Peter free, and the word of God triumphing."[14]

REFLECTION QUESTIONS

1. It can be confusing to see the name "Herod" used for several people. Clear up some of this confusion by reviewing and identifying those who are named Herod.
2. Why would Herod select the time of the Jewish Passover to carry out his plans to execute Peter?
3. Reread the definition of the spiritual gift of intercession. What people do you know, or do you know of, who might have this gift?
4. To what extent could you agree with Richard Foster that, "Certain things will happen in history if we pray rightly"? Why?
5. In this chapter we have explicit references to the real-life activity of angels. Have you ever had an experience that could be explained as a work of angels? Do you know anyone today who has?

13

ONWARD TO THE NATIONS

Acts 13

Till this point, cross-cultural mission to the Gentiles has been incidental in Luke's writings. Now Luke turns his full attention to systematic, evangelistic missionary outreach to the Gentile world of the first century, and by extension, to all peoples of the world ever since. The motto of the A.D. 2000 Movement, the history-making catalyst for world evangelization back in the 1990s, was: *A church for every people and the gospel for every person by the year 2000*. The theme of the rest of Acts is how the gospel can be firmly planted in every unreached people group of the world. Although there are yet some people groups to be reached, immense progress was made in the 1990s.

However, we should not carelessly equate that accomplishment with the end of history, the return of Christ or even the completion of the Great Commission. "Firmly planting the gospel in every unreached people group" is, nevertheless, an amazingly significant milestone for *cross-cultural* evangelism because when that happens every individual in the world will be able to hear the gospel from someone from their own cultural sphere. At that point, no more pioneer missions work will be left to do. This was the main goal of the A.D. 2000 Movement. Still remaining, of course, is the evangelistic task of people within each culture to evangelize every unsaved person, but by then the *mission task*, strictly speaking, would be over!

By way of review, keep in mind that this is not the first time Luke mentions Gentile evangelism in Acts. Peter blazed the trail when he evangelized the Gentiles in the house of Cornelius in Caesarea. This occurred in about the year A.D. 40, and Luke describes the event in Acts 10. The second incident was the ministry of the Cyprus and Cyrene Mission (CCM) in Antioch where Gentile churches were first planted. This occurred in about the year A.D. 45, and Luke writes about it in Acts 11. Now we come to the ministry of Paul around the year A.D. 47.

EXTENDING THE MISSION

[12:25] *And Barnabas and Saul returned from Jerusalem when they had fulfilled their ministry, and they also took with them John whose surname was Mark.*

In the last chapter, I pointed out that Acts 12 was like a parenthesis. It began with Barnabas and Paul taking relief funds from Antioch to Jerusalem, but the rest of the chapter tells of Peter's power encounter with King Herod. The end of the chapter closes the parentheses, and the last verse of Acts 12 actually belongs here with Acts 13. It opens with Barnabas and Paul returning to Antioch and young John Mark joining them. Mark's mother's house was the house of prayer in Jerusalem, and she, I suspect, was a personal intercessor for Peter. Who knows if Mary might have also been called to be a special intercessor for Barnabas and Paul now that her son Mark had joined their ministry team?

[13:1] *Now in the church that was at Antioch there were certain prophets and teachers: Barnabas, Simeon who was called Niger, Lucius of Cyrene, Manaen who had been brought up with Herod the tetrarch, and Saul.*

This passage of Scripture is so important for Christian missions that it becomes a topic of conversation in missiological circles just about as frequently as any other part of the Bible. Through the years, I have identified three questionable conclusions that some have drawn from this verse and the surrounding passage. Here are the three conclusions that I believe need to be reexamined:

1. Acts 13 marks the beginning of cross-cultural missions to the Gentiles.
2. The church at Antioch was an ethnically mixed local congregation.
3. The Antioch church was the missionary-sending agency under which Barnabas and Paul were sent out and to which they were accountable.

Let me explain.

Cross-cultural missions to the Gentiles did not begin here, but rather in Acts 11 when the missionaries from Cyprus and Cyrene went to Antioch with the express purpose of planting churches among the Gentiles in the Gentile quarters of the city. Previously, Hellenistic Jewish missionaries had gone to Antioch to plant messianic Jewish churches in the Jewish quarter. I explained this in considerable detail in chapter 10.

THE CHURCH AT ANTIOCH

It is easy to interpret the list of Barnabas, Simeon Niger, Lucius, Manaen and Saul as a selection of typical members of the church at Antioch. It is also easy to visualize the church at Antioch as if it were a fairly large multiethnic congregation of believers that met together on Sunday mornings for worship, heard the same sermon and developed a church program to serve the needs of its members. This is because our natural tendency is to relate "church" to the kind of local church that most of us attend from week to week.

This was far from the situation in Antioch. To review what we discussed in chapter 10, Antioch was a huge cosmopolitan city of 500,000. The Jews lived in a Jewish ghetto of only 25,000, and those among them who believed in Jesus and had become messianic Jews had been meeting with each other in homes for some 10 years before any Gentile churches were planted at all. The believers had no central location where they would all meet together on a regular basis, for as Jews they attended their own synagogues on the Sabbath. They abstained from pork, kept the Passover, married their children to other Jews, circumcised their male offspring and held the belief, perhaps with differing degrees of conviction, that Gentiles would need to be circumcised and become Jews in order to know God properly. They would not allow Gentiles either in their synagogues or in their homes. To eat in a Gentile home was unthinkable to them. They, like other Jews of the day, were notably ethnocentric, to put it mildly.

My understanding is that the CCM missionaries (as I have called them) evangelized the 475,000 Gentiles in various parts of the city, neighborhood by neighborhood. Again, they had no central church building, but rather, house churches. Antioch was a multicultural and multilinguistic city. In Antioch, as in cities throughout most of human history, residents who shared the same language, customs and marriage market tended to live in geographical proximity. How do I know this? I admit it is based on an assumption, namely, that Antioch would be a fairly normal city that followed predictable patterns of urban sociology and urban anthropology.

The Antioch churches were, therefore, basically homogeneous house churches or neighborhood churches. How many of the Antioch Gentile people groups, such as those of the Syrians, Greeks, Romans or any number of others, had networks of house churches growing among them we do not know. But whatever the number, the rule among them, with very few exceptions, if any, would be that the people who met regularly in any of the neighborhood house churches would have lived near each other and they would have been members of the same people group. On occasion, larger groups of them might have met together for specific purposes. Everett Harrison says, "It is likely that several groups met in homes throughout [Antioch], though we should not rule out the possibility that some public meetings for evangelistic purposes were held in halls."[1]

Keeping this picture in mind, Luke's phrase "the church that was at Antioch" (13:1) would include substantial numbers of neighborhood house churches, but not one master organization. Missiologist Dean S. Gilliland puts it this way: "The most important feature of the church was the multitude of small units, each of which met together, working out its new life in sharing blessings and working through problems. It is error to think even of Paul's urban churches as large single congregations."[2]

ANTIOCH'S PROPHETS AND TEACHERS

Church offices are now beginning to appear. In the Jerusalem church we have seen that the leaders first were the *apostles* (who then became mostly itinerant) and later *elders* who presumably were the residents of Jerusalem and to whom Barnabas and Paul delivered the offering for the poor donated by the church at Antioch. The churches had *prophets* as well, because Luke mentions, "In these days prophets came from Jerusalem to Antioch" (Acts 11:27).

This begins to flesh out what Paul later writes in Ephesians 4:11: "And He Himself gave some to be apostles, some prophets, some evangelists, and some pastors and teachers." Some call these "fivefold ministers," some label them "ascension gifts," but I like to see them as "governmental offices." Whatever the terminology, many now agree that not only do we read about these gifts and offices in the early church, but they are also fully operative today.

In Antioch, five people are listed as "prophets and teachers" (13:1). This implies the office of prophet and the office of teacher. A church office signifies that the church has recognized a particular spiritual gift that the Holy Spirit has given to a certain person, and it has authorized that person to minister with this gift in the church. Thus it can be assumed that these five had been given the spiritual gifts of prophecy and teaching. What is the difference? Here are the definitions found in my book *Your Spiritual Gifts Can Help Your Church Grow*:

> **Prophecy.** The gift of prophecy is the special ability that God gives to certain members of the Body of Christ to receive and communicate an immediate message of God to His people through a divinely anointed utterance.
>
> **Teaching.** The gift of teaching is the special ability that God gives to certain members of the Body of Christ to communicate information relevant to the health and ministry of the Body and its members in such a way that others will learn.[3]

In general, the prophets received new information from God while the teachers explained what was revealed to the church. It is not known which of the five in Antioch would have been prophets and which would have been teachers, or which might have been operating in both gifts simultaneously. William Ramsay thinks that a certain Greek construction might indicate that Barnabas, Simeon and Lucius were prophets, while Manaen and Saul (Paul) were teachers,[4] but few other biblical scholars see it exactly that way. My research on spiritual gifts shows that most Christians, especially leaders, have gift-mixes rather than solitary gifts, and that could well have been the case in Antioch.

If we read this passage rapidly, the fact might escape us that none of the five was a long-term resident of the city of Antioch. None ministered as an elder (or pastor) of one of the many house churches that were by then in full operation in Antioch, so the "prophets and teachers" (13:1) were not also called "elders." More than likely, they were what we would see today as the *foreign missionaries* who were helping to establish the national church. No information we are given would prevent us from supposing that the five were actually members of the CCM, the Cyprus and Cyrene Mission that I described in detail in chapter 10. Let's consider the five men one at a time.

Barnabas was a Hellenistic Jew born in Cyprus. He was one of the charter members of the Jerusalem church, and one of those who sold their property and donated the proceeds to the congregation (see 4:36-37). From that, it could well be taken that he was somewhat affluent. Being a Cyprian, Barnabas could easily have identified with the CCM missionaries who had gone from Cyprus to evangelize the Gentiles in Antioch (see 11:20). That might have been one reason why the leaders of the church in Jerusalem would have chosen him as the one to go to Antioch when they received the news that Gentiles were becoming believers there and that Gentile churches were rapidly forming.

It is not beyond reason to suppose that Barnabas, who must have left Jerusalem when the persecution came after Stephen's death because he was one of the Hellenists, could have been among those said to have gone from Jerusalem to Cyprus (see 11:19). If so, he could have helped plant the first churches among the Hellenistic Jews there, and they could have been some of the churches that supported the CCM. Barnabas, therefore, might have been a founder as well as a financial backer of the Cyprus and Cyrene Mission, which he would likely have joined as a field missionary when he arrived in Antioch.

Simeon was called Niger, the Latin word for black. Biblical scholars agree that he was probably from Africa, and he could well have been from the North African nation of Cyrene. He also could have been one of the original CCM missionaries to Antioch.

Lucius is said to be from Cyrene and even more likely a charter member of the CCM. Both Simeon and Lucius would have been Hellenistic Jews who had believed in Jesus as their Messiah. Some think they might have been converted in Jerusalem and left after Stephen's death, but no one knows for sure.

Manaen is said to have been "brought up with Herod the tetrarch" (13:1), possibly as a foster brother. Herod the tetrarch, who ruled over Judea and Perea, was the one who had John the Baptist beheaded. He and Manaen would have grown up in the palace of Herod the Great, which was in Caesarea. Manaen would have been a Jew because, as we have seen, Herod the Great constantly attempted to mask the fact that he was a proselyte and pretended that he was a full-blooded Jew. He would not have invited a non-Jew into his family. Kistemaker describes Manaen as "an influential person of royal descent."[5]

Saul was, of course, from Tarsus, not from Antioch.

All five of the *prophets and teachers* were therefore, according to my hypothesis, foreign missionaries who had been sent to Antioch on assignment. Because they had been ministering among the networks of house churches in Antioch, Luke can accurately describe them as being *in the church that was at Antioch*. If, as I suspect, they had planted a truly indigenous church, they would have by then turned the leadership over to the believers who were long-term permanent residents of Antioch, and they would not have made the mistake that many missionaries have made of attempting to serve as elders of the national church. The five, perhaps along with others, functioned as what we call today a "parachurch organization"—the Cyprus and Cyrene Mission.

In today's politically correct world, many attempt to showcase the church in Antioch as one big multiethnic congregation composed of Jews, Gentiles, whites and blacks. As I pointed out earlier, this is a highly questionable conclusion. The believers did not meet together as one congregation, but rather in homes located mostly in ethnically segregated neighborhoods. Consequently the house churches were, in all probability, culturally homogeneous units. The five foreign prophets and teachers would have had an itinerant ministry among the churches, but they were not natives of Antioch.

PIONEERING NEW FIELDS

[2] ***As they ministered to the Lord and fasted, the Holy Spirit said, "Now separate to Me Barnabas and Saul for the work to which I have called them."***

As a missionary team, the CCM members often would have withdrawn from the churches in Antioch for their own meetings. Waiting before the Lord in worship and prayer would have been a common experience for them. In this case they were also fasting. F. F. Bruce says, "There are indications in the New Testament that Christians were specially sensitive to the Spirit's communication during fasting."[6] As prophets, they would already have become accustomed to receiving direct revelation from God, so they had no problem in recognizing the word of the Holy Spirit to them clearly enough to put it in quotes: "Now separate to Me Barnabas and Saul for the work to which I have called them." Here is one more case, added to many we have already seen, of verbal instructions from God so specific that when the Antioch leaders later might have asked why they were sending Barnabas and Paul away, the correct answer would have been, "Because God told us to."

SODALITY VERSUS MODALITY

Keep in mind that Barnabas and Paul did not first become missionaries at this point. They were already missionaries, simply being reassigned. The process of hearing from God and reassigning the missionaries accordingly took place within what missiologists call the "sodality," or the CCM mission agency, not the "modality," or the Antioch church as such.

In 1974, missiologist Ralph D. Winter published a landmark essay called "The Two Structures of God's Redemptive Mission," laying the groundwork for subsequent modality-sodality theory.[7] In his essay, Winter established the fact that in biblical times, such as here in Antioch, the existing Jewish *synagogue* structure was largely adopted as the structure for local Christian churches, while the existing Jewish *proselytizing bands* were largely adopted as the model for missionary-sending organizations such as the CCM. The former he labels "modalities" and the latter "sodalities." For technical reasons, *sodality* seems to be a better term than *parachurch* because, in the broader sense, the sodality is legitimately part of the "church."

Winter convincingly shows that throughout history, the predominant structure for the extension of the kingdom of God into new mission frontiers has been the sodality, not the modality. Sodalities are apostolic; modalities are pastoral. Each has its essential place in the Kingdom, but for cross-cultural missions, God seems to have favored the sodality. This is why I believe it is important to understand that in Antioch the Holy Spirit evidently spoke to the *sodality* (the CCM) instead of the *modality* (the Antioch church) to "separate to Me Barnabas and Saul for the work to which I have called them" (13:2). That is the reason why I think it is inaccurate to say, as many attempt to do, that Paul and Barnabas were sent out by the *church* at Antioch.

You may be puzzled by this conclusion. It is not an attempt to demote the local church, but only to point out that, just as God can more readily speak directly to two or three elders of a church rather than to the entire membership, so also, when it comes to particulars of mission strategy, God more often speaks to apostolic teams rather than to home congregations.

COMMISSIONING WORKERS

[3] Then, having fasted and prayed, and laid hands on them, they sent them away. [4] So, being sent out by the Holy Spirit, they went down to Seleucia . . .

Fasting is again mentioned as a fairly routine spiritual discipline for the missionaries. Prayer and laying on of hands were an important part of the commissioning as well. Who laid on hands? As far as the text is concerned, the other three would have laid hands on Barnabas and Saul. Whether any others from either the sodality or the modality would have been invited to participate is a matter of conjecture. Most students of Acts think the church in general would have played some role. In all probability it did, but it should be seen as a secondary, not a primary, role.

Some scholars point out an interesting use of two Greek words for "to send" in this passage. Obviously, the chief sending agent was the Holy Spirit, and the Greek verb in the sentence "So, being *sent* out by the Holy Spirit" is *pempo,* which is usually a more proactive kind of sending or dispatching. The "send" in "they *sent* them away" is from the Greek word *apoluo,* which frequently means releasing something that has its own inherent source of energy. Thus it could be said that "they released them." Certainly here we have a combination of the two kinds of sending with the spiritual power for missionary activity coming ultimately from the Holy Spirit.

EAST CYPRUS AND THE SYNAGOGUES

[4] So, being sent out by the Holy Spirit, they went down to Seleucia, and from there they sailed to Cyprus. [5] And when they arrived in Salamis, they preached the word of God in the synagogues of the Jews. They also had John as their assistant.

Seleucia is the seaport that serves Antioch. From Seleucia, Barnabas and Paul went to Cyprus, an island about 60 miles away. Cyprus is about 140 miles long from east to west, and it was Barnabas's home territory. The principal city to the east is Salamis and the principal city to the west is Paphos.

In Salamis, Barnabas and Paul "preached the word of God in the synagogues of the Jews." This is about all we know for certain about their first stop on the missionary excursion. But it is important because it establishes a strategic pattern for most of Paul's subsequent evangelistic ministry. Whenever a city had a synagogue, Paul would begin his evangelistic work there. He apparently bypassed certain cities because they did not have a synagogue. Paul did this for several reasons.

First, Paul had a *theological reason*. The Abrahamic covenant has never been nullified. Paul later says, "For I am not ashamed of the gospel of Christ, for it is the power of God to salvation for everyone who believes, for the Jew first and also for the Greek" (Rom. 1:16). As things work out, the Jews as a people group, for the most part, push away the gospel, and the Gentiles are grafted in. Grafted into what? Grafted into the same roots coming from Abraham (see chapter 11).

Second, Paul had a *social reason*. The law of natural affinity would indicate that Paul would probably first seek out those of his own kith and kin. Wherever it might be in the Roman Empire, the Jewish community would be for Paul at most a moderate E-2 distance rather than the more radical E-3 distance.

Third, Paul had a *strategic reason*. Because Paul was called to be an apostle to the uncircumcision, his ultimate goal was to make disciples among *Gentiles* and to plant Gentile churches. To accomplish that goal, the best place to start at that point in history was the Jewish synagogue. As I have pointed out previously, three distinguishable groups of people were attached to most Jewish synagogues in the first century:

1. Jews who could trace their physical ancestry to Abraham
2. Proselytes who were born Gentiles, but who chose to convert and to become Jews instead
3. God-fearers who were also born Gentiles, but who chose to maintain their Gentile identity while associating with the synagogue as best they could so that they could follow Jehovah God

The God-fearers of the synagogue communities were by far the most receptive people to Paul's message as he traveled from place to place. Why this is true I will explain in detail when Barnabas and Paul arrive in "Antioch in Pisidia" (Acts 13:14). Meanwhile, we need to understand why they established such a pattern at the very beginning of their missionary journey.

The principle of targeting those who are already seeking is often overlooked by missionaries who sometimes assume that the likeliest converts will be those who have lost faith in their own religious culture. This may sometimes be true, but in the New Testament the major strategy is to seek the seekers.

"They also had John as their assistant" (13:5). This is John Mark, who may have been with them ever since they returned from Jerusalem to Antioch after taking the offering for the poor (see 12:25). Mark becomes important later when he and his cousin Barnabas precipitate a mission split.

WEST CYPRUS AND THE POWER ENCOUNTER

[6] *Now when they had gone through the island to Paphos, they found a certain sorcerer, a false prophet, a Jew whose name was Bar-Jesus,* [7] *who was with the proconsul, Sergius Paulus, an intelligent man. This man called for Barnabas and Saul and sought to hear the word of God.* [8] *But Elymas the sorcerer (for so his name is translated) withstood them, seeking to turn the proconsul away from the faith.* [9] *Then Saul, who is also called Paul, filled with the Holy Spirit, looked intently at him* [10] *and said, "O full of all deceit and all fraud, you son of the devil, you enemy of all righteousness, will you not cease perverting the straight ways of the Lord?* [11] *And now, indeed, the hand of the Lord is upon you, and you shall be blind, not seeing the sun for a time." And immediately a dark mist fell on him, and he went around seeking someone to lead him by the hand.*

Paphos was the capital of Cyprus in those days. Whether a synagogue was located in Paphos we are not told, but we have no reason to conclude that one did not exist and that Paul did not visit it first. Luke simply doesn't mention it. Why? Luke had something much more momentous to write about in West Cyprus. Living in Paphos was "the proconsul, Sergius Paulus, an intelligent man." With the Roman proconsul, in some sort of an established relationship, was "a certain sorcerer, a false prophet, a Jew whose name was Bar-Jesus."

Luke is setting the scene for one of the major episodes of spiritual warfare in the New Testament. John Stott remarks that Luke "brings before his readers a dramatic power encounter, in which the Holy Spirit overthrew the evil one, the apostle confounded the sorcerer, and the gospel triumphed over the occult."[8] Yale biblical scholar Susan Garrett puts it plainly: "The confrontation between Bar Jesus and Paul is also a confrontation between the Holy Spirit and the devil."[9]

What is a power encounter? A power encounter is a practical, visible demonstration that the power of God is greater than the power of the spirits worshiped or feared by the members of a given social group or by individuals. A prominent Old Testament example is seen when Elijah challenged the prophets of Baal on Mount Carmel. God visibly demonstrated His superior power by lighting the fire on the altar, and as a part of the aftermath the prophets of Baal were executed (see 1 Kings 18:20-40).

Strategic-Level Warfare?

Was the power encounter in West Cyprus an example of strategic-level spiritual warfare?

To review, the three levels of spiritual warfare most frequently encountered are *ground-level spiritual warfare,* which deals with casting demons out of an individual; *occult-level spiritual warfare,* which deals with the demonic forces behind witchcraft, sorcery, Satanism and other organized forms of the occult; and *strategic-level spiritual warfare,* which deals with confronting the territorial spirits that may control a city, a people group or some other human social network.

No one would question that, in agreement with John Stott, this story is one of the gospel triumphing over the occult. But could it possibly have reached higher than the occult level? This is a plausible question because of the relationship between the sorcerer and the highest-ranking political figure of the area, the Roman proconsul Sergius Paulus. Alliances between political leaders and the occult are extremely common today as well. They are not simply curiosities of history, as illustrated closer to home by the ongoing relationship that Mrs. Ronald Reagan maintained with an astrologer to advise her in arranging the president's schedule.

Much about this story we do not know, such as the precise identity of the spiritual principality who apparently was using Bar-Jesus as a human instrument to keep Sergius Paulus in darkness. But whatever the identity, the angel of darkness assigned to Sergius Paulus was much more than a standard rank-and-file demon. To underline the scale of this conflict, Susan Garrett points out, "Bar Jesus is closely linked with the figure of Satan."[10]

Sergius Paulus was open to the gospel. He was an "intelligent man" who "called for Barnabas and Saul and sought to hear the word of God" (Acts 13:7). This potentially could have been a major key to open the whole region to the kingdom of God. The chief opponent was Bar-Jesus, who "withstood them, seeking to turn the proconsul away from the faith" (v. 8). If Bar-Jesus failed, he would lose his job, because in a Christian environment there would be no more need for a court magician. More ominously, he was in danger that his spiritual masters, whoever they might have been, would more than likely turn against him because he had failed them and their ruler, Satan. He would have had good reason to be terrified of the punishments imposed by the kingdom of darkness.

What was at stake?

The Issue Was Power

The issue here was power; in this case it was neither truth nor morality. The lines were clearly drawn. In the visible world it was Paul versus Bar-Jesus. In the invisible world, as Susan Garrett says, "The human combatants Paul and Bar-Jesus in turn represent superhuman figures."[11] It was a clash of two kingdoms: the kingdom of God invading the kingdom of Satan. Because each side shared a common worldview that informed them of the interplay between the invisible world and the visible world, they well knew the rules of combat. The prize in the natural was the conversion of Sergius Paulus, but spiritually it could have been the opening of perhaps all of Cyprus to the gospel of Christ.

Paul was filled with the Holy Spirit (see 13:9) while his opponent, Bar-Jesus, was "full of all deceit and all fraud," explicitly a "son of the devil" (13:10).

Having the filling of the Holy Spirit, Paul was in intimate contact with the Father. In a power encounter of this magnitude it is essential to know for certain what the Father's will is at the precise moment. Paul's words "you shall be blind, not seeing the sun for a time" (13:11) should be taken as God's words spoken through Paul. Paul himself might even have been surprised at the words coming out of his mouth. Many Christian leaders can tell of occasions when they believed that what they were speaking had not been premeditated, but rather, they were words that were being given to them supernaturally.

God's power prevailed, and the sorcerer became blind for a period of time. The event, of course, was public, and the news would have spread far and wide in a short time. Jesus Christ would be seen by many to be the true Lord over Paphos and all of Cyprus.

Teaching by Word and Deed

[12] ***Then the proconsul believed, when he saw what had been done, being astonished at the teaching of the Lord.***

It is interesting that the trigger point for the proconsul's conversion was not so much what he *heard* as what he *saw*. He was "astonished at the teaching of the Lord," indicating that the kind of teaching Paul was doing was teaching both in word and in deed. One of the shortcomings of some Western missionaries in modern times has been their strong emphasis on the word and little demonstration of the deed. Fortunately, today's missionary force is now including many missionaries from the non-Western world. More and more frequently, we are receiving feedback from the field with words to this effect: "The Western missionaries brought us the knowledge of God, but the Global South missionaries are bringing us the power of God." The implication of the message was that the gospel is spreading much more rapidly now that visible demonstrations of God's power are accompanying the spoken message of the gospel.

The good news is that an increasing number of Western missionaries are now beginning to tune in to the kind of spiritual power demonstrated by the apostle Paul in West Cyprus. A deterrent in the past has been the failure of many of us to understand the awesome authority given to us by Jesus Christ through the Holy Spirit. Jesus said to His disciples, "Behold, I give you the authority . . . over all the power of the enemy" (Luke 10:19). Some believe this authority is over only the lower-ranking demons, but here in Cyprus we have seen that it was interpreted as power over Satan himself. Could we be bold enough to take what Jesus termed "*all* the power of the enemy" literally?

This is important for evangelism because, as Paul later wrote, the essential reason that the glory of Christ does not penetrate to unbelievers is that "the god of this age has blinded [their minds]" (2 Cor. 4:4). This pitches the battle on its highest plain because the "god of this age" is the devil himself. Here in West Cyprus, Paul was learning how to use this authority to get the blinders, imposed by Satan through Bar-Jesus, off of the eyes of Sergius Paulus. Susan Garrett asks how Paul could attempt to do such a thing, and then says, "The answer is that *Paul must be invested with authority that is greater than Satan's own* [emphasis hers]. In depicting Paul's successful unmasking and punishment of Bar-Jesus, Luke is saying that Paul could do the work to which he had been called because he possessed authority over all the power of the Enemy (cf. Luke 10:19)."[12]

SOME MISSION BUSINESS

[13] *Now when Paul and his party set sail from Paphos, they came to Perga in Pamphylia; and John, departing from them, returned to Jerusalem.*

Three significant changes take place in the affairs of the mission at this point.

Paul's name changes. Up till the power encounter with Bar-Jesus, Luke had been using the Jewish name Saul. From this point on, he uses the Roman name Paul. This will further emphasize that Paul's calling was that of a missionary to the Gentiles.

The leadership changes. Luke, up till this point, had always said, "Barnabas and Saul" (v. 7). Now for the first time we read, "Paul and his party." This signifies that Paul is regarded from here on as the leader.

John Mark resigns from the mission. Why did John Mark turn back? Depending on the biblical scholar you select, it could have been because he was homesick, because he didn't feel they should direct their ministry primarily at Gentiles, because he was afraid to travel through the dangerous Taurus Mountains where they were headed, or because his cousin, Barnabas, had taken a subordinate place in the mission to Paul. Since every reason I have mentioned is nothing more than an educated guess, it might not be out of order if I added one more.

My suspicion is that Mark's resignation could have come because he didn't feel called to the kind of high-level spiritual warfare he had just witnessed in Paphos. As the challenge of strategic-level spiritual warfare has been on the increase in churches today, beginning in the 1990s, it has become clear that now, as then, many good Christians and good Christian leaders do not want to have anything to do with it. This is perfectly normal. Gideon started with 32,000 men and, by God's direction, narrowed his army down to 300. The 300 were where God wanted them to be, and also the 31,700, who didn't go to the battle, were where God wanted them to be (see Judg. 6–7). If this pattern holds, it could well have been God's will that Mark be in Jerusalem rather than in south Galatia where they were heading. The fact that Paul didn't agree and later held it against Mark (see Acts 15:36-40) is incidental.

On to Turkey

[14] *But when they departed from Perga, they came to Antioch in Pisidia, and went into the synagogue on the Sabbath day and sat down*

Paul and his entourage would have traveled about 150 miles by ship and landed in the port of Adalia (today Antalya) in what we now know as Turkey. They continued 12 miles inland to Perga in the province then known as

Pamphylia. Perga was a Greek city featuring a large temple constructed to give honor to Artemis, one of the highest-ranking principalities in the Roman Empire, who had headquarters in Ephesus where she was also known as Diana of the Ephesians. Because some of the most instructive episodes of spiritual warfare in the ministry of Paul take place in Ephesus, we will postpone discussing Diana until we come to Acts 19.

Meanwhile, we could ask why "Paul and his party" (v. 13) didn't stop to preach and plant a church in Perga? Although we are not specifically told, a compelling enough reason would be that possibly Perga had no synagogue. Later Paul passes through Amphipolis and Apollonia, presumably for the same reason (see 17:1). In both cases, the synagogue is specifically mentioned as a reason why they did stop where they later did, namely, "Antioch in Pisidia" here in this text (13:14) and "Thessalonica" in 17:1.

We should also take note that although the temple to Artemis, or Diana, was located in Perga, and the most elementary spiritual mapping would presumably show that she was the territorial spirit ruling over the city, just knowing such a thing is not reason enough for engaging in strategic-level spiritual warfare. Paul was an accomplished spiritual warrior, but not trigger-happy. Obviously, God's will and His timing were different in Perga than in Paphos where God had directed Paul to engage in a high-level power encounter with Bar-Jesus. It is dangerous to the extreme to take on high-ranking demonic forces without the clear leading of the Lord and the filling of the Holy Spirit such as Paul had in West Cyprus.

Later, as we shall see, Paul did return and preach in Perga (see 14:25). Evidently the situation there had changed by then.

Antioch in Pisidia

They came to Antioch in Pisidia (13:14). This 100-mile trip on foot through rugged mountains would not have been easy. Among other things, it was known as a region infested with bandits who preyed on travelers. Some think that when Paul later said he had been "in perils of robbers" (2 Cor. 11:26), he could well have been reflecting on this particular trip. The name "Antioch" often causes confusion because it is the same name as the city of Antioch in Syria where Paul and Barnabas started this journey. Many cities were named Antioch in those days because a king named Antiochus had tried to immortalize himself by putting his name on as many cities as possible.

Why did Paul and Barnabas target "Antioch in Pisidia"? One reason could be that it was in Paul's home territory just as Cyprus had been Barnabas's home territory. Further, it was a leading city of the region and on a major trade route. But I think the most important determining factor was that a synagogue of the Jews was located in Antioch in Pisidia. Many receptive God-fearers would have been active in that synagogue.

It is also well to keep in mind that Antioch is in the region of Galatia. Soon after Paul ministered there, he wrote his first epistle to the churches, the Epistle to the Galatians. What we are about to see here has great missiological significance for the future, and this is a reason I will later include a whole chapter on the book of Galatians (chapter 15). What happens here in Antioch sets a pattern that all who engage in cross-cultural evangelism and missions need to understand as thoroughly as possible.

Paul and the others "went into the synagogue on the Sabbath day and sat down" (13:14). Then:

> [15] ***And after the reading of the Law and the Prophets, the rulers of the synagogue sent to them, saying, "Men and brethren, if you have any word of exhortation for the people, say on."***

It is good to remind ourselves that although Paul was an apostle of Jesus Christ, he was still a Jew. Furthermore, Paul was a rabbi of some prestige among first-century Jews. Because his family lived in Tarsus, about 250 miles to the east on the same trade route, Paul and his relatives would likely have been known or they would have had personal friends in the Jewish quarter of Antioch in Pisidia. It is not everyone who could claim to be a disciple of the famous rabbi Gamaliel. For these reasons, Paul was invited to speak.

The sermon Paul preached, which is Paul's first recorded sermon, is extremely significant. It is a long sermon as far as biblical sermons go. If measured by the number of Bible verses Luke dedicates to it, only two sermons in Acts are longer: Stephen's sermon to the Sanhedrin in Acts 7 (52 verses), and Peter's sermon on the Day of Pentecost in Acts 2 (36 verses). Paul's sermon here includes 26 verses. As was the case with the other two sermons, I will not reproduce it as a whole, but simply highlight some of the most significant features.

PAUL'S FIRST RECORDED SERMON

[16] ***Then Paul stood up, and motioning with his hand said, "Men of Israel, and you who fear God, listen: . . ."***

Paul addresses two audiences simultaneously: (1) "Men of Israel." These are Jews, including proselytes, who keep the law, circumcise their male children and strictly maintain a kosher kitchen. (2) "You who fear God." These are uncircumcised Gentiles who are attracted to the synagogue community and to God, but who have remained Gentiles and who have not promised to keep the whole law. They are not members of the synagogue per se.

By now, Paul has learned that *as far as his mission to plant Gentile churches as an apostle of the uncircumcision is concerned*, his primary audience in the synagogue community is the God-fearers. The ethnic Jews are also important, and some of them get saved, but in the long range this is a secondary audience. That is why, as we will see time after time, the bulk of the persecution against Paul and his colleagues comes from the ethnic Jews, not the Gentiles. *To win the God-fearing Gentiles in the synagogue community, Paul has to take the calculated risk of offending the traditional hard-core Jews.*

[17] ***The God of this people Israel chose our fathers, and exalted the people when they dwelt as strangers in the land of Egypt, and with an uplifted arm He brought them out of it.***

Paul stresses two important themes in his introductory remarks.

First, the Jews are God's chosen people. This is Paul's point of contact with his synagogue audience, his Jewish credentials. He speaks of "*our* fathers." And Paul elaborates on this through verse 22. By this, all should be certain that Paul is not anti-Semitic, although before he is through some of the Jews will begin wondering.

Second, God is a God of power. The phrase "with an uplifted arm" is at times translated "with mighty power." The time of the Exodus, to which Paul refers, was a period of some of the most concentrated displays of divine power in history, and Paul's audience would easily recognize this because they celebrated Passover every year.

God's New Plan for Salvation

After a brief review of Jewish history, Paul shows that the succession of Moses, Samuel, Saul, David and John the Baptist led directly to Jesus, who came "from this man's [David's] seed, according to the promise" (v. 23). This was a declaration that Jesus was the long-awaited Messiah.

And then came the real shocker:

> [26] *Men and brethren, sons of the family of Abraham, and* those among you who fear God, *to you the word of this salvation has been sent.*

Why was this a shocker? Because in this revelation of God's new plan of salvation, not only are the Jews included, as would be expected, but the Gentile God-fearers are also included: "those among you who fear God."

The nonnegotiable theological position of the Jews had been that, as the chosen people of God, they had been given an exclusive channel to God through the Mosaic law. Gentiles who also wanted to find God could do so only by becoming Jews through agreeing to adhere to the law. The former Gentiles, who were now proselytes among the Jews, had done that very thing. But the God-fearers had not yet made that radical step. Paul seemed to be suggesting what would be an outright heresy to the Jewish rabbis, namely, that Gentiles could be saved without first becoming Jews.

Here is the heart of the message:

> [38] *Therefore let it be known to you, brethren, that through this Man is preached to you the forgiveness of sins;* [39] *and by Him* everyone *who believes is justified from all things from which you could not be justified by the law of Moses.*

Paul speaks of "the forgiveness of sins." The Jews would consider this the Day of Atonement, which had to be repeated year after year because sins could not be forgiven once and for all. The remission of sins is a vital part of the gospel. Actually, Peter understandably mentions it more frequently than does Paul, for Peter is an apostle to the circumcision—the Jews. In his sermon on Pentecost, Peter spoke of repenting and being baptized in the name of Jesus Christ "for the remission of sins" (2:38), and at the house of Cornelius he said, "whoever believes in Him will receive remission of sins" (10:43). Peter, however, does not go as far as to risk raising the issue that "you could not be justified by the law of Moses" (13:39), although Paul, the apostle to the Gentiles, does. Paul would have known full well that many Jewish rabbis could not tolerate such a thought.

To help us understand this, imagine what would happen if someone suggested that the Daughters of the American Revolution should allow anyone at all to join their group, even recent immigrants! It is a foolish thought because it would violate the nature of the group. The Jews likewise revered their own historical DNA, and they felt that it counted for something in God's sight.

Paul also adds a further shocking truth: "everyone who believes is justified from all things." Paul's first recorded sermon bears down on one of Christianity's most important theological truths: *justification by faith*. This is a legal term that implies full acquittal. Once justification takes place it does not need to be repeated time after time. The record is wiped clean. Many would be asking, "Is this fair?" Yes, it is fair because Jesus paid the penalty for sin—death—even though He did not deserve it. Paul later puts it together by saying, "For the wages of sin is death, but the gift of God is eternal life in Christ Jesus our Lord" (Rom. 6:23). We don't deserve salvation, so it is all by grace. The Jews in Antioch, predictably, were having a difficult time absorbing these things, and the believers among them as well would not all come around quickly, as Paul's epistle to these same Galatians will later show.

Who can be justified? Paul was perfectly clear when he named his two audiences not once, but twice (see Acts 13:16,26), as being *both* Jews *and* God-fearers (Gentiles). Then he declared that *everyone* can be justified! The Jews' main message of salvation was "keep the Jewish law." Paul's new message of salvation was "believe." Humans constantly attempt to develop ways and means for them to save themselves by *works*. God, on the other hand, wants to save us by *faith*.

THE RESPONSE TO PAUL'S MESSAGE

[42] ***And when the Jews went out of the synagogue*** . . . [43] ***Now when the congregation had broken up, many of the Jews and devout proselytes followed Paul and Barnabas, who, speaking to them, persuaded them to continue in the grace of God.***

A two-pronged response came from the Jews. Some of the Jews, including the principal leaders, just "went out of the synagogue." But they were not passive. They soon took radical action against Paul and Barnabas both verbally and politically.

Many of the common rank-and-file Jews, however, believed in Jesus and were saved. This is the meaning of "persuaded them to continue in the grace of God." Some of the proselytes were also included among the new believers who would have become what we call today "messianic Jews."

The most enthusiastic and positive response, however, came from the Gentile God-fearers:

[42] *And when the Jews went out of the synagogue, the Gentiles begged that these words might be preached to them the next Sabbath.* [44] *And the next Sabbath almost the whole city came together to hear the word of God.*

The Gentile God-fearers were ecstatic—Paul's message was better than they could have dreamed! The God-fearers knew that Yahweh was the one true God and they wanted salvation. But they had not yet decided to bring themselves and their families to break social and cultural ties with their own people, become Jews and adhere to the Jewish law in order to merit that salvation. Now Paul comes along and removes the only major obstacle, telling them that through faith in Jesus Christ as the Messiah they could be saved without becoming Jews, without getting circumcised or without obeying the Mosaic law. This was truly good news, the root meaning of "gospel."

This good news would account for the God-fearers coming back on the second Sabbath, but they could have been only a small percentage of the Gentiles in Antioch. What, then, might account for the fact that *the next Sabbath almost the whole city came together to hear the word of God*?

Luke doesn't answer this question directly, so it is up to us to propose what known characteristic of the ministry of Paul and Barnabas could possibly have drawn a whole Gentile city to a public evangelistic service. It is reasonable to conclude that it might well have been that the missionaries characteristically did not minister only in *word*, but also in *deed*. After this ministry trip was over, Paul and Barnabas met with the Jerusalem Council. Luke's report of the council meeting states, "Then all the multitude kept silent and listened to Barnabas and Paul declaring how many miracles and wonders God had worked through them among the Gentiles" (15:12).

Paul's *words* might have been enough to convince the God-fearers, but it would have been the "miracles and wonders" that most likely would have attracted the rest of Antioch's Gentiles. These were not God-fearers. These were idol worshipers who were daily subjected to the fear of the evil spirits who surrounded them and who controlled much of their lives. They were not worried so much about their sins as they were worried about the demonic spirits. The God-fearers wanted justification by faith without the law. The pagans, by far the majority, wanted deliverance from the powers of darkness. Furthermore, they wanted physical healing. They were attracted to a miracle-working God. No matter which avenue they took, Paul was fulfilling his commission "to open their eyes and to turn them from darkness to light, and from the power of Satan to God" (26:18).

Paul and Barnabas planted a growing Gentile church so alive with the power of God that the believers in turn evangelized their whole area:

[48] *Now when the Gentiles heard this, they were glad and glorified the word of the Lord. And as many as had been appointed to eternal life believed.* [49] *And the word of the Lord was being spread throughout the region.*

The Jewish Uprising

[45] *But when the Jews saw the multitudes, they were filled with envy; and contradicting and blaspheming, they opposed the things spoken by Paul.* [50] *But the Jews stirred up the devout and prominent women and the chief men of the city, raised up persecution against Paul and Barnabas, and expelled them from their region.*

What had been happening in Antioch was not a trivial thing, and the Jewish leaders fully recognized the fact. They did what they could by "contradicting and blaspheming," but finally they appealed to the powers that be in the Gentile political structure and succeeded. They "expelled them from their region." The Jewish leaders had been thoroughly embarrassed by Paul's popularity, by hearing their theological nonnegotiables soundly contradicted and by the public display of the miraculous power of God that had not operated through them, but through the missionaries.

So Paul and Barnabas made a striking public declaration to the Jews:

[46] *Then Paul and Barnabas grew bold and said, "It was necessary that the word of God should be spoken to you first; but since you reject it, and judge yourselves unworthy of everlasting life, behold, we turn to the Gentiles."*

[51] *But they shook off the dust from their feet against them, and came to Iconium.*

This does not mean that as they moved from place to place Paul and his mission team no longer preached to Jews. On the contrary, the pattern of starting in the local synagogue established in Antioch in Pisidia was continued as a viable mission strategy. But because Paul ministered in similar ways in the future, the reaction was to be similar. The establishment Jews rejected his message with as much violence as they could muster, and the nucleus of the new churches he planted was largely made up of the God-fearing Gentiles. The new believers then moved out with the word of God in E-1, or monocultural, evangelism and the Gentile churches multiplied and grew.

But as far as the local situation in Antioch was concerned, the verbal declaration and the prophetic act of shaking dust off their feet, as Jesus had instructed His disciples to do in the face of rejection (see Matt. 10:14), was important to the nucleus of believers Paul and Barnabas left behind. Thus, Luke is able to report:

[52] *And the disciples were filled with joy and with the Holy Spirit.*

REFLECTION QUESTIONS

1. The church at Antioch was unlike many churches we are accustomed to today. Review the section that describes the Antioch church and list three or four important characteristics.
2. The words "sodality" and "modality" are new terms for many people. See if you can define them in your own words and then name several sodalities and modalities you know of firsthand.
3. Think of sorcerers such as Bar-Jesus. Are they really in touch with a supernatural power that can perform miracles, or are they skillful fakes such as some slight-of-hand illusionists you may know?
4. Work through the implications of a secular political ruler such as Sergius Paulus receiving power through an occult practitioner and a foreign missionary coming in and challenging that power. Do you think more such power encounters should take place today?
5. Why would Paul's message of justification by faith be good news to the God-fearers, but an incitement to riot for the ethnic Jews?

14

EXTENDING GOD'S KINGDOM UPSETS THE ENEMY

ACTS 14

Somewhere around this time, which was in late A.D. 47 or early 48, Paul was sick. When, a year or so later, he writes his Epistle to the Galatians and addresses it to these very churches, Paul says, "You know that because of physical infirmity I preached the gospel to you at the first" (Gal. 4:13). Luke does not record Paul's sickness in Acts, so it is impossible to pinpoint exactly what the disease was and why it might have forced Paul to go to this particular region. The climate of the area, which was the plateau of the Taurus Mountains at 3,600 feet, may have been a factor. Indeed, William Ramsay supposes that Paul might have become ill in Perga and left hastily to get to the higher and more healthy altitude of Galatia where Antioch of Pisidia was located.[1]

Whatever the full explanation might be, it is remarkable that Paul, in view of his infirmity, had the tremendous combination of energy and character to travel from place to place on foot, sleep wherever he could lie down, face both verbal and physical abuse and still lead an aggressive church-planting ministry across new frontiers. No wonder so many missionaries through the centuries could identify so closely with Paul. Many have similar biographies.

Through much tribulation, Paul pushes on to Iconium, Lystra and Derbe before turning back and revisiting the new churches.

ICONIUM

[1] *Now it happened in Iconium that they went together to the synagogue of the Jews . . .*

Iconium, which is called Konya today, is still in Turkey, about 80 miles east of Antioch of Pisidia. It ordinarily would have taken Paul, Barnabas and the others the better part of a week to make the journey along the well-traveled Roman trade route.

When they arrived in Iconium, they followed their normal pattern of locating the Jewish quarter, establishing themselves there among their own kind of people and attending the synagogue on the Sabbath. As we have seen, they previously did this in Salamis (see 13:5) and in Antioch (see 13:14). We do not know when Paul and Barnabas began to preach in the synagogue, but because they were in Iconium "a long time" (14:3), they likely did not begin preaching the very first Sabbath. It might have been awhile before they were actually invited to preach.

Their audience in the Iconium synagogue would have been made up, as before, of Jews—both ethnic Jews and proselytes—and of Gentiles or God-fearers, whom Luke chooses to refer to in this instance as "Greeks":

[1] . . . *and so spoke that a great multitude both of the Jews and of the Greeks believed.*

Although Paul is featured as the preacher in Antioch, here in Iconium, apparently, Barnabas also shares the pulpit. But it can be safely assumed that the message of both of them followed the lines of the model given for us in Antioch of Pisidia. The story of their ministry in Antioch took 36 verses for Luke to record, but he uses only 5 verses here for evangelizing Iconium, because he apparently believes he does not have to repeat what he had previously said. The next stop, Lystra, will be vastly different.

The results? Here Luke describes the large number of converts: "a great multitude both of the Jews and of the Greeks believed." Although Paul knew by now that the majority of believers in the nucleus of these new churches would ultimately consist of Gentile God-fearers, initially he also bore substantial fruit among ordinary ethnic Jews. Their unconverted leaders, however, perceived Paul and Barnabas as traitors to the faith of their fathers, so they predictably turned to their influential friends in the Gentile power structure of the city for help:

[2] *But the unbelieving Jews stirred up the Gentiles and poisoned their minds against the brethren.*

[3] *Therefore they stayed there a long time, speaking boldly in the Lord, who was bearing witness to the word of His grace, granting signs and wonders to be done by their hands.*

The opposition could not have reached a critical mass too quickly because Paul and Barnabas stayed there a long time. Exactly how long we do not know, but it was sufficient time to establish the nucleus of another healthy church. Their ministry while they were there bore much fruit because they ministered both in word and in deed.

Words Are Validated by Deeds

Luke describes Paul and Barnabas's ministry in word as "speaking boldly in the Lord." This effective preaching did not come about because Paul and Barnabas were extraordinary human orators. We are told of one occasion when a man fell asleep while Paul was preaching (see Acts 20:7-12; 1 Cor. 2:1-5). Nor was it because of their personal magnetism. Indeed, the most detailed physical description we have of Paul comes not from Acts, but from later history when an eyewitness resident of this city of Iconium, named Onesiphorus, is said to describe Paul as follows: "A man small of stature, with a bald head and crooked legs, in a good state of body, with eyebrows meeting and nose somewhat hooked."[2]

The reason Paul's message made such an impression was that he, along with Barnabas, preached "in the Lord." This was the power of God through the spoken word, to the extent that the same Onesiphorus also says of Paul: "Now he appeared like a man, and now he had the face of an angel."[3] This is another way of saying that the anointing of the Holy Spirit on Paul was at times so powerful, it could be seen as a tangible change in his facial countenance. I have Christian friends today who, like Onesiphorus, have a special ability to see with their physical eyes the power of the Holy Spirit resting on certain people. It is so evident to them, some have a difficult time realizing that not everyone else in the room can see the same evidence. I usually find myself in this latter company, much to the dismay and sometimes irritation of my friends who are seeing the power of the Holy Spirit in action so clearly.

But Paul and Barnabas also ministered in deed. The same Lord who was anointing them with powerful speech was "granting signs and wonders to be done by their hands." How was it that so many pagan Gentiles who apparently were not yet even in the God-fearer category were brought to Christ? Ministry in the word would have been sufficient for the conversion of many of the God-fearers because Paul and Barnabas brought just the good news they had been waiting for, as I explained in detail in the last chapter. But back in Antioch, practically the whole city came to the synagogue on the second Sabbath, not primarily because of the *word,* but because of ministry in *deed.*

A similar thing was happening here in Iconium. It is not that signs and wonders have power to save, but the signs and wonders—the deeds—were "bearing witness to the word of His grace." Without the signs and wonders, the unbelievers would not have listened so readily to the word, through which they were saved. It is unfortunate that many of today's preachers and missionaries have turned their backs on this clear biblical dynamic for evangelism.

Over the period of "a long time," here is what was happening:

> [4] *But the multitude of the city was divided: part sided with the Jews, and part with the apostles.* [5] *And when a violent attempt was made by both the Gentiles and Jews, with their rulers, to abuse and stone them,* [6] *they became aware of it and fled . . .*

Luke's statement that "a great multitude . . . believed" (v. 1), and the subsequent description of the division of the population of Iconium, give the impression that the percentage of the city that had become Christian before Paul and Barnabas left was significant. Nevertheless, the opposition prevailed. The phrase "to abuse and stone them" (v. 5) indicates nothing less than a murder plot against the missionaries. So when they heard through reliable informants that such a plot was about to be implemented, Paul and Barnabas did the prudent thing and left Iconium. They had accomplished their purpose of planting a solid church.

A DIFFERENT STRATEGY FOR LYSTRA

> [6] *They became aware of it and fled to Lystra and Derbe, cities of Lycaonia, and to the surrounding region.* [7] *And they were preaching the gospel there.* [8] *And in Lystra . . .*

Lystra was only about a day's journey on foot from Iconium. Paul and Barnabas might not have gone directly there, however, because some time or other they preached also "to the surrounding region," and they could have made a number of intentional detours to evade the pursuit of their enemies.

Nothing is said of a synagogue in Lystra, and none of the references I have been able to consult suggests that one might have been located there.

A scattering of Jews might have been living there, however, because Lystra is the place where Paul later links up with Timothy, whose mother and grandmother were Jewish. Paul and Barnabas likely would have sought out the Jews first, but in this case they undoubtedly sought them out primarily for social rather than strategic reasons. The absence of a synagogue would have also meant the absence of a significant group of God-fearers who would ordinarily have been Paul's primary target audience.

If their strategy of going to the synagogue first had been well established, why then stop at Lystra? No one knows for sure, but one possibility might have been that they were fleeing for their lives and did not have as much luxury of choice as they had when they had previously gone through Perga without stopping, for example. Another possibility might have been that God simply spoke directly to them in one way or another and told them they were to minister in Lystra and change their strategy accordingly. Behind this is the thought that our own missionary strategy, successful as it might prove to be, must always be seen as a means to an end, not as an end in itself. The end is to bring unbelievers into faith in Jesus Christ and extend the kingdom of God. If doing this requires an adjustment in strategy to make that happen, so be it.

The major adjustment that Paul made in Lystra was to assign ministry *in deed* a higher initial priority than ministry *in word*. The word would have been suitable for God-fearers, but, as in Iconium and Antioch, the pagan, non-God-fearing Gentiles would best be attracted first by the signs and wonders, and only after that to the explanation of the gospel of Jesus Christ as Savior and Lord.

The Lame Man Walks

[8] ***And in Lystra a certain man without strength in his feet was sitting, a cripple from his mother's womb, who had never walked.*** [9] ***This man heard Paul speaking. Paul, observing him intently and seeing that he had faith to be healed,*** [10] ***said with a loud voice, "Stand up straight on your feet!" And he leaped and walked.***

We have here in Lystra another specific example of "power evangelism," to use a modern term coined by John Wimber.[4] Power evangelism is evangelistic strategy based primarily on a visible manifestation of the power of God through signs, wonders, miracles and power encounters. Power evangelism was not mentioned specifically in Antioch because Luke's emphasis there was on Paul's spoken message. Nor does Luke mention signs and wonders in connection with the next stop on this missionary trip, Derbe. However, in Iconium, Luke specifies that God granted "signs and wonders" (v. 3), but he emphasizes them even more here in Lystra.

Everett Harrison concludes that miraculous manifestations "are mentioned [here] only in connection with the mission at Iconium and Lystra, but they must have occurred in the other two cities also."[5] Ernst Haenchen affirms that the wonders of God's power are "a part of God's witness to the Christian proclamation," and because of that, "when in what follows a special miracle is recounted, the reader knows that it is not an isolated event, an exceptional case, but a link in a long chain."[6]

Although Luke here emphasizes the deed, the word is not absent. The lame man first comes on the scene when "this man heard Paul speaking" (v. 9). He is described as "a cripple from his mother's womb, who had never walked" (v. 8). For those who have been active in the ministry of divine healing, as I have been for many years, the challenge of a person lame from birth comes as a rather extraordinary one. Although I have been involved in healing backs and legs, I have never as yet had the joy of seeing a cripple from birth leap and walk as a consequence of my ministry, although I have prayed for many. This is true of most of my friends. Yes, an Oral Roberts here and a John Wimber or Reinhard Bonnke there have seen them, but they also will admit that such a thing is extraordinary.

News of some of the greatest evangelistic harvest in history has come out of mainland China. Estimates have been in the thousands of conversions a day. Karen Feaver, who was part of a United States congressional delegation to Beijing, reports that Christian women who came in from Sichuan province told her, "Wherever we go, signs and wonders follow our sisters and brothers." They told her that in one meeting in which no one wanted to hear the gospel they were attempting to preach, a person who had been lame for 70 years got up and walked.[7] Such things actually do happen today, and the subsequent evangelistic effectiveness is great.

All Miracles Are Not the Same

All signs and wonders, whether healings or deliverances or nature miracles or power encounters or whatever, are not equal. They are all truly manifestations of the power of God, but some are much more dramatic than others.

Likewise, all conversions are produced by God's power, but some, as that of the apostle Paul himself, are more dramatic than most.

The healing of the lame man in Lystra was clearly one of those considered in the more dramatic category. Who knows how many boils or headaches or colds or fevers or slipped disks were also being healed through the ministry of the apostles? Who also knows how many people Paul and Barnabas prayed for who did not get healed (see 2 Tim. 4:20)? Luke, as all historians before and after, is selective. He chooses what to tell and also what not to tell. Most authors writing about signs and wonders, then and now, choose the successes, and among them the most dramatic successes, to relate to their readers. I did this, for example, when I wrote my book *How to Have a Healing Ministry in Any Church*, and John Wimber also did it in his book *Power Healing*.

On the other hand, both the late John Wimber and I have frankly admitted in our books that not all are healed, and we attempt to deal responsibly with the issues raised. In my book, I share the statistics that in my personal ministry, and also in Wimber's Vineyard Christian Fellowship, around 20 percent of those to whom we have ministered show no effects.[8] Although Luke doesn't mention the occasion in his Gospel, Matthew tells us that Jesus experienced such disappointments as well. When in Nazareth, "[Jesus] did not do many mighty works there because of their unbelief" (Matt. 13:58). In designing his Gospel, John carefully chose seven of Jesus' most astounding miracles around which to outline what we call the fourth Gospel, but he mentions no failures.

I say this to point out that simply because Luke does not choose to mention the failures in Paul's and Barnabas's ministry of signs and wonders, some mistakenly suppose that the apostles must have been 100 percent successful. Some of them then move from that rationale, by a kind of curious reasoning, to conclude that the fact that not all are healed today shows that healing ministries in particular and power evangelism in general, although prominent in the first century, are not to be included as part of our missionary strategy today. None of this was necessarily the case in Paul's time, nor do I think it is the case today.

Faith in Healing

Paul, "seeing that he had faith to be healed" (Acts 14:9), ministered directly to the lame man. What does this mean? Does this mean that divine healing will take place only when the sick person has enough faith to make it happen?

Obviously, several parallels can be drawn between healing this lame man in Lystra and healing the lame man at the Temple gate in Jerusalem in Acts 3. One of the differences, however, is that in Jerusalem nothing is said or implied that the faith of the lame man had anything to do with the healing.

To review what I mentioned at that point in discussing Acts 3, clearly a biblical relationship can be found between faith and divine healing, admitting also that the sovereign God at times chooses to bypass His ordinary *modus operandi* and heal apart from any known context of faith. The spiritual healing of Saul on the Damascus road would be an example of such divine intervention. But God *usually* moves in His supernatural power in response to faith.

The location of this faith, however, will vary from case to case. In Jerusalem, the faith was present in Peter and John, not in the lame man. When Jesus healed the centurion's servant, the faith was not in the sick servant but in an intermediary, the centurion. Here in Lystra the faith was, in fact, in the sick person, the lame man. To answer our question, then, in some cases the faith of the sick person is a factor in the healing process and in other cases it is not.

Paul had faith as well. He "said with a loud voice, 'Stand up straight on your feet!' " (14:10). Presumably guided by the Holy Spirit, Paul decided to use what we call today, for lack of a better term, a "command prayer." The most common form of healing prayer is petition, in which we ask God to do the healing by His Holy Spirit. Another form, which Paul used with the sorcerer Bar-Jesus in West Cyprus, is prayer of rebuke. The command prayer is risky, especially if done in public as we see here, because it presupposes that God has chosen to heal in this particular case and has directed the use of this form of prayer. Paul would have risked public embarrassment and a degree of discrediting his message if he had not heard from God correctly.

But Paul *had* heard from God and the lame man "leaped and walked"!

The Crowd's Reaction

[11] *Now when the people saw what Paul had done, they raised their voices, saying in the Lycaonian language, "The gods have come down to us in the likeness of men!"* [12] *And Barnabas they called Zeus, and Paul, Hermes, because he was the chief speaker.* [13] *Then the priest of Zeus, whose temple was in front of their city, brought oxen and garlands to the gates, intending to sacrifice with the multitudes.*

If Paul had been preaching in a synagogue, this incident would never have occurred. Monotheistic Jews would not have reacted the way these Gentiles did. Both Jews and Gentiles in the first century shared a worldview that allowed for the intervention of supernatural power in daily life, unlike many in our modern rationalistic world. They believed in the miraculous, in angels and in demons. But their spiritual bondages were different. As Paul later writes, the god of this age (Satan) had blinded their minds to the gospel (see 2 Cor. 4:4).

Satan blinded the Jews mainly by deceiving them into thinking so highly of the Mosaic law that they could not accept the notion of justification by faith. This became especially clear in Antioch of Pisidia. Satan blinded the Gentiles ordinarily by deceiving them into believing the lie that the demonic principalities who ruled over them and their cities were kindly and that they had the people's best interests in mind. This was especially clear here in Lystra.

Glorifying Principalities of Darkness

Two of the principalities of darkness to which the Lystrans had given special allegiance were the Greek deities Zeus (whom the Romans called Jupiter) and Hermes (whom the Romans called Mercury). The miracle of healing the lame man was so awesome in their eyes that, to explain how it must have happened, they went right to the top. In their minds, this was nothing the lesser spirits, whom they also served and to whom they sacrificed, could possibly have done. So they logically (according to their worldview) assumed that Zeus had appeared as Barnabas and Hermes had appeared as Paul. They were grateful for the healing, so they decided to honor the only power they believed could have been strong enough to have caused the miracle.

Do demonic forces ever do good things to people? Of course. Sick people treated by psychics in the Philippines actually get well, some through bloodless, physical surgery. Lonesome men and women find ardent lovers through voodoo in Haiti. Fortune-tellers in Japan warn clients of potential financial dangers and tell them how to avoid them. In Los Angeles, some distraught people learn the precise location of lost items through Santería. Demonic forces are not quaint superstitions of backward, unenlightened people. They are actual personalities who intervene in daily human life and who sometimes have amazing supernatural power. *Denying their existence does not neutralize their effectiveness*. And although many of their activities take the appearance of being good, such are only deceitful means used by the powers of darkness to accomplish their malignant ends.

What are these ends?

The devil and his forces are in the world to steal, to kill and to destroy (see John 10:10). Satan's perversity is usually underrated or totally invisible, even at the microscopic level where deadly germs constantly assault our immune systems. Just as God allows signs and wonders to point people toward eternal life, so Satan uses signs and wonders to point people to eternal death. That is why signs and wonders from God are also means, not ends. That is also why the *word* is not optional, but it must accompany the *deed*.

Deceived into thinking that the supernatural power that healed the lame man came from Zeus and Hermes, the Lystran priests were preparing to thank them through the usual means, blood sacrifice. The choice of oxen, rather than smaller animals, seems to indicate the unusual magnitude of the impression the miracle had on the community. To further impress the spirits, beautiful woolen garlands were hung on the bodies of the oxen before offering them to Zeus and Hermes. A large and public affair was taking shape.

Don't Glorify the Creature; Glorify the Creator!

[14] *But when the apostles Barnabas and Paul heard this, they tore their clothes and ran in among the multitude, crying out* [15] *and saying, "Men, why are you doing these things? We also are men with the same nature as you, and preach to you that you should turn from these vain things to the living God, who made the heaven, the earth, the sea, and all things that are in them,* [16] *who in bygone generations allowed all nations to walk in their own ways.* [17] *Nevertheless He did not leave Himself without witness, in that He did good, gave us rain from heaven and fruitful seasons, filling our hearts with food and gladness."*

History indicates that most Lystrans would have been bilingual. Lycaonian was their native tongue, but the trade language of that part of the Roman Empire was Greek. Paul and Barnabas had been preaching and conversing with the Lystrans in Greek. When the excitement about the miraculous healing swept the city, however, the Lystrans naturally reverted to their heart language, and Luke specifically tells us that "they raised their voices, saying in the Lycaonian language" (14:11).

The missionaries couldn't understand Lycaonian, so they may at first have been unaware of what was actually transpiring. If they had known, we can assume that they would have attempted to abort the pagan worship ceremony before it got as far as it did. It could have been the appearance of the oxen with their ceremonial garlands around their necks that tipped off the apostles about what was really happening.

As soon as Paul and Barnabas found out the meaning of the ceremony, however, they were appalled. They took immediate and decisive action. They wanted no part of any pagan sacrifice that involved them either as sacrificers or sacrificees. Although, as strangers, they had no special influence in the city, their temporary role as perceived incarnations of deity gave them enough authority to persuade the people not to follow through. It was no easy task, however, because at the end of the episode, Luke writes:

[18] ***And with these sayings they could scarcely restrain the multitudes from sacrificing to them.***

Three verses (14:15-17) constitute a brief summary of one of only two recorded messages that Paul preached to pagan Gentiles who were not God-fearers. The other verse will be revealed in Athens in Acts 17. Paul's main theme for the Lystrans could not be that Jesus is the Messiah fulfilling Old Testament revelation, because many of them had not so much as heard of the Old Testament. Paul's message here could be summed up in the words of Joshua: "Choose for yourselves this day whom you will serve" (Josh. 24:15).

Previously, the Lystrans had served Zeus, whom they had invited to be the patron deity over the city. A temple for the worship of Zeus stood right outside the city. They also worshiped the messenger of Zeus, Hermes, to whom they had erected a statue, dedicating the statue to Zeus. For who knows how long, the Lystrans had served these two territorial principalities of darkness along with all the other members of the hierarchy of evil under them who had been assigned by Satan to keep the Lystrans in spiritual blindness. This wasn't something marginal to their existence. As is common with animistic peoples everywhere, subservience to these dark angels was part of their conscious daily routine from morning to night. They had never known anything different. But the missionaries had come to offer them a better option.

When the Issue Is Power, Not Knowledge

The issue here is not knowledge. People who have an animistic worldview cannot be reasoned into conversion. The issue is power. Is this new God, the Father of the Lord Jesus Christ, more powerful than Zeus and Hermes? This is the question that Paul was addressing.

The reason Paul could address this issue of power was the healing of the lame man. Chances are, no miracle of this magnitude had previously been seen in Lystra. By stopping the sacrifice, Paul and Barnabas had succeeded in persuading the crowd that the power that had healed the lame man was not the power of Zeus and Hermes. From the Lystrans' point of view, if the supernatural power had not come from Zeus, who was the chief of all the gods of the Greek pantheon, it must have come from a yet higher source whom they were hearing about for the first time.

Who was this God who had so much power?

Paul revealed to them that God was "the living God, who made the heaven, the earth, the sea, and all things that are in them" (Acts 14:15; cf. Rev. 14:7). God was nothing less than the Creator—by implication, the Creator also of Zeus and Hermes. Paul's approach to the Lystrans was what Charles Kraft calls an "allegiance encounter."[9] In this instance it was not a "truth encounter," as it was in Antioch where the issue was grace versus law. Nor was it a "power encounter," as it was in West Cyprus with Bar-Jesus representing Satan versus Paul representing God. Here in Lystra God had shown His superior power, so the Lystrans were faced with the decision whether they should give up their allegiance to Zeus and Hermes and switch it to Jesus Christ.

Knowing the Old Testament and the gospel, the issue foremost in Paul's mind was that these Lystrans were glorifying the creature (Zeus and Hermes) rather than the Creator. Throughout the Bible, chapter by chapter and book by book, this is by far the sin that upsets God more than any other. It is no mere happenstance that the first two of the Ten Commandments deal with this issue: (1) "You shall have no other gods before Me" and (2) "You shall not make for yourself any carved image" (Exod. 20:3,4). Paul uses the same theme when he speaks to other pagan Gentiles later in Athens (see Acts 17:24-27), and then he elaborates on the theme in detail in Romans 1 where he says, "[They] worshiped and served the creature rather than the Creator" (Rom. 1:25). In a word, God despises idolatry more than any other sin.

What were the results? How many chose to serve God rather than Zeus and Hermes? How many took Paul's advice to "turn from these vain things" (Acts 14:15)? Luke, for some reason, does not stop to give us a church growth report here in Lystra as he does in many other places. What we do know from verse 20 is that some Christian disciples were made, and from subsequent visits of Paul to Lystra we also know that a solid church had been planted. We can only wish we had more information about the numbers.

PAUL IS RAISED FROM THE DEAD

[19] *Then Jews from Antioch and Iconium came there; and having persuaded the multitudes, they stoned Paul and dragged him out of the city, supposing him to be dead.* [20] *However, when the disciples gathered around him, he rose up and went into the city. . . .*

We may not know how many disciples had been made in Lystra, but the news of Paul's ministry there had apparently reached Iconium where Paul was still under sentence of death. The unbelieving Jews, both in Iconium and in Antioch of Pisidia, which was 100 miles away, were the instigators of the persecutions, convincing Gentile political leaders in both places that Paul and the others should be declared *persona non grata*. When they discovered Paul's whereabouts, they immediately traveled to Lystra and accomplished the same thing.

When the unbelieving Jews arrived in Lystra, they "persuaded the multitudes" that they should be allowed to carry out Paul's prescribed execution. Presumably, Paul was captured by the local security forces, and the Jews from Iconium and Antioch proceeded with their public stoning. Their purpose was to kill Paul as other Jews had done to Stephen.

Did they succeed? Was Paul really dead? The commentators I have access to assume that because Paul left Lystra alive the next day, he couldn't really have been dead. Awhile back, when we were looking at Peter raising Dorcas from the dead in Acts 9, I pointed out that a common explanation of reports of dead being raised today is that they could not have been truly dead, but they only *appeared* to be dead. I am not suggesting that such a thing as a mistaken diagnosis never occurs, and this may very well be the explanation in some cases; but not in all cases. I do not believe this was a false diagnosis.

Was Paul Really Dead?

It is safe to say that Dorcas was really dead, because Luke, a physician, tells us clearly that she was (see 9:37). Luke does not say this directly about Paul here in Lystra, however, so conclusions, accordingly, must be more tentative. My own conclusion from the information we have is that in all probability Paul was really dead, and that he was miraculously raised from the dead when the disciples gathered around him in prayer.

How do I come to this conclusion?

To start with, and most commentators would agree on this point, it is possible that a person can be dead and subsequently, through the supernatural power of God, be brought back to life. For example, Lazarus was raised by God's power after four days and his body smelled of rotting tissue. Paul raised from the dead is, therefore, at least within the scope of biblical possibilities.

Second, the Jews who were carrying out the execution presumably had prior experience in meting out capital punishment. They knew how to stone a person and they knew how to stone one to death. The fact that they had stoned Paul inside the city, then "dragged him [his body] out of the city," indicates quite persuasively that they were handling a corpse. We need not speculate whether these fanatical Jews knew the difference between death and life. No wonder they "[supposed] him to be dead." They knew the difference between a corpse and a live person.

The question remains: Why didn't Luke say so? I believe he did say so, indirectly. But apart from that, Luke was still a historian and, as we have seen on many occasions, he picks and chooses what he decides to put into print. The fact that he did not write about signs and wonders in Antioch of Pisidia, for example, is no reason to assume they did not happen there. Ernst Haenchen points out that one of the notable things about Luke's writings is his inclination toward "playing down these *pathemata*,"[10] or sufferings of the apostles. If this is true, it could be a reasonable explanation of Luke's desire to move on rapidly to the evangelistic ministry in the next stop, Derbe.

Luke may not have stressed Paul's sufferings, but Paul himself was not inhibited from writing about them, at least on occasion. Although we will never know for sure, it could well be that he flashed back to this event in Lystra when he later wrote to the Corinthians, "Once I was stoned" (2 Cor. 11:25), also affirming that he was "in deaths often" (v. 23).

Just as an aside, many associate Paul's out-of-the-body experience in the third heaven, which he relates in 2 Corinthians 12:2-4, with this execution by stoning in Lystra. However, Paul writes about that incident happening "fourteen years ago" (v. 2). Because he wrote 2 Corinthians in A.D. 54 or possibly as late as 57, and this visit to Lystra occurred no earlier than 47, the evidence does not seem to support this conclusion.

Imagine the joy of the new disciples in Lystra when they gathered around Paul's corpse, which had been dragged outside the city, and watched as "he rose up" (Acts 14:20)!

RAISING THE DEAD TODAY

It may help us in imagining such an incident to remind ourselves that similar things also happen today. Not long ago a friend of mine told me of an experience he had the previous week in Chicago. He was on the platform during an evening church meeting, and just as the time was approaching for him to deliver his message, a disturbance of some kind started near the rear of the large auditorium. Word came to the platform that a woman, well known in the congregation, had collapsed and was taken to a room near the church entrance. She was being attended by a medical doctor, also from the congregation, and the emergency paramedics had been called along with an ambulance. Right after my friend was introduced and had begun to speak, word came to the platform that the woman had died!

Few guest speakers have been faced with such a challenge. What could he say to a congregation, now swept by group trauma, with many weeping, handkerchiefs in hand? Rising to the occasion, my friend reminded the congregation that they all could be comforted because Jesus is the Resurrection and the Life. Their friend would be in Jesus' presence and ultimately participate in the resurrection of the dead. He called back the worship team, had the congregation stand, and began to lead a protracted time of worship and praise. He said to me later that it had not occurred to him at the time that the concept of Jesus as the Resurrection and the Life was also directly attached to the biblical passage telling of Lazarus being raised from the dead.

After 15 minutes or so of continuous praise, another message was delivered to the platform. They had removed the woman's body from the church and were laying it out on the stretcher to transport it to the morgue. As they did so, the woman opened her eyes and was very much alive! The congregation was ecstatic, just as the disciples in Lystra must have been, and God was glorified.

Although the woman had been pronounced dead by a medical doctor and the paramedics, some may suggest she never was really dead in the first place. Likewise, some commentators suppose that Paul was not really dead in Lystra. But at the end of the day, it doesn't really make that much difference. Whether Paul was dead or not, he was physically in critical condition. The brutal stoning had wounded his body considerably, causing cuts, bruises and possibly broken bones. The fact that "the next day he departed with Barnabas to Derbe" (14:20) represented, at the very minimum, an extraordinarily miraculous healing and restoration, which Luke also chooses not to emphasize. But the new disciples had been thoroughly convinced that the God they had decided to follow, instead of Zeus and Hermes, was a God of unsurpassed power who could save them and save their friends. They had turned "from darkness to light, and from the power of Satan to God" (26:18). The missionaries' goal had been accomplished and faith in Jesus Christ as Lord had been extended to Lystra.

DERBE

[20] . . . *And the next day he departed with Barnabas to Derbe.* [21] *And when they had preached the gospel to that city and made many disciples . . .*

Luke leaves many things to our imagination concerning the ministry of Paul and Barnabas in Derbe. Derbe was a city about 60 miles from Lystra. It would have been a journey of three days or so for the missionaries. Was a synagogue located in Derbe? How long did they stay? What was the nature of their ministry in Derbe?

We know for certain that "they . . . preached the gospel to that city." It is interesting that the city itself is mentioned as the target, although Paul was preaching to *people.* In recent times, cities have risen to the top of the agendas of many missionary strategists concerned with completing the Great Commission. Urban evangelism is receiving great attention. More and more Christian leaders, particularly those on the cutting edge of the growing movement for prayer and spiritual warfare, are becoming involved in taking their cities, to borrow the title of John Dawson's excellent book *Taking Our Cities for God.* This is not to ignore or downplay the value of reaching individuals or families for Christ, but it is to say that something in the heart of God desires entire cities to recognize Jesus Christ as Lord of all, turning to God and away from their former allegiances to such wicked spirits as Zeus and Hermes. Progress toward city transformation is being reported in various parts of the world.

Along those lines, it should be mentioned that societal transformation in general is now seen by many Christian leaders, including myself, as the major thrust of the Great Commission to disciple *nations*. God's desire that Adam should take dominion over all creation (see Gen 1:28) was frustrated in the Garden of Eden where Satan usurped Adam's authority. However, Jesus came as the Second Adam to reverse the process and see God's kingdom come on Earth as it is in heaven. Our assignment now is to push back the forces of evil with spiritual weapons, retake the dominion that Adam lost and see whole social units such as the city of Derbe come under the Lordship of Christ.

We can safely assume that the ministry of the apostles in Derbe followed the patterns previously laid down in Antioch, Iconium and Lystra. If Derbe had a synagogue, they would have started there, preaching to the God-fearers. If not, they would have approached the Gentiles with power evangelism, expecting signs and wonders to confirm the validity of the message of Jesus Christ. In any case "[preaching] the gospel to that city" would have involved ministries of both word and deed.

It is interesting that Luke mentions no persecution in Derbe. This could have been because of the brevity of his account, which is only 14 words long. But more likely, no persecution occurred because when Paul later writes to Timothy, he speaks of "persecutions, afflictions, which happened to me at Antioch, at Iconium, at Lystra" (2 Tim. 3:11). Here Paul mentions the other three cities, but not Derbe. It could have been that the absence of persecution allowed them to stay in Derbe for some time while things were cooling off in Antioch, Iconium and Lystra. In any case, what Everett Harrison says must have been true: "To have a peaceful mission here was a blessing after the stoning in Lystra."[11]

BACK TO ENEMY TERRITORY

[21] . . . *they returned to Lystra, Iconium, and Antioch,*
[22] *strengthening the souls of the disciples, exhorting them to continue in the faith, and saying, "We must through many tribulations enter the kingdom of God."*

Although they might have been in Derbe for a long enough time to let things settle down in the cities where they had been brutally persecuted, returning there would have been no easy decision. William Ramsay says, "New magistrates had now come into office in all the cities whence they had been driven."[12] Even so, the unbelieving Jews who had initiated the persecutions would still be there, at least in Iconium and Antioch. If they had persecuted once, what would keep them from doing it again? Returning so soon to these hotbeds of enemy opposition would have taken no little courage.

Why, then, would Paul and Barnabas do such a thing as to return to enemy territory? If they had pushed forward instead of retracing their steps, in a week or so they could have arrived in Tarsus, Paul's hometown. Wouldn't it have been much safer and more pleasant to spend some time with relatives and visit old friends in Tarsus?

Visiting Paul's hometown might have been more pleasant, but it would not have been good missionary strategy. What had taken place on this trip was not just routine church planting, but the sparking of people movements. At least Luke's language points in that direction. In Antioch, "almost the whole city came together to hear the word of God" (13:44). In Iconium, "a great multitude both of the Jews and of the Greeks believed" (14:1). In Derbe, they "made many disciples" (14:21). An indispensable part of people-movement strategy is post-baptismal care.

Classical missiologist Donald McGavran, the prime theoretician of people movements, says, "The quality of people-movement churches is uniquely dependent on post baptismal care. In these movements relatively large numbers of converts form new churches quickly. If they are neglected . . . a starved and nominal membership can be confidently expected." McGavran goes on to say that contrariwise, "If new congregations are nurtured with imagination and faithfulness, in ways that lead their members to a genuine advance in Christian living, solid congregations of sound Christians will result."[13] This is exactly what Paul and Barnabas had in mind when they decided to run the risk of retracing their steps.

KINGDOM WORK BRINGS CONFLICT

The one part of the teaching that Paul and Barnabas were giving to the new churches to "lead their members to a genuine advance in Christian living," as McGavran would say, is recorded by Luke as, "We must through many tribulations enter the kingdom of God" (v. 22). As I have said previously, preaching the kingdom of God must be recognized as an invasion of territories previously held by Satan in his kingdom of darkness. Taking people from darkness to light requires spiritual warfare. Satan does not release his captives without a fight. As in any other kind of warfare, spiritual warfare also involves conflict and casualties.

Jesus said the kingdom of heaven comes with violence "and the violent take it by force" (Matt. 11:12). When He told His disciples that He would build His church (see 16:18), He immediately warned them that it would involve spiritual warfare by saying, "And the gates of Hades shall not prevail against it" (16:18). Jesus then went on to say that the keys to advancing His kingdom would be "whatever you bind on earth will be bound in heaven" (16:19). The Greek word for "to bind," *deo*, is the same verb Jesus uses when He speaks of "binding the strong man" in Matthew 12:29.

In these cities in Galatia, Paul was discovering what the spiritual warfare associated with frontier evangelism would look like in practice. He later writes, "For we do not wrestle against flesh and blood, but against principalities, against powers, against the rulers of the darkness of this age, against spiritual hosts of wickedness in the heavenly places" (Eph. 6:12). Paul then describes the armor of God that we have been given through the Holy Spirit to move forward and push the enemy out of cities such as Iconium and Lystra. The analogy comes from the Roman legions that were constantly extending the borders of the Roman Empire. Their posture was always offensive. The defensive parts of the armor were only for protection, while openings were being made for cutting down the enemy with the sword. For the Christian, the sword of the Spirit is the Word of God (see 6:17).

Paul and Barnabas were teaching the new believers that even in the face of surefire opposition, they were not to huddle back in a defensive posture but they were to move aggressively against the forces of the enemy. And they did not hesitate to say that doing this would inevitably involve tribulation. Paul later prayed that the believers in Thessalonica "may be counted worthy of the kingdom of God, for which you also suffer" (2 Thess. 1:5). Paul told Timothy that "all who desire to live godly in Christ Jesus will suffer persecution" (2 Tim. 3:12). Extending God's kingdom definitely upsets the enemy.

INSTALLING THE ELDERS

[23] *So when they had appointed elders in every church, and prayed with fasting, they commended them to the Lord in whom they had believed.*

The first time through Antioch, Iconium, Lystra and Derbe, Paul and Barnabas's major goal was to win converts and form them into churches. The second time through Antioch, their major goal was to install the leadership of the churches. Few realize the critical importance of selecting leaders to assure that the fruit of evangelism is also fruit that remains. In many parts of the world today, evangelism is taking place with unbelievable rapidity, but those who give their lives to the Lord do not always become responsible members of local churches. They too often drift into nominality or dual allegiance, or they leave the Word of God and return to their idols.

The skills involved in selecting and training church leaders on the mission fields of the world are without question the most important skills that apostolically gifted missionaries can take to most fields today. Quite often the proper process is reversed—we *train* and then we *select.* Probably the greatest single error in mission field strategies today is to think that knowledge or training itself can replace the gifting of the Holy Spirit.

The Priority of Leadership

We have an excellent model of the high priority of church leadership here in the apostolic ministry of Paul and Barnabas. The timing is notable. Within a very short period of time they appointed elders. They did not set up a training institution and base leadership upon receiving a diploma. They did not require full maturity in the Christian life. They, as outsiders, did not assume the leadership themselves. They did not offer a financial subsidy to support the new leaders. I mention these things because all of the above are built into the very policies of some traditional missionary organizations.

What was Paul looking for when he visited the new churches? I believe that, as he later wrote in Romans, in 1 Corinthians and in Ephesians, he was looking for spiritual gifts. The people in the churches who by then had been recognized as having spiritual gifts, such as the gift of leadership or the gift of pastor or the gift of teaching or other gifts that would qualify them as elders of the local church, were the ones Paul and Barnabas would appoint. Keep in mind that by now the normal first-century pattern of networks of house churches spreading through the cities would have been in progress. None of the cities would have had only one local Christian congregation, but several. Each one needed leaders, and among all the churches as a group, certain people with gifts of apostle or gifts of prophecy would be recognized. At this time, however, they "appointed elders in every church" (14:23), that is, in every one of the local house churches.

Some may think that church leaders should not be appointed so hastily. In modern missions, however, our error has usually been waiting too long to appoint leaders of the national churches rather than doing it too hastily. It is of interest that a whole new genre of churches is arising today, in every part of the world, and especially in what is being called the Global South, that seem much more like the New Testament churches than the traditional churches and missions we have become used to. One characteristic of these churches, which I like to call "new apostolic" churches, is that few of their leaders have been trained in Western or Western-derived institutions. Most have been appointed to leadership as mature adults right from the grass roots, just as were the elders in Antioch, Iconium, Lystra and Derbe.

It will come as a surprise to some to learn that a rapidly growing number of modern cross-cultural missionaries are simple believers. The house churches of mainland China are a foremost example of these new apostolic churches. Many of their pastors are illiterate. Few have seen the inside of a college, or any kind of training institution, for that matter. Some have never even owned a Bible. But not only have they been multiplying churches across China at a remarkable rate, but they have also begun to tool up to move into other countries. Some, near the border of Russia, are learning the Russian language so that they can move out in cross-cultural missionary work. Others, in a Muslim region of China, are forming a grassroots mission agency to send out Chinese missionaries to the Muslim nations along the legendary Silk Road in what some call the "Back to Jerusalem" movement. One woman missionary from the Himalayas cannot read, write or count, but she *sings* the gospel and she has made thousands of converts from Hinduism.

By saying this, I am not disparaging quality education. As first a seminary professor and now Chancellor of Wagner Leadership Institute, I am personally dedicated to providing education for as many people as possible. At the same time, however, I fully recognize that God is not limited to seminary or Bible school graduates for the extension of His kingdom. God is not limited today, and He certainly was not limited in the first century. It is risky to assume that gifting alone, without training and impartation, is enough.

Risks in Selecting Church Leaders

On the other hand, is there a risk involved in installing national church leadership from the very start? Of course, but Paul was willing to take the risk. The results in Galatia were not all that good. As we will see in the next chapter, Paul had to write one of his most harsh and outspoken epistles to these leaders soon after he and Barnabas left. He then referred to them as "foolish Galatians!" (Gal. 3:1). But that did not reverse his missionary strategy. He kept appointing leaders in the new churches as he had done in Galatia.

When they ordained these elders as pastors of the local house churches, they always "prayed with fasting" (Acts 14:23). Paul would have depended a great deal on hearing from God through prayer regarding the people whom the Holy Spirit had gifted and chosen to lead the churches. Undoubtedly, some of the choices were easier than others because the elders had already been recognized as leaders, and the people in the congregations were gladly following them. Some may have been more difficult to choose. The choices would always have been made on the assumption that the local church members would have a consensus about who should be their leader. Paul and Barnabas would not have functioned as arbitrary spiritual overlords who superimposed their will on sometimes-reluctant churches. But they were apostles, and the Holy Spirit had anointed their apostolic authority.

BACK TO THE BASE: ANTIOCH

> [26] ***From there they sailed to Antioch, where they had been commended to the grace of God for the work which they had completed.*** [27] ***And when they had come and gathered the church together, they reported all that God had done with them, and that He had opened the door of faith to the Gentiles.*** [28] ***So they stayed there a long time with the disciples.***

This had been a strenuous term of missionary service, and Paul and Barnabas were ready for a furlough. They went back to Antioch of Syria and "stayed there a long time with the disciples." In Antioch was based the headquarters of what I have been calling the Cyprus and Cyrene Mission (CCM), which had sent them out and in all probability supported them. The missionaries would naturally have called together the believers from the many house churches in Antioch to share "all that God had done with them." They probably met frequently with them in various parts of the city. They were particularly eager to share that God *had opened the door of faith to the Gentiles* because it was here in Antioch that the first Gentile churches had been planted, as we saw in Acts 11.

Paul and Barnabas were in Antioch for about a year, and during that time the crucial theological issues, concerning whether Gentiles could truly be saved without being circumcised and becoming Jews, came to a head and needed to be resolved once and for all in the renowned Council of Jerusalem. More on that later.

REFLECTION QUESTIONS

1. The healing of the lame man in Lystra apparently was something other than an "ordinary" miracle. Is it proper to speak of some miracles as "ordinary" and others as "extraordinary"? Could you give examples from your own experience?
2. In evangelizing Lystra, on the cutting edge of missionary penetration were deeds such as healings and miracles rather than preaching sermons. Can you think of any place in the world today where the same thing might apply?
3. What is your opinion of whether or not Paul was actually raised from the dead? Why might your answer cause disagreement?
4. Persecution was severe for the missionaries on their trip. Think of missionaries today in dangerous areas of the world. When should they leave and when should they stay, despite the danger to themselves or to their families?
5. The way elders (or pastors) were named and put into leadership positions over the churches in the days of Paul and Barnabas was vastly different from the methods most churches use today. Is it best for us to maintain the status quo or should we make some changes? Do you think we have true apostles today?

15

SOLVING CONFLICTS IN A MULTICULTURAL CHURCH

ACTS 15 AND GALATIANS

It may seem unusual to find a chapter on Paul's Epistle to the Galatians in the middle of a commentary on Acts. No other commentator of whom I am aware does this, although Ernst Haenchen does allot four pages to Galatians in his commentary. I am including a whole chapter here, not to distract the reader from the sequence of events Luke is describing in the Acts of the Apostles, but to do just the opposite. I do not believe we can gain a full understanding of what Luke describes in Acts 15 without first being aware of the underlying situation that provokes calling an unprecedented summit meeting of church leaders at the Council of Jerusalem.

At the end of the last chapter, we left Paul and Barnabas on furlough in their home base of Antioch after serving their first term as missionaries in Cyprus and Galatia. They had planted at least four churches in Galatia in the cities of Antioch of Pisidia, Iconium, Lystra and Derbe. Because those churches were in all probability self-propagating churches, considerably more than four churches would most likely have been in existence in the region by this time. The churches were not only self-propagating, but as good indigenous churches, they were also self-governing. Paul and Barnabas had gone back to each of the churches and installed elders, which is another word for pastors. I mentioned then that it is sound missionary policy to appoint indigenous leaders in new churches, but that the risks involved should not be ignored. One of the risks is that because of the immaturity of the new elders, they can be more vulnerable than they might be later to being influenced by unhealthy deviations in doctrine and practice.

A WORST-CASE SCENARIO

What must have been Paul's worst-case scenario had unfolded in these new churches while Paul and Barnabas were on furlough. More rapidly than they would have expected, some church leaders from Jerusalem had visited the Galatian churches without the consent of either Paul or Barnabas and they began contradicting the essence of the message of salvation that Paul had preached to the God-fearers and other Gentiles.

This may well have been going on for several weeks or months without Paul and Barnabas knowing anything about it. The bad news surfaced when some of these people, or others who were affiliated with them in Jerusalem, finally arrived in Antioch where the missionaries themselves were staying. Here is how Luke describes it:

> [Acts 15:1] *And certain men came down from Judea and taught the brethren, "Unless you are circumcised according to the customs of Moses, you cannot be saved."*

This was the year A.D. 48. We need to recall that the first Gentile churches had been planted in A.D. 45 here in Antioch by what I have chosen to call the Cyprus and Cyrene Mission. Uncircumcised Gentiles at that time were professing to be true believers in Jesus Christ. This notion was so radical to the majority of born-again messianic Jewish brothers and sisters that it was totally unacceptable. Previous to that, no believers had been uncircumcised with the exception of the isolated incident in the house of Cornelius in Caesarea, which was so numerically insignificant that few had paid much attention to it.

In Antioch, however, it seemed as if a dangerous movement could be starting. The immediate response of the Jerusalem leaders had been to send Barnabas to Antioch to evaluate the situation. Barnabas liked what he saw, and he "encouraged them all that with purpose of heart they should continue with the Lord" (Acts 11:23). Barnabas stayed on in Antioch to minister to the newly saved Gentiles, and he then recruited Paul to come from Tarsus and to join the Cyprus and Cyrene Mission.

ETHNOCENTRIC CHRISTIANS

Apparently, however, the positive word that Barnabas had sent back to the leaders of the church in Jerusalem had not been unanimously accepted. As I have pointed out many times, the believers in Jerusalem were saved, they were growing in the Lord, they were filled with the Holy Spirit, they were people of prayer, they were generous with their material goods, and yet they remained monocultural, even ethnocentric, Jews. Salvation does not erase ethnicity, and the subsequent sanctification of ethnic biases and prejudices has seemed, all through history, to take longer than maturity in many other areas of the Christian life.

My point is that the controversial phenomenon of Gentile salvation was only three or four years old at this time—from A.D. 45, when the first Gentile churches were planted, to A.D. 48. The conflicts that had been surfacing were not at all surprising. It would have been more surprising if they had *not* arisen.

Paul was very upset with the ethnocentric messianic Jews from Jerusalem who came to see them in Antioch, and he told them plainly that they were wrong. He was even more upset when somehow the word got back from the new churches in Antioch of Pisidia, Iconium, Lystra and Derbe that some of these people called "Judaizers" had traveled that far and they had succeeded in deceiving some of the Gentile believers. The word "Judaizer" is not a biblical word, but it is commonly used to label those who were teaching young Gentile believers that to truly be saved they had to be circumcised and become Jews. Some Bible versions call them "the circumcision party." In my *New King James Version,* Luke describes them as "those of the circumcision who believed" (Acts 10:45).

Two Key Developments

Two extremely important developments took place at this time: (1) the face-to-face theological debate between Paul and the Judaizers in Antioch sparked the convening of the Jerusalem Council, which we will look at in the next chapter; and (2) the unsettling news from the new churches provoked Paul to write his first epistle, the Epistle to the Galatians, which we will discuss here in some detail. My intention is not to comment on the whole book of Galatians, but to highlight only those points that will help us understand Acts more thoroughly.

For those who may be aware of some of the academic issues relating to Galatians, it will be obvious that I am assuming what is known as the "South Galatian Hypothesis." This means that, in contrast to a North Galatian theory that puts the date of the Epistle to the Galatians much later, I believe that it was written to the churches in southern Galatia that Paul and Barnabas had just planted. Biblical scholar Ronald Fung assures us that, as far as the English-speaking world is concerned, the South Galatian Hypothesis "is followed by the majority of modern interpreters."[1]

Furthermore, I am aware that some scholars have not agreed that the troublemakers in the churches of Galatia were misguided Jewish believers. Some think they might have been unsaved Galatian Jews; some think they were Gentile believers; some think they were gnostics. Without discussing the pros and cons of these theories, as does Ronald Fung, I will simply affirm my agreement with his conclusion: "We take the Galatian agitators to be Jewish Christians who adopted a rigorist attitude towards Gentile Christians and sought to impose upon them circumcision and observance of the law as conditions necessary for salvation or—what amounts to the same thing—for a full Christian status."[2]

Judaizers Preach a Different Gospel

Several passages from Galatians put Paul's view of the problem in clear perspective:

> [Gal. 1:6] ***I marvel that you are turning away so soon from Him who called you in the grace of Christ, to a different gospel,***
> [7] ***which is not another; but there are some who trouble you and want to pervert the gospel of Christ.***

The message of the Judaizers was not just another legitimate option to consider, as some might regard being a Baptist or a Presbyterian or a Pentecostal today. It was much more serious than that. Paul calls it "a different gospel."

To understand why he does this, flash back to Paul's ministry in Antioch of Pisidia described earlier. In his sermon in the synagogue in Antioch (Paul's first recorded sermon), he preached that justification was by faith. He said they "could not be justified by the law of Moses" (Acts 13:39), but that forgiveness of sins comes through Jesus Christ and "by Him everyone who believes is justified" (v. 39). Salvation comes by faith, not by works, Paul said. This so infuriated the Jewish leaders in Antioch that they persuaded the municipal authorities to decree Paul's death by stoning. The Jews couldn't handle Paul's doctrine that Gentiles could be saved without first becoming Jews.

The foundational nucleus of the church at Antioch of Pisidia was made up of Gentiles who had become Christians and elders in the church without being circumcised. Then the Judaizers arrive after Paul leaves and they teach them that salvation by faith alone is incomplete. They argue that only through doing good works, such as circumcision and keeping the law, will God accept them into His family. No wonder Paul is furious:

> [Gal. 1:9] *As we have said before, so now I say again, if anyone preaches any other gospel to you than what you have received, let him be accursed.*

Strong language! The word "accursed" means to be delivered to destruction by God. It is the same word Paul later uses when he agonizes so passionately about the fact that the Jews in general were rejecting Christ, and he says, "I could wish that I myself were accursed from Christ for my brethren" (Rom. 9:3). To put it more bluntly, Paul was asking God to do away with these perverters of the true gospel!

Paul describes the Judaizers as:

> [Gal. 2:4] . . . *false brethren secretly brought in (who came in by stealth to spy out our liberty which we have in Christ Jesus, that they might bring us into bondage),* [5] *to whom we did not yield submission even for an hour, that the truth of the gospel might continue with you.*

Does Paul call into question the salvation of these Judaizers? The phrase "false brethren" might indicate it. The fact that they were "secretly brought in and came in by stealth" seems to point to some kind of conspiracy. Whatever the case, the Judaizers had an unusual amount of influence to which even Peter ultimately submitted. Paul does not say it in so many words, but we are here witnessing a powerful counterattack against the spread of the gospel by Satan's forces. If the enemy could be successful in undercutting the doctrine of justification by faith, he could effectively seal off the Christian movement as a mere Jewish cult limited forever to a tiny segment of the earth's population. He could have nullified Jesus' desire that "this gospel of the kingdom will be preached in all the world as a witness to all the nations" (Matt. 24:14).

PAUL VERSUS PETER

Paul's forthright description of his conflict with Peter regarding Gentile conversion is one of those examples of biblical honesty that gives us hope today. Despite many of the struggles we ourselves experience in attempting to live out our Christian faith, it is somewhat reassuring to know that apostles such as Paul and Peter did not always see eye to eye either. Paul had to be deeply upset when not only Peter, but also his missionary partner Barnabas, broke ranks with him during his furlough time in Antioch. Here is what Paul writes:

> [Gal. 2:11] *But when Peter had come to Antioch, I withstood him to his face, because he was to be blamed;* [12] *for before certain men came from James, he would eat with the Gentiles; but when they came, he withdrew and separated himself, fearing those who were of the circumcision.* [13] *And the rest of the Jews also played the hypocrite with him, so that even Barnabas was carried away with their hypocrisy.*

Why would Peter do this? Why would he change his behavior?

The first time Peter had eaten with Gentiles was in the house of Cornelius. This was in response to the clear vision God had given him by lowering a sheet filled with non-kosher food and inviting Peter to eat it. Then, when in Cornelius's house, he saw the Holy Spirit fall on the uncircumcised Gentiles and he heard them speak in tongues, as the apostles did on Pentecost. Peter went so far as to authorize their baptism (see Acts 10 and 11). For all we know, from that moment until the time Paul speaks of in Antioch, Peter ate with Gentiles whenever the occasion demanded. That is why Paul would write:

> [Gal. 2:14] . . . *I said to Peter before them all, "If you, being a Jew, live in the manner of Gentiles and not as the Jews, why do you compel Gentiles to live as Jews?"*

This provokes Paul to call Peter a hypocrite in public!

Peter's change had something to do with "certain men [who] came from James" (v. 12). This was James, the brother of Jesus, who by then had become the leader of the Jerusalem church. The apostles had by then begun their itinerant ministries and had given the church's responsibilities to the elders, one of whom was James.

Sometimes we are hesitant to understand that those believers, in what we often consider a model church in Jerusalem, were so ethnocentric, not to say racist. We would like to believe that the circumcision party, which taught that Gentiles had to make a racial decision to become Jews in order to be saved, was a tiny minority among the believers in Jerusalem. No concrete evidence shows that such was the case. On the contrary. If these Judaizers "came from James," they were sent by what we would call today the senior pastor. In all probability, James by then also had the office of apostle.

The Judaizers would have met with Peter in the Jewish quarter of Antioch, where they would have lodged, and they would have been circulating among the house churches of messianic believers and the synagogues on the Sabbath. Keep in mind that neither the city of Antioch nor the local house churches were integrated racially. The Judaizers would have said something to this effect: "Brother Peter, you are a very influential person. We in Jerusalem see you as one of the major apostles of the whole Jesus movement. When you were in Jerusalem with us you ate kosher food. But since you have come here to Antioch we know that you have visited so-called Gentile believers on the other side of town. You have not only participated in worship in Gentiles' houses, but we hear that you even sit down and eat with them. Don't you realize that this is controversial? Don't you realize that this can divide the Body of Christ? Some of the young believers have stumbled in their faith because of this. The church is confused. James and the other elders have sent us to help you see the harmful consequences of your behavior and encourage you to remain a true Jew as we are."

Whether this was the way the dialogue actually went or not, Peter was persuaded to change. "He withdrew and separated himself [from the Gentiles], fearing those who were of the circumcision" (v. 12).

Here was the root of the conflict between Paul and Peter. But each one brought to the situation an important personal viewpoint based on their respective prophetic callings.

The Prophetic Calling

Those who are familiar with Campus Crusade for Christ know that the first of the "four spiritual laws" is: "God loves you and has a wonderful plan for your life." The first part of fulfilling that wonderful plan is to bring a person into fellowship with God through Jesus Christ.

The second part of the plan of God for each person is to form him or her into a specific member of the Body of Christ through spiritual gifts, and then assign them to a specific ministry in the kingdom of God. This assignment is sometimes called a "prophetic calling." The word "prophetic" refers to the source of the calling, not the resultant ministry. The source is God and prophecy connotes divine-human communication. I can be secure in my calling to the degree that I am convinced it has come directly from God and is God's will for my life.

Notice how Paul referred back to such prophecy when he wrote to Timothy: "This charge I commit to you, son Timothy, according to the prophecies previously made concerning you" (1 Tim. 1:18). Both Paul and Timothy could agree on the direction Timothy was to take because they were convinced that it was God's will for his life, not some human plan.

The prophetic calling can come through a recognized prophet. It also can be a direct word from the Lord, as Paul experienced on the Damascus road. It can be an angel, as was the announcement to Mary that she would be the mother of Jesus. It can come through a group of leaders or prayer partners, which may have been Timothy's case: "Do not neglect the gift that is in you, which was given to you by prophecy with the laying on of the hands of the presbytery" (4:14). Or it can come in any number of other ways. We know how Paul received his calling, for example, but we do not have similar details concerning Peter.

Peter's Lose-Lose Predicament

The major point is that Paul and Peter each had received prophetic callings that were similar but also significantly different. Paul was called to be an apostle to the *Gentiles*; Peter was called to be an apostle to the *Jews*. Here is what Paul says:

> **[Gal. 2:7] . . . *the gospel for the uncircumcised had been committed to me, as the gospel for the circumcised was to Peter* [8] *(for He who worked effectively in Peter for the apostleship to the circumcised also worked effectively in me toward the Gentiles).***

Being sure of a prophetic calling is an important factor in any Christian leader's decision-making process. Unfortunately, many times a decision must be made in the context of a lose-lose situation. Some refer to this as being "between a rock and a hard place." No one likes to be forced to make a choice that cannot avoid offending some people, but Peter had been caught in such a predicament. The question was not whether his decision about eating with Gentiles would offend someone. The question was: Whom would Peter choose to offend?

In Antioch, Peter's decision would inevitably offend either Paul and the Gentile believers or James and the Jewish believers. When seen in that light, the choice for Peter would have been painful, but almost predictable. Peter's prophetic calling was "the apostleship to the circumcised" (v. 8). We cannot be surprised, then, when he felt that he should take the side of the Jews and no longer eat with the Gentiles.

Paul's Point of View

Predictably, Peter's decision irritated Paul immensely. He uses extremely strong language. "I withstood him to his face, because he was to be blamed" (v. 11). He labels Peter a hypocrite. These accusations were not made discreetly behind closed doors, but they were made in public: "I said to Peter before them all" (v. 14).

This was not a small thing to Paul because the very life and death of his evangelistic ministry to the Gentiles was at stake. The Judaizers were undermining the doctrine of justification by faith. Paul was speaking from his prophetic calling as an apostle to the uncircumcision. Paul had declared, "by Him [Jesus Christ] everyone who believes is justified from all things from which you could not be justified by the law of Moses" (Acts 13:39). However, Peter's friends in the Jerusalem church still strongly disagreed.

We have details on Paul's side of the story only. Because of this, many Bible students are understandably biased toward supporting Paul and condemning Peter for his actions. We also tend to be biased toward Paul because his doctrine of justification by faith apart from the law rightly has prevailed throughout Christian history, especially since the Protestant Reformation.

However, the conflict between Paul and Peter was not essentially a theological conflict. Peter had learned the rudiments of the theology of justification by faith not only from being with Jesus, but also while visiting the house of Cornelius. He asserted it publicly at the Council of Jerusalem, which was soon to be convened. The issue was not so much *theological* as *behavioral*, or what some would term *praxeological*. Let's try to see the situation through Peter's eyes.

Peter's Point of View

It is highly important at this time to try to reconstruct the overall unfolding of events that will allow us better to understand Peter's point of view.

The church in Jerusalem was in a critical point at this particular time, A.D. 48. The first wave of persecution had come in A.D. 32 following Stephen's speech. As we have seen, this persecution was directed against the believing *Hellenistic* Jews who had immigrated to Jerusalem from all over the Roman Empire. The believing *Hebrew* Jews, natives of Jerusalem, were exempted from the persecution.

Peace then reigned in Jerusalem for around eight years until Peter went to Cornelius's house in A.D. 40 and authorized the baptism of uncircumcised Gentiles. The apostles and Jerusalem church leaders cautiously accepted Peter's explanation, undoubtedly because they regarded his apostolic role so highly, and apparently this incident that took place in distant Caesarea did not provoke particularly serious problems among the Jerusalem believers themselves. As the word got out to the *unbelieving* Jews in Jerusalem, however, they became upset with Peter and the other apostles. In A.D. 42, King Herod took advantage of this tension and for political reasons initiated a new persecution, this time against the apostles. Herod killed the apostle James and almost succeeded in killing Peter. This pleased the Jews (see Acts 12:3).

Herod died two years later in A.D. 44, and following that the gospel spread rapidly among the Jews, much to the displeasure of the establishment. During the years after Herod's death, some of the Jewish Zealots, who were advocating a declaration of independence from Rome, had become influential in the political sphere. Meanwhile, the Hellenistic missionaries from Cyprus and Cyrene had gone to Antioch in A.D. 45 and planted specifically Gentile churches for the first time. The believers in Jerusalem had sent Barnabas, desiring to establish cordial relationships with them if possible. This provoked new harassment from the unbelieving Zealots in Jerusalem, who began accusing the believers of being soft on Gentiles.

Leaving the Church in the Hands of James

During this time, the apostles had begun moving out in their itinerant ministries, leaving the Jerusalem church in the hands of the elders, chief among whom was James, the brother of Jesus. From what we see in Galatians, James was by then leaning toward the stricter position on the circumcision of Gentile believers.

By the time of the overt disagreement between Paul and Peter in A.D. 48, we can well imagine that James and the other church leaders were emotionally worn down by the constant harassment they had been receiving. Understandably, they wanted peace as much as anything else. James apparently sent a message to Peter that his behavior, such as eating with Gentiles in

Antioch, was causing unnecessary turmoil in Jerusalem. Peter, feeling the emotional effects of harassment himself, thus apparently decided that preserving the peace of the Jerusalem church needed to be his highest priority at the moment, so he agreed to change his behavior.

This hypothetical reconstruction of the situation from Peter's point of view is not to excuse Peter for failing to live according to the doctrine he believed. Perhaps Paul was accurate in accusing him of hypocrisy. But at the same time, it may help us sympathize with some of the agony behind Peter's difficult decision.

The Church of Jesus Christ, through 2,000 years of history, has gone through much turmoil, similar to the turmoil taking place in the four years from A.D. 45 through A.D. 48. As I have said, the issue of Gentile circumcision is by all measurements one of the most crucial missiological challenges in the entire history of Christianity. We should not be surprised that some of the decisions that were made under such circumstances might have been unwise, and that some of the language used might have been harsher than intended. Thankfully, and to the glory of God, the disputes were responsibly dealt with and they were finally resolved in the approaching Council of Jerusalem.

The Epistle to the Galatians is Paul's personal response to these tumultuous events, previous to the Jerusalem Council. It is important to keep in mind that in his letter, Paul was addressing the Gentile churches he had planted during his first term as a missionary. He was not writing to the messianic Jews in Jerusalem. By writing to these churches, he was thereby fulfilling his personal prophetic calling. As he later said to King Agrippa, "I was not disobedient to the heavenly vision" (Acts 26:19).

GALATIANS IN A NUTSHELL

Paul, then, writes his first epistle in the midst of missiological turmoil. He is in the eye of the storm of a controversy of enormous importance. After the briefest of formal salutation, he immediately raises the issue at hand:

> [Gal. 1:6] *I marvel that you are turning away so soon from Him who called you in the grace of Christ, to a different gospel,* [7] *which is not another; but there are some who trouble you and want to pervert the gospel of Christ.*

Keeping in mind that the Judaizers had followed his trail and had tried to discredit his theology, Paul finds it necessary to establish his superior credentials as an apostle. He does this from the middle of Galatians 1 through all of chapter 2. Among other things, he mentions that the original apostles in Jerusalem had agreed with his prophetic calling to be an apostle to the Gentiles:

> [Gal. 2:9] *And when James, Cephas [Peter], and John, who seemed to be pillars, perceived the grace that had been given to me, they gave me and Barnabas the right hand of fellowship, that we should go to the Gentiles and they to the circumcised.*

As he wrote this, Paul must have felt serious frustration in realizing that the three apostles he mentioned, James (who by then had been killed by Herod), Peter and John, had later turned the Jerusalem church over to the elders under a different James, and that it was from there that these trouble-making Judaizers had come.

Having laid this foundation, Paul gets to the heart of his message and deals with the major problems arising from each of the two groups of people in the churches he had planted:

- Chapter 3 deals with the problems arising from those of the synagogue communities, namely, the Jews and former Gentile proselytes;
- Chapter 4 deals with problems arising from pagan Gentiles, including the God-fearers;
- Chapter 5 shows that both of the problems can lead to the works of the flesh as opposed to the fruit of the Spirit;
- Chapter 6 concludes with a personal note.

THE JEWISH PROBLEM: THE LAW

The God the Jews worshiped was Jehovah, the true God and Creator of the universe. For their whole lifetimes, and through generations in the past, they had been taught that God's will for them was to obey the Mosaic law. However, Paul and Barnabas had taught them that things changed when God sent His Son, Jesus, as the long-awaited Messiah. Jesus brought a new covenant that did not *destroy* the law but *fulfilled* it. Because Jesus died for all sins, the law was therefore no longer a prerequisite for salvation.

As messianic Jewish believers, they would have continued to keep the law, no problem. It was part of their native culture, given to them by God. But when they were born again, they understood that they were no longer *saved* by keeping the law, but by faith in Jesus Christ. The believing Jews had accepted this while Paul and Barnabas were there. But when the missionaries left and when the Judaizers later came, they began to change their minds and go back to the false doctrine that if they didn't keep the law they couldn't please God. This was so serious that Paul tells them they had been "bewitched."

[Gal. 3:1] *O foolish Galatians! Who has bewitched you that you should not obey the truth, before whose eyes Jesus Christ was clearly portrayed among you as crucified?* [2] *This only I want to learn from you: Did you receive the Spirit by the works of the law, or by the hearing of faith?* [3] *Are you so foolish? Having begun in the Spirit, are you now being made perfect by the flesh?*

The word "bewitched" from the Greek *baskaino* is a term that was used in the world of magic and the occult. The *New International Dictionary of New Testament Theology* says, "The meaning is to cast a spell by what is called the evil eye."[3] As F. F. Bruce explains, "Their new behavior was so strange, so completely at odds with the liberating message which they had previously accepted, that it appeared as if someone had put a spell on them."[4] This raised the possibility that these Judaizers who were going through the churches were not simply misguided and benign members of the Jerusalem church, but rather, they were perhaps cleverly disguised enemy agents empowered by Satan himself in an effort to abort the fulfillment of Jesus' Great Commission.

If the Judaizers were in fact demonized, the powerful curses they could have placed on these young believers could have subjected them once again to the law. Paul says:

[Gal. 3:10] *For as many as are of the works of the law are under the curse; for it is written, "Cursed is everyone who does not continue in all things which are written in the book of the law, to do them."* [11] *But that no one is justified by the law in the sight of God is evident, for "The just shall live by faith."*

What is wrong with the law? If you expect to get to God through the works of the law, you depend on human works and not faith. You depend on yourself for salvation, not on God.

THE GENTILE PROBLEM: EVIL SPIRITS

The Gentiles had never been in bondage to the Jewish law. The major reason that the God-fearers of the synagogue communities had not taken the step of becoming Jewish proselytes was that they did not want to submit to the law of Moses. The pain of circumcision was not the major deterrent, as some suppose. Much greater was the pain of inevitable social separation from their Gentile friends and relatives, because "the law," as it was then being interpreted, would not allow them to marry or eat with other Gentiles.

The Gentiles had been under a different bondage, that of the principalities and powers of an animistic culture. Paul puts it this way to them:

> [Gal. 4:3] ***Even so we [Jews], when we were children, were in bondage under the elements of the world.***

And later:

> [Gal. 4:8] ***But then, indeed, when you did not know God, you served those which by nature are not gods.*** [9] ***But now after you have known God, or rather are known by God, how is it that you turn again to the weak and beggarly elements, to which you desire again to be in bondage?*** [10] ***You observe days and months and seasons and years.***

The "elements" Paul mentions both in verse 3 and 9 is a translation of the Greek *stoicheia*. Kenneth Wuest says that this important word "refers to any first thing from which the others belonging to some series or composite whole take their rise. The word refers to first principles."[5]

THE TRAP OF DUAL ALLEGIANCE

Because Paul includes himself as also being under these "elements" in verse 3, *stoichea* probably has a dual meaning: (1) the original bondage of the *law* for Paul as a Jew, and (2) the original bondage of the *spirit world* for the Gentiles.

But then he becomes much more specific in verse 8 when he uses *stoicheia* in the context of "those which by nature are not gods," referring explicitly to demonic spirits; and he also says in verse 10, "You observe days and months and seasons and years," which points to the occult horoscope and all the other trappings associated with the pagan world of darkness. In other words, one of the dangers for the Gentiles in the churches of Galatia was to turn back to idolatry and yield to what missiologists call "dual allegiance."

In the last chapter, I pointed out that Paul's primary focus in preaching to the Gentiles in Lystra was an "allegiance encounter." Would they turn from Zeus and Hermes as former lords of their lives to Jesus Christ as their only Lord? The major question in their minds was whether Jesus had more power, and the healing of the lame man made it clear to anyone who wished to see that He, indeed, did.

An extremely common temptation among converts from animism is to cover all their bets and in times of crisis to draw on the powers of the demonic spirits while trying also to live a good Christian life. Missiologist Dean Gilliland tells of an unfortunate event during his ministry in Nigeria in which a pastor's wife was demonized, but neither the missionaries nor the other Nigerian church leaders could help her. The distraught pastor then took the only other recourse he could think of and consulted a witch doctor. Gilliland says, "It was sad to realize that here was a pastor whose desperation had brought him to trust again in 'those weak and pitiful ruling spirits,'"[6] in other words, the *stoicheia*.

WALKING IN THE SPIRIT

The Jewish believers in Galatia were in danger of allowing *the law* to substitute for the Spirit. The Gentile believers were in danger of allowing *demons* to substitute for the Spirit. Paul writes to them:

> [Gal. 5:16] *I say then: Walk in the Spirit, and you shall not fulfill the lust of the flesh.*

There are some objective ways to evaluate whether a person is walking in the Spirit or fulfilling the lust of the flesh.

> [Gal. 5:19] *Now the works of the flesh are . . .*

[Gal. 5:22] *But the fruit of the Spirit is . . .*

Dependence on the "elements of the world" (4:3), whether they take the form of the law of Moses or the principalities of darkness, will produce "works of the flesh." Faith in Jesus Christ promises, by His grace, to produce "the fruit of the Spirit."

ON TO THE COUNCIL

In instructing the believers in Galatia on holiness in their Christian lives, Paul is not forgetting the implications that the teaching of his enemies, the Judaizers, could have on future Gentile evangelism. To make circumcision a prerequisite for salvation would seal off the gospel from the unreached Gentiles around the world. That is why he says:

[Gal. 5:2] *Indeed, I Paul, say to you that if you become circumcised, Christ will profit you nothing.* [3] *And I testify again to every man who becomes circumcised that he is a debtor to keep the whole law.*

An implication here is that some of the Gentile believers were not only in danger of going back to "those which by nature are not gods" (4:8), but amazingly, the Judaizers might have been so strongly empowered by demonic forces that they were persuading Gentile Christians to consider physical circumcision. This never would have happened if Paul himself had been there in Antioch or Iconium or Lystra or Derbe. That is why Paul writes:

[Gal. 4:19] *My little children, for whom I labor in birth again until Christ is formed in you,* [20] *I would like to be present with you . . .*

We can safely assume that when the Judaizers had gone to Antioch of Syria, they were unsuccessful in deviating the Gentile Christians there because Paul was in fact present. Paul's confrontation with the circumcision party, his public rebuke of Peter and his writing the letter to the Galatians did not in themselves bring closure to the matters related to Gentile conversion. But these things did help to prepare Paul for the momentous summit meeting of first-century Christian leaders, the Council of Jerusalem, which Luke records in Acts 15.

REFLECTION QUESTIONS

1. We hold the church in Jerusalem in such high regard that it seems strange to read that it was a strongly ethnocentric church. Do you think the attitude of the Judaizers could compare to racism today?
2. Paul uses the term "a different gospel" and he combats it strongly in his Epistle to the Galatians. "Different" gospels have continued to appear through the years. Can you name some of them?
3. Explain in your own words why Paul would call Peter a hypocrite in public. If you were Peter, would you have continued to eat with Gentiles?
4. In Galatians, Paul writes partly to Jewish believers. What is their problem, and what is the solution?
5. Paul also writes partly to Gentile believers. What is their problem, and what is the solution?

16

THE FAMOUS JERUSALEM COUNCIL

ACTS 15

The famous Jerusalem Council was convened because of the success of what I have been calling the Cyprus and Cyrene Mission (CCM) in Antioch of Syria, and then because of Paul and Barnabas's first term as cross-cultural missionaries among the cities of Galatia. Had they failed to accomplish their goal of planting a network of Gentile churches, no controversy would have arisen at this time. The missionaries' success, however, precipitates a chain of events that ultimately breaks potential barriers for all future Christian missions. Jesus commanded His followers to "Go therefore and make disciples of all the nations" (Matt. 28:19). What happens in Jerusalem, missiologically speaking, is essential for that command to be fulfilled.

CONTEXTUALIZATION

The central missiological issue is that of *contextualization*. A church is established in one of the world's *ethne*, the Greek word for "nations." In obedience to Jesus, cross-cultural missionaries go out from one *ethnos* (or nation or people group) to another in order to plant churches. The new people group has its own culture, distinct from the culture of the sending church. At that point, the crucial questions of contextualization arise and they need to be dealt with as skillfully as possible, case by case.

In the new cultural context, what aspects of church life will be different? Which theological principles of culture A are nonnegotiable and must be maintained in culture B? Which theological principles, on the other hand, need to be reformulated, reworded or refocused in order to communicate true Christian beliefs to a different people group who have a different worldview? Will any behavioral patterns be different on the mission field? What about music, Bible translations, church government? What is essentially cultural and what is essentially Christian?

My reason for saying that these questions must be dealt with case by case is because we have no standard, universal answers to them. But a little thought will show that they are the most crucial issues cross-cultural missionaries will confront if their work is going to be everything God wants it to be. Missionaries, through the years, who have ignored these questions or who come upon the wrong answers to them, have been frustrated with minimal fruit for their labors. To put it bluntly, missiological ineptitude at the point of applied contextualization can result in lost people not being saved who otherwise would be saved.

When the first missionaries left one people group—the Jews—to plant churches in another cluster of people groups—the Gentiles—no one would have expected them to have anticipated the issues of contextualization. They were not graduates of a School of World Mission. They knew nothing of cultural anthropology. They were pioneers who would have to learn through ministry experience, by trial and error. The missionaries who went from Cyprus and Cyrene to the Gentile quarters in the city of Antioch, as well as Paul and Barnabas who evangelized Cyprus and Galatia, were trailblazers. They had no previous models to follow. Soon, when we see Paul and Barnabas addressing the Jerusalem Council, we will not hear theological discourses, but rather we will hear reports of their practical missionary experience.

FAULTY CONTEXTUALIZATION

[1] ***And certain men came down [to Antioch] from Judea and taught the brethren, "Unless you are circumcised according to the custom of Moses, you cannot be saved."***

This is the most blatant example of faulty contextualization recorded in the New Testament. In the last chapter, we looked at a detailed description of these Judaizers and their activities. Humanly speaking, their problem was that they were wearing cultural blinders. Questions of contextualization had never occurred to them. They assumed that good followers of Christ in Lystra would think like and act like good followers of Christ in Jerusalem. Those who would adopt the Judaizers' mindset have been all too frequent throughout the history of Christian missions. Many missionaries have uncritically superimposed their own highly culture-bound form of Christianity on converts in other cultures, never aware of the fundamental damage they might be doing. Most were good-hearted saints of God, although they were poor missiologists.

Paul's first confrontation with such inept missiologists came in Antioch. Not having worked through the relationships of Christianity to culture, they reflected the thinking of most Jewish believers of the day who, as missiologist Paul Pierson says, "assumed that of course pagans would be required to adopt their culture (which they believed to be superior) when they became followers of the Messiah."[1] Paul and Barnabas were incensed:

[2] ***Therefore, when Paul and Barnabas had no small dissension and dispute with them, they determined that Paul and Barnabas and certain others of them should go up to Jerusalem, to the apostles and elders, about this question.***

The confrontation described as "no small dissension and dispute" took place in Antioch, and rightly so. By then Antioch would have had the largest network of Gentile house churches of any place in the world. Why couldn't the dissension be resolved in Antioch?

HELP! CALL A SUMMIT MEETING!

For one thing, the dissension could not have been resolved in Antioch because the magnitude of the issues involved required a summit meeting where the consensus of the supreme leaders of the new Jesus movement could be attained under apostolic leadership. Ernst Haenchen reflects the virtually unanimous opinion of scholars when he says, "Chapter 15 [of Acts] is the turning point . . . the episode which rounds off and justifies the past developments, and makes those to come intrinsically possible."[2] Nothing less than the future unity of the Body of Christ was at stake here. F. F. Bruce adds, "There was a grave danger of a complete cleavage between the churches of Jerusalem and Judea on the one hand and the church of Antioch and her daughter-churches on the other."[3] This matter of whether the contextualization of the gospel could vary from people group to people group had to be resolved authoritatively and with the utmost clarity.

The church at Jerusalem, formed 10 days after Jesus' ascension into heaven on the Day of Pentecost, was then, and always will be, the mother church of the entire Christian movement. In A.D. 48, this was still a functional, not just honorific, title. It would not be functionally the mother church much longer. After the Council of Jerusalem, Ernst Haenchen says, "The only significance of Jerusalem for the further destiny of the Church is as a place of sacred memories."[4]

Having said that, there may be another less obvious, but equally plausible, reason why the debate on Gentile conversion had to be taken from Antioch to Jerusalem. It comes from Luke's statement that "[the Judaizers] determined that Paul and Barnabas and certain others of them should go up to Jerusalem." Consider the likely possibility that Paul and Barnabas were actually winning the debate in Antioch. Suppose the delegates of the circumcision party who were representing their colleagues in Jerusalem were indeed being persuaded that they were wrong? What if they were beginning to have serious doubts about whether Gentiles really needed to be circumcised in order to be saved?

If such were the case, the fact that the Judaizers were the ones who decided to take the discussion to Jerusalem would be easy to understand. They did not think they had the ability to return to Jerusalem and repeat to James, who by then had apostolic standing, and the others the persuasive arguments of Paul and Barnabas. They naturally would have said, "Please come back to Jerusalem with us and tell them just what you have told us here." If on the other hand the Judaizers had won the argument, they might have been most content to return to Jerusalem alone and take the credit.

SQUEEZING IN A DEPUTATION TOUR

[3] ***So, being sent on their way by the church, they passed through Phoenicia and Samaria, describing the conversion of the Gentiles; and they caused great joy to all the brethren.***

Paul, Barnabas and others started off for Jerusalem "being sent on their way by the church." It could have been that the networks of house churches in Antioch had some sort of an apostolic mechanism through which they could authorize Paul and Barnabas to serve as their official delegates to an ecumenical council. This, however, seems improbable to me because their recognition as apostles would in itself give them such authority, as long as they were representing the Gentile sphere to which they had been called.

"Being sent on their way" could also be taken to signify that the financial backing for the trip was provided through the believers in Antioch, most likely from the house churches in the Gentile quarters of the huge city. Apparently this was the custom, at least it was later when Paul wrote to the house churches in Rome asking them to help pay his way to Spain (see Rom. 15:24).

In chapter 5, when Paul and Barnabas were leaving Antioch for their missionary journey to Galatia, I argued that they were not sent out under the direct authority of the church, but that they were sent out by their mission—the CCM. I explained the structural difference between modalities (congregational structures) and sodalities (mission structures), pointing out that most cross-cultural missionary work throughout history has been done by sodalities. Within this framework I take the view that Paul and Barnabas did not seek or need the *authority* of the Antioch church, as if their resident apostolic authority were not enough. However, they certainly would have needed the financial *support* of the Antioch church, which they continued to receive.

Between Antioch and Jerusalem, Paul and Barnabas engaged in what many of today's missionaries would call a "deputation tour." Churches love to have informed missionaries visit because it stimulates their vision for the worldwide Christian movement and it keeps them from becoming narrowly parochial. It also helps generate prayer for the missionaries. Personal letters, newsletters, CDs, pictures or DVDs cannot substitute for a personal visit by the missionaries for whom the church has been praying.

Keep that in mind as Paul and Barnabas "passed through Phoenicia and Samaria" (Acts 15:3). We don't know for sure whom they were visiting there, but they were probably sharing the good news with the yet unconverted households of those who were following Christ. The churches they visited were not Gentile churches as were the ones they were working with in Antioch. The believers in these churches would have been circumcised and they would have been committed to obeying the Mosaic law. In Phoenicia, the churches would have consisted predominantly of Hellenistic Jews, and in Samaria, of Samaritans. The news of "the conversion of the Gentiles" came as good news to them, for Paul and Barnabas "caused great joy to all the brethren."

Apparently the theological issue related to Gentile circumcision in Antioch, and in other places, was not a particular problem in these churches.

Simple believers in local congregations are seldom on the cutting edge of theological disputes. They are usually more interested in hearing how the gospel—accompanied by power encounters, miracles, resurrections from the dead and other outworkings of power ministries—has transformed the lives of individuals and families. They want news of the expansion of the kingdom of God. Paul and Barnabas were probably exceptional missionary speakers, and the net result of their visits was positive and stimulating.

THE DEBATE STARTS

[4] *And when they had come to Jerusalem, they were received by the church and the apostles and the elders; and they reported all things that God had done with them.* [5] *But some of the sect of the Pharisees who believed rose up, saying, "It is necessary to circumcise them, and to command them to keep the law of Moses."*

When Paul and Barnabas and their entourage arrived in Jerusalem, arrangements had been made for the summit meeting. The news that Paul and Barnabas had agreed to go to Jerusalem may have reached Jerusalem any number of ways, one possibility being that the Judaizers who had confronted Paul in Antioch had returned directly to Jerusalem while the others were traveling at a slower pace, visiting the churches in Phoenicia and Syria.

"They were received by the church and the apostles and the elders." Naturally, the church and the elders would have been there. But the presence of the *apostles* is unusual if, as I suspect, they had by then set out for other places on their itinerant work. I believe that many of the original 12 apostles would have been there. Given the difficulties of travel in those days, the presence of some of those apostles in Jerusalem is a convincing indication that the leaders were fully aware of the transcendent significance of the approaching council.

JAMES: A "HORIZONTAL APOSTLE"

James of Jerusalem takes charge as the moderator. The fact that he could call together the apostles, including some or all of the original 12, reflects an anointing that I call that of a "horizontal apostle." Peter and Paul, in contrast, were "vertical apostles," exercising apostolic authority over a number of churches in their particular apostolic spheres. James had an important role as an elder of the church in Jerusalem, but he also had a God-given apostolic power of convocation. I doubt sincerely if either Peter or Paul could have called the meeting. For a starter, they didn't even like each other very much, as we have seen!

Luke does not choose to emphasize the spiritual activities that must have been associated with such a meeting. Therefore, our collective impressions of these events in books and sermons usually deal with the experiences Paul and Barnabas had on the mission field, the reactionary theology of "the sect of the Pharisees" and the mechanisms of how the Council of Jerusalem was conducted. Although these are of central importance, we must suppose that other gifts of the Holy Spirit, such as prophecy and intercession, had been activated. For example, part of "the church" that received Paul and Barnabas would have been the group of intercessors who met in the house of Mary, the mother of Mark (see 12:12). Knowing the desire of Satan to abort the whole Christian movement at this early stage, the spiritual warfare accompanying the Jerusalem Council must have been intense, and it is not beyond reason to suppose that the frontline engagement with the enemy was taking place in Mary's house as it did when Peter was delivered from prison.

An Open Forum

The first thing James did was open the floor and give opportunity for each one present to express their opinions. No one knows how long this took. It might have been several days. But it was very important that each one of the apostles be satisfied that their point of view had been heard and understood.

Paul and Barnabas "reported all things that God had done with them" (15:4). The response to their reports was probably quite different, however, from that of the churches in Phoenicia and Samaria. Luke does not say that these same reports caused "great joy" among the brethren in Jerusalem. Instead, he tells us that some people in the audience directly confronted them, telling them they were wrong! The members of "the sect of the Pharisees" were those who were supposed to be the experts on the Bible, which at that time was the Old Testament. They were the ranking theologians, the professionals.

There is little question that these theologians' knowledge of the Bible was accurate. But like any number of theologians today who also know the Bible well, they failed to tune in to some of the new things God was doing in their midst. They were not hearing what the Spirit was saying to the churches at that time. But they did represent a widespread bias among the leaders of the messianic Jewish movement of the day, namely, that non-Jews were not *fully* acceptable to God and, therefore, Gentiles could not be saved without first becoming Jews through circumcision, and all the other things that were standard to Judaism.

The results of the Jerusalem Council were not a foregone conclusion. It would not be a simple matter to gain a consensus among those leaders who had gathered in Jerusalem that what Paul and Barnabas had been doing and saying would be acceptable to all from now on.

Fortunately, the Pharisee believers, professionals that they were, could not intimidate Paul, who likewise had the credentials of a Pharisee as well as a former member of the Sanhedrin. And few of them, if any, would have had the seniority of a Barnabas who was nothing less than a charter member of the Jerusalem church. The sides seemed evenly matched, and all recognized and were willing to submit to the apostolic leadership of James for the occasion.

THE COUNCIL COMES TO ORDER

[6] ***So the apostles and elders came together to consider this matter.***
[7] ***And when there had been much dispute . . .***

The Jerusalem Council was a meeting of the apostles representing the church at large, the elders of the Jerusalem church and the missionaries and their colleagues from Antioch. "The church" (v. 4) in general had gathered to hear the missionaries' report previous to the council, but the deliberations on these momentous issues in the council itself were rightly left to the apostles and the elders.

Luke doesn't tell us, but I think that Simon Kistemaker would be correct when he suggests that "the council met for many days to discuss the matter at hand."[5] We, of course, do not have a log of all that took place during those days, but Luke summarizes the events by excerpting from three contributions: those of Peter, of Paul and Barnabas, and of James. There is no reason to assume that such as John and Matthew and Thomas and Bartholomew and others who might have been there would not have added their ministry reports and observations as well. But the major players for Luke were Peter and Paul.

Peter's Theology

[7] . . . Peter rose up and said to them: "Men and brethren, you know that a good while ago God chose among us, that by my mouth the Gentiles should hear the word of the gospel and believe. [8] So God, who knows the heart, acknowledged them, by giving them the Holy Spirit just as He did to us, [9] and made no distinction between us and them, purifying their hearts by faith."

Peter's *theology* was correct, although Paul had recently scolded him for failing to consistently apply what he knew. Paul had become seriously upset with Peter in Antioch when he decided to stop eating with the Gentile believers (see Gal. 2:11-14), because of the confusion it had caused there on Paul's turf. But now that Paul was in Jerusalem on Peter's turf, I wonder if Paul might not have seen it differently.

As I pointed out in the last chapter, Peter's catch-22 decision may have offended Paul and the Gentile believers in Antioch, but it was a carefully crafted strategic decision made to avoid confusion and potential division among the Jewish believers in the Jerusalem church under James. Because of that, Paul's opponents in the circumcision party in Jerusalem likely would have regarded Peter as their ally and, therefore, they would have been open to giving serious consideration to anything he said.

Peter said the right things. He did not begin with a philosophical discourse, but he reminded the council of his ministry in the house of Cornelius something close to 10 years previously. Peter's theology again was drawn from his ministry experience, as most sound theology is. Surely part of the reason why God sent Peter to Cornelius's house in Caesarea was not to prepare him for a lifetime of ministry to Gentiles—because his calling was to be that of an apostle to the circumcision—but to prepare him for this event, the Council of Jerusalem.

Not only had Peter taken the unprecedented action of authorizing the baptism of uncircumcised Gentiles in Cornelius's house in obedience to the leading of the Holy Spirit, but he had also immediately returned to Jerusalem and processed these very same issues with the leadership of the Jerusalem church. They were extremely upset at first, but before their discussion was finished, they had come to agree with Peter and said, "Then God has also granted to the Gentiles repentance to life" (Acts 11:18).

Here in the Council of Jerusalem, Peter relied on the same empirical evidence he had cited previously to validate the authenticity of the conversion of the Gentiles, namely, that those in Cornelius' house had spoken in tongues. This is implied in his assertion that "God, who knows the heart, acknowledged them, by giving them the Holy Spirit just as He did to us" (15:8). Back in Cornelius's house, Luke reports that the gift of the Holy Spirit had been poured out on the Gentiles also. For they heard them speak with tongues (10:45-46).

Peter's Conclusion and Advice

[10] ***"Now therefore, why do you test God by putting a yoke on the neck of the disciples which neither our fathers nor we were able to bear?*** [11] ***But we believe that through the grace of the Lord Jesus Christ we shall be saved in the same manner as they."***

Peter's conclusion was that the Gentiles did not need to obey the Mosaic law to be saved. His reference to "putting a yoke on the neck of the disciples" would have been understood by all present at the council as a reference to the Jewish law. F. F. Bruce tells us that in those days a Gentile who was converting to become a Jewish proselyte "by undertaking to keep the law of Moses, was said to 'take up the yoke of the kingdom of heaven.'"[6]

Peter goes right to the heart of the matter. If the yoke of the gospel as presented to them is too heavy to bear, most Gentiles will not be saved. This is not to say that the law is bad. Jewish converts would be expected to continue to obey the law of Moses to the best of their ability. Gentile converts also would find much good in the law of Moses that would contribute to their subsequent sanctification. But the law was not to be part and parcel of the initial presentation of the gospel of salvation. This would confuse *perfecting* with *discipling*, as some modern missiologists would say.

Donald McGavran, the founder of the church growth movement, puts it this way: "Antigrowth concepts arise from confusing perfecting with discipling."[7] In this, he is reflecting contemporary efforts to load onto the simple gospel of justification through faith in Jesus Christ any number of ethical demands favored by a given preacher. I have heard the gospel presented with caveats such as: If you want to be saved you must stop smoking or you must renounce polygamy or you must be baptized by immersion or you must give up racial biases, or, in our case in Jerusalem, you must be circumcised. Those matters are valid issues for the period of perfecting. When they are raised initially, the gospel does not move out cross-culturally in the way God intended it to.

If Peter, one of the most influential apostles of that day, had not been correct in his views of discipling versus perfecting, or of justification versus sanctification, or of faith versus works, the expansion of the Christian movement could have halted then and there.

Peter solidified his point by telling his colleagues what they already knew, namely, that even Jews could not be saved by the law because virtually all of them found it impossible to keep. The yoke of the law was something that "neither our fathers nor we were able to bear." Because the participants in the Jerusalem Council were all born-again believers in Jesus Christ, they knew in their hearts that they were saved by grace. But even so, many of them had not yet been able to break away from their inbred ethnocentricity.

If any of them had truly kept the law, Paul would have been counted among them. He says later in Philippians, "If anyone else thinks he may have confidence in the flesh, I more so . . . concerning the righteousness which is in the law, blameless" (3:4,6). However, looking back as a Christian, Paul counts keeping the law "as rubbish, that I may gain Christ and be found in Him, not having my own righteousness, which is from the law, but that which is through faith in Christ" (3:8-9).

Paul knew well that keeping the law apart from true repentance and faith was useless (see Rom. 9:31). Furthermore, by comparison to a knowledge of Christ, even the moral, ethical and spiritual content of the law was quite inferior.

The Missionaries Report Power Evangelism

[12] ***Then all the multitude kept silent and listened to Barnabas and Paul declaring how many miracles and wonders God had worked through them among the Gentiles.***

Apparently Peter's address had summarized the consensus that the council had reached after perhaps days of discussion. The gathering was now ready to listen to the missionaries who had actually been admitting uncircumcised Gentiles into their churches and baptizing them. No more debate is recorded.

In fact, from this point on, Peter drops out of the scene and Luke has nothing more to say about him in the rest of Acts.

A True Watershed

Reminding ourselves of the watershed nature of the Jerusalem Council, it might well be that Peter's influence there could be regarded as his major lifetime contribution to the kingdom of God. His ministry had many other notable aspects to be sure, but at least from the viewpoint of missiology, world evangelization and the fulfillment of the Great Commission, nothing Peter did had more far-reaching positive influence than this. He was a true trailblazer for the future spread of the gospel.

Granted that Luke uses a highly abbreviated account of the presentations Barnabas and Paul made to the members of the Council, his choice of "miracles and wonders" as the one theme to record in this historical account is notable. But what else would they have spoken about? Those who needed persuading would not like hearing about the new churches in Antioch, Iconium, Lystra and Derbe, because they were filled with uncircumcised Gentiles. They had already sent Judaizers throughout the area in an attempt to persuade the church leaders that they were wrong. They did not need another theological argument, especially from the pro-Gentile faction. Peter, an insider whom they trusted, had established a correct theological foundation.

Directing Attention to God's Power

The best thing Barnabas and Paul could have done would have been to direct the attention of the assembly away from churches, individuals, doctrines or behavior patterns and turn their attention to God and His power. I like the way Kistemaker puts it: "The emphasis does not fall on what Paul and Barnabas did during their missionary journey but on what God did through them."[8]

We do not know how long Paul and Barnabas talked, but it's unfortunate that history did not leave us a complete transcript of what they said. Certainly Acts 13 and 14 is a bare-bones account at best. Not only were "miracles and wonders" done through the apostles in the churches, but after they left, the Holy Spirit continued doing them through the new believers, including the uncircumcised Gentile disciples. In Galatians, Paul writes to them, "Therefore He who supplies the Spirit to you and works miracles among you" (3:5).

Among many other things, Barnabas and Paul would in all probability have told the Council about the following:

- The high-level power encounter in West Cyprus. This would have been a spellbinder to hear about Paul going eyeball to eyeball with the sorcerer Bar-Jesus in the presence of the proconsul, Sergius Paulus. As Susan Garrett says, "The human combatants Paul and Bar-Jesus in turn represent superhuman figures."[9] Paul is filled with the Holy Spirit while Bar-Jesus is filled with demonic powers of darkness. It is no contest. God demonstrates through Paul that His power is much greater than that of the enemy, and Sergius Paulus is saved (see Acts 13:6-12).

- The *signs and wonders* that were done in Iconium over *a long time*. Here is one place the missionaries might have filled in many details that Luke does not record (see 14:3).

- The amazing healing of the lame man in Lystra. Although this culture was accustomed to supernatural power, the magnitude of this miracle so exceeded anything they had known that they regarded Paul and Barnabas as incarnations of Hermes and Zeus, and the missionaries, therefore, had to deal with allegiance encounters (see vv. 6-18).

- Paul himself being raised from the dead in Lystra. Back in Antioch of Pisidia, Paul had announced that salvation was by faith in Jesus and not in the works of the law. This so infuriated the unbelieving Jews that they had the authorities sentence Paul to be executed by stoning. This incident must have impressed some on the Jerusalem Council, because the Pharisees there could have identified personally with the feelings those Jewish leaders had. The persecutors caught up to Paul in Lystra and stoned him to death, but through the prayers of the believers, Paul was raised from the dead (see vv. 19-20).

James Takes Charge

[13] *And after they had become silent, James answered, saying, "Men and brethren, listen to me . . ."*

At this point, James, the horizontal apostle and the convener of the Jerusalem Council, took charge. As a reminder, this James was not only the brother of

Jesus, but by now he was also the leading elder and a resident apostle in the Jerusalem church. He later wrote the Epistle of James, and he is referred to in history as "James the Just," undoubtedly because he had the spiritual gift of wisdom. He was wise enough, for example, to let all of the high-energy apostles who had gathered talk until they had nothing more to say. They finally "became silent."

James's procedure was not democratic; it was apostolic. He did not appoint a study commission to consider the matter and bring back a report a few days or months later as many of our churches do today. He did not even take a vote and declare that the majority had won the debate. He simply said, "Listen to *me*." And the room full of dignitaries did just that. They listened to James because they recognized James's apostolic anointing and the divine authority that it bore.

[14] ***Simon has declared how God at the first visited the Gentiles to take out of them a people for His name.***

James's combination of wisdom with apostolic authority was evident here in his concluding message. Notice that he wisely makes no reference to what Barnabas and Paul had said, but instead he refers to Peter's input. Those present who needed an attitude adjustment were mainly those who respected Peter, and who suspected Barnabas and Paul.

Apparently James, either during the council or before, had modified his own position. We see from Galatians that the Judaizers who went to Antioch of Syria and precipitated this whole controversy with Paul and Barnabas "came from James" (Gal. 2:12). Another possible explanation is that James might have sympathized with Paul's position from the start. But because he had no personal experience with Gentiles, he couldn't persuade the circumcision party, so he sent some of them to be persuaded by Paul. James had never eaten with Gentiles, but Paul had. However he arrived at it, James's conclusion now was that "God at the first visited the Gentiles to take out of them a people for His name" (Acts 15:14).

We shouldn't pass this by too rapidly. John Stott says, "[James's] statement is considerably more significant than it looks at first sight."[10] From the time of Abraham until now, the people of God had been chosen from among the Jews. James is now saying that the believing Gentiles, on their own merits, are accepted by God as if they were Israel. Such a statement would have confirmed the worst fears of the hard-core Judaizers present at the council, but no more arguments are recorded. Apostolic authority prevails, as it should.

The power of the Holy Spirit over this gathering must have been awesome in order to bring about such an agreement with the verdict of James, although Luke does not mention the presence of the Holy Spirit in his text. I can only speculate that the intercessors in Mary's house were once again winning the spiritual battle through prayer, as they had when Herod was planning to kill Peter.

To nail down his point, James goes immediately to the prophets, in this case Amos 9:11-12:

> [15] *And with this the words of the prophets agree, just as it is written:*
> [16] *"After this I will return and will rebuild the tabernacle of David which has fallen down. I will rebuild its ruins, and I will set it up,*
> [17] *so that the rest of mankind may seek the Lord, even all the Gentiles who are called by My name, says the Lord who does all these things."*

The major point James is attempting to make by citing this prophecy is that the notion of God's bringing Gentiles into the kingdom as His people was part of His long-range plan, not some precipitous change of plans at the time of sending Peter to Cornelius's house.

It is interesting that James does not quote Amos from the Hebrew Bible, but from the Greek translation called the *Septuagint* or *LXX*. James does this because it makes his point much more forcefully. We should not be surprised at this, because many of us do the same thing. If *The Living Bible*, for example, makes our point more clearly than the *New International Version* or the *King James Version*, we usually use *The Living Bible* for that particular matter. Many of the scholarly commentaries discuss James's use of the *LXX* in detail, and I recommend these commentaries to those who may be interested in knowing more about how the dynamic of quoting different versions of the Bible operates.

THE EPOCHAL CONCLUSION

James's conclusion constitutes the most important missiological statement ever made this side of Pentecost:

[19] Therefore I judge that we should not trouble those from among the Gentiles who are turning to God.

The way is open now for missionaries to take the gospel to every unreached people group in all six continents of the world and to seek God's leading on how the gospel will be contextualized for each one.

Some Diplomatic Concessions

James again exhibits his apostolic leadership and his gift of wisdom by suggesting how this history-making decision can be communicated to the churches while still maintaining the basic unity of the Body of Christ.

[20] But that we write to them [the Gentiles] to abstain from things polluted by idols, from sexual immorality, from things strangled, and from blood. [21] For Moses has had throughout many generations those who preach him in every city, being read in the synagogues every Sabbath.

The letter they wrote read:

[23] . . . To the brethren who are of the Gentiles in Antioch, Syria, and Cilicia . . .

The first thing the recipients of the letter would have looked for would have been what it said about circumcision, and much to their relief this was not made a requirement. They did not have to become Jews to be saved or to live a good Christian life. They could remain Gentiles forever. Keeping the law of Moses was unnecessary either for salvation or for sanctification.

At the same time, because those who had been Judaizers also deserved to have their opinions heard and reflected in the decisions of the council, some diplomatic concessions were made. The Gentiles were to be careful about the food they ate, abstaining from meat offered to idols and from strangled meat that still contained blood, or from the blood itself. They were also to live lives free from sexual immorality. Why immorality would have been included in the list of four is not entirely clear, except that Gentiles were, as a cultural characteristic, much more prone to immorality than Jews. In most of the New Testament lists of sins, immorality is placed on the top of the list. And in many of the pagan cultures, ritual immorality with temple prostitutes was a way of life, encouraged rather than condemned by society as a whole.

> [22] *Then it pleased the apostles and elders, with the whole church, to send chosen men of their own company to Antioch with Paul and Barnabas, namely, Judas who was also named Barsabas, and Silas, leading men among the brethren.*

We know nothing more about Judas except for this visit to Antioch. Silas, however, later joins Paul's mission for the next trip back through the churches of Galatia and beyond.

> [30] *So when they were sent off, they came to Antioch; and when they had gathered the multitude together, they delivered the letter.* [31] *When they had read it, they rejoiced over its encouragement.* [32] *Now Judas and Silas, themselves being prophets also, exhorted the brethren with many words and strengthened them.* [33] *And after they had stayed there for a time, they were sent back with greetings from the brethren to the apostles.* [34] *However, it seemed good to Silas to remain there.* [35] *Paul and Barnabas also remained in Antioch, teaching and preaching the word of the Lord, with many others also.*

Because the letter asserted that the Gentiles could maintain their own cultural identity and integrity and still be accepted as faithful followers of Jesus Christ, the Gentiles "rejoiced over its encouragement." The four conditions mentioned in the letter did not seem to cause any significant negative reactions. These matters are not listed as some new, automatic minimum requirements for salvation without faith, but simply matters of sensitivity in retaining a link with the Jewish followers of Christ.

Actually, after Paul had fulfilled his obligation of reading the letter to the churches he had previously planted (see 16:4), he himself did not seem to follow the guidelines of the dietary decrees. As we will see, his later writings, especially to the Corinthians, indicate this. He, of course, upheld the standard of sexual morality at all times.

Receiving Prophetic Ministry

The house churches in Antioch had become accustomed to having those who had the gift of prophecy circulate among them. The five leaders of the

Cyprus and Cyrene Mission were said to be "prophets and teachers" (13:1). Therefore, the prophetic ministry of Judas and Silas was not something unusual for them. Those who have the spiritual gift of prophecy are a great blessing to congregations and also to individual believers because they deliver personal prophecies from the Lord. As Paul later writes, "He who prophesies speaks edification and exhortation and comfort to men" (1 Cor. 14:3). My wife, Doris, and I have been greatly enriched in our spiritual lives and ministries over the years through the ministry of those who have the gift of prophecy, especially among our active team of personal intercessors. We keep a private "Prophetic Journal," preserving those prophecies that we regard as particularly significant.

The Reorganization of the CCM

Before Paul leaves for his next missionary trip, a major reorganization of the Cyprus and Cyrene Mission takes place. Because it fits more directly into the events of Acts 16, I will postpone commenting on this reorganization until we begin Paul's second term of service in the next chapter.

REFLECTION QUESTIONS

1. Discuss the meaning of "contextualization." From your knowledge of foreign missions in the past and what it is today, can you find some examples of mistakes in this area?
2. The debate about Gentile circumcision erupted in Antioch. Why, then, was the summit meeting called in Jerusalem?
3. How could it be possible that the highest-ranking theologians in the Jerusalem church, those of the sect of the Pharisees, could miss hearing what the Spirit was saying to the churches? Could the same thing be possible in our times?
4. A key to the positive outcome of the Jerusalem Council was Peter's speech. What parts of Peter's previous experience in the house of Cornelius were crucial in shaping his point of view?
5. Would you think it is an exaggeration to say that the Council of Jerusalem was the most important meeting of the Church in all of history? Why or why not?

17

GOODBYE, BARNABAS; HELLO, SILAS: REORGANIZING THE MISSION

ACTS 15 AND 16

After their furlough, Paul and Barnabas were prepared to set out on their second term of missionary service.

> [36] *Then after some days Paul said to Barnabas, "Let us now go back and visit our brethren in every city where we have preached the word of the Lord, and see how they are doing."*

Paul, by this time firmly recognized as the leader of the mission, decided that it was time to move out once again. The issues of Gentile circumcision had been settled in the Council of Jerusalem, and they could now go back and encourage the Gentile churches they had planted during their first term. The most natural thing would be for Paul and Barnabas, who had been through thick and thin together, to maintain their collegiality. But such was not to be, for Barnabas had some unexpected news to break to Paul.

> [37] *Now Barnabas was determined to take with them John called Mark.*

Apparently, Paul had not been aware of Barnabas's lingering desire to be affiliated with Mark once again. This condition, which for Barnabas had apparently become a nonnegotiable, seemed to take Paul by surprise. It caused quite an argument.

> [38] *But Paul insisted that they should not take with them the one who had departed from them in Pamphylia, and had not gone with them to the work.* [39] *Then the contention became so sharp that they parted from one another. And so Barnabas took Mark and sailed to Cyprus.*

I see this event from one perspective as a significant consolation for many of us in missionary work today. If the first missionary agency ever known, headed by such renowned apostolic leadership as Paul and Barnabas, suffered a mission split, we who suffer splits today join a rather distinguished company. I will never forget that in less than a year after Doris and I arrived in Bolivia as missionaries, our mission went through a serious split that forced us to move rather quickly from one place to another, much as Barnabas and Mark did. And, like the first missionary split, the fundamental causes were essentially personal differences between people who earnestly and honestly held differences of perspective about how best to do the work. My wife and I happened to be mere spectators, not direct participants in the dispute.

Let's pause a bit to analyze what might have happened to cause the split. As we do, it is good to keep in mind that the Body of Christ in general is characterized by both unity and diversity. Although some people may be disturbed by the proliferation of varieties of churches, denominations, mission agencies, apostolic networks and parachurch ministries, I do not share their dismay. By and large, as long as *spiritual* unity continues to be maintained, the more *organizational* diversity we have, the more we are likely to advance the kingdom of God.

John Mark

Although Mark's name is well known because he later became the author of one of the four Gospels, he is first introduced in Acts because his mother happened to be the leader of the prayer meeting that saved Peter from being executed by King Herod (see Acts 12:12). As the son of an intercessor, Mark must have been familiar with prayer and spiritual warfare firsthand. When Paul and Barnabas had delivered the offering from Antioch for the poor in Jerusalem, they invited John Mark to accompany them back to Antioch (see v. 25).

Mark was Barnabas's cousin, according to Colossians 4:10. This by itself could explain something of Barnabas's personal desire to work with him. It obviously would not be a totally adequate reason, however, to cause Paul to refuse to work with him.

Why would Paul so decisively refuse to allow Mark to rejoin his mission team?

As might be expected, most commentators raise this question, and as Luke does not give us reasons other than that Mark had deserted (see Acts 15:38), it is not surprising that each commentator would offer varying opinions. One commentator says that Mark had a character defect, another that he was not thoroughly dedicated to Christ, another that he unwisely might have reported to the elders in Jerusalem that Paul was allowing uncircumcised Gentiles to join the people of God, and yet another that he was not persevering enough to be a good missionary.

I have an alternate hypothesis, more directly related to the power ministries theme of Acts. Perhaps it was not a coincidence that Mark decided to go home right after the incident of high-level spiritual warfare involving the sorcerer Bar-Jesus in western Cyprus. Dramatic as the scene appears in Acts 13, I would not discount the possibility that Luke might even have understated it in his account. The episode could well have been similar to many reports my office receives from those doing frontline strategic-level spiritual warfare, describing events with superlatives such as "wild," "intense," "awesome" or "beyond imagination."

Mark Disliked War!

Mark's reaction could well have been like that of many today who witness raw confrontation with demonic principalities and powers for the first time. They are terrified by the reality and the blatant wickedness of the forces of darkness. They may believe in the theory that demonic forces could be at work, but they want nothing to do with them in practice. A good friend of mine, who at one time engaged in strategic-level spiritual warfare, tried it once at a power point of darkness in a foreign country and immediately fell ill because of a ferocious spiritual backlash and decided not to do it anymore. Now, he occasionally quarrels with those of us who continue to advocate aggressive confrontation of the forces of evil in the invisible world to prepare the way for effective evangelism.

Paul realized that his future ministry would involve more strategic-level spiritual warfare, although he had no way of knowing at that time of his coming encounters with such principalities as the Python spirit in Philippi or Diana of the Ephesians, and undoubtedly many others that Luke leaves unrecorded. For Paul to move into enemy territory with a team member who was timid and who might question the wisdom of Paul's approach, if indeed this describes John Mark, clearly would have been unwise. I would like to suppose that, in calmer moments, Paul and Mark would have agreed mutually that Mark simply was not among those called of God to Paul's particular kind of evangelistic ministry.

The Biblical Law of Warfare

If this were the case, and I repeat that it is merely a hypothesis, what I say should not be interpreted as implying that Paul was a member of a kind of spiritual elite—the frontline warriors—while Mark was in some sense lower in God's esteem and a spiritual wimp because he decided to stay home. Elitism in any phase of Christian ministry is a mindset that must be rejected at all costs, although many of us, me included, have tendencies in unguarded moments to fall into that trap. The best antidote, in my opinion, is a sound biblical understanding of spiritual gifts. The whole Body cannot and should not be an eye. Paul later writes to the Corinthians, "Those members of the body which we think to be less honorable, on these we bestow greater honor" (1 Cor. 12:23). I have elaborated on these things in detail in my book *Your Spiritual Gifts Can Help Your Church Grow.*

Meanwhile, a quick look at the "law of warfare" in the Old Testament gives us important insight into God's attitude toward those who choose to stay home rather than go to war. As the Israelites prepared for the war to take the Promised Land, God instructed the men who fell into any one of four categories to stay home: (1) those who had just built a new house; (2) those who had planted a new vineyard; (3) those who were engaged but not yet married; and (4) those who were "fearful and fainthearted" (see Deut. 20:5-8). Might Mark have fit into category number four? If he did, he should not be faulted.

A remarkable thing about Deuteronomy 20 is that it contains no hint that those who stay home for whatever reason are in any way inferior to those who go to war. The same applies to the 31,700 men who went home, leaving Gideon with only 300 men to fight the Midianites (see Judg. 7:1-6). When a similar situation later occurred in David's army, he said, "As his part is who goes down to the battle, so shall his part be who stays by the supplies; they shall share alike" (1 Sam. 30:24). There was nothing wrong with Mark staying home.

Mark Finished Well

To conclude the point, Mark subsequently finished well. Years later, when Paul was in the Roman jail toward the end of his career, Mark was with him, according to Colossians 4:10. And when he writes to Timothy, Paul says, "Get Mark and bring him with you, for he is useful to me for ministry" (2 Tim. 4:11). Mark eventually teamed up with Peter, and his mother Mary (who, incidentally, would also be Barnabas's "Aunt Mary"). The link was that, as I have mentioned, Mary in all likelihood served as Peter's personal intercessor (see Acts 12:5,12). To cap things off, Mark, arguably under Peter's influence, later wrote the Gospel of Mark and thereby gained a permanent position of honor in Christian history.

If Mark was fearful after the Cyprus power encounter, he later changed his attitude toward spiritual warfare. Throughout his Gospel, he deals openly with spiritual warfare and power encounters. Among other things, Mark addresses strategic-level spiritual warfare when he records the words of Jesus: "No one can enter a strong man's house and plunder his goods, unless he first binds the strong man. And then he will plunder his house" (Mark 3:27).

Good-bye, Barnabas

Paul and Barnabas had quite a dispute. As Eugene Peterson translates it in *THE MESSAGE*: "Tempers flared, and they ended up going their separate ways" (Acts 15:39).

What was the problem?

The problem between Paul and Barnabas was significantly different from the problem between Paul and Mark. In neither case are we dealing with a defined *doctrinal* issue as far as we know. In both cases, we are dealing with personalities and the way personal attitudes can translate to behavior in ministry.

An underlying and unresolved issue with Barnabas might well have been Paul's disappointment with him when Barnabas, at one point, had refused to eat with Gentiles in Antioch. Barnabas's doctrine on Gentile salvation was orthodox enough as shown by his planting, along with Paul, a series of Gentile churches, and his subsequent input to the Council of Jerusalem. But when Peter, who had previously eaten with Gentiles, stopped doing so after some Judaizers from the Jerusalem church showed up in Antioch, that was bad enough for Paul. Things became worse when Barnabas joined him, much to the consternation of Paul who forthrightly labeled Barnabas a hypocrite when he wrote the Epistle to the Galatians (see Gal. 2:13). Hypocrites are those who do not practice what they preach, and Paul had interpreted Barnabas's behavior in that very light.

Beyond that, their contrasting leadership styles may have been an even greater determining factor in the mission split. Let's look closer at these two personalities.

Barnabas as a Modality Leader

Barnabas stands out as a relational person, fundamentally people oriented. He had a strong need to like people, and probably to be liked by them and to get along well. His name, Barnabas, means "son of encouragement." God used him to encourage fellow believers through generous giving, to encourage Paul when he first went to Jerusalem as a new believer, to encourage uncircumcised Gentiles, to encourage Peter in Antioch, to encourage the leaders of the Jerusalem church, and to encourage his cousin Mark.

No one describes Barnabas better than does D. Edmond Hiebert, who calls him "one of the choicest saints of the early Christian church."[1] According to Hiebert, Barnabas "had a gracious personality . . . he excelled in building bridges of sympathy and understanding across chasms of difference which divided individuals, classes and races . . . he had a largeness of heart that enabled him to encourage those who failed and to succor the friendless and needy . . . he did have his faults and shortcomings, but those faults arose out of the very traits that made him such a kind and generous man—his ready sympathy for others' failings and his eagerness to think the best of everyone."[2]

According to this characterization, Barnabas clearly fits the profile of what some missiologists today would call a "modality leader," as opposed to Paul who would be seen as a "sodality leader." I explained the difference between modalities and sodalities in some detail when I was analyzing Acts 13. These technical terms, coined by missiologist Ralph D. Winter, relate roughly to what most of us today would call churches (modalities) and parachurch ministries or apostolic networks (sodalities).[3]

The modality is essentially a people-oriented structure, designed to serve the people who are a part of it. Peace and harmony are high values. *Being* is seen as superior to *doing*. Process is often more important than goal. Discipline is usually not strictly applied, especially when it might clash with contentment. Barnabas would fit here.

Paul as a Sodality Leader

On the other hand, the sodality is task oriented. People are also important in sodalities, but largely to the degree that they contribute to accomplishing the goal of the organization. Discipline is much higher, and people are eligible to be dismissed if they are found to be incompetent and thereby unable (or unwilling) to help accomplish the task. *Being* is important in sodalities, but *doing* is even more important.

According to Ralph Winter, both of these structures play important roles in bringing about God's redemptive purposes in the world. But they should not be confused. Essential differences would exist, for example, between First Baptist Church (a modality) and Wycliffe Bible Translators (a sodality). Throughout history, the structure that God has typically chosen to extend His kingdom across cultural boundaries into the unreached people groups of the world has been the sodality structure.

This brief explanation of a complex issue makes it easier to see that Barnabas would have been a type of modality leader while Paul would have been a type of sodality leader. Paul cared about people all right, but his personal drive came not so much from ministering to people as from accomplishing his assigned task. Paul said to the Philippians, "One thing I do, forgetting those things which are behind and reaching forward to those things which are ahead, I press toward the goal for the prize of the upward call of God in Christ Jesus" (Phil. 3:13-14). Toward the end of his life, Paul sums up his ministry career: "I have fought the good fight, I have finished the race" (2 Tim. 4:7). At one point, Paul was pragmatic enough to say, "I have become all things to all men, that I might by all means save some" (1 Cor. 9:22).

Now, back to the mission split in Antioch. Paul's consecrated pragmatism surfaces when he obviously seems to care less about hurting the feelings of Mark and Barnabas than he does about being certain in his own mind that his mission team is as highly competent and as qualified as possible to accomplish the formidable task just ahead of them.

It is important to recognize that Luke does not describe this mission split as the good guys versus the bad guys. Both are good, and at the end of the day, each will optimally be effective in ministering in areas that best fit the gifts and personalities God has given them. I suppose that about 80 percent of ordained clergy are like Barnabas and essentially people oriented, and only about 20 percent might be task-oriented sodality types like Paul. Nevertheless, the fact remains that most outreach and mission work get accomplished by the latter type. This may be one of the reasons Luke never so much as mentions Barnabas again after this volatile incident, although Paul graciously mentions him in 1 Corinthians 9:6.

I like the way F. F. Bruce optimistically sums up the situation: "The present disagreement was overruled for good: instead of one missionary and pastoral expedition, there were two."[4]

Hello, Silas

[40] ***But Paul chose Silas and departed, being commended by the brethren to the grace of God.***

Paul now needed to rebuild his mission team. He chose Silas (also called Silvanus) as the replacement for Barnabas. Where Silas happened to be at that time is unclear. He and Judas had previously been sent by the leaders in Jerusalem to bring the report of the Council of Jerusalem to the churches in Antioch, and then we read that "they were sent back with greetings from the brethren to the apostles" (v. 33). Acts 15:34 in the *New King James Version* seems to be confusing: "However, it seemed good to Silas to remain [in Antioch]." A strong scholarly consensus is that this verse must have been added later on to the original manuscript of Acts. So let's assume that Silas had gone back to Jerusalem with Judas and that Paul had called him from there to join his mission.

Why Silas? Why would Silas be a better partner for Paul at this stage of his career than Barnabas? One obvious reason was that Silas did not have a cousin Mark whom he insisted on bringing along. But other than that, I believe another more fundamental difference existed between Silas and Barnabas.

The difference did not lie in their personal characters or statures as mature Christian leaders. Both were recognized as leaders and highly respected by their peers. Both were members of the Jerusalem church, quite possibly charter members. Silas played an important role in the Council of Jerusalem. He is called one of the "leading men among the brethren" (v. 22), which many take to imply that he could have been an elder of the Jerusalem church.

It is not totally clear whether Silas was a Hebrew Jew or a Hellenistic Jew like Barnabas. My guess would be that because the Hellenistic believers had been driven out of Jerusalem after the murder of Stephen (see 8:1), leaving only the Hebrew church there, it would be unlikely that one of the elders of the Jerusalem church at that time would have been a Hellenist. If such were the case, it might have been to Paul's advantage to take a Hebrew leader from the Jerusalem church with him when he went back to visit the churches he had planted in Galatia. The Judaizers who had gone and messed things up in the Galatian churches had also come from Jerusalem, and Paul already had anticipated that he would have to engage in some potentially difficult damage control when he arrived. Silas would be an asset. As F. F. Bruce says, "But now, if any one should say, 'But what do they think, or practice, at Jerusalem?' reply could be made: 'Well, here is a leader of the Jerusalem church; he can tell you authoritatively what is thought or done there.' "[5]

A Prophet, Not an Apostle

An even more important difference between Silas and Barnabas, in my opinion, was that Silas was a prophet, not an apostle. Barnabas was an apostle, according to Acts 14:14: "When the *apostles* Barnabas and Paul heard this" (emphasis added). Subsequent centuries of mission history have revealed that in an active, dynamic mission organization there is ordinarily room for only one leader or apostle. There were not two Hudson Taylors in the China Inland Mission or two Dawson Trotmans in the Navigators or two Cameron Townsends in Wycliffe Bible Translators. It is not surprising, therefore, that Paul and Barnabas, both apostles, would only be able to minister in close contact with each other for a limited time period

Acts 15:32 mentions, "Judas and Silas, themselves being *prophets*" (emphasis added). Both apostles such as Barnabas and prophets such as Silas are essential in the Body of Christ when it is functioning as God designed it. "And He Himself gave some to be apostles, some prophets, some evangelists, and some pastors and teachers" (Eph. 4:11). The gift of apostle is essentially an authority-based gift. Here is my definition:

> The gift of apostle is the special ability that God gives to some members of the Body of Christ to assume and exercise general leadership over a number of churches with an extraordinary authority in spiritual matters that is spontaneously recognized and appreciated by those churches.[6]

Paul, considering his apostolic authority, would welcome a prophet as his colleague. A mutual recognition of spiritual gifts would assure both of them that there would be no questions concerning leadership of the mission as they worked together.[7]

One additional quality of Silas's that may or may not have been decisive in Paul's choice could have been that he was, like Paul, a Roman citizen. We learn this when they are later released from the Philippian jail and complain to the authorities, "They have beaten us openly, uncondemned Romans . . ." (Acts 16:37). When moving from city to city in the first-century Roman Empire, being able to claim citizenship had many advantages.

AVOIDING THE SYNDROME OF CHURCH DEVELOPMENT

[41] *And he went through Syria and Cilicia, strengthening the churches.*

I love Luke's brevity at this point. Paul thought it was necessary to revisit the churches that he and Barnabas had planted. He undoubtedly wanted Silas to see firsthand the work they had done and to introduce the church leaders in Derbe, Lystra, Iconium and Antioch to Silas. But Paul had no intention of making a career of nurturing these new churches, much as they undoubtedly would have liked him to stay around. By keeping his visits short and by moving out to the frontiers as quickly as possible, Paul avoided what some missiologists have called the "syndrome of church development."

The church-development syndrome, annoyingly common in missionary work today, emerges from a confusion of the goals of cross-cultural mission. Slowly and subtly, mission agencies begin to twist their priorities. They start with the vision of discipling the nations, but they later often fall into the trap of placing exaggerated emphasis on developing the new church or churches they have planted. Energies formerly invested in evangelism then become diverted into well-intentioned efforts to direct the inner spiritual and organizational growth of the new church. Missionaries originally called to be spiritual "obstetricians" find themselves functioning more and more as spiritual "pediatricians."

There is no question that the baby churches need nurture. The new believers definitely require instruction and pastoral care if they are not to be snatched away by the wolves. But pastoral care should *supplement* evangelism, not *replace* it, as is too often the case. Some missionaries do not realize how much attention they are giving to the 99 sheep that have been found as opposed to moving out to find the one that is lost. George Peters, a missiologist, laments, "The tragedy of the situation is that most evangelical missions are so overloaded with institutionalism that it becomes practically impossible to free personnel for the ministry of evangelism."[8]

Missionaries who follow Paul's excellent model wisely leave the nurturing to those appointed to be pastors and elders of the new churches, while they themselves persist in moving forward to reach the unreached. They will visit from time to time to provide apostolic guidance and to be a covering to the local church pastors. Locally the pastor is in charge, while translocally, the pastor is under the authority of and accountable to the apostle. Thus, like Paul, apostolic missionaries today can avoid the syndrome of church development.

TIMOTHY SIGNS UP FOR WARFARE: ACTS 16

[1] *Then he came to Derbe and Lystra. And behold, a certain disciple was there, named Timothy, the son of a certain Jewish woman who believed, but his father was Greek.* [2] *He was well spoken of by the brethren who were at Lystra and Iconium.* [3] *Paul wanted to have him go on with him. And he took him and circumcised him because of the Jews who were in that region, for they all knew that his father was Greek.*

The one thing Luke does stop for in his rapid-fire account of Paul's visits to the new churches is to tell of Timothy joining the apostolic team.

Timothy was a believer, in all probability converted along with his mother when Paul had first evangelized Lystra a couple of years previously. His father was a Gentile, but his mother was a Jew who had raised her child by giving him a thorough knowledge of the Old Testament (see 2 Tim. 3:15). In fact, Timothy's grandmother, Lois, and mother, Eunice, became believers before Timothy did (see 1:5). One of the reasons we think that Timothy may have been led to Christ by Paul himself is that several times in his Epistles Paul refers to Timothy as "my son."

During Paul's absence, Timothy apparently had matured as a Christian. "He was well spoken of by the brethren who were at Lystra and Iconium" (16:2). Iconium was a city about 18 miles, or one day's journey, from Lystra, so Timothy's reputation had spread beyond the boundaries of his hometown.

The reason I use the subhead "Timothy Signs Up for Warfare" is that his ordination to ministry and to missionary service apparently involved just that. Luke does not give us the details in Acts, but Paul later tells us about it when he writes one of his last Epistles, 1 Timothy. There, he says to Timothy, "Do not neglect the gift that is in you, which was given to you by prophecy with the laying on of the hands of the eldership" (4:14). The city of Lystra at that time would have had several house churches, each one pastored by one or more elders. It is likely that after Paul invited Timothy to join him and Silas in the mission, some elders of the house churches met with the missionaries and laid hands on Timothy.

That event, which today some would call an "ordination" or a "commissioning," would presumably have been a meeting characterized, among other things, by much prayer. Not surprisingly, prophecies from God would have been released. Paul could be referring to them when he writes to Timothy, "This charge I commit to you, son Timothy, according to the prophecies previously made concerning you, that by them you may wage the good warfare" (1:18). He also says to Timothy, "Fight the good fight" (6:12); and "You therefore must endure hardship as a good soldier of Jesus Christ" (2 Tim. 2:3); and "No one engaged in warfare entangles himself with the affairs of this life, that he may please him who enlisted him as a soldier" (v. 4). Such consistent military language hints strongly that when Timothy signed up for Paul's mission, he signed up for warfare.

WHY WAS TIMOTHY CIRCUMCISED?

Paul was known as the apostle to the uncircumcision. In his Epistle to the Galatians and in the Council of Jerusalem, he strongly argued that circumcision would not be necessary for salvation, and his viewpoint was accepted and has continued to be accepted by the Christian Church ever since. That is why it seems strange at first that Paul took Timothy "and circumcised him because of the Jews who were in that region" (Acts 16:3).

Obviously, Paul did not circumcise Timothy because it would have been necessary for his salvation. He had been saved for two years before he was circumcised. The reason for circumcision was not *theological*; it was *missiological*. If Timothy had simply stayed there in Lystra, he probably never would have been circumcised. Furthermore, if he had not been half Jewish, there would be no reason for him to be circumcised. He, in that case, would have been like the Gentile Titus of whom Paul says, "Yet not even Titus who was with me, being a Greek, was compelled to be circumcised" (Gal. 2:3).

But because Paul's *modus operandi* was to reside in the Jewish quarters in the unreached cities he was evangelizing and attend the synagogues, he had to flex in whatever way was necessary to avoid offending the Jews who lived there. Again, Paul's characteristic pragmatism came into play. As he said of himself, "to the Jews I became as a Jew, that I might win Jews; to those who are under the law, as under the law, that I might win those who are under the law" (1 Cor. 9:20). To use modern missiological language, Paul was "contextualizing" his behavior. His strategy was "seeker sensitive." He said, "I have become all things to all men, that I might by all means save some" (v. 22).

In Paul's future mission, the most receptive people awaiting him would be found in the synagogue communities. Only if Timothy were circumcised would he be admitted, along with Paul and Silas, into the synagogues and into the houses of the Jews. This social relationship was absolutely essential for the effective functioning of Paul's approach to evangelizing the cities to which God had called him at that time. By circumcising Timothy, Paul was not violating any doctrinal principle, nor was he ashamed of the gospel. As a good missionary, he was wise enough and flexible enough to remove beforehand any possible social or cultural or religious obstacle that might get in the way of spreading the gospel of the Kingdom.

THE JERUSALEM DECREES

[4] ***And as they went through the cities, they delivered to them the decrees to keep, which were determined by the apostles and elders at Jerusalem.***

The only other thing Luke chooses to mention about the visit to the new churches in Galatia concerns what some call "The Jerusalem Decrees." Let's refresh our memories:

> For it seemed good to the Holy Spirit, and to us, to lay upon you no greater burden than these necessary things: that you abstain from things offered to idols, from blood, from things strangled, and from sexual immorality (Acts 15:28-29).

When it comes right down to it, the Jerusalem Council was not primarily about idolatry or blood sausage or extramarital affairs. It was about whether Gentiles first had to become Jews to be saved. And the major symbol of that important issue was circumcision. The Council boldly decided that Gentiles could become part of God's people, the Body of Christ, without becoming Jews or being circumcised.

These "Jerusalem decrees," then, seem to be more in the nature of an amendment to the main motion by some who might have leaned in the opposite direction and who wanted to salvage the situation and keep the Jerusalem Council from possibly being viewed as anti-Semitic. In a conciliatory spirit, the Council thereby agreed to include some issues dealt with in the Jewish law in the letter they would send out to the churches.

Notice that the decrees were sent only to a limited number of churches, namely, those in "Antioch, Syria, and Cilicia" (v. 23). Judas and Silas were sent to deliver them to Antioch, and Paul and Silas were later to deliver them to the churches in Galatia (Cilicia). After this, we hear no more of the decrees. In fact, when Paul deals at length with the matter of eating meat offered to idols in 1 Corinthians, he does not so much as mention the Jerusalem decrees he had previously delivered to the Galatian churches, although abstaining from meat offered to idols was one of the prescribed items.

THE CHURCHES MULTIPLIED

[5] ***So the churches were strengthened in the faith, and increased in number daily.***

Here is another of Luke's characteristic church-growth reports. Even when Paul was not explicitly evangelizing, Luke is eager to indicate that his ministry helped multiply churches. Part of Paul's influence in the new churches was, undoubtedly, to stir them to evangelize the lost in their cities and their regions, and to plant new house churches in every neighborhood. No missiological principle is more important than saturation church planting, and Paul was doing his best to help make it happen. God had used Paul to light the fire, and then God sent him back to blaze the way.

God's kingdom was continuing to advance.

REFLECTION QUESTIONS

1. Think about the fact that all missionaries have experiences different from that of other missionaries. Name four or five missionaries whose ministries you respect, and describe their differing experiences.
2. Evangelizing the lost is a multifaceted undertaking. Do you agree that the *primary* facet is a spiritual battle? Explain your opinion.
3. Do you agree with the suggestion that John Mark may have returned home after the power encounter with Bar-Jesus on Cyprus because he did not feel called to high-level spiritual warfare? Why or why not?
4. See if you can define "modalities" and "sodalities" in your own words. In this context, would you personally identify more closely with Barnabas or with Paul?
5. Why should evangelistic missions try to avoid the "syndrome of church development"? Can you think of any missions today that honestly have avoided it?

18

TO EUROPE WITH POWER

ACTS 16

Did you ever have the experience of sensing that the Lord was leading you to do something really significant, even to the point of telling others about your decision, and then finding out that you were wrong? For many of us, myself included, the question is not whether such a thing has ever happened, but rather, how many times it might have happened!

One of the things I like best about Acts is that Luke, the author, is not inhibited about telling the story of the ministry of the apostles just like it was. I love it because it is a consolation to know that the great heroes of the faith in the first century were as capable of blowing it from time to time as we are today. If the apostle Paul had been perfect, I would have a difficult time identifying with him. But because he obviously wasn't perfect, I can say that if Paul, considering all his shortcomings, could be a faithful and productive servant of God, there is no reason why I can't, or why my students can't, or why my colleagues can't.

In the following case, Paul went through one of those experiences of missing what God was trying to say to him. Not just once, but twice!

TWO FALSE STARTS

[6] *Now when they had gone through Phrygia and the region of Galatia, they were forbidden by the Holy Spirit to preach the word in Asia.*
[7] *After they had come to Mysia, they tried to go into Bithynia, but the Spirit did not permit them.*

As we saw in the last chapter, Luke's customary way of relating the missionaries' visits to the churches they had previously planted is to do it relatively rapidly. The syndrome of church development was not allowed to establish a foothold. As they finished ministering to the churches in Galatia, Paul,

Silas and Timothy then set out, as good apostolic missionaries should, to reach more unreached people groups with the gospel. Their problem was that this time they went the wrong way!

It is safe to assume that Paul and his fellow missionaries did not set out for Asia haphazardly. That was not Paul's ordinary way of doing things. Much thought and much prayer must have gone into the decision to plant churches in Asia. Ernst Haenchen suggests, quite plausibly, that as far as Paul's human reasoning was concerned, he had learned from experience that *his primary evangelistic target would be the synagogue community in the Jewish quarters of the larger Greek-speaking cities*. Haenchen says, "With all his obedience to the will of God [Paul] yet did not neglect at each point to consider the situation exactly."[1] In this case, Asia Minor and the city of Ephesus would be a natural.

Not only would good missionary strategy affirm that Ephesus was a strategic target, but we cannot discount the fact that the missionaries would also have spent much time in sincere prayer. They would have been seeking God's specific leading, which they presumably would have concluded was Asia.

Picking up on what I have stressed several times throughout this commentary on Acts, God's servants in the first century frequently would have answered the question "Why are you doing what you are doing?" by responding with words to the effect: "Because God told us to." In most cases, this would be an accurate response. It certainly would have been, for example, when Paul and Barnabas left Antioch for their first term of missionary service, because "the Holy Spirit [had] said, 'Now separate to Me Barnabas and Saul for the work to which I have called them' " (13:2). Many other examples could be cited.

MISSING GOD'S WILL

I am a strong advocate of hearing from God and acting on what we hear today, just as it was done in the first century. But I am also aware that if this procedure is misused, it can become *presumption* rather than *providence*.

This story about Paul helps us arrive at a more balanced view. Suppose that, on the night before they left Lystra, someone asked the missionaries, "Why are you heading for Asia?" We, of course, do not know if Paul would have replied, "Because God told us to," but if he had, in that case he would have been wrong. I would rather imagine that Paul might have said what we ourselves should say in most similar situations: "*We sense* that this is the direction God wants us to go." If it later becomes evident that we missed God's will this time, we do not then need to attempt to explain why God might have said the wrong thing. We simply have to humble ourselves and admit that we happened to sense God's leading inaccurately. Missing God's will, then, is seen as *our* fault, not God's!

By what means "they were forbidden by the Holy Spirit to preach the word in Asia" (16:6) we do not know. From the way Luke says it, however, we could safely assume that if someone had asked Paul, "Why are you turning around?" he, in this case *accurately*, could have replied, "Because God told us we were going in the wrong direction."

It is important to understand that our well-laid human plans are sometimes changed by the Holy Spirit, as were Paul's, but that at other times *they can equally be obstructed by the devil*. Paul makes this clear when he later writes a letter to the church he would plant in Thessalonica, and says, "Therefore we wanted to come to you—even I, Paul, time and again—but Satan hindered us" (1 Thess. 2:18). Only by intimacy with the Father in prayer and maintaining the fullness of the Holy Spirit in our daily lives will we be able to discern whether we should turn around and go back because God wants us to, or whether we should courageously push on ahead because the obstacle has been placed in our way by the enemy.

Paul, Silas and Timothy went back, in this case to Mysia. Who knows if they might have found the first-century equivalent of a condominium on the shores of the Bosphorus to rest and recuperate from their setback. If they did, I could imagine they would have held a field-council meeting in Mysia and they might have drawn up a new set of detailed plans about why they should now set out to evangelize Bithynia. According to the criteria on which they might have previously chosen Ephesus, the Greek cities of Nicaea and Nicomedia in Bithynia would have been logical targets for church planting. There, they would find many "unreached peoples" in the true sense of the phrase. So "they tried to go into Bithynia, but the Spirit did not permit them" (Acts 16:7). Two strikes on the missionaries!

What now?

[8] *So passing by Mysia, they came down to Troas.*

By this time they could have been too upset to stop and rest in Mysia as they had done previously. The missionaries headed to Troas. But why there? Ernst Haenchen offers an interesting suggestion. If they were operating on the same assumptions we think might have pointed them first toward Asia and then toward Bithynia, they could now have targeted Greek cities in Greece itself. As Haenchen says, heading for Troas "does not yet mean that Paul now set out for Macedonia—he could have waited for a ship which would bring him and his companions directly to Greece."[2] If that is the case, poor Paul would have been up against a "three strikes and you're out" situation. It was time for God to step in more directly and be sure that the missionaries were headed in the right direction this time.

THE MACEDONIAN VISION

[9] ***And a vision appeared to Paul in the night. A man of Macedonia stood and pleaded with him, saying, "Come over to Macedonia and help us."***
[10] ***Now after he had seen the vision, immediately we sought to go to Macedonia, concluding that the Lord had called us to preach the gospel to them.***

God's initiative for directing the missionaries was now decisive. The indirect way didn't seem to work in this case, so a more tangible approach was in order. God, therefore, gave Paul a night vision. It is interesting how matter-of-factly Luke mentions that Paul had a vision. Those who have a first-century pre-Enlightenment worldview, such as Paul had, would not consider it unusual for supernatural beings—angels of darkness as well as angels of light—to communicate with human beings through visions and dreams. For example, Paul's conversion experience on the road to Damascus also included a vision in which he actually saw Jesus, as I explained in the chapter on Acts 9. Visions were such an assumed part of common life that there is no telling how many other visions Paul might have had between his conversion some 16 years previously and now. Luke would have had no particular reason to mention them.

But Luke does mention this vision because through it God was directing the penetration of the gospel for the very first time into Europe. I call this chapter "To Europe with Power" because it begins with a manifestation of divine power through the Macedonian vision, and immediately follows with an extraordinary power encounter with the Python spirit and a supernatural release from jail during the first European missionary target—Philippi.

Instead of Jesus appearing to Paul in the vision as He did on the Damascus road, this time God shows Paul a Macedonian man saying, "Come over to Macedonia and help us" (v. 9). This sovereign call of God also fits, to some extent, the missiological criteria we have mentioned on which Paul had been planning his evangelistic strategy—Greek-speaking cities that had large Jewish populations. In this case, the people of Macedonia, although ruled by the Romans, spoke Greek. The downside was that Philippi, the chief city of Macedonia, had only a small Jewish population, not a large one. Nevertheless, the missionaries "immediately [seek] to go to Macedonia" (v. 10).

WELCOME, DR. LUKE

Luke, the author of Acts, says that "after [Paul] had seen the vision, immediately *we* sought to go to Macedonia" (v. 10, emphasis added). Changing from the third person to the first person, from "they" to "we," indicates that at this point Luke apparently joins the missionary team.

Through the many years that I have studied the Acts of the Apostles, I have developed a human-interest hypothesis about the life of Dr. Luke that I have not yet found in any of the other commentaries. That, some might say, should be reason enough for me not to mention it. They base such an assumption on a notion that so many scholars have written so many commentaries on Acts—1,398 commentaries in English to be exact—that every possible explanation of events underlying the text must at some time or other have already been suggested.

However, I do not necessarily agree with this assumption. My personal conjecture is that each of the now-standard interpretations of the passages in Acts must have originated sometime in the past with a new suggestion by a certain individual or individuals who had not previously seen it in any of the then-existing commentaries. Based on that, I do not have any particular inhibition to keep me from stepping out from time to time and suggesting my own interpretation. I did just that, for example, when I hypothesized that the evidence in Acts 11 would indicate the possibility of *two* missions to Antioch, not just one. One mission was to the *Jews* living in Antioch and the other (which I called the Cyprus and Cyrene Mission [CCM]) was specifically targeting the *Gentiles*.

THE TASK OF BIBLICAL SCHOLARS

For those who are unfamiliar with the day-to-day task of biblical scholars, let me explain. These are highly educated people who have made a profession of studying and teaching the Bible. The immediate subject of their studies is 66 relatively short books, so it is a much more limited field than, say, astronomy, Chinese history or computer science. Furthermore, their scholarly predecessors have been studying and interpreting the same 66 books for almost 20 centuries. It is not surprising, then, that one of the desires of biblical scholars is to offer a first-time hypothesis that will throw some new light on the biblical text and that will hopefully elicit agreement from some other scholars in the field.

By doing this, these scholars are also mentally prepared for the eventuality that some erudite colleagues may disagree. A certain vocabulary is commonly used in such discussions. When one agrees with the new hypothesis, it is commonly lauded as "exegesis," meaning it appears to have been drawn from the biblical text. This is seen as legitimate. If one disagrees, however, it will frequently be termed "eisegesis," meaning that the hypothesis is apparently not demanded by the text, but that it has presumably been superimposed onto the text by the author. This is not regarded as entirely legitimate. Sometimes the boundary line between the two is not all that clear, and it boils down to a judgment call.

By way of illustration, consider the opinions of recognized biblical scholars regarding this passage in Acts 16:10, in which Luke begins to write in the first person, "we." Most scholars agree that the passage was written by Luke, but others suggest it may more likely be an insertion by Luke of something written by Paul, Silas or Timothy. Most scholars think that Luke met Paul in Troas, while others surmise that Luke might actually have been traveling with Paul ever since they left Antioch. And how did Luke and Paul meet? Here are some of the biblical scholars' hypotheses:

- Paul was sick in Galatia, so when he arrived in Troas he decided to seek medical assistance. Dr. Luke fit the bill.
- Luke looked for Paul because he had heard many stories of Paul's ministry of faith healing and was curious to know more about it.
- Luke was the actual Macedonian man whom Paul had seen in the vision, so Paul immediately recognized him when he finally saw Luke himself in Troas.
- Luke had previously talked to Paul about the challenge of Macedonia, thus priming Paul for the vision he was about to have.[3]

Would these suggestions be regarded as "exegesis" or "eisegesis"?

DID LUKE MARRY LYDIA?

Two of the major characters in this missionary episode in Philippi are Luke and Lydia. Luke, as I have already mentioned, was a physician and, like many physicians, he was in all probability cultured, well educated, widely traveled and wealthy. Lydia is described as "a seller of purple from the city of Thyatira" (v. 14), which casts her in the role of an international merchant. David Gill, a New Testament scholar, draws from several sources to suggest that Lydia was "of some standing" socially, a member of the "social elite," a seller of "luxury items or exotic merchandise, such as purple dye or perfumes"[4] and wealthy. In other words, like Luke, Lydia would be cultured, well educated, widely traveled and wealthy. They were both Gentiles. Could it be that they were both single? According to Bradley Blue, the fact that Lydia was the owner of her own large home makes it quite likely (although not certain) that she was single.[5]

Here is where the human interest comes in. After many exciting events in Philippi, which we will see in detail shortly, the last place we find the missionaries, Paul, Silas, Timothy and Luke, is in the house of Lydia where they had been lodged. But when they leave Philippi, the "we" suddenly changes to "they"! Luke obviously had stayed behind. Did he stay lodged in Lydia's house? Could they have decided to marry each other and help form the nucleus of that wonderful church in Philippi that later sent substantial financial gifts to Paul and his missionary team? When Paul later wrote a letter to the church at Philippi and mentioned his "true companion" (Phil. 4:3), could that be a reference to Luke? Several commentators, F. F. Bruce among them, think it might well have been Luke.[6]

Just a thought!

TARGETING THE SYNAGOGUE COMMUNITY

[13] ***On the Sabbath day we went out of the city to the riverside, where prayer was customarily made; and we sat down and spoke to the women who met there.*** **[14]** ***Now a certain woman named Lydia heard us. She was a seller of purple from Thyatira, who worshiped God. The Lord opened her heart to heed the things spoken by Paul.***

As I have mentioned, Philippi did not have a large Jewish population. It did not even have a synagogue. In those days, a proper synagogue required at least 10 adult Jewish males for its nucleus, and apparently that many Jewish males did not reside in Philippi. So instead of attending a synagogue, the Jewish women in Philippi customarily observed the Sabbath by gathering at a spot near the river to pray together. Although not a synagogue, such a gathering was, nevertheless, a functional substitute for a synagogue.

One of these women was Lydia, "who worshiped God." She was not a Jew, but a Gentile attracted to the true God of the Jews, the category known as "God-fearers." As we have previously seen, the typical synagogue community would likely be composed of Jews, proselytes and God-fearers. To review, proselytes had been born Gentiles, but they had broken their ties with their Gentile culture and they had officially converted to Judaism. From that point on, they were regarded by all, no longer as Gentiles, but as bona fide Jews. They were called "proselytes," however, to distinguish them from biological Jews. The God-fearers were also born Gentiles but they had not yet decided to take the very weighty and complicated step of cultural conversion through the outward circumcision of the males, baptism and adoption of the extensive cultural implications of Jewish law. They remained Gentiles, but they were admitted to the fringes of the synagogue community under certain restrictions.

Paul's Evangelistic Strategy

Paul's established evangelistic strategy was to head directly for the synagogue community in any new city on his ministry itinerary. He later did this in Thessalonica (see Acts 17:1), in Berea (see v. 10), in Athens (see v. 17), in Corinth (see 18:4) and in Ephesus (see 19:8). He went to the synagogues because there he would find many of the most receptive people for the gospel message he was bringing to them.

The ethnic Jews themselves were not particularly receptive, although we do have records of a number of them deciding to follow Jesus as Messiah as Paul went from city to city. Indeed, in Corinth two synagogue presidents, no less, were converted. Proselytes would be the least likely to convert because they had paid such a high personal price to become Jews that going back would not ordinarily be an attractive option. A serious problem for all Jews, whether ethnic Jews or proselytes, was Paul's willingness to admit Gentiles into the "people of God" without demanding circumcision, and all the rest. Strictly orthodox Jews could not so much as tolerate such a thought.

God-Fearers Were Ready for the Gospel

Those who were most receptive to the gospel were the Gentile God-fearers such as Lydia. Paul's message to them would have been something like: "Do you want to know and follow the true God? Are you here on the fringes of the synagogue community because you realize in your heart that the God whom the Jews worship is the true God? Have these synagogue leaders told you that to know Jehovah God and to be fully accepted by Him you first must be circumcised, become a Jew and obey the Jewish law? Well, I have come with good news for you. God loves you and He sent the Messiah, Jesus Christ, to die for you on the cross. Through faith in Jesus, God will forgive your sins, restore you to fellowship with Himself, and welcome you into His family. And all this while you remain a Gentile as you always have been."

The God-fearers had been waiting for exactly this kind of a message! When they heard and understood what Paul was saying, many of them opened their hearts to Christ and they were born again, accepting Him as the Lord of their lives and the Savior of their souls. Then, because they had not previously broken cultural and social contact with their fellow Gentiles, they could easily move among Gentiles who were not God-fearers and bring them the message of salvation. We have called this E-1 evangelism. At this point in particular, the mighty signs and wonders that ordinarily accompanied the preaching of the gospel message had maximum impact. First-century evangelism was consistently a combination of word and deed.

The result of this missionary strategy led to multiplying what were later to be called "Christian churches" that were predominantly Gentile churches. Paul's original commission from the Lord on the Damascus road involved this very thing. Jesus had said that He was sending Paul to the *Gentiles* "to open their eyes, in order to turn them from darkness to light, and from the power of Satan to God" (26:18). From that point onward, Paul understood himself as an apostle to the uncircumcised (see Gal. 2:7-8).

Lydia and Group Conversion

[15] ***And when she [Lydia] and her household were baptized, she begged us, saying, "If you have judged me to be faithful to the Lord, come to my house and stay." So she persuaded us.***

Not only was Lydia an outstanding example of a God-fearer prepared to receive the gospel, but all her household also came to Christ at the same time she did. Who were the people in her household? The lack of any reference to a husband is further indication that Lydia would likely have been single at the time. Whether she had previously been married is not known. If she had been, it would be expected that any children would have also been part of her household. Other close relatives might have been living with her. And because she was a woman of means, she would have had a household staff of servants or slaves. When Lydia as the head of the household decided to convert to Christianity, the rest of her household would naturally be expected to follow suit.

Group conversion is difficult for many Westerners to comprehend or to consider as fully legitimate. Worldwide, America has gained the reputation of being an extremely individualistic culture. Our frontier mindset and the expectation that all of us must pull ourselves up by our own bootstraps if we expect to be successful seems like a distorted value system to at least *two-thirds* of today's global population.

In most parts of the world, all *important* decisions are made by groups. Because only insignificant decisions are left to individuals, *when missionaries come with an individualistic gospel, it frequently seems as though it must be an unimportant issue to those they are trying to win.* Of course, Western missionaries often attach a *theological* reason to insisting that each person make his or her own decision. "Dare to be a Daniel; dare to stand alone" is the watchword of many. I recall that as a young man, I first decided whom I was going to marry, and *then* informed my parents. Although to us this may not seem like unusual behavior, to most people in the world it is utterly preposterous. People simply do not make such important decisions on their own.

The occasions in which many people have turned to Christ all at once throughout history have been by what missiologists call "people movements to Christ." They are defined as *multi-individual, mutually interdependent conversions.* That is what happened, quite naturally, in Lydia's household. The resultant professions of faith were just as valid as individuals being saved one by one in a Billy Graham meeting today.

We see major people movements occurring in China and India, for example, in our time. A people movement has been ignited among Korean-Americans, in which we find that 70 percent of Koreans living in the United States are Christians, compared to less than 20 percent of Koreans living in Korea. If, for example, we ever successfully evangelize our Native American population, it will certainly come largely, if not almost exclusively, through people movements in each tribal network. Lydia and her household experiencing group conversion should be more of a model for us today than it appears to be.

HIGH-LEVEL POWER ENCOUNTER

[16] *Now it happened, as we went to prayer, that a certain slave girl possessed with a spirit of divination met us, who brought her masters much profit by fortune-telling.* [17] *This girl followed Paul and us, and cried out, saying, "These men are the servants of the Most High God, who proclaim to us the way of salvation."* [18] *And this she did for many days. But Paul, greatly annoyed, turned and said to the spirit, "I command you in the name of Jesus Christ to come out of her." And he came out that very hour.*

The book of Acts contains four, possibly five, incidents of high-level spiritual warfare:

1. Peter's encounter with the sorcerer Simon Magus in Samaria, of whom was said, "This man is the great power of God" (8:10).
2. Paul's encounter with Bar-Jesus (or Elymas), who was employed as a medium by the Roman proconsul of Cyprus, Sergius Paulus (see 13:6-12).
3. The event here in Philippi in which Paul confronts the Python spirit (see 16:16-18).
4. Breaking the power of Diana of the Ephesians (see Acts 19), which we shall see later in chapter 21.
5. The fifth incident, which possibly fits into the same set, would be the encounter between King Herod, who ordered Peter's execution, and the prayer warriors in the house of Mary the mother of Mark (see 12:1-23).

As we study Acts, we see spiritual warfare on three levels: ground level, occult level and strategic level. I have defined each of them previously. We should keep in mind that these three categories are simply conceptual devices to help us understand more clearly some of the complex aspects of the battles in the invisible world. The lines between the three are not sharp and clear. Much of it overlaps and, furthermore, spiritual warfare on any one of the three levels has repercussions in varying degrees through the other two because we are invading the same kingdom of darkness.

A thoughtful question has been raised by some people about whether these four or five stories of spiritual warfare in Acts actually reach into the area of strategic-level spiritual warfare. It has been argued that the incidents involving people such as Simon Magus in Samaria, Bar-Jesus in Cyprus and the slave girl in Philippi could better be seen as ground-level, or, because all three were occult practitioners, perhaps occult-level spiritual warfare. And Paul himself, as we will see, never directly confronted Diana of the Ephesians. His encounter with the magicians in Ephesus would clearly have been considered occult-level spiritual warfare.

THE QUESTION OF AUTHORITY

The reason some raise these questions is because of a questionable theological assumption—namely, that Christians are given authority to deal with demons who are attached to a person, but Christians are not given similar authority to deal with evil spirits at other levels or in other spheres.

As readers of this commentary (as well as my *Prayer Warrior* series) will know, I disagree. I join those who take literally Jesus' words that He has given us authority "over *all* the power of the enemy" (Luke 10:19, emphasis added). It is also my opinion that Paul mentions the sword of the Spirit, the Word of God, in his description of our struggle with principalities and powers in Ephesians 6:12-18 because we are to use the sword in our struggle against them. It is my view that sound missiological strategy will take responsible, but aggressive, action to bind demonic strongmen, principalities, powers, territorial spirits, or whatever they might be called, who are serving Satan by keeping large populations as well as geographical areas in spiritual darkness. I also believe that such was Paul's understanding of Jesus' command to him "to open [the Gentiles'] eyes, in order to turn them from darkness to light, and from the power of Satan to God" (Acts 26:18).

In my opinion, Luke's accounts of Simon Magus, Bar-Jesus and the demonized slave girl in Philippi should each be understood as involving strategic-level spiritual warfare. I base this on the assumption that territorial spirits from time to time can and do choose to manifest themselves in the natural world by controlling certain human individuals.

Power encounters with Simon Magus and Bar-Jesus, for example, seemed to change the entire spiritual climates of regions such as Samaria and Cyprus, respectively. Luke reports that in Samaria "both men and women were baptized" (8:12) and in Cyprus "the proconsul believed, when he saw what had been done, being astonished at the teaching of the Lord" (13:12).

Such power encounters seem to involve something substantially different from what occurs in the ordinary ground-level deliverance ministries in which individuals are freed from afflicting spirits. In such cases, the ripple effect of personal deliverance might be felt among immediate family and friends, but that is far short of seeing entire geographical areas undergo spiritual transformation and increasing receptivity to the gospel of the Kingdom. At such a point, an accurate understanding of spiritual warfare becomes extremely significant for missiology and world evangelization.

I have chosen to develop the issue of strategic-level spiritual warfare at some length right here because this incident in Philippi is the clearest example we have in Acts of direct confrontation with a territorial spirit. Incidents later in places like Ephesus actually produce more evangelistic fruit, but they do not involve direct confrontation such as occurs here in Philippi.

A DEMONIZED SLAVE GIRL

> . . . a certain slave girl possessed with a spirit of divination met us, who brought her masters much profit by fortune-telling (v. 16).

The owners of this slave girl may not have known about, or cared little for, the supernatural forces at work, but they cared very much about the substantial income they were receiving through her services. How was it that they could make so much money through this fortune-teller?

The obvious answer is that this slave girl was good at fortune-telling. She knew certain things about the future, and she had built a sound reputation for accuracy. Any number of other fortune-tellers in Philippi must not have been making as much money because they simply weren't as good. The slave girl had not gained her stature in the occult community by making inaccurate pronouncements.

Another question that surfaces in some minds is whether this girl's ability was true supernatural power or just superstition. I have found this word "superstition" carelessly used by many otherwise thoughtful Christians. To say, for example, that consulting a spiritist medium such as this girl is "superstition" tends to imply that we are dealing with mere psychological issues rather than issues of real supernatural power. My dictionary says that "superstition" means "an irrational belief in or notion of the ominous significance of a particular thing, circumstance, occurrence."[7] The ordinary person thinks that superstition might be a fear of walking under ladders or black cats crossing our paths, something not worth paying much attention to because these are most likely figments of the imagination. The words on the paper slips in Chinese fortune cookies might be another example of this kind of superstition, but these certainly do not compare to the kind of fortune-telling the slave girl was practicing in Philippi.

This slave girl was serving as a channel for actual supernatural power. The demonic spirits of darkness in Philippi could reveal to her many things that would occur in the future simply because they at the time had considerable control over the entire society, and they had the power to determine much of what would happen in the future. John said, "The whole world lies under the sway of the wicked one" (1 John 5:19). He also writes that through Jesus "the true light is already shining" (2:8) and that those of us who are following Jesus "have overcome the wicked one" (v. 13). Only through the light of the world—Jesus Christ—can the control of Satan and his forces of darkness be weakened and dispelled. But before Paul and the other missionaries had arrived in Philippi, darkness had been in full control of much of the future. This is why fortune-telling in places like that could be amazingly accurate.

Also notice that if cities such as Philippi were indeed under the control of demonic beings, it might not be inaccurate to regard the higher-ranking ones as territorial spirits. And, as we shall see, the particular spirit empowering the slave girl happened to be one of the big ones. Those who understood the power of such demonic forces were not irrational or superstitious. Their rational minds had accurately perceived the reality of the spiritual power with which they were dealing—in this case, the Python spirit.

THE PYTHON SPIRIT

The slave girl in Philippi was demonized with a "spirit of divination" (Acts 16:16). Our English Bible versions translate the Greek *pneuma pythona* by using the *functional* name of this spirit, "spirit of divination" or "spirit of clairvoyance," instead of the *proper* name, "Python spirit." When we attempt to identify demonic beings in general, we frequently use one or the other.

In Latin America, for example, one of the most powerful and pervasive spirits is a spirit of religion well entrenched in the Roman Catholic church, which for centuries has kept multitudes in spiritual darkness by deceiving them into thinking they would be saved by their religion. "Spirit of religion" is the functional name of this high-ranking demon. However, its proper name, according to those experienced in spiritual mapping in Latin America, is "Queen of Heaven," mentioned in the Bible in Jeremiah 7:18. Working as a spirit of religion, the Queen of Heaven has apparently succeeded in disguising herself very skillfully as a counterfeit Virgin Mary, and she thereby delights in receiving the worship of millions.

Mentioning this is neither to deny that many Latin American Roman Catholics are sincere born-again Christians serving the Lord, nor to ignore the fact that the true historic Mary, mother of Jesus, is "blessed . . . among women" (Luke 1:28). It is simply to illustrate the difference between functional and proper names of demonic spirits by using a familiar case study.

In my opinion, it would have been better to translate *pneuma pythona* literally as "Python spirit." Simon Kistemaker argues that the best way to translate *pneuma pythona* into English is: "a spirit, namely, a Python."[8] This helps us form a clearer picture of why it is feasible to treat this as a case of strategic-level spiritual warfare. It helps us understand much more precisely what Paul was actually dealing with.

Who Was Python?

R. C. H. Lenski says that Python was "the mythical serpent or dragon that dwelt in the region Pytho at the foot of the Parnassus in Phocis and was said to have guarded the oracle at Delphi until it was slain by the god Apollo."[9] Delphi was the city in Greece in which a famous temple of Apollo was located, the seat of the Delphic oracle. Apollo was a powerful demonic spirit of prophecy who spoke on behalf of the great king of the gods, Zeus (Greek) or Jupiter (Roman).

Delphi was no ordinary Greek city. Here is how Everett Ferguson describes it: "According to legend Zeus wanted to determine the center of the earth, so he released two eagles from opposite ends of the world. They met over Delphi. The omphalos stone at Delphi marked the navel of the earth, and Delphi became the spiritual center of the Greek world." Ferguson goes on to say that Delphi was a "cult center of the earth goddess," "the center of Apollo's worship," and "The main attraction of Delphi was its oracle, located under the temple of Apollo."[10]

What was an oracle? An oracle was a religious institution focused upon an individual who had a satanically empowered gift of prophecy and who was sought out by many who wished to determine the will of the spirits. The oracle at Delphi was a priestess known as the Pythia because she was empowered by the Python spirit. According to Ferguson, she would only prophecy on the seventh day of each month when she would take a ceremonial bath, sacrifice a goat to Apollo, enter an underground chamber beneath the temple and sit on Apollo's tripod. Those who wished to receive her words would pay a high monetary price.[11]

A first-century spiritual mapper might well be inclined to designate Delphi as the seat of Satan for Greece. Paul had encountered this same Python spirit as the spirit of divination in the slave girl at Philippi. This is what makes me argue that we have a description of something more than simple ground-level spiritual warfare here in Acts 16.

Python's Theology Was Accurate

> This girl followed Paul and us, and cried out, saying, "These men are the servants of the Most High God, who proclaim to us the way of salvation" (v. 17).

We should keep in mind that these words are not those of the slave girl herself, but of the evil spirit that had taken control of her. The Python spirit's theology happened to be accurate. He recognized that the missionaries were true representatives of God, and that their message of salvation was true. Demons are inveterate liars, but not everything they say is a lie. Whether they speak the truth or falsehoods, however, their ultimate goal is to deceive. Sometimes they deceive by first building false credibility. The Python spirit spoke true theology and told true fortunes, enchanting people much as a spider would invite a fly into its web.

Mark tells of a similar spirit that once tried to entice Jesus by saying, "I know who You are—the Holy One of God" (Mark 1:24). But Jesus wasn't impressed. "Jesus rebuked him, saying, 'Be quiet, and come out of him!' " (v. 25). I like what James says about this: "You believe that there is one God. You do well. Even the demons believe—and tremble!" (Jas. 2:19).

Paul Pulls the Trigger

> And this she did for many days. But Paul, greatly annoyed, turned and said to the spirit, "I command you in the name of Jesus Christ to come out of her." And he came out that very hour (v. 18).

This example of a direct, high-level power encounter has two important aspects:

1. *Paul's method.* Paul addressed the spirit directly.
2. *Paul's timing.* Paul did not immediately cast out the spirit when it first manifested, but only after several days.

This raises two significant questions for us: (1) Should we, like Paul, address spirits directly, or only address God? And (2) If we should address the spirits, how long should we wait before confronting them?

Should We Address Spirits?

The question whether we should address spirits directly or whether we should only pray to God and ask Him to deal with them is often raised in discussions of strategic-level spiritual warfare.

Interestingly enough, this question is not ordinarily asked in relationship to ground-level spiritual warfare. The overwhelming consensus of those who are active in deliverance ministries involving power encounters is that demons can and should be told to leave. I just referred to Jesus' deliverance of the demonized man in the synagogue where He directly addressed the spirit, saying, "Be quiet, and come out of him!" (Mark 1:25).

I realize, of course, that some people approach individual deliverance from the viewpoint of the *truth encounter* rather than the *power encounter*. Even in cases where people seek freedom in Christ through truth encounter, however, they frequently end up informing the demons directly who they really are in Christ's kingdom, thereby serving the spirits an eviction notice, which the demons usually obey. A major proponent of this methodology is Neil Anderson, author of *Victory over the Darkness*.

One of the Scripture references many people use to argue that even if demons may be directly addressed on ground level, they should not be so addressed on the *strategic* level is Jude 9: "Yet Michael the archangel, in contending with the devil, when he disputed about the body of Moses, dared not bring against him a reviling accusation, but said, 'The Lord rebuke you!' "

Several things need to be mentioned in conjunction with Jude 9.

First, Jude 9 is not written in the context of methodologies of spiritual warfare, but it is a passage that teaches that we should never go beyond the bounds of whatever authority God has given us.

Second, Jude 9 condemns godless, immoral people (see vv. 4,8) who *slander* (rather than *rebuke* under Christ's authority) angelic beings.

Third, the text deals with addressing Satan himself, not addressing lesser spirits such as Python.

Fourth, it refers to Old Testament times before Jesus had given His disciples authority "over all the power of the enemy" (Luke 10:19). New Testament authority is quite different. Deliverance ministries are virtually unknown in the Old Testament because the victory over the demonic was not sealed until Jesus shed His blood on the cross.

Fifth, it is a strange text, based on something from the apocryphal book of First Enoch. The Old Testament tells us nothing of a "body of Moses." Granted, it is Scripture, but basing important teaching on Jude 9 would be as risky, for example, as basing important teaching on the passage in 1 Corinthians 15:29 that speaks of the custom of "baptizing the dead." For these reasons, I do not believe Jude 9 gives us sufficient evidence to choose to limit our proactive spiritual warfare to lower-ranking demons.

Paul's direct words to the Python spirit is evidence enough for many, myself included, that God does, indeed, direct us to speak with the authority of the name of Jesus to territorial spirits, and that it should be seen as acceptable Christian protocol to do so. Mary spoke directly to the angel Gabriel (see Luke 1:34), and Jesus spoke directly to the Legion spirit (see Mark 5:8-9). The psalmist also spoke directly to demonic principalities in Psalm 97:7, "Worship Him, all you gods," and in 29:1, "Give unto the Lord, O you mighty ones, give unto the Lord glory and strength."

Why Did Paul Wait?

It is puzzling to some that Paul allowed the Python spirit to manifest "for many days" (Acts 16:18) before casting it out. I am sure this is best explained by crediting Paul with following one of the most fundamental rules of strategic-level spiritual warfare: *proceed only on God's timing*. If it is true that God gives us the authority to deal with principalities and powers, it is equally true that we had better go into action only on cue from God Himself.

Jesus set the pattern for us when He said, "Most assuredly, I say to you, the Son can do nothing of Himself, but what He sees the Father do" (John 5:19). If Jesus had to check out His timing for ministry with the Father, so we much more should do the same. That is why prayer is important in spiritual warfare. Prayer establishes the intimacy we need with the Father so that He can communicate clearly to us and let us know exactly what His timing might be in each situation.

Although this is speculation, I personally think that it made good sense for God to have Paul postpone the final deliverance for several days while the tension about the fortune-teller was building and Paul was becoming "greatly annoyed" (Acts 16:18). Furthermore, it allowed the intercessors more time to weaken the spirit through prayer. This episode of strategic-level spiritual warfare was destined to affect the whole city of Philippi. Therefore, the more public the battle the better.

If Paul had cast out the Python spirit the first day, few probably would have known about it. But when it finally happened, it turned out to be a major public display of the power of God over the power of Satan, and the territorial spirit over Philippi was thoroughly embarrassed. The strongman had been bound in the name of Jesus. The way had been opened for the gospel to spread and for a powerful church to be planted.

A Vicious Counterattack

[19] ***But when her masters saw that their hope of profit was gone, they seized Paul and Silas and dragged them into the marketplace to the authorities.*** [20] ***And they brought them to the magistrates, and said, "These men, being Jews, exceedingly trouble our city;*** [21] ***and they teach customs which are not lawful for us, being Romans, to receive or observe."*** [22] ***Then the multitude rose up together against them; and the magistrates tore off their clothes and commanded them to be beaten with rods.*** [23] ***And when they had laid many stripes on them, they threw them into prison, commanding the jailer to keep them securely.***

Many avoid confronting spiritual powers of darkness because they fear a possible counterattack. Such fear is well grounded. The notion of Christian immunity to satanic attacks is a fanciful hope rather than an accurate evaluation of spiritual reality. Here we have a vivid example of missionaries engaging the enemy on a high level, undeterred by what must have been a frank appraisal of the potential risk involved. Paul was not a novice. He definitely was a spiritual warrior who did not love his life to the death (see Rev. 12:11). He would have been totally aware of the dangers!

In this case, the missionaries were arrested, beaten with rods and thrown into jail. Civil punishment by beating, or "caning" as some call it, is considered cruel and unusual punishment in the United States, and, therefore, it is hard for Americans to comprehend the intense physical agony Paul and Silas suffered as they were thrown into their jail cell. People in Singapore and other parts of the world where criminals regularly receive such physical punishment understand it well. Was binding the strongman over the city worth it?

The masters of the fortune-teller must have been influential citizens of Philippi, explained undoubtedly by their relationship with supernatural powers and bolstered by their considerable wealth. Their underlying motive for attacking Paul and Silas was financial. They "saw that their hope of profit was gone" (Acts 16:19). They were suddenly out of business. Why? Their fortune-teller could no longer tell fortunes accurately, and she may have been the first to admit it. The Python spirit who had given her the knowledge had left her. This in itself should dispel any remaining doubt that she had told correct fortunes because of the supernatural power she had channeled, and that we are not here reading about some irrational "superstition."

The public charges against the missionaries were, of course, along different lines. Political charges of confusion and civil unrest along with cultural charges of teaching illicit customs were brought against the missionaries. An anti-Semitic flavor was added in highlighting that they were Jews. It is interesting that neither Timothy nor Luke, who were not full-blooded Jews, were persecuted even though they were part of the same apostolic team.

WARFARE IS NOT FOR ALL

Christians should realize that suffering comes with the territory of being a Christian and serving God for the advance of His kingdom. Peter makes this clear when he wrote, "Beloved, do not think it strange concerning the fiery trial which is to try you, as though some strange thing happened to you; but rejoice to the extent that you partake of Christ's sufferings" (1 Pet. 4:12-13).

This is not a welcome Scripture for many of us. We tend to be more readily attracted to promises of health, freedom, prosperity and peace, all combining for a trouble-free Christian life. Some Christians even believe that they are *entitled* to all this. Such amenities are certainly part of God's kingdom and they are included in His promises, but they do not come easily. In order to attain them we must aggressively push back the enemy.

When Paul and Silas lay beat up and bleeding on the filthy floor of the Philippi jail, they probably had as much faith and were as doctrinally sound and were as filled with the Holy Spirit as Christians ought to be. But even with all of this, they had no trouble-free Christian life!

This is not to say that all Christians have a divine calling to penetrate the darkness of unreached people groups where Satan is still at the peak of his malignant power. Few of us will ever walk in the footsteps of Paul and Silas, although some will. Many believers are called by the same God to do other things. One pastor I know says that God has called His church to be a "bedroom" rather than a "battlefield." Some need protection rather than warfare, and they are reluctant to "duke it out with the devil." John Mark apparently was one of them. If he thought the battle with Bar-Jesus in Cyprus was bad, imagine how he might have reacted to confronting the Python spirit here in Philippi. Yet, Mark has gone down in history as a hero of the Christian faith.

Martin Luther said it well when he wrote the famous song "A Mighty Fortress Is Our God":

Let goods and kindred go,
This mortal life also—
The body they may kill;
God's truth abideth still:
His kingdom is forever![12]

THE SECOND POWER ENCOUNTER

[24] *Having received such a charge, [the jailer] put them into the inner prison and fastened their feet in the stocks.* [25] *But at midnight Paul and Silas were praying and singing hymns to God, and the prisoners were listening to them.* [26] *Suddenly there was a great earthquake, so that the foundations of the prison were shaken; and immediately all the doors were opened and everyone's chains were loosed.*

Humanly speaking, the situation was hopeless. Paul and Silas were not just in jail, they were also in the innermost cell, physically beaten, exhausted and bleeding with no medical attention, their hands chained and their feet in stocks. Although no visible way of escape was open to them, they had come to Europe with God's power and they knew that the major weapons in the spiritual battle they had engaged in with the enemy were prayer and praise.

Instead of giving up, they slept the best they could under the circumstances. At midnight not only were they wide awake but they were also singing praises to God! They did not complain that God had somehow let them down, but they exalted God for the privilege of serving Him and suffering for the advance of His kingdom. Praise should be seen as a form of prayer. Jesus told us to start our prayers by saying, "Hallowed be Your name" (Matt. 6:9), which is a word of praise to God. Paul and Silas were singing praises to an audience of one—God. The other prisoners were mere eavesdroppers.

Praise as a Powerful Weapon

Relatively few believers recognize that praise in itself is one of the most powerful weapons of spiritual warfare that we have at our disposition. Scripture says that God inhabits the praises of His people (see Ps. 22:3). The devil cannot long resist praises to God. In Philippi, the major spiritual battle against Python had been won. The forces of darkness were now harassing Paul and Silas with a caning and imprisonment, but they could not maintain their ground in the face of praise and worship. In this case, deliverance took place without any overt confrontation with the forces of darkness.

Deliverance came in the form of an unusual earthquake. I say unusual because I have lived in California, where I have experienced many earthquakes. How an earthquake could loosen all the chains of all the prisoners inside the jail without toppling the structure itself is a question that even the seismologists at the California Institute of Technology would have a difficult time explaining. Loosening one or two chains, maybe. But all the chains, without harming any of the prisoners? Only a very specific action of God synchronized with the general shaking of the earth could possibly account for what had happened. It was clearly an answer to prayer, not just a coincidental natural phenomenon. Once again, the power of God was seen in Philippi.

Consoling the Jailer

[27] ***And the keeper of the prison, awaking from sleep and seeing the prison doors open, supposing the prisoners had fled, drew his sword and was about to kill himself.*** **[28]** ***But Paul called with a loud voice, saying, "Do yourself no harm, for we are all here."*** **[29]** ***Then he called for a light, ran in, and fell down trembling before Paul and Silas.***

The jailer was ready to commit suicide, but Paul intervened and stopped him. For one thing, he would have no need to kill himself because none of the prisoners under his charge had left the jail. When the jailer went into the prison, he singled out Paul and Silas. Why? Out of all the prisoners in the jail, how did he know that Paul and Silas were key players in the drama that had unfolded?

The jailer must have been aware that some kind of extraordinary spiritual power was involved in this entire scenario. By the time he was taken to jail, Paul had gained a citywide public reputation for ministering in the power of God. Everyone, including the jailer, would have known about Paul's decisive victory over the Python spirit and the fury of the fortune-teller's masters who were responsible for Paul's being in jail. By now, the jailer would have been sure that Paul and Silas represented the true God, and he now wanted to have a part in what they were doing.

The Fruit of Warfare

[30] ***And he brought them out and said, "Sirs, what must I do to be saved?"*** **[31]** ***So they said, "Believe on the Lord Jesus Christ, and you will be saved, you and your household."*** **[32]** ***Then they spoke the word of the Lord to him and to all who were in his house.*** **[33]** ***And he took them the same hour of the night and washed their stripes. And immediately he and all his family were baptized.***

It is important, in my opinion, to keep reminding ourselves of the true purpose of strategic-level spiritual warfare. Binding territorial spirits is not an end in itself, but it is only a means to the end of freeing the captives under their control so that unsaved people can hear the gospel and be saved. As Paul later wrote, "But even if our gospel is veiled, it is veiled to those who are perishing, whose minds the god of this age has blinded, who do not believe, lest the light of the gospel of the glory of Christ, who is the image of God, should shine on them" (2 Cor. 4:3-4). No one was ever saved by binding the strongman. Salvation comes only through believing the gospel of Christ. But binding the strongman frees lost people to choose whether or not they will believe, though previously Satan had their minds blinded. In Philippi, Satan had apparently delegated this evil work to the Python spirit.

Group Conversion

Note that, as in the case of Lydia, we have here another example of group conversion. "Immediately he [the jailer] and all his family were baptized" (Acts 16:33). Presumably, the household group that was baptized included not only the relatives but also the slaves, whom in all probability they owned.

These new converts were baptized immediately. We are not told that Paul or any of the missionaries did the baptizing. It could well have been that the missionaries had assigned this to the Philippian believers, new in the faith as they were, so that baptisms would become a part of normal church life after the missionaries left. The best missionary strategy stresses incorporation of the new converts into local churches as quickly as possible.

Jesus tells His disciples, "Go therefore and make disciples of all the nations, baptizing them in the name of the Father and of the Son and of the Holy Spirit" (Matt. 28:19). If evangelism is equivalent to making disciples and not just preaching or passing out tracts, incorporation into the local church will not be seen as some afterthought but as part and parcel of the evangelistic strategy itself. This, I think, is what Jesus had in mind in the Great Commission just cited, and it was Paul's standard procedure on the mission field.

MOVING ON

[35] ***And when it was day, the magistrates sent the officers, saying, "Let those men go."*** **[37]** ***But Paul said to them, "They have beaten us openly, uncondemned Romans, and have thrown us into prison. And now do they put us out secretly? No indeed! Let them come themselves and get us out."***

God had opened the doors of the jail, but Paul did not become a fugitive. He chose to remain in the jail. When the authorities tried to free him, Paul demanded a public showdown. This was now a matter of civil justice. Roman citizens deserved a trial before punishment, but Paul and Silas, both Roman citizens, had been beaten and jailed illegally. The city leaders were obviously in trouble:

> [38] *And the officers told these words to the magistrates, and they were afraid when they heard that they were Romans.* [39] *Then they came and pleaded with them and brought them out, and asked them to depart from the city.*

After receiving the apology, Paul apparently did not think he should press charges of wrongful punishment. His time in Philippi was coming to a close and he was ready to move on.

> [40] *So they went out of the prison and entered the house of Lydia; and when they had seen the brethren, they encouraged them and departed.*

As I mentioned earlier in this chapter, it is rather fascinating that the last place we see the missionaries in Philippi is in Lydia's house, and when they leave, Luke's narrative suddenly switches from "we" to "they." Paul, Silas and Timothy continued their missionary work on new frontiers. Luke stayed behind in Lydia's house. Of course, the romantic notion I earlier suggested, namely, that Luke and Lydia might have married, cannot be definitively proved or disproved by the text itself. It is up to our individual imaginations!

REFLECTION QUESTIONS

1. Paul and his friends missed hearing accurately from God when they set out first for Asia and then for Bithynia. Can you think of similar experiences of your own when you found you were going in the wrong direction?
2. Talk about the possibility that Luke might have married Lydia in Philippi. On a probability scale of 1 to 10, where would you place it? Why?
3. What is your view on the authority given to believers over demonic powers? Is it limited to casting out demons from individuals or does it also involve higher demonic forces?

4. Warfare against the Python spirit in Philippi caused Paul and Silas great suffering. Are all Christians expected to follow their example? Discuss the reasons for your answer to this question.
5. It seems that the Philippian jailer's invitation to accept Christ applied not only to himself, but also to all those in his household. Do you believe that his wife, children and slaves could all be saved through a group decision rather than by each one making an individual decision?

19

YOU WIN SOME AND YOU LOSE SOME

ACTS 17

When Paul, Silas and Timothy were in Troas, God gave Paul a vision in which a Macedonian man said to him, "Come over to Macedonia and help us" (Acts 16:9). The next thing we know they have planted a church in Philippi, which indeed was one of the great cities of Macedonia. But Philippi was not the capital; Thessalonica happened to be the capital of the province of Macedonia.

PASSING THROUGH AMPHIPOLIS AND APOLLONIA

[1] *Now when they had passed through Amphipolis and Apollonia, they came to Thessalonica, where there was a synagogue of the Jews.*

The missionary team had been called to evangelize Macedonia, but after leaving Philippi, they passed through two significant Macedonian cities—Amphipolis and Apollonia—without stopping. Amphipolis was located 33 miles from Philippi, and Apollonia 27 miles farther down the same road. When they arrived in each of those cities, they in all probability found lodging at the local inn and spent at least one night in each, but then pushed on.

Some might wonder why they did not stop to evangelize and plant churches in Amphipolis and Apollonia. Paul's assignment as the apostle to the uncircumcision was to multiply Gentile churches, and these cities were, of course, full of unsaved Gentiles. It would seem logical to plant at least one church in every city they visited. But they didn't. This is not to say they might not have witnessed to some fellow travelers staying with them at the inn, or to people they might have met in the marketplace. But casual witnessing is a far cry from settling down to evangelize and plant a new church.

A plausible way of understanding this is to assume that Paul, Silas and Timothy were adhering to a sound principle of missiology called today "resistance-receptivity theory" or "the harvest principle."

THE HARVEST PRINCIPLE

Jesus established the foundation of the harvest principle when He sent His 12 disciples out on their own for the first time. Just prior to that He said, "The harvest truly is plentiful, but the laborers are few. Therefore pray the Lord of the harvest to send out laborers into His harvest" (Matt. 9:37-38).

Every farmer knows that harvest time is the part of the annual agricultural cycle when the maximum number of laborers is needed. Because the number of available harvesters is invariably limited, they must be deployed as wisely as possible. Farmers realize this and they make sure that their laborers are in fields where the harvest is ripe, not in green fields that have yet to ripen. That, obviously, would be a waste of their time.

Jesus used this analogy for evangelism. Just as different farm crops ripen at different times, so also different populations ripen for the gospel at different times. Missionaries, to the extent possible, should make sure they are present in ripened harvest fields. The bulk of evangelistic work should be done among receptive peoples. It is true that all peoples, whether receptive or resistant, need to receive a witness of Christ, but the greater investment of time, energy and money should be expended among the receptive.

When the 12 disciples went out, Jesus gave them amazingly specific instructions about their evangelistic targets. Three broadly defined people groups occupied the general area in those days: Jews, Gentiles and Samaritans. Jesus said, "Do not go into the way of the Gentiles, and do not enter a city of the Samaritans. But go rather to the lost sheep of the house of Israel" (10:5-6). Both Gentiles and Samaritans were lost and needed to be saved. Jesus came and would die on the cross for Gentiles and Samaritans as well as for Jews. But at that time they were not yet a ripened harvest field. The disciples would have wasted their time trying to reach them. Both groups later became receptive, and great harvests were eventually reaped among them. But not earlier. The disciples on Jesus' mission were to evangelize only Jews—"the lost sheep of the house of Israel."

But not all the Jews would be receptive either. Jesus told the disciples how to handle that situation as well. He said, "When you go into a household, greet it. If the household is worthy, let your peace come upon it" (vv. 12-13). This would describe the *receptive* Jews. And the *resistant*? "And whoever will not receive you nor hear your words, when you depart from that house or city, shake off the dust from your feet" (v. 14). Shaking off the dust was a public statement that they did not plan to return. Instead of returning to the resistant, they should push out to new frontiers and find those who are receptive—the ripened harvest fields.

HOW DO SPIRITUAL HARVESTS RIPEN?

How do harvests get ripe? Whether in agriculture or in evangelizing the lost, God is the only one who ripens the harvest. No human being ever manufactured a cauliflower or a persimmon or an ear of corn. Likewise, only the Holy Spirit prepares hearts to receive the gospel message. Paul said, "I planted, Apollos watered, but God gave the increase" (1 Cor. 3:6).

The harvest principle says, then, that good missionary strategy will be influenced by accurately perceiving the moving of the Holy Spirit upon unreached peoples as He is preparing them for hearing and accepting the message of salvation. Paul, Silas and Timothy were implementing that principle when they passed through Amphipolis and Apollonia without attempting to plant a church.

WHY THESSALONICA WAS RIPE

Thessalonica was riper for the gospel than either Amphipolis or Apollonia because it had a synagogue of the Jews. The missionaries' goal was to make Gentile disciples and, oddly enough, the most likely place to see that happen at that time was in the synagogue. I say "oddly enough" because in our day one of the *last* places we would expect to make Gentile disciples would be in a synagogue. As I explained in considerable detail in the last chapter, the major reason for this was that the most receptive people group in the cities of the Roman Empire was the Gentile God-fearers, and the place to find them and share with them was in the Jewish synagogue. This is exactly what Paul did.

[2] ***Then Paul, as his custom was, went in to them, and for three Sabbaths reasoned with them from the Scriptures,*** **[3]** ***explaining and demonstrating that the Christ had to suffer and rise again from the dead, and saying, "This Jesus whom I preach to you is the Christ."***

We shouldn't jump to the conclusion that Paul preached in the synagogue on the first three Sabbaths after arriving in Thessalonica. He left soon after preaching on the third Sabbath, so that supposition would have put him in Thessalonica for only about a month. But it appears that he was there longer than that. Let me explain.

When Paul later writes to the believers in Thessalonica, he reminisces about what had happened at that time. Among other things, he says, "For you remember, brethren, our labor and toil; for laboring night and day, that we might not be a burden to any of you, we preached to you the gospel of God" (1 Thess. 2:9). Paul and his friends had jobs, perhaps making tents, for apparently some period of time. Offhand, this sounds like more than a three-week visit.

Furthermore, we discover from the letter Paul later writes to the church in Philippi, "Now you Philippians know also that in the beginning of the gospel, when I departed from Macedonia, no church shared with me concerning giving and receiving but you only. For even in Thessalonica you sent aid once and again for my necessities" (Phil. 4:15-16). Two monetary gifts arrive from Philippi, perhaps largely from Luke and Lydia, while Paul is in Thessalonica, and this also appears to cover more than a period of three weeks.

While Paul was in Thessalonica, he was undoubtedly establishing many valuable contacts, building personal relationships and gaining credibility on which to launch his ministry in the synagogue itself when the proper time came.

The Church in Jason's House

[4] ***And some of them were persuaded; and a great multitude of the devout Greeks, and not a few of the leading women, joined Paul and Silas.***

A bit more detail of Paul's ministry in Thessalonica is provided in 1 Thessalonians 1:5: "For our gospel did not come to you in word only, but also in power, and in the Holy Spirit and in much assurance, as you know what kind of men we were among you for your sake." Notice the balance here, which ought to be a pattern for missionaries today as well. Paul, Silas and Timothy shared their faith in the following ways:

- *In word.* "For three Sabbaths [they] reasoned with them from the Scriptures, explaining . . . that the Christ had to suffer and rise again from the dead" (Acts 17:2-3). This was sound doctrinal preaching from the Old Testament, showing how it pointed to Jesus as the Messiah.

- *In power.* Not only were they explaining about Christ, but they were also demonstrating the truth. This once again is ministry in both word and deed, characteristic of the models we have found throughout the Acts of the Apostles. The power ministries of healing, deliverance, miracles, prophecies and spiritual warfare undoubtedly were fully active in Thessalonica, although by now they had become so much a part of the missionaries' routine that Luke does not find it necessary to mention them specifically.

- *In the Holy Spirit.* The missionaries' ministry was not of the flesh, but of the Spirit. It was characterized both by the *fruit* of the Spirit and by the *gifts* of the Spirit. Through the Holy Spirit, they were in close touch with the Father, and, therefore, they also could minister.

- *In much assurance.* They could be bold because they knew they were exactly where God wanted them to be and they were obeying God's orders. Paul ministered with deep conviction.

Not a Trickle, But a Multitude!

The net result of their ministry was not a mere trickle of converts, but "a great multitude." Here in Thessalonica, the converts appear to be mostly Gentiles, including the devout Greeks, who would have been the God-fearers, and also "not a few of the "leading women" (v. 4). These were undoubtedly upperclass women similar to Lydia of Philippi, possibly including some government functionaries. Paul had an outstanding nucleus for one of the most significant churches that he and his group would plant. Further affirming that they were largely Gentiles, Paul later writes that they had "turned to God from idols to serve the living and true God" (1 Thess. 1:9). Jewish conversion would not have involved turning from idols.

This church, like all the others Paul planted, *began as one house church,* in all probability meeting in the house of a man named Jason (see Acts 17:5).

Jason is a Greek name, so he was more than likely one of the God-fearers who heard Paul preach for three Sabbaths in the synagogue. Probably not long after Paul left, the number of house churches in Thessalonica began to multiply, spreading out from their base in Jason's house. The Thessalonian believers were aggressively evangelistic because Paul writes to them a few months later, saying, "For from you the word of the Lord has sounded forth, not only in Macedonia and Achaia, but also in every place" (1 Thess. 1:8).

Driven Out by Angry Jewish Leaders

[5] *But the Jews who were not persuaded, becoming envious, took some of the evil men from the marketplace, and gathering a mob, set all the city in an uproar and attacked the house of Jason, and sought to bring them out to the people.* [6] *But when they did not find them, they dragged* [7] *Jason and some brethren to the rulers of the city, crying out, "These who have turned the world upside down have come here too. Jason has harbored them, and these are all acting contrary to the decrees of Caesar, saying there is another king—Jesus."* [8] *And they troubled the crowd and the rulers of the city when they heard these things.* [9] *So when they had taken security from Jason and the rest, they let them go.*

The persecution of the believers began with the unconverted Jews. From what we can surmise, proportionately fewer Jews were present in the nucleus of the Thessalonian church than in some others. The Jews were envious, just as they were said to be in Antioch of Pisidia where Paul had planted one of his very first churches: "When the Jews saw the multitudes, they were filled with envy" (13:45). Here in Thessalonica, the Jewish leaders may have been envious for at least four reasons:

1. The Gentile God-fearers were leaving their synagogue to follow another Jewish leader—Paul.
2. The power of God in miracles and wonders was being manifested through Paul, and not through them.
3. Paul was not requiring circumcision for Gentiles to become saved, as the rabbis had been advocating through the years.
4. Paul declared, "This Jesus whom I preach to you is the Christ" (17:3). "The Christ" means the Messiah, and the rabbis in the

> synagogue were supposed to be the first to know when the real Jewish Messiah had arrived. Worse yet, when Paul declared that Jesus was the Messiah, the Jewish leaders came under a cloud of guilt because they, by identification, were to blame for killing Him. Paul mentions this in 1 Thessalonians, where he says the Jews "killed both the Lord Jesus and their own prophets" (2:15). If nothing else, this accusation alone could have incited the Jewish leaders to riot.

The charge against the missionaries, "Those who have turned the world upside down" (Acts 17:6), is not a backdoor commendation for effective evangelism, as many might think. F. F. Bruce suggests that it is much more serious than that. "The words imply subversive or seditious activity."[1] It was an ominous political charge, implying that the missionaries would advocate dethroning Caesar and installing a rival emperor. It was similar to the false accusation frequently leveled against many American missionaries today, me included, that we are secret CIA agents.

Although the missionaries were not found guilty, they, nevertheless, chose the more prudent action:

[10] ***Then the brethren immediately sent Paul and Silas away by night to Berea....***

THE FAIR-MINDED BEREANS

[10] ... ***When they arrived, they went into the synagogue of the Jews.*** [11] ***These were more fair-minded than those in Thessalonica, in that they received the word with all readiness, and searched the Scriptures daily to find out whether these things were so.***

Berea was about 40 miles southwest of Thessalonica. It was not a prominent city, as were Thessalonica and Philippi, but rather an out-of-the-way town. This may be why we have no later Epistle written by Paul to the church in Berea.

Luke mentions that only Paul and Silas left Thessalonica, so perhaps Timothy remained behind. If he did, he would have joined them later because he is mentioned being with them in Berea in verse 14.

The major reason they would have chosen Berea as their next evangelistic target would have been once again because of the Jewish synagogue there and the receptive God-fearers they would likely find in it. Some say Paul's missionary strategy was to target cities of great social, political and economic significance. This holds true only partially. Berea was no such city. More important to Paul than locating a city of great prestige *was the presence of a Jewish synagogue*, based on what I have described as the missiological principle of the harvest. That is where he would find the greatest number of Gentiles seeking God.

How long did the missionaries stay in Berea? We do not know exactly, but the chronology seems to indicate that it was probably for several months.

They had a much better time in the Berean synagogue than they did in Thessalonica. They were treated well, and even the Jews seemed receptive to the gospel of Christ. Luke says they were "more fair-minded" (v. 11). Why should this be? Perhaps because Berea was a smaller city and more laid back. It might not have had as much civic pride.

Was the Strongman Bound?

Also, the phrase "that they received the word with all readiness" (v. 11) seems to indicate that the spiritual atmosphere was a bit different in Berea. Somehow the forces of darkness that operate to blind the minds of those who do not believe (see 2 Cor. 4:3-4) did not seem to be as powerful here. Certainly it was nothing compared to what Paul would soon find in Athens. Knowing what we now know about the power of targeted intercession, it could have been that prayer warriors recruited in Philippi and Thessalonica were on the job and they had done some successful spiritual warfare against whatever territorial spirits might have been assigned to Berea.

To carry this one step further, it could have been that two of the women from the Philippian church, Euodia and Syntyche, had come along with the missionaries as intercessors. Paul says in his letter written later to the Philippians that these two women "labored with me in the gospel" (Phil. 4:3). Their role was much more significant than many commentators recognize. F. F. Bruce, for example, says that a very strong Greek verb is used here: "Whatever form these two women's collaboration with Paul in his gospel ministry may have taken, it was not confined to making tea for him and his circle—or whatever the first-century counterpart to that activity was."[2]

The verb *synathleo* means "contended" or "strived" or "fought at my side." D. Edmond Hiebert suggests that this verb "pictures these women as having served as Paul's fellow soldiers in the battle."[3] F. W. Beare puts these courageous women right on the frontlines of strategic-level spiritual warfare when he argues that Euodia and Syntyche were "pitted along with Paul 'against principalities and powers . . . against the spiritual hosts of wickedness in the heavenly places' of Ephesians 6:12, who employ the human opponents of the gospel as their tools."[4] I would, therefore, prefer to translate Paul's statement in Philippians 4:3 that these women were "doing spiritual warfare on my behalf."

Clarifying the possible role of Euodia and Syntyche does not prove, of course, that they were necessarily here in Berea with Paul and Silas. Their prayers at a distance from their homes in Philippi could also have been effective in pushing back the darkness from Berea. Nevertheless, on-site praying is to be preferred when it can be arranged. A trend in world Christianity traced back to Lausanne II in Manila in 1989, where it first occurred on a prominent level, is to recruit teams of experienced intercessors to pray 24 hours a day through what appear to be milestone events in the advance of the kingdom of God.

The role of personal intercessors, such as Euodia and Syntyche, in opening the way in the invisible world for the powerful working of God through ministries here in the visible world has been all but neglected in past decades. In my book *Prayer Shield*, I look into reasons for this and also report how things changed radically during the decade of the 1990s. Pastors, missionaries and Christian leaders of all kinds are now enjoying much more blessing in their ministries by having personal intercessors doing spiritual warfare on their behalf, as Euodia and Syntyche were doing for Paul and his team.

The Berean Church

One of the characteristics of the Bereans was that "they searched the Scriptures daily to find out whether these things were so" (Acts 17:11). The tone of this wording suggests that the Bereans' desire, as they read the Old Testament, was to go into more depth on the matters Paul was addressing, not doing it with the intention of refuting Paul or engaging in polemics. Paul was probably bringing to their attention Scripture passages to which they had not previously paid much attention. It appears that the rabbis in Berea were as willing to learn from the missionaries as were the common people. This humble desire to hear what God is saying is so commendable that even today Christians like to use the name "Berean Church" or "Berean Sunday School Class" or "Berean Bible School."

In contrast to Thessalonica, a higher percentage of Jews than usual probably participated in the nucleus of this new church. Nevertheless, Gentiles, beginning with the God-fearers, were undoubtedly the majority, as they were in the other churches Paul planted. Interestingly, in Thessalonica Luke makes a point of mentioning that "not a few of the leading women joined Paul and Silas" (v. 4), and here in Berea he also indicates that among the converts were "prominent women as well as men" (v. 12). From the first century until now, no matter where we go in the world, the backbone of Christian churches seems to be women. For whatever reason, it is axiomatic that year in and year out, more women than men are willing to give their hearts to Jesus Christ and serve Him with their lives.

MORE TROUBLE FROM HOSTILE JEWISH LEADERS

[13] ***But when the Jews from Thessalonica learned that the word of God was preached by Paul at Berea, they came there also and stirred up the crowds.*** [14] ***Then immediately the brethren sent Paul away, to go to the sea; but both Silas and Timothy remained there.***

The fair-minded Jews in Berea had no problem with Paul and his ministry until hostile Jews from Thessalonica arrived on the scene to stir up trouble. They must have arrived with considerable force. They began looking for Paul, possibly having a warrant for his execution from the capital city of Macedonia. Paul had known them all too well in Thessalonica, and he wanted nothing more to do with them. His friends helped him slip away under cover of darkness and catch a ship that was heading south on the Aegean Sea toward Athens. Perhaps because of the hasty escape, Silas and Timothy had no time to pack up and go along with him, so they stayed behind in Berea.

ATHENS: A STRONGHOLD OF DARKNESS

What a contrast between Berea—where people welcomed the missionaries, treated them well, searched the Scriptures, received the word of God, were born again and established a strong church—and Athens, in all probability the most impenetrable stronghold of darkness of all the cities that Paul ever set out to evangelize!

The city of Athens was so permeated with idolatry that the great apostle Paul came and went with minimal results. After the exciting harvests in Philippi, Thessalonica and Berea, Athens must have been an exceedingly depressing experience. From what we know about Paul, he would have preferred any day to be put in jail or to be driven out of town by angry opponents of the gospel rather than mocked and laughed at and effectively neutralized by sophisticated intellectuals.

From the viewpoint of evangelistic fruit, Athens will not play on Paul's highlight films. For many of us, however, it could have the redeeming feature of serving as a consolation. Many of us have also experienced meager or negative responses to good preaching, just as Paul did in Athens. If it could happen to Paul, there is no reason to think it couldn't happen to us from time to time also. Beyond that, Paul learned some important lessons related to engaging the enemy in Athens, and we can learn them as well.

A City Given to Idols

[16] ***Now while Paul waited for them at Athens, his spirit was provoked within him when he saw that the city was given over to idols.***

This is the only place in the New Testament where we find the Greek word *kateidolos*, translated "given over to idols." Descriptions of the idolatry of Athens abound in ancient literature. It was said that in Athens it was easier to find a god than a human being. Athens was called a "forest of idols." Some streets were so full of idols that pedestrians had difficulty getting through. One estimate reveals that more images were located in the city of Athens than in all the rest of Greece combined. The nearest thing I have found that might fit such a description today is Kyoto, Japan; but first-century Athens sounds even worse. No wonder Paul "was provoked within him"!

Athens' Personality

If cities can be said to have personalities, Athens would have boasted an extremely high IQ. For hundreds of years, Athens had been considered by many to be the intellectual center not only of Greece, but also of the whole world. It was the birthplace of the subsequent dominant philosophical tradition of the West.

Where did this brilliance originate? It certainly came largely from the demonic forces of darkness over the city. Some might reflect that the Greek knowledge could have been a product of human minds that were made in the image of God. This may be true, but the perverse *fruit* of those minds in Athens was anything but. James describes it as "wisdom [that] does not descend from above, but is earthly, sensual, demonic" (Jas. 3:15).

The idols in Athens were the visible front of the invisible spiritual forces that were actively shaping art, philosophy, education and daily life in the city. Not only that, but this influence also strongly radiated from Athens through the whole Roman Empire. The dominant culture was called "Hellenistic (or Greek) culture." Greek was the primary trade language in that part of the world, so much so that the entire New Testament was written in Greek, although mostly by Jews.

The Roots of Spiritual Darkness

Spiritual darkness over a city such as Athens is not something that just happens by a sort of unlucky roll of some cosmic dice. It is rooted in conscious decisions made by actual human beings. The population of Athens as a whole had voluntarily pledged allegiance to a variety of principalities of darkness, many of which can be identified by name.

For a starter, the name "Athens" was taken in honor of the goddess Athena (also called "Minerva" in Latin). Most cities in the ancient world had chosen to subject themselves and their fate consciously and intentionally to a so-called "patron deity" or deities. They are what we today would call the territorial spirits. Athena was the "Virgin goddess of wisdom, fine and skilled arts."[5] Thus, some of her functional names would have been "spirit of wisdom" and "spirit of art." Under her influence, Athens became both the intellectual center and the cultural center of the world.

Possibly Athena, like the Virgin Mary in Latin America, was another of the disguises of the powerful Queen of Heaven. She exercises such malignant power that even God is repelled by people who choose to serve her. Concerning those who sacrifice to the Queen of Heaven, the Lord says, "Therefore do not pray for this people, nor lift up a cry or prayer for them, nor make intercession to Me; for I will not hear you" (Jer. 7:16). This perhaps could explain why the prayers of intercessors such as Euodia and Syntyche, which apparently were effective in Berea, might have fallen on deaf ears in Athens.

Honoring Demonic Forces Through Festivals

The social life of Athens revolved around periodic celebrations—usually annual festivals—in honor of the multiple deities whom the people served. Of the scores of such events in Athens, eight of them stand out as being the most prominent:

1. *The Festival to Athena herself* (Minerva in Latin). This was called the Panathenaia and it was dedicated to what was likely the major territorial spirit over the city. It was held each summer.
2. *The Festival to Apollo* (who used the same name in Latin). Apollo was the spirit of machismo, of male beauty, of what would be epitomized today in the bodybuilding industry. His celebration, also in the summer, was called "The Great Sacrifice."

3-4. *The Festivals to Demeter* (Ceres in Latin). Demeter is Mother Earth, a spirit of fertility and likely a spirit of feminism, perhaps countering Apollo's spirit of machismo, and likely another deceptive adaptation of the Queen of Heaven. In early fall, the Eleusinian Mysteries were dedicated to her honor at the time grain was planted. Later in the fall, Demeter was invited to preside over the Thesmophoria, a fertility festival for women only.

5. *The Festival to Poseidon* (Neptune in Latin). Poseidon was served as the spirit of the sea and the spirit of earthquakes in midwinter.
6. *The Festival to the Dead, called Anthesterion.* This was a feast of flowers in early spring, honoring the spirit of death.
7. *The Festival of Dionysus* (Bacchus in Latin). This was a drunken orgy in late spring, dedicated to the spirit of the wine harvest.
8. *The Festival to Zeus* (Jupiter in Latin). Zeus was the highest of the principalities of the enemy, known also as the spirit of the sky and the spirit of weather. His ritual came at the beginning of each summer.

Each of these, and other festivals, were public displays of worship and sacrifice to these demonic beings. They seemed to be sending an engraved invitation to the demons to come and do their things in Athens for another year. They usually included the sacrifice itself, athletic and artistic contests, a procession of great pageantry through the streets that brought honor to the deities and mystery rites open only to those few individuals duly initiated into their secrets.

What was the real purpose of these festivals? Everett Ferguson says, "The festivals are dramatic testimony of the mutual interpenetration of religion and all phases of life in pagan antiquity."[6] The implication of this penetration into all phases of life underscores the challenge of separating the wholesome parts of a culture from those that serve the demonic outright. No wonder Paul calls Satan "the god of this age" (2 Cor. 4:4).

Serving the Devil from Morning to Night

The common people of Athens served the demonic spirits day in and day out. Each family had an altar to Zeus in the yard to protect the home; a pillar dedicated to Apollo to protect the family members; and a nonpoisonous snake in the pantry, representing Zeus, which ate the food offered to it each day. At every meal, they also offered food to Hestia, the spirit of the hearth, and they had a household altar on which they offered wine to Agathos Daimon, the "good demon." Good demon? Only those thoroughly deceived by the enemy could believe in any such thing, as some today tragically believe that certain kinds of witchcraft may be good for them.

Throughout the whole countryside, objects created by God would be used by the Athenians to give honor to a particular evil spirit: mountains, trees, rivers and winds.

The famous Greek philosophers also attributed their knowledge to spirit beings. For example, Socrates, a native of Athens, prayed to Pan, an outdoor spirit who had the legs and face of a goat: "O beloved Pan and all ye other gods of this place, grant to me that I may be made beautiful in my soul within, and that all external possessions be in harmony with my inner man. May I consider the wise man rich; and may I have such wealth as only the self-restrained man can bear or endure."[7] And Plato, also from Athens, wrote in his *Laws*, "There is also the priestly class, who, as the law declares, know how to give the gods gifts from men in the form of sacrifices which are acceptable to them, and to ask on our behalf blessings in return from them."[8]

Plato taught that "[a] demon [is] a destiny spirit somewhat like a guardian angel as a companion of man, or of cities as well as individuals."[9] This means that, for Plato, it would be desirable for both humans and cities to be demonized indefinitely. This same desire is reflected in some Native American cultures today in which young men are routinely expected to go through a sweat lodge or other ceremony to receive their lifetime demons. This, likewise, is reflected by New Agers who diligently seek, and encourage others to seek, their personal "spirit guide."

No Wonder Paul Was Provoked

Luke may well have been putting it mildly when he wrote that "[Paul's] spirit was provoked within him when he saw that the city was given over to idols" (Acts 17:16).

Paul had seen idolatry before, but nothing on the scale he saw in Athens. We must be clear, however, about what exactly was provoking Paul. This will not only help us understand what Paul was up against in Athens, but it will also help us greatly to confront many aspects of the world in which we live today, especially when we are called upon to engage in spiritual warfare.

Perhaps there were others, but I can see five things in the situation I have described in Athens that would especially provoke Paul and that should provoke us when we are up against such evil forces as well:

First, invisible spirits were behind the visible idols. The objects made of wood, stone, metal or clay called "idols" would not in themselves upset Paul too much. Later he would write, probably agreeing with something the Corinthians had written to him, "We know that an idol is nothing in the world" (1 Cor. 8:4). What would upset Paul more than the literal idol were the demonic spirits of the invisible world. These were frequently attached to visible idols and they were succeeding in keeping the minds of the people who served them blinded to the message of salvation Paul was bringing to them. Paul's primary focus was not on demons, but on people. Christ did not die to save demons, but to save people. The demons were provoking him because they were *obstacles* that had to be removed for the gospel to get through to the people.

Second, powerful strongholds were binding the population of Athens. Two major kinds of strongholds furnish excuses for the enemy to accomplish his malicious purposes. Paul later writes, "For the weapons of our warfare are not carnal but mighty in God for pulling down strongholds, casting down arguments and every high thing that exalts itself against the knowledge of God" (2 Cor. 10:4-5). The first kind of stronghold is "arguments" from the Greek *logizomai,* referring to human ideas or philosophies or attitudes or actions. The second is every "high thing," from the Greek *hypsoma,* referring to cosmic powers or spirits.[10] Athens as an intellectual center and as a religio-cultural center cluttered with idols had both of these strongholds firmly entrenched. These strongholds were effectively keeping the gospel of Christ from flourishing there, and Paul was understandably upset.

Third, the Athenians were serving the creature rather than the Creator. In Romans, Paul later puts his thoughts on this in words. He writes that "the wrath of God is revealed" (1:18) when human beings do not recognize the glory of God in His creation. The visible world was created so that "His invisible attributes are clearly seen, being understood by the things that are made" (v. 20). To put it clearly, God gets angry when He finds that people such as those in Athens "changed the glory of the incorruptible God into an image made like corruptible man—and birds and four-footed animals and creeping things" (v. 23). What a clear description of Athens! And God can become so angry at such things that He "gives them up" (see Rom. 1:24,26,28). Had He given up on some of the Athenians?

Fourth, the sacrifices in the idol ceremonies were being made to demons. Although it is true, as I have said, that an idol in itself is nothing, it is also true that an idol can serve as a medium through which an evil spirit (which *is* something) can actually harm a person in one way or another. Paul combines the two thoughts in 1 Corinthians 10 when he discusses the reasons for not eating meat in idol temples, or more likely in restaurants attached to them, in Corinth. He says that what the pagans offer to idols "they sacrifice to demons . . . , and I do not want you to have fellowship with demons" (1 Cor. 10:20). The idol is the *visible* while the demon is the *invisible* part of the same thing.

Michael Green, a New Testament scholar, offers a perceptive comment on this issue. He says that in the Early Church, "The more common attitude was . . . to pour scorn, indeed, on the form idolatry takes, but to take very seriously the demonic forces behind it. The demons were fed by the fat of the sacrifices, which was why it was particularly important for Christians to have nothing to do with the sacrificial system." He reminds us that the demons could be overcome by the power of Christ, and that "The Christian's business, therefore, was to wage total war upon them, relying on the victory of Christ."[11]

To put it another way, the people of Athens, while sacrificing to idols, were literally *taking communion* with demons and making covenant with them to continue their destructive control over their lives.

Fifth, the annual festivals to the high-ranking spirits were designed as occasions to renew and extend agreements previously made with the principalities that ruled the city.

Territorial spirits over cities gain their power only through decisions of human beings. Through the centuries, people groups experiencing collective trauma brought on by war, famine, epidemic, natural disaster or any other cause have often sought supernatural power to relieve their situation. Very few turn to the true God as they did in Nineveh (see Jon. 3:3-10). Most, because of their fallen human nature, turn rather to other sources of supernatural power, such as demonic principalities, for solutions to their problems.

Making Agreements with Demons

As George Otis, Jr., a missiologist, explains, "The overwhelming majority of peoples down through history have elected to exchange the revelation of God for a lie. Heeding the entreaties of demons, they have chosen in their desperation to enter into *quid pro quo* pacts with the spirit world. In return for a particular deity's consent to resolve their immediate traumas, they have offered up their singular and ongoing allegiance. They have collectively sold their proverbial souls."[12]

Once people, such as those in Athens, make such an agreement with evil spirits, how is this maintained? How is their demonic lease extended generation after generation? It is done principally through festivals and pilgrimages. George Otis, Jr., says, "These celebrations are decidedly not the benign, quaint and colorful cultural spectacles they are often made out to be. They are conscious transactions with the spirit world. They are opportunities for contemporary generations to reaffirm the choices and pacts made by their forefathers and ancestors. They are occasions to dust off ancient welcome mats and extend the devil's right to rule over specific peoples and places today."[13]

An interesting example of this occurred in Athens itself in 420 B.C. when a plague threatened to wipe out the city. In the face of this trauma, the people of Athens agreed to invite a spirit of psychic healing named Asclepius to save the city, which he gladly consented to do. I am not aware of the immediate price that Asclepius might have exacted for his services, but I am sure it was considerable. A. D. Nock comments, "The rise of Asclepius reflects also a tendency for a religion of emergencies to become prominent as contrasted to a religion of normality."[14] This is a confirmation of Otis's notion of traumas frequently precipitating the demonization of people groups or cities. Knowing this, Paul was deeply provoked by finding that practically the entire population of Athens was in captivity to the evil one.

Paul in the Athens Synagogue

[17] ***Therefore he reasoned in the synagogue with the Jews and with the Gentile worshipers . . .***

As was his custom, Paul went into the Jewish synagogue in Athens to share the gospel. Ordinarily, he would find some of the people in the synagogue most ready to hear and accept the message of salvation. But this apparently was not the case in Athens. Luke, who tells us of converts as frequently as he can, mentions nothing of either Jews or God-fearers in the synagogue being saved.

Why is this? Very few of the commentators I have consulted raise this issue, much less analyze the reasons. They generally believe that Paul's address to the Greek philosophers deserves our primary attention at this point. Simon Kistemaker, however, does make a brief, but plausible, suggestion concerning Paul's synagogue ministry: "We surmise that the membership in the synagogue in Athens was less than that of the synagogues in Berea and Thessalonica."[15] If this is the case, I would like to suggest three reasons why Paul would have seen meager response:

First, the thickness of the extraordinary cloud of spiritual darkness over Athens may have kept pagan Gentiles from becoming synagogue God-fearers in any significant numbers. True, Luke mentions "Gentile worshipers" in the synagogue there, but the numbers presumably would be nothing approaching those in the synagogues in Berea and Thessalonica. Furthermore, the idolatrous environment of the city would not have been particularly hospitable to Jews themselves (who despised idols), and, because Athens was not particularly known as a commercial center, relatively few Jews might have lived there.

Second, perhaps the Jews who had chosen to reside in Athens had developed a protective shield of tolerance, and the blatant idolatry of the city might not have bothered them that much. This certainly would have characterized them as liberal, rather than more orthodox, Jews. This in itself could have been the cause of a struggling synagogue that would have had little social strength.

Third, the constant festivals and pilgrimages that offered their sacrifices to the hosts of wickedness over the city would have served to empower the enemy to the extent that he had gained unusual ability to neutralize Paul's evangelistic efforts, both in the synagogue and in the marketplace.

Whatever the reasons, Paul became frustrated enough that he did something that was not his usual practice.

Paul in the Athens Marketplace

[17] *Therefore he reasoned . . . in the marketplace daily with those who happened to be there.*

Paul was desperate enough to try Plan B. He did not find the usual ripened harvest field among the God-fearers in the synagogue, so he decided to try going directly to the Gentiles. This had worked once on his first term when he and Barnabas went to Lystra, but there we saw a high-profile healing of a man lame from birth, which had opened the minds of the Gentiles. In Athens, however, we know of no such miracle, and approaching the Gentiles directly didn't work as expected.

[18] *Then certain Epicurean and Stoic philosophers encountered him. And some said, "What does this babbler want to say?" Others said, "He seems to be a proclaimer of foreign gods," because he preached to them Jesus and the resurrection.*

The Athenians insulted Paul by calling him a "babbler," which literally means a "seed picker." John Stott comments, "It would be hard to imagine a less receptive or more scornful audience."[16] It gets worse by verse 32 where, according to various translators, "some mocked" or "some laughed" or "some sneered" or "some scoffed." Eugene Peterson in *THE MESSAGE* puts it vividly: "Some laughed at him and walked off making jokes."

Paul's Speech on the Areopagus

[19] *And they took him and brought him to the Areopagus, saying, "May we know what this new doctrine is of which you speak?* [20] *For you are bringing some strange things to our ears. Therefore we want to know what these things mean."* [21] *For all the Athenians and the foreigners who were there spent their time in nothing else but either to tell or to hear some new thing.*

Undoubtedly, knowing ahead of time that his audience would be a hostile one, Paul decided to go all the way and address the philosophers who regularly gathered on the Areopagus, or "Mars Hill." All kinds of people were there, from the Epicureans who taught that we should eat, drink and be merry to get all the pleasure from life possible, to the Stoics who taught that we should submit ourselves patiently to whatever fate might bring through self-control, not pleasure-seeking. Tolerating all such philosophies was regarded as politically correct in Athens. As for Paul's ideas, the people in the marketplace were simply curious to see what this "seed picker" might have to offer. They literally had nothing better to do.

The Visible and the Invisible

Paul's central theme in talking to the idolatrous philosophers was the relationship between the visible and the invisible. It was a brilliant example of contextualization, beginning by his reference to their "UNKNOWN GOD" whom, Paul said, "you worship without knowing" (v. 23). This is a reference to the invisible Lord God who cannot stand to be represented by things made with human hands such as the forests of idols seen throughout Athens. The Creator never takes the form of the creature.

Paul said of this invisible Creator God: "Him I proclaim to you" (v. 23).

This God "made the world and everything in it" (v. 24). He sustains the world and "gives to all life, breath, and all things" (v. 25). He made all human beings.

[26] *And He has made from one blood every nation of men to dwell on all the face of the earth, and has determined their preappointed times and the boundaries of their dwellings,* [27] *so that they should seek the Lord, in the hope that they might grope for Him and find Him, though He is not far from each of us.*

God made all people from one blood; He designed a variety of human cultures; He set people in defined territories, and He did all this so that human beings could have fellowship with Him and enjoy Him forever.

Why didn't the Athenians know this God who was so close to them? It was essentially that they had chosen, rather, to worship idols and to submit themselves to creatures such as Apollo, Dionysus or Zeus. By doing so, they were breaking the first two of the Ten Commandments of the invisible true God whom Paul was preaching and to whom no idol could be dedicated.

Paul tries to communicate the futility of their idolatry by dealing with the visible. Here he points out two principal ways the creature is commonly glorified instead of the Creator. He mentions "temples made with hands" (v. 24), and "gold or silver or stone, something shaped by art and man's devising" (v. 29). Although the works of human hands can and often do glorify God, from long before Paul went to Athens until now, many human beings have chosen to use architecture and art to glorify the invisible powers of darkness rather than their rightful Creator. For example, a cursory reading of typical commercial tour packages for many nations of the world would show what I mean. They often feature sightseeing of buildings and works of art specifically and overtly designed to glorify demonic forces in a disproportionate way. This does not please God.

God, instead, is glorified by His creation. "His invisible attributes are clearly seen, being understood by the things that are made" (Rom. 1:20). Despite distortions of creation devised by people such as the Athenians, God has His purpose, a redemptive purpose, in all aspects of creation. Every person, every animal, every tree or stone or mountain, every angel, and every city or culture or people group has been designed by God and formed to display His glory when properly understood.

Paul asserts that God made a variety of cultural groups, which he terms "every nation of men" (Acts 17:26), in order "that they should seek the Lord" (v. 27). At that moment, Paul deeply desires that one of those groups, the Athenians, open their hearts to truly seek the Lord. To bring them to a point of decision, Paul drops a verbal bomb and tells them to repent!

[30] *Truly, these times of ignorance God overlooked, but now commands all men everywhere to repent.*

Paul was in no mood to invite debate or dialogue. He didn't compromise his message and say, "You are so wise that perhaps we can sit down and learn from each other." He didn't take an attitude of "tolerance." Rather, he forthrightly told them they needed to turn around and go in the other direction. He was telling them to repent of trying to shape the divine nature into art and architecture through fashioning idols and temples. They should worship the *invisible* God, not the *visible* objects fronting for demonic powers.

And Paul told them exactly why they should repent—because the God Paul preached is the judge of the whole world (see v. 31), and "He has given assurance of this to all by raising Him [Jesus] from the dead" (v. 31).

The Athenian philosophers had endured Paul until he mentioned the Resurrection. That was enough. Their tolerance had been stretched to the breaking point.

[32] ***And when they heard of the resurrection of the dead, some mocked, while others said, "We will hear you again on this matter."***

In other words: "Paul, don't call us, we'll call you!" They were not about to consider giving their ultimate allegiance to Paul's "UNKNOWN GOD" (v. 23).

You Win Some and You Lose Some

Was Paul's ministry in Athens successful?

The answer to this question could be yes or it could be no, depending on our understanding of Paul's goals.

If we understand that his goal was to deliver a speech that was theologically impeccable and yet skillfully contextualized to the culture of Greek philosophers, we would say that he was successful. Many students of Paul consider his address on Mars Hill as the finest of all his recorded speeches.

If we understand Paul's goal as winning a debate with the sophisticated intellectuals of what could be seen as the Harvard of the first century, we would say that he failed.

And if we understand that, more likely, his primary goal was to win people to Christ and to plant a strong church in Athens, Paul definitely was much less than successful. Only two converts are mentioned by name: "Dionysius the Areopagite, and a woman named Damaris" (v. 34). William Ramsay says, "It would appear that Paul was disappointed and perhaps disillusioned by his experience in Athens."[17]

Did Paul start a church in Athens? We have no Epistle written to the believers in Athens. Howard Marshall points out, "Whether a church was formed at this stage is doubtful; Paul describes some of his Corinthian converts as the 'first fruits of Achaia'"[18] (1 Cor. 16:15). Athens was in Achaia. By the time Paul wrote back to the church he was yet to plant in Corinth, Athens had apparently become a dim memory, and undoubtedly an unpleasant one at that.

WHAT DID PAUL LEARN?

I believe that Paul's experience in Athens, although far from a success in evangelism and church planting, would have been a valuable learning experience for him, and by application for us as well. Paul learned important lessons about (1) the awesome power of the enemy, and (2) missionary methodology.

None of the commentators I have checked raises the question of whether the demonic powers behind the idols and the festivals and the sacrifices in Athens could have been strong enough to frustrate Paul's evangelistic intentions in the city. I personally believe they could have been and they probably were more than Paul could handle. This is reminiscent of Jesus' ministry in His hometown of Nazareth. It is said, "He did not do many mighty works there because of their unbelief" (Matt. 13:58). Neither Jesus nor Paul did anything particularly wrong; they simply encountered powers that, at that particular time, were fortified enough to hold their position and to prevent the fullest penetration of the kingdom of God.

This is not intended to exalt demonic forces. Ultimately, as I have said many times, they have been, and will continue to be, overcome "by the blood of the Lamb" (Rev. 12:11). It is intended, however, to remind us of the real world of evangelism out there where Satan is deeply entrenched and fiercely determined to resist the gospel for as long as he possibly can. As I have said, we cannot win a war unless we accurately understand our enemy.

Methodologically, Paul's ministry in Athens seems to have been much word and little deed. In Thessalonica, Paul's method was both "explaining" and "demonstrating" (Acts 17:3). A church was planted in Lystra, where there was no synagogue at all and where they worshiped Zeus and Hermes, but this came in the wake of the miraculous healing of a lame man (see 14:8-18). No such miracle is recorded in Athens. Brilliant words, unaccompanied by visible examples of God's power, may avail little.

Finally, Paul goes from Athens to Corinth where he has a bit more time to reflect on the methodology he had just used. When he arrived in Corinth, he was ready to say, "And my speech and my preaching [in Corinth as contrasted to Athens] were not with persuasive words of human wisdom [as in Athens], but in demonstration of the Spirit and of power, that your faith should not be in the wisdom of men but in the power of God" (1 Cor. 2:4-5). As Richard Rackham comments, "At Athens St. Paul tried the wisdom of the world and found it wanting. . . . His disappointment at the failure of the former method to touch the frivolous Athenians no doubt kindled the fire with which he denounces the wisdom of the world in his first epistle to the Corinthians."[19]

Many times, missionaries in our day have perpetuated the kind of ministry that Paul used in Athens. We have tended to rationalize the gospel and present Christ to the lost on the weight of logical arguments. Most unbelievers, particularly in the Global South, and increasingly in the North, are not nearly as concerned about reason and logic as they are about power. They will believe the Word more readily if it is confirmed by the deed. Power ministries accompanying the gospel message of salvation in Christ have been severely underutilized in modern times.

Fortunately, this is changing, particularly now that in the years to come we will see more missionaries sent out by Third World churches than by the traditional Western churches. I recently read an inspiring report from Asian Outreach, a Third World mission agency based in Hong Kong. The word they had been receiving from the Asian people they were evangelizing was: "Western missionaries brought us the *knowledge* of God; now Asian missionaries are bringing us the *power* of God!" This may be too sweeping a generalization, but we Westerners must acknowledge that it makes an important point.

You win some and you lose some. Paul won in Thessalonica and Berea, but he lost in Athens. He left Athens disappointed, but he had learned valuable lessons that would help spread the Christian movement then and now.

REFLECTION QUESTIONS

1. In Paul's day, some of the most receptive people to the gospel message were Gentile God-fearers. Name some equally receptive groups of people in today's world, including in your own community.
2. It is likely that Euodia and Syntyche were personal intercessors for the apostle Paul. Can you think of anyone in your church who has a similar ministry for your pastor? Anyone outside your church who is called to pray for certain leaders?
3. The demonic forces in Athens were honored through certain holidays, festivals and pilgrimages. What do we do today that has a similar function? What part should Christians play in this?
4. How is it that invisible spirit beings relate to visible, lifeless forms such as idols? Can a sacrifice to an idol be a sacrifice to a demon?
5. Paul's speech on Mars Hill is regarded as a brilliant address. Why, then, did very little spiritual fruit come as a result?

20

CORINTH TO ANTIOCH TO EPHESUS

ACTS 18 AND 19

[18:1] *After these things Paul departed from Athens and went to Corinth.*

The journey from Athens to Corinth was about 50 miles due west. Both were famous cities in ancient Greece and, therefore, they had many things in common. But as far as Paul's missionary efforts were concerned, the differences were far greater. Here are some of the differences:

- Athens was a small city and had fewer than 10,000 people, while Corinth was large, having more than 200,000 people.
- Athens was an intellectual and cultural center, while Corinth was a commercial center that had sea trade to the Ionian Sea on the west and to the Aegean Sea on the east.
- In Athens Paul ministered alone (except for a possible short visit by Timothy), but in Corinth he had with him a missionary team.
- In Athens Paul focused on Gentile philosophers, while in Corinth he focused on Gentile God-fearers.
- In Athens Paul displayed brilliance in human wisdom; in Corinth he ministered with public displays of supernatural power.
- In Athens the *word* overshadowed deeds, but in Corinth *deeds* supported and confirmed the word.
- In Athens Paul reaped little fruit, while evangelistic ministry in Corinth produced a great harvest.

SPIRITUAL MAPPING

A further important difference between the two cities of Athens and Corinth was the difference in the apparent depth of demonic entrenchment. Areas or people groups that have not yet been penetrated by the gospel of Christ seem to display varying degrees of spiritual darkness. George Otis, Jr., says, "Regardless of their theology, any honest and moderately traveled Christian will acknowledge that there are certain areas of the world today where spiritual darkness is more pronounced. . . . The question is why? Why are some areas more oppressive, more idolatrous, more spiritually barren than others? Why does darkness seem to linger where it does?"[1]

Answers to these questions, which have previously been ignored by some and which have baffled others, are now becoming clearer through significant advances in the discipline of spiritual mapping. Even a novice spiritual mapper in the first century would have been able to recognize that darkness lingered over Athens more than over either Berea, Paul's previous stop, or here in Corinth. Luke tells us that in Athens "[Paul's] spirit was provoked within him when he saw the city was given over to idols" (17:16).

This is not to say that the pagan city of Corinth was without its territorial spirits and other hosts of wickedness that sought to keep its 200,000 people in spiritual captivity. A preliminary attempt to spiritually map Corinth might indicate that at least two powerful territorial spirits had been receiving the allegiance and worship of a great many of its people:

- ***Poseidon*** (Neptune in Latin). Poseidon was also worshiped in Athens, but more so here in Corinth. This was the spirit of the sea, a very important deity for the Corinthians to placate and to serve because Corinth had two seaports, located as it was on an isthmus. The sea was the primary source of its considerable wealth. Poseidon would have promised lucrative commerce in exchange for worship and sacrifices.

- ***Aphrodite*** (Venus in Latin). Aphrodite was a spirit of free love. Her temple, atop an 1,800-foot hill prominent in the city, was said to have featured 1,000 female slaves who served as temple prostitutes, readily available at no charge to all men who would glorify Aphrodite and agree to serve her. Few turned her down. Corinth was as well known in ancient Greece for unrestrained immorality as Athens was known for philosophy. Corinthian society itself promoted immorality as a *virtue*. In the Greek language of the day, the verb "to corinthianize" was synonymous with "to fornicate."

As a means of accomplishing his purposes of blinding people's minds against hearing the gospel, Satan is said to use the world and the flesh (see Eph. 2:1-3). Poseidon attracted people through the world (economic power), while Aphrodite drew them through the flesh (sex). And, although it was not another Athens, Corinth would have had a substantial presence of other demons who served their territorial superiors by personally and directly deceiving as many individual Corinthians as possible.

Because the Roman proconsul Gallio, whose historic dates are well known, was ruling Corinth at the time Paul was there (see Acts 18:12), we have a fairly certain time span for Paul's ministry in Corinth. He arrived in the fall of A.D. 50 and he left in the spring of A.D. 52.

PAUL, THE TENTMAKER

[2] *And he [Paul] found a certain Jew named Aquila, born in Pontus, who had recently come from Italy with his wife Priscilla (because Claudius had commanded all the Jews to depart from Rome); and he came to them.* [3] *So, because he was of the same trade, he stayed with them and worked; for by occupation they were tentmakers.*

Paul is frequently referred to in missionary circles as a "tentmaker," meaning a bivocational missionary. This implies that such missionaries earn their living by what is usually some sort of secular employment while also doing missionary work in the country or city in which they are employed. Some go as far as to assume that Paul *always* functioned as a bivocational missionary and, therefore, all of us who desire to follow Paul's example as a missionary should consider doing the same.

TENTMAKING IS FOR SOME, BUT NOT ALL

Tentmaking is a desirable and necessary option in some missionary work, but in my opinion it should not be seen as an overall principle or as an ideal course to follow. It is true that Paul frequently earned his own living while evangelizing and planting churches. Besides tentmaking in Corinth, he also did so in Thessalonica (see 1 Thess. 2:9) and in Ephesus (see Acts 20:34), and possibly in other places. He did it sometimes because it was a financial necessity, and it freed him from asking for material support from the new believers. But right here in Corinth, as we shall see shortly, Paul worked less and preached more as soon as money began to arrive from outside sources. For some reason, it seems that Paul was more reluctant to accept financial support from the Corinthians than from others (see 2 Cor. 12:13), although he had a basic right to accept it from all (see 1 Cor. 9:6).

In any case, Paul's secular work was always secondary to church planting. This is far different from many contemporary "tentmaking" missionaries who seldom get around to the arduous task of planting churches because of the competing demands of their secular vocations.

As was customary, Paul settled down in the Jewish quarter when he arrived in Corinth. How he found Aquila and Priscilla we are not told, but one reason he took lodging with them was that as fellow tentmakers they could offer him a job.

Luke doesn't mention it specifically, but historical evidence points to the likelihood that Aquila and Priscilla were already believers before Paul arrived. This derives from Luke's information that they had come from Rome "because Claudius had commanded all the Jews to depart from Rome" (Acts 18:2). A later statement from a Roman historian, Suetonius, leads many scholars to the same conclusion arrived at by F. F. Bruce: "Suetonius's statement, in fact, points to dissension and disorder within the Jewish community of Rome resulting from the introduction of Christianity into one or more of the synagogues of the city."[2] If this is true, one reason Paul would try to find them is obvious. They were probably charter members of the church in Rome, and therefore they would provide excellent support for new church planting in Corinth.

A REUNION WITH SILAS AND TIMOTHY

The last time Paul had seen Silas and Timothy together was when he was fleeing for his life from Berea. He had sent word for them to join him in Athens. Apparently Timothy did come (see 1 Thess. 3:1-2), but apparently he did not have an important enough role for Luke to mention this in Acts. There is a possibility that evangelizing Athens had not originally been a part of Paul's strategic planning.

We know that Paul landed in Athens simply because it is where the ship on which he escaped from the infuriated Jews in Berea had been headed. Then it says in Acts 17:16, "Now while Paul waited for them at Athens, his spirit was provoked within him." This might indicate a spur-of-the-moment decision. Be that as it may, here in Corinth we are told that now "Silas and Timothy had come from Macedonia" (18:5).

By now, undoubtedly, many more than three churches were located throughout Macedonia, but the chief centers of Christian activity would still have been Philippi, Thessalonica and Berea. Presumably, Silas and Timothy had recently been in contact with all three churches when they arrived. They brought with them to Corinth two things that Paul eagerly welcomed: money and news.

Luke does not specifically tell us here that they brought money, but Paul himself refers to it when he writes to the Corinthian believers three or four years later: "And when I was present with you, and in need, I was a burden to no one, for what I lacked the brethren who came from Macedonia supplied" (2 Cor. 11:9). It must have been a substantial sum of money. Luke and Lydia could well have been among the large donors, as well as the "prominent women" (Acts 17:12) mentioned as belonging to the churches in both Thessalonica and Berea, and others.

How substantial was the gift? The *New King James Version,* which I am using almost exclusively, is not as clear at this point as it might be. The *New International Version* is more accurate, so I will use it:

> When Silas and Timothy came from Macedonia, Paul devoted himself exclusively to preaching . . . (v. 5, *NIV*).

Because Paul's tentmaking was a stop-gap option used only when necessary, he was able to give it up and to minister full time when the money came from Macedonia. So it must have been a fairly large amount.

GOOD NEWS FROM THE NORTH

Silas and Timothy also brought good news from the churches up north, especially from Thessalonica (see 1 Thess. 3:6-9). We know this because while Paul was there in Corinth, he wrote both 1 Thessalonians and 2 Thessalonians. It is curious to me that Luke does not choose to mention any of the letters that Paul wrote. Paul actually wrote what are now 10 books of the Bible during the span of Acts, but Luke at the time apparently had no idea of the significance that Paul's letters would later have throughout history.

Those of us who have served as career missionaries know the joy that comes when we hear news that the churches we have planted are moving forward with the Lord. During the time he was in Athens, something had caused Paul to worry a great deal about the well-being of the Thessalonian believers. He had developed a worst-case scenario in his mind, as he admits in 1 Thessalonians 3:5: "For this reason, when I could no longer endure it, I sent to know your faith, lest by some means the tempter had tempted you, and our labor might be in vain." He had sent Timothy, who was apparently paying him a short visit in Athens, back to Thessalonica to find out what was happening.

Paul's worries were unfounded, much to his joy and encouragement. He writes to them from Corinth, "But now . . . Timothy has come to us from you, and brought us good news of your faith and love, and that you always have good remembrance of us, greatly desiring to see us, as we also to see you" (v. 6). The three kinds of news missionaries most like to hear were those brought by Timothy from the Thessalonian church:

1. Personal relationships continued strong. Their memories of each other were positive, and they wanted to get together again as soon as possible.
2. The fruit of the Holy Spirit was being manifested in the church. They were characterized by both "faith and love."
3. They were aggressively spreading the gospel throughout their region. "For from you the word of the Lord has sounded forth, not only in Macedonia and Achaia, but also in every place" (v. 8).

TO THE JEWS FIRST

[4] *And he reasoned in the synagogue every Sabbath, and persuaded both Jews and Greeks.* [5] *When Silas and Timothy had come from Macedonia, Paul [devoted himself exclusively to preaching*—NIV], *and testified to the Jews that Jesus is the Christ.* [6] *But when they opposed him and blasphemed, he shook his garments and said to them, "Your blood be upon your own heads; I am clean. From now on I will go to the Gentiles."*

By now, Paul's evangelistic strategy has become more highly predictable: He first goes to the synagogue to preach to the "Jews" (including both ethnic Jews and proselytes) and the "Greeks," who were the Gentile God-fearers who had been drawn to the synagogue.

For some time, the ministry seemed to go well. The word "persuaded" is from the Greek *peitho*, meaning to win another over to one's point of view. Paul was gathering converts both from among the Jews and from among the Gentile God-fearers. All seemed to be positive and peaceful.

Then something changed! Serious trouble started in the synagogue shortly after Silas and Timothy arrived with the money from the churches to the north and Paul then was able to give full time to his evangelistic ministry.

TROUBLE IN THE SYNAGOGUE!

But what had changed? It must have been something very controversial, not just the additional amount of time Paul would have had available for preaching between Sabbaths. Apparently what upset the Jews was related to the message that "Jesus is the Christ" or the very Messiah for whom the Jews had been waiting. The theological point behind this that would disturb the Jews the most was obviously the teaching of justification by faith, not by works.

Luke explained this in much detail when Paul did exactly the same thing in the synagogue in Antioch of Pisidia near the beginning of his first term of service. There, "the Jews . . . were filled with envy; and contradicting and blaspheming, they opposed the things spoken by Paul" (13:45). Here it likewise says that they opposed him and that they were "blaspheming." What angered them most was Paul's message that by faith in Jesus as Messiah "everyone who believes is justified from all things from which you could not be justified by the law of Moses" (v. 39).

From the Jewish point of view, this would undermine the bedrock on which they had traditionally built both their theological structure and their social community, namely, obeying the law of Moses as the only way to please God. They would immediately have understood that one of the implications of "everyone who believes" would be that Gentiles can be justified in God's sight and have their sins forgiven without being circumcised and becoming Jews. I can imagine that it would be a full-time job for Paul just to sustain the resultant theological dialogue, rabbi to rabbi, with the blaspheming Jewish leaders.

Paul was prepared to put up with such a dialogue for only so long. His goal was not to debate theology, but to evangelize. As time went on, it seems that Paul had less and less patience with his fellow Jews. This is demonstrated here first by Paul literally following Jesus' instructions to turn from those who reject the gospel and "shake off the dust from your feet" (Matt. 10:14). Paul "shook his garments" (Acts 18:6), which amounted to the same thing.

Second, Paul reminded them of the words of Ezekiel: "When I say to the wicked, 'You shall surely die,' and you give him no warning, . . . [he] shall die in his iniquity; but his blood I will require at your hand. Yet, if you warn the wicked, and he does not turn from his wickedness, nor from his wicked way, he shall die in his iniquity; but you have delivered your soul" (Ezek. 3:18-19). Such words would not be used either by Ezekiel or by Paul to win friends and influence people. Nevertheless, Paul said, "Your blood be upon your own heads; I am clean" (Acts 18:6). Paul's ministry in the Corinthian synagogue was history!

ALSO TO THE GREEKS

When Paul later wrote the book of Romans, he said that the gospel "is the power of God to salvation for everyone who believes, for the Jew first and also for the Greek" (1:16). In Corinth, it was now time to go directly to the Greeks.

[7] ***And he departed from there and entered the house of a certain man named Justus, one who worshiped God, whose house was next door to the synagogue.***

Not only were the Jews eager to get Paul out of their synagogue, but from Paul's own tactical point of view it would also be time to leave. At this juncture, Paul had gathered a good nucleus of Gentile God-fearers who had been attending the synagogue. His ultimate goal was to build a strong Gentile church in the Gentile city of Corinth, and these new believers could now move out among their unsaved friends and relatives in more aggressive E-1, or monocultural, evangelism. They would be most effective if they could then bring their new converts back to worship in a more familiar Gentile-flavored environment instead of into a Jewish synagogue that would have seemed strange and uncomfortable to them.

Paul, therefore, took his fledgling church from the synagogue to Titius Justus's house, which would be much more "seeker sensitive," as we would say today. Justus was a Roman, and probably a wealthy one at that, because his house next to the synagogue must have been a fairly large one. In all probability, he was also called Gaius (it was not unusual for Romans to have three names). We learn that Gaius was one of the few people Paul himself baptized in Corinth (see 1 Cor. 1:14). Also, when Paul returns to Corinth for a visit about six years later, he actually writes his Epistle to the Romans from Gaius's house where he is staying and where the church is still meeting (see Rom. 16:23). Suggesting that Justus and Gaius is the same person helps us understand several pieces of biblical information that otherwise might not be properly connected.

Although the church that met in Justus's house (undoubtedly only one of multiple house churches in Corinth) would be composed of predominantly Gentile converts, some believing Jews also formed a part of it. And one of them happened to be a Jewish celebrity:

[8] *Then Crispus, the ruler of the synagogue, believed on the Lord with all his household.*

CRISPUS'S HEADLINE CONVERSION

When Crispus "believed on the Lord," it must have been a headline conversion. I wish Luke had given us more details. Crispus and Justus (Gaius) were two of only three people in Corinth whom Paul baptized personally, all of them presumably VIPs. Was it significant that Crispus had not been converted while Paul was still preaching in the synagogue where Crispus was the president, but then he did accept Christ after Paul moved out? We should also take note that this was followed some time later by what was undoubtedly an equally high-profile conversion of Crispus's successor as president of the synagogue, Sosthenes. He is mentioned in Acts 18:1 as being merely a Jew, but then in 1 Corinthians 1:1 as being a believer in Jesus Christ.

Answers to questions concerning Crispus's conversion must, of course, be speculative but, in my opinion, it is a matter worth probing at least a bit. Could it be that a demonic spirit of religion had established a strong influence in the synagogue? Could strongholds there have afforded the demon a power to tempt Crispus to excessive pride in his authority? Might it be that the domain of that particular spirit was restricted to the synagogue building itself and that it could not extend to the house next door where Justus lived and where prayer had cleansed the spiritual atmosphere?

If this were the case, the very change in physical location of the church could have loosed Crispus and his family from a spiritual force of darkness over them and allowed him to go next door in order to hear and understand the glorious gospel of Christ.

Crispus's conversion may have been an illustration of the outworking of a statement that Paul makes later when he writes to the Gentile believers in Rome: "For I speak to you Gentiles; inasmuch as I am an apostle to the Gentiles, I magnify my ministry, if by any means I may provoke to jealousy those who are my flesh and save some of them" (Rom. 11:13-14). In Corinth, when Paul moved out and began speaking directly to Gentiles, a prominent fellow Jew and his family were apparently "provoked to jealousy" and then saved.

A further part of the explanation of why Crispus was converted after Paul left the synagogue could also lie in the varied emphases in Paul's ministry. As we have seen many times in Acts, beginning with Antioch of Pisidia, when evangelizing in the synagogues, Paul mostly used the persuasive power of the word—he particularly "testified to the Jews that Jesus is the Christ" (18:5). The message of justification by faith was offensive to the establishment Jews, but it was exactly the good news for which the Gentile God-fearers had been waiting, so Paul saw much fruit.

The rest of the Gentiles, however, who did not attend services in the synagogue had not been waiting for such a message. Pagan Gentiles spent much of their lives trying to appease the spirit world, and they were much more concerned about supernatural power than about theological arguments. That is why Paul's major emphasis outside of the synagogue would typically switch to power ministries in order to prepare people for the message that would follow. None of this is to say that either word or deed would have been absent in either situation, but it is a matter of emphasis. It could well have been that some miraculous event or events that Crispus began to witness next door in Justus's house had helped him cross over the line.

LUKE'S GROWTH REPORT

[8] . . . *And many of the Corinthians, hearing, believed and were baptized.*

In contrast to Athens, the nucleus of a solid church was established in Corinth. Both Jews and God-fearers formed the nucleus, but before long it was composed predominantly of formerly pagan Gentiles. They were baptized, but not by Paul. He later said to them, "I thank God that I baptized none of you except Crispus and Gaius, lest anyone should say that I had baptized in my own name. For Christ did not send me to baptize, but to preach the gospel" (1 Cor. 1:14,15,17).

Some of these church members, as they also were in Philippi, Thessalonica and Berea, were from the elite segments of society. This is worth mentioning because some have a tendency to exaggerate Paul's words to the Corinthians "that not many wise according to the flesh, not many mighty, not many noble, are called" (v. 26). Proportionately the upperclass may have been few, but they were not absent.

Bradley Blue, for example, suggests that "there were a considerable number of influential home owners who belonged to the Christian community at Corinth."[3] Blue reminds us that *house churches were the rule in those days*, and that in Corinth believers could have met regularly not only in the house of Titius Justus (Gaius), but also in houses belonging to Priscilla and Aquila, Stephanas (see v. 16) and Crispus. Blue says that these people "personify the type of affluence at Corinth. This is not to say that the majority of the believers were wealthy; however, it clearly indicates that there were congregants who had significant financial means at their disposal."[4]

A VISION AT A CROSSROADS

Paul was at a crossroads in Corinth. As a result of much experience, he knew well the ominous signs of serious persecution. Back in his first missionary term, he had been driven from Antioch of Pisidia and then from Iconium by mobs incited by angry Jews. They finally caught up to him in Lystra and stoned him to death, but God overruled and raised him from the dead. Earlier in this second term, similar bands of Jews had driven him from Thessalonica and from Berea up north in Macedonia. Now here in Achaia the same pattern was rapidly developing.

Paul's crossroads decision was: Should I leave Corinth or should I stay?

Many field missionaries today can immediately identify with Paul's situation. Danger has appeared on their horizon that could result in serious consequences, even death. Some would likely have been suggesting to Paul that the prudent thing for the kingdom of God would be for him to leave while there was still time. He himself must have been praying a good deal, asking God for direction in his precarious situation.

God answered Paul's prayer with a vision. This may seem unusual to many of us today who have been programmed by a Western worldview. Most of us, myself included, have never had God communicate to us through a vision. But for large numbers of people in the Third World today, as happened for first-century men and women, receiving a revelation from God through a vision was simply a part of the way life normally was. What did God say to Paul?

[9] *Now the Lord spoke to Paul in the night by a vision, "Do not be afraid, but speak, and do not keep silent;* [10] *for I am with you, and no one will attack you to hurt you; for I have many people in this city."*

Just so Paul would make no mistake, the Lord chose to speak to him eyeball to eyeball. He was told not to leave Corinth at that time, but to stay on, and (1) he was to keep preaching; (2) the attacks being planned would not hurt him; and (3) there would be much fruit for his ministry in Corinth. Paul, therefore, spent a year and a half in Corinth, longer than he usually stayed in one place. Undoubtedly, one of the reasons God told him to stay longer in Corinth was because an important decision to be made later by the Roman proconsul, Gallio, would have a strong influence on the subsequent spread of the gospel.

PAUL'S TRIAL IN GALLIO'S COURT

[12] *When Gallio was proconsul of Achaia, the Jews with one accord rose up against Paul and brought him to the judgment seat,* [13] *saying, "This fellow persuades men to worship God contrary to the law."* [14] *And when Paul was about to open his mouth, Gallio said to the Jews, "If it were a matter of wrongdoing or wicked crimes, O Jews, there would be reason why I should bear with you.* [15] *But if it is a question of words and names and your own law, look to it yourselves; for I do not want to be a judge of such matters."* [16] *And he drove them from the judgment seat.*

No one knows exactly at what point, during Paul's year and a half in Corinth, the trial in Gallio's court actually occurred. After the trial had ended, however, Luke says that Paul remained "a good while" (v. 18), so it probably was not toward the very end. In other words, this time when Paul left the city, he left voluntarily according to his own timeline, not just a few steps ahead of an angry lynch mob.

The whole Jewish community had become riled. Little wonder! Paul had first used his own credentials as a Jewish rabbi and had proceeded to upend their traditional Jewish theology. When he finally left the synagogue, instead of moving across town, he took the nucleus of his Christian church to Justus's *house* right next door. As if this weren't enough, their leader, Crispus, and his *whole family* (*household*) *then became disciples* of Paul. The Jews were by now more than ready to take some radical steps to see if they could get rid of the missionary they now hated.

The Jews' charge against Paul, "This fellow persuades men to worship God contrary to the law" (v. 13), is more crucial than it may seem to us at the first reading. Because the Jews knew very well that Gallio would not be concerned with violation of the *Jewish* law, they decided to accuse Paul of breaking the *Roman* law.

Here is the issue. As Bruce Winter points out, "The Jews attempted to force a confrontation between Christians and Roman authorities and did so in relation to the imperial cult."[5] By the time Christianity appeared, the Roman Empire had begun to deify its human emperors, and all Roman citizens were required by law to participate in the festivals and ceremonies that would honor them as gods. Christians, of course, believed in the one true God and, therefore, they conscientiously could not do such a thing. This became a serious problem toward the end of the first century and it remained so up to the time of Constantine in the fourth century, as students of church history well know. For more than 200 years, the Roman government was responsible for some of the most indescribable atrocities against Christians ever recorded. But this didn't seem to be a problem as yet in the period covered by the book of Acts. Why not?

Jews, like Christians, also worshiped only one God. The Romans had recognized this and had declared Judaism a *religio licita*, Latin for a "legal religion." As such, Jews were exempted from the requirements to participate in the imperial cult ceremonies. When Christianity came along, it began as messianic Judaism, and Christianity was therefore considered by the Roman authorities as simply a branch of Judaism. For years, at least up to the Council of Jerusalem, many Jews assumed the same thing.

But here in Corinth, the Jewish leaders had finally decided to draw the line and declare to the public that Christianity should not be considered a part of Judaism after all. The fact that Christianity was determined to include uncircumcised Gentiles as legitimate members of the family of the true God was something the faithful Jews could not tolerate.

It had occurred to the Jewish leaders that they could deal a crucial blow against Paul in particular and against Christianity in general if they could only get it declared a *religio illicita*, an illegal religion. This would force the Christians to begin to worship the emperor or to pay the penalty. For this to happen, they would first have to persuade Gallio, the highest Roman authority in Achaia, that Christianity was not, in fact, a part of Judaism. By taking this to Gallio, the Jews were playing for higher stakes than they themselves may have realized.

GALLIO'S HISTORIC DECISION

But Gallio threw the case out of court before Paul could even take the stand to defend himself. Galio noted that it involved no crime or fraud that had violated Roman law. He could no more understand theological nuances such as Gentile circumcision than many of us today could analyze differences between Sunni and Shiite Muslims. He wasn't interested enough to try to understand it. "The governor ruled it was beyond his legal jurisdiction to try the matter because it was an internal Jewish dispute."[6]

The Jews lost big in Gallio's court. As Bruce Winter says, "They secured the very ruling that no orthodox Jew wanted to hear! Christianity was a sect within Judaism and therefore *religio licita*."[7] F. F. Bruce adds, "It meant that for the next ten or twelve years, until imperial policy toward Christians underwent a complete reversal, the Gospel could be proclaimed in the provinces of the empire without fear of coming into conflict with Roman law."[8]

This meant that the large number of Greeks whom Paul had persuaded to follow Christ had been suddenly and unexpectedly rescued from torture and death. They may very well have been the ones who took out their wrath upon the one who had tried to harm them. If such were the case, it would also show that being born again does not instantly produce all the fruit of the Holy Spirit.

Adding Injury to Insult

[17] ***Then all the Greeks took Sosthenes, the ruler of the synagogue, and beat him before the judgment seat. But Gallio took no notice of these things.***

Perhaps by now, Paul and the Christian movement had gained a degree of social acceptance in Corinth, and public opinion might have favored Paul. Perhaps some anti-Semitism might have been surfacing as well. For whatever reason, Sosthenes, the Jewish ringleader, was thoroughly beaten. Physical injury was added to the judicial insult, and "Gallio didn't raise a finger. He could not have cared less" (Acts 18:17, *THE MESSAGE*).

TIME FOR A SECOND FURLOUGH

In modern missionary jargon, Paul served three terms as a career missionary. When he left Corinth, he had finished two of the three terms.

Barnabas was Paul's coworker on the first term when they planted churches in Cyprus, Antioch of Pisidia, Iconium, Lystra and Derbe. On their furlough, they returned to their home base of Antioch of Syria where whatever might have been equivalent to their mission headquarters would have been located. The most important event of the first furlough was a trip to Jerusalem for the historic Council of Jerusalem. On the second term, Silas, later Timothy, and for a time Luke accompanied Paul. After visiting the churches they had planted, they evangelized in Europe, planting new churches in Philippi, Thessalonica, Berea and Corinth. Paul had also ministered in Athens, and he paid a short visit to Ephesus on his way back to Antioch.

[18] ***Then he [Paul] took leave of the brethren and sailed for Syria, and Priscilla and Aquila were with him. He had his hair cut off at Cenchrea, for he had taken a vow.*** [19] ***And he came to Ephesus, and left them there; but he himself entered the synagogue and reasoned with the Jews.*** [20] ***When they asked him to stay a longer time with them, he did not consent,*** [21] ***but took leave of them, saying, "I must by all means keep this coming feast in Jerusalem; but I will return again to you, God willing." And he sailed from Ephesus.***

Silas and Timothy stayed in Corinth, but Paul took Aquila and Priscilla with him. They were to remain in Ephesus while Paul visited Jerusalem and Antioch, and they would lay the groundwork for his return. The three went to the Jewish quarter of the city to get Aquila and Priscilla settled. As we may recall, Paul had attempted to go to Ephesus two years previously, but the Holy Spirit had turned him around and had sent him instead to Europe (see 16:6-10). Now, apparently, God's timing for evangelizing Ephesus had almost arrived.

Paul naturally attended the synagogue, and there he came to know the Ephesian Jewish leaders. It seems that they had a good relationship with each other because they asked him to stay longer. But Paul wasn't ready for that as yet. The requirements of the vow he had taken gave him a good excuse to leave, but he promised he would soon return.

PAUL'S NAZIRITE VOW

What does it mean when it says, "[Paul] had his hair cut off at Cenchrea, for he had taken a vow" (v. 18)? The so-called Nazirite vow was a recognized Jewish ritual of thanksgiving. Paul was undoubtedly deeply grateful to God for the fruit of his second term of service, and particularly for the large church in Corinth and the legal victory in Gallio's court. Paul's vision that he would not be harmed and that he would have many converts had come true.

We don't know exactly when Paul would have started the period of the vow, but presumably it was sometime after the court case. During the vow, he would let his hair grow and abstain from wine, according to the Nazirite requirements in Numbers 6:1-5. Ordinarily, Paul would have continued to keep the vow until he arrived in Jerusalem and had his hair shaved off at the Temple there (see v. 18), then he would make an appropriate sacrifice. In Paul's day, however, the Jews had come to recognize the validity of the option of ending the vow and cutting off the hair somewhere other than in Jerusalem, but with the proviso that the hair would be delivered to the Temple and a sacrifice made within 30 days.

Why Paul would take that option and have his hair cut in Cenchrea instead of Jerusalem we do not really know.

Some might wonder why Paul would take a Nazirite vow in the first place. He may have had several good reasons:

1. We must keep in mind that Paul was still, and always would be, a Jew. He has become such a positive role model for Gentile Christians through the centuries that we are often prone to forget that. As we have just seen, it was also important for Paul to maintain the public image that Christianity could legally be regarded as a sect within Judaism. Whenever Paul went to a new

city such as Ephesus, he took up residence in the Jewish quarter. Now he was on his way to Jerusalem where many, he knew, had some questions about his Jewishness. A Nazirite vow may have been a visible way to attempt to put these thoughts to rest, and prove to whoever was interested that he was still a good Jew. Thus, he manifested the fact that the gospel was not only a Jewish way of life nor merely a Greek way of life. This, many Gentiles would soon forget.

2. For Jews, but not particularly for Gentile Christians, the Nazirite vow was a means of grace, similar to the way many of us view the Lord's Supper. It may have been a time for Paul to reestablish intimacy with the Father.

3. The Nazirite vow may have been a "prophetic act." The advent of the contemporary prayer movement toward strategic-level intercession and spiritual warfare has introduced many Christians to prophetic acts for the first time. I define it as follows: *A prophetic act is a visible, physical and public action by an individual or a group, in obedience to the immediate leading of the Holy Spirit, reflecting in the visible world important transactions taking place in the invisible world.*

Biblical examples of prophetic acts include Ezekiel lying on his left side for 390 days, then on his right side for 40 days (see Ezek. 4:4-6), or Joshua piling up rocks in the Jordan River for a memorial (see Josh. 4:7). Contemporary examples of prophetic acts might include Youth With A Mission sending teams of intercessors on the same day for "Cardinal Points praying" to the geographical northernmost, southernmost, easternmost and westernmost points of all six continents; or Pastor Bob Beckett driving two-by-two oak stakes into the ground on the borders of Hemet, California, to raise a prayer canopy over the city.

FAST-FORWARDING THE FURLOUGH

[22] *And when [Paul] had landed at Caesarea, and gone up and greeted the church, he went down to Antioch.* [23] *After he had spent some time there, he departed and went over the region of Galatia and Phrygia in order, strengthening all the disciples.*

Undoubtedly, a lot happened during the time period Luke describes in these two verses, but apparently not much that is of interest to him. For Luke, it is a time to fast-forward Paul's travels so that he can get back to the important business of evangelism and church planting.

Luke describes Paul's visit to Jerusalem by saying only that "he had landed at Caesarea, and gone up and greeted the church." In Jerusalem, Paul would have touched base with the elders and apostle James and he would have burned his hair and made a sacrifice at the Temple to fulfill his Nazirite vow. What else he did we do not know.

Then he would have walked 300 miles north to Antioch, the mission headquarters, staying there for "some time."

After that, Paul set out over land for Ephesus where Aquila and Priscilla would have by now established their tentmaking business, and prepared the way for church planting.

On the way to Ephesus, Paul again visited the young churches that he and Barnabas had planted on their first term in Derbe, Lystra, Iconium and Antioch of Pisidia. We don't know who might have been with Paul. Luke rushes through this time period rapidly as well. Luke's priorities seem to be similar to those of frontier missionaries throughout the ages who are called to reach the unreached, evangelize the unevangelized and win the lost. Typically, apostolic missionaries are more interested in:

- Making disciples than in perfecting disciples;
- Evangelizing the lost than in nurturing the saved;
- Pioneer missions than in pastoral care;
- Outreach than in church renewal.

Pointing this out does not at all mean that caring for believers and reviving the church are unimportant. God Himself tells us that these ministries are extremely important, and He calls many members of the Body of Christ to those kinds of ministries. He gives such missionaries the spiritual gifts of pastor, mercy, service, prophecy, teaching, administration, hospitality, and many other gifts.

Apostolic missionaries such as Paul will not neglect to care for the believers and the churches they are responsible for bringing into the Kingdom. Paul himself visited the churches in Derbe, Lystra, Iconium and Antioch no less than three separate times after he planted them. And Paul's nine Epistles later written to the churches brilliantly display his deep desire for their growth and their maturity in the things of the Lord. But because these Epistles are so prominent in the New Testament, some have concluded that Paul's chief priority must have been Christian nurture. My opinion is that Paul's chief priority never deviated from winning the lost and "going where Christ was not named."

By his selective way of compiling history, Luke seems to support the thesis that I detailed earlier, arguing that pioneer missionaries must always be on guard against succumbing to the "syndrome of church development."

APOLLOS'S MINISTRY IN EPHESUS AND CORINTH

[24] *Now a certain Jew named Apollos, born at Alexandria, an eloquent man and mighty in the Scriptures, came to Ephesus.* [25] *This man had been instructed in the way of the Lord; and being fervent in spirit, he spoke and taught accurately the things of the Lord, though he knew only the baptism of John.* [26] *So he began to speak boldly in the synagogue. When Aquila and Priscilla heard him, they took him aside and explained to him the way of God more accurately.* [27] *And when he desired to cross to Achaia, the brethren wrote, exhorting the disciples to receive him; and when he arrived, he greatly helped those who had believed through grace;* [28] *for he vigorously refuted the Jews publicly, showing from the Scriptures that Jesus is the Christ.*

Apollos is a well-known figure among Christians, although the only information we have of him is right here as well as several brief references to him in 1 Corinthians. We do know that he was a Jew from Alexandria, Egypt. Alexandria was the second-largest city in the Roman Empire after Rome, and it also had a large population of Jews. John Drane says, "There were probably more Jews living in . . . Alexandria in Egypt than there were in Jerusalem itself."[9] Apollos was eloquent and well educated and he knew the Old Testament thoroughly. He was a bold debater and an apologist. He knew much about Jesus, but he had received only John the Baptist's baptism. However, he was also a learner and he was willing to be instructed by Aquila and Priscilla in Ephesus.

Where do all these facts lead us? Mainly to frustration! Hans Conzelmann says it well, if wistfully: "If we only knew whether Apollos had become acquainted with Christianity while still at Alexandria!"[10] We must always elevate the Bible above our preconceived theories about what it should say. It is precisely when the Bible does not talk our language that we often have the most to learn!

THE MYSTERY OF APOLLOS

Let's try to construct a reasonable explanation. Christianity in the form of messianic Judaism did exist in Alexandria, supposing that the Hellenistic believers when driven out of Jerusalem went south to Alexandria as well as north to Antioch. Luke's story of the Ethiopian eunuch (see Acts 8:26-40) shows one way that the gospel indeed reached Africa. The fact that some missionaries later went out from North Africa (see 11:20) also indicates that churches must have been planted there. These believers, however, would have experienced the baptism of Jesus, so apparently Apollos had not been in touch with them, a viable possibility because of the huge Jewish population in Alexandria. So in Alexandria, some groups could well have followed Jesus and other groups could have followed John the Baptist.

How did John's disciples get there in the first place? Let's suppose that some Jews from Alexandria happened to be in Palestine during the time that John the Baptist was actively ministering. Some of them could have been baptized by John in the Jordan River, learned a good bit about Jesus, then returned home to Alexandria. Conybeare and Howson affirm that "Many Jews from other countries received from the Baptist their knowledge of the Messiah, and carried with them this knowledge on their return from Palestine."[11] Apollos could easily have been among the first or second generation of these disciples.

PAUL FINDS APOLLOS'S DISCIPLES: ACTS 19

As many would know, chapters and verses do not appear in the original manuscripts of the Bible. Most of the chapter divisions that have been subsequently introduced are very helpful, but this particular division between Acts 18 and Acts 19 seems to me to be in the wrong place. The following passage is best understood as a continuation of Acts 18:

> [19:1] *And it happened, while Apollos was at Corinth, that Paul, having passed through the upper regions, came to Ephesus. And finding some disciples* [2] *he said to them, "Did you receive the Holy Spirit when you believed?" So they said to him, "We have not so much as heard whether*

there is a Holy Spirit." [3] *And he said to them, "Into what then were you baptized?" So they said, "Into John's baptism."* [4] *Then Paul said, "John indeed baptized with a baptism of repentance, saying to the people that they should believe on Him who would come after him, that is, on Christ Jesus."* [5] *When they heard this, they were baptized in the name of the Lord Jesus.* [6] *And when Paul had laid hands on them, the Holy Spirit came upon them, and they spoke with tongues and prophesied.* [7] *Now the men were about twelve in all.*

When considered as a continuation of chapter 18, we can see clearly that these 12 were disciples of Apollos. E. M. Blaiklock agrees, saying, "Perhaps they were a remnant of Apollos' less-mature ministry in the city."[12] But were they true believers? The usual way Luke uses the word "disciples" from the Greek *mathetai* means what we call born again "Christians." But could they be real Christians without being baptized in the name of Jesus and without knowing anything about the Holy Spirit?

This is the kind of question many missionaries frequently face. The dividing line between those who are truly in the Kingdom and those on the outside is not always as clear as we would like. How about Jesus' own disciples after being with Him for one year? Were they Christians? They certainly had a great deal more to learn, including accurate knowledge about the Holy Spirit. Whether they were baptized in Jesus' name at that time we do not know.

NATIVISTIC MOVEMENTS

Groups of believers similar to Apollos's disciples are known by many as "nativistic movements." They usually begin without the influence of informed missionaries or evangelists. For example, years ago a pastor in Venezuela told me he had been traveling through the jungle when he suddenly came across a whole village of Christians. He knew that no preacher had ever gone to the area, but he learned that a young man from the area had taken some goods to the market in the city and had been given a Bible. When he returned, everyone in the village took an interest in this new book, and before long all had given their lives to Christ.

The pastor went on to explain that when he found these people, they had developed only three "heresies": (1) they worshiped on Saturday instead of Sunday; (2) they abstained from eating pork; and (3) they had killed all their dogs because their Bible said, "Beware of dogs" (Phil. 3:2)!

Examples run from this rather humorous incident to more serious ones, such as a committed believer in the house churches in China who, lacking sound instruction, sacrificed his son, desiring to imitate Abraham on Mount Moriah (see Gen. 22:1-14).

An important thing about such folks is that they are more than willing to change what they are doing wrong the minute they receive more accurate teaching, just as Apollos himself and Apollos's disciples did. This openness to the truth is one indication in itself that, although they may not be able to verbalize it, the Holy Spirit to some degree has been present in their lives.

RECEIVING THE HOLY SPIRIT

It is notable that Paul's examination of the orthodoxy of Apollos's disciples begins with a question about the third Person of the Trinity, the Holy Spirit. He then moves on to ask about the second Person, Jesus Christ. In response, they believed in the second Person and were baptized in Jesus' name; then they received the Holy Spirit.

Speaking in tongues was a common way to verify whether the Holy Spirit had come into a person's life. Back in Cornelius's house, "the gift of the Holy Spirit had been poured out on the Gentiles also" (Acts 10:45). How did they know? "For they heard them speak with tongues and magnify God" (v. 46). This later helped Peter convince the Jewish leaders in Jerusalem that Gentiles could be saved (see 11:17; 15:8).

Some, however, use this as a proof text for a doctrine that born-again Christians (not uninstructed disciples of Apollos) should all expect to receive the Holy Spirit as a second blessing after the first blessing of salvation, and that the invariable initial physical evidence is speaking in tongues. This is usually called "baptism in the Holy Spirit." Others, and I find myself part of this group, believe that Holy Spirit baptism ordinarily takes place as a part of conversion because Paul says, "For by one Spirit we were all baptized into one body" (1 Cor. 12:13). We prefer to call subsequent experiences "fillings of the Holy Spirit."

Whereas these differences of opinion, unfortunately, have become reasons for some serious divisions in the Body of Christ in the recent past, fortunately, the barriers they have created have been coming down rapidly. More and more we mutually agree that there may be several legitimate ways of understanding the same biblical evidence. No matter how we choose to interpret stories such as Paul's ministry to Apollos's disciples in Ephesus, on a deeper level we share an honest mutual desire to obey the Scriptures, serve our Lord, receive the maximum fullness and power of the Holy Spirit and get on with the task of winning our world to Christ. As a result, Christians around the world are clearly more united in heart, mind and spirit than they have been for centuries.

REFLECTION QUESTIONS

1. Paul earned his living in Corinth by making tents. What are the pros and cons of missionaries today holding down jobs as opposed to receiving outside financial support?
2. Paul generally preached first in the synagogue, concentrating on God-fearers, when he evangelized a new city such as Corinth. Why was this seen as good missionary strategy?
3. When persecution became strong in Corinth, God told Paul through a vision to stay on in Corinth. Have you or has anyone you know ever had such a direct personal word from God?
4. Paul's Nazirite vow is seen as a "prophetic act." What is your understanding of a prophetic act? Do we ever see such things today?
5. When Apollos's disciples received the Holy Spirit, they spoke in tongues. Does this always happen? Does it ever happen today? How important is this issue?

2 1

INVADING DIANA'S TERRITORY

ACTS 19

Acts 19 is my favorite chapter in Acts. Paul's ministry in Ephesus was by anyone's measurement the most outstanding success story of his missionary career. E. M. Blaiklock says it well: "Luke introduces what must have been the greatest triumph of Paul's life—the evangelization of the Province of Asia."[1]

As we have seen, Paul had set out to evangelize Asia once before, at the beginning of his second term of service. But at that time, Paul, Silas and Timothy "were forbidden by the Holy Spirit to preach the word in Asia" (16:6). The obvious reason for God closing the door on the first attempt was that the timing could not have been right. Often when we look back on such an incident, we never really know why the timing might or might not have been right. In such cases, we simply trust in the wisdom of a sovereign and omniscient God.

But for this ministry in Asia it could be plausible to speculate that Paul himself might not previously have been ready to tackle the formidable spiritual strongholds in Ephesus. When he first tried to go, Paul did not have the maturity, experience and the seasoning he subsequently acquired through:

- Dealing with the Python spirit in Philippi;
- Personally experiencing the virtually impenetrable cloud of spiritual darkness holding Athens in captivity;
- Gallio's decision in Corinth that Christianity was, indeed, a *religio licita*, a legal Roman Empire religion.

In Ephesus, Paul was to enter a spiritual battle of enormous magnitude. In this case (unlike the battle in Athens) he, by the power of God, would triumph, and, therefore, he would see churches multiplied not only in the city itself, but also throughout the whole province of Asia. It is fitting that we are about to see Paul's greatest victory because this is also the last recorded incident we have of Paul planting new churches.

The City of Ephesus

Ephesus was the third or fourth largest city in the Roman Empire after Rome, Alexandria and possibly Antioch of Syria. Clinton Arnold reports that population estimates "begin at a quarter of a million."[2] Ephesus was a city of elegant architecture. Around A.D. 20, Strabo wrote that "the city, because of its advantageous situation . . . grows daily, and is the largest emporium in Asia this side of the Taurus."[3] Administratively, Ephesus was a free Greek city within the Roman Empire. It handled its own internal affairs under the jurisdiction of a Roman proconsul.

Ephesus was also a principal center of magic for the ancient world. Bruce Metzger says, "Of all ancient Graeco-Roman cities, Ephesus . . . was by far the most hospitable to magicians, sorcerers, and charlatans of all sorts."[4] Magic, as many would know, is any process by which human beings become able to manipulate supernatural power for their own ends.

A Fetish Factory

One of the best-known objects used for magic in the ancient world was the "Ephesian writings." F. F. Bruce says, "The phrase 'Ephesian writings' was commonly used in antiquity for documents containing spells and formulae . . . to be placed in small cylinders or lockets worn around the neck or elsewhere about the person."[5] What Bruce is referring to are what are known throughout animistic cultures, such as in Ephesus, as fetishes.

Such fetishes are much more than just quaint artistic objects that may have some cultural significance. In many cases, they are vehicles through which powers of the spirit world are given varying degrees of freedom to operate in the natural world. For example, I once prayed for a woman to be healed and I saw nothing happen until God told me to have her remove the object she was wearing around her neck. After that the healing took place readily.

On another occasion, a missionary wife whom we were visiting in Japan had been suffering headaches and nausea beyond medical diagnosis. When my wife, Doris, and I learned that a standard procedure in the construction of Japanese buildings was to deposit an occult fetish in a strategic place, we thought that we might have a useful clue regarding the causal circumstances.

Not knowing exactly where the fetish might be, we escorted the missionary and her husband through every room in their rented house, breaking the power of any spirits present in each room in the name of Jesus and commanding them to leave the house. The headaches and nausea immediately disappeared. Obviously, the fetish was still present somewhere, but the spiritual power it had attracted was effectively neutralized.

Ephesus was known as the premier fetish factory of the Roman Empire. No wonder the silversmiths who manufactured many of them were ready to riot when the invisible world of darkness over Ephesus began to be torn apart as a result of the spiritual warfare initiated by the arrival of the apostle Paul!

Three Months in the Synagogue

[8] ***And [Paul] went into the synagogue and spoke boldly for three months, reasoning and persuading concerning the things of the kingdom of God.*** [9] ***But when some were hardened and did not believe, but spoke evil of the Way before the multitude, he departed from them and withdrew the disciples . . .***

Paul naturally had settled down with Aquila and Priscilla in the Jewish quarter of Ephesus, which was known to be a relatively large one. Luke doesn't tell us here that he made his own living, but Paul himself mentions that he did so when he later returns to teach the Ephesian pastors (see 20:33-35). Paul had left Aquila and Priscilla in Ephesus on his brief stopover between Corinth and Jerusalem (see 18:18), and presumably they had set up their tentmaking business before Paul joined them.

Spending three months in the synagogue and having relatively few problems with the traditional Jews was longer than usual. This problem-free time could probably be explained because Paul had succeeded in establishing good relationships with the Jewish leaders on his previous visit. Perhaps also Aquila and Priscilla had become active synagogue members while Paul was on furlough, and they undoubtedly continued to nurture those relationships.

Eventually, however, history repeated itself and the Jews in the synagogue turned against Paul. In Corinth, they did so because he was preaching that "Jesus is the Christ" (v. 5), and here in Ephesus it was because he was "reasoning and persuading concerning the things of the kingdom of God" (19:8). Same difference! It again boils down to the issue that faith in Jesus Christ is the only requirement for salvation, and, therefore, that Gentiles can be saved, as well as Jews, but without being circumcised or keeping the law of Moses.

Before the three months had ended, Paul had developed his nucleus of new converts. Luke says, "he departed from them [the synagogue] and withdrew the disciples" (v. 9). "Disciples," as I have mentioned, should ordinarily be taken as a synonym for "Christians."

It is not hard to imagine how upset the Jewish leaders would have been with this blatant case of what some today would call "sheep stealing." But this was Paul's normal pattern. In most cases, the initial growth of the new Christian church came at the expense of the Jewish synagogue. Although the synagogue leaders understandably would have been upset, the eventual outward persecution here in Ephesus, unlike what we saw in Thessalonica, Corinth and other places, does not originate with the Jews but with the pagan Gentiles.

Two Years Among the Gentiles

> [9] . . . *[Paul] departed from them and withdrew the disciples, reasoning daily in the school of Tyrannus.* [10] *And this continued for two years, so that all who dwelt in Asia heard the word of the Lord Jesus, both Jews and Greeks.*

Tyrannus, from the best we can understand, was a local teacher who had his own school facility. The Western text of the Greek New Testament tells us that Paul taught from the fifth to the tenth hour, or from 11:00 A.M. to 4:00 P.M. every day. Tyrannus would in all probability have been using the building in the mornings. The Ephesians kept a strict siesta. William Ramsay says, "Public life in the Ionian cities ended regularly at the fifth hour [11:00 A.M.]."[6] One historian reportedly commented that more people in Ephesus were asleep at 1:00 P.M. than at 1:00 A.M.!

Leadership Training

This is one of the clearest examples of formalized leadership training that we have in the New Testament, apparently something different from the ordinary teaching Paul and the pastors would do in their house churches or from house to house. This appears to be what we now would regard as a form of systematic equipping of the saints for the work of the ministry to which Paul refers in his later letter to the Ephesians (see Eph. 4:12). Many, if not most, of Paul's disciples would be workplace leaders who would be giving up their lunch hours and their siestas in order to take the training courses.

What would the curriculum have been like in such a school? Luke seems to suggest a cause-and-effect relationship between this and the fact that "all who dwelt in Asia heard the word of the Lord Jesus" (v. 10) before the end of two years. This means that the chief focus of the curriculum was likely to have been power evangelism and church planting.

Paul, then, was training and sending out church planters as rapidly as he could. This is not to be seen as a deviation in Paul's ministry from evangelism to Christian nurture. Paul was not hereby falling into the trap of the "syndrome of church development," which I have warned against from time to time. Pastoral care and the nurture of ordinary believers was also occurring in Ephesus, but that would be taking place in the house churches that would have been multiplying in considerable numbers throughout the city during Paul's two years in Ephesus. Paul would have been equipping those who had been called by God to expand the kingdom of God beyond their own families or churches.

Modern missionaries should take their direction from Paul's example. As I am writing this, more people are becoming Christians worldwide than ever before, in exponential proportions. With the exception of those called to begin work among the few remaining unreached people groups in today's world, there is no longer a great need for cross-cultural missionaries to do direct evangelism. Evangelism, in fact, is being done in most parts of the world much like evangelism was being done in the first century—excited new believers spreading their faith wherever they went. Some reports reveal that up to 35,000 people are being saved every day in China alone. The great missionary challenge in China for expatriate missionaries is not so much evangelism as it is leadership training.

By trained leadership, I do not necessarily mean those who have college and seminary degrees. The number of church planters who have such academic credentials is minuscule in proportion to the number of new churches being planted each day around the globe. By "training leadership," I mean doing what Paul was apparently doing in Ephesus—taking gifted believers whoever they might be, with whatever education they might have, providing for them the conceptual and practical tools they needed, imparting to them an anointing for power ministries, and sending them out to extend the kingdom of God. It paid off then and such a training design will pay off now.

Engaging in Spiritual Warfare

I would imagine that a significant part of the course content in Paul's school would also have focused on spiritual warfare. Whatever happened in Paul's ministry while in Ephesus would cause him later to write to the believers with these words: "For we do not wrestle against flesh and blood, but against principalities, against powers, against the rulers of the darkness of this age, against spiritual hosts of wickedness in the heavenly places" (Eph. 6:12). Clinton Arnold has found that the book of Ephesians contains "a substantially higher concentration of power terminology than in any other epistle attributed to Paul."[7]

A passage in 1 Corinthians seems to be an indication that Paul would likely have been involved in some particularly high-level spiritual warfare while he ministered in Ephesus. Actually, 1 Corinthians was written during the time Paul was still in Ephesus, and in it he remarks, "If, in the manner of men, I have fought with beasts at Ephesus" (15:32). F. F. Bruce explains that "in the manner of men" means "figuratively speaking."[8]

What, then, might Paul figuratively have meant? It could be that "beasts" refers to some human opponents, as many suspect. But I think that it is more likely that Paul meant he was engaged in battle with the dark angels of the city in strategic-level spiritual warfare. His language in his later letter to the Ephesians that "we don't wrestle against flesh and blood" would seem to bear out the latter interpretation.

Dealing with the Demonic

In the book of Acts, Luke gives only two examples of Paul's dealing directly with the demonic: the episode with the Python spirit in Philippi and this ministry in Ephesus. Would this mean that in Paul's evangelistic and missionary strategy, dealing with the demonic is largely secondary and sporadic and, therefore, that it is not very important for us today? This is what some who oppose strategic-level spiritual warfare have been arguing. But I do not believe it is a correct conclusion. Luke is characteristically selective about the places he chooses to emphasize one important aspect or another of Paul's ministry. Once doing that, he sees little need to repeat it each time it might have occurred.

The best example of this is Paul's message of justification by faith apart from the Jewish law. Most everyone would agree that this was a crucial part of his message wherever he went. But Luke gives us the details of this only once, namely, in Antioch of Pisidia (see Acts 13:38-39). We assume that Paul also preached justification by faith in Berea, Derbe or Thessalonica, for example, but not because Luke tells us he did. We can conclude, therefore, that the number of times Luke chooses to highlight a particular component of Paul's total ministry is not necessarily an indication of where it might have fit on his priority scale.

I think Michael Green, in his classic work *Evangelism in the Early Church*, has an insight that throws considerable light on this matter. He starts with Paul's testimony that in Thessalonica "our gospel did not come to you in word only, but also in power, and in the Holy Spirit and in much assurance" (1 Thess. 1:5). (We should note, by the way, that if all we had was Luke's account of this in Acts, these facts would have been hidden from us.)

Green points out that the Greek for "much assurance" is *plerophoria,* which includes two dimensions:

1. Powerful preaching. This is as far as many commentators go.
2. But Green also says, "There was another dimension to this power. It involved healings and exorcisms," which "continued throughout not only the apostolic church but into the second and third centuries, to look no further. Christians went out into the world as exorcizers and healers as well as preachers."[9] From this, we can conclude that power ministries, including dealing directly with the demonic in spiritual warfare, were so much part and parcel of the customary ministry of evangelists and missionaries that it would not necessarily merit specific mention in Acts every time it had occurred any more than justification by faith would.

History According to Ramsay MacMullen

Ramsay MacMullen, a Yale University historian, has developed a reputation as a foremost scholar of the Roman Empire. One of the historical phenomena all Roman Empire specialists are compelled to deal with was the incredibly rapid spread of Christianity, culminating with the conversion of the Emperor Constantine in A.D. 312. Christianity from then on became the dominant religion in the Roman Empire. MacMullen reports his research on this in a remarkable book, *Christianizing the Roman Empire.*

According to MacMullen, the chief factor accounting for the astounding spread of Christianity in the first four centuries was power ministries in the form of miracles and healings, but particularly as exhibited by dealing with the demonic. He says, "The manhandling of demons—humiliating them, making them howl, beg for mercy, tell their secrets, and depart in a hurry—served a purpose quite essential to the Christian definition of monotheism: it made physically (or dramatically) visible the superiority of the Christian's patron Power over all others."[10]

Although he doesn't use the term, Ramsay MacMullen has concluded that power encounters on levels higher than individual deliverance played a chief role in the vigorous spread of Christianity. Toward the end of the book, he summarizes his thesis by saying that the principal factors were "emphasis on miraculous demonstration, head-on challenge of non-Christians to a test of power, *head-on confrontation with supernatural beings inferior to God*, and contemptuous dismissal of merely rational, especially Greek philosophical, paths toward true knowledge of the divine"[11] (emphasis mine).

Ramsay then refers specifically to what we call strategic-level spiritual warfare by saying, "Where once [the saints and bishops] had driven devils only from poor souls possessed, now they can march into the holiest shrines and, with spectacular effect before large crowds, expel the devils from their very homes."[12]

Ephesus as a Battleground

Acts 19 is the only account of ministry in the Scriptures where we find references to all three levels of spiritual warfare:

1. Ground-level spiritual warfare—vv. 11-18
2. Occult-level spiritual warfare—v. 19
3. Strategic-level spiritual warfare—vv. 23-41

As I have mentioned repeatedly, we must always keep in mind that these are not three categories unrelated to each other. Rather, they are vitally interrelated in the spirit world in ways of which we may know very little. What we do know is that spiritual warfare on any one of the three levels can, and does, have varying degrees of influence on the other two.

Susan Garrett, a Yale biblical scholar, makes a careful study of the incident involving the seven sons of Sceva in her excellent book *The Demise of the Devil*. She argues strongly that the demon's victory over the seven sons of Sceva (which we would see as *ground-level*) was the factor that most contributed to the defeat of magic in Ephesus and the conversion of the magicians (which we would see as *occult-level*).[13] I would add that this, in turn, began the process of shattering the awesome power of Diana of the Ephesians (which we would see as *strategic-level*) without Paul so much as confronting this territorial spirit directly.

Let's now take a closer look at spiritual warfare on all three levels in Ephesus.

Ground-Level Spiritual Warfare

Luke's section on ground-level spiritual warfare, which refers to casting demons out of individuals, comes in two parts. First, Luke tells us how to do it, and second, Luke tells us how *not* to do it.

[11] ***Now God worked unusual miracles by the hands of Paul,***
[12] ***so that even handkerchiefs or aprons were brought from his body to the sick, and the diseases left them and the evil spirits went out of them.***

I love the way Luke uses the phrase "unusual miracles." The immediate implication is that if some miracles are *unusual,* then other miracles must be *usual* or *ordinary*. Compared to no miracles at all, any miracle might be regarded as unusual by some. But in places where the Holy Spirit is moving in a revival atmosphere and where miracles are not uncommon, we do find ourselves even today distinguishing unusual miracles from the ordinary ones.

In recent years, I have spent a good deal of time in Argentina where the renowned Argentine Revival was sustained for a remarkable 18 years through the mid-1990s. Argentine leaders found it necessary to create categories for various grades of miracles. For example, healings of ulcers, hernias, breast cancers and headaches were usual. Unusual miracles included a lung that had been surgically removed and had grown back after prayer, obese people losing weight (one woman lost 32 pounds) in healing services, and hair growing on the heads of bald men. Filling teeth supernaturally was so common in Argentina that in Carlos Annacondia's evangelistic rallies those who had only one or two teeth filled that night were not allowed to give public testimony. That was considered a "usual" miracle. Three or more teeth being filled was regarded as "unusual" enough to allow the recipient to take time on the platform and share the blessing with the audience.

I realize that some readers may not only be skeptical about reports that unusual miracles are occurring now, as they did in Paul's time, but also at this point they may be doubting Peter Wagner's credibility. One of my critics says in a book on the subject that he finds my field reports "preposterous." My response is that I have seen much of what I am reporting firsthand, and for the rest I have spoken extensively with many Argentine friends who are distinguished leaders, well educated, deeply spiritual, highly intelligent–in a word, credible witnesses. They are reporting exactly what they have seen.

Speaking of filling teeth, recent visits to Brazil, where divine dental work has also become common, have allowed me to see with my own eyes something even more unusual. Whereas in Argentina the teeth most frequently were being filled with a white substance that dentists could not identify, in Brazil the great majority were being filled or crowned with gold! On a recent visit to Brazil, I acquired a book wholly devoted to this phenomenon: *Dentes de Ouro: Os Sinais de Deus* (*Gold Teeth: Signs of God*) by Pastor Andres Aguiar. Many such stories are documented in the book.

Deliverance Through Handkerchiefs

Back to Ephesus. One of the unusual miracles was that even handkerchiefs or aprons were brought from his [Paul's] body to the sick . . . and the evil spirits went out of them (vv. 11-12).

Lest we also relegate such things as the use of handkerchiefs to a dim and perhaps irrelevant past, I have but to cite my friend William Kumuyi, pastor of the Deeper Life Bible Church in Lagos, Nigeria. Some 75,000 adults attend his local church on Sundays (with 40,000 children in a building across the street), and he has also planted more than 4,500 other churches throughout Nigeria. Considering these credentials, he was invited to be the speaker for our annual Fuller Seminary Church Growth Lectures in 1993. In one of his lectures he related this story.

Part of the usual weekly program in all of the 4,500 Deeper Life Bible Churches is a Thursday-night miracle meeting. On one of those nights, the pastor of an outlying church felt led to invite all those who had sick people at home to hold up their handkerchiefs, and he prayed a blessing of God's healing power upon them. They were to return home, place the handkerchief on the sick person and pray for healing in Jesus' name. He was unaware that the chief of a nearby Muslim village was visiting his church that night—the first time he had ever attended a Christian service. Although the Muslim did not have sick people in his home, he also held up his handkerchief and received the blessing.

Soon after the chief returned to his village, a nine-year-old girl died and he went to her home to attend the wake just before the burial. While there, he suddenly remembered the handkerchief, retrieved it, placed it on the corpse and prayed that she would be healed "in Jesus' name." Then God did an obviously "unusual" miracle and raised the girl from the dead! The chief called an immediate ad hoc meeting with the village elders who witnessed what had happened, then turned around and declared to his people, "For many years we have been serving Mohammed; but from this moment on our village will be a village of Jesus!" Needless to say, a Deeper Life Bible Church is now thriving in the village.

The experience in Nigeria is reminiscent of what Paul was seeing in Ephesus. Ministry was happening not only in word, but also in deed. I like what Susan Garrett says about Ephesus: These unusual miracles were "consistent with the message [Paul] preaches, indeed as part and parcel of that message."[14]

How Not to Do Ground-Level Warfare

[13] ***Then some of the itinerant Jewish exorcists took it upon themselves to call the name of the Lord Jesus over those who had evil spirits, saying, "We exorcise you by the Jesus whom Paul preaches."*** [14] ***Also there were seven sons of Sceva, a Jewish chief priest, who did so.*** [15] ***And the evil spirit answered and said, "Jesus I know, and Paul I know; but who are you?"*** [16] ***Then the man in whom the evil spirit was leaped on them, overpowered them, and prevailed against them, so that they fled out of that house naked and wounded.***

There is a right way and a wrong way to confront demons. Paul was doing it right, but the seven sons of Sceva did it wrong. The central issue here is the name of the Lord Jesus.

As all who minister deliverance on a regular basis know, the use of the name of Jesus is crucial. Jesus said, "If you ask anything in My name, I will do it" (John 14:14). He also said that among the signs that follow believers, "In My name they will cast out demons" (Mark 16:17).

The only authority we have to cast out demons does not reside inside of us naturally; it is delegated to us by Jesus. This is similar to the authority a United States ambassador would have in a foreign country. Ambassadors do not go to other countries in their own names; they go in the name of the president of the United States. And only those whom the president so designates can use his name effectively. If I went to the Japanese Foreign Ministry, for example, and announced that I have come in the name of the president of the United States, they would laugh at me.

This is exactly what happened to the seven sons of Sceva. The name of Jesus is no magic formula on the order of the "Ephesian writings," which presumably could be purchased in the neighborhood occult shop. Jesus had not authorized the seven sons of Sceva to use His name and, therefore, the power was absent. Jesus said that in the last days some will say, "Have we not . . . cast out demons in Your name?" And He will reply, "I never knew you" (Matt. 7:22-23). That is what He would have said to the sons of Sceva.

Because they used the Lord's name in vain, the seven sons opened themselves to a ferocious spiritual backlash that they would not soon forget. They were stripped, beat up and chased out of the house naked!

OCCULT-LEVEL SPIRITUAL WARFARE

[19] ***Also, many of those who had practiced magic brought their books together and burned them in the sight of all. And they counted up the value of them, and it totaled fifty thousand pieces of silver.***

Was there a significant relationship between the incident with the seven sons of Sceva and the conversion of the magicians? Susan Garrett thinks so, and she says that "the obvious answer is that in Luke's understanding, the Ephesians perceived the defeat of the seven sons to be a defeat of magic in general."[15] Clinton Arnold adds, "The overriding characteristic of the practice of magic throughout the Hellenistic world was the cognizance of a spirit world exercising influence over virtually every aspect of life . . . there can be no question that spirit beings were perceived as the functionaries behind the magic."[16] This means that, among other things, casting out demons from individuals on the ground level directly influenced the activity of the magicians on the occult level.

Burning Books

The major visible result of the spiritual warfare on the occult-level was a huge public book burning. How many magicians had come to Christ and were annulling their contracts with the spirit world we do not exactly know. But it must have been quite a few—so many that the meager information Luke gives us could reasonably be extrapolated into a possible people movement. Why do I say this?

Let's look at the value of the books and undoubtedly much other occult paraphernalia along with them. All together, they were worth "fifty thousand pieces of silver." Ernst Haenchen says that "a value equivalent to 50,000 days' wages goes up in flames."[17] If each piece of silver represents a day's wage, on a current U.S. scale of $10 an hour for eight-hour days, or $80 a day, it would total $4 million. Quite a book burning!

What should be our attitude toward book burning today? This question seems important in Luke's account because he stops to give reports of conversions right before:

> [18] ***And many who had believed came confessing and telling their deeds.***

As well as right afterward:

> [20] ***So the word of the Lord grew mightily and prevailed.***

A similar modern-day book-burning initiative in which the Word of the Lord grew mightily was the three-year evangelistic strategy implemented in Resistencia, Argentina, by Ed Silvoso's Harvest Evangelism organization not long ago. The evangelical community in Resistencia in those three years, and two more years following, grew some 500 percent—remarkable church growth in any nation! As part of the series of evangelistic rallies held at the end of the three-year period, a book-burning ceremony was held every evening, the first such activity I have been able to find on record in any part of Latin America.

Silvoso describes the event as follows: "In anticipation of an Ephesus-type response, a 100-gallon drum was set up to the left of the platform for the new converts to dispose of satanic paraphernalia. As people came forward, they dumped all kinds of occult-related items into it, many of them wrapped in newspaper. Before praying for the people, gasoline was poured on the contents of the drum, a match was struck and every evil thing inside went up in flames. Many times, spontaneous deliverances occurred throughout the audience when a specific fetish was burned and the spell was broken."[18]

Should We Do This More?

I wonder what new doors to evangelism might be opened in sophisticated, tolerant, politically correct America if Christians started expressing their faith by encouraging those who possessed artifacts of magic or unclean books to burn them publicly? Only one pastor I am aware of at the moment is doing this regularly. Pastor Donovan Larkins of Spirit of Life Christian Center in Dayton, Ohio, takes his congregation out every Halloween night for public book burnings, much to the consternation of the local authorities, as well as some of the other church leaders in his city. In his book *Up in Smoke*, Larkins says, "This type of public display is a witness of total rejection of Satan's kingdom and total allegiance to Jesus Christ and the kingdom of God!"[19]

Susan Garrett says something similar: "Luke's purpose . . . [was] to emphasize the sweeping victory of the Lord over the powers of darkness even in Ephesus, noted center of the magical arts."[20]

STRATEGIC-LEVEL SPIRITUAL WARFARE

The principal focal point of strategic-level spiritual warfare in Ephesus was Diana of the Ephesians, which is her Latin name, the Greek equivalent being Artemis. I am choosing to use the name "Diana" to follow the lead of the *New King James Version.*

It is important to know some details about this extraordinary principality of darkness. To begin with, the distraught silversmiths were saying:

> [27] ***So not only is this trade of ours in danger of falling into disrepute, but also the temple of the great goddess Diana may be despised and her magnificence destroyed, whom all Asia and the world worship.***
> [28] ***Now when they heard this, they were full of wrath and cried out, saying, "Great is Diana of the Ephesians!"***

The language here is exquisite: "great goddess . . . her magnificence . . . all Asia and the world worship [her]." She is said to be worthy of people crying, "Great is Diana of the Ephesians!" Clinton Arnold says Diana "was worshipped more widely by individuals than any other deity known to Pausanius."[21]

Diana as a Territorial Spirit

If we are indeed dealing with strategic-level spiritual warfare in this passage, it is necessary to explain why Diana may be regarded, not just as another demon, but as a territorial spirit. By territorial spirit, I mean a high-ranking member of the hierarchy of evil spirits delegated by Satan to control a nation, region, tribe, city, people group, neighborhood or any other significant social network of human beings.

Artemis had wide influence throughout the Roman Empire. F. F. Bruce makes reference to K. Wernicke who "enumerates thirty-three places, all over the known world, where Ephesian Artemis was venerated."[22] Even so, her chief location, which might have been called a seat of Satan, was Ephesus. Paul Trebilco, a New Zealand biblical scholar, says, "While Ephesus was the home of many cults, the most significant and powerful deity was Artemis of Ephesus."[23]

Why might we conceive of Diana as a territorial spirit over Ephesus? For one thing, "Artemis" is the name given to her by the Greeks, but it is not a Greek name. She was actually ruling Ephesus before the Greeks arrived.[24] For another, Diana's influence on all aspects of life in Ephesus was notable. Trebilco says, "It was the cult of the Ephesian Artemis which, more than anything else, made Ephesus a centre of religious life during our period. But the influence of the cult of Artemis extended beyond the religious sphere to the civic, economic, and cultural life of the city."[25] This fits our working definition of a territorial spirit.

Apropos to strategic-level spiritual warfare, which seeks to engage such spirits and challenge their authority, Trebilco says, "Any factor which sidelined Artemis would affect not only the religious, but also virtually all facets of life of the city."[26] In other words, part of effectively reaching Ephesus for God would necessarily include breaking the power of this all-controlling demon.

Some of the blasphemous names given to Diana were "greatest," "holiest," "most manifest," "Lady," "Savior" and "Queen of the Cosmos."[27] It is not farfetched to identify her—as we suggested in the case of Athena, the territorial spirit over Athens—with the infamous "Queen of Heaven" found in Jeremiah 7:16-18.

The Demonic Art and Architecture

As Paul stressed in his speech in the Athens Areopagus, two of the chief ways that humans frequently honor demonic spirits is through art and architecture. This was true in Ephesus. Diana's image, designed to glorify the creature rather than the Creator, was ubiquitous throughout the city. Unexpectedly, it was not pretty, but grotesque. She was endowed with no fewer than 21 breasts! It was more like an ugly Asian idol rather than a beautiful work of Greek art because, as I have mentioned, she had been worshiped in Ephesus even before the Greeks arrived. Clinton Arnold points out a significant characteristic: She was "the only divinity to depict visibly her divine superiority with the signs of the zodiac."[28]

The temple of Diana was anything but ugly. It was one of the most beautiful pieces of architecture in history, one of the seven wonders of the ancient world. It contained 93,500 square feet, four times the size of the Parthenon in Athens. It was supported by 127 columns, each one being 60 feet high and donated by a different king. Conybeare and Howson say, "The sun, it was said, saw nothing in its course more magnificent than Diana's temple. . . . It is probable that there was no religious building in the world in which was concentrated a greater amount of admiration, enthusiasm, and superstition."[29] In other words, the temple was a center of awesome spiritual power emanating from the invisible world of darkness.

Two major annual festivals honored Diana and reaffirmed to her and to the rest of the spirit world that the residents of Ephesus desired to continue to do her bidding for another year. One festival, the Artemisia, lasted a whole month. The other festival celebrated her birthday because supposedly she had been born near Ephesus. It was said that "this was one of the largest and most magnificent religious celebrations in Ephesus' liturgical calendar."[30]

The Riot

[23] ***And about that time there arose a great commotion about the Way.***

Considering that spiritual warfare was occurring at all levels, and victory after victory was being achieved by the forces of the kingdom of God, things could not long remain quiet in Ephesus. As John Stott says, "It was inevitable that sooner or later the kingly authority of Jesus would challenge

Diana's evil sway."[31] The magnitude of the riot is one more indication of Diana's territorial power. She was no ordinary demon.

> [24] *For a certain man named Demetrius, a silversmith, who made silver shrines of Diana, brought no small profit to the craftsmen.* [25] *He called them together with the workers of similar occupation, and said, "Men, you know that we have our prosperity by this trade.* [26] *Moreover you see and hear that not only at Ephesus, but throughout almost all Asia, this Paul has persuaded and turned away many people, saying that they are not gods which are made with hands.* [27] *So not only is this trade of ours in danger of falling into disrepute, but also the temple of the great goddess Diana may be despised and her magnificence destroyed, whom all Asia and the world worship."*

The problem was ostensibly an economic and a cultural one. But deeper than that, it was a spiritual problem. The territorial spirit who had gone unmolested for centuries was now beginning to lose her power! Why was she losing power? So many of the magicians whom she had controlled had been losing their battles in occult-level spiritual warfare against the Christians that control of the city was slipping out of her hands. Clinton Arnold says, "Although it has been claimed that the Ephesian Artemis was not by nature a goddess of magic, she does seem to have had a direct link with the magical practices of the time."[32] Her evil power could no longer control the local web of magic.

> [29] *So the whole city was filled with confusion, and rushed into the theater with one accord. . . .* [34] *. . . all with one voice cried out for about two hours, "Great is Diana of the Ephesians!"* [35] *And when the city clerk had quieted the crowd, he said: "Men of Ephesus . . .* [37] *For you have brought these men here who are neither robbers of temples nor blasphemers of your goddess.* [38] *Therefore if Demetrius and his fellow craftsmen have a case against anyone, the courts are open and there are proconsuls. . . ."* [41] *And when he said these things, he dismissed the assembly.*

The accusations against Paul were without substance. The city clerk of Ephesus justly cut through the emotional fog being raised by the silversmiths and dismissed the case.

CONFRONTING DIANA: FROM PAUL TO JOHN

During his ministry in Ephesus, Paul and his coworkers had succeeded in binding Diana, the territorial spirit, enough so that the gospel could spread vigorously. But they did this without directly confronting her (*these men* are not *blasphemers of your goddess*) or doing warfare in her temple (*neither robbers of temples*). Paul was not averse to doing such a thing because he had previously confronted the Python spirit in Philippi directly (see 16:18), but this was neither the time nor the place for a similar confrontation.

After the book of Acts closes and history picks up, we come to Scene II of this drama in Ephesus. Some years later, after Paul had left, the apostle John takes up residence in Ephesus. According to Ramsay MacMullen, the Yale historian, John, unlike Paul, eventually did enter directly into the famous temple of Diana to do strategic-level spiritual warfare. In the temple, he prayed this prayer: "O God . . . at whose name every idol takes flight and every demon and every unclean power: now let the demon that is here [i.e., Diana] take flight in thy name!"[33]

And what happened? History again tells us that when John took authority over Diana, her altar immediately split into pieces and half the temple crumbled to the ground! This is such an extraordinary report that some might question its historical reliability. Anticipating this, Ramsay MacMullen hastens to say, "I don't think the explanatory force of this scene should be discounted on the grounds that it cannot have really happened, that it is fiction, that no one was meant to believe it."[34]

Why did John take on Diana directly, but Paul did not? I think the answer is simple. God's timing is absolutely crucial for doing responsible strategic-level spiritual warfare, as I have often stressed. When Paul was in Ephesus, God did not assign him to do it because, for reasons we may never know, it was not yet time. Contrariwise, God did assign John to do it because it was then the proper time. It is likely that if Paul had tried what John did, he would have failed the same way the seven sons of Sceva did!

THE DEMISE OF DIANA

The one-two punches by Paul and John, as well as the prayers and aggressive spiritual warfare that must have been occurring among the believers in Ephesus before and after, had sealed the doom of the cult of Diana. An inscription written by a believer in Ephesus reads, in part, "Destroying the delusive image of the demon Artemis, Demeas has erected this symbol of Truth, the God that drives away idols, and the Cross of priests, deathless and victorious sign of Christ."[35]

Although records indicate that the worship of Diana still enthralled many people for at least 50 years after John faced her one on one, she didn't last much longer than that. Clinton Arnold finds that "the influx and expansion of Christianity eventually wrought the demise of the cult of the Ephesian Artemis."[36] Following that, Ephesus became the center of world Christianity for 200 years.

THE FIRST BLAZES IN EPHESUS AND ASIA MINOR

[17] *This became known both to all Jews and Greeks dwelling in Ephesus; and fear fell on them all, and the name of the Lord Jesus was magnified.* [18] *And many who had believed came confessing and telling of their deeds.* [20] *So the word of the Lord grew mightily and prevailed.*

We will want to remember once again that as the gospel spread across the city of Ephesus and its quarter-million inhabitants, the believers did not gather weekly in one huge megachurch. Instead, many house churches would have been meeting in many parts of the city, and those churches would have been multiplying under their own momentum. These would not have been confined only to Ephesus city, but they presumably would also be multiplying in the immediate suburbs such as Metropolis, Hypaipa, Diashieron, Neikaia, Koloe and Palaiapolis, according to Clinton Arnold.[37]

Paul's enemies also recognized that these churches were rapidly spreading into other cities in Asia. Demetrius the silversmith laments that "throughout almost all Asia, this Paul has persuaded and turned away many people" (v. 26).

From what we can surmise, Paul himself stayed in Ephesus city for the three years, training the church planters who would then move out into the other parts of Asia. Some evidence for this comes from the Epistle Paul later wrote to one of those cities—Colossae. In Colossians, Paul mentions that the Christians there had never seen him in person, and neither had the believers in another one of Asia's cities—Laodeceia (see Col. 2:1).

Who were the church planters who graduated from Paul's school? Many, if not most, we will never know, but we do have the names of some of the alumni: Epaphras (see Col. 1:7), Tychicus (see Acts 20:4; Eph. 6:21; Col. 4:7),

Trophimus (see Acts 20:4), Philemon (see Philem. 1:1) and Archippus (see Philem. 1:2).

What churches did they plant? Again, our list is not complete, but we can name several: Colossae, Laodeceia, Hierapolis, and those listed in Revelation 2–3: Smyrna, Pergamos, Thyatira, Sardis and Philadelphia. F. F. Bruce notes, "The province [of Asia] was intensely evangelized and remained one of the leading centers of Christianity for many centuries."[38]

Occupying Diana's Territory

I titled this chapter "Invading Diana's Territory" because it is the clearest biblical example I have found of a well-known territorial spirit being successfully engaged by the forces of the kingdom of God and thereby losing control of the territory. In this case, Paul had literally fulfilled the mandate he had received from Jesus on the Damascus road to turn Gentiles "from darkness to light, and from the power of Satan to God" (Acts 26:18).

Although it is true that the seat of Diana's power was Ephesus city, her territorial jurisdiction apparently extended throughout the whole province of Asia. Clinton Arnold affirms that "[Diana] was worshipped in . . . the cities of Colossae, Laodeceia, and Hierapolis" and that "the grandeur and fame of the temple of Diana was only exceeded by the influence of the cult itself, not only in Ephesus, but throughout all of Asia."[39]

Not everyone, perhaps including Clinton Arnold himself, would necessarily draw from this the conclusion that Diana was, indeed, a territorial spirit. Nevertheless, it looks very much that way to me, especially considering the suggestion that the magnificent temple of Diana, one of the seven wonders of the ancient world, was *surpassed* by the spiritual power of her cult throughout the province. Imagine the control this demonic ruler had freely exercised over the souls of millions of human beings throughout the centuries! This is exactly what is implied by the modern term "territorial spirit."

In this last recorded episode of Paul's church-planting missionary career, we see his most outstanding triumph. With the power and authority of Jesus Christ, he had invaded a territory that Satan had ruled from time immemorial. Paul was not wrestling against flesh and blood, but, as he later said, "against principalities, against powers, against the rulers of the darkness of this age, against spiritual hosts of wickedness in the heavenly places" (Eph. 6:12). As a result, Diana's territory was not only invaded, it was also conquered!

As I said earlier, Acts 19 is my favorite chapter in Acts. If the book of Acts truly is "A Training Manual for Every Christian," as I contend it is, no chapter in Acts could be more helpful for learning principles of evangelism and could be more encouraging regarding potential results for those willing to move into enemy territory by the power of the Holy Spirit!

REFLECTION QUESTIONS

1. Ephesus was a center of magic where fetishes were manufactured. What have you ever seen that could be identified as a fetish? Do these really have some kind of supernatural power?
2. Why was training church planters more important to Paul in Ephesus than personally traveling through the surrounding cities of Asia and conducting evangelistic crusades? How would you apply this to missions today?
3. How much weight should we put on the findings of historians such as Ramsay MacMullen? They do not carry the authority of Scripture, but what authority do you think they carry?
4. Do you think that reports of teeth being filled supernaturally in Argentina and Brazil are "preposterous," as one person says? Why or why not?
5. What would you think of Christian leaders in your city organizing and endorsing public burnings of evil items as they did in Ephesus? What would some of the sensible ground rules of such an initiative be?

22

A LONG TRIP TOWARD THE JERUSALEM JAIL

ACTS 20 AND 21

Beginning with Acts 20, Luke shifts gears decisively in his historical account of the spread of the gospel through the ancient world by the ministry of the apostles. In the remaining nine chapters of his book, Luke gives us very little additional information about missiology, church planting or power ministries. Not that these are entirely absent, for we do have some important things yet to learn about these crucial issues. But we will find that Luke's major emphasis is elsewhere, concentrating more on Paul's experiences of being jailed and defending himself in several courtroom-type scenes. In this respect, Luke concludes Acts much as he also does his Gospel.

Because of this, readers may have noticed that a relatively small number of pages remain in these final chapters. According to my calculations, I am devoting only 8 percent of my full commentary on Acts to chapters 20 to 28, which in turn comprise 32 percent of Luke's original work. As points of comparison, F. F. Bruce uses 26 percent of his commentary on Acts for these final chapters and John Stott 22 percent. But as a reminder, my chief purpose for writing number 1,399 English commentary on Acts is to highlight precisely the areas of missiology and power ministries that are not particularly stressed in the other 1,398 commentaries.

PAUL NEVER LOST HIS VISION

From this point on, Paul had to expend much energy to defend himself and the faith he represented. He spent a great deal of time in custody, but he never lost the vision that Jesus had given him on the Damascus road. We have seen that as a direct result of one of his final missionary tasks, the city of Ephesus became the center of world Christianity for the next 200 years! Here are some significant features of Ephesus:

1. Paul wrote 1 Corinthians from Ephesus.
2. Timothy succeeded Paul in Ephesus. Paul wrote 1 and 2 Timothy to him while Timothy was in Ephesus (see 1 Tim. 1:3).
3. The apostle John later took up residence in Ephesus and wrote 1, 2 and 3 John from there, as well as the Gospel of John. I could well imagine that the school that Paul had started in Tyrannus's building had included both Timothy and John on the faculty, as well as many others as the years passed.
4. Paul also made plans for his future there:

[19:21] ***When these things were accomplished, Paul purposed in the Spirit, when he had passed through Macedonia and Achaia, to go to Jerusalem, saying, "After I have been there, I must also see Rome."***

Visiting the established churches in Achaia (which would include its capital, Corinth) and in Macedonia (which would include Philippi, Thessalonica and Berea) was important for Paul. But, avoiding the "syndrome of church development," which we have mentioned from time to time, his true vision was for Rome, which he had never visited. Not only that, but we later also learn that Rome, in Paul's mind, was considered just a stopping-off place because Christian churches had already been planted and they were multiplying in Rome. He really wanted to pioneer the kingdom of God in Spain.

In his letter to the Christians in Rome, Paul says, "For this reason I also have been much hindered from coming to you. But now no longer having a place in these parts, and having a great desire these many years to come to you, whenever I journey to Spain, I shall come to you" (Rom. 15:22-24). Paul also tells the Romans that he hopes they will provide financial support for his projected missionary work in Spain: "I hope to . . . be helped on my way there by you" (v. 24).

No one knows for sure whether Paul ever made it to Spain. But whether he did or not, he never lost his vision for frontier missions. As F. F. Bruce puts it, "[Paul] looked around for fresh worlds to conquer."[1]

ENCOURAGING FRIENDS: ACTS 20

[1] After the uproar [in Ephesus] had ceased, Paul called the disciples to himself, embraced them, and departed to go to Macedonia. [2] *Now when he had gone over that region and encouraged them with many words, he came to Greece* [3] *and stayed three months. . . .*

From this account, it looks as though Paul would have gone directly from Ephesus to Philippi (Macedonia). But such is not the case. Luke chooses not to mention that Paul first went back to Troas where he originally had received the Macedonian vision to go to Philippi and other parts of Europe for the first time (see 16:8-9). We learn this not from Acts, but from Paul himself when he later writes 2 Corinthians: "Furthermore, when I came to Troas to preach Christ's gospel, and a door was opened to me by the Lord, I had no rest in my spirit, because I did not find Titus my brother; but taking my leave of them, I departed for Macedonia" (2:12-13).

First, then, he went to Troas to preach and there he found good receptivity—an open door to the gospel. But Paul also expressed a bit of frustration when he didn't meet Titus there as expected. As we read Acts, it seems strange that Luke does not mention Titus at all. He is well known to us because a letter later written to him by Paul has become one of the books of our New Testament. This is a puzzle to many. William Ramsay says, "The complete omission of Titus' name must be intentional." But no one seems to know why. "It is equally hard to explain on every theory," adds Ramsay.[2]

Paul then set out for Macedonia and the city of Philippi where he had previously sent Timothy and Erastus from Ephesus (see Acts 19:22). It seems that he stayed there quite a while, possibly a year and a half, according to F. F. Bruce.[3] This is an unusually long period of time to spend in an already existing church, given what we have said about the need to avoid the "syndrome of church development." Why would Paul have done this?

It could be that Paul moved in with Luke and Lydia, that he became very comfortable there, that he had his material needs cared for without making tents and that he enjoyed some leisure time while also meeting with and instructing the believers. He wrote his second letter to the Corinthians while he was in Philippi.

But this does not sound like what we would usually expect of this restless frontier missionary whom we have been following. Another possible explanation as to why Paul stayed in Philippi so long seems more feasible to me. Toward the end of his letter to the Romans, Paul writes, "For I will not dare to speak of any of those things which Christ has not accomplished through me, in word and deed, to make Gentiles obedient in mighty signs and wonders, by the power of the Spirit of God, so that from Jerusalem and round about to Illyricum I have fully preached the gospel of Christ" (15:18-19). This sounds more like what we have come to expect of Paul, and the interesting thing is that he specifies "Illyricum."

Illyricum is the province to the north of Macedonia, occupying much of the lands of the former Yugoslavia. Luke doesn't mention it in Acts, and nowhere else do we find a reference about exactly when Paul might have preached in Illyricum. It might have happened here. It would seem reasonable to surmise that Paul could have used Philippi as a base from which he moved out to plant churches throughout the regions north of Philippi. It could well have been the time when Paul reached his northernmost evangelistic targets.

Luke does not tell of this either, but it turns out that Titus had actually been in Corinth, and that he and Paul were reunited here in Philippi (see 2 Cor. 7:5-7) instead of in Troas as Paul had first expected. Could Titus have joined Paul in evangelizing Illyricum? Possibly so.

FUND-RAISING IN CORINTH

When Paul left Philippi, it is likely that Timothy and Erastus accompanied him to Corinth. Whether he had also visited churches in Thessalonica and Berea while in Macedonia we do not know, but the words "when he had gone over that region" (Acts 20:2) sound as if he might have. One purpose could have been to raise funds, as we shall soon see. In any case, Paul spent the winter of A.D. 56-57 in Corinth, undoubtedly encouraging the believers as he had done in Macedonia.

Paul had the gift of apostle, and, thereby, he had a great deal of authority over the churches in his sphere. Simon Kistemaker observes, "Paul was the spiritual father of the believers in the Gentile world, and he addressed them as his spiritual children."[4] The church in Corinth, from the evidence we have in 1 Corinthians, had become one of the most messed-up churches with which Paul had to deal. In that letter, written from Ephesus, Paul had clearly laid out two options for them: "What do you want? Shall I come to you with a rod, or in love and a spirit of gentleness?" (4:21).

The answer was that the Corinthians themselves wisely had decided to clean up their act before Paul got there, and Titus brought this good news to Paul while he was still in Philippi. The good news prompted Paul to write 2 Corinthians, in which he said, "God . . . comforted us by the coming of Titus, and not only by his coming, but also by the consolation with which he was comforted in you, when he told us of your earnest desire, your mourning, your zeal for me, so that I rejoiced even more" (7:6-7).

We also learn from 2 Corinthians that Paul was on his way to Corinth to raise funds. The believers in Jerusalem were struggling. The scenario we read about in Acts 2, where the believers "sold their possessions and goods, and divided them among all, as anyone had need" (v. 45), had changed radically when the wealthier Hellenistic Jewish believers had been driven out of Jerusalem as a backlash from Stephen's ministry (see 8:1), leaving only the poorer Hebrew Jewish believers. Paul refers to them when he says, "Now concerning the ministering to the saints" (2 Cor. 9:1).

SOME PRINCIPLES OF FUND-RAISING

Paul's visit to Corinth prompted some of the most detailed principles of fund-raising we have in the Scriptures. If we follow Paul's lead, we will keep three things in mind:

1. *Let Christians know what others are doing.* It seems that Paul did not believe donation records should be kept secret. He told the Corinthians that the churches in Macedonia, although they were poor, had given generously to the fund. "For I bear witness that according to their ability, yes, and beyond their ability, they were freely willing" (2 Cor. 8:3). This is not designed to put individuals or churches in competition with one another. The intention is to build each other's faith.

2. *Giving is like sowing seed.* The more you sow, the more you reap. "He who sows sparingly will also reap sparingly, and he who sows bountifully will also reap bountifully" (9:6). Is this a teaching about prosperity? If prosperity means greediness and the desire to have money to support an opulent lifestyle, it certainly does not. But if prosperity means having sufficient resources for

living, plus much more to advance the kingdom of God, it apparently means just that. I like the way the *Good News Bible* translates 2 Corinthians 9:8: "And God is able to give you more than you need, so that you will always have all you need for yourselves and more than enough for every good cause."

3. *Giving causes joy.* "God loves a cheerful giver" (v. 7). I am well acquainted with many Christians who are generous givers, contributing much more than the expected tithe, or 10 percent of income, to "every good cause." I have not yet found one of them who is not a cheerful giver nor have I found one for whom God has not provided all the necessities of life. Many of them are subsequently able to live more comfortable lives than the more stingy believers around them. In most cases, increased giving causes increased cheerfulness and increased cheerfulness causes increased giving.

FLEEING THE JEWS AGAIN

> . . . And when the Jews plotted against him as he was about to sail to Syria, he decided to return through Macedonia (v. 3).

The Jews in Corinth, who were previously unsuccessful in having Paul accused of breaking the Roman law by Gallio, now set out on a more direct approach to attack Paul. They decided to take the law into their own hands. Paul, therefore, changed his plans and did not head directly for Jerusalem as he originally intended to do. William Ramsay says, "With a shipload of hostile Jews, it would be easy to find opportunity to murder Paul."[5]

Paul might have also had a word directly from God in making this decision. Although we do not have it in our version, another ancient text of the New Testament, which scholars do not ignore, says, "The Spirit told him to return through Macedonia."

Back in Philippi (Macedonia), a regional leadership meeting is taking place. Seven people from a variety of churches in the area have gathered to prepare to take their relief funds to Jerusalem. The seven then continued on to Troas while Paul and Luke stayed for a time in Philippi. We know that Luke was there because the passage from Acts once more shifts to the first person "we" at this point:

[5] *These men, going ahead, waited for us at Troas.*

A WEEK AT TROAS

[7] *Now on the first day of the week, when the disciples [in Troas] came together to break bread, Paul, ready to depart the next day, spoke to them and continued his message until midnight.*

Many of the commentators who write about this passage draw the conclusion from the phrase "the first day of the week, when the disciples came together to break bread" that by this time in A.D. 57, Sunday worship had become normal for Christians. The traditional worship day for the Jews, of course, was Saturday—the Sabbath or the last day of the week. Although Seventh-day Adventists and others continue to keep the Sabbath, most Christians conduct their primary worship services on Sunday.

The roots of Sunday worship, interestingly enough, go back largely to custom and consensus rather than to explicit biblical mandate. In the particular case of Troas, it could be argued at least as strongly that the only reason the Christians met on the *first* day of the week was that Paul's ship was scheduled to sail the *second* day of the week. It could well have been a farewell party, highlighted perhaps by the Lord's Supper.

Some, I know, may be uncomfortable with this observation. But the two other biblical passages frequently cited to justify Sunday worship, 1 Corinthians 16:2 and John 20:19, furnish, at best, circumstantial evidence subject to shades of interpretation.

In any case, it is known that Christians eventually decided that they should worship on Sunday to honor the Lord's resurrection on the first day of the week. It is also true that this occurred in a Roman social setting where Sunday, not Saturday, was the day off each week. In any event, by the end of the first century, Sunday was being called the "Lord's Day," according to *The Didache*, an ancient record of the apostles' teachings (*Didache 14:1*). Whether this was the practice at the time of the meeting in Troas, however, is questionable.

RAISING THE DEAD

[8] *There were many lamps in the upper room where they were gathered together.* [9] *And in a window sat a certain young man named Eutychus, who was sinking into a deep sleep. He was overcome by sleep; and as Paul*

continued speaking, he fell down from the third story and was taken up dead. [10] *But Paul went down, fell on him, and embracing him said, "Do not trouble yourselves, for his life is in him."* [11] *Now when he had come up, had broken bread and eaten, and talked a long while, even till daybreak, he departed.* [12] *And they brought the young man in alive, and they were not a little comforted.*

This is the last of nine examples we have in the Bible of the dead being raised. For the record, here they are:

1. Elijah raises a young boy (see 1 Kings 17:17-24).
2. Elisha raises a young boy (see 2 Kings 4:32-37).
3. Jesus raises a widow's grown son (see Luke 7:11-16).
4. Jesus raises Jairus's daughter (see Luke 8:49-56).
5. Jesus raises Lazarus (see John 11:43-44).
6. Jesus Himself is raised (see Luke 24:6).
7. Peter raises Dorcas (see Acts 9:36-42).
8. The believers in Lystra raise Paul (see Acts 14:19-20).
9. Paul raises Eutychus (see Acts 20:9-12).

Bible-believing Christians have little reason to doubt that dead people are still being raised today. Reports of this occurring have been coming in from many places by credible witnesses, perhaps not daily, but certainly regularly. I mentioned earlier that I met one evangelist in Nigeria who, when I asked him, had forgotten exactly how many people he had raised from the dead! Jesus commanded His disciples to raise the dead the very first time He sent them out on an evangelistic tour (see Matt. 10:8). He then ordered His disciples to teach their converts to do all that He had commanded them (see 28:20), presumably, including raising the dead. Both Peter and Paul did just that, and undoubtedly many others as well in the first century. Interestingly, we have more *biblical* evidence for Christians raising the dead through the power of the Holy Spirit than we have for worshiping on Sunday.

THE PASTORS' SEMINAR FOR ASIA

[16] *For Paul had decided to sail past Ephesus, so that he would not have to spend time in Asia . . .* [17] *From Miletus he sent to Ephesus*

and called for the elders of the church. [18] *And when they had come to him, he said to them . . .*

On his way to Jerusalem, Paul wanted to conduct a leadership training seminar for the pastors of the Ephesian churches. Apparently, he did not care to socialize with the believers in general, so he bypassed the city of Ephesus and stopped at Miletus, a two-day journey by land to the south. This, by the way, is the only example we have in Acts of Paul's teaching to Christians in general, in this case, specifically to leaders. All other examples of Paul's speeches are directed to evangelize unbelievers, either Jews or Gentiles, or to defend himself in front of government officials and accusers.

Unlike the challenges many of us face today, marketing this seminar was relatively easy. All it took was Paul's announcement that the seminar would be held. The reason for this was Paul's recognized position as an apostle—a position that carried with it an extraordinary amount of spiritual authority, including powers of convocation.

Modern readers often do not understand that Paul led a *pastors'* seminar as opposed to a seminar for lay elders, and this is confusing because many English Bible versions, such as the *New King James Version,* which we are using, translate the Greek *presbyteros* as "elders," certainly a legitimate translation. But so many of our churches are structured today with an ordained senior pastor who works with a board of lay elders that "elders" has come to take on another meaning for us. Let me explain.

Three Greek words, all used by Paul in his seminar here in Miletus, refer to the pastors whom he had called together:

> . . . [Paul] called for the elders of the church. "Therefore take heed to yourselves and to all the flock, among which the Holy Spirit has made you overseers, to shepherd the church of God . . . (vv. 17,28, emphasis added).

- **elders** = *presbyteros.* This is the standard word for elders, and the root from which we get the name "Presbyterian Church." It is a church government in which the lay elders rule the local congregation.
- **overseers** = *episkopos.* We usually translate this as bishops, meaning those who supervise a number of pastors. This is the root word for the "Episcopal Church."

- **shepherd** = *poimen*. Using the metaphor of the caretaker of sheep, we usually translate this as "pastor."

The point to note here is that all three of these words refer to the same people whom Paul is teaching, so that at least to a significant extent, we can consider them synonyms for each other rather than thinking that they represent three different offices in the church. Despite certain individual nuances, these three words denote the top leaders of local churches (i.e., the pastors) as opposed to another important kind of church leader called "deacons." The two are clearly differentiated in 1 Timothy 3, where Paul first lists the qualifications of a bishop (see 3:1-7) and then the qualifications of a deacon (see vv. 8-13).

The House Churches of Ephesus

The leaders who walked for two days from Ephesus to Miletus to attend the seminar were, to sum it up, the pastors of the multiple house churches in Ephesus city, and undoubtedly from the immediate outlying suburbs. Paul refers to the house churches as he speaks to them when, recalling his three-year ministry there, he says he would go from house to house (see Acts 20:20). It is easy for us in the twenty-first century to forget that no such things as church buildings, as we now know them, existed in the Early Church. Bradley Blue says, "The gathering of Christian believers in private homes (or homes renovated for the purpose of Christian gatherings) continued to be the norm until the early decades of the fourth century when Constantine began erecting the first Christian basilicas."[6]

It is important, not just for understanding the nature of Paul's seminar in Miletus, but also for understanding church planting in the book of Acts in general, to look closely at the word "church," which we translate from the Greek *ekklesia*. Few have helped us more on this subject than Robert Banks in his excellent book *Paul's Idea of Community*. Although some may conclude that all the Christians in a large city such as Ephesus would occasionally, if not regularly, meet together, Banks does not agree. He says, "There is no suggestion that Christians ever met as a whole in one place."[7]

Although it is hard to read the details of our twenty-first century back into the first century, it is not farfetched to say that those whom Paul was teaching in his seminar would be the functional equivalent of what we regard today as ordained ministers. Each one would have been in charge of a relatively small congregation meeting in someone's home. I can well imagine that by this time some 200 such congregations might have been meeting in greater Ephesus, considering its population of 250,000 people, in addition to the adjoining suburbs.

Paul's Teaching

How long would this seminar have lasted? One day? Two days? Suppose, just to make a point, it was a one-day seminar and Paul taught for six hours that day. That means he would have taught for 360 minutes. But Luke summarizes Paul's teaching in Acts 20:18-35, which can be read out loud in 2 minutes and 10 seconds. In other words, we have here less than one-half of 1 percent of Paul's teaching content, even assuming it was a short one-day seminar. So from one perspective, we could say we have ended up with but a brief summary of the high points that seemed important to Luke. Or, from another perspective, we could say we trust that the Holy Spirit, who inspired Luke as he was writing Acts, guided Luke supernaturally to select the exact items that would be the most important for the leaders of the church through the ages. Let's move on this latter assumption.

As I read it, it looks as though the seminar could have been divided into four sessions, all of which are important for Christian leaders in all places at all times:

Session 1: Striving for a servant's heart (Acts 20:17-21). Just before coming here to Miletus, Paul had written his letters to the Corinthians. In these letters, he makes two statements that every Christian leader who serves as a role model for others should also be able to make:

"I do not even judge myself. For I know nothing against myself, yet I am not justified by this; but He who judges me is the Lord" (1 Cor. 4:3-4). As Paul honestly examined his own life, he could find nothing wrong. This is the basis on which he could later say, "Therefore, I urge you, imitate me" (v. 16). He was not reluctant to use his own life and testimony as a model for Christian leadership. How could the leaders attain this?

[18] . . . *You know, from the first day that I came to Asia, in what manner I always lived among you,* [19] *serving the Lord with all humility, with many tears and trials which happened to me by the plotting of the Jews."*

Paul regarded himself as a slave, serving the Lord. In many other places, he also refers to himself as a slave (see, for example, Rom. 1:1). Coming from a society in which many of the pastors themselves would undoubtedly either have owned slaves or have been slaves themselves at the time,[8] they would have known exactly what he was talking about. They knew that taking the attitude of a slave would invariably produce humility. As they served the Lord, they should expect that their service would have its ups and downs. Paul spoke of "many tears and trials," of enemies he had and they also would have. He later writes back to them, reminding them that the real enemies are not flesh and blood, but the supernatural principalities and powers of darkness behind human agents (see Eph. 6:12).

Session 2: Counting the cost of discipleship (Acts 20:22-24). Paul knew his troubles had not ended, but that many more awaited him when he would arrive in Jerusalem:

> [22] ***And see, now I go bound in the spirit to Jerusalem, not knowing the things that will happen to me there,*** [23] ***except that the Holy Spirit testifies in every city, saying that chains and tribulations await me.***

As he had experienced on many other occasions, Paul received word from the Holy Spirit that he was to go to Jerusalem. If asked, he could have replied that he was going to Jerusalem because "God told me to." But was this leading of God toward a health, wealth and happiness direction? Obviously not. It was to "chains and tribulations."

At this point, Paul would have taught the pastors that they must realistically count the cost whenever they accept an assignment to Christian leadership. Pastoring a church is not easy. All of them will have some price to pay, and for some it will be the ultimate price of life itself. Paul was ready to model this also by saying, "nor do I count my life dear to myself" (v. 24).

Session 3: Guarding against counterfeits (Acts 20:25-31). One quality of Christian leaders is to be able to discern truth from falsehood. The devil will certainly attempt to introduce deception both from without and from within:

> [29] ***For I know this, that after my departure savage wolves will come in among you, not sparing the flock.*** [30] ***Also from among yourselves***

men will rise up, speaking perverse things, to draw away the disciples after themselves.

The magicians were burning their books, and Diana of the Ephesians was on the defensive, so the pastors in Ephesus could expect all manner of attacks, some blatant and some more subtle. As part of the seminar, Paul would have given them instructions on how to deal with such evil infiltrations. The good news is that apparently the pastors learned their lesson well and courageously applied what they knew. The message Jesus gives to the Ephesians many years later, recorded by John in Revelation, says, among other things, "I know your works, your labor, your patience, and that you cannot bear those who are evil. And you have tested those who say they are apostles and are not, and have found them liars" (2:2).

Session 4: Turning the church over to the nationals (Acts 20:32-35). Many of those who attended Paul's leadership seminar would have been people he had previously trained as church planters in his school in Tyrannus's facility. He most probably would have taught them what we call today "indigenous church principles," an extremely important missiological concept. Donald McGavran, a renowned missiologist, says, "Stoppage [in church growth] is avoided by using a pattern of church growth that is indefinitely reproducible with the resources available to a given church."[9] Paul indicated that one way he had helped this process was by not loading his personal expenses onto the new churches:

[33] *I have coveted no one's silver or gold or apparel.* [34] *Yes, you yourselves know that these hands have provided for my necessities, and for those who were with me.*

At the same time, Paul taught that pastors of local churches should be compensated for their services: "Let the elders who rule well be counted worthy of double honor, especially those who labor in the word and in doctrine. For the Scripture says, 'You shall not muzzle an ox while it treads out the grain,' and, 'The laborer is worthy of his wages' " (1 Tim. 5:18).

THE NEED TO EVALUATE PROPHECY: ACTS 21

As Paul continues his trip to Jerusalem, he runs into two incidents in which it seems that prophetic words delivered to him by others might contradict the word he himself had received from the Holy Spirit that he should go to Jerusalem even if "chains and tribulations await [him]" (Acts 20:22). One incident occurs in his stopover in Tyre (see 21:1-6), and the other one during a longer stay in Caesarea (see vv. 7-14).

The incident in Tyre:

> [4] *And finding disciples, we stayed there seven days. They told Paul through the Spirit not to go up to Jerusalem.*

And the incident in Caesarea:

> [10] *And as we stayed many days, a certain prophet named Agabus came down from Judea.* [11] *When he had come to us, he took Paul's belt, bound his own hands and feet, and said, "Thus says the Holy Spirit, 'So shall the Jews at Jerusalem bind the man who owns this belt, and deliver him into the hands of the Gentiles.'"* [12] *Now when we heard these things, both we and those from that place pleaded with him not to go up to Jerusalem.*

In both of these cases, Paul already knew that God had told him to go to Jerusalem, and he also knew that he would face serious problems once he arrived there. Yet, words such as these must have been quite disturbing to him. Could it be that he had heard from God inaccurately? Could it be that God had changed His mind?

In Tyre, it might have been fairly easy for Paul to judge that the believers could have heard accurately from God about the dangers, and then they could have allowed their own love for him to shape their application of what they had heard. Their revelation "through the Spirit" (v. 4) could be explained by Luke's use of the Greek *dia* ("through"), which can mean "as a consequence of" what the Spirit had told them, as opposed to a similar Greek word *hupo,* which Luke chose *not* to use and which would have implied that the Holy Spirit was the direct source of telling Paul not to go.[10]

But the situation in Caesarea with Agabus is a bit more complex. Agabus was a recognized prophet in the churches. Furthermore, he was known to be accurate, as we saw earlier when he prophesied a famine that actually came to pass (see 11:28). Agabus apparently went to Caesarea specifically to bring this prophetic word to Paul.

This prophecy, however, did not turn out to be all that accurate. Agabus introduced it with a prophetic act that would ordinarily serve to dramatize the event. He prefaced it by saying, "Thus says the Holy Spirit" (21:11). And the prophecy itself had two parts:

1. "So shall the Jews at Jerusalem bind the man who owns this belt" (v. 11). As it turns out, Paul is later bound, but not by Jews; he is bound by Romans (see v. 33).
2. "So shall the Jews . . . deliver him into the hands of the Gentiles" (v. 11). As it turns out, the Jews have no intention of delivering Paul to the Gentiles, but, rather, they attempt to murder him themselves. The Romans (Gentiles) actually rescue him *from* the Jews (see vv. 31-33).

How can we explain this prophecy? It would not seem to be sufficient to explain it by arguing that only the *details* might not have been accurate, while the *essence* of Agabus's prophecy was accurate. Wayne Grudem points out, "This explanation does not take full enough account of the fact that these are the *only* two details Agabus mentions–they are, in terms of content, the heart of his prophecy."[11]

STEPS TOWARD EVALUATING PERSONAL PROPHECY

Christian leaders who believe that the spiritual gifts of the New Testament, such as prophecy, are still actively functioning in the Body of Christ today may often face situations illustrated by Paul and Agabus. I know that I find myself in a similar position many times because, in my role as an international prayer coordinator, I am in close contact with intercessors and prophets who love me and pray for me.

Here are some useful steps, which I have developed over a period of time, to evaluate personal prophecy:

We cannot take all the words, purportedly from the Holy Spirit, that come our way equally at face value. If we allowed all of them equally to direct our attitudes, our decisions and our actions, we would quickly find ourselves moving in many different directions at the same time, and our leadership effectiveness could thereby be neutralized.

Our decisions and our activities as leaders must ultimately be based on what we ourselves sense the Spirit is saying to us, *not what He may be saying to* others. I like Stanley

Horton's comment on the word Paul received from the believers at Tyre: "In other words, because of the prophecy of bonds and imprisonment, the people voiced their feelings that he should not go. But Paul refused to let them force their feelings on him. So he still obeyed what the Holy Spirit directed him personally to do, that is, go on to Jerusalem."[12] If we are true leaders, the buck will necessarily stop with us. We will take full personal responsibility before God and before our followers for every decision we make, while being grateful to prayer partners and prophets for their ongoing love and concern.

The Holy Spirit, however, does frequently use the prophetic ministry of others to guide us toward our decisions. This is the central value of personal prophecy. How, then, do we know which words we should take seriously and which we should ignore? In my opinion, our starting point must be the character, reputation and gifting of the person who offers the prophecy. Agabus obviously passed this test.

It is also important to keep in mind three distinct steps in receiving a prophetic guidance:

1. The *revelation* itself
2. The *interpretation* of the revelation
3. The *application* of the interpretation to real life

Getting back to the problem Paul had with Agabus. Consider, in light of these three steps, Wayne Grudem's response: "The best solution is to say that Agabus had a '*revelation*' from the Holy Spirit concerning what would happen to Paul in Jerusalem, and gave a prophecy which included his own *interpretation* of this revelation"[13] (emphasis added). Having said this, it is clear that Paul himself had to make the final *application*. As in Tyre, he believed that his personal word from the Lord directing him to go to Jerusalem overruled any other opinion that might have come to him through his dear friends and colleagues, gifted as they might be. When he made that known, the others involved appropriately recognized that Paul was correct, and Luke says "we ceased [giving Paul advice], saying, 'The will of the Lord be done' " (21:14).

THREE INHERENT LIMITATIONS

Recognize the inherent limitations of personal prophecy. Bill Hamon, a well-respected prophetic leader, says, "However it may be worded, a personal prophecy will always be partial, progressive and conditional."[14] Prophecies are *partial* because each one touches only a relatively small segment of our lives. Prophecy is *progressive* because it "unfolds and expands gradually over the years, with each prophetic word adding new information and revelation."[15] It is *conditional* because its fulfillment "requires the proper participation and cooperation of the one who receives the prophetic word."[16]

The human factors involved in interpretation and application of personal prophecies can be sifted and tested through agreement. If several responsible people are receiving the same or similar words, the accuracy is more probable.

For several years, my wife, Doris, and I have been keeping what I call a "prophetic journal," which has now reached over 200 single-spaced pages. In it, I record only certain prophecies directed to Doris and me that we have sifted out from many others, believing they merit special consideration in our prayers for direction. Much of what is recorded there could not be made public for a number of reasons. But, as an example of what I am saying, our very important decision to accept the invitation to coordinate the United Prayer Track of the A.D. 2000 and Beyond Movement back in 1991 came largely as a result of many directional prophetic words given to Doris and me through our trusted intercessors.

For example: Before the invitation came, one person said, "You are now about to face the greatest challenge of your life. It will be a challenge almost beyond belief, but you are to believe the unbelievable." When the invitation came, another person said, "This is not like anything else I've felt. I feel the glory of the Lord around A.D. 2000. Whatever this movement is, get on it! This is a God-ordained program; it is where God is moving right now!" And another one said, "A.D. 2000 is a strong stream of God's movement in these days; you should be a part of it." Still others agreed, and we thereby became part of what turned out to be an extremely fruitful time of ministry through the decade of the 1990s.

In obedience to the Lord, Paul, likewise, had no choice but to move on to Jerusalem and the Jerusalem jail.

REFLECTION QUESTIONS

1. What do you think of the suggestion that in raising funds for Christian work we might compare what some give to what others give? Can this be abused?

2. When it comes right down to it, how much biblical justification do we have for worshiping on the first day of the week as opposed to keeping the Sabbath?
3. Why would some people doubt that God at times raises dead people to life today just as He did in biblical times?
4. The churches in the first century were all house churches. Do you think it is either unbiblical or unwise to meet in church buildings today?
5. Do you agree that some prophets today hear the voice of God? What are the potential benefits of such ministry? What cautions would you offer?

23

WHAT TO DO WITH THIS TROUBLEMAKER?

Acts 21 to 26

Paul's last visit to Jerusalem was not the best of experiences. Coming off his tremendous success in the evangelization of Ephesus and Asia and ending up in jail in Jerusalem was a shocking change. For many other Christian leaders since Paul, however, moving from an extraordinary high to a depressing low has not been unknown. In such situations, looking back to the way that Paul handled his unpleasant experience has been a strong encouragement. Paul managed it splendidly, although, sadly, this trip to Jerusalem marked the beginning of the end, not only of Paul's active ministry but of his life.

We cannot help but wonder why Luke gives so much space in Acts to this experience in Jerusalem. I like the way George Ladd analyzes it: "Luke devotes five and a half chapters to an account of Paul's last visit to Jerusalem. Why does this story merit so much space?" Ladd points out that, unlike what we have seen in Acts so far, "No new churches were established; no theological or ecclesiastical problems solved. No positive gains came from this visit."[1]

After raising the question, Ladd then goes on to propose an answer: "The importance of these chapters is found in their illustration of Israel's rejection of the Gospel."[2] As we have followed Paul's ministry, we have seen many local incidents of the Jews rejecting the gospel, accompanied by varying degrees of violence. But I think Ladd is right in suggesting that the final rejection must come in Jerusalem, just as the Gospel of Luke places the final rejection of Jesus in the same city.

PLANS THAT DIDN'T WORK OUT

Paul thought that God was leading him to evangelize Spain, and that Rome would be his sending base for that mission. By this time, Paul had written his Epistle to the Romans and he had stated these goals very clearly. He said, "Whenever I journey to Spain, I shall come to you. For I hope to see you on my journey, and to be helped on my way there by you, if first I may enjoy your company for a while" (Rom. 15:24).

He then told them he was first going to Jerusalem to deliver the offering to the poor Jews that was given by the Gentile believers in Macedonia and Achaia. In light of what is in store for Paul here in Jerusalem, amid many false accusations, it is significant to know his real heart on the crucial matters of Gentile believers and how they relate to Jews. He writes to the Romans, "For if the Gentiles have been partakers of their spiritual things, their duty is also to minister to them in material things" (v. 27). Paul wanted harmony in the Body of Christ.

But this time, Paul's plans did not work out as he wished. He said to the Roman Christians, "When I have performed this and have sealed them this fruit, I shall go by way of you to Spain" (v. 28). Not that he was unaware of the dangers of going to Jerusalem, even at that time. He had asked the Roman believers for personal intercession: "That you strive together with me in prayers to God for me, that I may be delivered from those in Judea who do not believe, and that my service [the offering] for Jerusalem may be acceptable to the saints" (vv. 30-31). Nevertheless, Paul still expected to "come to [the Romans] with joy by the will of God, and may be refreshed together with you" (v. 32).

Indeed, Paul eventually did go to Rome, but not under the conditions for which he had asked the Romans to pray.

A WELCOME AND A WARNING

[17] *And when we had come to Jerusalem, the brethren received us gladly.* [18] *On the following day Paul went in with us to James, and all the elders were present.* [19] *When he had greeted them, he told in detail those things which God had done among the Gentiles through his ministry.* [20] *And when they heard it, they glorified the Lord. . . .*

This was Paul's welcome to Jerusalem by the church leaders there. It was cordial, and well it should have been. Paul brought with him what must have been a substantial monetary gift from the Gentile churches to help the poor believers in Jerusalem. It seems a bit strange that Luke doesn't mention this, although he refers to it later when he tells of Paul's defense before Festus, and Paul says, "Now after many years I came to bring alms and offerings to my nation" (24:17).

It is important to observe that Paul and Luke "went in to James." And "all the elders were present." This is particularly significant because James is, quite clearly, in a category different from the elders, who were the pastors of the house churches. James is now recognized as an apostle, and his apostolic sphere comprises the Hebrew churches in Jerusalem and probably throughout the region as well. Keep in mind that this is James, the brother of Jesus, who convened the Council of Jerusalem (see Acts 15) and not one of the 12 original apostles.

As this scenario unfolds, we need to recognize that Paul, although he himself was a full-blooded Jew who could trace his genealogy back to Abraham with the best of them, must have been quite thin on patience with his fellow Jews by this time. He had just barely escaped with his life from the Jews in Corinth. Other Jews had driven him out of Berea and Thessalonica. They had attacked him in Antioch of Pisidia, in Iconium, and they had incited a mob to stone him to death in Lystra. His attitude toward unbelieving Jews could not have been the most positive.

But it was a two-way street. The attitude of the Jews, even including some of the Jewish *believers*, was not that positive toward Paul either. At least from the way Luke tells the story, the Jerusalem elders moved Paul quickly from his agenda of praising God for blessings on the Gentiles to their own agenda without so much as a cordial transition:

> . . . And they said to him, "You see, brother, how many myriads of Jews there are who have believed, and they are all zealous for the law" (v. 20).

The elders' warning to Paul begins here. The issue they raise is keeping the law of Moses. Because of the Jerusalem Council about eight years prior to this, the question of *Gentiles* obeying the law was no longer debated (see v. 25). Nor was there a problem with the messianic Jews in Jerusalem who were still keeping the law as they were expected to do. But how about the minority of Jews in the majority Gentile churches that Paul had been planting? Here is the thorny issue:

[21] *"but they have been informed about you that you teach all the Jews who are among the Gentiles to forsake Moses, saying that they ought not to circumcise their children nor walk according to their customs."*

Paul found himself being accused of teaching Jewish believers to stop following the Jewish law. This in all probability blindsided him, for such teaching, as we see clearly in his Epistles, was not part of the way he actually believed or taught. As is all too frequently the case, a false accusation, blown out of proportion and propagated by enemies of the gospel, can be devastating.

The orthodox Jewish mentality contains no categories to assimilate the statement from a Jew like Paul that "I have become all things to all men, that I might by all means save some" (1 Cor. 9:22). This may be simple enough for us Gentiles to say, but for Paul, his commitment to that principle set him on the road that ultimately led to his death.

As a stopgap, the church elders persuaded Paul to attempt to defuse the criticism by identifying with some Jewish believers who were fulfilling a Nazirite vow like the one Paul took toward the end of his first visit to Corinth. He did so (see Acts 21:23-24,26), but not to much avail.

The crisis came when some Jews from Asia, probably Ephesus, spotted this missionary, whom they had learned to hate while in the Jewish Temple. They undoubtedly thought they might be able to get away with some things here in Jerusalem that they would not have dared to attempt in Ephesus, so they captured Paul, falsely accused him and illegally commenced to beat him to death. At that moment, the Roman authorities stepped into the picture, rescued Paul from what amounted to a lynch mob just in time and took him into protective custody.

Paul had arrived at the Jerusalem jail!

PAUL ON THE DEFENSIVE

Instead of going right to Rome as he had planned, Paul was now forced to spend no less than two years in Jerusalem and in nearby Caesarea explaining himself, his ministry, his theology and his patriotism to both Jews and Gentiles. As a preliminary overview, here are the five major incidents recorded by Luke throughout this lengthy episode. How many other such incidents, if any, took place, and that Luke did not record, we do not know.

1. Paul lets a hostile Jewish crowd in Jerusalem know who he is and why he went to minister to Gentiles in the first place (see 21:37–22:23).
2. Paul meets with the Jewish Sanhedrin to address their concerns (see 22:30–23:11). He is then escorted to Caesarea.
3. In Caesarea, the Roman governor, Felix, calls a court session and Paul's accusers come from Jerusalem (see 23:34–24:27).
4. Felix's successor, Governor Festus, calls a similar court session, again with Jewish accusers from Jerusalem (see 25:1-12).
5. When Festus's friend King Agrippa comes to Caesarea to visit, they invite Paul in to state his position once again (see 25:13–26:32).

WHY WERE THE JEWS SO VITRIOLIC?

The Roman commander who sent soldiers to rescue Paul was named Claudius Lysias (see 23:26). Fortunately, he turns out to be a fair and just military officer. He at first thought Paul was one of the fugitives from justice for whom his agents had been searching; but after this was straightened out and Paul's true identity was established, Lysias granted Paul's request to address the mob of Jews who had been trying to murder him.

The unruly crowd calmed down somewhat when Paul switched from the Greek language he had been speaking to Claudius Lysias to Aramaic ("Hebrew" in the *New King James Version*), which was the mother tongue of this crowd of Jerusalem Jews. He started by saying:

[22:1] *Brethren and fathers, hear my defense before you now.*

It is important to remember that Paul's audience here would have included messianic Jewish believers as well as unbelieving Jews. This is not to imply that the believers among them would have participated in the effort to beat Paul to death, but it is worthy of note that they did not overtly oppose the effort either. Why?

Perhaps they were too few to have any influence, although the elders had just told Paul "how many myriads of Jews there are who have believed" (21:20). No one really knows exactly how many believers were in Jerusalem at that time or what percentage of the population they might have been. But it must have been quite significant, considering that at least 5,000 Jewish male believers were there 25 years prior to this time (see 4:4), with the total probably nearer 15,000. Some have ventured to estimate that the number of messianic believers by this time might have been approaching 100,000, although naturally they wouldn't all have been in the city of Jerusalem.

If, in fact, a large number of believers were in Jerusalem at this time, their failure to defend Paul in any known or effective way could possibly indicate that they were unwilling to take a public stand on the validity of Paul's missionary work to the Gentiles. Although they would undoubtedly maintain their formal theological agreement with the Jerusalem Council when meeting alone with Paul (see 21:25), it could well be that in a public forum like this, they found themselves facing a battle they did not want to fight with their nonbelieving Jewish friends and relatives. Their Jewish ethnocentrism was still a strong characteristic of their worldviews.

It could have been that the believers' identity as messianic *Jews* was more important to some of them than their unity with the Gentile segments of the Body of Christ. By this time, they could have come to value highly, perhaps too highly, their peaceful social relationships with other Jews in the city. It is not unusual now, and it might not have been unusual then, for a Christian community, over a span of 25 years, to accommodate to the culture around it so much that it forfeits some of the sharp edges of its theological commitments in order to remain in the comfort zone.

A. J. Mattill, Jr., is quite blunt about this matter when he writes, "The Jerusalem church knew that if it declared its solidarity with Paul [by doing certain things], it would destroy the possibility of its own mission among the Jews, indeed, would risk its own destruction at the hands of Jews who could not tolerate any preaching of freedom from the Law."[3]

The patience of the Jews came to an end when Paul, in telling of his experience with Jesus on the Damascus road, said:

> [21] *Then [Jesus] said to me, "Depart, for I will send you far from here to the Gentiles."* [22] *And they listened to him until this word, and then they raised their voices and said, "Away with such a fellow from the earth, for he is not fit to live!"* [23] *Then, as they cried out and tore off their clothes and threw dust into the air,* [24] *the commander ordered him to be brought into the barracks . . .*

CAN CHRISTIANS BE RACIST?

It is safe to assume that those who were calling for Paul's execution were the unbelieving Jews in the crowd. They, of course, had never agreed to the findings of the Council of Jerusalem; indeed, they in all probability knew nothing about it. What exactly was the issue that so infuriated them? I like the way John Stott says it: "In their eyes proselytism (making Gentiles into Jews) was fine; but evangelism (making Gentiles into Christians without first making them Jews) was an abomination." Now notice very carefully Stott's next phrase, which goes below the surface to the heart of the matter: "It was tantamount to saying that Jews and Gentiles were equal, for they both needed to come to God through Christ, and that on identical terms."[4]

Another way of putting this is that the Jews in Jerusalem at that time were quite racist. They considered their own race superior to non-Jews. Even slaves, the lowest rung on the social ladder, who were Gentiles, would be forced by their Jewish masters to become Jews. Joachim Jeremias says, "Gentile slaves of both sexes who became the property of a Jew were made to accept baptism. . . . If the slave were a woman this baptism signified *conversion to Judaism*; male slaves had to complete this conversion by submitting to circumcision" (emphasis his).[5]

The question that naturally comes to our minds is: How about the Christians, or messianic Jews, as they were called in Jerusalem? Wouldn't they be different from the others? We would wish the answer was yes. But suppose we ask the same question about ourselves—let's say those of us who are white Christians in America today? Does being Christian exempt us from participating in what is clearly the number one national American sin: racism? After studying this issue for some time, my reluctant conclusion is no, Christians are not exempt from racism, I'm ashamed to say, because I am one of them. I would hope that the fruit of the Holy Spirit enables us to handle our inbred racism with a bit more grace than do some of our non-Christian counterparts, but that does not exonerate us from our share of the national sin, nor does it excuse us from taking concrete and positive steps toward meaningful repentance and reconciliation.

Having admitted that, we can look back on the believers in Jerusalem without a holier-than-thou attitude. Here was the apostle Paul, whom we revere as perhaps the Christian leader second in importance only to Jesus, being beaten with the intent to kill on the streets of Jerusalem. And as Mattill puts it, "But where were the Jewish Christians? They could have helped because of their faithfulness to the Law and the Temple, but they sat idly by."[6] Paul's body had been saved by the Roman soldiers but his spirit must have been devastated.

CITIZENSHIP HAS ITS ADVANTAGES

The Roman commander, Claudius Lysias, was both surprised and perplexed at what was happening. He wanted to find out the truth from Paul, so he ordered a centurion to tie Paul and beat him thoroughly before the interrogation. This was not an unusual way to treat suspects in those days, except for Roman citizens. Knowing this:

> [25] . . . *Paul said to the centurion who stood by, "Is it lawful for you to scourge a man who is a Roman, and uncondemned?"* [26] *When the centurion heard that, he went and told the commander, saying, "Take care what you do, for this man is a Roman."* [29] *Then immediately those who were about to examine him withdrew from him; and the commander was also afraid after he found out that he was a Roman, and because he had bound him.*

We may wonder why Paul invoked his Roman citizenship here, while he and Silas did not do so when they were being flogged before going to jail in Philippi. A likely explanation is that in Philippi a close personal bond had existed between the members of the nucleus of the new church and Paul, who had led most of them to Christ. Paul probably thought that using his citizenship credential to avoid physical persecution would be a bad role model for fellow Christians who did not enjoy such citizenship.

But Jerusalem was not Philippi! At this point, as we have seen, Paul's personal relationship with the local believers was not all that cordial, and claiming an exemption from scourging would have little or no direct influence on the local Christian or the messianic community.

Furthermore, Paul's behavior was not characterized by a martyr complex. As a reading of 2 Corinthians 11 will confirm, he had suffered more than his share of physical and emotional crises in his ministry. He had known prophetically before coming to Jerusalem that trouble was in store for him, and in contemplating that he said, "nor do I count my life dear to myself" (Acts 20:24). Nevertheless, he did not consider suffering in itself a desirable thing when it could legitimately be avoided. So he did what was a good way to avoid it. Roman citizenship had its advantages.

DIVIDE AND CONQUER

[30] *The next day, because he wanted to know for certain why he was accused by the Jews, [the commander] released him from his bonds, and commanded the chief priests and all their council to appear, and brought Paul down and set him before them.*

When Claudius Lysias realized that he was not going to get the information he wanted by beating and interrogating Paul, he went to Plan B and called the Jewish Sanhedrin into session. The Sanhedrin was meeting in the same room where it had heard Stephen's argument more than 20 years earlier, and where, in all likelihood, Paul himself had participated in council deliberations as a member of the Sanhedrin. As we may recall, Stephen first raised the issues about whether people could be saved apart from the Jewish law and the Jewish Temple, and he ultimately gave his life for his radical ideas. What has changed? Here is Paul standing in exactly the same place with the Jewish leaders wanting to add him to the honor roll of Christian martyrs. It was the same issue, the sin of racism being at the root.

From time to time, it is good for us to remember that even the greatest heroes of the faith are human beings and they are susceptible to the same temptations and sins as the rest of us. As a part of this meeting with the Sanhedrin, the high priest, Ananias, and Paul get into a personal tiff, and Paul loses his cool:

[23:3] *Then Paul said to him, "God will strike you, you whitewashed wall! For you sit to judge me according to the law, and do you command me to be struck contrary to the law?"*

This would not have been a good thing to say to anyone, much less the high priest. But Paul didn't realize he was talking to the high priest. As soon as it was brought to his attention, he admitted his impropriety and apologized (see vv. 4-5).

Paul was a Pharisee, and probably a member of the Sanhedrin itself at one time. But whether he had been or not, he knew well that the Pharisees were a strong minority in the Sanhedrin, serving alongside the majority Sadducees. He also knew that, although they were both Jews, they had sensitive doctrinal differences. The Sadducees were similar to what we would today call "theological liberals" because they denied, among other things, the resurrection of the dead and the reality of the spirit world. Whether he had premeditated it or not we are unsure, but Paul skillfully connected his viewpoint to the resurrection of the dead and, thereby, set the Pharisees and Sadducees off on a theological debate. He had decided to divide and conquer.

For some of the Pharisees, winning their argument against the Sadducees suddenly became more important than condemning Paul, and they said:

> [9] *We find no evil in this man; but if a spirit or an angel has spoken to him, let us not fight against God.*

The battle heated up so much that for the third time the Roman soldiers rescued Paul:

> [10] *Now when there arose a great dissension, the commander, fearing lest Paul might be pulled to pieces by them, commanded the soldiers to go down and take him by force from among them, and bring him into the barracks.*

As Paul went from incident to incident, he must have felt more and more discouraged. He still had his life, although his body would have been severely bruised from the beating the Jews had given him before the Roman soldiers stepped in. His plans of warm fellowship with the believers in Jerusalem, followed by a positive send-off to Rome and Spain, had by then vaporized. Remembering that his chains and imprisonment had been prophesied before coming to Jerusalem would have been little consolation. In the midst of all this, Jesus did a wonderful thing. He appeared to Paul personally!

JESUS APPEARS

> [11] *But the following night the Lord stood by him and said, "Be of good cheer, Paul; for as you have testified for Me in Jerusalem, so you must also bear witness at Rome."*

This is just what Paul needed most to regain the physical, emotional and spiritual fortitude he would need to carry him through the rest of this trying experience. It was not the only time Jesus appeared to Paul since his personal introduction to Him on the Damascus road. When Paul returned to Jerusalem after his conversion and when he was in danger again of being captured by the Jews, Jesus had appeared and warned him to leave (see 22:18). In Corinth, when the Jews there were taking Paul to Gallio's court, Jesus appeared to him in a vision and told him he would not be harmed (see 18:9-10). It could well be that other such incidents occurred that Luke did not record.

Interestingly, some people doubt that the spiritual gift of apostle could still be in operation today. One of the arguments to support that position is that true apostles have all seen Jesus in person (based precariously on Acts 1:21-22), so we could not have any more apostles today because Jesus is now in heaven.

But Paul was certainly an apostle, and he bases that office, among other things, on having seen Jesus (see 1 Cor. 9:1). Paul, however, never saw Jesus in person during His earthly ministry. The Jesus whom Paul saw, then, must have been the risen Christ who came and appeared to him personally, as in the incidents just mentioned. If this is true, there is therefore no theological reason why Jesus couldn't or wouldn't do the same thing in other times and at other places. Although such a thing has not happened to me personally, some trusted friends of mine have given me their word that it has happened to them. In fact, I once did some informal research among apostles and found that around 20 percent of them say they have seen Jesus personally.

This by itself, of course, does not qualify each person who ever sees Jesus to claim to be an apostle. To me, the notion that seeing Jesus personally would be a nonnegotiable prerequisite for receiving the gift of apostle is not a good argument, but even if it was, it would not neutralize the possibility of true apostles serving the Church today. Although we do not always use the name, I believe the function and the office of apostle have always been with the Church through the ages. Churches belonging to the rapidly growing New Apostolic Reformation now openly recognize the gift and office of apostle as I explain in detail in my textbook on the movement, *Churchquake!*

ANGRY JEWS ON A HUNGER STRIKE

[12] ***And when it was day, some of the Jews banded together and bound themselves under an oath, saying that they would neither eat nor drink till they had killed Paul.*** [13] ***Now there were more than forty who had formed this conspiracy.***

Paul leaves Jerusalem and ends up in Caesarea because the plans of the Jews to kill him, rather than subside, only gain momentum. The oath of a hunger strike by more than 40 of the radical Jews signaled to the Romans that if they were going to protect Paul and give him a decent trial, they had better get him out of Jerusalem to a safer place.

Claudius Lysias, the military commander, did a wise thing. He put together a large detachment of foot soldiers and cavalry, which escorted Paul to Caesarea where the Roman governor, Felix, lived and worked. Lysias sent a letter along, explaining the situation, but notably without a formal accusation. By rights, Felix should, therefore, have released Paul, but he didn't want to risk the Jews being upset with him. So he gave Paul comfortable accommodations in the palace that Herod the Great had built, and where Felix himself also had his residence.

PAUL'S FIRST REAL TRIAL

We mentioned earlier that Paul had to defend himself in public five separate times during these two years in Jerusalem and Caesarea. It might be stretching it to describe his appearance before the Sanhedrin as a legitimate trial, so this event with Felix could be considered the first trial.

[24:1] *Now after five days Ananias the high priest came down with the elders and a certain orator [attorney] named Tertullus. These gave evidence to the governor against Paul.*

Three accusations were brought against Paul, and he responded to all three. Let's look at them:

Accusation Number One

[5] *For we have found this man a plague, a creator of dissension among all the Jews throughout the world . . .*

Felix would have paid close attention to this accusation because the Roman government was constantly on the vigil to detect any kind of political unrest or uprisings. Another translation of "plague" could be "troublemaker," and I have introduced this word in the title of this chapter, "What to Do with This Troublemaker?" Tertullus, the attorney, wanted Felix to see Paul as a potentially dangerous political reactionary.

Response Number One

[11] . . . *because you may ascertain that it is no more than twelve days since I went up to Jerusalem to worship.* [12] *And they neither found me in the temple disputing with anyone nor inciting the crowd, either in the synagogues or in the city.* [13] *Nor can they prove the things of which they now accuse me.*

Paul's major achievement here was to put his accusers on the spot in court, challenging them to produce witnesses to verify that he was responsible for stirring up a disturbance in Jerusalem during the last 12 days. They must have been embarrassed when they could not provide these witnesses.

Accusation Number Two

[5] . . . *[Paul is] a ringleader of the sect of the Nazarenes.*

We should keep in mind that the word "Christian" at this time was being used only for Gentile believers, and perhaps only as a term of ridicule. Messianic Jews back then, and even some today, prefer to avoid the term for themselves. This is the only time believers were called "Nazarenes" in Scripture. It sounds fairly natural to us today, however, considering the worldwide spread of the Church of the Nazarene, which is headquartered in Kansas City, Missouri.

The legal tactic that Tertullus was using here was to try to cast the Nazarenes into the mold of a *political* movement that Felix might see as a danger to the public welfare. He may not have known that Felix was well informed about Christianity, also known as "the Way" (see v. 22).

Response Number Two

[14] *But this I confess to you, that according to the Way which they call a sect, so I worship the God of my fathers, believing all things which are written in the Law and in the Prophets.*

Paul definitely identified himself with the movement, although note that he did not identify himself either as a *Nazarene* or a *Christian*. But he went on from there to affirm, as Gallio also had concluded in Corinth, that "the Way" was not a political party, but rather a fulfillment of Judaism itself, in which it was firmly rooted.

Accusation Number Three

[6] ***He even tried to profane the temple . . .***

The Romans had given the Jews—as a *religio licita*, a legal religion—jurisdiction of the internal affairs in their Temple. If they could prove that Paul had tried to desecrate the Temple, Paul would have been in serious trouble.

Response Number Three

[17] ***Now after many years I came to bring alms and offerings to my nation,*** [18] ***in the midst of which some Jews from Asia found me purified in the temple, neither with a mob nor with tumult.*** [19] ***They ought to have been here before you to object if they had anything against me.***

Instead of desecrating the Temple, they did just the opposite. Paul had entered the Temple to purify himself, thus affirming his own personal commitment to Temple worship and to the God of the Jews. His reason for coming to Jerusalem was to bless the Jewish people. If the Asian Jews had an accusation, according to Roman law, they would have to be present in person to press charges.

The upshot of the trial was not a "hung jury" but a "hung governor," so to speak. He had no grounds on which to accuse Paul, but at the same time he did not want to offend the Jews. So he postponed a final decision instead of releasing Paul as he should have done.

A RERUN FOR GOVERNOR FESTUS

[27] ***But after two years Porcius Festus succeeded Felix; and Felix, wanting to do the Jews a favor, left Paul bound.***

When Festus took office as the governor, he personally went to Jerusalem for a briefing on Paul's case, then he held a trial in Caesarea similar to that of Felix's trial. The upshot of this trial was that Festus wanted to take Paul back to Jerusalem to face the Sanhedrin. Paul was not foolish. He was aware that going to Jerusalem would in all probability end his life, so he decided to go over Festus's head and appeal to Caesar:

> [25:10] *So Paul said, "I stand at Caesar's judgment seat, where I ought to be judged. To the Jews I have done no wrong, as you very well know.* [11] *... I appeal to Caesar."* [12] *Then Festus, when he had conferred with the council, answered, "You have appealed to Caesar? To Caesar you shall go!"*

If nothing else, Paul now had his ticket to Rome!

SATISFYING AGRIPPA'S CURIOSITY

> [13] *And after some days King Agrippa and Bernice came to Caesarea to greet Festus.* [14] *When they had been there many days, Festus laid Paul's case before the king, ...* [22] *Then Agrippa said to Festus, "I also would like to hear the man myself." "Tomorrow," he said, "you shall hear him."*

Agrippa, great-grandson of the notorious Herod the Great, was a Jew and he had gained considerable influence among the Jewish community. More out of curiosity than anything else, he requests that Paul be brought in for a hearing. This was not as much a trial, having the accusers present, as an assembly called together to listen to Paul's account of what had been happening.

The details of this hearing add little to what we have already discussed in other places. Among other things Paul relates what is the third account of his conversion on the Damascus road in the book of Acts, and in it he emphasizes his call to evangelize the Gentiles and "to open their eyes, in order to turn them from darkness to light, and from the power of Satan to God" (26:18).

The passage also includes the much-preached verse:

> [26:28] *Then Agrippa said to Paul, "You almost persuade me to become a Christian."*

Not to ruin any sermons, but many biblical scholars believe that a more accurate rendering of what Agrippa was really saying to Paul was, "In a short time you are trying to persuade me to act as a Christian."[7] I remember Ralph

Winter paraphrasing this and imagining that Agrippa might really have been saying, "Are you trying to make me into a 'Messiah nut'?"

Paul never lost his evangelistic passion, even when finishing his fifth public defense against false charges. His reply to Agrippa is classic:

> [29] *And Paul said, "I would to God that not only you, but also all who hear me today, might become both almost and altogether such as I am, except for these chains."*

Both Festus and Agrippa agreed that Paul was innocent and that if he had not appealed to Caesar he could have gone free. But, as we know, it was God's will that Paul go to Rome, and even if the conditions were not what he might have wished, he was ready for the trip.

REFLECTION QUESTIONS

1. The end of Acts depicts very graphically the Jewish rejection of the gospel. What is the state of affairs today? Do you think this will change?
2. Why did the Jewish believers in Jerusalem seem to give Paul a warm welcome and then begin to quarrel with him? Why didn't they take Paul's side when he was arrested?
3. Review the section under "Can Christians Be Racist?" Express your own feelings not only about the first century, but also about the twenty-first century.
4. When Paul was at a personal low point, Jesus appeared to him in person. Have you ever heard of something like that happening to someone you know?
5. Why wasn't the word "Christian" being applied to Jewish believers in Paul's day? What do you think is the preference of Jewish believers today?

24

DESTINATION: ROME

ACTS 27 AND 28

Paul's long-standing plan to go to Rome, dramatically altered by his imprisonment, would not have been primarily to introduce the gospel, to evangelize and plant churches, as he had done in many other cities. Others had already served as the pioneer church planters in Rome, for Christianity was by then solidly established in the capital of the Roman Empire.

CHRISTIANITY IN ROME

How many house churches might have been located in Rome by this time we have no way of knowing exactly, but it is likely there were quite a few. In the Epistle that Paul wrote to these Roman believers a few years previously, he mentioned some house churches by name. For example, Priscilla and Aquila, who had shared their tentmaking business with Paul in Corinth and Ephesus, had by then returned to Rome and they hosted a church in their home (see Rom. 16:3-5). He also mentions the "household of Aristobulus" and the "household of Narcissus," which may also indicate house churches (see vv. 10-11). Then Paul speaks of the "brethren who are with" Asyncritus, Phlegon, Hermas, Patrobas and Hermes, possibly a unit of its own (see v. 14), and others as well.

The Roman Christians, largely, it would seem, because of their strategic location in the capital city, had such a powerful testimony that Paul could say, "I thank my God through Jesus Christ for you all, that your faith is spoken of throughout the whole world" (1:8). If all roads led to Rome, then all roads would also lead out of Rome, and the gospel could and did spread along them.

It is true that Paul had expressed to them his desire to "have some fruit among you" (v. 13). He had also said, "I am ready to preach the gospel to you who are in Rome" (v. 15). But these statements could easily be understood as expressing a vision for ministry to believers as well as evangelistic ministry to unbelievers. Paul, as a pioneer missionary, would minister to believers as the need presented itself, but not as his career goal. I mention this because later in the same letter Paul said to the Romans, "And so I have made it my aim to preach the gospel, not where Christ was named, lest I should build on another man's foundation" (15:20). Clearly, someone else had already laid the foundation in Rome.

Athens, as we have seen, was known far and wide for its idolatry and philosophy, Corinth was known for its immorality and wealth, and Ephesus was known for its magic. Rome, in turn, was known for its extraordinary political power over a large part of the world.

John Stott gives us a vivid summary of the political accomplishments of Rome: "It treated its conquered subjects and their religions with comparatively humane tolerance; it somehow managed to integrate Romans, Greeks, Jews and 'Barbarians' into its social life; it protected the Greek culture and language; it inculcated respect for the rule of law; it gained a reputation for efficient administration and postal communication; and it facilitated travel by its ambitious system of roads and ports, policed by its legions and its navy, so preserving for the benefit of all the long-standing *pax romana*."[1] Certainly the hand of God must have been behind the government of Rome to prepare the way for sending His Son, Jesus, so that the message of salvation could spread so rapidly.

Equally important to the spread of Christianity, we may recall, was the very significant minority population of Jews in the Roman Empire and specifically the many "Corneliuses" or Gentiles who were called "devout persons" or "God-fearers." To the credit of the Jews, an authentic godliness was present in many synagogues that both attracted and to some extent actually welcomed these God-fearers as a marginal element in their midst. The Jews, of course, would have been happier with Gentile "proselytes," who had made a complete cultural switch including circumcision. But it is easier to understand how Christianity spread so rapidly when we recognize that its initial base was established among the million or so God-fearers in the Roman Empire. Their faith and understanding of the Old Testament had come through the synagogues found throughout the nations.

In any case, Roman justice had allowed Paul to escape with his life from the furious Jews at Jerusalem, and the Roman transportation system was ready to carry him, this time by sea, to the capital city.

LUKE SHIPS OUT WITH PAUL

[27:1] And when it was decided that we should sail to Italy, they delivered Paul and some other prisoners to one named Julius, a centurion of the Augustan Regiment. [2] So, entering a ship of Adramyttium, we put to sea, meaning to sail along the coasts of Asia. Aristarchus, a Macedonian of Thessalonica, was with us.

Luke begins this episode with the statement "And when it was decided that we should sail to Italy." The "we" means that Luke was again with Paul. The last time Luke used "we" was after arriving in Jerusalem, but before Paul had his meeting with the elders of the Jerusalem church. Luke does not indicate that he was with Paul during all the trouble with the Jews in Jerusalem, leading to his rescue by the Roman authorities, and the two years as a prisoner in Herod's Palace in Caesarea. Some scholars speculate that Luke could have remained in the Caesarea area doing research for his two-volume work, which we now know as Luke and Acts. It also could have been that he spent a good part of that time back home in Philippi. Whatever the case may be, Luke was with Paul once again when the time came to sail to Rome.

How would Luke have secured passage on this ship among the prisoners who were being taken to Rome? The vessel evidently was one of those huge grain freighters that regularly carried wheat to Rome from Egypt, the so-called breadbasket of the Roman Empire. Some biblical scholars speculate that Luke, as well as Aristarchus from Thessalonica, posed as slaves owned by Paul and thus were allowed to go along with him to care for his needs. Others suggest that Luke may have hired on as the ship's physician. Perhaps an even more likely assumption could be that such a large ship would not necessarily limit the number of passengers it carried to a group of Roman prisoners, but it might also have accommodated others who simply booked passage and paid their respective fares.

Who were the other prisoners? I think William Ramsay helps us by pointing out that they were undoubtedly quite different from Paul, who was "a man of distinction, a Roman citizen who had appealed for trial to the supreme court in Rome."[2] And the other prisoners? "[They] had been in all probability already condemned to death, and were going to supply the perpetual demand which Rome made on the provinces for human victims to amuse the populace by their death in the arena."[3]

This observation also serves as a reminder to us that the Rome to which Paul was headed may have been a brilliant political phenomenon, but it had its dark side as well. A populace that would consider watching fellow human beings suffer cruel and traumatic deaths as a primary spectator attraction in its public stadiums must have been influenced, more than most, by powerful spirits of violence and death. This undoubtedly would have had ominous ramifications throughout society as a whole.

PAUL'S FIRST WORD FOR THE SHIP'S OFFICERS

> [9] *Now when much time had been spent, and sailing was now dangerous . . . Paul advised them,* [10] *saying, "Men, I perceive that this voyage will end with disaster and much loss, not only of the cargo and ship, but also our lives."*

Winter was approaching rapidly, and with it the notorious stormy weather in that part of the Mediterranean Sea. The officers of the ship were well aware of this when they harbored to survive one of the early storms in a place called Fair Havens, on the southern shores of the Island of Crete. The officers, however, wanted to take the risk of pushing ahead a bit farther to the port of Phoenix. If they had to spend their winter on land, they were anxious to move on to a more luxuriously equipped harbor.

Paul, however, knew that this was a poor decision and that it would end in disaster for them all. Where did Paul get this information? He could have drawn on the human experience he had accumulated by sailing frequently on ships in and around the Mediterranean Sea, and this is the most common interpretation in the commentaries on Acts.

It does seem odd, however, that Paul, who was a tentmaker by trade, not a sailor, would have matched his nautical wisdom against that of professional sailors who had spent most of their lives at sea. It would be similar to my attempting to offer technical advice to a commercial airline pilot because I travel 100,000 miles a year in the air.

Another much more likely possibility is that Paul had received a prophetic word from God concerning this trip. After they pushed off and the problems that Paul warned against had begun, Paul then received a second word, this one specifically attributed to a voice from God through an angel. If

Paul's second word was clearly supernatural, it does not seem farfetched to suppose the first one could also have been supernatural.

There is no reason to expect that a ship's crew of unbelievers would have any inclination to attach some sort of divine directive to the advice of a landlubber passenger. If the crew had been believers, however, one might have had other expectations. And in those days, when the prophetic ministry was much better understood than it is in many places today, a believing crew might well have put aside its professional expertise and listened to the word from God through the apostle.

I mention this because, unfortunately, in all too many of our churches today, such prophetic words are not given due credibility, and the consequences of substituting technical know-how for God's direction are similar. Unfortunately, many church leaders would take an approach similar to what the sailors took:

[11] *Nevertheless the centurion was more persuaded by the helmsman and the owner of the ship than by the things spoken by Paul.*
[12] *And because the harbor was not suitable to winter in, the majority advised to set sail from there . . .*

The word "majority" can be misleading. Although those of us who live in a democratic society know that the majority can be, and often is, wrong, we frequently insist on making important decisions in our churches on the basis of 51 percent or more of the votes. This is especially unwise when God Himself is trying to say something to the Church contrary to the opinion of most, as He evidently was doing on the ship on which Paul was sailing.

Fortunately, Christianity worldwide seems to be moving strongly toward a more biblical view of basing church decisions on the voice of God rather than on the wisdom of professionals, when they face a choice. This is not to imply that the wisdom of professionals in our churches is not important. Indeed, most day-to-day decisions are made through consecrated human wisdom, taking into account the way the majority feels about an issue. I believe, however, that churches, like sailors, should be prepared for the exception to the rule when a divine word contrary to the majority opinion comes through a servant of God, such as the apostle Paul, or from those who have a recognized prophetic ministry today.

THE STORM AND PAUL'S SECOND WORD

This story reminds me of Jonah. Jonah also ignored a word from God, and to get his attention, God placed him in the midst of a life-threatening storm at sea. It worked in the case of Jonah, and it also worked on the ship from Adramyttium.

> [14] . . . *a tempestuous head wind arose, called Euroclydon.* [18] . . . *we were exceedingly tempest-tossed* . . . [20] *Now when neither sun nor stars appeared for many days, and no small tempest beat on us, all hope that we would be saved was finally given up.*

The professional sailors were now willing to listen to Paul. Their hope was gone! And this time Paul is more specific in indicating that his prophetic word comes directly from God.

> [21] . . . *Paul stood in the midst of them and said, "Men, you should have listened to me, and not have sailed from Crete and incurred this disaster and loss.* [22] *And now I urge you to take heart, for there will be no loss of life among you, but only of the ship.* [23] *For there stood by me this night an angel of the God to whom I belong and whom I serve,* [24] *saying, 'Do not be afraid, Paul; you must be brought before Caesar; and indeed God has granted you all those who sail with you.'* [25] *Therefore take heart, men, for I believe God that it will be just as it was told me.* [26] *However, we must run aground on a certain island."*

One thing many will notice about this second prophecy is that it differs from the first at a key point. In the first prophecy, Paul said that if they sailed from Fair Haven they would lose their lives. This time, he says their lives will be spared. One way this could be explained is to suppose, as many do, that the first word was not prophetic at all, but simply human advice. This is possible, but I lean toward seeing them both as prophetic. How, then, would I explain it?

A Conditional Prophecy

Some may recall that earlier, when I discussed the need to evaluate prophecies such as Paul was receiving on his way to Jerusalem, I said we should keep in mind that personal prophecies are (1) partial, (2) progressive and (3) conditional. A reasonable explanation of this event, then, is to postulate that the first word Paul received about all the passengers losing their lives if the ship had sailed was conditional. We are not told explicitly what the conditions might have been. But those who have had experience in prophetic ministries and who have monitored the way prophecies are ordinarily fulfilled report that a frequent condition, if not the most frequent, is prayer. Brother Andrew, for example, has written an excellent book on intercessory prayer, which has the striking title *And God Changed His Mind*, emphasizing this idea.

Theologically speaking, a sovereign God is never double minded. But the sovereign God, for reasons that obviously please Him, has designed His world so that certain things happen in history contingent on certain decisions and actions of human beings. He changed His mind about destroying Nineveh in Jonah's time, for example, when Nineveh repented. Here, I believe, Paul was instrumental in fulfilling a condition that allowed his fellow passengers, in this case 276 of them (see 27:37), to live through the shipwreck rather than die.

This condition, I strongly suspect, was intercessory prayer. For one thing, the power of intercessory prayer is much more awesome than we often think, as I argue in my book *Praying with Power*. For another thing, consider the words the angel spoke to Paul: "indeed God has granted you all those who sail with you" (v. 24). Clearly, the statement that God had "granted" the lives of the fellow passengers to Paul could best be understood by supposing that Paul had indeed asked God for them. Otherwise it is difficult to explain. These other prisoners, for example, were not, nor ever would be, Paul's in any literal sense of the word. Whether any were ever converted, we have no way of knowing except that Luke is usually inclined to mention conversions in his narrative when they do occur.

It seems likely that Paul, having compassion characteristic of the fruit of the Spirit, had asked for God's mercy on them all, and had received it. History belongs to the intercessors, as Walter Wink might say.

The Shipwreck

[41] *But striking a place where two seas met, they ran the ship aground; and the prow stuck fast and remained immovable, but the stern was being broken up by the violence of the waves.* [43] *But the centurion . . .*

commanded that those who could swim should jump overboard first and get to land, [44] *and the rest, some on boards and some on parts of the ship. And so it was that they all escaped safely to land.*

The prophecy is fulfilled! Not only did the passengers survive the shipwreck itself, but one more thing: Those who were prisoners could easily have been killed by their guards! According to Roman custom, if prisoners escaped, their guards would have been subject to receive their allotted punishment, in this case, possibly thrown to the lions in the Coliseum. But the centurion put a stop to that in deference to his most distinguished prisoner, the apostle Paul, and their lives had been spared from not one, but two potential causes of death through Paul's prayers.

MIRACLES ON MALTA

[28:1] *Now when they had escaped, they then found out that the island was called Malta.* [2] *And the natives showed an unusual kindness; for they kindled a fire and made us all welcome, because of the rain that was falling and because of the cold.*

Back in those days, it would not have been unusual for the occupants of a wrecked ship to have been taken as slaves by those who lived on the land. But in this case, perhaps because of the presence of the Roman centurion and his soldiers, the natives showed warm hospitality instead.

Five years pass from the time Paul is arrested in Jerusalem to the end of the book of Acts. In the seven-and-one-half chapters Luke uses to tell of this experience (about 27 percent of Acts), explicit accounts of power ministries are few and far between in comparison to the other three-fourths of the book. The same is true of evangelism and church planting. This may suggest a relationship between the two, at least for Luke.

Although miracles, healings, tongues and prophecies are important ongoing ministries in established churches, for missionaries such as the apostle Paul and for missiology in general, they are much more important on the frontiers of the expansion of the kingdom of God. God uses them to validate the spoken message. Luke previously has stressed this many times by using words such as those describing the ministry of Philip in Samaria as an example: "And the multitudes with one accord heeded the things spoken by Philip, hearing and seeing the miracles which he did" (8:6). Luke also records the report of Paul and Barnabas to the Jerusalem Council by saying, "Then all the multitude kept silent and listened to Barnabas and Paul declaring how many miracles and wonders God had worked through them among the Gentiles" (15:12). Many other examples of such power evangelism can be found.

Now in the final chapter of Acts, although this is not another story of evangelism and church planting, Luke reminds us that the supernatural power of God continues to be manifested by using two vivid anecdotes. Here is the first anecdote:

[3] *But when Paul had gathered a bundle of sticks and laid them on the fire, a viper came out because of the heat, and fastened on his hand.* [4] *So when the natives saw the creature hanging from his hand, they said to one another, "No doubt this man is a murderer, whom, though he has escaped the sea, yet justice does not allow to live."* [5] *But he shook off the creature into the fire and suffered no harm.* [6] *However, they were expecting that he would swell up or suddenly fall down dead. But after they had looked for a long time and saw no harm come to him, they changed their minds and said that he was a god.*

Saved from a Snakebite

Although scholarly debates consider whether or not the final words of Mark are part of the original Greek, the words of Jesus there at the conclusion of the Gospel of Mark relate exactly to Paul's experiences on Malta. According to most ancient manuscripts, Jesus said, "Go into all the world and preach the gospel to every creature. . . . And these signs will follow those who believe . . . they will take up serpents; and if they drink anything deadly, it will by no means hurt them; they will lay hands on the sick, and they will recover" (Mark 16:15-18).

The clearest example we find of the fulfillment of these words is Paul's snakebite next to the bonfire. It is interesting to see how some interpret this miraculous event. Although he disagrees with them, Simon Kistemaker reports, "Some scholars think that the reptile was a common grass snake that, although it may strike a man, does not harm him."[4] On this premise, it is difficult to explain the expectations of the Malta natives who undoubtedly were thoroughly familiar with the species. They thought for sure Paul would die. If they recognized it as a miracle, we can hardly do less.

Unfortunately, many modern Christians have absorbed so much of the rationalistic mentality of our Western culture that whenever they confront a situation that can be explained either by a miracle of the grace of God or by scientific cause and effect, they seem to prefer the latter. Luke, although he was a physician, obviously tells this story to glorify God through highlighting His healing power.

A HEALING SERVICE IN PUBLIUS'S HOUSE

This is the second of Luke's two power ministry anecdotes:

> [8] ***And it happened that the father of Publius lay sick of a fever and dysentery. Paul went in to him and prayed, and he laid his hands on him and healed him.*** [9] ***So when this was done, the rest of those on the island who had diseases also came and were healed.***

Publius was the "leading citizen of the island" (v. 7), the political head of Malta at the time. He invited some of the stranded passengers, including at least Luke and Paul, to spend three days at his home, which undoubtedly would have been well appointed. Publius's father happened to be sick with a serious illness, which could likely have been what has since come to be recognized as "Malta fever."

Before Paul laid hands on the man for healing, Luke says that Paul prayed. For what would Paul have been praying? He likely would have been asking God if it was His will that Publius's father be healed at that particular time. The words of Jesus come to mind: "Most assuredly, I say to you, the Son can do nothing of Himself, but what He sees the Father do; for whatever He does, the Son also does in like manner" (John 5:19). Before ministering in a situation requiring a miracle, Jesus would have made sure it was His Father's will. Much more, then, would Paul need to do the same. We also recall that when Peter raised Dorcas from the dead, "[he] put them all out, and knelt down and prayed" (Acts 9:40).

Apparently, Paul received a heavenly green light because he then laid hands on Publius's father, as Jesus had said believers were to do. The man was healed, and not surprisingly the word was spread around the area. It wouldn't have taken long for the people on Malta, which is only 18 miles long and 8 miles wide, to hear the good news about the miracle. Before long, a healing line of sorts apparently had formed outside of Publius's home, and Paul found himself in the midst of a large healing service.

WHEN *ALL* ARE HEALED

From the way Luke tells it, extraordinary healing power must have been present, for all who came apparently were healed.

Although it happened frequently with Jesus, it is rare today to see *all* the sick healed during a healing service. But at times, not all were healed in Jesus' ministry either. For example, Jesus was frustrated with His ministry in His own hometown of Nazareth when He couldn't do many miracles there "because of their unbelief" (Matt. 13:58), and Jesus healed only one out of a great multitude of sick people at the pool of Bethesda (see John 5:1-9).

The apostle Paul, who evidently had the gift of healing, had previously failed also. When he later writes a letter to Timothy, he says, "Erastus stayed in Corinth, but Trophimus I have left in Miletus sick" (2 Tim. 4:20). It would be hard to imagine that Paul hadn't prayed for Trophimus's healing. Nevertheless, he did not get well.

This time on Malta, however, it was not that way. And the people naturally were most grateful. They showered Paul, Luke and the others with gifts, providing all they needed to continue their journey to Rome in relative comfort. It seems that Paul was not reluctant to receive love offerings in gratitude for his healing ministry.

THE LAST LAP

> [11] ***After three months we sailed in an Alexandrian ship whose figurehead was the Twin Brothers, which had wintered at the island.*** [13] . . . ***we came to Puteoli,*** [14] ***where we found brethren, and were invited to stay with them seven days. And so we went toward Rome.***

Puteoli was the Italian harbor at which they terminated the grueling sea journey. Rome lay about 120 miles north by land. Apparently, the gospel had been spreading well in Italy, for Puteoli had a church by then and apparently Julius allowed the missionaries to spend a week there. During that time, they sent word to the believers in Rome that Paul was on his way:

[15] *And from there, when the brethren heard about us, they came to meet us as far as Appii Forum and Three Inns. When Paul saw them, he thanked God and took courage.*

Much to Paul's joy, the believers from many of the Roman house churches had come to meet him on the road and to accompany him to Rome.

SETTLING IN AT ROME

[16] *Now when we came to Rome, the centurion delivered the prisoners to the captain of the guard; but Paul was permitted to dwell by himself with the soldier who guarded him.*

Staying in his own home gave Paul the freedom to meet with and minister to many people in Rome. He had come because the Jews in Jerusalem had first tried to kill him, then they attempted to have him convicted by the Romans of a crime. Neither action had been successful. Now he was to stand trial before Caesar. One thing he naturally would want to know as soon as possible was how he faired with the Jews in Rome. Rome had a large Jewish population, perhaps some 40,000 at the time.

Because Paul could not live in his usual residence in the Jewish quarter and begin attending the synagogue, as was his custom, this time he had to call for the Jewish leaders to come to him:

[17] *And it came to pass after three days that Paul called the leaders of the Jews together. . . .*

He would, undoubtedly, have been greatly relieved by their comment:

[21] *Then they said to him, "We neither received letters from Judea concerning you, nor have any of the brethren who came reported or spoken any evil of you.* [22] *But we desire to hear from you what you think; for concerning this sect, we know that it is spoken against everywhere."*

Paul's sessions with the Roman Jews turned out the way most of his prior ministry to the Jews had gone. He spoke to them about salvation through faith in Jesus as Messiah, and some believed. But, as usual, communication broke down when the matter of the Gentiles surfaced. Jews in Rome could not handle, any better than other Jews, the fact that God through Jesus Christ had invited Gentiles to share the same salvation, and that Gentiles could have it on the basis of faith in Jesus without first becoming Jews. They could not imagine that Gentiles could be considered equal to Jews in God's sight.

[28] ***"Therefore let it be known to you that the salvation of God has been sent to the Gentiles, and they will hear it!"*** **[29]** ***And when he had said these words, the Jews departed and had a great dispute among themselves.***

Two Years Preaching the Kingdom of God

[30] ***Then Paul dwelt two whole years in his own rented house, and received all who came to him,*** **[31]** ***preaching the kingdom of God and teaching the things which concern the Lord Jesus Christ with all confidence, no one forbidding him.***

The book of Acts ends where it began—preaching the kingdom of God. Acts begins with Jesus gathered with His disciples, before Paul was a believer, "speaking of the things pertaining to the kingdom of God" (1:3). Thirty years later, the kingdom of God had indeed spread into many parts of the Roman Empire through Peter, John, Stephen, Philip, Barnabas, Paul, Silas, Timothy, Luke and many others whose names we will never know.

The fulfillment of Jesus' desire that His followers "make disciples of all the nations" (Matt. 28:19) had started with great power and determination. It has continued through almost 2,000 years, and now for the first time in history some missiologists are saying that there is light at the end of the tunnel. It is not beyond the realm of possibility that the Great Commission can actually be fulfilled in our generation!

And while we probably do not fully understand what God has in mind for the "fulfillment" of that commission, we can be sure that it includes the presence and power of the gospel to be within access of every soul in every language on Earth. That particular goal is achievable in the foreseeable future.

Furthermore, to the degree that we use Acts as our missionary training manual, that possibility can become even more readily a reality!

REFLECTION QUESTIONS

1. On the ship, the word Paul heard from God could have prevented a disaster. Why is it so hard to make some people believe that God really speaks true things to people today?
2. Do you think our churches would be better off if we made more room for the gift of prophecy? What would this take?
3. A poisonous snake bit Paul, and he didn't die. Some churches today actually handle poisonous snakes in their services to demonstrate the power of God. What do you think of that?
4. For two years, Paul, under arrest, ministered to those who came to visit him. Knowing what we know about Paul, what do you think would have been his major themes?
5. This concludes our study of Acts. In light of what we have seen, name two or three things you think we should be doing more in our churches today than we have been doing.

ENDNOTES

Chapter 1: God's Training Manual for Modern Christians

1. Simon J. Kistemaker, *New Testament Commentary: Exposition on the Acts of the Apostles* (Grand Rapids, MI: Baker Books, 1990), p. 53.
2. Cf. Stanley M. Horton, *The Book of Acts* (Springfield, MO: Gospel Publishing House, 1981), pp. 21-22.
3. Cf. Paul E. Pierson, *Themes from Acts* (Ventura, CA: Regal Books, 1982), pp. 10-14.
4. For further information on the New Apostolic Reformation, see my books *Churchquake!* (Regal Books), *Changing Church* (Regal Books) and *Apostles Today* (Regal Books).
5. F. F. Bruce, *The Book of Acts* (Grand Rapids, MI: William B. Eerdmans, 1988), p. 30.
6. D. Edmund Hiebert, *Personalities Around Paul* (Chicago, IL: Moody Press, 1973), p. 67.
7. Ibid., p. 74.
8. Bruce, *The Book of Acts,* p. 30.
9. Pierson, *Themes from Acts,* p. 11.

Chapter 2: How Jesus Attracted 120 Followers

1. Donald A. McGavran, *Understanding Church Growth* (Grand Rapids, MI: William B. Eerdmans Publishing Co., Third Edition, 1990), p. 163.
2. Ibid., p. 155.
3. Ibid., p. 156.
4. Gerhard von Rad, *Genesis: A Commentary,* tr. John H. Marks (Louisville, KY: Westminster Press, 1961), p. 148.
5. Bernhard Anderson, "The Babel Story: Paradigm of Human Unity and Diversity," *Ethnicity,* edited by Andrew M. Greeley and Gregory Baum (New York: The Seabury Press, 1977), p. 68.
6. C. Peter Wagner, *Your Spiritual Gifts Can Help Your Church Grow* (Ventura, CA: Regal Books, 1979, 1994, 2000), p. 189.
7. A. C. Bouquet, *Everyday Life in New Testament Times* (New York: Charles Scribner's Sons, 1953), p. 16.
8. John A. Broadus, *Commentary on the Gospel of Matthew* (Philadelphia, PA: American Baptist Publishing Society, 1886), p. 211.
9. E. A. Judge, *The Social Pattern of the Christian Groups in the First Century* (London: Tyndale, 1960), p. 15.

Chapter 3: History's Most Powerful Prayer Meeting (Acts 1)

1. Ken Blue, *Authority to Heal* (Downers Grove, IL: InterVarsity Press, 1987).
2. Don Williams, *Signs, Wonders and the Kingdom of God* (Ann Arbor, MI: Servant Publications, 1989).
3. Ray S. Anderson, ed., *Theological Foundations for Ministry* (Grand Rapids, MI: William B. Eerdmans Publishing Co., 1979), p. 7.
4. Colin Brown, *That You May Believe: Miracles and Faith Then and Now* (Grand Rapids, MI: William B. Eerdmans Publishing Co., 1985), p. 97.
5. Thomas A. Smail, *Reflected Glory: The Spirit in Christ and in Christians* (London: Hodder and Stoughton, 1975), p. 70.
6. John R. W. Stott, *The Spirit, the Church and the World: The Message of Acts* (Downers Grove, IL: InterVarsity Press, 1990), p. 41.
7. George Otis, Jr., *The Last of the Giants* (Grand Rapids, MI: Fleming H. Revell Company, a division of Baker Book House Company, 1991), p. 144.
8. Some of the literature dealing with strategic-level spiritual warfare includes John Dawson, *Taking Our Cities for God* (Altamonte Springs, FL: Creation House, 1989); Cindy Jacobs, *Possessing the Gates of the Enemy* (Grand Rapids, MI: Fleming H. Revell Company, 1991); George Otis, Jr.,

The Last of the Giants (Grand Rapids, MI: Fleming H. Revell Company, 1991) and *Informed Intercession* (Regal Books, 1999); and four contributions of mine: *Engaging the Enemy*, *Warfare Prayer*, *Breaking Strongholds in Your City* and *Confronting the Powers*, all published by Regal Books.

Chapter 4: The Spiritual Explosion at Pentecost (Acts 2)

1. Donald A. McGavran, *Understanding Church Growth* (Grand Rapids, MI: William B. Eerdmans Publishing Co., Third Edition, 1990), p. 26.
2. Ibid., p. 30.
3. Reprinted from Joachim Jeremias, *Jerusalem in the Time of Jesus* (London: SCM Press, 1969), p. 84.
4. C. Peter Wagner, *Your Spiritual Gifts Can Help Your Church Grow* (Ventura, CA: Regal Books, 1979, 1994, 2000), p. 219.
5. Simon J. Kistemaker, *New Testament Commentary: Exposition on the Acts of the Apostles* (Grand Rapids, MI: Baker Book House Company, 1990), p. 78.
6. Stanley M. Horton, *The Book of Acts* (Springfield, MO: Gospel Publishing House, 1981), p. 106.
7. Hermann Haarbeck, "Word, Tongue, Utterance," *The New International Dictionary of New Testament Theology*, Colin Brown, ed. (Grand Rapids, MI: Zondervan Publishing House, 1971, 1978), Vol. 3, p. 1080.
8. McGavran, *Understanding Church Growth*, p. 123.

Chapter 5: One Hundred Thirty Converts a Day Can Shake a City (Acts 3 and 4)

1. Ralph D. Winter, personal correspondence, June 4, 1999.
2. Otto Betz, "Exousia," *The New International Dictionary of New Testament Theology*, Colin Brown, ed. (Grand Rapids, MI: Zondervan Publishing House, 1976), Vol. 2, p. 607.
3. Richard B. Rackham, *The Acts of the Apostles: An Exposition* (London, England: Methuen & Co. Ltd., 1901), p. 44.
4. Donald A. Hagner, "Sadducees," *The Zondervan Pictorial Encyclopedia of the Bible* by Merrill C. Tenney, ed., vol. 5 (Grand Rapids, MI: Zondervan, 1975, 1976), p. 213.
5. Ibid., p. 214.
6. Rackham, *The Acts of the Apostles*, p. 45.
7. Hagner, "Sadducees," p. 215.
8. Ernst Haenchen, *The Acts of the Apostles: A Commentary* (Louisville, KY: Westminster Press, 1971), p. 189.
9. I. Howard Marshall, *Acts* (Grand Rapids, MI: William B. Eerdmans Publishing Co., 1980), p. 98.
10. F. F. Bruce, *The Book of Acts* (Grand Rapids, MI: William B. Eerdmans Publishing Co., 1988), p. 91.
11. Ibid.
12. Simon J. Kistemaker, *New Testament Commentary: Exposition on the Acts of the Apostles* (Grand Rapids, MI: Baker Book House Company, 1990), p. 151.

Chapter 6: Follow These Signs to Salvation (Acts 4 and 5)

1. John Stott, *The Spirit, The Church and the World* (Downers Grove, IL: InterVarsity Press, 1990), p. 107.
2. Everett F. Harrison, *Acts: The Expanding Church* (Chicago, IL: Moody Press, 1975), p. 91.
3. William Sanford LaSor, *Church Alive* (Ventura, CA: Regal Books, 1972), p. 73.
4. Stanley M. Horton, *The Book of Acts* (Springfield, MO: Gospel Publishing House, 1981), p. 72.
5. Harrison, *Acts: The Expanding Church*, p. 98.

Chapter 7: Should Foreigners Run the Church? (Acts 6)

1. R. C. H. Lenski, *The Interpretation of the Acts of the Apostles* (Minneapolis, MN: Augsburg Publishing House, 1934), p. 239.
2. Donald A. McGavran, *Understanding Church Growth* (Grand Rapids, MI: William B. Eerdmans Publishing Co., 1990), p. 67.
3. I. Howard Marshall, *The Acts of the Apostles* (Leicester, England; Inter-Varsity Press, 1980), p. 125.

4. Simon J. Kistemaker, *New Testament Commentary: Exposition on the Acts of the Apostles* (Grand Rapids, MI: Baker Book House Company, 1990), p. 220.
5. Ibid.
6. Marshall, *The Acts of the Apostles*, p. 125.
7. Ernst Haenchen, *The Acts of the Apostles: A Commentary* (Louisville, KY: The Westminster Press, 1971), p. 266.
8. Hans Conzelmann, *History of Primitive Christianity* (Nashville, TN: Abingdon Press, 1973), p. 57.
9. Kistemaker, *New Testament Commentary: Exposition on the Acts of the Apostles*, p. 224.
10. Derek Tidball, *The Social Context of the New Testament* (Grand Rapids, MI: Zondervan Publishing House, 1984), p. 55.
11. John Stott, *The Spirit, the World and the Church* (Downers Grove, IL: InterVarsity Press, 1990), p. 122.
12. Tidball, *The Social Context of the New Testament*, p. 55.
13. Conzelmann, *History of Primitive Christianity*, p. 58.
14. Reprinted from Joachim Jeremias, *Jerusalem in the Time of Jesus* (London: SCM, 1969), p. 204. Used by permission of Augsburg Fortress.
15. Haenchen, *The Acts of the Apostles: A Commentary*, p. 264.
16. Richard Belward Rackham, *The Acts of the Apostles: An Exposition* (London: Methuen & Co. Ltd., 1901), p. 87.
17. Ibid.

Chapter 8: Samaria: Preaching on the Other Side of the Tracks (Acts 6, 7 and 8)

1. F. F. Bruce, *Commentary on the Book of Acts* (Grand Rapids, MI: William B. Eerdmans Publishing Co., 1988), p. 124.
2. Charles Van Engen, *God's Missionary People* (Grand Rapids, MI: Baker Book House Company, 1991), p. 26.
3. Ernst Haenchen, *The Acts of the Apostles: A Commentary* (Louisville, KY: Westminster Press, 1971), p. 295.
4. Everett F. Harrison, *Acts: The Expanding Church* (Chicago, IL: Moody Press, 1975), pp. 129-130.
5. Bruce, *Commentary on the Book of Acts*, p. 162.
6. Ibid.
7. C. Peter Wagner, *Your Spiritual Gifts Can Help Your Church Grow* (Ventura, CA: Regal Books, 1979, 1994, 2005), p. 164.
8. Ibid., p. 189.
9. John Wimber and Kevin Springer, *Power Evangelism* (San Francisco, CA: HarperSanFrancisco, 1985, 1992).
10. See Carlos Annacondia, *Listen to Me, Satan!: Exercising Authority Over the Devil in Jesus' Name* (Lake Mary, FL, 1998).
11. Jack Hayford, *The Beauty of Spiritual Language* (Dallas, TX: Word Inc., 1992), p. 92.
12. Reprinted by permission from *The Demise of the Devil* by Susan Garrett, copyright © 1989 Augsburg Fortress, p. 37.
13. Ibid., p. 75.
14. Ibid.
15. Paul E. Pierson, *Themes from Acts* (Ventura, CA: Regal Books, 1982), p. 67.
15. Garrett, *The Demise of the Devil*, p. 65.
17. Ibid., p. 74.

Chapter 9: Meet Paul—The Greatest Missionary of All Time (Acts 9)

1. John Stott, *The Spirit, the Church and the World: The Message of Acts* (Downers Grove, IL: InterVarsity Press, 1990), pp. 168-169.
2. Richard N. Longenecker, *Paul: Apostle of Liberty* (New York: HarperCollins, 1964), p. 32.
3. F. F. Bruce, *Paul: Apostle of the Heart Set Free* (Grand Rapids, MI: William B. Eerdmans Publishing Co., 1977), p. 43.

4. Jack W. Hayford, *Glory on Your House* (Grand Rapids, MI: Chosen Books, 1991), pp. 63-67.
5. Sharon E. Mumper, "Where in the World Is the Church Growing?" *Christianity Today* (July 11, 1986), p. 17.
6. Jim and Lyn Montgomery, "I Myself Will Drive Them Out," *DAWN Ministries* newsletter (February 1994), p. 1.
7. Edward F. Murphy, "Church Growth Perspectives from the Book of Acts" (Ph.D. diss., Fuller Theological Seminary, 1979), p. 283.
8. Jack Deere, *Surprised by the Power of the Spirit* (Grand Rapids, MI: Zondervan Publishing House, 1993), pp. 88-96.
9. John White, *When the Spirit Comes in Power* (Downers Grove, IL: InterVarsity Press, 1988), p. 24.
10. Hayford, *Glory on Your House*, p. 139.
11. Simon J. Kistemaker, *Exposition of the Acts of the Apostles* (Grand Rapids, MI: Baker Book House, 1990), p. 335.
12. Richard Belward Rackham, *The Acts of the Apostles* (London: Methuen & Co., Ltd., 1901), p. 133.
13. F. F. Bruce, *The Book of Acts* (Grand Rapids, MI: William B. Eerdmans Publishing Co., 1954; revised edition, 1988), p. 188.
14. Clinton E. Arnold, *Powers of Darkness* (Downers Grove, IL: InterVarsity Press, 1992), p. 158.
15. Bruce, *Paul: Apostle of the Heart Set Free*, p. 81.
16. Bruce, *The Book of Acts*, p. 192.

Chapter 10: Peter Blazes the Trail to the Gentiles (Acts 9, 10 and 11)

1. C. Peter Wagner, *Church Planting for a Greater Harvest* (Ventura, CA: Regal Books, 1990), p. 11.
2. C. Peter Wagner, *Your Spiritual Gifts Can Help Your Church Grow* (Ventura, CA: Regal Books, 1979; 1994, 2005), p. 189.
3. Donald A. McGavran, *Understanding Church Growth* (Grand Rapids, MI: William B. Eerdmans Publishing Co., 1970; 1980; third edition revised and edited by C. Peter Wagner, 1990), p. 241.
4. Ibid., p. 227.
5. Carl Lawrence, *The Church in China* (Minneapolis, MN: Bethany House Publishers, 1985), pp. 76-77.
6. F. F. Bruce, *The Book of Acts* (Grand Rapids, MI: William B. Eerdmans Publishing Co., 1954; revised edition, 1988), p. 58.
7. John Stott, *The Spirit, the Church and the World: The Message of Acts* (Downers Grove, IL: InterVarsity Press, 1990), p. 185.
8. Bruce, *The Book of Acts*, p. 208.

Chapter 11: Planting the First Gentile Church (Acts 11)

1. F. F. Bruce, *The Book of Acts* (Grand Rapids, MI: William B. Eerdmans Publishing Co., 1954; revised edition, 1988), p. 224.
2. Simon J. Kistemaker, *Exposition of the Acts of the Apostles* (Grand Rapids, MI: Baker Book House, 1990), p. 417.
3. W. J. Conybeare and J. S. Howson, *The Life and Epistles of St. Paul* (London: Longmans, Green and Co., 1875), p. 103.
4. I. Howard Marshall, *The Acts of the Apostles: An Introduction and Commentary* (Leicester, England: InterVarsity Press, 1980), p. 201.
5. Kistemaker, *Exposition of the Acts of the Apostles*, p. 418.
6. Bruce, *The Book of Acts*, p. 225.
7. Kistemaker, *Exposition of the Acts of the Apostles*, pp. 418-419.
8. R. C. H. Lenski, *The Interpretation of the Acts of the Apostles* (Minneapolis, MN: Augsburg Publishing House, 1934), p. 450.
9. See Charles Van Engen, *God's Missionary People* (Grand Rapids, MI: Baker Book House, 1991).
10. William Sanford LaSor, *Church Alive* (Ventura, CA: Regal Books, 1972), p. 167.
11. Stanley M. Horton, *The Book of Acts* (Springfield, MO: Gospel Publishing House, 1981), p. 140.

12. Kistemaker, *Exposition of the Acts of the Apostles*, p. 423.

Chapter 12: The Power of Herod Versus the Power of Prayer (Acts 12)

1. Everett F. Harrison, *Acts: The Expanding Church* (Chicago: Moody Press, 1975), p. 189.
2. Ibid., pp. 189-190.
3. Richard Belward Rackham, *The Acts of the Apostles* (London: Methuen & Co., Ltd., 1901), p. 176.
4. Joachim Jeremias, *Jerusalem in the Time of Jesus* (Philadelphia, PA: Fortress Press, 1969), p. 331.
5. Ibid., p. 332.
6. Ibid., p. 333.
7. C. Peter Wagner, *Your Spiritual Gifts Can Help Your Church Grow* (Ventura, CA: Regal Books, 1979, 1994, 2005), p. 70.
8. Richard J. Foster, *Celebration of Discipline* (San Francisco: HarperSanFrancisco, 1988), p. 35.
9. Walter Wink, *Engaging the Powers* (Minneapolis, MN: Fortress Press, 1992), p. 299.
10. John Stott, *The Spirit, the Church and the World: The Message of Acts* (Downers Grove, IL: InterVarsity Press, 1990), p. 209.
11. Gary Kinnaman, *Angels Dark and Light* (Ann Arbor, MI: Servant Publications, 1994), p. 20.
12. Ibid., p. 52.
13. C. Peter Wagner, *Warfare Prayer* (Ventura, CA: Regal Books, 1992), p. 33.
14. Stott, *The Spirit, the Church and the World*, p. 213.

Chapter 13: Onward to the Nations (Acts 13)

1. Everett F. Harrison, *The Apostolic Church* (Grand Rapids, MI: William B. Eerdmans Publishing Co., 1985), p. 186.
2. Dean S. Gilliland, *Pauline Theology and Mission Practice* (Grand Rapids, MI: Baker Book House, 1983), p. 209.
3. C. Peter Wagner, *Your Spiritual Gifts Can Help Your Church Grow* (Ventura, CA: Regal Books, 1979, 1994, 2005), p. 267.
4. William Mitchell Ramsay, *St. Paul the Traveller and the Roman Citizen* (London: Hodder and Stoughton, 1925), p. 65.
5. Simon J. Kistemaker, *Exposition of the Acts of the Apostles* (Grand Rapids, MI: Baker Book House, 1990), p. 454.
6. F. F. Bruce, *The Book of Acts* (Grand Rapids, MI: William B. Eerdmans Publishing Co., 1954; revised edition, 1988), pp. 245-246.
7. Ralph D. Winter, "The Two Structures of God's Redemptive Mission," *Missiology: An International Review* (January 1974), pp. 121-139.
8. John Stott, *The Spirit, the Church and the World: The Message of Acts* (Downers Grove, IL: InterVarsity Press, 1990), p. 220.
9. Susan R. Garrett, *The Demise of the Devil* (Minneapolis, MN: Fortress Press, 1989), p. 80.
10. Ibid.
11. Ibid.
12. Ibid., p. 84.

Chapter 14: Extending God's Kingdom Upsets the Enemy (Acts 14)

1. William Mitchell Ramsay, *St. Paul the Traveller and the Roman Citizen* (London: Hodder and Stoughton, 1925), p. 93.
2. This comes from *Acts of Paul* 3.3, referenced by F. F. Bruce, *The Book of Acts* (Grand Rapids, MI: William B. Eerdmans Publishing Co., 1954; revised edition, 1988), p. 271.
3. Ibid.
4. See John Wimber and Kevin Springer, *Power Evangelism* (San Francisco: HarperSanFrancisco, 1985; revised edition, 1992).
5. Everett F. Harrison, *Acts: The Expanding Church* (Chicago: Moody Press, 1975), p. 219.
6. Ernst Haenchen, *The Acts of the Apostles* (Philadelphia, PA: The Westminster Press, 1971), p. 423.

7. Karen M. Feaver, "What Chinese Christians Taught a U. S. Congressional Delegation," *Christianity Today* (16 May 1994): 34.
8. C. Peter Wagner, *How to Have a Healing Ministry in Any Church* (Ventura, CA: Regal Books, 1988), pp. 243-244.
9. For the important distinction between "power encounter," "truth encounter" and "allegiance encounter," see Charles H. Kraft, "Allegiance, Truth and Power Encounters in Christian Witness," *Pentecost, Mission and Ecumenism Essays on Intercultural Theology*, ed. by Jan A. B. Jongeneel (Frankfurt am Main, Germany: Peter Lang, 1992), pp. 215-230.
10. Haenchen, *The Acts of the Apostles*, p. 434.
11. Harrison, *Acts: The Expanding Church*, p. 225.
12. Ramsay, *St. Paul the Traveller*, p. 120.
13. Donald A. McGavran, *Understanding Church Growth* (Grand Rapids, MI: William B. Eerdmans Publishing Co., 1970; 1980; third edition revised and edited by C. Peter Wagner, 1990), pp. 247-248.

Chapter 15: Solving Conflicts in a Multicultural Church (Acts 15 and Galatians)

1. Ronald Y. K. Fung, *The Epistle to the Galatians* (Grand Rapids, MI: William B. Eerdmans Publishing Co., 1988), p. 2.
2. Ibid., pp. 7-8.
3. J. Stafford Wright, "Magic, Sorcery, Magi," *The New International Dictionary of New Testament Theology* Vol. 2, ed. Colin Brown (Grand Rapids, MI: Zondervan Publishing House, 1976), p. 559.
4. F. F. Bruce, *The Epistle to the Galatians: A Commentary on the Greek Text* (Grand Rapids, MI: William B. Eerdmans Publishing Co., 1982), p. 148.
5. Kenneth S. Wuest, *Galatians in the Greek New Testament for the English Reader* (Grand Rapids, MI: William B. Eerdmans Publishing Co., 1946), pp. 113-114.
6. Dean S. Gilliland, *Pauline Theology and Mission Practice* (Grand Rapids, MI: Baker Book House, 1983), p. 195.

Chapter 16: The Famous Jerusalem Council (Acts 15)

1. Paul E. Pierson, *Themes from Acts* (Ventura, CA: Regal Books, 1982), p. 115.
2. Ernst Haenchen, *The Acts of the Apostles* (Philadelphia, PA: The Westminster Press, 1971), p. 461.
3. F. F. Bruce, *The Book of Acts* (Grand Rapids, MI: William B. Eerdmans Publishing Co., 1954; revised edition, 1988), p. 287.
4. Haenchen, *The Acts of the Apostles*, p. 462.
5. Simon J. Kistemaker, *Exposition of the Acts of the Apostles* (Grand Rapids, MI: Baker Book House, 1990), p. 543.
6. Bruce, *The Book of Acts*, p. 290.
7. Donald A. McGavran, *Understanding Church Growth* (Grand Rapids, MI: William B. Eerdmans Publishing Co., 1970; 1980; third edition revised and edited by C. Peter Wagner, 1990), p. 123.
8. Kistemaker, *Exposition of the Acts of the Apostles*, p. 549.
9. Susan R. Garrett, *The Demise of the Devil: Magic and the Demonic in Luke's Writings* (Minneapolis, MN: Fortress Press, 1989), p. 80.
10. John Stott, *The Spirit, the Church and the World: The Message of Acts* (Downers Grove, IL: InterVarsity Press, 1990), p. 24.

Chapter 17: Goodbye, Barnabas; Hello, Silas: Reorganizing the Mission (Acts 15 and 16)

1. D. Edmond Hiebert, *Personalities Around Paul* (Chicago: Moody Press, 1973), p. 62.
2. Ibid.
3. For those who would like more information about modality-sodality theory, I recommend Ralph D. Winter's groundbreaking essay "The Two Structures of God's Redemptive Mission," *Missiology: An International Review* (January 1974): 121-139; and the chapter "Why Bill Bright Is Not Your Pastor" in my book *Leading Your Church to Growth* (Ventura, CA.: Regal Books, 1984), pp. 141-166.

4. F. F. Bruce, *The Book of Acts* (Grand Rapids, MI: William B. Eerdmans Publishing Company, 1988), p. 302.
5. F. F. Bruce, *The Pauline Circle* (Grand Rapids, MI: William B. Eerdmans Publishing Company, 1985), pp. 25-26.
6. C. Peter Wagner, *Your Spiritual Gifts Can Help Your Church Grow* (Ventura, CA: Regal Books, 1979; revised edition, 1994), pp. 181-182.
7. On the question of Silas's apostleship, some may suppose that Paul refers to him as an apostle in 1 Thessalonians. Paul starts the Epistle with "Paul, Silvanus [Silas], and Timothy" (1:1), and then says later, "Nor did we seek glory from men, either from you or from others, when we might have made demands as apostles of Christ" (2:6). This most probably should be taken as an editorial "we," not a technical designation of Silas as an apostle. Some may disagree.
8. George W. Peters, "An Analysis from Africa," *Africa Pulse,* no. 2 (March 1970): 2.

Chapter 18: To Europe with Power (Acts 16)

1. Ernst Haenchen, *The Acts of the Apostles: A Commentary* (Philadelphia, PA: The Westminster Press, 1971), p. 486.
2. Ibid., p. 487
3. These hypotheses are compiled by Ernst Haenchen, ibid., pp. 489-490.
4. David W. J. Gill, "Acts and the Urban Elites," *The Book of Acts in Its Graeco-Roman Setting,* ed. David W. J. Gill and Conrad Gempf (Grand Rapids, MI: William B. Eerdmans Publishing Company, 1994), pp. 114-115.
5. See Bradley Blue, "Acts and the House Church," ibid., pp. 184-185.
6. See F. F. Bruce, *Paul: Apostle of the Heart Set Free* (Grand Rapids, MI: William B. Eerdmans Publishing Company, 1977), p. 221.
7. *Random House Webster's College Dictionary* (New York: Random House, 1992), p. 1342.
8. Simon J. Kistemaker, *Exposition of the Acts of the Apostles* (Grand Rapids, MI: Baker Book House, 1990), p. 594.
9. R. C. H. Lenski, *The Interpretation of the Acts of the Apostles* (Minneapolis, MN: Augsburg Publishing House, 1934), p. 662.
10. Everett Ferguson, *Backgrounds of Early Christianity,* 2nd ed. (Grand Rapids, MI: William B. Eerdmans Publishing Company, 1987; revised edition, 1993), p. 200.
11. Ibid., pp. 168-169.
12. Martin Luther (1483-1546), "A Mighty Fortress Is Our God." Public domain.

Chapter 19: You Win Some and You Lose Some (Acts 17)

1. F. F. Bruce, *Paul: Apostle of the Heart Set Free* (Grand Rapids, MI: William B. Eerdmans Publishing Company, 1977), p. 225.
2. F. F. Bruce, *The Pauline Circle* (Grand Rapids, MI: William B. Eerdmans Publishing Company, 1985), p. 85.
3. D. Edmond Hiebert, *Personalities Around Paul* (Chicago: Moody Press, 1973), p. 166.
4. F. W. Beare, *A Commentary on the Epistle to the Philippians* (London: Adam & Charles Black, 1959), p. 145.
5. Everett Ferguson, *Backgrounds of Early Christianity* (Grand Rapids, MI: William B. Eerdmans Publishing Company, 1987; revised edition, 1993), p. 143.
6. Ibid., p. 151.
7. Ibid., p. 136.
8. Ibid., p. 141.
9. Ibid., p. 185
10. J. Blunck says, "The NT use of *hypsoma* probably reflects astrological ideas, and hence denotes cosmic powers." "Height, Depth, Exalt," *The New International Dictionary of New Testament Theology,* ed. Colin Brown (Grand Rapids, MI: Zondervan Publishing House, 1976), vol. 2, p. 200.

11. Michael Green, *Evangelism in the Early Church* (Grand Rapids, MI: William B. Eerdmans Publishing Company, 1970), p. 131.
12. George Otis, Jr., "An Overview of Spiritual Mapping," *Breaking Strongholds in Your City*, ed. C. Peter Wagner (Ventura, CA: Regal Books, 1993), p. 40.
13. Ibid., p. 42.
14. Cited by Ferguson, *Backgrounds of Early Christianity*, p. 173.
15. Simon J. Kistemaker, *Exposition of the Acts of the Apostles* (Grand Rapids, MI: Baker Book House, 1990), p. 626.
16. John Stott, *The Spirit, the Church and the World: The Message of Acts* (Downers Grove, IL: InterVarsity Press, 1990), p. 284.
17. William Mitchell Ramsay, *St. Paul the Traveler and the Roman Citizen* (London: Hodder & Stoughton, 1925), p. 252.
18. I. Howard Marshall, *The Acts of the Apostles: An Introduction and a Commentary* (Grand Rapids, MI: William B. Eerdmans Publishing Company, 1980), p. 291.
19. Richard Belward Rackham, *The Acts of the Apostles: An Exposition* (London: Methuen & Company, Ltd., 1901), p. 320.

Chapter 20: Corinth to Antioch to Ephesus (Acts 18 and 19)

1. George Otis, Jr., "An Overview of Spiritual Mapping," *Breaking Strongholds in Your City*, ed. C. Peter Wagner (Ventura, CA: Regal Books, 1993), p. 36.
2. F. F. Bruce, *The Book of Acts* (Grand Rapids, MI: William B. Eerdmans Publishing Company, 1954; revised edition, 1988), p. 347.
3. Bradley Blue, "Acts and the House Church," *The Book of Acts in Its Graeco-Roman Setting*, ed. David W. J. Gill and Conrad Gempf (Grand Rapids, MI: William B. Eerdmans Publishing Company, 1994), p. 172.
4. Ibid., p. 177.
5. Bruce W. Winter, "Acts and Roman Religion: B. The Imperial Cult," *The Book of Acts in Its Graeco-Roman Setting*, vol. 2, pp. 98-99.
6. Ibid., p. 100.
7. Ibid., p. 101.
8. Bruce, *The Book of Acts*, p. 354.
9. John W. Drane, *Early Christians* (San Francisco: HarperSanFrancisco, 1982), p. 19.
10. Hans Conzelmann, *History of Primitive Christianity* (Nashville, TN: Abingdon Press, 1973), p. 160.
11. W. J. Conybeare and J. S. Howson, *The Life and Epistles of St. Paul* (London: Longmans, Green and Co., 1875), pp. 364-365.
12. E. M. Blaiklock, *Acts: the Birth of the Church* (Grand Rapids, MI: Fleming H. Revell Company, 1980), p. 189.

Chapter 21: Invading Diana's Territory (Acts 19)

1. E. M. Blaiklock, *Acts: The Birth of the Church* (Grand Rapids, MI: Fleming H. Revell Company, 1980), p. 185.
2. Clinton E. Arnold, *Ephesians: Power and Magic* (Grand Rapids, MI: Baker Book House, 1992), p. 6.
3. Quoted in Paul Trebilco, "Asia," *The Book of Acts in Its Graeco-Roman Setting*, ed. David W. J. Gill and Conrad Gempf (Grand Rapids, MI: William B. Eerdmans Publishing Company, 1994), pp. 305-306.
4. Bruce M. Metzger, "St. Paul and the Magicians," *Princeton Seminary Bulletin* 38 (June 1944): 27.
5. F. F. Bruce, *Paul: Apostle of the Heart Set Free* (Grand Rapids, MI: William B. Eerdmans Publishing Company, 1977), p. 291.
6. William Mitchell Ramsay, *St. Paul the Traveller and the Roman Citizen* (London: Hodder & Stoughton, 1925), p. 271.
7. Arnold, *Ephesians: Power and Magic*, p. 1.
8. Bruce, *Paul: Apostle of the Heart Set Free*, p. 295.

9. Michael Green, *Evangelism in the Early Church* (Grand Rapids, MI: William B. Eerdmans Publishing Company, 1970), pp. 188-189.
10. Ramsay MacMullen, *Christianizing the Roman Empire* (New Haven, CT: Yale University Press, 1984), p. 28.
11. Ibid., p. 112.
12. Ibid., p. 113.
13. Susan R. Garrett says, "I will argue . . . that Luke uses the story of the seven sons of Sceva . . . to advance the theme of the ongoing Christian triumph over Satan, and, consequently, over magic." *The Demise of the Devil* (Minneapolis, MI: Fortress Press, 1989), p. 90.
14. Ibid., p. 91.
15. Ibid., p. 95.
16. Arnold, *Ephesians: Power and Magic*, p. 18.
17. Ernst Haenchen, *The Acts of the Apostles: A Commentary* (Philadelphia, PA: The Westminster Press, 1971), p. 567.
18. Ed Silvoso, *That None Should Perish* (Ventura, CA: Regal Books, 1994), p. 50.
19. Donovan A. Larkins, *Up in Smoke: Why I Conduct Public Book Burnings* (Dayton, OH: Victory Press Publications, 1994), p. 44.
20. Garrett, *The Demise of the Devil*, p. 97.
21. Arnold, *Ephesians: Power and Magic*, p. 20.
22. F. F. Bruce, *The Book of Acts* (Grand Rapids, MI: William B. Eerdmans Publishing Company, 1988; revised edition, 1954), p. 375.
23. Trebilco, "Asia," *The Book of Acts in Its Graeco-Roman Setting*, p. 316.
24. Bruce, *The Book of Acts*, p. 373.
25. Trebilco, "Asia," *The Book of Acts in Its Graeco-Roman Setting*, p. 316.
26. Ibid., p. 329.
27. Ibid., pp. 317-318.
28. Arnold, *Ephesians: Power and Magic*, p. 21.
29. W. J. Conybeare and J. S. Howson, *The Life and Epistles of St. Paul* (London: Longmans, Green and Co., 1875), p. 423.
30. Trebilco, "Asia," *The Book of Acts in Its Graeco-Roman Setting*, p. 321.
31. John Stott, *The Spirit, The Church and the World: The Message of Acts* (Downers Grove, IL: InterVarsity Press, 1990), p. 308.
32. Arnold, *Ephesians: Power and Magic*, p. 22
33. MacMullen, *Christianizing the Roman Empire*, p. 26.
34. Ibid.
35. Ibid., p. 18.
36. Arnold, *Ephesians: Power and Magic*, p. 28.
37. Ibid., p. 6.
38. Bruce, *The Book of Acts*, p. 366.
39. Arnold, *Ephesians: Power and Magic*, p. 20.

Chapter 22: A Long Trip Toward the Jerusalem Jail (Acts 20 and 21)

1. F. F. Bruce, *The Book of Acts* (Grand Rapids, MI: William B. Eerdmans Publishing Company, 1954; revised edition, 1988), p. 371.
2. William Mitchell Ramsay, *St. Paul the Traveller and the Roman Citizen* (London: Hodder & Stoughton, 1925), p. 59.
3. Bruce, *The Book of Acts*, p. 381.
4. Simon J. Kistemaker, *Exposition of the Acts of the Apostles* (Grand Rapids, MI: Baker Book House, 1990), p. 712.
5. Ramsay, *St. Paul the Traveller and the Roman Citizen*, p. 287.
6. Bradley Blue, "Acts and the House Church," *The Book of Acts in Its Graeco-Roman Setting*, ed. David W. J. Gill and Conrad Gempf (Grand Rapids, MI: William B. Eerdmans Publishing Company, 1994), p. 120.

7. Robert Banks, *Paul's Idea of Community* (Peabody, MA: Hendrickson Publishers, 1994), p. 32.
8. S. Scott Bartchy, *First-Century Slavery and 1 Corinthians 7:21* (Missoula, MT: The Society of Biblical Literature, 1973), p. 73. It might come as a surprise to many modern readers to suppose that slaves in first-century Ephesus could have been pastors, because our primary paradigm for slavery is African slaves in America. Slavery in the Roman Empire was quite different. S. Scott Bartchy says, "The person in slavery in the first century worked, but his working was not the specific way in which he could be distinguished from the rest of his society." A slave was often "an administrator of funds and personnel and an executive with decision-making power."
9. Donald A. McGavran, *Understanding Church Growth* (Grand Rapids, MI: William B. Eerdmans Publishing Company, 1970; 1980; third edition revised and edited by C. Peter Wagner, 1990), p. 218.
10. See Stanley M. Horton, *The Book of Acts* (Springfield, MO: Gospel Publishing House, 1981), p. 244.
11. Wayne A. Grudem, *The Gift of Prophecy in the New Testament and Today* (Westchester, IL: Crossway Books, 1988), p. 97.
12. Horton, *The Book of Acts*, p. 244.
13. Grudem, *The Gift of Prophecy in the New Testament and Today*, p. 100.
14. Bill Hamon, *Prophets and Personal Prophecy* (Shippensburg PA: Destiny Image Publishers, 1987), p. 145.
15. Ibid., p. 147.
16. Ibid., p. 152.

Chapter 23: What to Do with This Troublemaker? (Acts 21 to 26)

1. George Eldon Ladd, *The Young Church: Acts of the Apostles* (Nashville, TN: Abingdon Press, 1964), p. 78.
2. Ibid., p. 79.
3. A. J. Mattill Jr., "The Purpose of Acts: Schneckenburger Reconsidered," *Apostolic History and the Gospel*, ed. W. Ward Gasque and Ralph P. Martin (Grand Rapids, MI: William B. Eerdmans Publishing Company, 1970), p. 116.
4. John Stott, *The Spirit, the Church and the World: The Message of Acts* (Downers Grove, IL: InterVarsity Press, 1990), p. 348.
5. Joachim Jeremias, *Jerusalem in the Time of Jesus* (Philadelphia, PA: Fortress Press, 1969), p. 348.
6. Mattill, "The Purpose of Acts," *Apostolic History and the Gospel*, p. 116.
7. See Simon J. Kistemaker, *Exposition of the Acts of the Apostles* (Grand Rapids, MI: Baker Book House, 1990), p. 906.

Chapter 24: Destination: Rome (Acts 27 and 28)

1. John Stott, *The Spirit, the Church and the World: The Message of Acts* (Downers Grove, IL: InterVarsity Press, 1990), p. 383.
2. William Mitchell Ramsay, *St. Paul the Traveller and the Roman Citizen* (London: Hodder & Stoughton, 1925), p. 314.
3. Ibid.
4. Simon J. Kistemaker, *Exposition of the Acts of the Apostles* (Grand Rapids, MI: Baker Book House, 1990), p. 948.

SCRIPTURE INDEX

1 Chronicles 21:1; 124
1 Chronicles 21:8; 124
1 Corinthians 1:14; 413
1 Corinthians 1:14-17; 415
1 Corinthians 1:22; 68
1 Corinthians 2:1-5; 284
1 Corinthians 2:4-5; 103
1 Corinthians 3:6; 383
1 Corinthians 4:3-4; 459
1 Corinthians 4:21; 452
1 Corinthians 6:19; 135
1 Corinthians 8:4; 395
1 Corinthians 9:1; 172, 477
1 Corinthians 9:6; 347, 408
1 Corinthians 9:20; 352
1 Corinthians 9:22; 346, 352, 470
1 Corinthians 10:13; 109
1 Corinthians 10:20; 396
1 Corinthians 12:9; 84, 117, 137, 197
1 Corinthians 12:10; 69, 197, 237
1 Corinthians 12:13; 52, 95, 159, 426
1 Corinthians 12:23; 343
1 Corinthians 12:28; 237
1 Corinthians 13:1; 70
1 Corinthians 13:2; 137, 234
1 Corinthians 14:2; 69
1 Corinthians 14:3; 339
1 Corinthians 14:5; 70
1 Corinthians 14:9; 69
1 Corinthians 14:13; 70
1 Corinthians 14:24-25; 110
1 Corinthians 14:39; 70
1 Corinthians 15:6; 17
1 Corinthians 15:24-26; 20
1 Corinthians 15:26; 205, 256
1 Corinthians 15:29; 372
1 Corinthians 15:32; 433
1 Corinthians 16:2; 455
1 Corinthians 16:15; 402
1 John 2:8; 368
1 John 2:13; 368
1 John 3:8; 21
1 John 5:19; 20, 368
1 Kings 17:17-24; 456
1 Kings 18:20-40; 270
1 Kings 18:38; 62
1 Kings 19:5-8; 251
1 Peter 4:12-13; 374
1 Peter 4:14; 236
1 Peter 4:16; 81, 236
1 Peter 5:8; 109, 168
1 Samuel 30:24; 343
1 Thessalonians 1:5; 434
1 Thessalonians 1:8; 386
1 Thessalonians 1:9; 385
1 Thessalonians 2:9; 384, 407
1 Thessalonians 2:15; 387
1 Thessalonians 2:18; 357
1 Thessalonians 3:1-2; 408
1 Thessalonians 3:5; 410
1 Thessalonians 3:6-9; 409
1 Timothy 1:18; 312
1 Timothy 3:1-7; 458
1 Timothy 4:14; 351
1 Timothy 5:18; 461
1 Timothy 6:15; 33
2 Corinthians 2:11; 57
2 Corinthians 2:12-13; 451
2 Corinthians 4:3-4; 378, 388
2 Corinthians 4:4; 20, 68, 172, 185, 272, 290, 394
2 Corinthians 7:5-7; 452, 453
2 Corinthians 8:3; 453
2 Corinthians 9:1; 453
2 Corinthians 9:7; 454
2 Corinthians 9:8; 454
2 Corinthians 10:4; 185
2 Corinthians 10:4-5; 395
2 Corinthians 11; 474
2 Corinthians 11:9; 409
2 Corinthians 11:23; 295
2 Corinthians 11:25; 295
2 Corinthians 11:26; 274

2 Corinthians 11:32-33; 189
2 Corinthians 12:2-4; 295
2 Corinthians 12:13; 408
2 Kings 4:32-37; 456
2 Peter 3:9; 29, 247
2 Thessalonians 1:5; 300
2 Timothy 3:11; 298
2 Timothy 3:12; 300
2 Timothy 3:15; 350
2 Timothy 4:7; 346
2 Timothy 4:11; 19, 344
2 Timothy 4:20; 288, 493
Amos 9:11-12; 336
Colossians 2:15; 21, 185
Colossians 4:10; 341, 344
Colossians 4:14; 18, 19
Daniel 9:20; 89
Daniel 10:1-14; 253
Deuteronomy 17:15; 243
Deuteronomy 18:2; 106
Deuteronomy 20:5-8; 343
Ephesians 2:1-3; 407
Ephesians 2:2; 20, 185, 252, 461
Ephesians 4:11; 237, 262, 348
Ephesians 4:12; 431
Ephesians 5:18; 52
Ephesians 6:12; 24, 185, 252, 300, 389, 433, 447, 460
Ephesians 6:12-18; 366
Ephesians 6:21; 446
Exodus 3:2; 62
Exodus 17:8-14; 252
Exodus 20:3-4; 293
Exodus 34:22; 60
Ezekiel 3:18-19; 412
Ezekiel 4:4-6; 421
Galatians 1:1; 182
Galatians 1:6-7; 308, 315
Galatians 1:9; 309
Galatians 1:11-12; 188
Galatians 1:14; 168
Galatians 1:16; 189
Galatians 1:17; 188
Galatians 1:18; 188
Galatians 1:18-19; 191
Galatians 1:21; 235
Galatians 2:1; 229
Galatians 2:3; 352
Galatians 2:4; 309
Galatians 2:7-8; 312, 363
Galatians 2:8; 184
Galatians 2:9; 195, 316
Galatians 2:11-14; 310, 330
Galatians 2:12; 335
Galatians 2:13; 345
Galatians 2:20; 178
Galatians 3:1; 303
Galatians 3:1-3; 317
Galatians 3:5; 333
Galatians 3:10-11; 317
Galatians 3:28; 29
Galatians 4:3; 318
Galatians 4:8-10; 318
Galatians 4:13; 282
Galatians 4:19-21; 320
Galatians 5:16; 319
Galatians 5:19; 319
Galatians 5:22; 104, 320
Galatians 5:22-23; 136
Galatians 5:23; 320
Genesis 1:28; 32, 298
Genesis 10:5; 32
Genesis 11:1; 32
Genesis 11:4; 32, 33
Genesis 11:7; 32
Genesis 12:3; 28
Genesis 22:1-14; 426
Hebrews 1:14; 251
Isaiah 6:6-7; 62
Isaiah 14:14; 255
Isaiah 24:21; 252
James 2:19; 370
James 3:15; 392
James 4:2; 247
James 4:7; 109
James 5:16; 248
Jeremiah 1:1; 106
Jeremiah 7:16; 392
Jeremiah 7:16-18; 442
Jeremiah 7:18; 369
Jeremiah 32:6-15; 106
Jeremiah 33:3; 57
Job 1:22; 109

Job 2:3; 109
Job 2:10; 109
John 1:13; 171
John 1:41; 37
John 1:43-44; 137
John 1:44; 72
John 1:49; 37
John 3:8; 62
John 4:5-43; 41
John 4:9; 37, 151
John 4:21; 149
John 4:24; 149
John 4:25; 156
John 4:35-36; 60
John 4:39-42; 159
John 5:1-9; 117, 493
John 5:19; 86, 373, 492
John 6:2; 86
John 6:64; 86
John 6:66; 86
John 7:5; 58
John 7:15; 96
John 10:10; 22, 244
John 11:43-44; 456
John 12:20-22; 40
John 12:31; 20
John 14:12; 45, 63, 115, 145
John 14:14; 438
John 16:7; 24, 55
John 18:36; 21, 101
John 20:19; 455
John 20:21; 53
John 20:30; 158
John 20:31; 158
Jonah 3:3-10; 397
Joshua 4:7; 421
Joshua 13:14; 106
Joshua 24:15; 292
Jude 9; 371-372
Judges 6-7; 273
Judges 7:1-6; 343
Leviticus 11:2; 212
Leviticus 11:4; 212
Leviticus 11:43; 212
Luke 1:3; 18
Luke 1:26-38; 251
Luke 1:28; 369
Luke 1:34; 372
Luke 3:16; 62
Luke 4:6; 20
Luke 4:16-19; 102
Luke 4:18; 105
Luke 4:18-19; 22
Luke 7:11-16; 456
Luke 7:20-23; 103
Luke 7:22; 205
Luke 8:2-3; 58
Luke 8:49-56; 456
Luke 9:49-50; 114
Luke 10:1; 114
Luke 10:9; 114
Luke 10:19; 22, 272, 366, 372
Luke 10:20; 117
Luke 10:30-37; 41
Luke 10:38; 41
Luke 11:13; 95
Luke 11:20; 54
Luke 11:21-22; 54
Luke 12:34; 77
Luke 21:12-13; 95
Luke 22:41; 245
Luke 23:21; 89
Luke 24:6; 456
Luke 24:19; 43
Luke 24:47; 53
Luke 24:49; 23, 48, 49, 56
Luke 24:53; 56
Mark 1:24; 370
Mark 1:25; 371
Mark 5:8-9; 372
Mark 5:18; 40
Mark 5:19; 40
Mark 5:37; 203, 344
Mark 5:40; 203
Mark 7:24-30; 211
Mark 9:38-39; 114
Mark 12:24; 91
Mark 14:33; 80
Mark 16:15; 53
Mark 16:15-18; 103, 491
Mark 16:17; 438
Mark 16:18; 117, 186

Matthew 3:2; 21, 102
Matthew 4:17; 102
Matthew 4:23; 21
Matthew 6:9; 376
Matthew 6:10; 21, 47, 101
Matthew 6:19; 104
Matthew 6:33; 104
Matthew 7:22-23; 439
Matthew 8:5-13; 41, 211
Matthew 8:10; 86
Matthew 9:27-31; 86
Matthew 9:37-38; 61, 382
Matthew 10:1; 22, 85
Matthew 10:5-6; 41, 124
Matthew 10:6; 67
Matthew 10:7; 21
Matthew 10:8; 201, 205, 456
Matthew 10:11; 67
Matthew 10:14; 67, 281, 412
Matthew 11:11; 21
Matthew 11:12; 21, 23, 300
Matthew 12:26; 21
Matthew 12:28; 111
Matthew 12:29; 24, 54, 300
Matthew 13:58; 117, 288, 403, 493
Matthew 15:24; 27, 40, 41
Matthew 15:32-39; 41
Matthew 16:16; 47
Matthew 16:18; 22, 24, 47
Matthew 16:18-19; 159
Matthew 16:19; 24, 54, 216
Matthew 16:22; 55
Matthew 16:23; 24, 55, 108
Matthew 17:1; 80
Matthew 17:2; 171
Matthew 17:20; 247
Matthew 18:19; 57
Matthew 21:22; 247
Matthew 22:39; 104
Matthew 23:15; 228
Matthew 24:14; 16, 33, 53, 101, 309
Matthew 26:73; 39
Matthew 28:19; 29, 41, 124, 184, 322, 378, 495
Matthew 28:19-20; 12, 22
Nehemiah 1:6; 89
Philemon 1:1-2; 447
Philemon 24; 19
Philippians 2:5-8; 35
Philippians 2:13; 87
Philippians 3:2; 426
Philippians 3:4; 332
Philippians 3:5; 168
Philippians 3:6; 332
Philippians 3:8-9; 332
Philippians 3:13-14; 346
Philippians 4:3; 361, 388
Philippians 4:15-16; 384
Psalm 22:3; 376
Psalm 24:1; 20
Psalm 29:1; 372
Psalm 97:7; 372
Psalm 99:2; 148
Psalm 118:22; 96
Revelation 2–3; 447
Revelation 2:2; 461
Revelation 7:9; 29
Revelation 12:11; 374; 403
Revelation 12:12; 73
Revelation 14:7; 293
Revelation 20:14; 205
Revelation 21:1; 20
Revelation 21:4; 205
Romans 1:16; 26, 27, 38, 74, 192, 268
Romans 1:20; 401
Romans 1:24; 256, 396
Romans 1:25; 293
Romans 1:26; 396
Romans 1:28; 396
Romans 6:23; 205, 278
Romans 8:11; 95
Romans 9:3; 309
Romans 9:1-5; 28
Romans 9:31; 332
Romans 11:13-14; 414
Romans 11:20; 28
Romans 11:25; 28
Romans 12:6; 237
Romans 15:20; 484
Romans 15:22-24; 450
Romans 15:24; 326, 468
Romans 15:26; 130
Romans 16:23; 413

SUBJECT INDEX

10/40 Window, 53
120 Fellowship, 12
Abraham, 5, 20, 28, 66, 88, 150, 151, 268, 335, 426
Acts, chronology of, 228-229
A.D. 2000 Movement, 259, 465
A.D. 2000 United Prayer Track, 465
Aereopagus (Mars Hill), 31, 399, 400, 402, 443
Agabus, 236-237, 462-464
Agrippa, 81, 168, 182, 236, 240, 243, 253, 315, 471, 481-482
Aguiar, Andres, 437
Aland, Kurt, 442
Alexandria, 126, 130, 184, 223, 423-424, 429, 493
allegiance encounter, 293, 319, 334
Allen, Leslie, 13
American Indians, 129
Ananias, 52, 172, 178-182, 186-187, 191, 236, 475, 478
Ananias and Sapphira, 106-110
Anderson, Bernhard, 33
Anderson, Neil, 371
Anderson, Ray, 44-45
angels, 70, 91, 118, 149-150, 157, 164, 209-210, 214, 245, 249-256, 270, 292, 312, 358, 372, 401, 433, 476, 486, 488-489
guardian, 253-254, 394
animism, 319
Annacondia, Carlos, 157, 436
Anthesterion, 393
Antioch, 36, 38, 154, 293, 294, 298, 299, 356, 360, 419, 429
church at, 81, 170, 190, 192, 219, 222, 240 259-269, 273-275, 278-287, 301-315, 320-338, 341, 344-347, 353
city of, 19, 27, 136, 220, 223-240, 349, 359 405, 421-422, 424
in Pisidia, 268, 273-275, 281-283, 290, 294, 295, 305, 307, 308,334, 386, 411, 414, 415, 419, 422, 434, 469
anti-Semitism, 37, 419
Aphrodite, 406-407
Apollo, 224, 232, 369-370, 393, 394, 400
Apollos, 383, 423-427
disciples of, 425, 427
apostle(s), 18, 22, 27, 36, 38, 43, 47, 48, 50, 58, 66, 68, 72, 75-76, 78, 83, 91, 92, 94, 95, 97, 100, 104, 106-107, 111-112, 114, 117-120, 122, 124, 126, 128, 131-141, 144-146, 150, 153-154, 158, 160-162, 168, 172, 178, 183-184, 190-191, 195-197, 200-201, 211-212, 219, 222, 233, 235, 237-238, 241-245, 251, 252, 262, 269, 275, 276, 277, 285, 288, 292, 295, 298, 303, 310-314, 316, 324, 326-330, 332, 333, 335, 338, 347, 348, 350-352, 355, 363, 381, 414, 449, 455, 457, 461, 469, 477, 487
gift of, 196, 302, 348, 452, 477
horizontal, 327, 334
vertical, 327
workplace, 19
apostolic anointing, 335
authority, 172, 303, 327, 335-336, 349
missionaries, 350, 356, 422
teams, 266, 350, 374
Appalachia, 39
Appollonia, 274, 381, 383
Aquila and Priscilla, 407-408, 415, 419, 422-423, 430, 483
Arabia, 7, 188-190, 208
Arabs, 20, 189-190, 208
Argentina, 63, 175, 186, 195, 256-257, 436-437,440
armor of God, 300
Arnold, Clinton, 185, 429, 433, 439, 442, 443, 444, 4456
Artemis (see Diana of the Ephesians)
Artemisia, 443
ascension gifts, 262
Asian Outreach, 114
Athena, 392-393, 442
Athens, 31, 184, 185, 292, 293, 362, 388, 390-408, 410, 414, 419, 428, 442, 443, 484

authority, 20, 22, 51, 85, 94, 96, 119, 130, 136, 179, 252, 253, 272, 298, 326, 348, 350, 366, 372, 413, 439, 442, 443, 447
apostolic, 172, 303, 326, 327, 335, 336, 349
divine, 164, 335
spiritual, 73, 76, 133, 457
to heal, 84
Azusa Street revival, 68
Bacchus, 393
Banks, Robert, 458
baptism, 37, 51-52, 65, 75-76, 148, 158, 159, 160, 163, 186, 208, 215, 217, 299, 310, 314, 330, 362, 378, 423, 424-425, 426, 473
Bar-Jesus, 24, 52, 162, 204, 269-274, 289, 293, 334, 342, 365-367, 375
Barnabas, 106-108, 137, 154, 190-192,200, 221, 228-229, 233, 237, 239, 241,260-270, 273-275, 278-286, 288-293, 297, 299-301, 303-306, 310, 314, 316, 317, 322-329, 332-335, 338, 340-341, 344-349, 356, 399, 419, 422, 491, 495
Beare, F. W., 389
Beckett, Bob, 421
Beelzebub, 24, 54
Berea, 362, 387-392, 398, 404, 406, 408, 409, 415, 419, 434, 450, 452, 469
Berlin Declaration, 68
biblical scholars, 14, 15, 18, 32, 103, 218, 226, 228, 263, 264, 359-360, 481, 485
task of, 359
binding and loosing, 54
binding the strongman, 24, 54, 300, 374, 378
Blaiklock, E. M., 425, 428
Blue, Bradley, 361, 415, 458
Blue, Ken, 44
Bolivia, 11, 63, 82, 341
Bonnke, Reinhart, 115, 155, 287
Bouquet, A. C., 36
Brazil, 74, 437
Broadus, John A., 39
Brother Andrew, 489
Brown, Colin, 45
Bruce, F. F., 12, 13, 18, 22, 94, 145, 154, 167, 182, 189, 190, 207, 214, 223, 226, 265, 317, 324, 331, 347, 348, 361, 387, 388, 408, 418, 429, 433, 442, 447, 449, 450, 451
burning books, 440-441, 461
Cabrera, Omar, 186
California, 12, 113, 171, 180, 376, 421
Campus Crusade for Christ, 311
Cardinal Points praying, 421
Carey, William, 44
Ceres, 393
Cessationism, 49, 144-145
China Inland Mission, 348
China, 74, 114-115, 173, 195, 199, 200, 201, 287, 302, 348, 364, 426, 432
Chinese, the, 20, 114
Chinese Americans, 127
"Christians," 81, 236, 425, 431
Christians, ethnocentric, 134, 261, 306-307, 310
Church, 23-25, 33, 37, 38, 47, 68, 75, 79, 92, 98, 105, 110, 122, 145, 158, 178, 181, 216, 315, 325, 351, 487
division, 139-140, 426
growth, 13, 17, 18, 22, 24, 38, 48, 75, 92, 93, 111, 123-124, 139, 172, 178, 180, 220-221, 232, 234, 294, 331, 461
planting, 46, 155, 161, 195, 222, 228, 232, 239, 299, 353, 403, 408, 422, 432, 449, 458, 490-491
churches, new apostolic, 69, 78, 302
circumcision, 37, 65, 148, 208, 217, 240, 241, 308-309, 318, 320, 329, 337, 351, 353, 362, 386, 484
Gentile, 230, 243, 315, 326, 418
party, 307, 310, 330
civil disobedience, 97, 118-119
Claudius Caesar, 236, 407-408
Claudius Lysias, 471, 474-475, 478
Commissioning, 182, 367
Constantine, 417, 434, 458
contextualization, 67, 81, 322-323, 400
faulty, 323
Conybeare, W. J., 224, 424, 443
Conzelmann, Hans, 137
Corinth, 362, 396, 402, 403, 405-410, 412-417, 419-420, 423, 424, 428, 430-431, 450, 452-454, 469-470, 477, 480, 483, 484, 493
Cornelius, 27, 52, 71, 134, 150, 159, 160, 165, 195-196, 206-211, 213-217, 219, 220-221, 227, 230, 232, 233, 239-240, 241, 259, 277, 306, 310, 313, 314, 330-331, 336, 426

Council of Jerusalem, 27, 149, 191, 212, 239, 240, 254, 304, 305, 313, 315, 320, 325, 331, 340, 347, 351, 419, 469, 473
Crete, 486, 488
Crispus, 413-415, 417
Cyprus, 24, 27, 36, 39, 106, 127, 204, 222-223, 226-228, 233, 260, 264, 267, 269-272, 274-275, 289, 293, 305, 314, 323, 334, 341, 342, 344, 365-367, 375, 419
Cyprus and Cyrene Mission (CCM), 227, 232, 259, 263, 264, 265, 303, 306, 322, 339, 359
Damascus, 52, 118, 166-173, 175, 177-179, 182, 186-190, 197, 229, 235-236, 242, 289, 312, 358, 447, 449, 447, 477, 481
Daniel, 89, 253, 364
Daphene, 224, 232
David, 124, 276, 277, 336, 343
Dawson, John, 89, 297
Day of Atonement, 277
deacons, 138, 144, 458
death, 20, 21, 26, 51, 101, 102, 108, 110, 119, 145, 152, 153, 160, 169, 177, 178, 187, 192, 202, 205, 206, 216, 226-227, 229, 240, 249, 255, 256, 257, 264, 278, 291, 294, 295, 308, 313, 314, 334, 374, 415, 418, 469, 470, 471, 485, 486, 490
  spirit of, 243-244, 256-257, 393
Deere, Jack, 44, 48-49, 145, 174-175
deliverance, 14, 22, 26, 48, 78, 102, 111, 114, 157, 219, 280, 287, 367, 371-372, 373, 376, 435, 437, 438, 441
Demeter, 393
demonic affliction, 109
  beings, 368, 369, 393
  deliverances, 111, 157
  forces, 255, 270, 274, 290, 342, 366, 368, 393, 396, 401, 403, 433
  influence, 109, 243
  manifestations, 157
  obstacles, 257
  oppression, 109
  powers, 334, 401, 403
  principalities, 32, 224, 244, 342, 372, 397
  spirits, 157, 368, 369, 394, 413, 434, 443
demonization, 109, 397
demons, 24, 25, 26, 46, 48, 54, 58, 78, 91, 111, 114, 117, 144, 145, 157, 160, 161, 218, 250, 270, 272, 290, 319, 366, 370, 371, 372, 393, 395, 396, 397, 407,435, 438-439
Derbe, 282, 285, 287, 295, 297, 298-299, 301, 302, 307, 320, 333, 349, 350, 419, 422, 434
Diana of the Ephesians, 24, 224, 232, 274, 343, 365-366, 428, 436, 441-447, 461
  temple of, 274, 443
Dionysus, 393, 400
discipleship, cost of, 460
discipling, 75, 331-332, 349
  and perfecting, 331-332
Dorcas, 25, 201-204, 207, 221, 294, 295, 456, 492
Drane, John, 423
du Plessis, David, 69
dual allegiance, 318-319
earth goddess, 370
Edwards, Jonathan, 175
Egypt, 38, 39, 149, 150, 173, 276, 423, 485
elders, 94-95, 98, 146, 237, 238, 241, 262, 263, 265, 266, 301-303, 305, 308, 310, 314, 316, 324, 327, 329, 338, 342, 348, 350, 351, 352, 422, 438, 457, 461, 468, 469, 470, 471, 478, 485
Elijah, 62, 248, 251, 270, 456
Elisha, 456
elitism, 343
Elymas, 25, 162, 204, 232, 269, 365
Ephesus, 24, 26, 162, 170, 274, 356, 357, 362, 366, 367, 405, 407, 419-424, 427, 428-438, 441-447, 450, 451, 452, 456-459, 461, 467, 470, 484
Erastus, 451, 452, 493
ethnocentrism, 472
Eunice, 350
Euodia, 388, 389, 392
evangelism, 12, 33, 38, 49, 129, 178, 194-195, 230, 256, 257, 272, 285, 301, 342, 349, 350, 378, 382, 387, 403, 422, 441, 448, 473, 490-491
    cross-cultural, 67, 143, 164, 226, 275
    E-1, 33, 34, 37, 40-42, 65, 143, 224-225, 281, 363, 412
    E-2, 34, 64-65, 143, 165
    E-3, 34, 143, 165, 184
    frontier, 300
    Gentile, 259, 320
    individual, 122

international, 141
monocultural, 33, 35, 143, 184, 224, 281, 412
power, 123, 158, 286, 288, 298, 332, 432
prayer, 57, 156
public, 157
urban, 297
evangelist, gift of, 84, 155, 157, 218, 246
evangelists, 34, 66, 131, 156, 205, 225, 425, 434, 456
cross-cultural, 156
E-1, 35, 185
E-3, 230
monocultural, 34, 156
national, 35
Philip the, 137, 155
evil spirits, 58, 103, 157, 256, 279, 318, 366, 397, 436, 438, 442
exorcism, 434
Ezekiel, 13, 412, 421
falling under the Spirit, 171, 174-175
fasting, 78, 186, 209, 212, 253, 265, 267, 301, 303
Feaver, Karen, 287
Felix, 170, 471, 478-480
fellowship, 5, 50, 69, 76-77, 79, 128, 222, 311, 316, 363, 396, 400, 476
Ferguson, Everett, 369-370, 394
Festus, 469, 471, 480-482
fetish(es), 199, 429-430, 441
fivefold ministers, 262
fortune-telling, 365, 367-368
fortune-tellers, 290, 367, 373-374, 377
Foster, Richard, 247
four spiritual laws, 311
frontier evangelism, 300
Fuller, Harold, 131
Fuller Seminary, 11, 12, 13, 16, 44, 45, 113, 180-181, 183, 437
fund-raising, 452, 453
Fung, Ronald, 307-308
Gabriel, 251, 372
Gaius, 413, 415
Galatia, 273, 275, 282, 300, 303, 305, 307, 308, 319, 320, 322, 323, 326, 338, 348, 352, 353, 355, 360, 421
Galileans, 37, 39, 40, 42, 64, 66, 68, 72, 96, 125, 147
Gallio, 407, 416-420, 428, 454, 477, 480
Gamaliel, 91, 120, 167-168, 275
Garrett, Susan, 162, 163, 164, 269, 270, 271, 272, 334, 435, 438, 439, 441
Gentile church(es), 81, 170, 192, 219, 220, 224, 228, 230-233, 235, 239-240, 259, 261, 264, 268, 276, 280, 281, 304, 306, 314, 315, 322, 326, 340, 363, 381, 412, 468, 469
circumcision, 230, 243, 315, 326, 340, 418
conversion, 165, 195, 217, 325
evangelism, 165, 259, 320
salvation, 307, 344
Gideon, 273, 343
Gill, David W. J., 361
Gilliland, Dean S., 262, 319
giving, 105-106, 345, 453-454
God-fearers, 165, 207, 208, 268, 275, 276, 277, 279, 280, 283, 284, 286, 292, 306, 316, 318, 362, 363, 383, 386, 388, 390, 398, 399, 405, 411, 412, 414, 484
Graham, Billy, 155, 246, 364
Great Commission, 13, 29, 49, 53, 73, 90, 143, 398, 333, 378, 495
Green, Michael, 396, 434
Greig, Gary, 44
group conversion, 364-365
Grudem, Wayne, 44, 463, 464
Haenchen, Ernst, 12, 134, 140, 152, 287, 305, 324, 325, 356, 357, 358, 440
Hagner, Donald, 91
Hamon, Bill, 464
Harrison, Everett, 12, 106, 153-154, 240, 241, 262, 287, 298
Harvest Evangelism, 256, 440
harvest principle, 382-383
Hayford, Jack, 160, 171, 176
healing, faith for, 86
gift of, 137
power, 84, 163, 437, 492, 493
prayer, 87, 289
service, 436, 492-493
hearing God, 56, 109, 171, 174, 175-176, 212, 266, 303, 356

Hebrews, 7, 18, 28, 37, 38-39, 64, 66, 90, 93, 107, 124-130, 132-134, 137, 139, 140, 143, 145, 146, 167, 235
Hellenists, 7, 37-39, 64-66, 89, 93, 107, 124-140, 143, 145, 146, 147, 154, 158, 167, 191, 223-227, 264
Hermes, 289-294, 297, 298, 319, 334, 403, 483
Herod Agrippa, I, 240, 243, 253
Herod Agrippa, II, 240
Herod Antipas, 240, 244
Herod the Great, 240, 242-243, 256, 264, 478, 481
Hiebert, D. Edmond, 18, 345, 389
hillbillies, 39, 48, 68, 69, 97, 125, 139, 147
Hindus, 6, 211
Holy Rollers, 69
Holy Spirit, 15-16, 22-23, 24, 39, 43, 49, 55, 61, 63, 65, 70-75, 85, 96, 97, 99, 106, 107, 109, 122, 137, 145, 148, 159, 160, 162, 164, 187, 192, 197, 210, 213, 215, 235, 237, 246, 248, 249, 250, 265, 352, 355-357, 378, 383, 384, 385, 419, 421, 424-426, 428, 434, 436, 457, 459, 460, 462-464
    anointing of, 284
    baptism of, 51-52, 62, 159-160, 426
    filled(ing) of, 52, 54, 56, 60, 71, 95, 100, 110, 112, 131, 134-135, 151, 152, 159-160, 179, 186, 217, 230, 234, 241, 269, 271, 274, 281, 307, 334, 375, 426
    fruit(s) of, 104, 136, 410, 418, 473
    gift of, 69, 216, 230, 301, 303, 328, 331, 426
    power of, 24, 45-46, 52, 53, 54, 60, 74, 77, 84, 88, 90, 112, 116, 143, 153, 156, 206, 216, 218, 220-221, 284, 336, 427, 448, 456
    presence of, 135
    work(s) of, 43, 157
Homogeneity, 29, 33
Hong Kong, 127, 404
Horton, Stanley M., 15, 71, 110, 113, 232, 464
house church(es), 200, 230, 261-263, 265, 302-304, 311, 324-326, 338, 351, 353, 386, 413, 426, 431, 432, 446, 458, 469, 483, 494
Howson, J. S., 224, 424, 443
humility, 459-460
hyphenated ethnics, 127
hypocrites, 345
Iconium, 281, 282-287, 294, 298-302, 305, 307, 320, 333, 334, 349, 350, 415, 419, 422, 469
identificational repentance, 89
idolatry, 123-124, 293, 319, 353, 391, 395, 396, 398, 401, 484
idols, 301, 337, 352, 353, 385, 391-392, 395-396, 398, 400, 401, 403, 406, 446
Illyricum, 452
indigenous church(es), 135, 265, 305
Indonesia, 74, 194, 202
intercession, gift of, 50, 246, 248
intercessors, 50, 214, 246, 248-249, 252-253, 328, 336, 339, 373, 388-389, 392, 421, 463, 465, 489
intercessory prayer, 489
Irian Jaya, 199
Isaiah, 62
Jacobs, Cindy, 89, 115, 256
Jairus's daughter, 203, 205, 456
James, brother of Jesus (see James of Jerusalem)
    brother of John, 191, 241
    of Jerusalem, 58, 242, 254, 310, 314, 327, 335
    son of Alphaeus, 191
    son of Zebedee (see James of Jerusalem)
    the Just (see James of Jerusalem)
Japan, 64, 290, 391, 429
Jeremias, Joachim, 65, 93, 140,242, 473
Jerusalem, 7, 15, 23, 27, 39, 40, 41-42, 47-48, 51, 55, 56-57, 58, 60, 62, 64, 65, 66, 71, 72, 76-78, 80-82, 89, 90-94, 96-98, 101, 102-106, 108, 110-112, 114, 116, 118-120, 122-131, 133-135, 137-141, 143-151, 153-155, 158, 161, 164-165, 166-170, 172, 173, 177, 179, 184, 187, 188, 190-192,194, 197, 200, 201, 206, 208, 215, 217, 218, 220-227, 229, 232-237, 239-242, 244, 249-250,253-255, 260, 262, 264, 269, 272-273, 289, 306-307, 310, 311, 313, 314-317, 322-335, 341-342, 344-345, 347-348, 419-424, 426, 430, 449-454, 457, 460-465, 467-474, 476-481,484, 485, 488, 490, 494
Jerusalem Council (see Council of Jerusalem)
Jerusalem Decrees, 352-353
Jesus, monocultural ministry, 35, 196
Jewish Zealots, 314

Job, 109
Joel, 73-74, 77, 237
John, 17, 18, 20, 25, 37, 38, 39, 80-82, 84, 86-88, 94-98, 117-119, 153, 158, 159, 161, 195, 197, 198, 203, 212, 215, 233, 241, 260, 267, 288, 289, 316, 329, 445-446, 450
John Mark (see Mark, John)
John the Baptist, 21, 37, 51-52, 62, 102-103, 154, 195, 205, 240, 244, 264, 276, 423-425
Jonah, 488
Joseph, 149, 150
Joseph (and Mary), 58, 191
Joseph Barsabas, 39, 107, 126
Joshua, 252, 292, 421
Judaizers, 307-309, 311, 313, 315-317, 320, 323, 325, 327, 333, 335-337, 344, 348
Judas Iscariot, 39, 111, 125
Judeans, 37, 39, 66, 125
Judge, E. A., 40
Jupiter, 290, 369, 393
justification by faith, 278, 280,309, 313, 411, 414, 433-434
Kenya, 34, 213
kingdom of God, 5, 19-23, 29, 46-49, 51, 54-57, 76, 100-105, 110-112, 116, 139, 153, 156-158, 161, 165, 201, 204-205, 221, 231, 257, 266, 270, 271, 286, 298, 300, 311, 333, 341, 389, 403, 415, 430, 432, 443, 447, 450, 454, 490, 495
Kingdom, keys to, 53, 300
Kingdom, signs of, 100-104, 106, 110-112, 116, 205
Kinnamin, Gary, 250-251
Kistemaker, Simon J., 12, 15, 70, 95, 127, 137, 177, 224, 226, 227, 236, 264, 329, 333, 369, 398, 342, 491
Korea, 78, 225, 364
Korean-Americans, 225, 364
Kraft, Charles, 48-49, 113, 293
Kumuyi, William, 437
Ladd, George Eldon, 467
Lake Avenue Congregational Church, 12
Larkins, Donovan, 441
LaSor, William, 107, 229
last days, 73-74, 77, 439
Lausanne II in Manila, 182, 389
Lawrence, Carl, 200
Lazarus, 40, 205, 295, 296, 456
leadership, apostolic, 76, 136, 324, 329, 337, 341
  gift of, 301
  priority of, 301
  servant, 136
  styles, 345
  training, 431, 432, 457
Legion spirit, 372
Lenski, R. C. H., 12, 123, 227, 369
Levites, 91, 106, 125, 140
Lois, 350
Longenecker, Richard, 167
Los Angeles, 68, 225, 231, 290
Lucius, 260-264
Luther, Martin, 44, 375
Lydia, 361-365, 378-379, 384, 385, 409, 451
Lystra, 204, 282, 283, 285-298, 300-302, 305, 307, 319, 320, 323, 333, 334, 339, 350-351, 356, 399, 403, 415, 419, 422, 456, 469
Macedonian vision, 358, 451
MacMullen, Ramsay, 434-435, 445
magic, 116, 162, 317, 429, 436, 439, 441, 444, 484
Malta, 490-493
Manaen, 260-264
Mark, John, 247, 260, 269, 273, 341, 343, 375
Mars Hill (see Aereopagus)
Marshall, Howard, 12, 93, 125, 134, 226, 402
martyr complex, 474
Mary and Martha, 40
Mary, mother of Jesus, 56, 58, 312, 369, 372
Mary, mother of Mark, 105, 247, 248, 249, 328, 344
Mary Magdelene, 58
Matthias, 39, 58, 72, 111
Mattill, A. J., Jr., 472-473
McGavran, Donald A., 30-31, 38, 61, 75, 124, 166, 199, 299, 331, 461
Mercury, 290
Messianic Jews, 80-81, 93, 118, 127, 132, 170, 178, 201, 218, 222, 230, 261, 269, 307, 469, 472-473, 479
    ethnocentric, 307
Messianic Samaritans, 156, 158, 161, 178, 211
Metzger, Bruce, 429

Michael, 253, 371
Miletus, 456-459, 493
Minerva, 392, 393
miracles, 14, 45-46, 78, 84, 85, 111, 115-116, 117, 118, 132, 136, 145, 155-158, 162, 163, 197, 200-204, 221, 223, 234, 279, 286, 287-288, 327, 332, 333, 385, 386, 435, 436-438
  gift of, 198
  healing, 84, 115
  on Malta, 490-491
  purpose of, 115-116
  usual and unusual, 78, 436-438
missiologists, 30, 53, 122, 131, 135, 163, 216, 225-226, 228, 266, 319, 324, 331, 345, 364, 495
missiology, 13, 15, 19, 23, 27, 30, 31, 33, 44, 49, 122, 138, 141, 168, 180, 183-184, 199, 220, 227, 232, 233, 367, 382, 449, 490
missionaries, 7, 27, 35, 61, 63, 67, 131-132, 138, 154, 156, 174, 223, 226, 227, 229, 231, 235, 260, 261, 265, 266, 268, 272, 279-280, 282, 285, 292, 297, 301, 303, 306, 314, 319, 322-324, 326, 329, 332-334, 337, 341, 349, 356-359, 364, 368, 373-374, 378, 379, 382-385, 387-390, 404, 407,410, 424-425, 434, 490, 493
  apostolic, 350, 356, 422
  Assemblies of God, 231
  CCM, 228-231, 233, 261, 264
  cross-cultural, 35, 131, 141, 166, 302, 322, 432
  E-3, 36
  field, 11, 16, 415
  foreign, 128, 263, 265
  frontier, 422-423
missionary, gift of, 34, 156, 196, 218-219, 228
mission split, 269, 341, 345, 346
modality, 266-267, 345, 346
modalities, 266, 326, 345
modality-sodality theory, 228, 266
monocultural, 33-35, 65, 131, 143, 156, 185, 195, 196, 224, 281, 307, 412
Mosaic Law, 277, 279, 290, 316, 326, 331
Moses, 62, 88, 124, 146-147, 150, 218, 252, 276, 306, 323, 371-372
Mother Earth, 393
multicultural church, 133, 305
Munck, Johannes, 12
Murphy, Edward F., 174
Muslims, 6, 66, 70, 89, 173, 199, 202, 302, 418, 437-438
Native Americans, 364, 394
nativistic movements, 425
navel of the earth, 369
Navigators, 348
Nazarenes, 479
Nazirite vow, 420-422
Neptune, 393, 406
New Age, 54, 161, 395
New Apostolic Reformation, 69, 237, 477
New York City, 167
Nigeria, 74, 205, 319, 437-438, 456
Ninevah, 489
Nock, A. D., 397
North Africa, 7, 226, 227, 264, 424
Onesiphorus, 284
oracle at Delphi, 369-370
ordained ministers, 19, 180, 458
ordination, 351
Orthodox Jews, 167, 208, 211, 214, 362, 398, 418, 470
Otis, George, Jr., 53, 397, 406
Outreach 38, 49, 79, 131, 259, 346, 422
Overcome, 54
Overseers, 457
Palau, Luis, 155
Pan, 394
parachurch ministries, 341, 345
  organization, 228, 265
paradigm shift, 112-115, 189
pastors, 34, 57, 77, 78, 225, 238, 248, 262, 302, 303, 305, 348, 350, 389, 430, 431, 456-458, 460, 461, 469
Paul, out-of-the-body experience, 295
pax romana, 484
Pentecost, 3, 12, 25, 42, 57, 58, 60, 65, 67, 70-71, 73-76, 80, 83, 87-89, 92-93, 95, 98, 100, 104, 106, 111, 125, 126, 130, 135, 159-160, 216-217, 275, 277, 325, 336
  event, 70, 160
people groups, 20, 29, 31-34, 37, 55, 122, 128, 147-148, 152, 184, 185, 225, 229-231, 259, 323, 356, 375, 397, 406, 432
people movements, 199, 200, 364, 365

perfecting and discipling, 75, 331-332, 422
personal intercessors, 50, 248, 260, 339, 389
Peters, George, 350
Peterson, Eugene H., 344, 399
Pharisees, 37, 48, 91, 97, 118, 168, 228, 235, 241, 327, 328, 334, 475-476
Philip, 7, 25, 27, 36-38, 40, 71, 117, 136-137, 143, 154-158, 161-165, 196-167, 200, 201, 207, 211, 221, 233, 250, 490, 495
Philippi, 19, 24, 47, 251, 342, 358-359, 361-362, 365-358, 370, 373-376, 378-379, 381, 384-385, 387-389, 409, 415, 419, 428, 433, 445, 450-454, 474, 485
Phoenicia, 222, 223, 325, 326, 327, 328
Pierson, Paul E., 15, 23, 163, 324
Plato, 394
Poseidon, 393, 406, 407
post-baptismal care, 299
poverty, 83, 104-105, 130
power encounter, 25, 52, 62, 123, 204, 232, 240, 244, 249, 250, 252, 253-255, 257, 260, 269-271, 273, 286, 287, 293, 327, 334, 344, 358, 365, 367, 371, 375, 435
  evangelism, 123, 156, 286, 288, 298, 432, 491
  ministries, 14, 15-16, 23, 25, 45, 49, 74, 78, 111, 112, 122, 144-145, 173-174, 175, 183, 202, 221, 232, 234, 327, 385, 414, 432, 434, 449, 490
praise, 11, 47, 49, 50, 56, 58, 78, 98, 194, 296, 376
prayer, 13, 16, 47, 50, 56-59, 61, 70, 76, 78, 80, 87, 98, 111, 115, 116, 133, 159, 180, 185, 186, 187, 198, 202, 203, 209, 211, 212, 214, 222, 239-240, 245-254, 257, 260, 265, 267, 289, 295, 297, 303, 307, 312, 326, 334, 336, 341, 351, 356-357, 361, 365, 373, 376, 388, 389, 392, 413, 416, 421, 436, 445, 463-465, 468, 489
  evangelism, 57
  intercessory, 489
  Lord's, 21, 101, 104
  meeting, 43, 52, 55, 56-59, 78, 80, 232, 245, 252
  of rebuke, 289
  partners, 248, 252, 464
priests, 62, 90, 91, 96, 98, 111, 118, 139, 140, 141, 148, 179, 187, 291, 446, 475
Prince of Persia, 253
Princeton Seminary, 33, 144
principalities, 32, 53, 161, 185, 232, 244, 256, 274, 290, 292, 300, 320, 342, 366, 372, 392, 393, 396, 397, 433, 447
principalities and powers, 21, 53, 185, 252, 342, 366, 372, 389
prophecy, 62, 70, 73-74, 77, 84, 110, 145, 151, 160, 181, 237, 263, 312, 328, 336, 339, 351, 369-370, 422, 461, 463-465, 488, 490
  conditional, 465, 488-489
  evaluating, 463
  gift of, 180, 219, 237, 263, 338-339, 370
  limitations of, 464
  personal, 463-464
prophet(s), 43, 73, 88, 90, 151, 163, 181-182, 215, 236-237, 253, 260, 262-263, 265, 269-270, 275, 312, 336, 338-339, 348-349, 387, 462, 463-464, 479
prophetic act(s), 281, 421, 463
  calling(s), 311-312, 313, 315, 316
  ministry, 339, 464, 487
proselytes, 27, 65, 148, 155, 165, 207, 208, 242, 268, 276, 277, 278-279, 283, 316, 318, 362, 411, 484
prosperity, 375, 444, 453
Protestant Reformation, 44, 313
psychics, 290
Publius, 492-493
Puteoli, 493
Pythia, 370
Python spirit, 24, 162, 342, 358, 365, 368-378, 428, 433, 445
Queen of Heaven, 369, 392, 393, 442
racism, 129, 473, 475
Rackham, Richard, 91, 140, 178, 242, 403
raising the dead, 84, 103, 201, 203, 205, 206, 296, 455-456
Ramsay, William Mitchell, 263, 282, 299, 402, 431, 451, 454, 485
Reagan, Mrs. Ronald, 270
Reconciliation Walk, 89
religio licita, 417-418, 480
repentance, 29, 53, 75, 89, 119, 151, 218, 330, 332, 425, 473
resistance/receptivity, 67

Resistencia, 256-257, 440
Roberts, Oral, 287
Roberts' Rules of Order, 133
Roman Catholic, 58, 369
Roman Empire, 5, 36, 64, 126, 127, 207-208, 223, 268, 291, 300, 383, 392, 417, 423, 428-430, 434, 443, 483-485, 495
Rome, 7, 19, 36, 51, 91, 130, 223, 240, 254, 314, 326, 349-350, 355, 407-408, 414, 423, 429, 432, 450, 451, 467-468, 470, 476, 481, 482, 483-486, 493-495
Sadducees, 37, 90, 91-92, 93, 95, 97, 101, 117-118, 120, 140, 141, 146, 476
Samaria, 7, 15, 23, 41, 51, 60, 71, 90, 92, 98, 110, 124, 138, 141, 143, 150-151, 153-162, 164-165, 170, 192, 194, 196, 206, 220-222, 233, 241, 325-326, 328, 365-367, 490
Samaritan woman, 23, 41, 149, 151, 156
Samaritans, 25, 27, 29, 36-38, 41, 42, 71, 124, 137, 143, 149, 151, 155, 156, 158, 159, 161, 163, 178, 196, 200, 211, 216, 220, 233, 240, 382
San La Muerte, 256-257
Sanhedrin, 39, 92, 94-98, 100, 118-120, 139, 146, 150, 151-152, 170, 221, 242, 245, 275, 329, 471, 475-456, 478, 481
Santería, 290
Satan, 91, 118, 120, 153, 158, 179, 236
  seat of, 232, 370, 442
Saturday worship, 222, 425, 455
Saul of Tarsus, 118, 158, 179, 236
Septuagint, 126, 167, 336
Sergius Paulus, 269-272, 334, 365
Seventh Day Adventists, 455
sheep stealing, 431
shepherd, 457-458
shipwreck, 183, 489
signs and wonders, 26, 44-45, 73, 74, 98, 111-115, 144, 145, 200, 202, 221, 232, 283, 284-285, 287-288, 291, 295, 298, 334, 363
Silas, 251, 338-339, 340, 347-349, 351-353, 356-357, 360-361, 373-377, 379, 381-384, 387, 389-390, 408-411, 419, 428, 474, 495
Silk Road, 302
Silvoso, Ed, 256-257, 440
Simeon, 260, 261, 263, 264
Simon Magus, 365-367
Simon the Sorcerer, 71, 156, 161-163
Simon the Zealot, 58
Simson, Wolfgang, 173
Singapore, 374
Smail, Thomas A., 46
Socrates, 394
sodality, 266, 267, 345, 346
sodalities, 228, 266, 326, 345, 346
Sosthenes, 413, 418-419
South Africa, 76, 130
Spain, 326, 450, 467-468, 476
spirit guide, 395
spirit of death, 243-244, 256-257, 393
  divination, 365, 367, 368, 370
  religion, 369, 413
  violence, 486
spiritual gifts, 34, 69, 84, 117, 133, 155, 157, 196, 197, 201, 263, 301, 311, 343, 349, 422, 463
    mapping, 256, 274, 369, 405-406
    warfare, 14, 16, 23-24, 53-54, 73, 89, 161-162, 164, 185, 204, 249, 252-253, 256, 270, 273-274, 297, 300, 328, 341-342, 344, 365-367, 369-372, 376-377, 385, 388-389, 395, 421, 430, 433-436, 439-445
Spiritual Warfare Network, 183
Springer, Kevin, 44
Stephen, 117, 134, 136-137, 141, 143-155, 158, 169-170, 177, 190-192, 200, 206, 221-222, 226-227, 229, 234, 240, 242, 264, 275, 294, 313, 348, 353, 475, 495
stoicheia, 318-319
Stott, John R. W., 12, 51, 105, 138, 166-167, 208, 250, 257, 269, 270, 335, 399, 443, 449, 473, 484
Strabo, 429
strongholds, 20, 53, 185, 395-396, 413, 428
strongman, 24, 54, 373, 374, 378, 388
Sunday worship, 261, 425, 455, 456
supernatural power, 45, 48, 52, 84, 95, 98, 145, 188, 196, 221, 232, 255, 289, 290, 291, 293, 334, 367-368, 374, 397, 405, 414, 429
superstition, 290, 367-368, 374
synagogues, 5, 128, 132, 146, 148, 166, 170, 187, 188, 200, 207, 208, 222, 227-231, 261, 267-268, 311, 337, 352, 362, 398, 408, 414, 479, 484

syndrome of church development, 349, 355, 423, 432, 450
Syntyche, 388-389
Tarsus, 38, 167, 184, 191, 192, 234, 235, 264, 275, 299, 306
Taylor, Hudson, 348
teachers, 91, 189, 260, 262, 263, 265, 339, 348
teaching, gift of, 263
Ten Commandments, 101, 2983, 400
tentmaking, 407-409, 422, 430, 483
territorial spirits, 161, 163, 183, 204, 270, 274, 366-367, 368, 372, 377, 388, 392, 393, 394, 406, 442, 444, 445, 447
Tertullus, 478-479
theology, 13, 28, 44, 45, 48, 76, 91, 188, 190, 195, 218, 313, 315, 406, 411
    cessationist, 69
    Jewish, 207, 417
    of harvest, 61
    of mission, 169
    Old Testament, 33
    Paul's, 13, 235, 470
    Peter's, 195, 330
    Python's, 370
    reactionary, 328
    search, 61
Theophilus, 18, 43, 84
Thesmophoria, 393
Thessalonica, 274, 300, 357, 362, 381, 383-388, 390, 391, 398, 403, 404, 407, 409, 410, 415, 431, 434, 452, 469, 485
Third Wave, 15, 16, 69, 113
Thomas, 35, 329
Thomas, James and Jaime, 63
Tidball, Derek, 138, 139
timeline, 7, 41, 53, 73, 228
tithe, 77, 106
Titius Justus, 415
Titus, 352, 451-453
tongues, 25, 29, 48, 60, 63, 87, 221, 490
    gift of, 70
    speaking in, 68-72, 103, 160, 217-218, 232, 310, 331, 425-427
Tower of Babel, 32
Townsend, Cameron, 348
Trebilco, Paul, 442
Trinity, 24, 45-46, 55, 61, 205, 426
Trophimus, 447, 493
Trotman, Dawson, 348
truth encounter, 293, 371
Turkey, 167, 223, 273, 282
Tyrannus, 431, 450, 461
unclean food, 211-213
unreached peoples, 19, 35, 357
Upper Room, 12, 17, 27, 42, 49, 50, 56, 57, 61, 72, 98, 106, 126, 201, 202, 455
Van Engen, Charles, 150, 228
Venezuela, 425
Venus, 406
Vineyard Christian Fellowship, 113, 288
Virgin Mary, counterfeit, 369
visible and invisible, 400
visions, 73, 74, 174, 209, 212, 215, 358
von Rad, Gerhard, 32
voodoo, 290
Wagner, Doris, 50, 82, 249, 257, 341, 465
Wang, David, 114
warfare, spiritual (see spiritual warfare)
Warfield, Benjamin Breckinridge, 144
Wernicke, K., 442
Wesley, John, 174
West African, 174
White, John, 174-175
Williams, Don, 44
Wilson, Sam, 82
Wimber, John, 44, 49, 113, 115, 156, 180, 286-288
Wink, Walter, 248-249
Winter, Bruce W., 417-418
Winter, Ralph D., 6, 81, 224, 266, 345-346, 481-482
world evangelization, 11, 30-31, 42, 53, 63, 81, 83, 182, 183, 196, 199, 226, 259, 367
Wuest, Kenneth, 318
Wycliffe Bible Translators, 346, 348
Yugoslavia, 452
Zeus, 126, 289-294, 297, 298, 319, 334, 369, 393, 394, 400, 403
Zimmerman, Thomas, 69

STUDY NOTES

STUDY NOTES

STUDY NOTES

STUDY NOTES

STUDY NOTES

STUDY NOTES

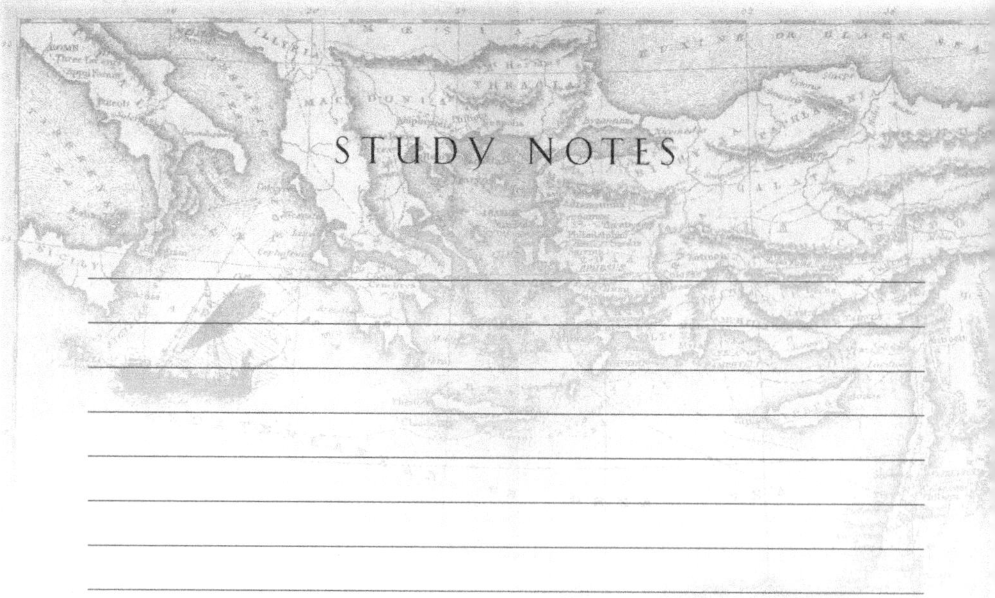